Teaching with
The Norton Anthology of World Literature

SECOND EDITION

VOLUMES D, E, F

1500 TO THE MODERN WORLD

A Guide for Instructors

Teaching with
The Norton Anthology
of World Literature

SECOND EDITION

VOLUMES D, E, F
1500 TO THE MODERN WORLD

A Guide for Instructors

Paula Berggren
BARUCH COLLEGE
with the Editors

W · W · NORTON & COMPANY
New York · London

The text of this book is composed in Fairfield Medium
with the display set in Bernhard Modern.
Composition by PennSet, Inc.

ISBN 0-393-97811-7 (pbk.)

W. W. Norton & Company, Inc., 500 Fifth Avenue, New York, N.Y. 10110
www.wwnorton.com

W. W. Norton & Company Ltd., Castle House, 75/76 Wells Street,
London W1T 3QT

1 2 3 4 5 6 7 8 9 0

Contents

Vernacular Literature in China

WU CH'ENG-EN

Monkey

Backgrounds

Like Rabelais's *Gargantua and Pantagruel, Monkey* is a sprawling novel, though one held together by the theme of the pilgrimage to India to get the Buddhist scriptures. The novel begins with Monkey's miraculous birth from a stone egg and takes him through his gradual acquisition of magic powers and rule of the other monkeys at the Mountain of Flowers and Fruit. As Monkey becomes more and more arrogant, he makes trouble in Heaven. None of the deities can subdue him until the god Erh-lang and his brothers come, and with the help of the Taoist Sage Lao Tzu they capture him. Monkey has, however, stolen Lao Tzu's magic elixir; when they try to execute him, his body proves impervious to everything. At last Monkey is subdued by the Buddha and imprisoned underneath the Mountain of the Five Elements.

Five hundred years later the Boddhisattva Kuan-yin travels east to China in search of someone to undertake the pilgrimage to India and fetch the scriptures. Hsüan Tsang is chosen and, in the selections in the anthology, gathers his disciples and begins his adventures. The greater part of the novel involves dangers encountered and overcome along the way. At the end of the novel the group reaches India, acquires the scriptures, and is conveniently flown home to China by Buddhist magic.

Monkey is very different from earlier Chinese works in this anthology, and this difference is to a large degree a function of a difference in language. Written Chinese is divided roughly into "literary" or "classical" Chinese and "vernacular" Chinese. Many assume that "classical" Chinese represents something like the spoken language of the first three centuries B.C. As time went on and spoken Chinese evolved, "classical" Chinese remained the standard of writing—and in most cases was probably aurally comprehensible, as biblical English is. For instance, most stories dating from the T'ang Dynasty, such as "The Tale of Ying-ying," are written in classical Chinese. However, the written texts of some Buddhist stories from that period use compounds and grammatical particles that are recognizably related to the modern spoken language. From the thirteenth century on, stories could be written in either classical or vernacular Chinese. The two linguistic registers represented very different narrative sensibilities. Classical stories (usually called "tales," in some imperfect analogy to the distinction between tales and short stories in the West) were usually shorter, stylistically terse and placing great weight on particular phrasing. Vernacular stories, imitating the manner of oral storytelling, delighted in detailed description, lively dialogue, and speculation on the motivation of characters. In a classical story a small gesture would be pregnant with meaning, while in a vernacular story the narrator often would explain such a gesture fully.

Although there were a few attempts at novels in classical Chinese later in the tradition, the novel was essentially a vernacular form. The novel first developed out of storytelling cycles, of which *Monkey* was one. A story cycle on the history of the breakup of the Han Dynasty emerged as the novel *The Romance of the Three Kingdoms,* while another cycle on heroic bandits of the Sung Dynasty became *Shui-hu chuan,* variously translated as "Water Margin," "Men of the Marsh," or, in Pearl Buck's famous retelling, "All Men Are Brothers."

Arthur David Waley, not inappropriately, calls *Monkey* a "folk novel." Although Wu Ch'eng-en may have been responsible for its final form, the present version is the outcome of cumulative retelling. Only in the eighteenth century can authorship be properly associated with novels in the way it is with poetry and essays. Prose fiction was a low-status activity, and before the eighteenth century, known literary men were often unwilling to have their names associated with a novel. Novels were usually published under pseudonyms, and not only is it difficult to find the historical writer behind the pseudonym, that author is not always the real author of the novel. A second problem, and one not unfamiliar to the student of the early novel in Europe, is that novels were commercially very successful: once a successful novel appeared, many other publishers soon issued the work in altered, reduced, or expanded versions. While the publishing history of works of classical poetry and essays is easy to trace, the history of editions of novels is often an intricate scholarly puzzle. Thus not only authorship but even the "original" text of a novel is often a matter of debate. In any case, by the seventeenth century and the publication of the erotic novel of manners *The Golden Lotus* in 1617, while problems of authorship and text remain, the Chinese novel ceases to be a retelling of traditional material and develops original plots.

In Chinese the phrase "monkey of the mind" refers to the mind's ungovernability—its constant speculations, stratagems, and shifts. The metal fillet, which the Boddhisattva Kuan Yin gives to Hsüan Tsang to control Monkey, is an excellent figure for external discipline (by his very nature Monkey is incapable of any internal discipline greater than accomplishing the task at hand). Much of the energy of the story grows out of the conflict between the mission, to which the reader subscribes, and Monkey's inherent rebelliousness, which the reader also approves. These two values—consistent purpose and the resistance to purpose—can never be perfectly reconciled. The fillet, the image of external compulsion, becomes the only means to hold together these two powerfully opposed forces in the story. Eventually Monkey comes to share fully in the pilgrimage, but it is a conversion accomplished through coercion.

This same conflict reappears in Monkey's eternal resourcefulness, which is the very stuff of the narrative, and the predestined Buddhist plot, which underlies not only the larger narrative but also many of the particular episodes. Monkey always finds a way to rescue his master, only to discover that all events were foreordained.

Classroom Strategies and Topics for Discussion

1. Discuss the issues of liberty and devotion to the pilgrimage, which demands the constraint of freedom, in the character of Monkey.

   [Monkey is utterly devoted when he is "into" a project. Note that to distinguish the real Tripitaka from the false one in the Cock-crow Kingdom, he asks Tripitaka to recite the spell that tightens the fillet on his head.]

2. In the episode involving the Cock-crow Kingdom (and throughout *Monkey*) there is a level of immediate narrative and a level of Buddhist retribution narrative. Nothing is what it seems on the surface, and part of the process that occurs in the narrative is stripping away appearances to true shapes and true causes. Discuss how this process works in the episode involving the Cock-crow Kingdom.

   [There is the immediate revelation of one level of the story by the ghost to Tripitaka. Monkey believes this revelation immediately because it promises excitement. The prince is persuaded by a ruse based on false appearances. When the prince tests this information with his mother, he discovers the false-king's avoidance of intimacy with the queen. The scene in the throne room is a wonderful theater of true and false appearances, with the wizard changing shapes. But the most significant episode occurs when the final imposture is exposed and the disciples set off to do battle with the wizard. At the point when they are about to achieve victory, the Boddhisattva Manjúsrī appears. He reveals that the wizard is actually his lion and that the entire event was due to a misdeed of the king. The narrative has all been predestined.]

Comparative Perspectives

1. Many of the readings in this anthology describe the experience of pilgrimage. In what ways may we compare *Monkey* with, as appropriate, Dante's *The Divine Comedy,* Chaucer's *The Canterbury Tales,* Saikaku's *The Barrelmaker Brimful of Love,* Bashō's *The Narrow Road of the Interior,* Thomas Mann's *Death in Venice,* Aimé Césaire's *Notebook of a Return to the Native Land?*

2. The earnest Tripitaka's disciples all have animal forms. What other works have you read in which animal characters take on major roles? How do different authors use such creatures to comment about human nature?

3. Compare the relationship of Monkey and Tripitaka to that of Don Quixote and Sancho Panza. How are the roles of servant and master reversed in these novels? What qualities makes one more "serious" than the other?

Further Reading

See the reading suggestions in the anthology, p. 9

K'UNG SHANG-JEN

The Peach Blossom Fan

Backgrounds

Understanding *The Peach Blossom Fan* requires a basic knowledge of the history of China in the seventeenth century. Early in the century the Ming Dynasty was clearly in decline. Power fell into the hands of an imperial eunuch, Wei Chung-hsien, who controlled the secret police and ruthlessly suppressed the reformist party made up of Confucian intellectuals. Juan Ta-ch'eng, one of the main villains in the play, had belonged to Wei Chung-hsien's party and was made Wei's "foster son." When the Emperor Ch'ung-chen came to the throne in 1628, Wei's party was purged, which is why Juan Ta-ch'eng initially appears in the play living privately in Nanking.

Rebellions were breaking out all over the country, the most serious being that of Li Tzu-ch'eng in North China. At the same time, the Manchus, a non-Chinese people on China's northeastern frontier, had consolidated their own state and created a formidable military machine. In 1644 Li Tzu-ch'eng's forces took the capital at Peking, and the Emperor Ch'ung-chen hanged himself. Wu San-kui, the Ming general stationed at the frontier fortifications that held the Manchu armies out of China, was, as legend has it, enraged because Li Tzu-ch'eng's generals took his favorite concubine. As a result Wu San-kui opened the passes and welcomed the invading Manchu army, which quickly defeated Li Tzu-ch'eng's forces and drove him out of Peking. The Manchus then began their conquest of the rest of China.

With the emperor dead and the crown prince missing, the question of the Ming succession was uncertain. The general isolation of members of the imperial house ensured that few could recognize them. Imperial princes and pretenders appeared everywhere. Nanking was officially the "Southern Capital" of the Ming, though it had long since ceased to be a place of real political power. A faction in Nanking, supported by the retreating Ming armies, set up the Prince of Fu as emperor. The ineptness, political squabbling, and opportunism of the "Southern Ming" regime led to a series of military disasters and defections as the Manchu moved inexorably southward. After they took Nanking and put an end to the regime, the Manchus were established as the Ch'ing Dynasty, though they had to spend many more decades putting down rebellions and chasing down pretenders.

Aware of China's power to assimilate non-Chinese regimes, the Manchus attempted to maintain a strict ethnic distinction between themselves and their Chinese subjects. Perhaps the most drastic cultural reminder of foreign rule was the requirement that all male Chinese wear the "queue," the long single braid of hair, in the Manchu style. Aware of the simmering hostility of many of their Chinese subjects, the Ch'ing authorities were sensitive to any slight and any sign of Ming loyalism. On the other side, the fate of the Ming became an almost obsessive concern for Chinese intellectuals in the second half of the seventeenth century. It is in this context that *The Peach Blossom Fan* tells the story of the Southern Ming, carefully avoiding wounding the dangerous sensitivities of the Ch'ing authorities.

If contemporary history is one parameter of *The Peach Blossom Fan*, theater and role-playing is another. Seventeenth-century China was a theater-loving society; and as in the West, the metaphor of theater became a primary means to reflect on society and the roles of individuals within society. Juan Ta-ch'eng was not only a political opportunist, but also the foremost dramatist of his day, writing romantic comedies that seemed, to K'ung Shang-jen, to be the very embodiment of bad art, an indulgence in small-scale intrigue that was blind to larger social and political realities. K'ung Shang-jen took drama very seriously, seeing it as the contemporary form in which effective history could be written. In *The Peach Blossom Fan*, then, the Southern Ming regime is clearly compared to theater; it is a stage-managed affair, with an emperor who loves theater. On the other side are the courtesans and performers, such as Fragrant Princess and the storyteller, Liu Ching-t'ing, who actually become the heroes and heroines they learn to play. Toward the end of the play, the characters begin to desert the stage of Nanking.

Classroom Strategies

The headnote to the selection (pp. 71–74) suggests some of the issues that might be explored in class. *The Peach Blossom Fan* is an exceptionally well-constructed play and suffers from excerpting more than do most long Chinese works.

Fragrant Princess is originally a nameless adolescent girl. She is given a name and a role to play; in playing that role, she truly becomes her character and draws others in. Her "mother," Li Chen-li, becomes a true self-sacrificing mother, rather than simply the madam of a brothel. Hou Fang-yü becomes (or would become) a true husband and a noble figure, rather than a weak-willed young man who has purchased the virginity of a courtesan. Liu Ching-t'ing, the storyteller, becomes the kind of character he tells about in his stories. And, as suggested in the second topic below, even Juan Ta-ch'eng truly becomes a villain, because that is the role assigned to him. Only Yang Wen-ts'ung, the painter, stands above the unfolding drama, ready to intervene to complicate the story and keep it going.

Topics for Discussion

1. Consider the relationship between art and true feeling, comparing Fragrant Princess's singing lesson in scene 2 and her long lament at the beginning of scene 23. Why does Yang Wen-ts'ung paint the bloodstains into flowers later in scene 23?

   [In the singing lesson given by Su K'un-sheng, a passionate aria is interrupted constantly for the sake of "technique," calling attention to its artificiality. Fragrant Princess is literally "learning her role," but instead of learning to be an "actress," she learns to be the romantic heroine that actresses play. In the beginning of scene 27, she "is" the character she was supposed to learn to play. Yang Wen-ts'ung is attracted to the color of the blood, and there is a peculiar juxtaposition of art, with its own concerns of form and color, and the traces of human pain and suffering. Yang Wen-ts'ung intends only to "decorate" the fan, but Fragrant Princess awakes and recognizes in it her "portrait," the image of her fate.]

2. Contrast (in scene 7) Hou Fang-yü's initial response to Juan Ta-ch'eng's proposal with that of Fragrant Princess. Relate this to the question of Juan Ta-ch'eng as a villain.

   [Eventually in the play Juan Ta-ch'eng does become a true theatrical villain, but in the early scenes of the play he seems flawed and compromised, while also willing to compromise in order to be accepted by Nanking society. Other characters in the play "cast" him as a villain, and he eventually lives up to his role. In the scene in which Fragrant Princess rejects the trousseau, Hou Fang-yü is also willing to compromise at first; but Fragrant Princess, the romantic heroine, forces young Hou to be the romantic hero.]

3. Consider the role of the low, comic characters, especially at the beginning of scene 3, the end of scene 6, and the beginning of scene 7.

   [As in Shakespeare, Chinese plays use socially "low" characters to undercut the "high" characters and portray their problems and concerns from a different perspective. The ceremony in the Confucian temple, whose gravity and purity is supposedly undermined by the presence of Juan Ta-ch'eng, is initially shown from the point of view of the servants, taking stock of the ritual implements. Just as Li Chen-li reminds her daughter, the romantic heroine, how much things cost, the servants remind the audience how much the ceremony is grounded in commodities. The bawdy banter at the end of the wedding in scene 6 is more than simply the sexual good humor that was supposed to accompany weddings; it reminds the audience that this lofty scene of love is occurring in a brothel. Hou Fang-yü's "purchase" of Fragrant Princess's virginity is concealed under the fiction of the "gifts" provided by Juan Ta-ch'eng through Yang Wen-ts'ung—we are even told how much they cost. However, at the end of scene 6, we see sex as an explicitly commercial transaction. At the beginning of scene 7 the comic song of the maid reminds the audience of another fact of the brothels, namely, how it all comes down to bodily fluids and the uncertainty of paternity in such indiscriminate mixing.]

4. Discuss the question of theatricality in regard to scene 40.

[Chang Wei begins by conducting a ceremony for the dead Emperor Ch'ung-chen, after which there is a vision of the Ming martyrs and the villains all getting their just rewards. This brings the political "play" to a conclusion. Chang Wei is about to give a sermon on detachment, when the recognition scene between Hou Fang-yü and Fragrant Princess occurs. This scene was a staple of Chinese romantic comedies, but it is familiar enough in the Western tradition that students should be able to recognize it for what it is—the long-separated lovers rediscovering one another. Suddenly Chang Wei steps in and destroys the fan, in which so much feeling has been invested. Hou Fang-yü and Fragrant Princess seem intent on playing the end of their version of the play, enumerating their debts to the other characters; when Chang objects, Hou Fang-yü replies with the "happily ever after" pieties linked to the Confucian family. At this point Chang Wei tells them what this is—a bad performance of a play—and he reminds them that there is no world out there in which they can live happily ever after. Students do not like the sudden conversion of the lovers at this point, finding it somehow unnatural; "natural" here is nothing more than the powerful drive toward the conclusion of romantic comedy.]

Comparative Perspectives

1. What is there in the nature of playwriting that leads so many playwrights to question their art? Note that the villain of *The Peach Blossom Fan* writes plays. Compare the theatrical manipulations contrived by many of the major characters in *Hamlet*, including those of the protagonist himself, who writes a speech for the court performance of *The Murder of Gonzago*. Compare the condemnation of the shirking playwright in *Six Characters in Search of an Author*.

2. Hamlet warns Polonius to treat the visiting players well, for actors "are the abstracts and brief chronicles of the time." How is the warning reflected in the roles assigned to actors in the Chinese literature of the seventeenth century (*The Peach Blossom Fan*, *The Story of the Stone*)?

3. Note the treatment of political dissidents in *The Peach Blossom Fan*, and the burning of books to which tyrannical new rulers resort in hoping to solidify their power. Discuss responses to this threat against literary production in other texts you have studied, such as the *Popol Vuh* or Akhmatova's *Requiem*.

Further Reading

See also the reading suggestions in the anthology, p. 74.

Dolby, William. *A History of Chinese Drama*. 1976.

CAO XUEQIN (TS'AO HSÜEH-CH'IN)

The Story of the Stone

Backgrounds

The Story of the Stone is something like a cross between Proust, Jane Austen, and Thomas Mann's *Buddenbrooks*. Students may have the greatest difficulty with the unfamiliarity both of the society and of the details of daily life, of which there are a great many.

The Cao family had been a wealthy "bannerman" family, originally Chinese bondservants of the Manchu ruling house who were entrusted with major administrative duties when the Manchus conquered China. Cao Yin, Cao Xueqin's grandfather's brother, had been the textile commissioner in Suzhou and Nanjing, which meant, in effect, that he had control of a significant part of the Chinese silk trade. The family had grown immensely wealthy, and Cao Xueqin's father had inherited the post at an early age. Cao Xueqin's father lost a significant part of the family wealth in a political purge, and the family, in fallen circumstances, had moved to their mansion in Beijing. *The Story of the Stone* seems to have been something like a family project; manuscript versions circulated among the Caos and their friends, with commentators, apparently members of the family, adding interpretive judgments and suggestions for revision, measuring the events in the novel against their memories of the family history. Thus, while the novel does not address the question of memory internally as Proust's novel does, its composition and continual revision was a family project of memory.

Like many traditional Chinese novels, *The Story of the Stone* opens with a framing narrative in which the events of the novel are predestined. Much Chinese writing of the sixteenth through eighteenth century was concerned with *ging*, a broad term encompassing the full range of feeling from "sentiments" to "passion" and linked particularly to romantic love. Both Buddhism and Taoism, in different ways, sought *wuging*, "absence of passion," a detachment that recognizes all feeling as illusory. One means to achieve such enlightenment was to experience the full intensity of human feeling until all feeling was purged.

The opening allegory of Stone, which becomes a tangible object within the narrative, and the occasional appearance of the mendicant Buddhist and Taoist in the narrative remind the reader that on one level the events of the story are unreal. Bao-yu's name means "precious jade," and his surname Jia is homophonous with another Chinese character meaning "false" or, by this period, "fictive." Later in the novel Jia Bao-yu meets a young man his own age who looks very much like him named Zhen Bao-yu, which can be translated "Genuine Precious Jade." By the end of the novel the passions and losses that our Bao-yu has experience lead him to renounce the world and go off with the Buddhist and the Taoist. Thus, on one level, the novel is framed as an enlightenment narrative. This element of unreality is, however, effectively balanced by the novel's intense engagement in the concrete world and in the passion of the moment.

The question of gender is a strong motif in the novel. Bao-yu is "effeminate," not in the modern sense of the world but in its older usage, referring to a man who likes the company of women, takes on some of their characteristics, and is also sexually or romantically interested in them. In contrast, "masculine" characters prefer the company of other men and are characterized by a stylized roughness. In childhood, Bao-yu prefers the company of girls, finding in them a purity and sensibility missing from the crude company of boys. In early adolescence, he occasionally takes part in male gatherings, but even there he clearly prefers young men of sensibility, such as the boy actor Bijou, who gets Bao-yu into a good deal of trouble. Most of the males in the novel are represented as crude, violent, or hypocritical.

The world of women represented in the novel is one of enclosed intensities of feeling and sensibility—loves, kindnesses done, wounded feelings. This partially protected world is, however, never safe. Power can intrude from the outside, as when Jia Zheng almost whips Bao-yu to death. Authority is also dangerous from within, as when Lady Wang's anger drives the maid Golden to suicide. Unlike the world of Jane Austen, which the Garden in some ways resembles, Cao Xueqin's idyllic world is a very fragile one.

The literary self-consciousness of the novel's opening chapter is reinforced by the importance placed by the leading characters in the central, tragic love story on poetry. In Jane Austen's fictional world, to continue the comparison suggested above, an exchange of letters often allows characters to articulate and express feelings they could not easily acknowledge in person. The selections here illustrate the way in which poems carry the depth of the emotional attachment shared by Bao-yu and Dai-yu. In chapter 34, for example, Bao-yu sends a couple of his used handkerchiefs to Dai-yu, presumably as an excuse for Skybright to go between the two. Dai-yu recognizes this unusual offering as a gift of self and inscribes them with three poems. The third of her poems, rich with intertextual references, alludes to the doomed love of two imperial consorts.

The anthology then jumps to chapters 96 and 97, making it easy to see the morbid juxtaposition of teardrops, verses, and blood, mingled effusions of the self that fuel the immolation that prefigures Dai-yu's pathetic death. She burns the handkerchiefs that had absorbed Bao-yu's bodily fluids and had borne her poems as Dai-yu prepares to die. In chapter 98, not printed in the anthology, we learn that Dai-yu expires at the very moment the unwitting Bao-yu is married to the levelheaded and less literary Bao-chai.

Another way to approach the novel is to raise the question of hierarchy and power in the family, and to weigh it against the equalizing force of personal feelings. Bao-yu is at once the pampered male successor and someone who does try often to relate to others on an equal level—though that may be impossible.

On all levels there are those with less status vying for greater status. Lin Dai-yu's sense of her marginality in the family and her jealousy of the self-assured Bao-chai lead her sometimes to use Bao-yu's affection for her as a weapon. The hatred of Jia Huan, the son of a concubine, for his half-brother, the pampered Bao-yu, festers like a wound. And competition is frequently represented in stylized form, such as the song-composition competition at the gathering of young males, an act that reveals not only personality but gradations of sensibility. Beneath this idyll of childhood and the edenic Garden lurk forces constantly struggling to define a pecking order and to rise in that pecking order.

Classroom Strategies and Topics for Discussion

1. Comment on the role of hierarchy and authority within the family. How does Bao-yu fit in?

   [Bao-yu is the person for whom others exercise power. Even though he tries to hide his own authority, it is always present. One of the most serious moments is when, in a fit of rage, he kicks Aroma and wounds her. But he is never comfortable with his authority. There are conflicting hierarchies of age, gender, and status. Bao-yu's father should exercise absolute authority, but that power is circumvented by his mother, Grandmother Jia.]

2. Comment on the triangle formed by Bao-yu, Dai-yu, and Bao-chai.

Comparative Perspectives

1. Like *Monkey*, *The Story of the Stone* has been interpreted as a Buddhist allegory. How do the first chapter of the novel and the names of the characters contribute to this reading? Compare Cao Xueqin's management of "levels of interpretation" to Dante's in *The Divine Comedy* or to Thomas Mann's in *Death in Venice*.

2. Discuss the way references to literature and theater reveal character and character relationships in *The Story of the Stone*, and compare the use of such devices in Canto 5 of Dante's *Inferno*, *The Tale of Genji*, or *Madame Bovary*.

3. In the literature of late Imperial China, the life of servants comes clearly into view. How many social gradations may be discerned in this world? What did it mean to be a maid in a household like the Jia Rong compound? How does the novel treat the fate of Golden? Compare the role of servants in the literature of the European Enlightenment (Dorine in *Tartuffe*, Cacambo in *Candide*).

Further Reading

See also the reading suggestions in the anthology, p. 148.

Hsia, C. T. *The Classic Chinese Novel: A Critical Introduction.* 1968.

Li, Wai-yee. *Enchantment and Disenchantment: Love and Illusion in Chinese Literature.* 1993.

Yu, Anthony C. *Rereading the Stone: Desire and the Making of Fiction in Dream of the Red Chamber.* 1997. A superb study of the novel's self-reflexive awareness of its status as fiction; theoretically informed but not theory-driven, with an exhaustive bibliography.

The Ottoman Empire:
Çelebi's *Book of Travels*

EVLIYA ÇELEBI

The Book of Travels

Backgrounds

Evliya nearly always begins his description of a town with an account of how it got its name, followed by a few historical notes about its conquest by the Ottomans, then some administrative notes. In the case of Boudonítza, he is at a loss for the etymology of the name and none too clear about the history of conquest. All he can say is that it was "wrested from the hands of the French and Venetians" by Gazi Ömer Bey during the campaign that won Morea (Peloponnesus) for the Ottoman state. He gives a law of Sultan Suleyman I as authority for his statements about the administration, and he may actually be quoting from such a document, but no great reliance can be put on the details. Evliya is aware of, and distressed by, the decline in administrative probity in his own time, and when he refers to rules laid down over a hundred years before, his intention is usually to suggest that current conditions are sadly deficient.

It is clear that Boudonítza in Evliya's time was a poor and rather neglected town, even as it is now. If Evliya had not set his imagination to work, there would be less to say about it than about the more prosperous villages in the vicinity. He tells us that the position of judge for the administration of Islamic law is worth a hundred and fifty *aspers* (this is a silver coin—a direct descendant of the small silver coins of the Byzantine empire, and by Evliya's time almost as debased and worthless). That sum represents a poor living indeed, and it is not surprising that Evliya's fantastic tale includes a picture of the judge as a grasping miser. There is a commander of the local feudal levy, who probably has nothing to do at all, because there are no working fiefs any longer, and a captain of Janissaries, who is there to keep some small degree of order when traveling squads of Janissaries on detached assignment arrive to be quartered and maintained at the cost of the local populace. There are three officials in charge of commercial matters: one a sort of market inspector, one to collect the annual taxes from the non-Muslim population, and one to levy transit dues, since Boudonítza's one asset is its position on the only major land route from Northern to Central Greece. In the fortress there is supposed to be a garrison of one hundred men who will have been sent out by the central government. Castle garrisons normally were made up of some nonlocal population, in the belief that they were less likely, in that case, to make common cause with a local rebellion. Evliya finishes by saying with gentle sarcasm that the "great magnates" of the town are all poor.

Classroom Strategies

A single assignment.

Topics for Discussion and Writing

Until the bloody fighting between Serbs and Bosnians broke out in 1991, we in the West had been in the habit of thinking of the Islamic world as entirely separate from our own, but here we see Muslims and Christians sharing the same community and even, rather surprisingly, making common cause against an official that both find oppressive.

It is tempting to dismiss the miracles that Evliya recounts with such enthusiasm, but the belief in miracles was as widespread among Europeans as it was among Muslims (cf. Geoffrey Chaucer in volume B). Moreover, it continues to the present day as a recurrent feature of popular belief. In Evliya's account, the miracle has gained an institutional sanction by its association with the sufi cloister. It also provides an explanation for the conversion of the formerly Christian population to Islam that is more appealing than such alternatives as coercion on the part of the Muslims or economic opportunism on the part of the Christians.

The inclusion in *The Book of Travels* of passages that are so clearly fantastic raises once again the question of the uncertain boundary between truth and fiction in Islamic prose literature (cf. Sa'di's *Golestan*). From our point of view, it is a hybrid text: a mixture of truth and fiction, a genre popular in premodern Europe as well as Islam.

Comparative Perspectives

1. Although Voltaire surely had never read *The Book of Travels*, he could almost be accused of having its catalogue of outrageous and miraculous deeds in mind in his skewering of the conventions of travel literature. Compare Evliya's description of his experience in the city of Boudonítza with Voltaire's account of Candide's travels. What kind of stylistic gestures distinguish Evliya's piety from Voltaire's satire?

2. Evliya explains that Boudonítza was vulnerable to the attack of the pirate Captain Giorgio because the corrupt judge had trampled on the rights of the "tributary subjects," non-Muslims who were expected to pay taxes while they lived under Islamic rule. What other works have you studied that show the tolerance of non-Muslims that traditional Islamic practice dictates?

3. The articles left behind by pilgrims to the shrine of Saint Veliüllah
    and the "apparatus and paraphernalia" of the dervishes figure im-
    portantly in Evliya's narrative. Discuss the different attitudes toward
    property in some of the pilgrimage stories that you have read.

    [Examples include *The Canterbury Tales* and *The Narrow Road of
    the Interior*.]

Further Reading

See also the reading suggestions in the anthology, p. 284.

Robert Dankoff, ed. and trans. *Evliya Chelebi in Bitlis: The Relevant Section of the Seyahatname*. 1990. With commentary and an introduction
by Dankoff.

The Enlightenment in Europe

JEAN-BAPTISTE POQUELIN MOLIÈRE

Tartuffe

Classroom Strategies and Topics for Discussion

The biggest problem for students who are reading *Tartuffe* for the first time is likely to be the expectations they bring to the play. If they anticipate characters with realistically conceived psychologies, and events closely resembling what might occur in ordinary life, they will be bewildered and irritated. It is important, therefore, to explain in advance that the play depends on the particular forms of artifice we call *convention*.

In the first place, it relies on the set of *dramatic* conventions associated with the comedy of manners. These conventions include the use of type characters, figures differentiated by role rather than by psychology. Students can probably identify many of the types in *Tartuffe* themselves, once alerted to the presence of type characters: the hypocrite, the clever maid, the blustering young man, the foolish but tyrannical father, the naive young girl, and so on. Equally conventional is the structure of the plot, dependent not on plausibility but on the design of providing pleasure (including particularly the pleasure of surprise) by its ingenuity and of demonstrating the restoration of a just social order and the punishment of deviants from that order.

The play also assumes a set of *social* conventions. These have to do with the kind and degree of authority exercised by the father of a family. A father, for instance, has absolute power over his daughter's marital choices; he may be argued with but not refused. A wife's chastity is of paramount importance to her husband. A son's economic status depends entirely on his father's will. Thus the father's role in the family resembles the king's in the country—a point of some importance to the ending of *Tartuffe*.

It is especially useful in teaching this play to read aloud sequences with different members of the class assuming different roles. Only thus will students realize the brilliance of the verse, the wit of the language (e.g., "You deserve to be tartuffified") and rhymes (e.g., "fossil" and "docile")—effects approximating in English the dramatist's achievement in French—the speed and economy with which Molière conveys necessary information and moves the plot along, the sheer *fun* of language and event.

The first scene is a good place to start, both for reading aloud and for

15

analysis. Mme. Pernelle's initial haste ("Come, come, Flipote, it's time I left this place": students should think about how the entrance would be staged, with everyone rushing to keep up with Mme. Pernelle), when contrasted with her leisure for denunciation, extending to everyone in the household except Tartuffe, of course creates comedy. One might ask whether it has also a serious point. It announces a theme that runs through the play: the degree to which people are driven by their own obsessions to be blind to the needs of others. If students are asked for examples of this pattern, they will probably mention Tartuffe and Orgon (perhaps the brilliant scene in which Orgon hears of his wife's illness but concerns himself only with "poor Tartuffe"), but Damis, Mariane, and Valère are also relevant. What else does the first scene accomplish? It introduces the presence of Tartuffe they get from this scene; later in the discussion, they might pursue the ways that this impression is elaborated and modified as the play goes on. And the scene sketches, mainly from Mme. Pernelle's distorted point of view, characteristics of the play's persons. What notion does one get of each? It introduces Dorine as a young woman exceptionally willing to state her own opinions. Does one trust her view or Mme. Pernelle's more fully? What aspects of their accounts of other people make them seem more or less trustworthy?

Many individual scenes of the play reward similar analysis. Particularly rich are the farcical scene between Valère and Dorine (II.4) and the seduction scene, with Orgon under the table (IV.5). Analysis of almost any scene can lead to investigation of the play's larger issues. A few general points worth pursuing: *Is* this comedy in fact antireligious, or does it only attack corruptions of religion? (Opinions may differ here; the point is to get students to support their opinions by reference to the text.) In Act IV, Scene 3, Elmire remarks, "My taste is for good-natured rectitude." Is "good-natured rectitude" the implicit value advocated by the play? How does the concept of rectitude relate to the common sense consistently exemplified by Cléante? (Cléante's role is worth extended discussion. What, exactly, does his common sense involve? What sort of view of human nature does he seem to have? Why does Orgon refuse to pay attention to him?) How serious a criticism of society does this play offer? In other words, is its purpose only to entertain, or does it aspire to educate as well?

In working out answers to such questions, it is worth thinking about what causes characters to be deluded. The ridiculous misunderstanding between Valère and Mariane comes partly from the wish of each to have the other acknowledge need or desire first. If Valère proclaimed his love when Mariane was actually willing to marry someone else, he would appear weak; conversely, if Mariane says she won't marry Tartuffe because she loves Valère, she gives him the upper hand. Similar issues of power emerge in every situation. Orgon feels himself powerful in his role of benevolent patron to Tartuffe; he must believe in Tartuffe's goodness in order to believe in his own magnanimity. Tartuffe, to take the most obvious example, gains power by proclaiming his weakness and humility. This common element in the characters' motivation is worth emphasizing because it calls attention to the fact that the play lights up issues of perennial concern, not simply those inherent in a society with religious and political structures quite different from our own.

Some time should be spent on the question of plot and how it works here. Tartuffe's will to power (including the power of wealth) and Orgon's determination to indulge him are the motivating forces producing an intertwined sequence of events that seem inevitable, given the premises. Students might be asked at what points in the play they were surprised by what happened next. Any answers to this question would be worth pursuing, to try to ascertain whether surprise reflects a real failure of plausibility or a failure of expectation. The most likely moments of surprise are Tartuffe's attempt to seize the house, after he is unmasked and one expects all problems to be solved, and the final intervention of the king. Both are particularly useful to discuss. The first surprise derives from our expectations of comedy: we anticipate no really serious problems, and we assume that difficulties will be readily resolved in a comic scheme. Molière's extra twist serves as a reminder that the problems announced in this play *are* in fact serious—and perhaps as a reminder that in the real world they are not so easily solved.

The matter of the king is more complicated. To twentieth-century sensibilities, this may seem an arbitrary intervention or a piece of gross flattery; and perhaps it cannot be fully justified. But it can at least be argued that the introduction of the king as a force in the action serves as a reminder that the family is a microcosm for larger patterns of social organization. Order must be restored in the family for order to operate in the kingdom; and it is only by the exercise of authority, in this play, that order exists.

Topics for Writing

1. The function of the mother-in-law (Mme. Pernelle).
2. The importance of seeing in *Tartuffe*.
3. The voice of reason in *Tartuffe*.
4. What kinds of emotion are important in the play?
5. Secrets and secrecy in *Tartuffe*.

Comparative Perspectives

1. Compare the kinds of conventions employed by Molière and by Brecht in *The Good Woman of Setzuan* or by K'ung Shang-jen in *The Peach Blossom Fan*. How do characters speak? Are these plays aiming for "realism"? How would you describe the relationship between the reality of a stage performance and our perception of actual events in our own lives?
2. Who possesses "common sense" in Molière's theater and other literary works of the Enlightenment that you have read? Compare the way class status contributes to the experience of passion in Chinese literature of the same period.

Further Reading

See also the reading suggestions in the anthology, pp. 305–06.

Gaines, J. F. and M. S. Koppisch, eds. *Approaches to Teaching Molière's* Tartuffe *and Other Plays.* 1995. A volume in the MLA series.

Gossman, L. *Man and Masks.* 1963. Looks at Molière in his historical situation, with emphasis on his continuing relevance to the present as well as on the way he embodies ideas important in his own time.

Guicharnaud, J., ed. *Molière: A Collection of Critical Essays.* 1964. Exemplifies diverse approaches and includes a particularly valuable group of seven essays under the rubric "The Art of Comedy."

Hubert, J. *Molière and the Comedy of Intellect.* 1962. Particularly useful for teachers: studies the playwright's "achievement as a creator of dramatic and poetic forms," emphasizing the inner coherence and the moral vision of Molière's work as a whole. The chapter on *Tartuffe*, "Hypocrisy as Spectacle," is rich in insight.

Jagendorf, Zvi. *The Happy End of Comedy.* 1984. Treats Molière's comedies in relation to Shakespeare's and Ben Jonson's.

McBride, R. *The Sceptical Vision of Molière.* 1977. Organized around the idea of paradox, with an introductory section about the relation between Molière as moralist and as comic artist, followed by a detailed study of how the playwright's thought is embodied in his comedy.

Walker, H. *Molière.* 1971. This introductory volume in the Twayne series provides a brief biography, thematically organized analysis of the plays, and valuable bibliography.

JEAN RACINE

Phaedra

Classroom Strategies and Topics for Discussion

Even if they have already read Molière, students may have trouble with the artifice and formality of Racine. To encounter characters who make pronouncements about their feelings in blank verse, with none of the comic relief familiar from Shakespeare, often proves a forbidding experience. The problems that preoccupy these characters seem remote from common twentieth-century life; the personages on the stage do not invite easy identification from the audience. But all is not lost. Although students should probably be told at the outset enough about seventeenth-century tragic convention to understand that they are to look at and learn from these characters, not instantly perceive them as analogs for the self, in fact it is possible to find in the long run important points of contact between the constructed world whose inhabitants concern themselves with conflicts of love and virtue and our own time and experience.

To achieve such a result demands attention to the play's detail. Although it is possible to read the entire drama as a single assignment, it lends itself well to a two-part division: the first three acts, then the final two. A good place to start discussion is with Phaedra's first important speech—her explanation to Oenone, in Act I, of the source of her distress. Reading this speech aloud facilitates talk about the function of the play's sonorous verse. Even in translation, one can feel how the dignity and control of language and meter provide a counterpoint for the chaotic emotion they render. The dramatist is always in control, although the characters are not necessarily able to keep a sense of mastery, and the poetic authority of Racine's voice (behind Phaedra's) affirms the possibility of restored human order—that possibility clearly announced at the play's ending.

But the content of Phaedra's speech also deserves attention. Her initial characterization of her love for Hippolytus as "My ills" sets the tone for her utterance as a whole, with its emphasis on evil, pain, and misery. Students might be asked to find the metaphors in this passage. The imagery emphasizes war and sickness: metaphors that run through the play. You might ask where else such metaphors occur; the answers will help students see how imagery creates and emphasizes unity. This speech also brings up the large question of Phaedra's responsibility for her own and other people's suffering. She sees herself as helpless ("Venus fastens on her helpless prey"); is she? This is not, of course, the kind of question that has a preestablished answer, but students should be urged to find evidence for their position on either side. If they believe that Phaedra's love has overcome her with no possibility for her to resist, is she to be held responsible for her further acts, for confessing her love to Hippolytus and condoning Oenone's terrible lie about him? How does one determine human responsibility in a world governed by gods and goddesses? Are we to take these deities simply as projections of human feelings? If so, Phaedra *is* responsible. In that case, does she become villain rather than victim? The problem of moral responsibility is a powerful issue in the play, as in our lives. One way of understanding Phaedra's insistence that Venus is to blame is to recall our modern tendency to see criminals as "sick" rather than wicked, ourselves as formed by our heredity and environment rather than our wills. But no matter how much we blame our parents for what is wrong with us, we are left with a residue of feeling that it is all our fault. So is Phaedra. Discussion of the final two acts of the play should obviously involve attention to how Phaedra's suicide modifies our sense of her disclaiming responsibility.

Oenone's speech in response to Phaedra's revelation (after the interruption of Panope) brings up further large issues. The nurse speaks, typically, in a voice of common sense. She invokes public opinion, a mother's obligation to her child, tactics for appealing to Hippolytus. Of course her advice proves fatally wrong. Does this fact suggest anything about the value attached to "common sense" in the play? Why does common sense seem altogether irrelevant to the characters' real problems? To investigate such questions leads one to understand the insistent claims within the play that human dilemmas must be comprehended first of all in moral rather than in pragmatic terms. Oenone does not think primarily about right and wrong; Phaedra tries to, but often fails. Yet right and wrong remain the crucial issues of this drama.

To speak of "right and wrong" brings up the whole matter of "virtue," allegedly Hippolytus's defining characteristic. A teacher might ask why Hippolytus is so completely vulnerable. The answer must surely involve the character's claim to virtue. He knows himself to be good and believes goodness to be sufficient protection; the innocent, he fancies, must triumph. But he is wrong—not only mistaken because he inhabits a corrupt world, but mistaken because his smugness about his own virtue involves ignoring the claims and the feelings of other people. Oenone observes to Phaedra, "You must give up, since honor is at stake, / Everything, even virtue, for its sake" (III.3); she values the reputation of virtue more highly than the thing itself. She is wrong too: neither honor nor virtue is sufficient in itself.

Such general formulations are less important than the means of reaching them: by close attention to the language of the text, which provides material for many kinds of formulation. Other large questions that discussion might engage include why and how the past is important in this play. The past figures as both public history (the history of rulers and governments) and private (the history of families, frequently and emphatically alluded to). It is also involved in allusions to gods and goddesses: in the background is a history of relations between deities and mortals. Such stress on the past emphasizes the fact that here no act occurs in isolation. People cannot act independently of other people, as Hippolytus must tragically learn, and they cannot cut themselves loose from what has happened before them. Why is there so much stress in the play on Theseus's womanizing? Sometimes this seems an aspect of his heroism; sometimes it seems a flaw. Hippolytus's attitude toward it emphasizes both his own inadequacy and his moral superiority. It underlines the whole problem of sexual feeling that lies at the heart of the drama. Sexuality appears to be the primary source of human vulnerability: it gets Theseus into trouble; it kills Phaedra and Hippolytus; it makes Aricia miserable. It seems to lie outside the control of reason—a fact that must be taken into consideration in any discussion of the function of reason as an ideal in this action. How do issues of power become part of issues of love here? Private politics reflects public. Not only do actual and potential sexual alliances literally affect government, but they too involve complex patterns of dominance and submission that can be traced through the play. And finally, what about the play's ending? Does one believe in the reconciliation that Theseus proposes? How does one feel about Phaedra's final "purity" (the last word she speaks)? Again, there is no "right" answer, but discussion of such problems calls attention to the fact that the play demands, and usually receives, complicated emotional responses from its readers. Such responses reveal that the problems it engages remain dilemmas that concern us all, even though we typically put them in less elevated terms.

Topics for Writing

1. The role of Oenone.
2. The meaning of Hippolytus's death.
3. Theseus as a father.
4. The emotional effect of any single speech and how it is achieved (for example, Phaedra's speech to Hippolytus, II.5.90–131; Hippolytus to Aricia, V.1.11–47).
5. Phaedra as a strong woman.
6. Phaedra as a weak woman.

Comparative Perspectives

1. Hippolytus fears Phaedra, "the child of Minos and Pasiphaë." Show how her heritage is linked to the treatment of sexuality in this neoclassical play, and discuss the way it expresses an Enlightenment view of irrational desire. Contrast the imagery associated with other seductive females, such as Manago in *Bewitched* or Keats's Belle Dame sans Merci.

   [Racine, like his model, Euripides, treated Phaedra's passion as a derangement, typified by the imagery of monsters, bulls, and dragons. The frightening vision of Manago in her demonic form emphasizes the monstrosity of her desire. Keats's beautiful lady is no less fatal, but as a figment of the Romantic imagination recycling the conventions of Arthurian romance, she is a creature of fairyland enchantment rather than brute passion. If your students have read Malory's *Morte Darthur* or Marie de France's *Lanval*, comparisons would be instructive.]

2. Theseus, Phaedra, and Hippolytus are the actors in a tragic triangle oddly like the one that traps Melville's Captain Vere, Mr. Claggart, and Billy Budd. Discuss the roles played by the key figures (choose any pair or write a long essay discussing all three): the paternal Theseus/Vere; the predatory Phaedra/Claggart; the innocent Hippolytus/Billy. How does an analysis of their motives and personalities clarify the difference between Racine's view of good and evil and Melville's? How are subtle psychosexual conflicts addressed by each author?

   [Racine draws on the ancient classical tradition, Melville on the biblical; their moral universes differ, although their plots share many assumptions. Venus has Phaedra in her clutches; what impels both Claggart and Vere in their fixations on the Handsome Sailor is not so clearly delineated or, perhaps, understood.)

Further Reading

See also the reading suggestions in the anthology, p. 364.

Burnley, A. M. *Lilith Raging: The Gender Crisis and Alienation in the Theatre of Jean Racine.* 1989. Strong feminist interpretation.

Cloonan, W. *Racine's Theatre: The Politics of Love.* 1977. A study of the conflict between the personal emotion of love and the socially accepted ideal of glory that examines the "quest for reconciliation between personal needs and the legitimate obligations which society must impose upon its members."

Goldmann, L. *Racine.* Trans. A. Hamilton. 1972. A Marxist analysis that reviews biographical data and studies the development and structure of Racine's drama.

King, R. *Racine: Modern Judgments.* 1969. Includes pieces on structure, detail, style, and tradition.

Turnell, M. *Jean Racine, Dramatist.* 1972. A thorough and illuminating study of the "dramatic experience" Racine provides, with attention to versification and staging as well as theme and structure.

Weinberg, B. *The Art of Jean Racine.* 1963. An investigation of Racine's dramatic development that demonstrates how the art of each play builds on that of its predecessors.

SOR JUANA INÉS DE LA CRUZ

Reply to Sor Filotea de la Cruz

Classroom Strategies and Topics for Discussion

Perhaps the most interesting aspect of Sister Juana's polemical *Reply*, from the point of view of modern readers, is its use of autobiography as an element of argument. A class discussion of the work can profitably be organized around this topic.

Such a discussion might start with a question about what the author is arguing for in the essay as a whole—or, as usefully, what she is arguing against. Students may conclude that she wishes to defend the right of women to learning; alternately, that she wants to defend herself against charges of presumption, impiety, or unwomanliness. Other formulations of the grounds of argument are possible, but all will probably fall into one or the other category: arguments about Sister Juana's own role, or arguments about the position of women in general. The relation between the two categories—Sister Juana in particular, women in general—provides a way to focus discussion.

The first few pages of the *Reply* consist mainly of apologies, couched in a tone of extreme deference ("my clumsy pen"; "your most learned, most prudent, most holy, and most loving letter"). What purpose do they serve in the piece as a whole? Whether or not they are asked to make such a judgment, students are likely to volunteer that Sister Juana does not sound "sincere." Such a comment supplies a useful opening. Is it possible that Sister Juana doesn't *wish* to sound sincere, that she is heavily ironic in her insistence on her own comparative inadequacy and she wants the irony to show? She thus dramatizes the posture of humility expected of women and suggests her own discontent with it. Increasingly as her essay continues, the reader is forced to realize the discrepancy between her elaborate pose of ignorance and her rhetorical skill.

The autobiographical section of the *Reply* begins with Sister Juana's assertion of her "vehement . . . overpowering" inclination toward learning. It concentrates mainly on her intellectual life—but the intellectual and the emotional merge for this writer, and in a sense that merging is the subject of the autobiography. Students can be asked to locate the various ways and places in which the writer conveys her intense feelings about learning. Does she also communicate emotions about other matters? What is she trying to establish in her "autobiography"? Most autobiographies dwell on a sequence of experience; Sister Juana appears less concerned with experience than with character. She primarily wants us to know not what she has done or what has happened to her but what kind of person she is. What kind of person *is* she? If students disagree on this matter, the disagreement can be made the starting point for detailed discussion not only of what kind of character emerges from this narrative but of the strategies Sister Juana uses for conveying character.

Autobiography in effect merges with argument at various points—for example, in the paragraph in which Sister Juana speaks of the inspiration she has found in books and lists the gifted women who appear in the Bible. Such a passage not only tells us of Sister Juana's reading and her reaction to it; it also contributes to a larger argument about the capacities and rights of women. You might invite your students to locate other passages in which the writer's personal experience—particularly her experience of books—is recorded in ways suggesting her views about the nature of women.

Sister Juana's career is obviously an unusual one, and she presents herself as a phenomenon among women. What makes her "special"? The question is worth considering in some detail: perhaps one might conclude that her intellectual enthusiasm and capacity are no more remarkable than is her relative lack of interest in the ordinary social life of the convent. Her revelation of genuine passion also helps to define her specialness: the sheer intensity of her feeling, and her willingness to make it known, differentiate her from other women.

But if Sister Juana differs dramatically from others of her sex, the question recurs: How does her autobiography relate to her argument about the status of women in general? A remarkable aspect of the *Reply* is its combination of assertions of uniqueness with the implication that many women, given the opportunity, might display comparable capacities. Indeed, the repeated allusions to the author's inadequacies emphasize her insistence that many women, despite social restrictions, have demonstrated their ability to rule, to teach, to write. She narrates her own struggles to learn as part of an argument that women should routinely receive opportunities for education. What makes her "special," she implicitly argues, is not her intellectual gifts so much as her will to develop them. Her desire for learning—which she alludes to as a "torment" and as an "ungovernable force"—drives her to surmount the limitations imposed on women.

The *Reply* makes a powerful case for the value of learning in itself—a value equally great for men and for women. Love of wisdom, Sister Juana maintains, constitutes a ground for persecution: people hate the person who claims intellectual authority, who demonstrates intellectual vitality. But the writer herself has been willing to endure obloquy for the sake of her endless mental activity. How does she make the reader feel that the pleasure of thought and writing is worth the pain of social disapproval? It might be worth drawing attention to the passages in which children are playing spillikins. Both provide instances of Sister Juana's indefatigable spirit of inquiry; they exemplify the nature of intellectual inquiry in general at the same time that they tell us of this woman's special ways of pursuing it.

Topics for Writing

1. Examine Sister Juana's use of specific detail as an element in her argument.
2. What is Sister Juana's attitude toward the power of language? How does she convey this attitude? How important is it in her argument as a whole?
3. What is the dominant emotion of the *Reply*? Self-pity? Pride? Anger? Write a paper maintaining the primary importance of one emotion in Sister Juana's essay.
4. Discuss the functions of biblical allusion in the *Reply*.
5. Write an essay in which you use some element or elements in your own experience as the foundation for a serious argument.

Comparative Perspectives

1. As a child, Sister Juana reports, she asked her mother to dress her in boy's clothing and send her to study at the university. How did she manage to acquire her education? Compare the fate of the fictional sister of Shakespeare in Virginia Woolf's *A Room of One's Own*. How does Woolf's motive differ from Sister Juana's? Why did Woolf prefer not to document the few remarkable women who gained knowledge by their own efforts?
2. Sister Juana cuts off her hair to force herself to learn more quickly, although she knows that among young women, "the natural adornment of one's hair is held in such high esteem." Finally, she enters the convent (where women had their heads shorn). What other works have you read that emphasize the importance of a woman's hair? Why does it seem to have so much symbolic value in such a range of cultures and times?
   [Examples include *Paradise Lost, Hedda Gabler, The Love Song of J. Alfred Prufrock.*]
3. *The Sultan's Dilemma* is set in the seventeenth century, the same

time period during which Sister Juana lived. What attitude toward a
learned woman do we see in the play?

Further Reading

See also the reading suggestions in the anthology, p. 404.

Apart from the Twayne volume cited in the anthology, virtually all the
available English-language material on Sister Juana occurs in the context
of broader discussions.

Anderson-Imbert, Enrique. *Spanish-American Literature: A History.* Revised by Elaine Malley. Vol. 1. 1969. Sets Sister Juana's writing in its
historical context.

Henriquez-Urena, Pedro. *Literary Currents in Hispanic America.* 1945.
Given as the Norton Lectures at Harvard, these essays offer a good introduction to Sister Juana in relation to her contemporaries and her
successors.

Montross, Constance M. *Virtue or Vice?: Sor Juana's Use of Thomistic
Thought.* 1981. A fairly technical study of Sister Juana's theological position.

Torres-Rioseco, Arturo. *The Epic of Latin American Literature.* 1942. Another general treatment, which sets Sister Juana in her literary context.

JONATHAN SWIFT

Gulliver's Travels

Classroom Strategies and Topics for Discussion

Students may well be bewildered by the sometimes bland, sometimes
ferocious tone of *Gulliver's Travels*, part IV, and by such questions as:
What is Swift attacking? Why? What does it have to do with us? and,
most troubling of all, How can we be sure?—exactly the questions that
have disturbed generations of critics. It may be useful at the outset to
point out that a minimal definition of satire is "attack by indirection" and
to discuss the possibility that one important satiric function, often, is to
generate just the kind of trouble the students are presumably experienc-
ing. *Gulliver's Travels* creates uncertainty partly because of society's constantly changing assumptions about what is important, what is *good*, for
human beings. Swift concerns himself with such fundamental values. If
he can make his readers inquire about their own assumptions, as well as
about how matters should be, he has achieved part of his aim. His kind of
satire does not produce certainties; it produces difficulties.

One can profitably organize discussion around a series of large and obvious questions, with special attention to the need to support hypotheses
from the text. First of all, what is the relation between the Yahoos and humankind? In answering (or attempting to answer) this question, one must
consider the development of Gulliver's attitude toward them. At the out-

set, he says, "I never beheld in all my travels so disagreeable an animal, or one against which I naturally conceived so strong an antipathy" (p. 439). This response suggests that the Yahoos belong to an alien species. But Gulliver's convictions change, influenced partly by the assumptions of his Houyhnhnm hosts, who believe him to be of the Yahoo kind. The episode in which the young Yahoo girl pursues Gulliver with lustful intent might suggest that they belong to a single species. By the end, Gulliver believes all the rest of humanity to be Yahoos, but appears to exempt himself. He is, at any rate, a Yahoo educated in a way no other human being has enjoyed. If we accept Gulliver's view, we must understand this volume of *Gulliver's Travels* as constituting an unrelenting and total attack on humankind.

The problem of how far we can accept Gulliver's view must be dealt with fairly early in the discussion; it will certainly come up in the course of considering the Yahoo question. Evidence for Gulliver's state of mind after his sojourn with the Houyhnhnms comes from the book's final chapters and from the prefatory letter to Gulliver's cousin Sympson (which students should be urged to read, or to reread, *after* reading the narrative proper). The question can be formulated as one of delusion: is Gulliver deluded after his journey? Does his attack on pride only conceal his own pride, his overweening desire to escape the limits of the human situation? In trying to decide how far we can accept his judgment (e.g., his judgment that human beings are Yahoos), one must try to assess the forces possibly operating to distort his judgment: for example, the pressures inherent in the master-slave relationship in which he finds himself.

The obvious corollary to the Yahoo question is the Houyhnhnm question. Whether or not people and Yahoos are the same, do Houyhnhnms represent an ideal for humanity? Considering this matter implies not only further speculation about Gulliver's dependability but direct assessment of the evidence. What are the characteristics of this race? Most salient, of course, is their allegiance to reason. They believe that reason is sufficient guide for a reasonable being. Is this conviction relevant to the realities of human existence? How does one respond to their lack of literature, to their difficulty in finding subject matter for conversation (Gulliver provides useful material for their talk), to such activities as their threading of needles, to their attitudes toward their young? If one has negative responses to any of their manifestations of commitment to reason, do such responses declare something wrong with them or something wrong with us?

The part of the book dealing with Gulliver's activities and responses after leaving the Houyhnhnms deserves particularly close attention. What does it mean, in Swift's satiric structure, that he is wounded by the arrow of savages? Certainly this fact suggests that man in the state of nature is brutal and far from being governed by reason and benevolence. But the character of the Portuguese captain also demands attention. Here is a civilized man, acting with generosity and sympathy in the face of Gulliver's boorishness. Does the existence of such a man refute the identification of humanity with the Yahoos? What differences does it suggest between humanity and the Houyhnhnms? If Gulliver seems wrong (misguided) in his response to the captain's kindness, how does this fact bear on our assessment of his judgments?

The answers for this series of questions are largely indeterminate, and this fact itself must become an issue for discussion. It brings up a historical problem: does our difficulty in ascertaining where Swift stands come simply from the time that has elapsed since he wrote? One must suspect that shifts in general assumptions between the eighteenth century and the twentieth century help to account for the problematic aspects of this satire, but the difficulty in determining the exact scope of the attack is also partly built into the text. The historical problem, however, also creates an opportunity to raise the question of how far Swift's satire remains relevant to our own time, in which wars and lawyers and doctors and politicians continue to provide manifestations of folly and vice and in which questions about the human capacity for reason and virtue continue to present themselves.

One problem about teaching *Gulliver's Travels* (it is a problem in teaching everything, of course—but particularly here) is that of time. The general issues sketched above are peculiarly compelling, and they are *essential* to minimal understanding of the narrative. But Swift's local effects also deserve attention. If time permits, it is useful to take up such episodes as Gulliver's early conduct toward the Houyhnhnms (his assumption that they are to be won by bracelets and mirrors) and his recital to his master about the nature of civilized life. Students need to understand that in the structure of the narrative, Gulliver's account demonstrates considerable distortion and exaggeration, attributable to his desire to impress his master in various ways; and also that, in the structure of the satire, it exemplifies exactly the kind of distortion that generates emotional power. If it is not always clear what designs *Gulliver's Travels* has on the reader in the most general sense, it is clear that it attacks specific corruptions of eighteenth-century English society in a way that makes it relevant to our own.

A Modest Proposal

Classroom Strategies and Topics for Discussion

Virtually every teacher has at least one anecdote about trying to teach *A Modest Proposal* to a class whose members insisted on taking it straight, unable to comprehend the nature of Swift's irony. As the horrors of the modern age multiply, it becomes harder and harder to appeal to universal standards of decency, to insist that of course we all know that no one would seriously consider eating children. Human skin has been made into lampshades; why shouldn't babies be made into meat? The problems of teaching this work, then, are clear-cut: to help students find the clues to Swiftian irony, and to make them understand what as well as how the satirist attacks.

One way to start is with the character of the speaker. What sort of person does he seem to be? Undergraduates can readily be brought to recognize his self-image as a practical, sensible man, fond of statistics ("three, four, or six children") and of economic solutions ("a fair, cheap, and easy method"), not devoid of vanity (he would like to have his statue set up as a preserver of the nation), both self-confident and ambitious (see the third paragraph). Students should be asked to read the opening paragraphs with particular care, and asked what is the first word that begins to make one suspicious about this projector. For most readers, it is "dam," in the fourth paragraph, with its suggestion that the speaker thinks of human beings, if they are poor, as identical with lower animals. One can trace further evidence of the projector's inhumanity, his incapacity to imagine the poor (or at least the Irish poor) as beings like himself, throughout the satire.

The speaker objects to his friend's proposal of butchering starving adolescents on the grounds that it might be censured as "a little bordering upon cruelty." Why does he not think of his own proposal as cruel? This topic is worth extended consideration. One can examine the various ways in which the projector demonstrates the need for drastic measures; the cruelty of the existing state of things, he implicitly and explicitly argues, far exceeds that of his scheme for remedying the situation. Particular attention should be paid to the italicized paragraph of "other expedients" that Swift would in fact advocate. What are these expedients like? It should be noted that they combine the practical and the moral; that they demand clear perception, concerted action, and steady moral awareness. The speaker's doubt that there will ever be a sincere attempt to put them in practice therefore suggests that Swift is criticizing the Irish people as well as their English oppressors.

This text of course provides abundant opportunity for talking about the classic problems of satire. Students might be interested to discuss the question of whether such writing as this implies any real purpose of reform or whether it constitutes only attack; they might wish to talk about how the satire makes them feel, and why. (Indeed, such an apparently naive approach to the work might be a profitable way to start.)

Topics for Writing

1. The importance of Gulliver's initial situation (how he is cast ashore) to the narrative.
2. How Gulliver sees himself.
3. A specific object of attack and how it is criticized.
4. Why are horses (rather than some other species) made creatures of pure reason?
5. A definition of a Yahoo.
6. A modest proposal for our time.
7. Has Swift any hope for Ireland?

Comparative Perspectives

1. Like the readers of this anthology, Gulliver constantly finds himself in contact with strange worlds. What marks of cultural difference does he distinguish in the Houyhnhnms and the Yahoos that make them unlike their counterparts in England? How good an observer is he? Do you find yourself confronting similar signs of difference in any of the works you have been reading this semester? Give some examples and compare your criteria for evaluating what you have discovered with those used by Gulliver.
2. "The Houyhnhnms have no letters, and consequently, their knowledge is all traditional," Gulliver declares in the middle of chapter IX, but he praises their poetry. Writing in the 1700s, Swift may very well have had an opinion of this critical pronouncement quite different from ours. What works of oral cultures prove that poetry can exist without "letters"?
3. Impressed by the truthfulness of a society that lacks a word for "lie," Gulliver takes great pains in his conclusion to set himself apart from other travelers whose descriptions of their voyages "impose the grossest falsities on the unwary reader." Is factual accuracy always the best measure of truth? Have you read any travel accounts in this anthology that challenge Gulliver's strictures here? Why do their writers sometimes say *the thing that is not*?

   [If possible, compare *Monkey*, Çelebi's *Book of Travels*, as well as Voltaire's *Candide*.]
4. Compare the implicit depiction in *A Modest Proposal* of the way government bureaucracies function with the suggestion in *Tartuffe* that the Prince personally intervenes in the minutiae of judicial administration, or with the treatment of political events in *The Peach Blossom Fan*. How would you characterize the attitudes toward the prospect of just rule in each text?

Further Reading

See also the reading suggestions in the anthology, p. 433.

Donoghue, D. *Jonathan Swift: A Critical Introduction.* 1969. An interpretation that seeks to avoid relying on irony as the governing mode of Swift's work. Offers a detailed exegesis of *Gulliver's Travels* as "an anatomy of human pride."

Ehrenpreis, I. *Swift: The Man, His Works, and the Age.* 3 vols. 1962–83. The definitive critical biography. Vol. 3, *Dean Swift*, contains detailed treatments of *Gulliver's Travels* and *A Modest Proposal*: accounts of their composition and publication as well as critical analysis.

Quintana, R. *The Mind and Art of Jonathan Swift.* 1956. An accessible introduction to Swift. Provides both biographical data and a critical survey of thought and technique.

Reilly, E. J., ed. *Approaches to Teaching Swift's* Gulliver's Travels. 1988. Immensely useful, pedagogically focused collection of essays.

ALEXANDER POPE

The Rape of the Lock

Classroom Strategies and Topics for Discussion

This fanciful narrative of trivial pursuits uses its account of a belle's pleasures and conflicts to suggest the moral flaws and the aesthetic values of early eighteenth-century English social life. Its allusions to epic imply intent to comment on the preoccupations of a society—not, of course, "society" in its largest sense, the community of humankind, but the limited aristocratic society of eighteenth-century London, concerned with appearance and with luxury rather than with genuine accomplishment, cut off from realities of human suffering, yet miniaturizing the same desires that drive the heroes of the *Aeneid* or the *Iliad*. One problem you face is to ask students to discover connections between eighteenth-century London society and its twenty-first-century American counterpart.

The glittering smoothness of Pope's verse, concealing complexities of thought, sometimes creates the illusion that the poetry is easy to read. It is not, of course, given its density of meaning, but first-time readers have to be shown that it's worth struggling with. You might find it useful to spend time working on a single short passage: for example, the toilette scene at the end of canto I (lines 121–48). By exploring in depth the implications of such a phrase as "the sacred rites of Pride" (line 128), you can demonstrate what close attention Pope's language demands and what rewards it offers. Why are these rites "sacred"? And why, for that matter, are they "rites"? As students begin to realize how completely Belinda (and her society, and ours, and we ourselves) has ritualized everyday procedures, they come to understand why the trivial receives so much emphasis in the poem and in our own lives. The necessity for putting on makeup is never questioned in Belinda's world, as the order of religious rituals is never questioned. The sequence of rouge and powder and eyeshadow is unvaried, unchallenged. Like other "rites," this one of makeup provides a stay against confusion, an assertion of continuity and of power. Such rites are "sacred" because they participate in a religion of self-love belonging not only to Belinda herself but to the community in which she participates. And they are *called* "sacred" in the poem to remind us of other more significant rites that they trivialize.

If it is possible to spend two class hours on this poem, students might be asked to read it in its entirety for the first meeting, which could concentrate on close reading of a relatively short sequence; the class might read the poem again for the second meeting, and then engage in a more general discussion of the poem as a whole.

Students often find the couplet structure monotonous and uninteresting. The best way to disabuse them of the notion that Pope engages in a kind of automatic writing is to ask each to compose a single couplet. The experience of trying to condense meaning into two rhymed pentameter lines usually proves both chastening and enlightening.

Sometimes students assume that *The Rape of the Lock* is as trivial as its subject matter. But of course the trivial can be highly revealing, in Pope's time and in ours. A character who mingles Bibles and love letters on her dressing table bears some resemblance to the student who reads Milton while listening to rock music: incompatible commitments jostle in all our minds. To call attention to such jostling does not imply the commentator's frivolity, but it is usually necessary to spend a good deal of time demonstrating how Pope enforces his criticism of a group that has lost its sense that some values are preferable to others, as well as time talking about why mere "silliness" matters in the moral scheme.

Students can become quite involved in the problem of how to ascertain the poet's precise targets of attack. The famous couplet, "The hungry judges soon the sentence sign, / And wretches hang that jurymen may dine" (III.21–22) provides an obvious example of satiric attack, in which the extreme discrepancy between the motivation of judge and jury and the fate of the "wretches" they condemn calls attention to something wrong in society. Discussion might move from this sort of obvious satiric instance to other kinds of discrepancy: between staining one's honor and one's dress, for example, or between the stately elephant and the comb to which its tusks are converted. Pope's discrepancies typically alert the reader to "something wrong"; figuring out just what is wrong and why often proves a valuable enterprise.

One more difficulty troubling to many readers of Pope is that of ascertaining positive value in *The Rape of the Lock*. What does the poet believe in? This is by no means a simple question to answer, but it is a useful one to confront. Clarissa's counsel of good sense provides one standard by which to judge the deviations from the sensible that pervade the poem, but it is not the only standard. Why is the lock taken up into the heavens, why does the poem conclude with stress on its own permanence, and why is Belinda's world evoked with such poetic beauty? The answers to all these questions are surely related: the poet, too, appears to believe in the aesthetic, in the necessity and the lastingness of the art that transforms the trivial into the stuff of poetry (or of constellations).

Topics for Writing

These develop readily from the kinds of discussion suggested above. A few possibilities:

1. The function of Clarissa's speech.
2. The importance of the Sylphs.
3. The concept of manhood in *The Rape of the Lock*.
4. What is wrong with Belinda?
5. Why the Cave of Spleen?

An Essay on Man

Classroom Strategies and Topics for Discussion

Students—like other people—often have trouble with the very idea of a philosophic poem: the notion of the "philosophic," they seem to feel, opposes that of the "poetic." The teacher's problem, then, is to demonstrate (or to help the class discover) how Pope reconciles the two modes—a task made more difficult by the fact that *An Essay on Man*, unlike *Paradise Lost*, presents no sustained characters.

As usual, a good place to start is at the beginning, with the introductory section. Students can be asked to locate Pope's images: maze, wild, garden, field, "Nature's walks," "Folly" and "Manners" as birds to be hunted. Then they can discuss how the images' implications expand. Why, for example, is the garden "tempting with forbidden fruit" (line 8)? The world is thus made analogous to Eden, and humankind, by implication, is in danger of recommitting the original sin of Adam and Eve. Thinking about the rest of epistle I, students might speculate about what this sin constitutes, how it might be repeated. As the epistle develops, it increasingly emphasizes the human tendency to pride (and the degree to which this tendency often seems inherent in the very act of presuming to philosophize). Eve too, as readers of *Paradise Lost* may remember, was victimized by pride: the desire to assume a place closer to that of Deity. The introductory section of *An Essay on Man* thus foretells the epistle's argument in specifically metaphoric terms. Reminded of the particular allusion to *Paradise Lost* in line 16, students may wish to reflect about how *vindicate* differs from *justify*, Milton's word: what a different (more combative, more skeptical) universe the change of a verb implies. Enough time should be spent on this section (the development of the hunting metaphor, with its casual tone and purposeful rhetoric, also repays attention; and the conversational, almost joking tone of the opening couplet) for the class to realize that Pope has established a situation and an atmosphere not at all predictable for philosophic verse, and that he has done so by relying on traditional poetic devices.

Students will probably be eager to discuss, even to argue about, the nature of Pope's thought. It is valuable to trace the argument as it develops, section by section, through the epistle, pausing on the question of how connections are made between one point and the next. A useful way to link Pope's method with his subject is to look for persuasive devices. How does the poet seek to convince his audience of the rightness of his view? Aspects of the poem likely to attract comment in this connection include the use of example, both brief images ("die of a rose in aromatic pain" [line 200]) and more extended vignettes (the poor Indian or the lamb licking the hand of its slaughterer), and of the sheer power of sound and rhythm as persuasive devices (the concluding passage, for instance). Discussion of the poem's shifting tone would also be appropriate. If asked, after talking about such matters, whether Pope relies more heavily on intellectual or on emotional arguments, students are likely to agree at least that emotional persuasion forms an important part of his agenda: that he works, in this respect, more like what they might expect of a poet than what they might expect of a philosopher.

Another fruitful subject for discussion is the relationship, or series of relationships, established between the narrator and the reader. The section numbered I, for instance, begins in a measured, reasoned tone suggesting the opening of a set of intellectual propositions. By the end of the eighteen-line section, the narrator is beginning to insult the reader by calling attention to that reader's insignificance in the universe ("Is the great chain, that draws all to agree, / And drawn supports, upheld by God, or thee?" [lines 33–34]); the next section, emphasizing humankind's pettiness, begins, "Presumptuous Man!" Alternations of didacticism, insult, a kind of cooperative reasoning (see section V), and inspirational rhetoric (section VIII) continue through the poem, shifting with bewildering rapidity. Asked to think about this technique in relation to Pope's purposes here, students might conclude that the poet's rhetorical agility calls attention to exactly the problem the epistle's title announces: "The Nature and State of Man, with Respect to the Universe." The dilemma about humanity's nature and state involves the poet as speaker and the reader as listener: neither poet nor reader, it seems, can securely know his or her position. Sometimes the poet appears to understand everything; sometimes he shares the humility he enjoins for the reader; sometimes he substitutes awe for comprehension. Always he dramatizes the human position.

Specific passages worth special attention include the short sequence on the passions (lines 165–72), interesting to discuss as exemplifying Pope's emotional and ideological commitment to necessity for action: the passions may be good or bad in themselves, but they *function* for good because they make things happen. The lines beginning "All are but parts of one stupendous whole" (267–80) are important for defining Pope's view of the universal scheme in terms that will be useful if you teach Wordsworth.

Topics for Writing

1. Why the poor Indian?
2. How the satiric impulse is expressed in *An Essay on Man*.
3. A specific image and how it works.
4. What does Pope mean by "order"?
5. The function of animals in the poem.

Comparative Perspectives

1. Although Pope goes back to the classical tradition in these works, he also invokes a vernacular world. How would you compare his treatment of domestic and everyday life with that of Dorothy Wordsworth in *The Grasmere Journals*, Flaubert in *Madame Bovary*, or with that in the Chinese works of this period, especially the detail

of an aristocratic family's routine in *The Story of the Stone*? What kinds of details do they single out? Do they view ordinary life as laughable, serious, or dull?

2. How committed are Pope and Cao Xueqin to the traditional values and sense of order (classical and Christian on one hand, and Confucian on the other) against which their characters are measured? What balance of ancient and modern does each seem to prefer?

3. Compare Pope's attitude toward evil with that expressed by Machiavelli in *The Prince* by discussing the reference to Cesare Borgia in *An Essay on Man* (line 156) in relation to "New Princedoms Gained with Other Men's Forces and through Fortunes," in which Machiavelli describes Cesare Borgia's political and military tactics (Volume C, pp. 2521–29).

Further Reading

See also the reading suggestions in the anthology, p. 492.

Griffin, De. *Alexander Pope: The Poet in the Poem.* 1978. Uses biographical data to help understand the positions taken by the speakers in Pope's poems.

Guerinot, J., ed. *Pope: A Collection of Critical Essays.* 1972. Provides a survey of critical approaches useful to the student.

Jackson, W., and R. P. Yoder, eds. *Approaches to Teaching Pope's Poetry.* 1993. A volume in the MLA series, with several relevant articles.

Spacks, P. *An Argument of Images.* 1972. Interprets Pope's imagery in comparison with his poetic predecessors and successors.

FRANÇOIS-MARIE AROUET DE VOLTAIRE

Candide, or Optimism

Classroom Strategies and Topics for Discussion

Its combination of metaphysical and social satire makes *Candide* both exciting and problematic. What is the connection between pointing out the barbarities of war and of organized religion (themes also of Swift in *Gulliver's Travels*) and calling attention to the possible fatuities of philosophic optimism (by exaggerating and simplifying ideas like those in *An Essay on Man*)? How does Voltaire persuade us to tolerate, and even to laugh at, recitals of incredible horror? If such questions are too large and forbidding for students (or anyone else), answers to them can at least be approached by discussing specific aspects of *Candide*.

To begin with the first chapter: a useful exercise is to try collectively to separate sentences with satiric bite from those (like the first) that seem intended quite seriously. There will probably be dispute about at least a few examples—a development that can profitably lead to questions about how one decides. Even if everyone agrees about everything, the group can discuss how they know what is straightforward and what satiric. Such discussion should include consideration of the matter of assumed common standards. We all agree, presumably, that for a woman to weigh three hundred and fifty pounds is not sufficient reason for her to be respected, and that the congruity of noses and spectacles is not part of the order of nature. What is worth emphasizing is that we share these assumptions, and many others, with Voltaire, and that he can and does draw on them in constructing his satiric fiction: moreover, that without at least some vestige of such shared standards, we would be unable to recognize satire. This point is important for students to understand, both because it helps them to realize that the gap between the eighteenth and twentieth centuries is not in every respect so great as they imagine and because it is absolutely fundamental to an understanding of satire.

Candide's experiences in the Bulgar army typify central patterns of Voltaire's work. You might call the class's attention to the enormous speed of the narrative (other sequences of the fiction would of course work equally well to demonstrate this aspect of Voltaire's technique). Detailed discussion of effects generated by this speed is likely to prove profitable. For instance, it's worth pointing out that the failure to linger over gruesome details helps to suggest that they are not too serious after all. Their lack of apparent "seriousness" of course depends on their emphatic fictionality: because the narrator himself seems unconcerned, seems to think these things don't matter much, we are reminded that they belong to the realm of imagination. If they had really happened, they would horrify the narrator and the reader alike. The speed of movement also has a comic effect: the sheer incongruity between the dreadfulness of what allegedly happens and the gusto and rapidity with which reports of the dreadful pile up makes us smile. Consideration of this sort of effect enlarges understanding of the workings of satire, which typically depends on exaggeration and unmistakable distancing from the actual to enforce its comments. In this connection, it is perhaps worth inquiring whether the literal horrors of twentieth-century war, far in excess of anything Voltaire has imagined, have any effect on our response to Voltairean satire.

A large question that will both interest students and draw them closer to the workings of this fiction concerns the functions of sex in the narrative. What purpose does the stress on sexual feeling and action serve? As in *Phaedra*, although of course with tonality as different as possible, sexuality makes people vulnerable. It is a form of feeling all men and women share, a defining aspect of animal nature but also, in some of its specific expressions, of human nature. The relation between animality and humanity is a recurrent theme of *Candide*; students might be asked to find examples of it. In this respect and others, the sexual expressiveness of men and women epitomizes kinds of paradox that interest Voltaire. Sexuality involves both weakness and strength, pleasure and pain, physical disease and psychic health, human connection and violation, and so on. Students can find instances of apparently contradictory values associated with sex, and can move from these to a realization of how *Candide* constructs a notion of humanity far too complicated to be contained in a Panglossian scheme of things.

What keeps one reading this narrative? Voltaire generates genuine suspense, not so much about his characters as about the workings of his imagination. What will he think of next; what further excess will he conjure up? What explanation will he find for the fact that the old woman has only one buttock? Our interest in the operations of the satirist's fancy intensifies satiric effect: as we realize that we are enjoying images of rape, murder, treachery, violence, we are presumably led to reflect on the real occurrences of such phenomena in our own world, on how we respond to them (when, for example, they are reported on TV), and on the implications of our capacity to tolerate horrors when they happen to other people.

But another point that should be discussed is the incursions of realism into this text. In what ways, to what extent, does Voltaire rely on realistic insights? In chapter 14, Candide laments, "Cunégonde, brought from so far, what will ever become of you?" Cacambo responds, "She'll become what she can . . . women can always find something to do with themselves; God sees to it; let's get going" (p. 540). Cacambo's kind of practicality accepts the limitations of a fiercely competitive world and acknowledges the need for dealing with the given. (His attribution of women's instinct for self-preservation to God is another matter, more closely related to Voltaire's satiric pattern.) The kind of comment we might call "realistic" is here typically a general observation on human nature or habits drawn from the exaggerated experience of the protagonists. Students can easily multiply examples. In this way—by offering generalizations of which we recognize the cogency—Voltaire keeps his satire rooted in truths we can acknowledge. (Again, the matter of shared assumptions between author and reader is relevant.)

Increasingly toward the end of the tale, the narrative dwells on human corruption (e.g., the shooting of admirals, the deposing of kings, the various operations of avarice, lust, envy, and competitiveness). In the last chapter, "Pangloss asserted that he had always suffered horribly; but having once declared that everything was marvelously well, he continued to repeat the opinion and didn't believe a word of it" (p. 579). By the time we are told directly that Pangloss does not believe his own philosophic contentions, we have been brought to realize that philosophic optimism (here parodied as the view that everything is for the best in this best of all possible worlds) itself amounts to one of the constructions human beings make to protect themselves from reality—like Pococurante's belief that nothing is of value and Candide's declarations of love for Cunégonde; and like the human propensity for war, thievery, and rape, all of which constitute modes of asserting or acquiring power and importance. Political arrangements and philosophic beliefs, the work has shown, have a good deal in common.

Topics for Writing

1. Could Voltaire satirize Hitler?
2. An exercise in Voltairean satire (i.e., student attempts in the mode).
3. What Candide learns.
4. A moment of comedy and how its effect contributes to the satire.
5. The function of some minor character.
6. The relation of the conclusion to the beginning.

Comparative Perspectives

Like many of the travelers depicted in this anthology, Candide has an entourage. What literary purpose is served by making a traveler one of a group? How does the tone of a travel narrative differ when the protagonist forges on alone, as in the case of *Gulliver's Travels*? See also comparisons suggested to Çelebi, *The Book of Travels*; Frederick Douglass, *Narrative of the Life of an American Slave*; Kawabata, *Snow Country*.

Further Reading

See also the reading suggestions in the anthology, p. 519.

Aldridge, A. *Voltaire and the Century of Light.* 1975. The biographical treatment emphasizes both personality and thought, "combining the methods of comparative literature and the history of ideas."

Torrey, N. *The Spirit of Voltaire.* 1938. Provides a biographical treatment with emphasis on Voltaire's intellectual life and development.

Wade, I. *The Intellectual Development of Voltaire.* 1969. Supplies an exhaustive examination of Voltaire's intellectual life.

Waldinger, R., ed. *Approaches to Teaching Voltaire's* Candide. 1989. This collection of essays by many authors, published by the MLA, is designed to help teachers in the classroom.

The Rise of Popular Arts in Premodern Japan

IHARA SAIKAKU

The Barrelmaker Brimful of Love

Backgrounds and Classroom Strategies

The Barrelmaker Brimful of Love comes from a collection of novellas titled *Five Women Who Loved Love*. It was published in 1686, four years after Saikaku's first novel, *The Life of a Sensuous Man,* and thematically it represents a departure.

Saikaku's so-called love novels (*kōshoku-mono*), the bulk of his fiction to date, had treated love life in the pleasure quarters. In writing *The Life of a Sensuous Man,* Saikaku drew heavily on popular guidebooks to the red-light district that reviewed the allure and accomplishments of certain prostitutes of note: once the hero, Yonosuke, is old enough to become a regular customer, the women he pursues are professionals. The same is true for Saikaku's second novel, a sequel called *The Sirens' Mirror* (1684), in which the hero, Yonosuke's son, follows in his father's footsteps. *The Life of Wankyū the First* (1685), Saikaku's third novel, chronicles the misadventures of an actual townsman of Saikaku's day, who ran through the family fortune patronizing his favorite courtesan.

With *Five Women Who Loved Love,* however, Saikaku moved to a bigger stage, and a much more freighted subject: illicit love, where the women are not professionals. Students will be puzzled by the story included in the anthology if they do not understand the conception of love and attitudes toward sex in seventeenth-century Japan. At the time, the function of marriage was procreation, and romantic love was not even an assumption. For the upper classes (the samurai and the remnants of the aristocracy), marriages were arranged with attention to political and economic considerations. To a certain extent (at least financially), this would also have been true for the more prosperous members of the merchant class. Perhaps only the humble townspeople, who had no particular privileges to protect, could afford to let an element of sexual attraction affect the practical process of betrothal. (We see this in *The Barrelmaker Brimful of Love.*) Once married, at all levels of this Confucian society, a wife was to be a mother, not an object of romantic or erotic attachment, and certainly not a free agent sexually or any other way. The one arena in which sensuality and its more troublesome offshoot, love, had social and legal sanction was the demimonde. In the officially licensed red-light districts that sprang up in each of the new cities, any man with the money could find sexual freedom and a simulation at least of romantic affection.

But anyone who tried to find that freedom outside the licensed quarters—including all "ordinary" women—was flirting with disaster. It is worth looking at the relevant sections of the legal code governing Saikaku's society:

> Item one. Illicit intercourse. For persons engaging in, or attempting, such with their master's daughter, the penalty: death. Subject at the master's request to pardon or commutation to banishment.[1]
>
> Item two. Illicit intercourse. For persons committing adultery with their master's, or teacher's, wife, the penalty for both parties: death.
>
> Item three. Illicit intercourse. For those who propose adultery or send love letters to their master's wife, the penalty: death or banishment. Go-betweens may be pardoned.
>
> Item four. Illicit intercourse. For accessories to adultery with a master's wife, the penalty: death.
>
> Item five. Abduction. In accordance with previous examples, for those guilty of such, the penalty: death.

While illicit sexual relations were not automatically punished if both the man and the woman were of the same social status and had committed no criminal offense, in many cases, including that of *The Barrelmaker Brimful of Love,* the one led to the other. Chozaemon is executed because a life had been taken, even though Osen committed suicide. (In the case of a failed double suicide, the lover who survived was often executed anyway.) Several government edicts decreed that a husband who caught his wife in flagrante delicto had the legal right to execute both wife and lover on the spot. If Osen's affair seems rash to us, the more so once we've read the law, her speedy suicide does not. It isn't shame or remorse prompting her; it is an understanding of her legal fate.

Only a year earlier Saikaku had published his first novel based on the life of a real person (*The Life of Wankyū the First*), whose notoriety made the book a provocative bestseller. *Five Women Who Loved Love* was even more incendiary. Its five adulterous heroines were all explicitly modeled on actual contemporary women. It may be hard for students to grasp fully the sensation this created in an age before newspapers or the equivalent of *People* magazine. It will undoubtedly require background information of the sort provided above, plus an imaginative leap, before students can begin to comprehend Saikaku's daring. After all, no matter how much effort we try to exert, can we picture ourselves in a world so rigid and hierarchical that there is no equality (at least between classes) and no recognized social mobility? Saikaku is iconoclastic not only for introduc-

---

1. The daughter's punishment was to be handcuffed and turned over to her parents.

ing physicality and sexual attraction as literary subjects (even *The Tale of Genji* [in volume B, pp. 2182–2270], that great amatory novel, focuses on emotions rather than bodies); he is the first to write about the danger of sex and, still more radical, the yearning that ordinary people felt to follow their own will.

What, then, are we to make of the tone of this work? The narrator's detachment keeps us at a distance. Saikaku's subject is the human comedy, and he is more interested in creating a tableau of character types than in fashioning three-dimensional individuals. For his choice of topics—material and physical desire—and for his comedian's sense of specific detail Saikaku is often described as a realist. Students should be able to point out examples of this on almost every page of the story. The cooper's offer of courting gifts, including "a set of Nara-hemp clothes of second quality," or the picture of Osen in bed between two men—the cooper on one side caressing her waist, a fellow servant on the other fondling her toes—are only two of the many instances of humor derived from detail.

But students should also be able to describe why Saikaku's "realism" is that of a caricaturist. An interesting discussion can result from comparing Saikaku with Flaubert (pp. 1088–1301 in volume E) and the European Realist movement. How can two writers with such different aims both be realists? And what is literary realism?

Topics for Discussion and Writing

1. Following from the discussion above, how can the motivation for Osen's affair with Chozaemon be considered realistic?
2. Saikaku's point of view has been described as that of someone looking through the reverse end of a telescope. What do you think about this comparison?
3. Selecting examples of Saikaku's use of detail from each of the five chapters, analyze how they function to create both an illusion of realism and a comic effect.
4. The narrator takes a long time getting to the main event. Could the fact that the story is based on an actual incident be a reason for this? How? What other reasons might there be for the story's structure?
5. Discuss characterization. Is it possible for a character to be two-dimensional and still exhibit individuality?

Comparative Perspectives

1. When Osen is introduced to the reader, she is an innocent; gradually, however, she becomes "a woman who loved love." Describe the degrees by which her metamorphosis occurs.

   [Saikaku surrounds her with "demons in human form who play havoc with the lives of ignorant men."]

   What is the tone of the concluding paragraph? Compare Saikaku's depiction of her with, as appropriate, Voltaire's portrait of Cunégonde, Flaubert's of Emma Bovary, or Zhang Ailing's of Liusu in *Love in a Fallen City*. How fully do we enter into each heroine's inner consciousness? What impact does psychological intimacy or distance have on our sense of a character's moral agency?

2. Like Bashō, Saikaku writes of pilgrimage. Judging from the contrast between these two contemporaries, into what different categories do pilgrimage narratives fall? Discuss some similarities between Saikaku's use of pilgrimage in *The Barrelmaker Brimful of Love* and Chaucer's in *The Canterbury Tales*.

   [Consider pilgrimage as a license to relax sexual morality, and as an invitation to writers to explore details of middle-class life, dead-pan ironies.]

Further Reading

See also the reading suggestions in the anthology, p. 590.

Danly, Robert Lyons. *In the Shade of Spring Leaves*. 1992. For the influences of Saikaku's linked poetry on his fiction see pp. 109–32.

Drake, Christopher. "The Collision of Traditions in Saikaku's Haikai." *Harvard Journal of Asiatic Studies* 52, no. 1 (1992), pp. 5–75.

———. "Saikaku's Haikai Requiem: *A Thousand Haikai Alone in a Single Day*, the First Hundred Verses." *Harvard Journal of Asiatic Studies* 52, no. 2 (1992), pp. 481–588.

MATSUO BASHŌ

The Narrow Road of the Interior

Backgrounds and Classroom Strategies

As the headnote (pp. 603–06 in the anthology) points out, there is more to haiku than seventeen syllables. This, in a nutshell, is the suggested theme if haiku are to come alive for students and so transcend their image as fortune-cookie verse or Zen doggerel.

Strictly speaking, the history of haiku does not begin until the late nineteenth century, when the poet Masaoka Shiki (1867–1902) coined the term to denote an independent poetic form deriving from medieval comic linked verse. After civil war erupted in Japan in the twelfth century (see *The Tale of the Heike*, volume B, pp. 2300), the political and economic stability of the aristocratic order were not the only things to fragment. Court poetry, the *tanka* (see the *Kokinshū*, volume B, pp. 2163–74, and the comments on it in the volume of this guide that covers A, B, and C), also splintered. By the fifteenth century, the predominant verse form was a kind of chain poetry comprising seventeen- and fourteen-syllable fragments of the old thirty-one-syllable *tanka*. These fragments combined to create the momentary effect of a classical poem before recombining in perpetual mutation, through thirty-six, one hundred, or even a thousand links.

Such poetic chains were almost always group efforts, where a chorus of poets submerged individualistic expression to the demands of joint composition. The literary jam sessions began as pastimes or party games but quickly developed rules guaranteed to ensure artistic results. The first rule was that each verse in a sequence stand on its own, the second rule that it also combine with the preceding verse to create a unified poetic statement. Scores of other rules governed semantic and thematic requirements, so that as the sequence progressed it would be assured variety and continued change. The end product was to be a sequence that recapitulated the entire classical tradition, representing all the categories established by the imperial collections of court poetry (love, seasons, laments, and so forth): a flow of intense poetic moments against more subdued "background verses," progressing through various forms of association. "The essence of a linked-verse sequence, then, is a dialectical movement that produces now a prosaic scene, now a more striking one, here a simple extension, there a complete change in interpretation, setting off exclamations against sighs and speaking for a host of people including travelers, lovers, old men recluses, peasants, and emperors—all in a symphonic structure that contains the poems within a formal whole while resisting comprehensive interpretations."[1]

It will help to look at an example. Here are the first five links of a one-hundred-verse sequence, one of the most famous, *Three Poets at Minase,* produced in 1488 by three poets Bashō greatly admired, Sōgi (1421–1502), Shōhaku (1443–1527), and Sōchō (1448–1532):

> Some snow still remains
>   as haze moves low on the slopes
>   toward evening.
>
>   Sōgi

> Flowing water, far away—
> and a plum-scented village.
>
>   Shōhaku

> Wind off the river
>   blows through a clump of willows—
> and spring appears.
>
>   Sōchō

> A boat being poled along,
> sounding clear at break of day.
>
>   Sōgi

1. Steven D. Carter, *Traditional Japanese Poetry,* Stanford, Calif., 1991, pp. 305–06.

Still there, somewhere:
the moon off behind the mist
traversing the night.

Shōhaku[2]

According to convention, the first stanza by Sōgi combines with the second by Shōhaku to create a five-line, thirty-one-syllable *tanka*, the traditional poetic form (see *The Man'yōshū*, volume B, pp. 2152–60, and the
comments on it in the volume of this guide that covers A, B, and C. But
there is always a fissure in this new kind of poetry. Originally, of course,
the other poets (and those in attendance) had to wait for Shōhaku to pen
his stanza and "complete" the poem. The reader is aware of this gap as
well. The white space is there for a reason: the two stanzas are discrete
thoughts. They juxtapose to create new meaning, but the union is never
so complete as to remove the forward movement of anticipation. The perfect literary analog of the Buddhist law on the impermanence of life,
linked poetry was inherently unpredictable, unstable, and given to rupture. No sooner has Shōhaku's stanza "completed" Sōgi's poem than it, in
turn, is "completed" by Sōchō's contribution.

As the headnote describes, when anthologies of linked poetry began to
appear in the fourteenth century, it became the custom to devote a special section to particularly stellar opening stanzas. Over time, these first
stanzas, called *hokku*, came to be viewed as poetic units with a life independent of the sequences that they had once introduced. Some poets began to write just *hokku*, without bothering to participate in the joint
venture of linked-verse composition; others competed in contests pitting
one clever *hokku* against another. Slowly in this way, *hokku* took on the
trappings of autonomous poems. The logical conclusion of this trend was
the decision by Masaoka Shiki to distinguish between true *hokku*, the
opening stanzas of linked poetry, and *haiku*, the term he invented to refer
to seventeen-syllable verses intended solely as self-contained poems.
(*Haiku* is a contraction of *haikai*, meaning "comic linked verse," and *ku*,
meaning "verse," "stanza," "poem.")

Bashō, writing in the seventeenth century, comes somewhere in the
middle of this spectrum. He would not have distinguished between the
two kinds of *hokku*, as Shiki does. Nor would he have been able to forget
the many conventions of linked poetry, for he was himself a practitioner.
With the two strands so completely interwoven, one might say that Bashō
had the best of both worlds. Sometimes, for example, when spontaneity
seized him, he would write a *hokku* prompted by some aspect of nature
that impressed him or some incident he had witnessed. Later he would
use it as the opening for a linked-verse sequence. No doubt more than a
few of his contemporaries did the same.

Bashō, however, was the one to raise the seventeen-syllable form we

2. Ibid., p. 307.

now call *haiku* to its real poetic potential. *Haikai* had been in many ways a game of wordplay, despite all the rules. It took pride in its humor, by which *haikai* distinguished itself from a more sober strain of linked poetry (*renga*). Bashō kept the gentle humor, but he also explored possibilities that until now had lain dormant in the form. He combined slang and unconventional topics with the traditions of classical Japanese poetry; he drew on his knowledge of Chinese literature; he experimented with heterodox syllabication, writing *hokku* in eighteen, nineteen, or more counts; he infused conventional poetic associations with a fresh vision, and aristocratic sensibilities with popular concerns; he saw the short poem as both a moment apart and belonging to a larger context. Most important, while he never completely abandoned the playfulness of comic linked verse, he used *hokku* as a vehicle for a truthful exploration of the meaning of life.

Instances of many of these achievements will be found in Bashō's most distinguished composition, *The Narrow Road of the Interior*. The footnotes to the text can be used as a guide to pointing out examples. You can show students how Bashō, for all his innovations, remains faithful to—and steeped in—the classical tradition by working through his references or allusions to earlier Japanese poetry. See especially in volume D: p. 611, notes 5, 6, and 7; p. 614, notes 4 and 5; p. 615, note 2; p. 616, note 2; p. 617, note 8; p. 618, note 9; p. 621, note 4; p. 622, note 7; p. 623, note 2; p. 624, note 4; not to mention his allusions to other venerated works of Japanese literature, for example, *The Tale of Genji* on p. 628, note 5, and *The Tale of the Heike* on p. 610, note 8; p. 613, notes 6 and 1; p. 616, note 7; p. 625, notes 8 and 1; or to the esteemed (because even older) Chinese literary and historical tradition: p. 608, notes 9 and 2; p. 611, note 3; p. 613, note 9; p. 616, notes 4 and 8; p. 619, note 7; p. 621, note 1; p. 622, note 6; p. 623, notes 9 and 3; and p. 624, note 5. If students read the *nō* plays in volume B (pp. 2350–70), a discussion of intertextuality similar to that outlined in this guide (pp. 286–88 in the volume covering A, B, and C) is most germane. Evidence that Bashō conceived of his *hokku* as links in a sequence is implicit throughout. If he had viewed these poems as entirely self-contained, there would be no prose narrative. Further evidence of this is suggested by the translator's comment in note 96.

It is a commonplace that among the other things Bashō managed to unite were a sense of the momentary and a sense of the eternal. The following poem (on p. 620 in the anthology) will serve as an example:

> Ah, tranquility!
> Penetrating the very rock,
> a cicada's voice.

This is one of Bashō's most famous *haiku*. He sets it up by describing how he and his traveling companion had arrived at their hostel before sundown, then climbed the crag above to view a well-known temple, "a serene, quiet seat of religion" (p. 620). It is the height of summer, quiet indeed in the late afternoon heat. "Not a sound emanated from the temple buildings at the summit . . . but we skirted the cliffs and clambered over the rocks. . . . The quiet, lonely beauty of the environs purified the heart." And then—the screech of a cicada, a sound so shrill it seems to sink into the surrounding landscape. The silence of the scene is paradoxically magnified. The poem breaks into two parts ("Ah, tranquility!" and "Penetrating the very rock, / a cicada's voice"), and the two parts interpenetrate: the tranquility only makes the cicada's cry louder, and the shrill hum of the insect punctuates the silence.

Through the centuries commentators have gone to town with this poem. An eighteenth-century scholar: "Not a single sound was heard at this quiet place, except the voice of the cicadas that was so forceful that it seemed to seep into the rocks. As the poet listened to it, his thoughts became collected and his mind attained tranquility. The poem's meaning goes beyond the words and points toward the profound secrets of Zen."[3] Another eighteenth-century critic: "Cicadas' cries are a metaphor for men's earthly desires. The poem suggests how such desires disappear in the court of Buddha's law."[4] You will note that these two commentaries construe cicada to be plural. Number is not usually marked in Japanese, and is not marked here, so that both interpretations are possible. Two twentieth-century commentators debated whether cicada should be taken as singular or plural. "If my sensibility is reliable, there should not be many cicadas here."[5] "I disagree. The whole mountain is filled with the cicadas' screech."[6] Much ink has flowed over the question of how many cicadas are trilling. "I'd rather have many cicadas in this scene," weighs in another twentieth-century scholar. "It is a little dark and cool out there [?], and the cicadas' cries are sounding in unison."[7] A more interesting, if gnomic reading: "In the word 'penetrating' we sense motion in stillness, and stillness in motion. Bashō, with his consummate art, captured this oneness of motion and stillness in a short poem."[8] Many critics have seen in this poem something approaching the ineffable:

What Bashō felt on hearing the cicadas' cries "seeping into the rocks" was probably a mysterious kind of loneliness emanating from his absorption into the unified, serene chirping of the cicadas. It was not the type of sad, empty feeling that we experience when we cannot obtain what we seek in our daily lives. Nor was it the kind of helpless feeling we have when, all alone, we ponder over life's frightening aspects. This was the type of loneliness we feel when we encounter nature at its fullest moment and touch on its motionless motion—when we sense the movement of the Prime Mover that does not move. It is at once "loneliness" and "stillness." Or, more precisely, it is a pure "apprehension of nature" before it branches into those two emotions.[9]

3. Makoto Ueda, *Bashō and His Interpreters: Selected Hokku with Commentary*, Stanford, Calif., 1991, p. 249.
4. Ibid.
5. Ibid.
6. Ibid.
7. Ibid.
8. Ibid.
9. Ibid., pp. 249–50.

And finally, perhaps most satisfying for its simplicity, " 'Cicada's voice' is a symbol. Through it, Bashō listened to the stillness of nature, to the rhythm of nature."[10]

One thing that is clear from the commentaries is Bashō's absolute success in manipulating nature's smallest and most fragile creatures. The cicada is evanescence, or vulnerability, itself—a tiny yardstick that, for all its inadequacy, measures the unbounded. The ephemeral and the infinite intersect. We feel a communion with nature and yet a new sense of insignificance. Time and again Bashō creates this effect, and students will enjoy identifying their favorite examples.

Topics for Writing and Discussion

1. Do you agree that the best *haiku* fuse the eternal and the changing? Could the failure to do so be one reason that many *haiku* seem banal or precious?
2. How do Bashō's *haiku* comment on the Buddhist concept of impermanence?
3. Bashō's poetry may seem modern, but in what ways is his a conservative sensibility?
4. Despite its air of spontaneity, *The Narrow Road of the Interior* is the product of contrivance. What evidence can you detect of this?
5. Describe the literary persona that Bashō creates for himself.

Comparative Perspectives

1. To what extent do the details that pilgrims choose to record about their experiences on the road convey the essence of the religion practiced by the traveler? Compare the Christian pilgrimage undertaken by Dante in *The Divine Comedy,* or the Mahayana Buddhism that impels the journey to the West in *Monkey*, with the Zen Buddhist principles guiding Bashō's journey.

   [Look, perhaps, at the rare anecdote in which Bashō mentions overhearing the whispers of the old man and the concubines in the room next door. When the women ask him to be their guide the next day, Bashō politely turns them down. The Zen Buddhist does not believe in ameliorating action in the world. Contrast the instinct for camaraderie and the sheer curiosity typical of other pilgrimage literature.]
2. Compare Bashō's response to the difficult natural landscape he must cover in his journey to the North with the descriptions of European Romantic writers of their travels.

   [Where Wordsworth articulates the nature of his disappointments and epiphanies, the spare *haiku* of Bashō leaves the reader to unravel his meaning. Note the difference between "But there's a Tree,

10. Ibid., p. 250.

of many, one, / A single Field which I have looked upon, / Both of them speak of something that is gone" (*Ode on Intimations of Immortality,* lines 52–54; on p. 797 in volume E of the anthology) and the cicada or the frog of Bashō's most celebrated poems: in each case, the poet fixes on an isolated element in the landscape, but the Englishman interprets in terms of his own sensibility what the Japanese observer distills. Yet Bashō on Ojima Beach imagines human shapes in the island formations, and, like Wordsworth discerning the presence of "hermits" around Tintern Abbey, comments on the presence of "recluses" from whose huts smoke rises.]

3. How would you compare the Buddhist-Taoist sensibility in T'ao Ch'ien's *Substance, Shadow, and Spirit* or Han-shan's Cold Mountain poems with Bashō's sense of transcience and loss?

Further Reading

See also the reading suggestions in the anthology, p. 590.

Sato, Hiroaki, and Burton Watson, ed. and trans. *From the Country of Eight Islands: An Anthology of Japanese Poetry.* 1981. Pp. 278–309. Hiroaki Sato's translations of Bashō's *haiku* into one-line poems come very close to capturing the pace of the originals.

Shirane, Haruo. "Matsuo Bashō and the Poetics of Scent." *Harvard Journal of Asiatic Studies* 52, no. 1 (1992), pp. 77–110. An interesting treatment of *haikai* principles of linking as practiced by Bashō.

UEDA AKINARI

Bewitched

Backgrounds and Classroom Strategies

Why do we enjoy ghost stories? What is the fantastic? What is verisimilitude? In Japanese culture, how has the blurring of the line between the two traditionally made them part of a continuum? Reading stories of the supernatural somehow prompts large questions. You may want to address them as part of the discussion of *Bewitched.*

You might begin by asking students to define the fantastic as a literary genre. For this, the theoretical formulations of Tzvetan Todorov are a valuable reference. In *The Fantastic: A Structural Approach to a Literary Genre* (1975), Todorov cites various generic characteristics: a hero who feels a contradiction between two worlds, one real, one unreal; the violent intrusion of mystery into the context of daily life; ordinary people suddenly confronted by the inexplicable; a rupture in acknowledged order.

All four characterize Akinari's narrative. At the first sight of Manago, Toyo-o's reaction is "utter amazement" (section 1), and "his heart leaped with excitement" (section 2). We know from the second paragraph of the story that Toyo-o is "a handsome youth" (section 1), handsome enough, presumably, to have encountered beautiful women before. His bewilderment, then, signals the prescribed rupture in the acknowledged order. Thus the hero is plunged into Todorov's contradiction between two worlds. Manago seems real but also "bewitchingly voluptuous" (section 1) and "almost otherworldly" (section 2). By the time that Toyo-o has gone looking for her the next day (section 3)—first frustrated because no one in the neighborhood has ever heard of her, then astonished when her house replicates his dream—he is every bit the common man of Todorov's formula suddenly confronted by the inexplicable. He correctly concludes that hers could not be the home of an ordinary person. But he lacks the discipline to think things through, content to believe for the moment that wealth or office account for the difference. Here and repeatedly, the hero hovers between the real and the unreal, and solves his dilemma simply by willing the fantastic to be normal. Finally, however, the brutal intrusion of mystery comes in section 8 when, accused of stealing the sword that Manago has given him, Toyo-o leads authorities to her "house," only to find a shell of the splendid edifice he remembers.

> What had appeared to Toyo-o as imposing pillars on the front gate of Manago's house were sagging with rot; the roof tiles were mostly broken, fallen to the ground. The yard was overgrown with weeds. There were no signs of anyone living in the house. Toyo-o was amazed, to say the least. . . . The inside of the building was in a greater state of ruin and desolation than the outside. As they approached the inner courtyard they found what must once have been a lavishly built garden. The pond had dried up, the flowering plants were dead. Wild bushes and weeds flourished everywhere. A lone pine tree, broken by strong winds, looked ghastly.
>
> Opening the latticed door leading to the main hall, they felt a raw-smelling spectral gust of wind and fell back in fearful excitement. Toyo-o, struck with amazement at the change, could not utter a word.

Inside the house, in a filthy room, sits a beautiful woman. When they approach her she disappears with a thunderclap, which literally bowls the men over.

Neither Toyo-o nor readers should be completely surprised by these developments. We have allowed ourselves to reach the point of believing, or nearly believing, in something whose existence, or normality, much of the narrative evidence would refute. An instructive question is why we as readers go along with Toyo-o when he chooses to ignore the evidence. Ask students what hints the narrator gives us, and Toyo-o, that Manago is not of this world. By the time she vaporizes in section 8 the significant suggestions include her larger-than-life appearance and a sensuousness described very specifically as "bewitching" and "otherworldly." It occurs to Toyo-o that he has never heard of such a beauty living in the vicinity— odd under any circumstances but especially when she claims to have lived there a long time (section 2). And when he first encounters her dripping wet—the image of sensuality—why was she out walking on a deserted beach in a rainstorm (sections 1, 2)? He asks the right questions but accepts any answer, or at least any answer from a creature as adroitly mendacious as this one.

Other clues: What does Toyo-o's dream indicate (section 3)? When he goes looking for Manago the next day, why can't he find her house in the neighborhood (section 3)? Why does her maid just happen to appear (section 3)? Would an ordinary woman tell her maid, "Don't let him leave the house," or employ a maid, for that matter, who shoves visitors into rooms from which they can't escape (section 3)? What really happened to Manago's husband—was there one (section 4)? If her husband was assistant to the governor why doesn't anyone remember him (section 6)? How can Manago know that Toyo-o is the man she will devote her life to (section 4)? What does her sudden anger mean (section 4)? Isn't it odd that someone in a humble fishing village, even a minor official, would have owned so valuable a sword (sections 4, 5)? When told point-blank that no one with the name of Manago's "dead husband" was ever employed by the governor, how can Toyo-o still depend on her testimony to exonerate him (section 7)?

In both her subsequent reappearances, Toyo-o is again similarly deceived. We are too, if only because we choose to be—so integrated are we into the world of the protagonist. Yet we hesitate, a reader response that becomes in Todorov's schema an essential aspect of the fantastic. Todorov argues that such narratives provoke an unresolved hesitation between the marvelous (a fictional category where the magical or supernatural are accepted as the norm in a world apart from our reality) and the uncanny (stories whose incredible events might have natural or psychological explanations within our own world). Taking students through the subtleties of Todorov's argument can yield a stimulating discussion, especially when we consider that in premodern Japan ghosts, possession, and the general existence of a spirit world were considered everyday phenomena. Refer students to *Evening Faces* (in volume B, p. 2204), where the jealous spirit of a rival love kills Genji's new inamorata, and to the ghosts and demons who appear in the nō plays *Atsumori* and *Dōjōji* (in volume B, pp. 2350–55; 2361–70). Does this make Manago more "real"? Does it make Akinari's narrative more realistic? Can we always expect literature to be a transcription of external reality?

Hesitating between Todorov's two poles—the marvelous and the uncanny, both further problematized by Japanese culture—if we incline to an interpretation that entertains the possibility of natural or psychological explanations, can we read *Bewitched* as a tale of sexual fear, or of the toils of excessive desire? If we do, are we merely imposing a reality, thereby depriving a genre of its force?

To close, consider Todorov's definition of the fantastic, for which he posits the necessary fulfillment of three conditions:

> First, the text must oblige the reader to consider the world of the characters as a world of living persons and to hesitate between a natural and a supernatural

explanation of the events described. Second, this hesitation may also be experienced by a character; thus the reader's role is so to speak entrusted to a character, and at the same time the hesitation is represented, it becomes one of the themes of the work—in the case of naive reading, the actual reader identifies himself with the character. Third, the reader must adopt a certain attitude with regard to the text: he will reject allegorical as well as "poetic" interpretations. (p. 33)

Topics for Discussion and Writing

1. Discuss the point of view Akinari has chosen for *Bewitched* and its advantages for a story of the fantastic. What effect does it have on the reader? Do you agree with the headnote in the anthology that Akinari is "an Alfred Hitchcock of the supernatural"?
2. In what ways could Toyo-o be called an easy target? Would you describe his portrayal as sympathetic?
3. Toyo-o succeeds in escaping Manago only when he ceases to flee. Why does he decide on this course of action and what significance can we attribute to it?
4. How would you appraise Akinari's characterization of Manago?
5. Trace Akinari's borrowings from the *nō* play *Dōjōji*. How do the stories and characters in the two works differ? How do emotion and obsession figure in both?
6. If you have read *The Tale of Genji*, discuss the evidence for concluding that in premodern Japan the supernatural was considered "natural."
7. Discuss atmosphere as a component of Akinari's brand of the fantastic.

Comparative Perspectives

1. Explore the attitudes of relatives and friends who learn that Manago is a serpent: priests approach such demonic manifestations as phenomena that can be understood and dealt with. There is no reason to doubt the old man's explanation that the serpentine beauty embodies a monstrous lust that fastens itself to a good-looking young man. Compare this view of the supernatural as natural with the similar approach to the many demons who appear in *Monkey*, or in The Fisherman and the Demon in *The Thousand and One Nights*. How would you contrast the tone of these narratives?
2. In *The Metamorphosis*, Kafka lets readers share the point of view of Gregor Samsa, transformed into a dung beetle. One of Akinari's sources for his story, the *nō* drama *Dōjōji*, gives insight into the suffering of the woman transformed into a snake. Whose perspective does Akinari focus on in *Bewitched*? How would you compare the transformation of Manago with that of Kafka's Gregor?

Further Reading

See also the reading suggestions in the anthology, p. 631.

Morris, Ivan. *The World of the Shining Prince: Court Life in Ancient Japan*. 1964. On the question of the supernatural in premodern Japan see "Superstitions," pp. 123–40.

Todorov, Tzvetan. *The Fantastic: A Structural Approach to a Literary Genre*. 1975.

Revolution and Romanticism in Europe and America

JEAN-JACQUES ROUSSEAU

Confessions

Classroom Strategies and Topics for Discussion

The aspect of Rousseau's autobiographical writing likely to interest students most, even in a fragmentary selection, is the author's determination to create a mythology of the self. Class time can profitably be occupied in tracing elements in Rousseau's systematic development of a self-image that coincides with his notion of what a man should be. Most important, perhaps, is his emphasis on his "passions" as defining a central aspect of his nature. You might ask students to locate occurrences of the word and the concept of passion. The writer claims for himself "unique" knowledge of the passions as a child-reader; he celebrates his own passion for music; he characterizes himself as "a man of very strong passions," which take total command of his personality; he suggests that no one has ever possessed passions "at once more lively and purer" than his own; he boasts his "lively and tumultuous passions"; and so on. Everyone has passions (meaning strong feelings), of course; why does Rousseau believe his own feelings so important? As students speculate about this question, it would be worth suggesting that they think back to the eighteenth-century texts they have read, and the very different valuation of the passions expressed or hinted in them. In *Phaedra*, for example, passion is the enemy of reason and of civil order; in *Gulliver's Travels*, part IV, it belongs only to Yahoos. If *An Essay on Man* indicates that passion generates action, it also suggests the need for restraint. Such reminders will emphasize that Rousseau's self-glorification on the basis of his own intense and uncontrollable passions implies a new value system. Possible answers to the question about why Rousseau assigns such importance to his passions include the hypothesis that strong feelings are associated with "naturalness" and with authenticity. Even when Rousseau says of himself that he is marked by "sluggishness of thought" along with his "liveliness of feeling," he describes himself as a man whose thought readily becomes inextricably mixed with feeling; the resulting "agitation" testifies once more to his status as a being uncorrupted because uncontrolled.

Other aspects of his personality that Rousseau emphasizes include his imagination, his attachment to nature, his commitment to impulse, and his interest in the common people. Each of these characteristics could also become subjects of discussion that might dwell on how this writer differs from his eighteenth-century predecessors. Possibly even more fruitful would be an examination of the idea of uniqueness in the *Confessions*. The book opens, of course, with the author's claim of absolute distinction ("If I am not better, at least I am different" [volume E, p. 664]). In book II, however, Rousseau observes, "I have been reproached with wanting to pose as an original, and different from others. In reality, I have never troubled about acting like other people or differently from them" (p. 670). And in book VI, instead of asserting his difference, he *wonders* about whether others share his ideas. Is it possible to reconcile these claims? One can, of course, emphasize the verb "pose" in the second sequence: Rousseau doesn't want to *pose* as an original, he simply *is* one. But the question of posing or acting is a useful one to bring up in connection with the *Confessions*. Is all Rousseau's self-presentation perhaps a form of posing? His wondering about other people acknowledges the mystery of uniqueness. In fact, no one can possibly know whether he or she is different from everyone else. So to claim difference, as Rousseau does at the outset, necessarily involves a kind of posing. But is that necessarily a bad thing? Such questions can obviously lead to consideration of the perplexing problem of what autobiography as a genre implies.

Rousseau himself directly brings up the problem of autobiographical narrative in the selection quoted from book VI. He suggests the difficulty of communicating the source of feeling, the impossibility of making narrative equivalent to memory. Students may be asked to assess the degree to which he in fact solves these problems. Does he convincingly evoke feeling and memory? If so, how?

Topics for Writing

A useful paper assignment is to ask students to write a fragment of their own "confessions." Other possibilities:

1. The place of imagination for Rousseau.
2. Rousseau's evocation of Paris.
3. A description of Rousseau as a child.

Comparative Perspectives

1. As self-contemplating wanderers and lovers of nature, Rousseau, Bashō, Wordsworth, and Whitman share many personal preferences, but their cultural backgrounds are quite distinct. How important to each of these gigantic figures are other people? How fully does each identify with his country and its principles? Is Rousseau a "Swiss" or "French" writer in the sense that Bashō is quintessentially Japanese, Wordsworth is "English," and Whitman is "American"?
2. Rousseau wishes to "dispose of Nature in its entirety as its lord and

master," and exults in his power to express the sensations he draws from it. How does his pleasure in appropriating the natural world for his own delectation compare with the approach to nature observed in the lyrics of some of the later Romantic poets, such as Bécquer or Leopardi, or that in the lyrics of China and Japan?

3. Compare Rousseau's account of his perverse pleasure in the corporal punishments he received from Mademoiselle Lambercier with Keats's reference to "aching pleasure" (line 23) in *Ode on Melancholy*. In what way are these Romantic sentiments?

Further Reading

See also the reading suggestions in the anthology, p. 663.

Crocker, L. *Jean-Jacques Rousseau*. 2 vols. 1963. An exhaustive and perceptive treatment of Rousseau's life and works.

France, P. *Rousseau, Confessions*. 1987. A critical study entirely focused on the *Confessions*.

Gremsley, R. *Jean-Jacques Rousseau: A Study in Self-Awareness*. 1961. Provides psychological analysis of Rousseau's personality.

Guéhenno, J. *Jean-Jacques Rousseau*. Trans. J. and D. Weightman. 2 vols. 1966. Another excellent critical biography (its treatment of the *Confessions* is confined to Vol. 2).

Havens, G. *Jean-Jacques Rousseau*. 1978. In the Twayne series. A rather pedestrian but useful general introduction.

JOHANN WOLFGANG VON GOETHE

Faust

Classroom Strategies and Topics for Discussion

As the "type characters" in Molière are likely to create problems for student readers, so are the personages of Goethe's *Faust*. You can simplify the task of reading this work (probably in two assignments, the first one ending just before the first appearance of Margaret, p. 733), by explaining that *Faust* can best be read as a philosophic poem. Its characters exemplify positions rather than display developed personalities. Such positions, however, can be very complex indeed; a good place to start discussion of the play is by trying to elucidate together the set of attitudes and assumptions that Faust himself embodies.

What, first of all, about his attitude toward knowledge? Those who know Marlowe's *Doctor Faustus* or other versions of the Faust legend may anticipate that the protagonist will seek intellectual grasp or comprehension of the universe. In fact, it is Faust's rather foolish and obtuse assistant, Wagner, who "should like to know all." Faust, on the other hand, proclaims that "We can know nothing." He adds immediately, "It burns my heart" (p. 684). Does he mean that the knowledge he has gained all seems irrelevant to his purposes? or that none of it means anything? or what? Detailed analysis of his first speech will announce the chief problems of his role. *Why* can he not presume to make use of his learning, or open his mind to improve humankind? No answer is immediately given in the text; students should be urged to support speculations based on later passages and actual textual evidence. They may well conclude—even on the basis of the first speech as a whole—that Faust cannot use his learning or improve humankind because learning has nothing to do with reality and because people exist only in individual isolation.

As the first speech continues, it becomes ever clearer that Faust wishes not to gain more knowledge but to escape the knowledge he has acquired. He wants to stop "rummaging in phrases," to unite himself with nature, "casting dusty knowledge overboard," to participate in the world rather than deal with "skeletons" (books and theories). A useful question is how the concepts that seem important to Faust compare with those apparently important to Rousseau. Nature and imagination are key ideas here too; the common people are valued (in the scene where Faust walks in the village), and so is feeling. But Faust dwells on these ideas in more meditative and detailed fashion than does Rousseau. Rousseau assumes their authority; Faust comes closer to arguing it. The question of his heroic stature is perhaps best postponed until students have finished reading the entire play, but it is worth inquiring even at the outset what kind of impression his passionate investment in his own convictions makes on first-time readers.

An important early piece of action is Faust's near-suicide. What impels him to kill himself? One way of answering this question (there are of course others, and students should be encouraged to find them) is to say that he cannot tolerate the gap between his capacity to imagine and his capacity to act. He can conceive of great possibilities for himself, but the realities of experience and of other people keep frustrating them. (This source of pain is best articulated in the soliloquy beginning "Hope never seems to leave those who affirm" [p. 689].) The choir of angels he hears saves him from self-destruction; why? Its meaning seems concerned less with religion than with memory—"these chords, which I have known since infancy." Memory involves reminiscences of past faith and, perhaps, of past community.

Faust, like Rousseau, considers himself unique, superior to others. Mephistopheles presents himself as "the spirit that negates," and Faust, accepting him, implicitly denies himself association with his kind. An important issue for class discussion of the first reading assignment is Faust's pact with the devil. Why does he voluntarily accept death and damnation if ever he stretches himself on a bed of sloth? This is a complicated and important question. In assessing why Faust in effect equates sloth and death, students should be urged to think, for example, of the scene in which he amends the Bible, denying the power of the Word as originating force, replacing Word with Mind, then with Force, then with Act. As

Faust says shortly after making his compact, "Restless activity proves a man." A little later, he makes it clear that he values no effect that fails to result in "new strength within." The class should consider such statements (and others) as evidence for the high value Faust attaches to *effort* and *force* and *action* as defining characteristics of the truly human. His aspiration involves the need constantly to *do*, without much regard for what the doing specifically involves.

When Margaret enters the play, its emphasis changes. Discussion of the second assignment might begin with the figure of Margaret. In her first appearance, she seems rather spunky ("I . . . can go home without your care" [p. 733]), but once Mephistopheles begins plotting on Faust's behalf to get her, she loses obvious force of character. What is her function in the play? Neither great beauty nor great intelligence is assigned her; she epitomizes virtue but falls easily to Faust. One way of understanding her is as a projection of Faust's desires. What does he want in a woman? He rhapsodizes over the neatness of her room; he praises her as an "angel." If he himself wants to act and desire without ceasing, he appears to wish for a woman who will do neither except in response to him. Margaret fills his needs because she so readily makes him the center of her universe (he is already the center of his own). But at the end of Part I, she transcends his construction of her. Is her refusal of his rescue attempt psychologically and morally plausible? The question admits of much debate. One can at least argue that her reaffirmation of the moral authority of her religion and her community both fits with her previously demonstrated need for self-subordination and shows how, in the play's logic, a sense of guilt (which Faust is only beginning to develop) can be liberating. Certainly the voice from above that pronounces her "redeemed" suggests that her misery results in a happy ending.

Obviously important to the structure and the argument of *Faust* is Mephistopheles, worth attention both for the way that his moral position is established and elaborated and for the relation of that position to Faust's. A crude way to put the contrast between him and Faust might be to suggest that he always takes a cynical view of experience, while Faust often takes an idealistic one. Discussion of this point might begin with investigation of the dialogue just before the scene in Martha's garden, where Faust, in Mephistopheles's summary of his viewpoint, speaks his "soul's profoundest love" and his devilish companion suggests that such talk is only a way to "Deceive poor Gretchen" (p. 743). Faust protests his truth and declares his flame of love "everlasting"; Mephistopheles insists that he, the cynic, is right; Faust concludes, "You are right, because I have no choice." Faust believes himself to be making only a verbal concession; he doesn't deeply acknowledge his companion's rightness. But one brilliant aspect of this play is the way it demonstrates the partial accuracy of many points of view. Faust's conviction of the absolute authenticity and authority of his own feelings is from one viewpoint naive and self-centered; from another, it affirms the value of the emotional capacity that presumably helps to differentiate humanity from the lower animals.

Conversely, Mephistopheles's cynicism is entirely too easy—everything in experience is obviously susceptible to his kind of criticism; the value of feeling and aspiration can in the nature of things never be proved. But it also calls attention to the equivalent "easiness" in Faust's protestations. Students can be led toward an understanding of the relationship of cross-commentary between Faust and Mephistopheles by beginning with an apparently simple but engaging question: How do you feel to- ward Mephistopheles? The next question, obviously, is: Do your feelings change? If so, when, and why? The various answers generated by such questions will lead the group back to the text to look particularly at the various sequences of dialogue between Faust and his betrayer.

Other issues worth attending to include the importance of the super- natural in the play (What is gained by casting this drama in terms of God and devil? Could the same story be told as well in other terms?) and the functions of the various minor characters.

Topics for Writing

1. Why the witches?
2. How does the figure of Martha clarify that of Margaret?
3. Is Faust a hero?
4. How does Margaret affect Faust?
5. The importance of feeling.
6. The importance of imagination.
7. What nature means in this play.

Comparative Perspectives

1. Goethe draws on many works in the Western literary tradition in shaping the issues he raises in *Faust*. Compare his treatment of the relationship between God and Satan in conversation with the open- ing chapters of Job; compare Goethe's Mephistopheles with Mil- ton's Satan (see the references to the earlier poem on p. 763); or review the medieval lyrics in volume B by poets such as Walther von der Vogelweide and the Archpoet to show how Goethe re-creates the late-medieval world in his *Faust*.
2. Why is Gretchen shown at her spinning wheel? Note the conversa- tion "at the well" about Barbara, who used to stay out late while other girls stayed home "spinning away." How do nineteenth- century musical settings of this moment, most notably Schubert's song "Gretchen am Spinnrade," illuminate the girl's state of mind by mimicking the undertone of the relentlessly spinning wheel? How does this reflect a Western motif quite different from the meaning of spinning and wheels in Hindu and Buddhist art?
3. The headnote to *Faust* in the anthology (pp. 678–80) reminds us that Goethe excelled as "a poet, dramatist, novelist, and autobiogra- pher," and also pursued a varied career in diplomacy, science, and law. Most of these occupational categories could be applied to Wole

Soyinka as well. As did Goethe in *Faust*, Soyinka has enriched the theatrical vocabulary of his time in *Death and the King's Horseman*. Compare and contrast the way each playwright introduces folk motifs, music, and elements of the supernatural to explore the dilemmas that beset his protagonist. If *Faust* and *Death and the King's Horseman* were written as realistic plays, would we view their protagonists differently?

Further Reading

See also the reading suggestions in the anthology, p. 680.

Dieckmann, L. *Johann Wolfgang Goethe*. 1974. In the Twayne series. Particularly good, "intended as a guide to close reading," and offering a chapter on *Faust*.

Fairley, B. *Goethe as Revealed in His Poetry*. 1932; reprinted 1963. Includes two chapters on *Faust*, one arguing that the entire play rather than merely its hero must be understood as dramatizing a process of development, the other on *Faust* as a manifestation of Goethe's lyricism.

Friedenthal, R. *Goethe: His Life and Times*. 1965. Concentrates on the poet's life and his social and historical context rather than on his works.

McMillan, D. J., ed. *Approaches to Teaching Goethe's* Faust. 1987. Varied and useful essays.

Stearns, M. *Goethe: Pattern of Genius*. 1967. Predominantly biographical in emphasis, also offers detailed analysis of *Faust*.

WILLIAM BLAKE

Songs of Innocence and of Experience

Classroom Strategies and Topics for Discussion

In teaching Blake, as with all lyric poets, you must spend a good deal of time—probably most of the available time—attending to local effects. But large matters also deserve attention. It is often useful to students (because it provides a kind of orientation that helps in reading individual poems) to point out in advance that Blake's lyrics are marked by their mixture of social and metaphysical awareness. If students have heard this suggestion before they read the assignment, they may be prepared to begin discussion by pointing out specific examples of the combination. (Good ones occur in *The Little Black Boy*, *The Chimney Sweeper* [both versions], *London*, and *And Did Those Feet*.) Then the class can talk about how Blake achieves this unusual merging of concerns and how successful it is. Such discussion will lead naturally to detailed investigation of individual lyrics. Here are a few useful questions for some of the poems.

INTRODUCTION

It is enlightening to consider the "Introduction" to *Songs of Innocence* and that to *Songs of Experience* together, seeking similarities and contrasts between them. Both poems define a poet's role. How does that role differ in the two poems? Matters worth attention are the poet's subject matter and tone in each case ("happy" songs—the word occurs three times, along with related terms like "pleasant glee," "laughing," "joy"—about a Lamb or about "chear," versus visionary songs from a "weeping" Bard who sings in order to appeal to "the lapsed Soul"); the kinds of communication anticipated (to "Every child" or to Earth and the Soul); the imagined function of poetry (to create emotional effect, to redeem the fall of man). Students might be asked about the differences in the level of diction and syntactical complexity and about the effects generated by these differences. Finally, you might inquire what kind of volume each introduction appears to introduce.

THE LAMB

This lyric is useful as a basis for discussing what "innocence" means in Blake's mythology. The lamb, as students should know or be told, is a traditional symbol of Christ. It is also, like the little child, associated with innocence. What is the effect of the childlike diction and repetition in this poem? They create a kind of incantatory effect that almost forces the reader to attend to the speaker's sense of a wondrous universe. The simplest phenomenon, to a child's sensibility, can seem astonishing; Blake tries to recreate the feeling of innocent astonishment. Innocence thus becomes a mode of perception—as it appears to be in all the poems of the volume. Discussion can move on in this way to other poems: what is the perspective of innocence in each case? How does it work?

EARTH'S ANSWER

The combination of abstract and concrete diction here may interest students. Such phrases as "grey despair" and "Starry Jealousy" (extremely difficult to explicate) exemplify the way that Blake tries to make abstractions part of the physical world. This is a difficult poem to understand. It is valuable, therefore, to show students that they probably understand more than they think they do. You might go through the lyric, stanza by stanza, asking what impression each leaves. Most readers will comprehend the general situation—this is a lamentation by imprisoned Earth. To what does it "answer"? The *Introduction*, just before, ends with an appeal to Earth to "Arise" and participate in a process of redemption. This answer involves Earth's explanation of why she cannot arise—because of emotional, not political, enemies that oppose love and growth.

THE TYGER

The poem is convenient to consider in conjunction with *The Lamb* as a transformation of the same sense of wonder into terms of experience rather than innocence. What kind of emotion does it generate in the reader? What is the effect of the peculiar syntax in line 12 ("What dread hand? & what dread feet?")? How does the rest of the poem account for the change in verb in the last lines of the first and the last stanzas ("could" to "dare")?

Topics for Writing

1. One of Blake's characters (e.g., the chimney sweeper, the child on the cloud, or the speaker in any of the poems).
2. What is the city like?
3. Blake's use of nature.

Comparative Perspectives

1. By the eighteenth century, many European writers indicate their disapproval of the colonial oppression of native peoples, but the references are often oblique and fleeting. By the beginning of the nineteenth century, the antislavery movement has gained strength and the tone of these references changes. Compare, as appropriate, Pope's "poor Indian" (*An Essay on Man*, epistle I, line 99), Candide's encounter with the maimed slave who works in the sugar mill (chapter 19), and Blake's Little Black Boy. What lessons do we learn about authorial perspective when we set any of these beside the *Narrative of the Life of Frederick Douglass, An American Slave* or the poems of Caribbean writers of the twentieth century?
2. What view of nature do we see in Blake's *Introduction to Songs of Experience* and in *Earth's Answer*? Who or what seems to be responsible for "the darkness dread & drear" of the world? Compare the reasons in Leopardi's *To Himself* for declaring "The world is mud" (p. 847). How does the industrialization of the Western World during this period contribute to the difference between European poetry and the lyrics of Bashō?

Further Reading

See also the reading suggestions in the anthology, p. 782.

Frye, N. *Fearful Symmetry*. 1947. Sees Blake as developing a unified myth through his poetry. (See Hirsch, cited in the anthology, for an opposing view.)

Gleckner, R. *The Piper and the Bard*. 1959. Treats *Songs of Innocence* and *Songs of Experience* as dividing naturally into groups organized by common images and themes.

Gleckner, R. F., and M. L. Greenberg, eds. *Approaches to Teaching Blake's* Songs of Innocence and Experience. 1989. Another invaluable collection.

O'Neill, J., ed. *Critics on Blake.* 1970. A work specifically intended for undergraduates. Includes a smattering of criticism from 1803 to 1941 as well as several later essays; its essays concentrate on *Songs of Innocence* and *Songs of Experience.*

WILLIAM WORDSWORTH

Classroom Strategies and Topics for Discussion

As some students may know already, William Wordsworth has a special position as the announcer of Romanticism in England (in the preface to *Lyrical Ballads*). You should probably suggest before they begin reading that they will find in his poetry an even more emphatic stress on nature than Rousseau and Goethe offered, and equivalent attention to the importance of the self and its feelings. Students might also be alerted in advance to the significance of memory and of childhood as Wordsworthian themes. A few suggestions about the two long poems follow.

LINES COMPOSED A FEW MILES ABOVE TINTERN ABBEY

As so often with poetry, it is illuminating to read a passage aloud at the outset and to talk about the effect of the verse form. If students have just been reading Blake, they will hardly be prepared for the leisurely, ruminative rhythms of the blank verse, which by its very movement helps to establish the contemplative tone of the poem. Talking about the introductory section (lines 1–21), you might inquire about the speaker's attitude toward appearances created by human beings as opposed to those of nature. The orchard tufts that "lose themselves / 'Mid groves and copses" epitomize a pattern as the poet subsumes human artifacts into the natural world, making the hedgerows seem like bits of wood, the farmhouse smoke seem like a hermit's smoke, and so on. Observation of this fact prepares readers for the complicated attitude toward the human that develops as the poem goes on. One can trace throughout the poem the ways in which the speaker approaches and retreats from connection with the human: he speaks of acts of kindness and of love, but immediately moves on to something "more sublime"—a mood that enables him to forget the body, become all soul, and see into the life of things. The "fretful stir" of the third section suggests real antipathy to the human. Nourishment comes from the natural ("in this moment there is life and food / For future years" [lines 64–65]); Nature guards the heart and soul and moral being. But the poem is resolved by an address to his sister. The ending is worth dwelling on: Does it in fact resolve the problems the poem has established? What are those problems? One of them, certainly, is the speaker's relation to others of his kind. Another is the loss implicit in growing up (students can be asked to find evidence for this notion). Yet another is the difficulty of preserving in memory what is lost in experience. How does the final section answer these problems? Or does it only evade them? How convincing is Wordsworth's evocation of nature as a moral force? How does his vision of "something far more deeply inter-fused" (line 96) compare with the evocation of universal "oneness" at the end of the first epistle of *An Essay on Man*?

ODE ON INTIMATIONS OF IMMORTALITY

To a considerable extent, the themes of this poem duplicate those of *Tintern Abbey*. Students may find it interesting to begin by trying to locate ideas that the two poems hold in common, going on to analyze ways in which differences in expression and context have the effect of altering meaning. Specifically, it may be valuable to compare the sense of past versus present in the poems, and the function of nature, which here appears to be more emotional than moral. The word "glory" (along with "glories" and "glorious") occurs at least seven times in this ode. "There hath past away a glory from the earth," line 18 proclaims. Considering the different occurrences of the word and its cognates, what does "glory" appear to mean here? It will not be possible to define it precisely, but a group can talk about its associations (with royalty, with divinity, with splendor, beauty, radiance, for example) and about the range of meanings suggested by the word's various uses in the ode. It might be hypothesized that the word's value for the poet comes partly from its vagueness and its breadth of association. The poem is trying to articulate something that cannot be precisely located; it tries to make the reader understand this "something" by playing on the reader's feelings. A passage particularly repaying close attention is the account of human development in stanzas VII and VIII. What does this theory of development involve and imply? It glorifies the preconscious and deprecates maturity; it implicitly argues that human association (the heavy, freezing weight of "custom") contains the seed of the soul's destruction. Compared with the view of *Tintern Abbey*, this seems more extreme, more somber. What about the resolution of this poem? Is it more or less satisfactory than that of its predecessor? Does it solve the emotional problems that have been evoked? Why is the last word "tears"? Does that fact suggest anything about the atmosphere of this ending as opposed to the other?

Topics for Writing

1. Sunshine and clouds in *Immortality*.
2. An impression of the "sister" in *Tintern Abbey*.
3. The morality of *Tintern Abbey* (or of *Immortality*).

Comparative Perspectives

1. How would you compare the view of the city in the selections by an-cient writers with those expressed by writers such as Swift (Dublin in *A Modest Proposal*), Rousseau (from book IV), Blake (*London*), and Wordsworth? Each of these writers has a unique perspective on city life. Explore the various dissatisfactions they articulate and

think about the way Aeschylus treats Athens in the *Oresteia*, or the Psalmist speaks about Jerusalem.

2. Explain the role of childhood in the theory of poetic inspiration that animates *Tintern Abbey* and *Immortality*. Compare Wordsworth's idealization of youthful percipience with the approach taken by other writers to the impressionability of the young, including Cao Xueqin, Rousseau, Proust, Pirandello, Ichiyō, Faulkner, and Munro.

Further Reading

See also the reading suggestions in the anthology, pp. 791–92.

Bewell, A. *Wordsworth and the Enlightenment*. 1989. An anthropological approach to Wordsworth and his historical context.

Davies, H. *William Wordsworth*. 1980. A highly readable biography, with splendid plates.

Davis, J., ed. *Discussions of William Wordsworth*. 1965. An exceptionally useful collection of essays that exemplifies many points of view.

Ferry, D. *The Limits of Mortality*. 1959. A study of Wordsworth's major poems that places those included in the anthology in the context of the poet's other work.

Hall, S., with J. Ramsey, ed. *Approaches to Teaching Wordsworth's Poetry*. 1986. Pedagogically invaluable essays.

Noyes, R. *William Wordsworth*. 1971. In the Twayne series. Provides thoughtful criticism as well as a biographical introduction and bibliography.

DOROTHY WORDSWORTH

The Grasmere Journals

Classroom Strategies and Topics for Discussion

There are at least four ways of using Dorothy Wordsworth's *Grasmere Journals* in the classroom, and since they are complementary rather than mutually exclusive, it is worth considering them all. Traditionally, critics have combed through the sister's journals to find insights into her brother's poetry; more recently, feminist scholars have trained on the same materials a psychoanalytic lens; general readers have always been fascinated by the journals as sources of wonderful "inside information" about an extraordinary group of people who changed the course of English literature; and most important, perhaps, as the headnote in the anthology stresses, students of the Romantic era can focus on documents that reveal a remarkable sensibility confronting the issues of mind and nature that lie at the heart of so much Western literature of the early nineteenth century.

Probably the most famous example of William Wordsworth's transmutation of Dorothy Wordsworth's perceptions is *I Wandered Lonely as a Cloud,* in which the daffodils so exquisitely described by Dorothy in her journal entry for Thursday, April 15, 1802, become the subject of one of his best-known poems. William Wordsworth recollects the daffodils in tranquillity, musing on the value they impart to him, self-declared "a poet," when he is far from the original scene. If you have read *Tintern Abbey* with your students, you may want to send them back to that poem to find the reference, in lines 25–31, to the kind of moment when such a memory was important to him.

Dorothy uses her journals, as that word implies, to record the dailiness of experience as it is being lived, generally preferring the "we" to the "I," although she certainly does specify when she alone makes a judgment: "I never saw daffodils so beautiful." Significantly, she looks at them without thinking of the profit she might realize from them, more concerned to render an accurate description of the veritable colony of flowers that she discovers in their own habitat. Yet it is she who invents the famous, witty anthropomorphic characterization of the dancing flowers, "some of whom rested their heads upon these stones as on a pillow for weariness."

In other words, although she often represses the first personal singular, Dorothy is far more than the possessor of the "wild eyes" (*Tintern Abbey,* lines 119, 148) on which William Wordsworth grew to rely; she has her own idiosyncratic imagination. She never simply records; she too transforms what she sees. In this case, her imputation of "weariness" to the gay flowers bespeaks her own preoccupation with such exhaustion. No one can read the entries in her journals without noting the frequency of her (and her brother's) headaches, bouts of amnesia, and recurrent, if brief, sieges of (probably dyspeptic?) illness.

You may be surprised by the sympathy that your students will express for these symptoms of anxiety and by how interested they are likely to be by the family story that at least to some degree precipitates them. You may want to point out that the journal entries in the anthology were all written in anticipation of the forthcoming marriage of William Wordsworth to Dorothy's close friend Mary Hutchinson, of whom the brother and sister think at the end of April 15, 1802, the day of the daffodils (pp. 803–04). The day before, the point at which the anthology picks up the entries, Dorothy is "ill out of spirits—disheartened": Is this because William has just returned from visiting Mary and fixing the day of their wedding (October 4, 1802), an event so traumatizing that Dorothy was unable to attend it, devoted though she was to both the bride and the groom?

Should you choose to dispense information of this sort, you may want also to identify the "Annette" with whom so many letters are exchanged as Annette Vallon, the young French woman who was the mother of William's daughter, Caroline. Before the marriage to Mary took place, Dorothy and William went to Calais to spend about a month with Annette and Caroline. (Originally, Dorothy had expected that William would marry Annette, whom he met during his tour of France in the early 1790s; although it became clear that neither partner wished to resume and formalize their relationship, the Wordsworths remained supportive. Years later, Caroline named a daughter "Dorothy" in honor of her beloved aunt.)

None of this biographical data, however, need be brought into the classroom. Another approach to integrating the life that Dorothy's journals describe to the poetic enterprise that she shared with Wordsworth and Coleridge (also an important presence in these excerpts) is simply to ask your students about the relation between the small events of an apparently uneventful existence to the development of intellectual and moral consciousness. For one thing, you can use Dorothy Wordsworth's journals to initiate your students into the role that reading literature plays in writing literature. Once your students have seen these entries from *The Grasmere Journals*, with their references to Spenser's *Prothalamium* (Sunday, April 25) and Milton's sonnets (Friday, May 21), they should understand why the influence of Milton and Spenser can be detected in Wordsworth's poems.

Even more rewarding is to investigate with your class the way the blandness of the activities engaged in here nevertheless excited complicated responses. If Dorothy Wordsworth's extreme modesty contrasts with the "egotistical sublime" of her brother, the way she interprets events is no less compelling than his more self-involved thought process. For instance, the random encounter with the local population that gives rise to Dorothy's self-deprecating insight into the shared laughter of the "two sisters at work" at the expense of the brother and sister with whom they "had some talk" on April 16, 1802, seems to have no effect on her brother, intent on finishing his poem.

Whatever one makes of the mysteries of these journals, which were never intended for the kind of inspection to which they have now been subjected, we cannot but be grateful for the fineness of the observations they preserve. Perhaps no better example of this may be found in these selections than in the entry for Friday, May 14, 1802 (not included in the anthology), a day of a late-season storm. Early in the day, William seeks "an epithet for the cuckow." After dinner, Dorothy kneads bread, mends stockings, and watches the strange night:

> The woods looked miserable, the coppices green as grass which looked quite unnatural and they seemed half shrivelled up as if they shrunk from the air. O thought I! what a beautiful thing God has made winter to be by stripping the trees and letting us see their shapes and forms.

The unexpectedness of the conclusion that she draws from the desolate scene reveals the modern artist latent in the careful homemaker. Dorothy Wordsworth's appreciation for the stripped-down shapes and forms of the created world should help each of us see afresh the surroundings in which we live.

Topics for Writing

1. Keep a journal for twenty-four hours and record with as unblemished an eye as possible the shapes of what you see and the events in which you participate, and then compare your account with one of Dorothy Wordsworth's journal entries. How has life changed since the beginning of the nineteenth century? What habits of your own mind can you discover from your work? What can you now appreciate about the details that recommend themselves to Wordsworth's consciousness?

2. Is there such a thing as a feminine sensibility? Citing evidence from *The Grasmere Journals,* try to distinguish between observations and preoccupations that derive from the social role Dorothy Wordsworth played and those that reflect the quality of her intellect and imagination.

Comparative Perspectives

1. The journal has proved a fruitful genre for women who may have lacked the support to launch careers as authors but nevertheless found sufficient leisure to record the minutiae of daily existence. Although Dorothy Wordsworth's record of her daily walks and bread-baking may seem far removed from the experiences of a woman like Sei Shonagon, they share a love of poetry and a keen eye for beauty in unexpected places. Choose an example from each woman's diary that illustrates her attentiveness to aesthetic matters, then compare and contrast your selections.

2. A great deal of contemporary fiction about women evinces a kind of quiet suffering not unlike Dorothy Wordsworth's. Compare the sources of Wordsworth's buried pain with the emotions that trouble the protagonist of Clarice Lispector's *Daydreams of a Drunken Woman* or of Ingeborg Bachmann's *The Barking.* Analyze these women from different perspectives: how would the Freud who failed in his treatment of Dora view their problems? How would Virginia Woolf?

Further Reading

See also the reading suggestions in the anthology, p. 802.

Homans, Margaret. *Women Writers and Poetic Identity.* 1980. While it deals primarily with the small number of poems that Dorothy Wordsworth wrote, this book makes many observations that are useful in regard to her journal writing as well.

Levin, Susan M. *Dorothy Wordsworth & Romanticism.* 1987. Informed by contemporary psychological and linguistic critical insights, this valuable book contains a good bibliography and perceptive comments, some noted above.

Wordsworth, Dorothy. *The Grasmere Journal.* 1987. A beautifully produced edition of the complete journal, richly illustrated with maps and
contemporary drawings by artists like Constable, Harden, and Turner.
Introduction by Jonathan Wordsworth.

SAMUEL TAYLOR COLERIDGE

Classroom Strategies and Topics for Discussion

Coleridge's poetry is likely to interest students through its capacity subtly to differentiate states of emotion and also compellingly to suggest the
nature of an emotional condition. If undergraduates think his tone sometimes overwrought, they often can be brought by close attention to the
text to understand the precision of his poetic effects and how richly they
are used in poetic structures.

KUBLA KHAN

An absolutely surefire way to engage student attention is to raise the
problem of automatic writing brought up by Coleridge's account of this
poem's composition. You should point out that the footnote on page 813
calls attention to the dubious authenticity of this account, but then go on
to invite speculation about why the notion of the poet as inspired creator
is so compelling to the imagination. Why should we like to think that poetry issues from unconscious depths, without effort, discipline, or rewriting? Certainly this view contradicts ordinary experience of what it is like
to write anything at all; good writing, most people find, is hard work. It is
then valuable to point out how the vision of the poet as natural seer
comes into the poem itself. You might inquire about the "damsel with a
dulcimer" and how she figures in *Kubla Khan,* and about the "I" at the
poem's end and what others are alleged to "cry" about him. What do the
final lines ("For he on honey-dew hath fed, / And drunk the milk of Paradise") mean and imply? The poet here emerges as an awe-inspiring figure,
set apart from others, mysteriously dangerous, nourished in other ways
than ordinary mortals, possessed of essentially magic powers ("And all
who heard should see them there"). Another kind of question worth pursuing in relation to this poem is the power of scene to evoke feeling. Students can be asked to specify the various individual scenes summoned up
by description and to talk about the kinds of emotion they call forth.

DEJECTION: AN ODE

The poem is worth going through stanza by stanza, to specify what is
happening in each stanza and how each relates to its successor. If time
forbids such detailed examination, here are a few matters to investigate.
What is the relation between the conversational tone of the opening lines
and the rhetorical intensity of, say, stanza III? In other words, how does
the speaker make plausible his movement from one tone to the other? In
effect he documents that movement in the course of stanza I: the casual

observation about the weather leads him to think about the prospect of bad weather that would fit with his mood; by stanza II it has become apparent that the remark about the weather was in the first place only an effort to disguise the mood of depression. How is *scene* used in this poem (perhaps in comparison to *Kubla Khan*)? Here too one can trace precise correlations between scene and feeling. Special attention should be paid to the idea that the human experiencer gives meaning to nature, announced at the end of stanza III and the beginning of stanza IV; students might be asked to trace the intertwining of subjective and objective through the poem. What is the meaning of "Reality's dark dream" (line 95)? The speaker seems to have in mind fantasies stimulated by the dark realities around him; the rest of stanza VII specifies such fantasies. What psychic purpose do they serve? They enlarge the reference of the depression that tends to isolate the person who feels it; in the development of the poem, they prepare for the invocation in stanza VIII, which declares the speaker's capacity to concern himself with others. Finally, what is the role of the "Lady" in the poem and how does it compare with the role of the "Sister" in *Tintern Abbey*?

Topics for Writing

Writing topics can develop from any of the questions suggested above; it is also often useful to ask students to write about the function of a single image and how it is developed in the poem. See also "Topics for Writing" for Shelley, below.

Comparative Perspectives

1. Compare the reflections on art and the supernatural in *Dejection: An Ode* to those expressed in Mahfouz's *Zaabalawi*.

   [Coleridge's poems are interesting embodiments of a famous modernist's dictum that Romanticism is "spilled religion," whereas Mahfouz's work reflects a culture in which the aesthetic and the spiritual seem inextricably bound.]
2. Coleridge claims that the fragmentary *Kubla Khan* resulted from a narcotized state. Set its imagery alongside some of the Chinese poems in celebration of wine (for instance, Li Po's *Bring in the Wine*), and comment on how different uses of inebriation mark different ideas about the nature of poetry and the role of the imagination.

Further Reading

See also the reading suggestions in the anthology, p. 812.

Bygrave, S. *Coleridge and the Self: Romantic Egotism.* 1986. A psychologically focused essay.

Hill, J. *A Coleridge Companion.* 1983. Supplies a biographical sketch as well as invaluable background and interpretation for *Kubla Khan* and *Dejection: An Ode.*

Watson, G. *Coleridge the Poet.* 1966. Concentrates on the achievement of the poems, with considerable analysis of individual texts.

PERCY BYSSHE SHELLEY

Classroom Strategies and Topics for Discussion

One aspect of Shelley's poetry likely to interest undergraduates is his combination of lyric impulse with political and social passion—a version of the same linkage found in Blake.

ENGLAND IN 1819

This sonnet is a useful place to start discussion—partly because it is likely to contradict any expectations students might come with about Shelley as a poet. In the next to the last line of the sonnet, *graves* become a summarizing image for all the phenomena previously evoked. The point of the grave appears to be that a "glorious Phantom" may burst out of it. But graves are also, above all, places where someone (or, by extension, something) is buried. In what sense can kings, princes, armies, and the rest be said to bury something? In other words, how does the metaphor of graves enlarge or illuminate what has come before? Among other things, all the realities Shelley has evoked seem in his view to represent ends to hope, belief, or possibility; this is one reason his tone is so angry. Before all the early references are summed up as constituting "graves," however, they are also characterized by a wealth of individual metaphors. What are some of these metaphors? Students will presumably mention *dregs, mud, leeches, sword, book, statute.* Do these metaphors have anything in common? Typically, they reduce something human to something nonhuman, thus preparing for the final reduction of everything to the grave. A line students are likely to find particularly difficult, because of its extreme condensation, is line 10: "Golden and sanguine laws which tempt and slay." (The footnote helps, but not a whole lot.) It is worth spending some time on elucidation here, working out what it might mean to imagine laws as tempting and slaying. Do golden laws tempt and sanguine ones slay? Or are laws in general being imagined as both golden and sanguine? What kinds of laws might tempt? How do they slay? A particular reason for attending to this line is that it is likely to lead to a perception of how relevant Shelley's indictment might be to our own time.

ODE TO THE WEST WIND

How does the high value attached to *energy* in this poem compare with the valuing of energy in *Faust*? One might remark, in this connection, the degree to which Shelley attaches the idea of energy to that of *purpose*. What is the relation between the poet's dwelling on description and his apparent belief that the poet can provide "the trumpet of a prophecy"? It might be argued that the luxurious descriptions here exemplify an important aspect of the poet's power: to evoke, to make real, to generate the force of incantation. These are the methods he (or, for that matter, she) can use to inspire and to prophesy.

A DEFENCE OF POETRY

How does the emphasis on power in this essay compare with the stress on energy in *Ode to the West Wind?*

Topics for Writing

The exercise on an image suggested for Coleridge would work well here too. Other possibilities:

1. Compare Shelley and Coleridge on dejection.
2. Use the *Defence* as a means of characterizing one of the other Romantic poets.

Comparative Perspectives

1. *Ode to the West Wind* makes frequent allusions to many of the same masterpieces of world literature that appear in the anthology. How many can you identify?

    [Shelley's adaptation of *terza rima* and the poem's opening image of fallen leaves clearly allude to Dante's *Divine Comedy* and the rich epic tradition that the Italian master drew on. The comparison of clouds to a "fierce Maenad" will be appreciated by students who know about the Dionysian sources of Greek tragedy. "I fall upon the thorns of life, I bleed!" invokes Christ's crown of thorns. In turn, in its evocation of seasonal change and tone of desperation, the poem stands as a source for Tennyson's *In Memoriam* and Eliot's *The Waste Land.*]
2. In *A Defence of Poetry*, Shelley admits the possibility of a moral gap between the human beings who write poetry and "that spirit of good of which they are the ministers." As you read the biographical introductions to the writers you are studying this term, do you note any such contradictions? Need an artist be a good person to create good art?

Further Reading

See also the reading suggestions in the anthology, p. 820.

Chernaik, J. *The Lyrics of Shelley.* 1972. Contains new texts of many Shelley poems and offers thoughtful readings of the lyrics in the anthology.

Duerksen, Roland. *Shelley's Poetry of Involvement.* 1988. Shelley as social commentator.

Reiman, D. *Percy Bysshe Shelley.* 1969. Provides an excellent short general biography and critical introduction, with useful bibliography.

White, N. *Shelley*. 2 vols. 1940. The standard biography, monumental and exhaustive.

Hall, Spencer, ed. *Approaches to Teaching Shelley's Poetry*. 1990. Another useful MLA volume.

JOHN KEATS

Classroom Strategies and Topics for Discussion

If students enjoy poetry at all, they usually like Keats for the incantatory and evocative power of his verse (although they would not necessarily put it that way). Class time can usefully be spent on trying to elucidate how he achieves his effects. For example (a few poems):

LA BELLE DAME SANS MERCI

This narrative poem begins with a question, a statement of a problem. How is the question finally answered; that is, what, exactly, *does* ail this knight? How has the woman injured him? Or is it his total absorption in love that has damaged him? What about the kings, princes, and warriors who appear to him—what exactly do they warn him about? Such questions will emphasize the fact that one element in the poem's power is the presence of what is *not* said, the suggestions of a narrative behind the explicit narrative, which the reader must figure out. Descriptively, there is considerable stress on seasonal signs of cold and on the contrast with what has gone before (the withered sedge and silent birds call to mind their opposites). How does this technique reiterate the poem's theme? Certainly the denuded form of external nature echoes the sense of psychic deprivation the knight feels, and it underlines the fact that his deprivations depend on his previously having—or thinking he had—what he now lacks.

ODE ON A GRECIAN URN

In many ways the representations on the urn appear superior to what real life has to offer. What are some of these ways? One might mention the degree to which art offers stimulus to the imagination (unheard melodies, which must be imagined, are sweeter than those actually heard; and the sequence of questions emphasizes the imaginative inquiry set in motion by the sight of the urn's shapes); the impossibility of disappointment for characters embedded in artistic form; and, most important, the permanence of art, comparable to eternity. Increasingly, the poem stresses this element of permanence and its effect on mortals. What kinds of effect does it have? Specifically, what does it mean that the urn can "tease us out of thought" (line 44)? Perhaps it makes us feel rather than think; perhaps it makes us surpass thought, entering a realm of intuitive knowledge; perhaps, as other lines suggest, it helps us avoid ordinary kinds of thought by removing us from commonplace experience. The ode's final lines can of course supply much matter for debate. The fundamental question here, beyond what it means to identify beauty and truth, is why this should be sufficient knowledge for humankind.

ODE TO A NIGHTINGALE

What sort of "happiness" is it that creates numbness and heartache? This is a point worth dwelling on, trying to define the sort of emotion Keats here wishes to evoke—by no means an easy matter. What is the poem's attitude toward ordinary human experience (stanza III)? How does the function of art as suggested in this poem differ from that implicit in *Ode on a Grecian Urn*? Art, here, is epitomized by "Poesy" (line 33), whose "viewless wings" carry the hearer of the nightingale's song to imaginative union with the bird. The "dull brain" (line 34) creates obstacles to such fusion, as "thought" appears to generate problems in the previous poem. Here too, then, art enables mortals to transcend their limitations, but by a rather different process from that suggested by *Grecian Urn*. What is the importance of death in the poem? The poet declares himself "half in love with easeful Death" (line 52) and imagines death while listening to the bird as a rich and satisfying experience, but also imagines it as a state of deprivation in which he would "become a sod" (line 60). The bird's power, like that of the urn, comes partly from the possibility of imagining it as free of the threat of death—not, of course, in its own literal body, but because nightingales have always existed and will continue to exist and to become the substance of imagination. So there seems to be a contrast here between two views of death: the literal death that makes people and birds alike into mere pieces of earth, and an imagined death that becomes itself a form of fulfillment. Why is the "self" unsatisfactory in the final stanza? The self seems a being deprived of imagination because it exists in isolation, separated from the bird that has enabled the speaker to transcend his own sense of limitation.

TO AUTUMN

In relation to this poem of lush description, possibly the most useful question is the simplest and most obvious: How does it make you feel? If students can specify emotional responses, one can work backward from such responses to their stimuli in the text. It's essential to pause on the personification of Autumn in the second stanza, to inquire how that works in the poem. Autumn becomes a person deeply enjoying the experiences and the sense of luxurious ease that only this time of year offers. The "music" of autumn, specified in the final stanza, has less obvious power than "the songs of Spring" (23). What is attractive about this kind of music? One might wish to mention its multiplicity, both of source and of sound, and the impression it gives of the unity of all nature.

Topics for Writing

1. The function of nature in a single poem.
2. A comparison between a Keats poem and one by Shelley.
3. A single emotion that attracts the speaker—and why.

Comparative Perspectives

1. *La Belle Dame sans Merci* is one in a long line of texts from many cultures and eras that express a masculine fear of a demonic female. Compare Keats's indirect depiction of this creature's power to other treatments of this theme.

   [Possibilities include the Sirens who tempt Homer's Odysseus, the lady in *Sir Gawain and the Green Knight,* and their more recent counterparts, including, perhaps, Phaedra and Hedda Gabler. What relation does the victim or would-be victim have to the seductress? Why is the beleaguered male in any of these examples singled out for attack? What makes him vulnerable?]

2. Keats's evocation of the five senses puts him in the company of a wide range of poets especially attuned to the nuances of sensation.

   a. How does the finish of Keats's full stanzas reflect the all-too-human world, where, beauty notwithstanding, "youth grows pale, and spectre-thin, and dies"? Contrast the fleeting, luxurious details of the mystical Urdu texts (compare, for example, "beaker full of the warm South" in *Ode to a Nightingale,* line 15, with "the wave of the wine trembles with envy" and the resolution of this idea in the last line of Ghalib's *Ghazal X.*)

   b. Compare the sensual worlds of Baudelaire, Mallarme, Verlaine, Rimbaud, and the Surrealists with that described by Keats in *Ode on Melancholy.* Discuss the paradoxically energetic refusal of the sensual pleasures that lead to oblivion in the first stanza of Keats's *Ode:* "No, no, go not to Lethe . . ." Compare the attitudes toward "fertile idleness and fragrant leisure" in Baudelaire's *Her Hair* (line 24), or the witty critique of sensory categories in a poem like *Anna Blume* by Kurt Schwitters.

3. How does Keats's *Ode on a Grecian Urn* (based on his viewing of classical Greek vases) reflect a view of the complexity of human experience that we recognize from Homer's poems and the shield of Achilles in particular?

   [The two sides of heroic life are present in both poets' works: peace and war, wedding and funeral.]

Further Reading

See also the reading suggestions in the anthology, p. 826.

Dickstein, M. *Keats and His Poetry: A Study in Development.* 1971. Supplies a particularly detailed reading of *To a Nightingale.*

Evert, W. H., and J. W. Rhodes, eds. *Approaches to Teaching Keats's Poetry.* 1991. A volume in the MLA series.

Gittings, R. *John Keats.* 1968. Gittings attempts to provide factual substantiation for every detail of the poet's life; Bate and Ward (cited in the anthology) offer critical as well as biographical interpretation.

Vendler, H. *The Odes of John Keats.* 1983. Offers brilliant, exhaustive interpretations of all the odes.

Watkins, Daniel P. *Keats's Poetry and the Politics of the Imagination.* 1989. Keats as social commentator.

CONTINENTAL ROMANTIC LYRICS: A SELECTION

This selection of French, German, Italian, Spanish, and Russian lyric poems greatly expands the pedagogical possibilities for teaching the Romantic period. As is the case with all the selected lyrics grouped throughout the anthology, these poems may be approached in many different ways. The headnote speaks of the grand Romantic themes that cross national boundaries; you may select one of them—time, death, nature, or love—for comparative study that will quickly reveal how differently each poet responds to a similar problem. Or you may want to look at the works of Russian writers of the period (adding the lovely poem by Bunina to a class on Pushkin), for example, or the Spanish poets (Bécquer and de Castro), with an eye toward teaching some of the work of their compatriots later in the semester. Equally important is the explicit way in which so many poets of the nineteenth and twentieth centuries wrestle with the idea of poetry itself, making it their ultimate subject; this point is easily made by noting references in these lyrics to nightingales and swans or the song of the wind, all of which represent the spirit of poetry that Romantic writers seek to incorporate into their very being.

If you have not yet concentrated on the short lyric as a distinct genre, you should choose a few of the more complex poems in this selection and work through them with your students in great detail, examining the way idiosyncratic speaking voices capture the play of mind as they twist and turn through their subjects. *Et nox facta est* by Victor Hugo, *The Lake* by Lamartine, *To Sylvia* and *The Village Saturday* by Leopardi, and *Yearning for Death* by Novalis would be particularly good choices for this kind of extended treatment. You might also consider using a single poem to complement a narrative that you are studying, either to indicate how widespread certain conventional assumptions were within the Romantic period or to juxtapose works from different periods with each other, to show your students how certain thematic preoccupations may be treated differently in different times and places.

The comparative questions at the end of each entry below will suggest some fruitful combinations; you will doubtless discover more as you plan your course.

Friedrich Hölderlin

Classroom Strategies and Topics for Discussion

As with so many Romantic works, your presentation of these four well-known poems may be facilitated by references to the author's life's experience. The headnote explains that the young Hölderlin "found work—not very successfully—as a tutor." In 1796–97, he fell deeply in love with Susette Gontard, the mother of the children he taught in his second such assignment. In this, the great love affair of Hölderlin's life, he found his poetic voice, addressing a number of poems to her as "Diotima" (honor of Zeus). This was a requited affair, and Susette wrote many letters that have been preserved. Herr Gontard fired Hölderlin, not surprisingly. In a two-volume epistolary novel, *Hyperion: Or the Hermit in Greece,* published in 1797–99, many of the dilemmas the young poet faced are explored through his fictional protagonist, Hyperion, a modern Greek who goes to study in Germany in the wake of a failed political revolution in Greece. Hyperion falls in love with a woman called Diotima, and one of the crises he faces is her untimely death. Thus Hölderlin's fascination for the Greek classics and his personal struggles shape his writing career.

THE HALF OF LIFE

Composed 1803–04, when Hölderlin was thirty-three years old, *The Half of Life* may be compared to the beginning of Dante's *Inferno,* for it is a midlife retrospective. The beauty of the images in the first stanza of the poem (Keatsian in their sensory richness) gives way in the second stanza to the expectation of barrenness to come, a vision of the second half of life, a time of aging and decay. You may want to spend some time discussing the disjunction between the two stanzas, which seem so diametrically opposed to each other, without any transitional gestures linking them. The poem's pessimism is deep (and accurately prefigures the rapid descent into madness that effectively silenced Hölderlin only a short while after this poem was written).

If the first stanza is, as one critic has suggested, about "merging," with the image of the swans, traditional symbols of the soul, dipping their heads in the mirroring water, the second is about "isolation." The coming of winter will erase the natural beauty of youth, replacing it with human artifacts that separate and mute the human observer. "Walls stand / Speechless and cold, in the wind / The weathervanes clatter." You can make much of these images, and the weathervanes in particular cry out for comment. Are we subject to the whims of the elements, turning without control? What good does it do for humankind to measure the direction and velocity of the wind? How do such objects deface the landscape?

HYPERION'S SONG OF FATE

In Hölderlin's novel, Hyperion writes this poem after receiving a letter from the dying Diotima. Recalling ideas as old as Homer about the un-

bridgeable distance between the mortal and the immortal, the poet rumi-
nates on "the celestials" who walk "up there in the light / on floors like
velvet" to the accompaniment of soft winds and a heavenly harpist. In this
imagined luxury the gods enjoy their "fateless" existence and flowers
never die.

The third and last stanza turns to the tragic human lot; blindness contrasts to the calm gaze of eternal beings. The very shape of the poem,
each stanza indented so that it looks like a downward precipice, expresses
its meaning, a device that your students will surely want to discuss.

BREVITY

This short poem exemplifies its title. The frigid cold that marked the
second stanza of *The Half of Life* returns here, as does the quirky imagination that characterizes misplaced effort as "swimming at sundown."
The futility of song with which the poem opens is picked up again at its
close, with another unusual image: "the annoying nightbird" makes its
impression not for any song that it may utter but for its visual intrusion
and its pesky motion, flitting and "blocking your vision."

TO THE FATES

Both *Brevity* and *To the Fates* are strictly Asclepiadean odes, a Greek
model that Hölderlin frequently followed. They are characterized by four-
line stanzas, with two longer lines followed by two shorter ones, the first
two marked by heavy caesuras. One critic speaks of the impact of Hölderlin's "falling rhythms and marked pauses" in these odes, which even in
translation can be perceived. As with *Hyperion's Song of Fate*, that sense
of fall is powerful. If you have been doing metrical analyses with your students, these are excellent texts for detailed study.

These poems, written in the last two years of the eighteenth century,
are haunted by the fear of a man not yet thirty that his time was running
out. The classical past burdens his imagination, as does the evanescence
of the seasons. Hölderlin seems to see himself as one of those fallen warriors of ancient myth for whom the proper obsequies have been omitted,
so that his soul will not find rest "even in Orcus below." Yet the poem
concludes with a positive thought. Unlike the inhabitants of the Homeric
underworld, or an Orpheus without his lyre, Hölderlin will have had his
godhood if only he can write his poems. It is painful to realize that his
days for writing poetry were numbered, and worse, that unlike Keats,
Heine, and so many other poets who died young, Hölderlin suffered from
a dementia that left him in just the kind of "shadow world" he speaks of
in this ode, alive but stripped of his sanity and his music.

Topics for Writing and Comparative Perspectives

1. Discuss the importance of the classical past in Hölderlin's poetry.
   [To focus this more particularly, you might ask your students to

compare Shelley's *Ode to the West Wind* with Hölderlin's *To the Fates*, in terms both of their form and of their attitudes toward time.]

2. What is the importance of the way a poem looks on the page? Comment on *Hyperion's Song of Fate*.

[A good juxtaposition would be to compare and contrast the visual effects sought by the Dadaists, focusing especially on the selections in the anthology by Tristan Tzara (volume F, pp. 2112–13).]

3. Compare Hölderlin's depiction of the "annoying nightbird" in *Brevity* with Keats's nightingale and discuss the significance of bird imagery in lyric poetry.

[If you have read some of the medieval lyrics in volume B of the anthology, you may want to revisit some of them, especially the anonymous *Song of Summer*, for their loving evocations of birds and their songs.]

4. Compare the evocation of autumn as the harbinger of death in *The Half of Life* with the attitude toward the rich harvest in Keats's *To Autumn* or Tagore's *Last Honey*.

Further Reading

Constantine, David. *Hölderlin*. 1988. An excellent introduction for the English-speaking reader, written by a veteran teacher who knows how to present matters relating to rhythm and form. His analysis of the odes is particularly worth reading.

Santner, Eric L. *Friedrich Hölderlin: Narrative Vigilance and the Poetic Imagination*. 1986. A sophisticated literary discussion of Hölderlin's proclivity for "paratactic composition." See especially the detailed analysis of this quality of "side-by-sideness" in *The Half of Life*, pp. 81–91.

Unger, Richard. *Friedrich Hölderlin*. 1984. An overview of the life and times of the poet, in the Twayne series.

Novalis (Friedrich von Hardenberg)

YEARNING FOR DEATH

Classroom Strategies and Topics for Discussion

Another writer who found his vocation in mourning the loss of a beloved girl and then died young himself, Friedrich von Hardenberg (who became Novalis) typifies the popular image of the Romantic poet. Identified with "The Blue Flower," a symbol of the unattainable that he introduced in his unfinished novel, *Heinrich von Ofterdingen*, Novalis represents a conservative Germanic ideology. If you choose to teach the three German poets in this selection together, you will be able to draw significant distinctions among Hölderlin, Heine, and Novalis. All three were born in the same tumultous decade, but were from different back-grounds; not surprisingly, each developed a unique sensibility and voice. Of the three, Novalis most fixedly pursues the quest for transcendence.

A good way to begin your examination of Novalis's role is by noting the privileged atmosphere in which he was raised. (Hölderlin, whom Novalis knew, was of middle-class origins, and Heine, a Jew and a revolutionary spirit, exiled himself from Germany.) Carefully educated at home, the young Novalis went off to the University of Jena, where in the company of his closest friend, Friedrich Schlegel, he frequented the home of August Wilhelm Schlegel and his wife. Thus he was, in effect, present at the cre-ation of German Romanticism and knew the leading figures of the move-ment, including Goethe and the great dramatist Schiller, with whom Novalis studied history at Jena.

Goethe actually visited the deathbed of the young woman to whom Friedrich von Hardenberg had become engaged. In many ways, that doomed courtship shaped von Hardenberg's short life. Like Dante, he fell deeply in love at first glance with a girl who was to become his poetic in-spiration. This process began when he saw Sophia von Kuhn in Novem-ber 1794, when she was not yet thirteen and he was some ten years older. In 1795, their engagement was announced; when she was barely fifteen, Sophia died. As Dante's Beatrice had a richly suggestive name, so did Sophia. As Sophie, she was the youngster whom he adored; as Sophia, af-ter her death she became the symbolic embodiment of the wisdom that is deeply identified with Christian mysticism.

The choice of Novalis for a poetic name also deserves elucidation: the family had an estate named Grossenrode in Hannover, from which they took the name "von Rode." Latinized, this became "de Novali," and, as Hiebal explains in the study mentioned in the headnote, "seems to have meant 'one who clears new land'—a pathfinder or a pioneer?" The pioneer who chose this name had only three years in which to write the works on which his reputation is based. Sophia died in March 1797; a month later, one of his brothers died. Novalis eventually wrote six Hymns to the Night, of which the poem printed in the anthology is the last. With it, the painful contemplation of death and the loss of Sophia yields to the love of Jesus, "the sweet bride" who will never fail.

The title Yearning for Death seems to have been assigned to this poem (the only one of the Hymns written entirely in verse) by Schlegel, after the death of Novalis; its mood, as Hiebal points out, is actually more pur-posefully directed to reunion with Christ. As the poem begins, we are traveling, already embarked for the cool, "everlasting Night." The world is "alien" to human beings, as line 11 indicates: "To our Father's house we would return." Contemplating the past when God was a presence in this world (the German Vorzeit, translated here as "the times forgone," occurs four times in rapid succession, beginning with line 18 and then repeated at the head of the three central stanzas beginning at line 19), Novalis sketches the vitality of the primitive world. We are back at the beginning of the universe, it would appear, when man is created in "the lofty image that [the Father] bore" (lines 23–24). This quasi-historical survey of the olden days alludes to scenes of martyrdom, both that of "children toward God's kingdom going / [who] For death and torment strove" (lines 27–28) and that of the savior, "Refusing not the smart and pain, / That it might be our dearer gain" (lines 35–36). Since the world is no longer a place where these sacrifices would be meaningful, "temporal life" is equated with "hot thirst" that cannot be slaked (line 39). Our dead (like Sophie) have been buried; indeed, it is from these dead that the impulse to move on surges:

> Methinks from far distance sounded
> An echo of our sorrow.
> Perhaps our loved ones likewise longing
> Have wafted us this sigh of longing.

Interestingly, to give oneself over to Jesus one moves downward, the easier direction presaged by the poem's opening lines. One needs only to "sink" to be embraced by God, not to attempt the arduous upward climb prescribed in other visionary verses. By depicting a maternally nurturing Father God who has lived among men and women and offers Jesus to them as a bride, Novalis emphasizes the availability of salvation. To reach it is to "return": nothing needs to be invented to deserve to go home. This sense of return is reinforced in the original German: "the dark earth's womb" of line 1, *der Erde Schoss*, anticipates the last two words: *Vaters Schoss*, the "Father's arms," or more precisely, "the Father's womb," the receptacle in which humankind is formed and comforted.

Topics for Writing and Comparative Perspectives

1. Contrast the significance of up and down in *Yearning for Death* with that expressed in *Hyperion's Song of Fate*. How does the poet's religious vision enter into the sense of movement in each poem?
2. Compare the representation of the great Romantic themes Night and Death in Novalis's *Yearning for Death* with that in Heine's *Ah, Death Is Like the Long, Cool Night*, Hugo's *Et nox facta est*, Keats's *Ode to a Nightingale*.
3. Compare the evocation of the life of Jesus Christ on earth in *Yearning for Death* with Tagore's sketch of the life of Buddha in *At midnight* on p. 1676, volume F. Discuss the ways in which each poet makes palpable divine concern for humanity by his choice of language and tone.

Further Reading

See also the reading suggestions in the anthology, p. 838.

Reynolds, Simon. *Novalis and the Poets of Pessimism*. 1995. An attractive, small volume with a black-and-white reproduction of Franz Gareis's

1799 oil painting of the long-haired, bright-eyed poet, it includes James Thomson's translation of *Hymns to the Night,* set against a facing version of the original.

Anna Petrovna Bunina

FROM THE SEASHORE

Classroom Strategies and Topics for Discussion

With Bunina, the tradition of women's poetry in Russia may be said to begin; at the same time, in terms of her stylistic development, she is a transitional figure. Her early work was regarded as neoclassical, while *From the Seashore* clearly deals in a Romantic idiom. Partly because of her sex, partly because of the support she received from Aleksander Shishkov (known as a traditionalist), Bunina earned the scorn of Pushkin, who, according to Catriona Kelly, derided her work as "a crying example of the worthlessness of poetry before Romanticism." Bunina seems to admit as much in a witty poem (not in the anthology) called *Conversation between Me and the Women*: in this imaginary dialogue, the women reprimand her for ignoring their concerns, while Bunina, the "me" of the poem, admits to having written odes about great men to advance her own career.

In *From the Seashore,* however, a purer voice emerges. You may want to call to your student's attention the time-honored image of a harmonious cosmos with which this poem begins. The sea and the sky seem one continuous entity, and the tremulous sense of peace in the landscape seems to travel from one unit of existence to another, from the shore to the tree-tops, where the birds nest. As the headnote indicates, this mood is echoed by an image of domestic tranquillity as we move indoors, where children, like the birds, "nestled / Modestly in the corners."

Ask your students to trace the way Bunina appeals to the different senses in establishing the calm that is soon to be shattered: from the silence comes the sound of the "golden harp," calling up a specific image of a middle-class music room in which Lina, a particular woman, joins in another example of harmonious connection. Color is also described in just enough detail so that we feel in the presence of a real scene: from the beautiful sunset of a moonless twilight to the glowing "rose" flame leaping across the hearth and the "dark silver" smoke, we have a powerful visual image of rich contentment.

What happens to the fire? How does the sixth stanza transform the particularity of this happy family gathering to a more abstract distillation of heat? How does the seventh turn the flowing liquid sea arid? How does the rippling movement of the opening translate to "heaving"?

This modest poem expresses a keen eye for detail that carefully prepares for its disruptive conclusion. The effortless flowing of sea from sky cannot help the "poor woman," cold and parched, who requires the fire to "flow" and the sea to "churn" if she is to recover the health that has been leached out of her and the poem in its final stanzas.

Topics for Writing and Comparative Perspectives

1. Compare the opening of Bunina's poem with that of *Tintern Abbey*: why do so many Romantic writers attach significance to the apparent connectedness of sea, landscape, and sky?

   [You might want to mention the opening of Genesis as perhaps the archetypal site for this sense of cosmic integration—a state of being into which, significantly, God quickly proceeds to introduce difference.]

2. Many great poems document their authors' various experiences of fatal illness. Compare the tone of Bunina's *From the Seashore* to that of Heine's *Ah, Death Is Like the Long, Cool Night*, Rosalía de Castro's *The Ailing Woman Felt Her Forces Ebb*, Rubén Darío's *Fatality*, or Alfonsina Storni's *Departure*. How explicit are the references to physical suffering? Is the writer accepting or bitter?

3. Compare and contrast the experience of nature and death in Bunina's *From the Seashore* and in Anna Akhmatova's *Requiem*, discussing the way the enormities of twentieth-century politics transform the poetry of personal grief.

Further Reading

Kelly, Catriona, ed. *An Anthology of Russian Women's Writing, 1777–1992*. 1994. The source of the quotation cited above, this groundbreaking volume presents two of Bunina's poems. The introduction discusses the broader topic and may be useful if you plan to teach Anna Akhmatova's poetry as well.

Alphonse de Lamartine

THE LAKE

Classroom Strategies and Topics for Discussion

Like so much Romantic poetry, *The Lake* can lead you into a discussion of the relationship between autobiography and art. As the footnote on p. 842 of the anthology indicates, this poem, based on a specific recollection of time Lamartine spent on Lake Bourget with Julie Charles, was written in August 1817. Julie died in December 1817; although she was already ailing when these verses were composed, to read them as a tribute to a lost beloved anticipates the event. In them, the poet seizes on a personal experience and transforms it into a symbolic meditation, as the headnote puts it, "on nature and time." His private suffering is not his primary subject, as the first stanza makes clear. It is rather the human confrontation with eternity, on a boat traversing "time's vast ocean" instead of a real Alpine lake.

Lamartine stands at the very beginning of the French Romantic tradition; the formal characteristics of *The Lake*, regular quatrains of perfect alexandrines, could as easily belong to a neoclassical poem. The poem is famed for its rhythmic and melodious qualities, well caught by the English translator in lines 59–60. Many of its themes, particularly in the four stanzas that begin "O time, suspend your flight! and you, blessed hours, / suspend your swift passage" in which the speaker ostensibly quotes his beloved, have deep roots in the Western tradition. The "voice so dear" echoes Ovid's *Amores*, with the famous cry to the horses that draw the chariot of the night, "Lente, lente currite noctis equi," as well as the aubade, in which the lady bewails the coming of the dawn that will drive her lover from her bed.

What Lamartine brings to these conventions is an urgency and a universality of sweep that was enormously appealing to his generational peers. His *Meditations Poetiques,* the short volume of which *The Lake* is the centerpiece, was one of the great best-sellers of French literary history. The poem records the ambivalence with which the Romantics viewed nature. On the one hand, *The Lake* is the most famous Continental example of the "pathetic fallacy," the tendency to attribute human emotions to the natural world; on the other, it presents an alien, if majestic, landscape, a stage set against which the speaker's emotions play themselves out rather than a specifically visualized place.

The first three quatrains establish the landscape frame; the next six (lines 13–36) recall the scene a year before. You might ask your students to contrast the stormy landscape of the metaphysically grand third stanza, with the water breaking against the rocks' "torn flanks," and the calm of the fourth and fifth, in which the speaker and his beloved sail together. The shores (again, as if they were human), prospectively enchanted by her voice, provide an eerie aural accompaniment of "strains unknown to earth" as an undercurrent to Julie's eloquent plea to the night. Her words establish the imagery that the speaker recapitulates in the beginning of the poem and effect the transformation from actual experience to metaphor: the ocean is time.

In the following three stanzas, the speaker challenges the universe, in grand heroic style: note the prevalence of question marks and exclamation points. You could have your students trace the personification of the great abstraction—"jealous," thieving, and indiscriminate time—and the speaker's effort to rally nature to stand for him against time by preserving the memory of happiness. Then, in the last three stanzas, an erotically charged landscape is invoked, as the poet, now using the third person to celebrate "their love" transforms his recollected love affair into an objective value that will be preserved in the lake and its environs, whether in peace or in storm, on "glad slopes" or "savage rocks," and thus transcend both the threat and the promise of the changeable surroundings. Elevated and presumably ennobled by his love, he ends magnanimously, on a note of benediction.

Topics for Writing and Comparative Perspectives

1. In *The Lake,* like Wordsworth in *Tintern Abbey,* Lamartine returns to a place where he was once happy. Compare and contrast the two

poets' reasons for valuing the landscapes of their choice and the poetic prayers with which they end their poems.

[Wordsworth's focus on the imaginative sustenance he derives
from hedgerows and hills memorializes a poetics of intellectual activity that contrasts with Lamartine's more passionate quest for immortality.]

2. Compare Lamartine's presentation of time in *The Lake* with that of
   Novalis in *Yearning for Death*; of Keats in *To Autumn*; or of Tennyson in *Tithonus*.

   [Note that Julie distinguishes between those for whom time is a
   burden—see lines 25–28—and those for whom it should be prolonged.]

3. Two of the most famous poems in French literature use the image
   of a boat on the water but to very different effect. Compare and
   contrast poetic point of view and/or landscape description in Lamartine's *The Lake* and Rimbaud's *Drunken Boat*.

   [Each of these poems defines the sensibility with which it is associated: see the helpful headnote to Rimbaud in the anthology,
   pp. 1411–13.]

4. Compare Lamartine's image of the boat in which he and Julie
   drifted in a sublime scene with Tagore's very different *Golden Boat*,
   a domesticated image of a power beyond human control. To what
   degree do the boats—one in which two lovers sit, one which collects
   the farmer's harvest and passes him by—reflect the difference between a Western anthropocentrism and an Indian view of a power
   in the universe that transcends the human sphere?

Further Reading

See also the reading suggestions in the anthology, p. 842.

Levi, Anthony. *Guide to French Literature: 1789 to the Present*. 1992.
Contains a short, informative article about Lamartine.

Heinrich Heine

Classroom Strategies and Topics for Discussion

Of the three German poets represented in this selection of Romantic
lyrics, Heine is the best loved and most frequently quoted, in large part
because his poems seem very simple; a great many of them have been set
to music and generations of German speakers have grown up with these
lieder. From our students' point of view, Heine's poems offer a wonderful
introduction to some major nineteenth-century preoccupations because
they seem at first so unthreatening, yet yield so much when discussed at
length.

[A PINE IS STANDING LONELY]

The spirit of Northern Romanticism breathes through this poem: reproductions of Caspar David Friedrich's paintings will allow you to present visually the kind of austere, vaguely mysterious landscape captured
here. Asking about the way Heine personifies the pine tree leads you into
a discussion of the idea of nature as a virtually human presence for so
many of the Romantic poets. Why is the pine "lonely"? The bare, snowbound plateau symbolizes a kind of emotional dormancy very close to
death—the ice and snow, the speaker tells us, "enshroud" him, yet the
pine tree is sleeping, not dead, and he dreams of an exotic palm tree, also
"lonely and silently mourning."

In eight brief lines, the poet paints an archetypal tragedy. We are all
solitary, longing for something quite beyond reach. Diametrically opposed
to each other, the two trees can never meet. Note the juxtaposition of
Northern and *Eastern*, rather than *Southern*; Heine's poetry abounds in
details like this, words or ideas that don't quite match one's expectations
and therefore require some thought. There are also many Asian references in Heine's work. Here, a Middle Eastern palm tree may conjure up
a cultural divide—perhaps it is not too extreme to read in the gulf separating the pine and the palm something of the cleavage between Heine's
Germanic and Judaic heritages.

[A YOUNG MAN LOVES A MAIDEN]

It may be helpful to work out the complications of the artless first
stanza: A loves B, B loves C, C loves D, and "these two haply wed." The
angry B marries E, and poor A is left inconsolable. Notice too that C and
D marry "haply"—not "happily." The formula for comedy, boy loves girl
and so on, has no place here; as the last stanza suggests, perhaps the formula was never accurate to begin with. Your students will probably want
to talk about this poem at some length. Indeed, the last stanza makes a
good argument for the study of literature. The old stories when deeply felt
are always new.

[AH, DEATH IS LIKE THE LONG, COOL NIGHT]

Heine is another Romantic poet who suffered terribly from a long, in-
curable illness; unlike others in the anthology (see especially Bunina and
de Castro), he does not see death as a threat. You may want to link this
beautiful poem with the more objectified situation of the pine and the
palm tree: note the reiterated contrast between cold and hot, between
death and sleep—perennial themes to which Heine returns again and
again throughout his work.

The slight disconnection between the two stanzas invites the reader to
supply the missing link. Mentioned without self-pity, the poignancy of the
nightingale singing "in dreams" seems to be the product of the poet's hallucination. Why this gleaming vision should appear to the poet, "tired of
light," is left to our imaginations. Working this through with your class

should offer a good opportunity to talk about the frequently drawn analogy between lyric writers and nightingales. Why should the capacity to sing be enhanced by the dark? How does that notion fit the Romantic exaltation of the fanciful and irrational?

[THE SILESIAN WEAVERS]

In addition to the short, deceptively simple songs of the sort cited above, Heine wrote a number of explicitly political poems. Deeply influenced both by the events of the day (when he wrote this poem, Heine had established a friendship with Karl Marx) and by the classical past, Heine may well be combining references to two kinds of textile workers in this poem. The dislocations caused by the Industrial Revolution are behind the protests of the Silesian weavers against "intolerable working conditions during June 1844," as the footnote will inform your students. In threatening both God and king, the weavers enunciate Heine's radicalism. They may also evoke the three fates of ancient mythology—the Parcae, who spin, measure, and cut the threads of life. Certainly the heavy rhythms of the poems proclaim that fate will vindicate the brutalized workers.

Yet another meditation on death, this poem predicts the downfall of Prussian tyranny. It also incorporates the odd reversals of expectation with which Heine so frequently plays. The flower, the emblem of life, is "crushed in a day," while the worm, the agent of death, feeds fat "on rot and decay."

In summary then, you can demonstrate to your class that Heine's reliance on simple sentence structure, obvious rhymes, and naive diction establishes a tension reiterating that implicit in the poem's double consciousness. On the one hand, he appears to offer simple, confident assertions. On the other, the confidence is subtly undermined by the implications suggested above. The effort to state simple truths, like the effort to love, is a difficult endeavor; and, like its counterpart, it may finally prove inadequate. Hearing these poems can reinforce an understanding of how the music of the verses actually conveys this double sense. If you or a colleague speaks German well, one or two of the shorter poems read aloud in the original will remind your students that many poetic effects are not easily got at through discussion.

Topics for Writing

1. Compare any two lyrics by Heine in their use of imagery.
2. Discuss the concept of death implied in one of Heine's poems.
3. How does the idea of the past figure in Heine?

Comparative Perspectives

1. Although Shelley refers to poets as the "unacknowledged legislators of the World" in A Defence of Poetry, Romantic poets, himself in-

cluded, often tackle specific political content in their works. How does Heine's use of ballad form in *The Silesian Weavers* differ from Shelley's use of the sonnet in *England in 1819?* What other poems that you have read resemble Heine's way of tackling social problems through verse? [Good choices include Rubén Darío's *To Roosevelt,* Pablo Neruda's *I'm Explaining a Few Things,* and—to mark a distinct shift in the poet's ambitions—Aimé Césaire's *Notebook of a Return to the Native Land.*]

2. Like many of the writers of the Romantic era, Heine often turns his personal experience into poetry. Compare the experiences that apparently underlie both *Ah, Death Is Like the Long, Cool Night* and Keats's *Ode to a Nightingale.*

Further Reading

See also the reading suggestions in the anthology, p. 844.

Brod, Max, *Heinrich Heine: The Artist in Revolt.* 1957. A study of the poet's literary career.

Fairley, B. *Heinrich Heine: An Interpretation.* 1977. Scholarly and thorough.

Kohn, Hans. *Heinrich Heine: The Man and the Myth.* 1959. Short lecture offering suggestive definitions of Heine's characteristics as a poet.

Liptzen, Sol. *The English Legend of Heinrich Heine.* 1954. A lucid account of the shifts of Heine's literary reputation in England.

Perraudin, M. *Heinrich Heine.* 1988. A general critical study.

Roche, M. W. *Dynamic Stillness.* 1987. Treats the importance of quietness as a theme in Heine and other major German poets.

Rose, William. *The Early Love Poetry of Heinrich Heine: An Inquiry into Poetic Inspiration.* 1962. As the title suggests, this work concentrates on analysis of Heine's early lyrics and of their sources.

Spencer, H. *Heinrich Heine.* 1982. A fairly elementary introduction in the Twayne series. Useful bibliography.

Giacomo Leopardi

Classroom Strategies and Topics for Discussion

Petrarch and Leopardi are generally considered the preeminent lyric poets of Italy. Petrarch, of course, is world famous; Leopardi is less well known, partially because Romanticism was never as central to Italian culture as was the humanism that we associate with Petrarch. Short-lived, unlucky in love, the celebrator of his regional landscape, Leopardi fits the pattern of the Romantic poet in many ways. In other ways, however, he plays against type: a scholar and intellectual of the first rank, he wrote more prose than poetry (there are only thirty-four poems in the *Canti*, his major work in the genre, from which the selections in the anthology are drawn). Most interesting, perhaps, is his attitude toward nature, which he came to see as the great enemy of human happiness. In *Tintern Abbey*, Wordsworth claims that "Nature never did betray / The heart that loved her" (lines 122–23). The philosophical poetry of Giacomo Leopardi explores precisely the opposite of that sentiment.

THE INFINITE

This early poem, written in 1819, is set on Mount Tabor in Leopardi's hometown, the northern Italian city of Recanati. Leopardi often climbed this hill, to which he had access from the back gate of his family's garden. Thus the poem begins by acknowledging the habitual affection in which he holds the spot, so "dear" as is "the hedge which hides away / The reaches of the sky." But this is no nostalgic reflection on happy childhood days. With that reference to the hedge, *The Infinite*, unlike many other lyrics in this selection, posits discontinuity as its point of departure: the human being is isolated in and alienated from a terrifying universe.

The central lines of *The Infinite* allude to one of the most famous statements in Pascal's *Pensées*: "The eternal silence of those infinite spaces terrifies me." Perhaps not yet convinced that this is the fundamental truth about the universe, Leopardi ends the poem with a suspended judgment. The vibrancy of the wind and the live sound of the present seem to counter "the dead seasons" and the "more than human silences" that surround him.

TO HIMSELF

The latest of the poems in this selection, *To Himself* was written in 1833, when Leopardi was bitterly unhappy in the aftermath of a deeply felt but unrequited love. The uncharacteristically short lines and lack of metapors express formally the bleakness that the poem describes. The poet addresses not merely himself but his heart, here considered more a motor than the locus of love. "Rest, rest, forever. / You have beaten long enough."

In the following sentence, the word translated as "vacuum" is in Italian *noia*, a recurring and crucial term for Leopardi, akin to, but even bleaker than, Baudelaire's *ennui*. In its existential inclusiveness, it balances the earthier specificity of the short declaration to which it leads: "The world is mud." The ending here is Sophoclean in its hard-eyed sense of the unremitting cruelty of human life: "The only gift / Fate gave our kind was death." Leopardi is now convinced that nature is the root of all our troubles—the definitive judgment of the final lines offers no hope of any kind. "The boundless emptiness" is in the original *l'infinita vanita*, and thus carries with it a theological force. All is vanity.

TO SYLVIA

It can be rather hard on students to expose them to too much unremitting despair; the two longer poems in this selection offer a slightly softer view of a still-deplorable situation. *To Sylvia,* written in April 1828, pays tribute to an idealized image of a village girl who died young. Although her "perpetual song" (line 8) is from the start set against the insistence in the first stanza on the evanescence of her "mortal lifetime," the nostalgic recollections of Sylvia at her "woman's tasks" give us an image of the teenaged Leopardi turning away from his scholarly labors in his father's library to listen to her song and look around him at the beauty of the natural landscape.

The accusation against nature is all the more bitter because of this sense of disappointed hope: "why / Do you not keep the promises you gave? / Why trick the children so?" That line deserves full discussion with your class. From Rousseau on, childhood is a sacred component of the Romantic understanding of life. To violate it is one of the cardinal sins. Time, too, is a villain here, depriving Sylvia of her allotted years: "Before winter struck the summer grass" (line 36), before her natural "flowering" (line 39), she has been deprived of life.

To Sylvia concludes with as many questions as final judgments. If the sadness that the poet feels is not merely a response to Sylvia's premature death, by choosing to focus on her the poet avoids the totalizing vision of *To Himself.* Looking at the original Italian confirms this personalizing, rather than universalizing, of despair. The "stark sepulchre" is *una tomba ignuda,* "an unmarked grave"—both a sign of Sylvia's individual fate and a reminder of the way that we all must go.

THE VILLAGE SATURDAY

Written in 1829, during a period when Leopardi had returned home (which he did not leave until he was twenty-four years old and allowed to go to Rome—like Recanati, a conservative place of which his father approved), this sad, lovely poem finds some positive value in the passing of time, for the transition from Saturday to Sunday brings peace to the hard-working inhabitants of the village and happy memories prevail. Woman's archetypal task, spinning, is here undertaken by an old woman (in *To Sylvia,* it is the doomed girl who weaves) who regales her neighbors with stories of time past. The landscape darkens, but illuminated by "the whitening of the moon," the site spells beauty and contentment.

The earlier poems find silence fearful; here, "happy chatter" and the carpenter's almost biblical activity punctuate the Saturday evening as it turns to a Sunday, the welcome seventh day. To be sure, *noia* awaits: this is the word translated as "tedium" in line 40, which predicts the coming return to "habitual travail." And, as in *To Sylvia,* a child is apostrophized. This youngster seems to be enjoying his "flowering time," but the speaker warns of what will inevitably become of "the great feast of life." Yet the poet holds his tongue. The mood is gentler, more accepting, less fierce than in the two shorter poems; the outlook, however, remains bleak.

Topics for Writing and Comparative Perspectives

1. Discuss the significance attributed to sounds and silence in Leopardi's poems.
2. Choose examples of landscape description in Leopardi's poems and explore their relevance to his angry statements about nature, "the ugly force." How would you compare his view of the lonely hill in *The Infinite,* or the darkening shadows in *The Village Saturday*, with the hopeful evocation of the English landscape in Wordsworth's *Ode on Intimations of Immortality* (note the importance of that last word), or of the Swiss lakeside in Lamartine's *The Lake*?
3. What is the young poet's relation to Sylvia? Compare the respectful distance that separates him, on his ancestral balcony, from this village girl with the way Goethe's Faust imposes himself on Gretchen.
4. Discuss Leopardi's depictions of women weaving or spinning.
   [Compare the classical Fates alluded to in Heine's *Silesian Weavers,* or Gretchen in *Faust.*]
5. Leopardi's skill in turning a local vignette into a thought-provoking poem in *A Village Saturday* is matched by several of the selections in the anthology by Rabindranath Tagore. Compare and contrast the use of authentic, daily detail in one of Tagore's poems.
   [Good choices include *I Won't Let You Go* and *Hide and Seek.*]
6. Compare *To Himself* with Ruben Darío's *Fatality.* Is there a difference between Leopardi's accusation that Nature "orders universal ruin" and Darío's characterization of "the flesh that tempts us with bunches of cool grapes"? Does Leopardi's "vacuum" seem the same as Darío's "terror"?
   [You may find it helpful to remind your students that questions like these do not lead them to pat responses, but rather invite them to speculate by bringing detailed readings of the poems in question to support their findings.]

Further Reading

See also the reading suggestions in the anthology, p. 846.

Carsaniga, G. *Giacomo Lombardi: The Unheeded Voice.* 1977. A reassessment that places Leopardi in his social and historical context.

Grennan, Eamon, trans. *Leopardi: Selected Poems.* 1997. See the helpful introduction by John C. Barnes and the translator's comments. Like those of Casale in *A Leopardi Reader,* these translations are accompanied by the Italian originals.

Nelson, Lowry, Jr. "Leopardi First and Last." In *Italian Literature Roots and Branches.* G. Rimanelli and K. J. Atchity, ed. 1976. Study of Leopardi in relation to his literary predecessors.

Wilkins, Ernest Hatch. *A History of Italian Literature.* 1954. The chapter on Leopardi places the poet in his literary context.

Victor Hugo

Et nox facta est

Classroom Strategies and Topics for Discussion

As one of the great exemplars of the Romantic movement in Europe, Victor Hugo merits attention not only for the remarkable range of his individual accomplishment but also for his consistent embodiment of the principles of Romanticism. Glorification of imagination (indeed, of consciousness); attention to the phenomena of the natural world; indignation over social oppression; interest in the illuminations provided by detail; an effort to reimagine and resee the everyday—such manifestations of the Romantic spirit appear everywhere in Hugo. Any of them might provide a starting point for investigation of *Et nox facta est*.

Et nox facta est offers an intricate treatment of consciousness. Students will think at first that "consciousness," in this poem, alludes only to Satan's mental states; and indeed Satan's emotional progress provides an appropriate starting point for investigation. If your class has read *Paradise Lost* (in volume C of the anthology), comparison with Milton's Satan—who, like Hugo's, declares his hatred of the sun—is one way to elucidate the problem. It can be argued that Hugo's defier of God is a more nearly sympathetic figure than is Milton's. At any rate, you might offer this hypothesis to the class and invite them to support or refute it by reference to the text. But the question of how one is invited to feel about Satan can also be considered without reference to Milton. How do such adjectives as "aghast" and "dumbfounded" and "sad" make one feel about Satan? How does one respond to his desperate flight after the dying star, to his "Quiver" at the growing of his "membraned wing," to his shivering at the loss of two suns? These instances of apparent invitations to pity must be considered in relation to such terms as "bandit" and "monster" and to Satan's declaration of hatred for God; certainly no case can be made for sympathy or pity as *adequate* responses to this being. Hugo insists that one understand Satan both as victim and as villain and that one reflect about the relation between the two reactions.

Thus the poet invites alternative states of consciousness in the reader. He also tacitly contrasts Satan's state with God's ("absorbed in being and in Life"); the meaning of the perverted archangel depends on awareness of the state from which he has fallen. Finally, providing a complicated retrospect on the entire poem, Hugo's concluding section introduces the question of the writer's consciousness and its meaning. Students should be asked to speculate about the importance of this section (lines 214–31) in the poem as a whole. It calls emphatic attention to the fact that the narrative we have just read is and must be entirely a product of imagination, since it alludes to "Cycles previous to man, chaos, heavens," about which no human being can possibly have direct knowledge. The "sage," the "thinker," the "wise man"—in other words, the poet—undertakes a superhuman moral search, "further / Than the facts witnessed by the present sky." His effort is described in heroic terms. What is the connection between his grand, impossible, necessary undertaking and that of Satan, which the poem has just described? This question cannot be answered with certainty, but speculation about it is sure to prove fruitful in leading to an understanding of the mysterious, dangerous power that the Romantics believed inherent in the poetic act.

Topics for Writing

1. In what respects is Hugo's Satan a heroic figure? Describe in detail how the impression of his heroism is developed through the course of *Et nox facta est*.
2. What is the importance of the white feather in *Et nox facta est*? Consider the allusions to feathers and to wings of various sorts in the poem as a whole; do not rely on the explanatory footnote as a guide to the feather's *significance*.

Comparative Perspectives

Western and Islamic writers return again and again to the figure of Satan, from perspectives as varied as the eras in which they live. Compare and contrast the diabolical figures in, as appropriate, Job, the Koran, Dante's *Inferno*, Goethe's *Faust*, or Milton's *Paradise Lost*, with Hugo's fallen devil. How and why do different historical periods reinterpret this character?

Further Reading

See also the reading suggestions in the anthology, p. 850.

Grant, Elliott M. *The Career of Victor Hugo*. 1946. A useful literary biography.

Guerlac, S. *The Impersonal Sublime: Hugo, Baudelaire, Lautreamont*. 1990. This treatment of Hugo in conjunction with other important French poets emphasizes his modern aspects.

Houston, J. P. *The Demonic Imagination: Style and Theme in French Romantic Poetry*. 1969. The section on Hugo relates his "demonic imagination" to that of other French Romantic poets.

Porter, L. *The Renaissance of the Lyric in French Romanticism*. 1978. Places Hugo in his immediate literary context and stresses his importance as lyricist.

Swinburne, Algernon. *A Study of Victor Hugo*. 1886. An important English poet reacting to an important French poet.

Gustavo Adolfo Bécquer

Classroom Strategies and Topics for Discussion

[I Know a Strange, Gigantic Hymn]

I Know a Strange, Gigantic Hymn, the first poem in Bécquer's posthumously published *Rimas,* introduces the poet's themes and "these pages," the volume itself, which (like so much Romantic poetry) is devoted to an impossible task. The challenge is to capture the ineffable. The opening stanza suggests that poetry has a salvific function, bringing light where there has been darkness, and the poet seeks a language that unites human feelings and senses. Immediately, however, the difficulty of his task is acknowledged: human beings cannot get beyond their "impoverished language," for there is "no cipher," no secret code of writing or sign, to accomplish the synaestheic union that will render this great universal truth and speak to the particular beloved. In this brief and elegant set of quatrains, Bécquer announces his preoccupations.

[Nameless Spirit]

Nameless Spirit, the fifth of the rimas, more fully explores the implications and difficulties of these preoccupations. Here, the spirit of poetry itself, "Espíritu sin nombre," speaks, expressing the age-old tension between forms and ideas first articulated, perhaps, by Plato and Aristotle. The spirit takes many substantial forms from nature. This poem can be read in minute detail with your students, who will be able to delineate the fleeting and brilliantly imagined states in which the poetic spirit can be identified. In the second stanza, the spirit, beautifully voiced, moves in the cosmos; in the third through the fifth, it assumes the shape of many transient emanations of the natural world, from moonlight to cloud, from snow to seafoam.

In the sixth stanza, the spirit seems to move closer to human actions. Appropriating one of the central Romantic images, Bécquer makes this nameless spirit "a note in the lute," without telling us whether there is a musician. This resembles the aeolian harp, the passive instrument through which the wind itself makes music. If perfume resides by nature in the violet, it may also be extracted by human effort; and the tombs and the ruins that flame and ivy momentarily inhabit are by definition built by human hands but at the same time are emblems of human mutability and failure.

Through line 36, the spirit expresses a full range of emotions, again lodged in cosmic and natural entities, coming closer to the world in which we live in the exquisite image beginning on line 37, as it swings, like a spider or even a monkey, between the trees. Evoking the world of classical antiquity and Germanic folklore, the spirit takes on a more literary consciousness as it inspects the overt and covert sites in which mythic creatures have their being. The spirit reasserts its consciousness of human history in looking "for the now obliterated / traces of the centuries" (lines 53–54), training its "pupil" on "the whole of creation" (59–60).

In a triumphant finish, poetry offers itself as the link between form and idea, between Heaven and Earth, and names the poet as its vessel. Rare indeed is the Romantic statement that speaks with such confidence; this exhilarating poem expresses the highest aspirations of an age in love with poetry, nature, music, and the seeing eye, the "pupil" that can read order and beauty in the endless varieties of life.

Topics for Writing and Comparative Perspectives

1. Bécquer wrote a series of prose *leyendas* (legends) as well as the dozens of poems published in *Rimas*. Find evidence in *Nameless Spirit* of his awareness of the legends of old and consider why so many Romantic artists were fascinated by mythic visions of natural beings.

   [Consider juxtaposing the selections by Bécquer with Goethe's *Faust*, especially the *Study* scene in which Mephistopheles has the spirits serenade Faust, to "dazzle him with dream shapes, sweet and vast" (p. 708). Would Bécquer agree that the poetic visions they conjure are "an ocean of untruth"?]

2. Compare Bécquer's idealistic claims for poetry with those of his Romantic predecessors Shelley (*Ode to the West Wind* in particular) or Coleridge (*Kubla Khan*); or contrast them with the vision of poetry as "disheveled" musicality in Paul Verlaine's *Art of Poetry* or the sense of poetry's limits and powers in the *Lament for Ignacio Mejías Sánchez* by the great Spanish poet of the twentieth century, Federico García Lorca.

3. Elsewhere in his poetry, Bécquer speaks of the power of the "pupil," or eye. Why is the power of sight so important a theme in Romantic poetry?

   [A good comparative essay might ask this in connection with Wordsworth's philosophic effort in *Tintern Abbey* to distinguish the work of eye from that of ear; or with the brilliant imagery of Aimé Césaire's *Sun Serpent* and *Day and Night,* which make pure visual sensation primary.]

4. Ruben Darío was an admirer of Bécquer's; in *I Seek a Form*, the later poet seems to be revising his precursor's *I Know a Strange, Gigantic Hymn*. Compare and contrast the two poems, considering the hopes each has to find a language adequate to his vision. Comment on Bécquer's reference to the "cipher" unable to capture the hymn and Darío's chase after "the word that runs away." How does the linguistic and imagistic range of these poems seem to counter the failed quest that they each deplore?

Further Reading

See also the reading suggestions in the anthology, p. 856.

Bynum, B. Brant. *The Romantic Imagination in the Works of Gustavo Adolfo Bécquer.* 1993. This useful contextualization of Bécquer's work within the frame of European Romanticism provides a good basic bibliography of critical writings about the period and offers a reading of *Nameless Spirit* on pp. 45–48. Quotations from Spanish primary and secondary texts are not translated.

Turk, Henry Charles. *German Romanticism in Gustavo Adolfo Bécquer's Short Stories.* 1959. Although none of the specific works discussed are in the anthology, Turk's broad introduction considers the degree to which Bécquer's work may have been directly influenced by German philosophical and poetic traditions.

Rosalía de Castro

Classroom Strategies and Topics for Discussion

[As I Composed This Little Book]

This opening poem sets the tone for this moving series of verses. De Castro was a champion of her native region, Galicia, and her earlier verses had been written in Galician. In *Beside the River Sar,* she writes in Castilian, Spain's language of high culture, but likens her work to "the prayers and rituals of belief," verses that children commit to memory and that speak to a popular audience.

Yet the critic César Barja has called de Castro "the most modern of Spanish poets of the nineteenth century," pointing to her "subordination of verse to poetry, to inner rhythm." Keeping this in mind, you might ask your students to notice the shifting line lengths that the translator has been careful to preserve. No rigid metrical pattern is imposed on her poems, which respond to the pressures of thought rather than to the exigencies of form.

[Mild Was the Air]

The first stanza of *Mild Was the Air* offers a particularly striking example of this fluidity: the short, soft opening lines record an inevitable event; the final couplet expands to accommodate the watching mother's painful contrast of the child's peaceful passing with her own bitter response. Note, too, the shifting point of view throughout this poem: third person yields to second, as the speaker addresses both herself and her dead child, working out of her grief in the conclusion to return to the more objective third person, and the shorter final line: there is nothing to be done. "It is the earthly way."

[A Glowworm Scatters Flashes]

Articulating a horror of science that reminds the English-speaking reader of Tennyson's in *In Memoriam,* de Castro here cites the brevity of a firefly's glow and the distance of a star, beautiful emanations of the natural world that bring no comfort to the distressed. Like Tennyson, who finds the proto-Darwinian assurance that nature was "careful of the type" of little use to human beings when she was "so careless of the single life" (p. 900), de Castro deplores human ignorance in the face of the profound questions of life and death, scientific advances notwithstanding. Explaining phenomena like glowworms or distant stars is "vain" (line 6), a matter of information rather than knowledge. Her fear is that God is absent in a universe so cold.

In stanza 2, she kneels, uncertain of what kind of icon is set before her. What is the "Deity" of which she speaks in the third stanza? The idol that she worships, the "image rudely carved," appears to be the dead child lying in a cemetery surrounded by carved angels in "lofty marble niches," whose flesh she returned to dust in *Mild Was the Air*. The angelic message, however, offers little sympathy. Rather, it accuses her of a virtually pagan insolence for daring to dispute the decisions of an unfathomable God.

[The Feet of Spring Are on the Stair]

A Tennysonian concern for the evanescent individual is heard again in this poem. The celebration of springtime coupling in the opening lines is oddly expressed in the quasi-scientific reference to "atoms," treated here as if they were unique beings. Beginning with a traditional evocation of spring's beauty, this short lyric quickly ends with the harsh certainty that "Summer masters Spring" and heat dries up new life.

[Candescent Lies the Air]

De Castro's treatment of the images of nature so typical of Romantic rhetoric is both subtle and simple. The last poems in the selection take the familiar seasonal theme and give it a surprising twist. As noted above, her praise of spring, like its duration, is short-lived, and again the shifting line lengths seem to echo the swift passage of which the final stanza speaks. As hinted in the poem discussed above, De Castro's summer is cruel, scorching and stifling. The brook turns "noisome," and the insect sounds are "a low death-rattle." Conventional notions of time are undercut: "The midmost hour of day / Is best called night." Winter would be preferable to the "sorry" summer that spells death.

[The Ailing Woman Felt Her Forces Ebb]

Rosalía de Castro died on July 15, 1885, after enduring years of pain. It is hard not to think of her suffering in the intense Spanish summer heat in *The Ailing Woman Felt Her Forces Ebb*, which stresses the incongruity of "the ailing woman," never explicitly identified with the poet herself, dying by inches in an inappropriate season, out of harmony with her own being, it would seem, as with the natural world. In this final poem, the great Romantic themes that she has touched on all come together, reinforcing the sense that all the assumptions that made the nineteenth-century poets worship nature have been violated—time and the seasons are out of joint.

Topics for Writing and Comparative Perspectives

1. Rosalía de Castro's poems treat winter as a kinder time than spring or summer. Explain why this should be so, and compare her view of the connotations of weather changes and the seasons with that of other poets whose work you have studied.

   [Good choices include Shelley in *Ode to the West Wind*; Heine in *Ah, Death Is Like the Long, Cool Night*; Lamartine in *The Lake*; or T. S. Eliot in *The Waste Land*.]

2. Discuss the relation of form to content in the poems of Rosalía de Castro. In what sense is she a precursor of the modern attitude toward verse forms observable in the work of twentieth-century poets like Akhmatova, Alfonsina Storni, or García Lorca?

3. Compare and contrast the portrait of a woman dying in these poems with Flaubert's description of the death of Madame Bovary. How does the difference between the two help us understand the contrast between Romanticism and realism, and between the resources of the poet and those of the novelist?

Further Reading

See the suggestion in the anthology, p. 859.

ALEXANDER SERGEYEVICH PUSHKIN

The Queen of Spades

Classroom Strategies and Topics for Discussion

One provocative aspect of Pushkin's great story is the way a reader's expectations are systematically manipulated and violated. To trace the ways in which anticipation is generated, only to be thwarted, may help students realize the artistry of this narrative.

What does the opening scene lead one to expect? A story about gambling, perhaps, about winning and losing. Its central character, one might think, will be Tomsky, the only person who speaks at any length and the one who offers judgments on others ("Hermann's a German: he's cautious—that's all"). After he tells the story of his grandmother, none of the responses suggests that those who make them will have any narrative importance. Chapter 2 in its first section divides the interest between Tomsky's grandmother and the girl Lisaveta, promising a romantic fairy tale on the order of *Cinderella*—the poor abused underling will find her prince. When Hermann reappears, at the chapter's end, we may suspect that he will be the prince, although his intense interest in money already has disturbing overtones. Chapter 3 begins by suggesting a sexual denouement but ends with the countess's death; the tale has changed direction once more. Chapter 4 exposes Hermann in his full heartlessness and leads one to expect that this will be a story of complete frustration; no one will achieve what she or he desires. Chapter 5 turns into a ghost story, focusing our interest on whether the dead countess has revealed the truth; chapter 6 leaves that question unresolved (has she deliberately named the wrong third card or has she by supernatural intervention switched the cards?). The "Conclusion," contradicting all previous suggestions, gives everyone but Hermann—and Hermann is, after all, the principal character—his or her heart's desire.

Why does Pushkin adopt such techniques of playing with the reader? Students may find it interesting to ask why we have the kinds of successive expectations suggested above. When we try to locate a story's main character on the basis of who has the most to say, when we allow ourselves to expect a romantic story or a sexual one or to focus our attention on exactly how a ghost has dealt with a human being, we demonstrate the degree to which we read every piece of writing in relation to other literary works we have experienced. Not what we know about life but what we know about literature leads us to think that Lisaveta might find her Prince Charming; we may not "believe" in ghosts, but we've all read enough ghost stories to know the kinds of questions one should ask about the operations of such beings. Pushkin, by manipulating our expectations, calls attention to their nature. He thus suggests the possibility that in reading a work of fiction we both expect and want something quite different from what we find in our actual lives. Of course, the characters Pushkin creates also want, within the fiction, something different from what their lives offer them. Everyone dreams of a way of escaping from the dissatisfactions of his or her existence. Hermann—who intentionally calls Tomsky's tale of his grandmother a "fairy-tale"—in his actual confrontation with the old woman says to her, "The happiness of a man is in your hands." His imagination has indeed created for him a world of happiness dependent only on the winning of money; his earlier doctrine that "economy, moderation and industry . . . are my three winning cards" has vanished in fantasy. A young man of "fiery imagination," Hermann exemplifies in extreme form what the story's other characters also reveal—that imagination disguises harsh or boring actuality by projecting into the future the fulfillment of desire. When Hermann entreats the countess "by the feelings of a wife, a lover, a mother" to grant his request, he suggests that even authentic tender feelings can become merely instruments of the imagination's insatiable hunger, words to be invoked rather than emotions to be experienced. Pushkin arouses the reader's desires in various ways only to frustrate them; he assigns satisfactions to his characters in almost random fashion, as though to mock longings for a universe controlled by justice.

This way of investigating *The Queen of Spades* implies that the story has dark social and moral implications. The point, of course, might be argued; you can inquire of students whether they believe Pushkin to be offering a serious social indictment. What human qualities and social arrangements does the story criticize? What evidence does it provide for the author's outrage at, perhaps, human self-deception, self-absorption, heartlessness? or at the maneuverings for wealth and position that society encourages? or at inequities of rank and power? How does Pushkin enforce his attitudes?

Students may find it useful to reflect on the narrator's importance in this fiction—and the reader's. Since the story reveals the emotional and moral inadequacies of all its characters, it in effect makes a hero of the storyteller, who alone demonstrates his awareness of what is really going on in a corrupt society. And this storyteller, through the manipulations of the reader discussed above, brings that reader to comparable awareness. If he denies us the obvious sorts of literary satisfaction, he provides a kind of moral satisfaction by placing us, finally, in a position of superiority to the characters. Our consciousness has been altered; we have been made to understand something. And the narrator's consciousness has guided us to understanding.

The story repays close attention to detail; almost any paragraph can be analyzed as attentively as a lyric poem to reveal its structural relation to the whole. A deceptively simple way of engaging student interest in Pushkin's larger purposes is to concentrate on his use of concrete detail. For example, you might wish to consider the description of the furniture in Lisaveta's bedroom and in the countess's, Lisaveta's clothing and the countess's, or the various allusions to flowers.

Topics for Writing

1. Discuss the importance of Tomsky as a character in the story.
2. How appropriately does the "Conclusion" conclude the narrative? Consider how each of its details has been prepared for in the fiction as a whole.
3. Analyze the character of Lisaveta, making sure to support your analysis by specific reference to the text.
4. Discuss the importance of Hermann's moralizing in The Queen of Spades as a whole. Why do you think Pushkin conceives him as a German?

Comparative Perspectives

1. Compare the appearance of the countess's ghost in the midst of Pushkin's realistic world with the intrusion of the supernatural in ancient classical literature. Do we doubt the existence of ghosts in works such as the Oresteia or the Aeneid? Could the countess be only a figment of Hermann's imagination? In what sense may we view even Hermann himself as a creation of Lisaveta's?
2. Why does Pushkin tell us that Hermann's first letter to Lisaveta Ivanovna is "taken word for word from a German novel"? Would a character in a Japanese or Chinese story be admired or dismissed for borrowing from a literary source in this way? How is the idea of originality perceived differently in different cultures and eras?
   [It would be interesting to compare the influence of old books on the Christian humanists, for whom imitation was a beloved peda-

gogical exercise, or on a character like Don Quixote, with the emphasis on originality in the post-Enlightenment West.]

Further Reading

See also the reading suggestions in the anthology, p. 864.

Barta, P., and U. Goebel, eds. *The Contexts of Aleksandr Sergeevich Pushkin.* 1988. A collection of essays that attempts to place Pushkin in his historical and literary setting.

Lavrin, Janko. *Pushkin and Russian Literature.* 1947. A short study primarily concerned with the historical background and setting of Pushkin's work, this establishes a useful context in which to consider the writer.

Magarshack, David. *Pushkin.* 1967. A biography with emphasis on its subject's literary development.

Petrie, Glen. *The Fourth King.* 1986. Critical exegesis of Pushkin's accomplishment in many genres.

Simmons, Ernest J. *Pushkin.* 1937. A sound biography offering little literary analysis.

Todd, W. *Fiction and Society in the Age of Pushkin: Ideology, Institutions, and Narrative.* 1986. As the title suggests, this study examines the social implications of Pushkin's fiction.

ALFRED, LORD TENNYSON

Classroom Strategies and Topics for Discussion

The narrative interest of the Tennyson poems included in the anthology should involve student readers. Even *In Memoriam A. H. H.* implicitly tells a story about the domination and then the weakening of grief; the two shorter poems, *Ulysses* and *Tithonus*, more vividly elucidate narratives of human feeling. *Ulysses*, the more readily comprehensible of the two, is a good place to start.

Ulysses

Students might be asked what they think the purpose of the poem is. The answer most likely to emerge, finally, is that it both establishes and celebrates a particular kind of human character. What seems to be the precipitating cause of Ulysses' monologue? He appears to be at a point of decision about his life; Tennyson's rendering reveals how and why he proposes to change course. What, exactly, do we learn or deduce about Ulysses' character? This is of course the most obvious subject of discussion, but it is a fruitful one, as students find support in the poem itself for their understanding of its central character. Related, and almost equally important, is the question of what makes Ulysses a hero in Tennyson's view. If students have read the *Odyssey* (in volume A of the anthology), they will remember Homer's version of Ulysses' character and will realize that it only tangentially coincides with Tennyson's. The poem's final line, of course, epitomizes the attitudes here held up for admiration. The contrast with Telemachus (lines 33–43) is worth dwelling on. What, precisely, does Ulysses mean by "his work" and "mine"? How does he make the reader feel about the opposition between them?

In Memoriam A. H. H.

A large question that can focus the entire discussion of the poem is how Tennyson manages to unite public (social, intellectual, theological, scientific) and private concerns in what purports to be an extended record of his grief over a personal loss. (Since the potential selfishness of dwelling on one's own feelings concerns many adolescents and adults alike, the question is one of large interest.) Finally in *In Memoriam*, the dead young man, Hallam, becomes representative of a higher human species approaching realization, but originally his importance comes only from his close friendship with the poet. To trace the stages by which his significance is enlarged, and the correlation between this enlargement of meaning and the diminishment of grief, is probably sufficient enterprise for any class.

A few more local issues that may prove illuminating (and that often can call attention to larger problems): The Prologue purports to be a statement of faith, but in fact it expresses great uncertainty. How is uncertainty conveyed? It is worth noting a sequence of ambiguous verbs: "thinks" (line 11), "seemest" (line 13), "know not" (line 15), "cannot know" (line 21), "trust" (line 23). Also relevant are the contrast between the assertions of faith, or the appeals to God (e.g., "Let knowledge grow from more to more," line 25), and the statements of fact (e.g., "They are but broken lights of thee," line 19; "these wild and wandering cries," line 41). As students attend to the varying rhetoric of this piece of the poem, they should come to see that it establishes a kind of drama, an internal conflict between faith and perception that in fact runs through the poem as a whole (and can be traced, if there is time).

Section 3: Personified Sorrow dominates this section; her "whisper" epitomizes one aspect of the speaker's struggle. Why does the speaker perceive what she says as both sweet and bitter? This allegation suggests that he finds perverse comfort in the notion that all of nature simply duplicates the sense of futility that he himself experiences, given his loss. It is particularly important because it provides one answer to the question of how Tennyson unites small and large concerns; here he demonstrates the psychological pattern by which human beings can make the universe subordinate to their own feelings, turning nature itself into an objectification of personal emotion. What is the effect of the final stanza? It emphasizes the continuing ambiguity of the speaker's responses; he cannot decide whether it is comforting ("natural good") or destructive ("vice of blood") to allow himself this kind of interpretation.

Section 5: This section raises the question of poetry and its function. What is its function in this passage? Concealment is emphasized more than revelation: poetry's discipline helps to numb pain and to obscure the intensity of feeling. Why is it "half a sin" to write poetry about this subject? By implication, because it falsifies in being unable to reveal all. Students might be asked to seek other passages in which the poet speaks about the function of poetry.

Section 21: Here the function of poetry comes up again, in relation to imagined responses to it. Why does the poet imagine various others reacting to his poem? Perhaps he is thus suggesting his own doubts about what he is doing. The specific things that are said are worth examining and summarizing: that such dwelling on grief fosters weakness in others, that it constitutes self-indulgence and seeking after fame, that concern with the private has no validity in a time of public upheaval and of dispute over the revelations of science. How is the problem of negative response resolved? The poet claims the spontaneity and naturalness of his song, and his compulsion to sing it; he cannot help himself, as a bird cannot help itself. If students are asked whether this resolution seems adequate, they are likely to say no—and probably they would be right. The weakness of the resolution is part of the continuing structure of doubt; the poet cannot yet fully justify what he is doing.

Section 95: This section contains the moment of revelation that most clearly resolves the problems previously articulated. What is the importance of the natural setting? Earlier, nature in a large, abstract sense seemed to echo the poet's sense of futility; now specific details of nature generate a sense of calm. But it could be argued that the most significant fact here is that the speaker is now able fully to notice what lies outside him; he is no longer locked in his own grief. What is the stimulus to the visionary experience? Looking at the leaves (in the sixth stanza), the poet is reminded of natural cycle and of the fact that even fallen leaves may remain green, as Hallam's memory remains green for him. The speaker thinks specifically of the dead man and of his qualities of character; this leads to the revelation. What does that revelation consist of? The poet announces that it cannot be fully stated in words (yet another glance at the problem of poetry's function), but he conveys a recognition of universal pattern making sense of time, chance, and death, those apparent obstacles to human happiness. Then he returns to the natural scene. Why? The calm continues, but it is a calm involving movement and process; dawn comes to foretell the day, symbolizing the new day of acceptance and possible happiness in the poet's experience.

Topics for Writing

1. Science in *In Memoriam*.
2. An analysis of one section of *In Memoriam*.
3. The use of animals in *In Memoriam*.
4. Water in *In Memoriam*.
5. Tithonus and Ulysses as characters.

Comparative Perspectives

1. *In Memoriam* is a poem of struggle in which Tennyson seemingly
   wills himself into believing in a Christian God. This anthology includes the record of similar struggles in the literature of two major
   Islamic writers who seem more successful than Tennyson in their
   quest, partly on account of the genres and syntax available to them.
   Compare the mood and imagery of the *Ghazals* of Ghalib, as translated by several different poets, with Tennyson's poetic strategies, or
   compare the first-person narrator of Mahfouz's *Zaabalawi* with the
   voice of *In Memoriam*. What social and intellectual concerns im-
   pede Tennyson's quest?
   [A question like this, of course, invites a subjective response. In
   Tennyson's hands, the quatrain may perhaps be too self-enclosed a
   form to relieve his sense of loss and crisis. By contrast, the fluidity
   and ambiguity of Ghalib's technique, as described in the headnote,
   offer a sense of openness and possibility that Tennyson has to strain
   for in sequences like "Ring out, wild bells." Mahfouz's protagonist,
   on the other hand, seems temperamentally open. He begins in hope
   and no discouragement cancels out that hope.]
2. If Arthur Hallam died too young, Tithonus lives to be too old. Compare Tennyson's contemplation of the cruelty of these complementary states with Keats's reflections on death in his odes, or with
   Rosalía de Castro's treatment of the seasons in *Candescent Lies the
   Air,* or Heine's in *Ah, Death Is Like the Long, Cool Night,* or with
   the fierce and specific verses of García Lorca's *Lament for Ignacio
   Sánchez Mejías.*

Further Reading

See also the reading suggestions in the anthology, p. 885.

Bloom, H., ed. *Alfred Lord Tennyson.* 1985. Miscellaneous, often
provocative essays.

Culler, A. D. *The Poetry of Tennyson.* 1977. Supplies a particularly fine
treatment of *In Memoriam,* analyzing the poem's form and thought and
giving detailed accounts of specific poetic effects.

Kissane, J. *Alfred Tennyson.* 1970. In the Twayne series. Centers on treatments of the poet's work in various genres: lyric, narrative, and drama.

Tennyson, C. *Alfred Tennyson.* 1949. The standard, thorough biography.

ROBERT BROWNING

Classroom Strategies and Topics for Discussion

The question likely to interest students most in any reading of dramatic
monologue is that inherent in the form: how does an imagined character

reveal himself or herself without any apparent intention of doing so? The question, in relation to the bishop ordering his tomb, has two obvious aspects: what do we learn of his personal history, and what do we learn of his character?

The two matters, of course, are closely connected. From line 3 ("Nephews—sons mine . . . ah God, I know not!") on, the reader is increasingly forced to realize the interdependence of history and character. The fact that the bishop does not know the nature of his relationship to the men around the bed reveals that he has had promiscuous relations with women—a revelation both of character and of experience. As students call attention to the details that show the bishop's nature and uncover his past, you can ask them to think more deeply about the implications of almost any line. The clergyman's lack of knowledge about his children, for instance, speaks of more than his promiscuity: it suggests his lack of concern for human ties in general, in his failure to keep track either of his women or of their offspring.

Lines especially worth attention include line 14 ("Saint Praxed's ever was the church for peace),” an example of a trick frequently repeated in the poem. The speaker appears to declare something he values—"peace"—only to reveal as he goes on that he has done everything possible to contradict this value: he has fought every inch of the way. Then there is the bishop's description of his setting, particularly the columns of "Peach-blossom marble": how does the description reveal him? The conjunction of "Peach-blossom," "red wine," and "mighty pulse" (lines 29–30) suggests the degree to which he attributes vitality to the realm of sensuous satisfaction, conveying more affection for stone than for women (or putative offspring). Lines 56–61, about the frieze the dying man images, are also worth attention: they demonstrate his detailed aesthetic awareness and how that dominates any religious feeling, as religious and pagan references mingle for the sake of an imagined spectacle in stone.

Specific questions about the bishop's character may lead students more deeply into the poem. For example, in what terms does he understand other people? His interpretation of Gandolf and of his "sons" suggests that he can grasp the nature of others only by thinking them like himself. (Of course, the poem offers no evidence that they are *not* like himself: we see only through the bishop's eyes, and through his eyes everyone emerges as grasping and competitive.) What is the bishop's attitude toward language? He appears to be an obsessive talker, but he also thinks about language: for example, "marble's language, Latin pure, discreet" (line 98). Language becomes for him an aesthetic phenomenon like marble itself, and a woman's "talking eyes" (line 96), which speak a nonverbal tongue, seem no more appealing than "Choice Latin, picked phrase" (line 77).

The last line of the poem reiterates line 5; how has its meaning and effect changed, given all that has come between its two occurrences? As we learn more and more about the bishop, we realize that he thinks of a

woman as like a piece of lapis lazuli or a statue: her value, too, is purely
aesthetic. The only ground for envy he can imagine concerns the possession of aesthetic objects.

At the end of the poem, the bishop appears to have achieved a certain
peace, as he rests in "the church for peace" (line 14). What accounts for
his apparent emotional shift? He knows that his sons will follow not his
will but their own, that he will not have the tomb he desires; he knows
that he is dying. But his past aesthetic triumphs continue to comfort him:
even if he possesses nothing now to arouse Gandolf's envy, he possesses
his past, his perceptions, and the memory of his perceptions. He contents
himself at last with what he securely has.

My Last Duchess, which appears to constitute a less complicated narrative, provides a particularly useful focus for discussion because it allows
students to tease out meanings from the apparently direct and simple.
Questions of character are obviously at issue in this poem. Although a
teacher may wish to begin discussion by making sure students understand
the situation and the past happenings that have taken place (To whom is
the duke speaking, and why? How did the duchess die? What does she
look like in the portrait?), such concerns quickly lead to more subtle matters of characterization. What was the duchess like as a person? This obvious question can generate intense classroom exchange, as it leads to the
related problem of the duke's nature. Why does the poem emphasize
works of art so insistently? Is there any relation between the duchess's
portrait and the bronze statue of Neptune (line 54)? Does the word "fair"
(line 52) have any special importance by the time the duke uses it here?
What is his attitude toward money?

Finally, students may find it interesting to contemplate why Browning
would choose to tell his story in verse rather than prose. The narrative
could provide the substance of a short story or even, conceivably, a novel.
Here, though, the story is told in retrospect and allusively. What are the
advantages and disadvantages to such a method? How does the use of
couplets contribute to the poem's meaning and impact?

"*Childe Roland to the Dark Tower Came,*" a more obviously difficult
poem, also tends to generate lively controversy—usually over the fundamental issue of what the poem is *about*. It probably should be acknowledged at the outset that no definitive answer to this question is likely to
present itself: critics have debated for many years whether the poem has
allegorical meaning. You might direct discussion by asking students to
specify what, exactly, the poem allows its readers to *know* (e.g., we know
that someone is looking for something; we know that he has been searching for a long time; that many before him have failed in the quest; that he
follows the cripple's advice). Many facts emerge from the narrative; what
crucial facts remain missing? Students may decide that they feel deprived
of important information about what the point of the quest is, why so
many have undertaken it, what the Dark Tower "stands for." Next they
might think about why the poet would choose to omit so much information. In other words, what poetic effects are achieved by the omissions?

One way of trying to define the poem's mood and its effect on the reader is to trace the speaker's uncertainties, which multiply steadily as the poem goes on, from his doubt about whether the cripple lies through his doubt about his own fitness, his questions about whether the horse is alive or dead—on and on. How do these uncertainties affect the reader?

Discussion of the poem's ambiguities may lead to larger issues about the workings of poetry. Students may wish to discuss whether definable meaning is essential to a poem, whether creating a mood is sufficient goal for a poet, what besides clear meaning determines poetic impact.

Topics for Writing

1. The five senses in *The Bishop Orders His Tomb.*
2. The importance of conflict in the poem.
3. Why I admire the bishop.
4. Why I feel contempt for the bishop.
5. Why the duchess's portrait is behind a curtain.
6. The duke's "skill in speech" (cf. lines 35–36).
7. The importance of the title to *"Childe Roland to the Dark Tower Came."*
8. The similes in *"Childe Roland to the Dark Tower Came."*

Comparative Perspectives

1. The intense subjectivity of much nineteenth-century poetry reaches an apogee in the dramatic monologues of Tennyson and Browning. Why did the Romantic and Victorian poets excel in monologue but not in drama? Why is this essentially a *Western* poetic genre? What categories of post-Enlightenment culture produce the egotistical sublime?

   [The intense self-absorption of Browning's speakers makes this a particularly rewarding question to pursue and opens up vistas into the self-reflexive works of the great modernists, notably Proust and Joyce.]

2. What is happening in *"Childe Roland to the Dark Tower Came"*? How would you compare this version of a quest narrative with the medieval poems it imitates and the modern searches it anticipates?

   [If they have read *Sir Gawain and the Green Knight* and portions of Dante's *Inferno*, students may be asked how Browning amalgamates the two but adds a distinctly modern note when he has nature "peevishly" despair of the burnt-out landscape (stanza XI). In the context of other selections from this anthology, this last reference shares some of Tennyson's Darwinian anguish, but Browning may also be seen here as an experimental anticipator of Robbe-Grillet. Like *The Secret Room,* "Childe Roland" stretches conventions and rhetorical postures as if to gauge how elastic they may be, without any genuine concern for "meaning."]

Further Reading

See also the reading suggestions in the anthology, pp. 909–10.

Bloom, H., and A. Munich, eds. *Robert Browning: A Collection of Critical Essays.* 1979. Useful for suggesting varied critical approaches.

Burrows, L. *Browning the Poet.* 1969. Presents itself as an introductory study; it contains a useful detailed reading of *The Bishop Orders His Tomb.*

Thomas, D. *Robert Browning: A Life Within Life.* 1982. A well-written biography.

FREDERICK DOUGLASS

Narrative of the Life of Frederick Douglass, An American Slave

Classroom Strategies and Topics for Discussion

This personal account of self-discovery, survival, and escape translates into narrative terms the linked concern with the social and the emotional to be found in the work of such poets as Blake and Shelley. Douglass's story has obvious historical interest, but it also generates vivid awareness, still relevant today, of the emotional realities of oppression. Although students may find Douglass's language on occasion uncomfortably high-flown, they will probably be caught up in the drama of his efforts to escape conditions that appear inescapable.

Because the shift to prose narrative constitutes such a startling change from the poetry that surrounds this work in the anthology, it is probably useful to begin by talking about autobiography as a form. Students can be either told or asked about what it means to tell a story of the self. The important point here is that telling such a story involves imaginative activity comparable to that involved in writing a poem. The facts of a life are given, but the appropriate way of imagining the self is not. The autobiographer must decide, consciously or unconsciously, how to present him- or herself—as hero or victim, as unique individual or as representative of a group, as defined principally by childhood experience or as self-creator. Selections must be made among the many events remembered; one cannot set down *everything*. Such self-imagining and such selection form the story. Another way of putting the same truth is to point out that many different stories can be told of any individual; students might be asked to think about how many different life stories they can imagine for themselves.

As for Douglass's story, it divides itself naturally into two teaching units, the first one extending to the beginning of chapter X (p. 967). It is useful to ask students when they read to try to decide what the center of each chapter is, in terms of narrative or emotional interest. Following are a few suggestions, chapter by chapter, of how classroom discussion might be focused.

CHAPTER I

It is worth spending some time on the first paragraph, concentrating on the question of what that paragraph establishes, how it prepares us for the book that succeeds it. Points worth mentioning include: the stress on deprivation, on what the narrator does *not* know; the linkage of slaves to the natural cycle (they locate their birthdays by planting-time, etc.); the degree to which the narrator identifies himself with his social class; the mention of contrast between the situation of blacks and that of whites as a source of consciousness; the definition of the narrator as someone who figures things out (his way of estimating his own age). The tone is matter-of-fact, yet emotion permeates the paragraph. Where does it come from? You might comment on the emphasis on the negative (no knowledge, no memory, want of information, "could not tell," not allowed, etc.) and on the explicit reference to early unhappiness. The episode in the chapter receiving the greatest emotional stress is Douglass's concluding account of watching the whipping of his aunt. Why, one might ask, does this episode merit such extended attention? It is directly stated to be "the first of a long series of such outrages"; in other words, it has representative meaning. It announces themes that the rest of the text will reiterate—not only the irresistible power and brutality of white masters but the degree to which sexual issues are interwined with those of slavery. And it suggests the way in which Douglass as a child felt himself directly implicated in the persecution he saw, not for altruistic but for selfish reasons: "I expected it would be my turn next."

CHAPTER II

This chapter concerns Colonel Lloyd and his household; its most emphatic detail has to do with the songs the slaves sing. "To those songs," Douglass writes, "I trace my first glimmering conception of the dehumanizing character of slavery." Can we understand why the songs affect him thus? Douglass stresses the mixture of joy and sadness in the songs; the joy is associated with going to the Great House Farm. There is pathos, thus, in the very cause of joy, pathos in the fact that slaves achieve their satisfaction out of such impoverished stimuli. The importance of the invariable undertone of deep sadness is of course primary: Douglass insists that there is no joy without sadness in the slaves' lives, but that in spite of their oppression they manage to find causes for qualified happiness.

CHAPTER III

The episode of the two Barneys is central here. Why? The arbitrary punishment meted out to them by an unjust master, whose concern is greater for his horses than for the slaves who care for those horses, epitomizes the dehumanization of slavery.

Chapter IV

The series of murders toward the chapter's end best expresses the theme. It is worth commenting on the relation of chapters II, III, and IV to one another—a steadily intensifying emphasis on slavery's injustice. Why, the class might be asked, has Douglass thus far said so little about himself, except as observer? Obviously, he wishes to insist as forcefully as possible on his identification with his people: whether or not he is actually murdered, he participates emotionally in the plight of the victims.

Chapter V

"I look upon my departure from Colonel Lloyd's plantation as one of the most interesting events of my life," Douglass writes. Why? He attributes to this event the possibility of his subsequent escape, and he attributes the event itself to the interposition of Providence. Why is this important? It places the narrative as a whole in a religious context and suggests in a muted way an issue that will later become explicit: how can Christians reconcile themselves to slavery?

Chapter VI

The key event of this chapter, and perhaps of the book as a whole, is the abortive reading lessons Douglass receives from his mistress (see the headnote, pp. 920–22). Their importance is directly stated in the text and is quite obvious but nonetheless worth discussing. Why does the chapter end with the story of Mary's mistreatment? Douglass wishes to emphasize that even in the best possible situation for slaves, injustice and oppression remain, and remain impossible to withstand.

Chapter VII

This chapter dwells almost entirely on reading and on the degree to which learning to read from white children intensified Douglass's consciousness of the intolerable difference of situation between him and his white contemporaries. The most important theme here is the way the child moved from consciousness of his particular plight to awareness of generalizations that could be made about it. Why is the capacity to generalize perceived as a source of strength? The boy's interest in the term *abolition*, his reading of *The Columbian Orator*, even his conversation with the Irishmen all enlarge his comprehension. The ability to go beyond himself, to understand himself in a social context, is crucial to Douglass's self-freeing. Students might be asked about the relation between his interest in books and his ability to figure out how to learn to write. Both aspects of his character declare his capacity to make use of what lies outside himself, a capacity of enormous value to him.

CHAPTER VIII

This chapter reports Douglass's enforced leaving of Baltimore and of his relatively kind master. Its central episode, however, is the partly imagined story of his grandmother, who, if she now lives, "lives to remember and mourn over the loss of children, the loss of grandchildren, and the loss of great-grandchildren." Douglass goes on to envision, however, her solitary death, and to insist that a righteous God will punish those responsible for such a situation. Why is this episode so important in the narrative economy? Talking about this problem will provide a way of discussing the degree to which this autobiography builds itself up by the use of symbolic events, events not necessarily directly autobiographical. If one tries to describe what kind of person Douglass is (and the effort to do so makes a useful classroom exercise), it is necessary to dwell on the fact that he is a symbol-maker, someone who sees experience in symbolic terms. Just as the whipping of his aunt symbolizes for him one aspect of injustice, the isolation of his grandmother symbolizes another. Her alienation in old age, however, assumes special symbolic importance because, as this book increasingly makes clear, the sense of community among slaves is their greatest resource; isolating the old woman in the woods deprives her of this community. Douglass's way of writing resembles a poet's method of creating events: he uses individual happenings to stand for kinds of happening and to evoke the emotion associated with other events of the same order.

CHAPTER IX

Now Douglass finds himself at the mercy of a hard master. This chapter is very short; at its heart is the matter of Southern Christianity. Why does Douglass linger on this aspect of his culture? He thus finds another way to emphasize the injustice of his situation: it is injustice considered in relation to the human obligation to God as well as that to other people. He is gradually enlarging the scope of his concern and his claim.

CHAPTER X

In this first chapter of the second assignment, the scale of the narrative changes. Chapters X and XI together occupy almost as much space as the nine preceding chapters. All the rest, from one point of view, is background; now the autobiographer moves toward the crucial—the absolutely central—event of his escape, showing what emotional forces made escape feel like a necessity and what contributed to making it a possibility. Chapter X summarizes the narrator's experience with three different masters. Its central episode is the failed attempt at escape, important both in relation to what led up to it (the increasingly intense abuse in Douglass's life) and what it leads to (increased determination to escape successfully). But it is worth asking also about the importance of other events, most notably the "magic root" that protects Douglass from being whipped, the Sabbath school he establishes, and his experience as a caulker in Baltimore. An effort should be made to establish both his intensifying sense of personal integrity and independence and his increasingly emphatic sense of community.

CHAPTER XI

Now the escape actually takes place, but this chapter, more than any previous one, emphasizes emotional rather than external event—an effect made more emphatic by the author's deliberate suppression of the literal details of his escape. Instead, he talks about his feelings. It is useful to discuss which feelings are most important: the sadness at the thought of breaking the ties of affection with his slave friends, exhilaration at freedom, suspicion of white and black men alike, wonder at the prosperity of the North, excitement at earning his own money. And time can profitably be spent on delineating the relation between these emotions and those earlier evoked in the book—to what extent these feelings confirm or develop from earlier ones.

APPENDIX

Here Douglass makes most explicit the larger meaning of his narrative. He claims not to be talking about a single life but to be discussing a problem with its bearing on religious professions and practice. Yet the *Narrative* ends with his reassertion of his own name and identity. The large question of how this book integrates its concern with the individual and with the social must be confronted finally—in writing or in class discussion.

Topics for Writing

1. A single episode and how it relates to the whole.
2. What kind of man was Douglass?
3. A way in which this narrative relates to late-twentieth-century problems.
4. The importance of songs and hymns.
5. A single character (apart from Douglass) and his or her importance in the story.
6. What whipping means in this narrative.

Comparative Perspectives

1. While a slave, Douglass witnessed and sometimes engaged in violent action, and his *Narrative* is a revolutionary document. Does it achieve revolutionary status by advocating violence as a means of transforming an evil system? How do the cruel treatment of his own aunt, described at the end of chapter I, and his conflict with Mr. Covey (chapter X) lead him to an understanding of the nature and sources of violence? How much do the proprieties of his era and the vocabulary at his command permit him to articulate about that un-

derstanding? Compare and contrast the depiction of violence in the works of other socially committed writers like Kamau Braithwaite and of postmodernist writers such as Alain Robbe-Grillet.

2. At the end of chapter II, Douglass says that the "wild songs" of slaves express and relieve their unhappiness. In *A Defence of Poetry*, Shelley proclaims that "Poetry is the record of the best and happiest moments of the happiest and best minds." To what degree is their disagreement resolved if we view "wild songs" and poetry as fundamentally different means of expression? Could one argue that the two forms are similar and that the contradiction suggested in this juxtaposition is more apparent than real? Drawing on the reading you have done this semester, define poetry and song and explain the emotions that seem to produce them.

Further Reading

See also the reading suggestions in the anthology, p. 922.

Huggins, N. *Slave and Citizen: The Life of Frederick Douglass.* 1980. Offers a short but comprehensive biography for the general reader, with a bibliography of historical sources.

Preston, D. J. *Young Frederick Douglass: The Maryland Years.* 1980. Concentrates on Douglass's youth, with a section on his late-life return to Maryland; Preston provides a thorough, lucid account.

Stepto, R. "Narration, Authentication, and Authorial Control in Frederick Douglass's Narrative of 1845." *Afro-American Literature: The Reconstruction of Instruction,* ed. R. Stepto and D. Fisher. 1978.

Stone, A. "Identity and Art in Frederick Douglass's Narrative." *College Language Association Journal* 17. 1973, pp. 192–213. Two essays that explore Douglass's work as narrative and specifically as autobiography.

Sweet, L. *Black Images of America, 1784–1870.* 1976. Places Douglass's thought in the context of intellectual history, with stress on his concept of nationality.

WALT WHITMAN

Classroom Strategies and Topics for Discussion

Song of Myself

The notion of the self as inherently fascinating dominates much literature of the Romantic period. One may think, for example, of the Rousseau of the *Confessions*, or of the character of Faust. Since college students themselves are in a developmental stage of intense self-concentration, concerned with defining and understanding their own identities, they are likely to be readily interested in the problems of what it might mean to write a "song of myself"—and what in fact it *does* mean in Whitman's version. Does any notion of the self emerge from the selections printed in the anthology? Certainly one would have to comment on the idea of the self as infinitely inclusive, not defined by difference (as most of us define ourselves) but by comprehension. It is worth pausing to specify some varieties of comprehensiveness here suggested: geographical, political, vocational, sexual ("I am the poet of the woman the same as the man" [21.4]), emotional. Are these claims of vast inclusiveness equivalent to Rousseau's insistence on his uniqueness? It might be argued that Whitman, on the contrary, tries to unite himself with all the rest of humanity—all the rest, that is, of American humanity. Yet, paradoxically, such an attempt at union underlines the speaker's specialness—he alone has the capacity for such inclusiveness. It might be worth pausing to discuss what the poet's notion of containing all kinds of people within himself really means. It is obviously not literal. Does he, perhaps, mean that he has a large capacity for sympathy and empathy? Is this another way of celebrating the poetic imagination, directed now not toward birds and urns but toward other human beings?

One way of getting at important aspects of *Song of Myself* is to inquire in what ways it might be peculiarly American. Published only five years after *In Memoriam*, it of course reflects a very different sensibility. The difference can be explained in terms of Tennyson's and Whitman's personalities, but also in relation to the divergences between English and American culture in the mid-nineteenth century. Obvious answers to the question about "American" aspects of the poem might begin with the specific geographic allusions that abound. Almost equally apparent are the references to American occupations—planter, raftsman, fancy man, rowdy, and the like. It is yet more illuminating to note Whitman's enormous emphasis on the idea of democracy. This is both explicit ("I speak the pass-word primeval, I give the sign of democracy" [24.10]) and implicit, in the reiterated idea of the equality of humankind. (Why should the "primeval" be associated with democracy? The poet appears to imply that democracy constitutes the natural state of humanity—a favorite notion of the Romantics.) Whitman's diction is often insistently American: "Shoulder your duds dear son" (46.15). (Students might be asked to seek other instances of especially "American" language.) And his verse form deviates dramatically from the developed conventions of English poetry, deliberately risking prosiness, working in leisurely rhythms. Even the idea of unity through diversity, here imagined as epitomized in a single person, can be understood as an American concept, a personalized version of a national ideal.

Out of the Cradle Endlessly Rocking

This extended lyric particularly invites comparison with previous Romantic poetry. An obvious point of connection is Whitman's use of nature. How does the speaker's attitude toward the birds compare with say, Keat's toward the nightingale? Whitman appears to be more interested in evoking the birds in themselves, imagined in terms of the birds' situation rather than only in relation to the speaker's needs. The bird song, for Whitman, has more specific emotional meaning and more detailed narrative background. The speaker's sense of identification with the bird is more emphatic. The experience he reports has taken place in the distant past; Keats creates the illusion that he speaks of the present. (This is a point worth dwelling on: what differences are generated by the speaker's different locations in time? It is interesting to consider the relative poetic values, and the different poetic functions, of immediacy versus the impression of meditated meaning.) Both poems stress emotional contrast; both stress the melancholy of the birdsong. Death becomes in both lyrics an important issue: what is the difference in their treatment? (It might also be valuable to compare Whitman's musings on death here with Shelley's in *Stanzas Written in Dejection.*) To Whitman, death seems to comprise a kind of literary temptation ("The word of the sweetest song and all songs," line 180), a "delicious" word, the "key" to all poetry—but not even at the level of fantasy an invitation to suicide. Students might be asked to look for the evidence the poem supplies of its speaker's great vitality. He identifies his own energy with that of his impulse to write verse ("A thousand warbling echoes have started to life within me, never to die," line 149), and he defines himself, in Faustian fashion, with infinite wanting ("The unknown want, the destiny of me," line 157; "O if I am to have so much, let me have more!" line 159). Knowledge of death, in his apparent view, is necessary to the capacity for full expressiveness of life. Why does he evoke the sea as "savage old mother," "fierce old mother," "some old crone rocking the cradle"? The idea of the sea as mother of humanity, the origin of all life, is a Romantic commonplace, but Whitman through his adjectives suggests a common source for life and death: the principle of life contains, inextricably mingled, that of destructiveness.

Topics for Writing

1. Whitman's relation to his reader (in a single poem).
2. The personality the poet creates for himself (in a single poem).
3. The importance of a single image from nature.
4. Whitman's optimism.

Comparative Perspectives

1. Explore the ways in which Whitman defines a sensibility that is both indisputably American and inimitably personal in *Song of Myself.* Compare the attitudes and verbal devices that contribute to this definition with the means by which other modern writers create aesthetic philosophies that similarly combine idiosyncratic and national characteristics.

   [Good choices include Baudelaire's *Paris Spleen,* Tanizaki's *In Praise of Shadows,* Yeats's *Easter 1916* or *Lapis Lazuli,* or Akhmatova's *Requiem.*]

2. Whitman is hardly the first to associate his own vocation with the song of the solitary bird, as he does in *Out of the Cradle Endlessly Rocking*; this call is heard, as the headnote points out, by Keats, in *Ode to a Nightingale,* and it found sympathetic ears at least as long ago as Vālmīki, poet of the *Rāmāyaṇa.* But he may be one of the last to embrace this symbol wholeheartedly. How is Whitman's use of this poetic convention more complicated than that of earlier writers? [Discuss the emotional complexity that Whitman hears in the "aria" of his "brother." What is the significance of those two words? What is beginning to happen to the age-old sense of nature as a reliable source of beauty and inspiration? Such questions could lead into the study of a modernist such as Rilke, or Stevens, or Yeats, for whom art has a status separable from or superior to nature.]

3. Although many politically engaged Latin American poets of the twentieth century harbored strong resentment against North American politics and culture, they revered the work of Walt Whitman. What is there about Whitman's poetry that immunizes him against this resentment?

Further Reading

See also the reading suggestions in the anthology, p. 982.

Allen, G. *Walt Whitman Handbook.* 1946. Provides useful biographical and critical background.

Asselineau, R. *The Evolution of Walt Whitman.* 2 vols. 1960–62. Consists of a biographical volume subtitled *The Creation of a Personality* and a critical volume on *Leaves of Grass* called *The Creation of a Book.*

Kummings, D. D. *Approaches to Teaching Whitman's* Leaves of Grass. 1990. Stimulating collection representing varied approaches.

Price, K. M. *Whitman and Tradition.* 1990. Study of literary influences.

Waskow, H. *Whitman: Explorations in Form.* 1966. Attempts to "define individual poems by showing how they work, and to define Whitman's poetry by demonstrating the relationship among the various ways of working."

Woodress, J., ed. *Critical Essays on Walt Whitman.* 1983. Includes nineteenth- and twentieth-century responses to the poet and supplies an excellent survey of issues relevant to understanding his work.

HERMAN MELVILLE

Billy Budd, Sailor

Classroom Strategies and Topics for Discussion

The sheer suspense of this psychological narrative will keep students involved in reading the story, but—like professional critics—they will probably have trouble with its complexities and ambiguities. As the head-note (on pp. 992–94 of the anthology) suggests, such "trouble" can itself supply a source of interest. In any case, it is helpful, before the first assignment (the narrative naturally divides at the end of chapter 17, p. 1023), to suggest that readers concentrate on trying to fathom the characters of Billy, Vere, and Claggart, and on thinking about the voice of the storyteller, what it's like and what it contributes to the story's effect. The first discussion may well concentrate on just these matters.

The obvious first question for a class, though, is why Melville includes at the beginning the detailed account of the black sailor in Liverpool. This is, of course, only the first of many "digressions" apparently designed to insist on the broad implications of Billy's story. Billy belongs to a type, the narrator suggests; we should understand what happens to him in relation to the function of that type. The black sailor is the center of his companions' attention; he seems to have an enviable role and to foretell just such a position for the hero of this story. The episode is worth returning to at the end of the discussion of *Billy Budd*, as a good example of Melville's irony.

Subtle and important points can emerge from class conversation based on such apparently simple and straightforward questions as What is Billy like?, What is Claggart like?, etc. In arriving at a consensus on such matters, it is obviously important not to let the discussion stray too far from the text. Students might wish to talk about the imagery used to characterize Billy. On the one hand, he resembles "a dog of Saint Bernard's breed," or an "upright barbarian"; on the other, he turns out to be the kind of barbarian Adam may have been before the Fall. How does one reconcile the apparently degrading and the apparently exalted metaphors associated with Billy? Is it possible that to be a barbarian or a dog might be a good thing, given the nature of civilized society? In chapter 16, Billy is said to be ignorant, simpleminded, unsophisticated. Such qualities precipitate his destruction. Are they therefore to be condemned? Like all questions associated with *Billy Budd*, these have no definitive answers, but pursuing them will help readers realize the complexity of the narrative.

The characterization of Vere also presents difficulties. What are we to make of the explanation of his being called "starry Vere"? The matter-of-fact account of the epithet associates him with a long tradition of English heroism, but also suggests that the adjective is a kind of joke. Is it a good thing or a bad one that he loves books? (This manifestly unanswerable question is worth raising because his scholarly nature becomes relevant later on.) Students should particularly note the stress on his social conservatism, and the imagery ("a dyke against those invading waters") associated with it.

You should make sure that students understand the nature of Claggart's job on the ship, to which Melville gives considerable stress. It becomes important that he is the officer in charge of discipline. The storyteller suggests that he is impossible to characterize adequately ("His portrait I essay, but shall never hit it," p. 1008). Why? Worth noting particularly is the emphasis on covert suggestions of "something defective or abnormal" about him, suggestions summed up, on the social level (they are also relevant on the psychological level), by the persistent stories of a criminal past. What is the source of the antagonism Claggart feels for Billy? Speculation about this matter provides much of the substance of chapter 12; does this speculation resolve anything? What would it mean to say that this is the fundamental antipathy of evil for good? Can we believe in this sort of antipathy? Would the Bible support such belief?

The voice of the storyteller in some ways presents the greatest difficulties of all. Passages that should be considered in assessing it include the observation at the end of chapter 2 that Billy is not a conventional hero and his story no romance (what does *romance* mean here? is the narrator simply claiming realism for his tale?); the apology for digression at the beginning of chapter 4, with the association between digression and sinning (why? is this simply a joke? does it raise questions about the nature of "sin" in the story itself?); and (particularly important) the discussion in chapter 11 about Claggart's antipathy, a discussion that suggests and rejects the possibility of inventing an explanation. This last sequence implicitly insists that the storyteller does not finally have control over his story, and other passages echo the point. It makes a claim of truth for the narrative, and it argues that reality is more "mysterious" than invention. Students should be asked how they respond to such a claim. Does it make them trust or distrust the narrator? It certainly could be argued that the storyteller goes out of his way to hint that he is not a dependable or adequate guide through the intricacies of his own story; why should he do such a thing? Perhaps he is trying to make his readers reflect on the final incomprehensibility of their own experience, and of all human experience, and to tell us that the difficulties of his story correspond to those of life.

The second class should perhaps begin with renewed discussion of the imagery associated with Billy. There is, of course, increasing stress on biblical reference, most of which associates Billy with innocence or virtue. Melville renews his allusions to Billy as child, as barbarian, and as dog; he adds, at a crucial moment (just before the hanging), the singing bird. How does this imagery control or affect our developing impression of Billy? Does it convey the storyteller's clear judgment? Students will be interested in the large moral questions raised by the second half of *Billy Budd*. For example, does Billy receive a fair trial? Both possible answers to this question should be fully explored. If Captain Vere's arguments are taken with full seriousness, the answer will probably be yes; if one believes that morality rather than legality or practical considerations should operate in legal proceedings, the answer will be no. In Melville's account, considerable stress is placed on the influence of Vere's "unshared studies," which, along with his superior intellectuality, differentiate him from the other men. Is the point that Captain Vere's is the more well-thought-out position? If this *isn't* the point, what is?

The problem of the storyteller's role also recurs more emphatically in the second half of *Billy Budd*. For example, he claims not to know what happened in the final private interview between Billy and Captain Vere; he can only "conjecture." This device reiterates the claim of truth for the narrative; it may also renew the reader's uneasiness. It is worth asking once more why the narrator, the inventor of characters and action alike, should disclaim his own authority. Do the questions he implicitly raises about authorial authority extend to other kinds of power? Or does one come to believe in the truth of the story he tells? Another question about the way the story is being told may arise with the "digression" after the hanging: what is the point of introducing these speculations about why Billy's body didn't move? Do they suggest something supernatural about his death? Does the reader find him- or herself trying to come up with other explanations? Do we believe that the problem matters at all?

A few more large questions that might prove stimulating: Do the three principal characters conduct themselves in the crisis in ways you would anticipate from their characterizations in the first half? Claggart is the villain, but he alone does not cause Billy's death. Who or what should be blamed? Captain Vere? "Society"? War? Chance? How do you feel about Billy at the end? Is he saint or simpleton? Can you think of comparable instances, in public or in private life, of conflicts between legality and justice that are very difficult to adjudicate?

Topics for Writing

Most of the questions that have been raised here would provide good material for essays, whether or not they have been discussed in class. (Since this work is so richly interpretable, everyone can have individual opinions differing from ones arrived at collectively.) Some other possible topics:

1. Why does the action occur during the French Revolution?
2. Billy as a passive hero.
3. Billy's effect on others.
4. Captain Vere: the tragedy of the educated man.
5. Claggart's motives.

Comparative Perspectives

1. Works as different as *Antigone, Narrative of the Life of Frederick Douglass, The Guest, The Sultan's Dilemma,* and *Things Fall Apart* tackle a question similar to the ones Melville puts here: When should the law be obeyed? What is the relationship between law and justice? How does the tone of the work in question guide us to varying responses to these problems?
2. The British composer Benjamin Britten turned both *Billy Budd* and *Death in Venice* into operas, helping us see that both texts describe the disturbing attraction felt by a quasi-paternal authority figure for a very young man. Compare the emphases of Melville and Mann in

dealing with these feelings. Both writers draw heavily on classical and biblical allusions rather than examine these situations in explicitly psychological terms. What difference does half a century make in the presentation of this theme in the two works? How does Freud's effort to analyze "Dora" expose some of the complicated sexual attitudes that may underlie the tensions in these two short novels?

[If time and context permit, listening to key portions of the leading tenor roles—Vere and Aschenbach—would be a rewarding exercise.]

Further Reading

See also the reading suggestions in the anthology, p. 994.

Miller, E. *Melville*. 1975. Both biographical and critical, stressing Freudian interpretation.

Parker, H. *Reading* Billy Budd. 1990. Focused on the difficulties of interpretation and their significance.

Stafford, W. *Melville's* Billy Budd *and the Critics.* 1969. Offers an enormous amount of useful information, containing texts of Melville's story and of the play made from it; an essay on the Hayford-Sealts text; and a collection of early and recent criticism from several points of view including treatments of characters, sources, digressions, tradition, theological implications, and a valuable bibliography.

EMILY DICKINSON

Classroom Strategies and Topics for Discussion

First-time readers of Emily Dickinson typically have trouble understanding why such tiny poems should be taken seriously. Because Dickinson makes no loud claims for herself, because her lyrics do not elaborate their emotional arguments, perhaps even because of their eccentric punctuation, students may make the mistake of thinking these are easy and obvious poems. Your first task, therefore, is to demonstrate how much goes on beneath the surface of apparently simple verse—and for this purpose, there is no substitute for close attention to a specific text. A class can easily spend an hour exploring implications of a single short poem; to do so provides the best way to demonstrate the complexity of Dickinson's achievement.

If time limitations forbid such leisurely analysis, you may use a more general approach. You could point out, for example, that at least five of Dickinson's lyrics here printed deal centrally with death (216, 449, 465, 712, 1564). Beyond this theme, the five poems have little obviously in common. Yet it is illuminating to compare them with one another—say, 216 and 712. Do they share any images? Students might notice immediately that both suggest connections between graves and houses: "Al-

abaster Chambers," "a House that seemed / A Swelling of the Ground."
Are these associations reassuring or disturbing? This question should generate considerable discussion—possibly even controversy. The solidity,
beauty, security of alabaster, satin, stone (216, first stanza) might be cited
as forms of positive suggestion; and the apparent affinity to nature of the
"House" in 712. On the other hand, the fact that the alabaster chambers
remain untouched by morning and noon (with the past participle repeated for emphasis) is more ambiguous. One could argue that being
untouched by diurnal sequence implies existence beyond time, transcendence—or, with very different emotional tone, that it implies the cessa-
tion of experience. Similarly, the "Centuries" that have elapsed since the
speaker in 712 set out on her journey with Death may convey the positive
associations of "Immortality" or the terrifying possibilities of "Eternity."
Does the speaker convey a consistent attitude toward death in each case?
The effect of 216 depends on the contrast between the first and second
stanzas. Is that contrast mainly between the ignorance of breeze, bee, and
birds and the "sagacity" of the dead? Perhaps so—but the sagacity has already "perished," so "the meek members of the Resurrection" in their
sleep can oppose no wisdom to the "ignorant cadence" of the birds.

The noun "Resurrection" in 216, like "Immortality" in 712, suggests a
Christian view of the afterlife. Does anything else in either poem sub-
stantiate this view? The predominant images, in both cases, are secular—
in 216, details of tomb, coffin, and natural world; in 712, items of
clothing and scenes that recapitulate stages of human life. Why, then, the
Christian allusions? Generations of critics have debated this problem, and
no definitive answer is likely. Students might, however, find it interesting
to think about the degree to which both poems achieve their effects by
juxtaposing incongruous points of view without mediating between them.
The most obvious example is the imagining of Death as a gentlemanly figure stopping his carriage for a lady and of the journey through eternity as
an exercise in civility. To think of gossamer and tulle in relation to death,
or of horses and eternity, also strains the imagination by invoking sharply
different focuses of perception. The abstractness of "Immortality" contrasts with the concretely imagined scene of two figures in a carriage. To
think of the dead as "members of the Resurrection" conflicts with thinking of them in their graves; to turn attention to what happens in the air
makes it hard to think simultaneously of what happens underground; and
to sum up the dead as having embodied "sagacity" violates the expectations that the poem has established.

The techniques students will discover by trying to figure out the relation of these two poems recur in many others. In other lyrics too they can
find unpredictable juxtapositions of abstract and concrete and of opposed
perspectives; gaps in meaning that both demand and elude interpretation
(What, for example, is the relation, on the narrative level, between the
"House" before which the travelers pause in 712 and their continued
journey? What does the grave have to do with eternity?) and the shock
value of unexpected words (e.g., "omnipotent" in 585, "infirm" in 1129,

"enabled" in 1207, "Pangless" in 1564). The effect of the punctuation is worth discussing: often a dash at the end of a poem suspends meaning, implying that a thought or feeling is only interrupted, not completed; often a dash in the middle of a line forces a pause that demands attention for a phrase suddenly made fresh by being perceived as a small, contained unit. And you may wish to call attention to Dickinson's slant rhymes ("away" and "civility," "chill" and "Tulle"). True rhymes in a quatrain structure create effects of finality, order, closure. These near-rhymes, like the dashes, suggest that matters cannot quite be closed off, that no statement comprehends the significance of any phenomenon.

Rhetoric, rhythm, and punctuation reiterate the same implications of open meaning. These poems demand active involvement from their readers. Their predominantly simple language, their way of contemplating the ordinary until it becomes strange (think of the buzzing fly in 465), suggest that everyday experience also invites active involvement, active interpretation—and that all meaning depends on interpretation. One can imagine the dead as buried or as resurrected (or as both at once); one can imagine a train as an animal or a star (585). Such acts of imagination make the world simultaneously comprehensible and mysterious.

Topics for Writing

1. Animal life in Emily Dickinson.
2. A "feminine" aspect of Dickinson's poems.
3. Who is the speaker, and what is she like (in any poem)?
4. Dickinson's sense of humor.

Comparative Perspectives

1. Compare the attitude toward human consciousness and its power or weakness relative to nature in "The Brain—is wider than the Sky—" (632) with Coleridge's *Dejection: An Ode* or Leopardi's *The Infinite*. Which poet is more confident of the mind's ability?
2. One might say that Emily Dickinson writes an American equivalent of the medieval Persian poet Jalâloddin Rumi's *Robais*, pithy short lyrics that open the reader's mind to a mystical contemplation of the apparently commonplace. Compare Rumi's meditations on the shortcomings of language in [*Listen, if you can stand to*], or the comment "I've lived too long where I can be reached" in [*What I most want*], with Dickinson's "Tell all the Truth but tell it slant" (1129) or "He preached upon 'Breadth'" (1207). Why do poets so often question the efficacy of words?
3. How does Dickinson's unsentimental treatment of the familiar imagery of birds (as in 328 or 1084) contrast with the lusher poems of Keats and Whitman discussed above? Does she seem more like the Romantic or the modernist poets in this regard?

Further Reading

See also the reading suggestions in the anthology, p. 1051.

Fast, R. R., and C. M. Gordon, eds. *Approaches to Teaching Emily Dickinson's Poetry*. 1989. An exceptionally useful and varied collection.

Pollak, V. *Dickinson: The Anxiety of Gender*. 1984. Analyzes the life and work with emphasis on her experience as a woman.

Sewall, R. *The Life of Emily Dickinson*. 2 vols. 1974. A thorough, readable, and interesting biography.

————, ed. *Emily Dickinson: A Collection of Critical Essays*. 1963. A group of essays illuminating in their diversity.

Urdu Lyric Poetry in
North India

GHALIB

Ghazals

Backgrounds and Classroom Strategies

One aspect of Urdu *ghazal* poetry that might need further contextualization is the role of this literature in the complex interface among Islamic, Indian, Moghal, and other elements that characterizes Indian civilization after the coming of Islam to the subcontinent.

In the introductory chapter of his book *The Golden Tradition* (one of the readings suggested on p. 1065 in the anthology), Ahmad Ali shows that, although poets in Muslim kingdoms in central India (Bijapur and Golconda) were the first to write Urdu *ghazals*, it was in Delhi, especially under Bahadur Shah, the last Moghal emperor and himself a *ghazal* poet, that the Urdu *ghazal* flowered. However, because of the turbulent events that took place in Delhi in the eighteenth and nineteenth centuries, including the sack of Delhi by the Persian king Nadir Shah in 1739 and the Indian revolt against the British in 1857, Lucknow, the capital of the north Indian province of Oudh, became Delhi's rival as a center for Urdu poetry.

In the nineteenth century, during Ghalib's lifetime, modern Hindi—written in the Sanskrit (Devanagari) script and containing a mainly Sanskritic vocabulary—was still evolving as a language, and both Hindus and Muslims commonly used Urdu in everyday speech and writing (in the Perso-Arabic script), as well as in literature. Urdu poetry was thus an integral part of the culture of north India in the nineteenth century, shared by Hindus and Muslims alike. The situation has changed considerably in the twentieth century, with Hindi being used and promoted as the common language of north Indian speech and literature, while Urdu has been adopted as the national language of Pakistan, which was founded as a homeland for the Muslims of the subcontinent when India became independent from British rule in 1947. Thus it is that two of the preeminent Urdu poets of this century, Muhammad Iqbal (1877–1938) and Faiz Ahmad Faiz (1922–1984), are the national poets of Pakistan.

The cultural function of *ghazal* poetry is an important topic for classroom discussion. Throughout the history of the form, not only pro-

fessional poets but intellectuals of various persuasions have composed
ghazals. Urdu poets often functioned as teachers (*ustād*) of versification
for their aristocratic patrons. In private communication and in social
gatherings, the *ghazal* couplet has always functioned as a kind of code
language, an artistic means of conveying thoughts and ideas in a complex,
enigmatic, veiled fashion. The cultural ambience of *ghazal* repartee is a
major theme in Mirza Ruswa's *Umrao Jan Ada* (translated under the title
The Courtesan of Lucknow), the first novel in modern Urdu. Ruswa depicts Umrao Jan, an aging courtesan, remembering her life and, in particular, the scintillating *ghazals* she exchanged with her former lovers. In the
course of the narrative Umrao Jan and her creator, Mirza Ruswa, themselves quote *ghazal* couplets as they muse about the fading splendor of
Lucknow culture. Students might benefit from reading a short excerpt
from this novel. *Ghazal* poetry and the cultural dilemmas surrounding the
partition of India are significant themes in Anita Desai's novel *Clear Light
of Day* (1980), and the primary focus of her novel *In Custody* (1987) is on
the culture of Urdu poetry. The recent film version of *In Custody* (in English), available on videotape, is a splendid teaching tool for a unit on
Urdu poetry. Desai's novel and the film illuminate the integral part the
Urdu *ghazal* plays in north Indian culture. See also the poems of Agha
Shahid Ali, a modern Indian poet writing in English, on Urdu poetry.

   You might open a discussion about form by asking the students what
formal traits of the *ghazal* allowed it to become a highly valued form of
communication in Indian culture. For instance, how do the stock images,
the strict rhyme scheme, and the short couplets contribute to the *ghazal*'s
effectiveness in this respect? Discussion might also focus on the accessi-
bility of *ghazal* poetry to a modern audience. Despite the cultural specificity of the *ghazal*'s imagery, and the formal and romantic tone of the
form, it is clear from the American poets' translations that they have
found the *ghazal*—or at least Ghalib's *ghazals*—accessible to them as poets as well as readers. Many modern readers have found Ghalib's couplets
startlingly modern, enigmatic in a manner akin to the verses of the German poet Rilke, and resonating in their brevity with the fragmented quality conveyed by much modern poetry, which itself reflects the fragmented
nature of modern society as a whole. It is not accidental that nineteenth-
century Western scholars criticized *ghazal* poems for what they perceived
as a lack of unity, whereas twentieth-century readers feel perfectly comfortable with the relative autonomy of each couplet and with the shifts in
mood from one couplet to another within a single *ghazal*. In this context
it is important to remember that connoisseurs usually quote a single couplet by itself.

   One should not, however, emphasize the separateness of the couplet at
the expense of the *ghazal* as a whole. By all means, encourage students to
look for resonances among the couplets in each poem. Note, for instance,
the play of water and air in Ghazal V, or the variations on fire, desert, and
garden in Ghazal XIX. How does Ghalib use the stock imagery of flowers
and wine in his poems? In the book from which the American *ghazal*

translations have been taken, editor Aijaz Ahmad provides a literal translation and notes for each *ghazal*, followed by translations of the poem by
several poets. Students might find it illuminating to compare several
translations of a single poem and to discuss questions of form, feeling,
and cultural as well as literary aspects of translation.

Comparative Perspectives

1. The final couplet in Ghalib's Ghazal V suggests that the rose functions in the poem as an image of openness and plenitude (motifs
   that recur in Ghazal VIII as well, although not in connection with
   the flower). Writers have frequently endowed the rose with symbolic
   significance, and understanding the different ways they have used it
   helps us understand their idiosyncratic visions and concerns. What
   properties of the rose lend themselves to various poetic appropria-
   tions?

   [Good choices include Dante's architectural account of the petals
   of the Mystic Rose in Cantos 31 and 32 of *Paradiso*; Pope's reference to the heady scent of the rose in *Essay on Man*, Epistle I (lines
   199–200); Blake's personification of "The Sick Rose" in *Songs of Experience*; Lorna Goodison's summary reference to the generally accepted excellence of the flower in *To Us, All Flowers are Roses*.]

2. Ghazal XII, in Adrienne Rich's translation, fuses the poet and the
   poem in a remarkable identification of sound and grief. Use this
   ghazal to discuss the focal role of the poetic persona in this complex
   poetic tradition (as in the usual insertion of the poet's signature).
   This habit of imprinting the self on the poem does not necessarily
   mean that the *ghazal* as a form is more "sincere" than other less self-
   referential lyric traditions. Explore the degree to which the poet's
   "real" voice emerges in other lyrics in the anthology.

   [In the works that initiate the Western tradition, Homer's epics,
   the narrative voice is generally obscured once the Muse has been invoked. By contrast, the putative creators of the two great Indian
   epics, Vyāsa and Vālmīkī, are actors in the stories they tell. The
   T'ang poets seem to turn autobiography into poetry, but, like the Petrarchan sonneteer, they do so within well-understood conventional
   norms. Where might one place poet X (this exercise should work
   with almost any choice) along a continuum beginning with the totally self-effacing voice of ritual poetry like the *Night Chant* and
   ending with the insistently self-identifying poet like Walt Whitman?
   How much does individual temperament contribute to this equation? How much is it a function of cultural practice or period style?]

Further Reading and Viewing

See also the reading suggestions in the anthology, p. 1065.

Ali, Agha Shahid. "A Butcher," "In Memory of Begum Akhtar," "Homage
to Faiz Ahmad Faiz." In *The Half-Inch Himalayas*. 1987.

Desai, Anita. *Clear Light of Day.* 1980.

———. *In Custody.* 1984.

Ivory, James. *In Custody.* A Merchant Ivory film, based on the novel; available on videotape.

Ruswa, Mirza. *The Courtesan of Lucknow (Umrao Jan Ada).* Translated by Khushwant Singh and M. A. Husaini. 1961.

Realism, Naturalism, and Symbolism in Europe

GUSTAVE FLAUBERT

Madame Bovary

Backgrounds

Madame Bovary is the story of Emma, a young woman living in Normandy in the 1840s. She has received a convent education that has filled her head with romantic dreams of luxury and love. She marries a country doctor, Charles Bovary, an awkward, dull, but honest and loving young man, and bears him a daughter. Quickly disappointed and bored by her marriage, she resists the advances of a shy student, Léon, but then becomes depressed and revives only when Charles manages to move into a larger village, Yonville. There she quickly succumbs to the advances of a dashing landowner, Rodolphe. She wants to elope with him, but he deserts her in the last moment. On a trip to Rouen where she attends the opera, she again meets Léon, now a law clerk, and becomes his mistress. Her clandestine meetings and the luxuries she purchases involve her in debt to a local, usurious merchant. When he presses her and all attempts to get help from her lovers fail, she commits suicide by arsenic poisoning. Only after her death does Charles discover her infidelities.

Flaubert wrote the novel after his return from a trip to the Levant, deliberately choosing a low and commonplace subject and a heroine whose vulgarity he despised. He felt he had to make a new beginning as all his early writings had been lyrical and romantic. He worked assiduously at the novel, describing his slow progress and his "agonies of composition" in letters to his friend Louise Colet.

Flaubert's treatment of sexual encounters, frank for his time, and his description of the ceremony of extreme unction caused an attempt by the government of Napoleon III to suppress the book as obscene. The defense won acquittal on the argument that the story actually shows the wages of sin and even metes out harsh punishment for Emma's adulteries. The success of the book was thus assured. What Flaubert wrote, however, was neither a salacious book nor a warning against adultery but a supreme work of art, which today is generally regarded as the first modern novel, clearly set off by its objectivity from the earlier moralizing novels of writers such as Balzac, Dickens, and Thackeray.

Classroom Strategies

Flaubert divided the novel into three parts, which can be taught in three assignments. If necessary, part 2 may be divided after chapter VIII (which ends on p. 1180) and part 3 after chapter VI (which ends on p. 1267), making five assignments.

The main difficulties of the book come from defining the author's ambiguous attitude toward Emma, which obviously includes condemnation of her lying, her lust, and her improvidence, satire on her romantic illusions, and compassion for her sufferings. As the headnote indicates, Flaubert's point of view is not as detached and completely objective as the reputation of the book may suggest. The story begins in the schoolroom with a teller who speaks of "we" as if he were one of the boys in the class, but then the point of view shifts to omniscience: much that is represented could not possibly have been seen or felt by Madame Bovary. Occasionally Flaubert comments disapprovingly on her "hard-hearted and tight-fisted peasant nature" or her "corruption." But at the end, in his description of the extreme unction, he solemnly pronounces forgiveness even for her sensuality and lust. One must keep alert throughout for shifts in perspective of this kind. For example, the ball at the castle of the Marquis (chapter VII of part 1) is drenched in the atmosphere of Emma's own dreams and longings. The agricultural fair on the other hand, which has been called "polyphonic" in reproducing the speeches of the pompous officials alternating with the lovetalk of Rodolphe, is viewed not through Emma's eyes but with the satirical and ironic detachment of the author.

Other valuable points for discussion are the satirical picture of the whole society (particularly as represented in the odious pharmacist Homais, who is the target of Flaubert's dislike of the ideas of progress, science and democracy) and the character of Charles Bovary, who opens and closes the book and whose final judgment, "It was decreed by fate" (p. 1300), is endorsed by the author even though Rodolphe finds it slightly ridiculous.

The technique of building the book around striking pictorial scenes should also be discussed. The ball, the agricultural fair, the ride in the woods, Emma receiving Rodolphe's letter and climbing to the attic, the opera (*Lucia di Lammermoor*) in Rouen, the visit to the Cathedral, the cab ride, the scenes in the hotel with Léon, and finally the suicide print themselves indelibly on one's memory, and it pays to ask by what means Flaubert has accomplished this. Often small details are used almost symbolically, as in the little scene of Charles and Emma having supper, he eating boiled beef, she drawing knife lines on the oilcloth on the table: a scene used by Erich Auerbach in *Mimesis* to stress the novelty of Flaubert's impersonal realism. Or to take another example: the wooden napkin rings of Binet and the whirr of the lathe, which saves Emma from falling to her death. Such details serve to point out the estrangement between husband and wife while emphasizing also the role of little things, the chances of life.

Topics for Discussion and Writing

1. Discuss the character of Emma and the author's attitude toward her.

2. Discuss the social picture and social types of the novel: the husband-physician, the landowner, the law clerk, the pharmacist, the merchant-usurer, the beggar, etc.

3. Discuss Percy Lubbock's statement in *Craft of Fiction* that this is "the novel of all novels which no criticism of fiction can overlook" (p. 60). In comparison with other novels you have read, what features do you discover in it that might justify Lubbock's praise?

4. Discuss the implied philosophy of life or scale of values. Do you agree with Martin Turnell (*The Novel in France*) that this novel is "an onslaught on the whole basis of human feeling and on all spiritual and moral values"? Think also of the "positive" figures: Emma's father, the pharmacist's apprentice, the old peasant woman at the agricultural fair who got for fifty-four years of service a medal worth twenty-five francs, or of Dr. Larivière, who comes too late to save Emma.

5. Discuss some particularly clearly visualized episodes such as the agricultural fair and the scene in the Cathedral. Both contrast the trivial lovetalk with the pompous rhetoric of an official or a guide. What is the effect of this?

6. Ask how far the story transcends its local setting in time and place and, particularly, how far its scenes, persons, actions, emotional and mental attitudes may be applied to our own time. Emma is sometimes thought of as a typical dreamer like Don Quixote, but in fact the two are very different. Don Quixote takes action, however foolish, while Emma can only plan a trip to Italy. Homais has become the type of the conventional small-town man who has accepted all the commonplaces of nineteenth-century progress, faith in science, and democracy, and he is, in the last words of the book, rewarded with the order of the Legion of Honor. Do we still find this type today?

Comparative Perspectives

1. Like Flaubert, Molière ran afoul of authority for his depiction of religion.

    a. Compare the treatment of French Catholic mores in *Madame Bovary* with Molière's portrait of Tartuffe. Which do you think poses a greater challenge to ecclesiastical control?

    b. How convincing do you find Molière's defense of the stage in the three prefaces to *Tartuffe*? Compare Flaubert's strategy of speaking not in his own voice, but through the debates between Homais and the abbé Bournisien in the discussion of theater in part two, chapter XIV.

2. Like St. Augustine and like Rousseau, Emma is deeply influenced

by her reading. Describe the fiction and poetry that move her and
analyze your own responses to such material. If reading matter can
corrupt, is the fault in the text or in the reader?

   a. Note Emma's love of Walter Scott (and the power and limits of
her response to the performance of *Lucia di Lammermoor* in part
two, chapter XV) and Romantic poetry (see the reference to Lamartine's *The Lake* in part three, chapter III).

   b. Footnote 8 on p. 1248 mentions Flaubert's attitude toward a
"stilted romantic sensibility." Does that mean he rejects Romanticism in all its forms? Discuss some elements of *Madame Bovary* that
seem romantic you and compare them to elements you have observed in your study of nineteenth-century lyric poetry.

3. The death of Emma Bovary and the death of Ivan Ilyich are among
   the most famous scenes in nineteenth-century fiction. Compare and
   contrast the kinds of details singled out by Flaubert and Tolstoy, two
   masters of realism, and comment on the points they make about the
   nature of the characters who are dying. For a wider-ranging examination of tone, look at some other literary death scenes (of Hector
   in the *Iliad*, for example, of Dai-yu in *The Story of the Stone*, or of
   Aschenbach in *Death in Venice*). In each case, examine the values
   implicit in the author's descriptive techniques and show how they
   guide the audience to make judgments about the deceased.

4. The ball scene in which Emma waltzes for the first time introduces
   her to the world of the senses, a world in which women drink wine
   and make assignations with lovers. In *The Tale of Genji* and *The
   Story of the Stone*, gatherings at which poetry is shared serve as the
   occasion—and metaphoric vehicle—for initiations such as Emma
   undergoes at the dance. Although adulterous relationships occur in
   all three narratives, the ways in which sexuality is described seem to
   involve different cultural codes. Comment on the literary priority
   given to the pressure of bodies in the Western novel in contrast
   to the emphasis on communing through verse in the great Asian
   novels.

5. Flaubert's empathizing with Emma Bovary's longings does not obscure the novel's ruthless anatomizing of the bored housewife, a literary type that has become a staple of modern women's fiction.
   Contrast the limits of Emma Bovary's self-awareness with the capacity for critical self-scrutiny exhibited by characters like Clarice
   Lispector's heroine in *Daydreams of a Drunk Woman*. Do women
   understand their lives in ways that male writers cannot?

Further Reading

See also the reading suggestions in the anthology, p. 1088.

Auerbach, Erich. *Mimesis: The Representation of Reality in Western Literature*. Trans. Willard Trask. 1953. "In the Hotel de la Mole" has lumi-
nous pages.

Bart, Benjamin F., ed. *Madame Bovary and the Critics: A Collection of Essays.* 1966.

James, Henry. *Notes on Novelists.* 1914. Throws doubt on the choice of subject.

Levin, Harry. *The Gates of Horn: A Study of Five French Realists.* 1963. The chapter "Flaubert" gives a general appraisal of *Madame Bovary.*

Lubbock, Percy. *The Craft of Fiction.* 1921. In chapters 5 and 6, Lubbock stresses the role of telling and the point of view.

Porter, Laurence M., and Eugene F. Gary, eds. *Approaches to Teaching Flaubert's* Madame Bovary. 1995. One of the volumes in the MLA series.

Steegmuller, Francis. *Flaubert and* Madame Bovary. 1939; new ed. 1950. Good on the biographical background and the genesis of the book.

Turnell, Martin. *The Novel in France.* 1950. Criticizes Flaubert from a moral point of view.

FYODOR DOSTOEVSKY

Notes from Underground

Backgrounds

Notes from Underground consists of two distinct parts. First comes the monologue of a lonely, spiteful former clerk who lives in a garret in St. Petersburg and states his hatred of humanity, progress, science, and determinism. Next follows a kind of memoir in which the same man reminisces about events in his earlier life. An attempt at self-assertion has led to his jostling an officer; an intrusion into the company of former schoolfellows has resulted in humiliating altercations and finally in a visit to a brothel. There he in turn humiliates the prostitute Lisa by depicting her future terrible fate. Deeply moved and determined to change her life, Lisa calls on the Underground Man, only to find him engaged in a disgraceful scene with his servant. Newly humiliated, he seeks vicarious revenge by sexually assaulting the girl and forcing money on her. She flees, throwing the money away. The Underground Man remains in his hole, alienated, mortified, disgusted with himself and everything around.

The story, written in 1864, reflects the beginning of Dostoevsky's conversion to a conservative creed. He had, as explained in the headnote (see pp. 1301–06 in the anthology), taken part in an underground circle, which the government of Tsar Nicholas considered subversive, but which was mainly a discussion group interested in the utopian socialism of Fourier. Dostoevsky was arrested, tried, taken to be shot, but reprieved at the place of execution to ten years penal servitude in Siberia. Four years he spent in a stockade in chains and six as a common soldier on the frontier of China. He returned to Petersburg in 1859, a changed man.

Notes from Underground is a departure from Dostoevsky's early manner as a social novelist and anticipates the later great novels beginning with *Crime and Punishment* two years later.

Classroom Strategies

Two assignments or three. Part II can be divided after chapter V (which ends on p. 1354), if three are desired.

The first part, the monologue, presents difficulties to students in that it contains a searing attack on the assumptions of their tradition. The whole Enlightenment cherished by the West—including the ideas of perpetual progress, of scientific truth, of a well-organized, rational society "in pursuit of happiness"—is not only questioned but jeered at. Students are apt to discount the whole diatribe because it is put into the mouth of a despicable being, who himself declares that he is motivated by resentment at his failure in human relations. Such a dismissal would be an enormous mistake: the Underground Man is right in Dostoevsky's eyes in asserting human freedom, which seems to him the essential prerogative of our species. He feels that he is robbed of it by deterministic science, which forbids him to argue that two plus two may be five, and by the utopian schemes of socialist world-improvers who would force humanity into an artificial collective paradise. Through the mouth of his unlovely speaker, Dostoevsky attacks all rationalism, all utopianism, all illusions about natural goodness. He does not believe that men and women follow their enlightened self-interest as the utopians hope. Rather, in his view, they are creatures of passion, even senseless and destructive passion. The human species is bloodthirsty, and history is a record of butcheries. Our nature, as history shows, craves chaos and destruction, even suffering and pain. The intellectual position of the Underground Man can be seen as an anticipation of existentialism, which in the writings of Jean-Paul Sartre and Albert Camus asserted indeterminism, the freedom of the will, and choice. It can also be seen as curiously prophetic of the terrifying inhumanities we have witnessed in our own century.

Topics for Discussion

The whole question of optimism versus pessimism about the fate of mankind will properly take center stage. Questions about the brutalities of humankind both past and present will make for exciting debate. Our own modern fear of totalitarianism is raised as the Underground Man revolts at the thought that the individual soul might become a member of an "ant heap," a "mere cipher," a "piano key," an "organ stop" (as he says in many variations).

The second part, in particular, raises psychological questions: Dostoevsky depicts a personality dominated by resentment, who doubts the stability of human personality and who himself oscillates between pride and humility, the desire to humiliate others and the hardly concealed desire of being humiliated. The scenes with Lisa are the best illustrations.

A literary question is raised by the dramatic monologue, which at times is almost like a stream of consciousness, in its relation to the confessions of the second part, which buttress and justify the tone and content of the first part. The parody of the rescue of a prostitute is the most striking example. The whole story, told by an "antihero," may at first strike us as purely negative; yet it is one of the paradoxes of Dostoevsky's art that he uses his most doubtful characters as spokesmen for his most cherished ideas. Though Dostoevsky complained of the suppression of a chapter by the censor, hinting at a religious solution that he found later, we may at this stage of our knowledge of Dostoevsky's writings remain baffled by the blind alley in which the Underground Man has lost himself.

A further point of discussion is raised by the peculiarly Russian setting of the person and events of the story. Dostoevsky considers the Underground Man, in his alienation from society, to be representative of the generation of the forties and the fifties. The story particularly attacks the utopianism of such novels as that by Nikolay Chernyshevsky, *What Is to Be Done?* (1863), which much later was highly admired by Lenin, and which jeers at the materialist progress reflected in the Crystal Palace at the London Universal Exhibition, which Dostoevsky saw in 1862. Polemics against Russian radical critics of the sixties color the speech of the Underground Man. The nature of the reflections on Romanticism, which here means "dreaming" or vague "idealism," and the picture of the stratified society (clerks, bureaucrats, military officers, prostitutes) date the story to the same extent as the wet snow and the fog localize it in a Petersburg winter.

Topics for Writing

1. Discuss the attack on the idea of progress, on the natural goodness of humankind, on the benefits of science, and on rationalism and optimism generally.

   [Clues to possible answers are suggested in the headnote and in "Topics for Discussion," but may be different for different students.]

2. Discuss the view that humanity's history shows our cruelty: that we *want* to suffer and inflict pain. Do not exclude current and recent history.

   [In psychiatry the term "sadomasochism" would describe this condition. In the story, the scenes with Lisa are perhaps the best examples.]

3. Discuss humanity's "terrifying freedom." Are you convinced by the argument against determinism and for complete individualism, even caprice? Are you any more convinced by the converse of these views? Why or why not?

4. What does the term "Underground Man" imply?

   [In Russian, *podpolie* means "below the floor." The Underground Man is compared to a mouse living in a cellar-hole, but the actual protagonist lives in a garret with a servant. The answer is suggested by the whole tone of resentment, isolation, and alienation.]

Comparative Perspectives

1. The protagonist of Dostoevsky's *Notes from Underground* labels himself an antihero who couldn't resist writing about himself, despite his sense that "a novel needs a hero." What does he mean by this? What neurotic needs drive antiheroic figures? Are such characters peculiar to nineteenth- and twentieth-century art, or can you think of other examples?

   [Examine the narrator's own definition of his antiheroic state— being "estranged from life"—to open up many vistas. Achilles arguably fits this definition. What has changed over time is the vocabulary available for analyzing compulsive, self-destructive behavior, not the impulse behind it; in contemporary literature, examples abound. Possibilities include Hermann in Pushkin's *The Queen of Spades*, Gregor in Kafka's *The Metamorphosis*, Eliot's J. Alfred Prufrock, and the Misfit in O'Connor's *A Good Man Is Hard to Find*.]

2. Must two times two equal four? Explain the Underground Man's critique of reason and compare it with other challenges to what seems to him a dead and mechanistic way of dealing with the world.

   [Possibilities include Swift's *Modest Proposal* as well as his account of life among the Houyhnhnms; Blake's *Mock On, Mock On, Voltaire, Rousseau*; Tzara's *Dadaist Disgust* (in the *Dada Manifesto 1918*); and Borges's *The Garden of Forking Paths*.]

Further Reading

See also the reading suggestions in the anthology, p. 1306.

Carr, Edward Hallett. *Dostoevsky, 1821–1881: A New Biography*. 1931. Sober and factual.

Dostoevsky, Fyodor. *Notes from Underground*. Trans. and ed. Michael R. Katz. 2nd ed. 2001. Contains a section of modern criticism.

Frank, Joseph. *Dostoevsky: The Seeds of Revolt, 1821–1849*. 1976.

———. *Dostoevsky: The Years of Ordeal, 1850–1859*. 1984.

———. *Dostoevsky: The Stir of Liberation, 1860–1865*. 1986. The period of *Notes from Underground*.

———. *Dostoevsky: The Miraculous Years, 1865–1871*. 1995.

Jones, Malcolm V. *Dostoevsky: The Novel of Discord*. 1976. A good recent introduction.

Simmons, Ernest J. *Dostoevsky: The Making of the Novelist*. 1940. Provides a reliable digest of Russian scholarship.

SYMBOLISM

The four poets gathered under "Symbolism" may be taught as a group—major poets who are also heralds of twentieth-century modernism—or as individual authors to be compared and contrasted with others in the anthology. In addition, you may wish to select single poems to set against others with similar themes: the familiar Romantic themes of love, art, nature, and beauty, for example, reappear with a new twist in Symbolist poetry. You could compare Romantic melancholy as in Coleridge's *Dejection: An Ode*, Heine's *A Pine Is Standing Lonely*, or Leopardi's *To Himself* with Baudelaire's *Spleen* or Verlaine's *Autumn Song*; visionary scenes such as Coleridge's *Kubla Khan*, or Bécquer's *Nameless Spirit* with Rimbaud's impersonal *Illuminations* and Mallarmé's *Saint*; and evocations of the seasons such as Rosaliá de Castro's *Candescent Lies the Air* or Lamartine's *The Lake* with Baudelaire's *Song of Autumn* and *Spleen LXXVIII*, (Verlaine's *Autumn Song* or Lu Xun's *Wild Grass*.) In a broader perspective, you might bring up symbolic voyages, such as Dante's *Divine Comedy*, and compare Baudelaire's *The Voyage* and Rimbaud's *The Drunken Boat* or Tagore's *The Golden Boat*; or launch a discussion about the nature of literature and the role of the poet, comparing Shelley's *A Defense of Poetry* with Baudelaire's anti-Petrarchan love poem, *A Carcass*, Verlaine's counter-canonical *Art of Poetry*, or Derek Walcott's complex *North and South*.

The period introduction discusses the distinction between the short-lived Symbolist Movement of 1886 and its great predecessors. Without belaboring the distinction between the Symbolist "school" and its precursors, it is worth remembering that Baudelaire, Rimbaud, Verlaine, and Mallarmé were born over a span of thirty-three years (1821 to 1854), never formed a movement, and have been grouped by literary historians because their work as a whole marks a revolution in modern poetic language. Although you will probably not stress the formal aspects of this revolution in class, it may be useful to summarize some of its leading characteristics. (They will return as familiar echoes when you embark on modernist works.) Where Romantic literature emphasizes subjective feeling and personal lyricism (the Romantic "I"), Symbolist literature tends to convey the same emotion in abstract or impersonal terms: a mood is not proclaimed by its subject but portrayed as an imaginary landscape, or in a series of brilliant but impersonal images. Instead of depending on a narrative thread and linear argument, the Symbolists' extremely pictorial style uses image clusters, breaks in continuity, and blank spaces on the page to defer conclusions and multiply *implied* meanings. Internal connections are highly developed, suggesting further and mysteriously hidden relationships: these poetic connections include verbal ambiguities and allusions, musical patterns and echoes, multiple reflected images, and textual self-reflexivity—that is, a sense that on some level the poem describes its own status as a created object rather than any referent in the real world. Symbolism rejects realistic representation, crosses genres, and breaks with traditional forms because it believes in the *total* work of art, a multidimensional creation that imparts a special transcendental knowledge. In summary, nineteenth-century literary Symbolism has little to do with the conventional definition of symbol as a specific substitution of one unit for another (e.g., A = B; a rose = love). Instead, it proposes techniques of suggestion and internal reference that evoke, or *symbolize*, a larger realm of mystery. In Mallarme's words, "To *name* an object is to suppress three-quarters of the enjoyment of the poem, which consists in guessing little by little: to *suggest* it is my dream. The flawless practice of this mystery constitutes this symbol."

Further Reading

Balakian, Anna, ed. *The Symbolist Movement in the Literature of European Languages.* 1982. Provides a unique collection of theoretical and literary-critical essays by international scholars.

CHARLES BAUDELAIRE

The Flowers of Evil *and* Paris Spleen

Backgrounds

His contemporaries would have been amazed to know that Charles Baudelaire, a dandyish Parisian poet and art critic whose disturbing *Flowers of Evil* earned him a court fine in 1857, would continue to inspire writers, critics, and even rock groups for more than a century after his death. Baudelaire's fascination with questions of good and evil, his passion to explore the unknown (especially forbidden topics), his combination of crude realism and escapist dreams, and the insistent sensuality of his tormented love relationships strike chords in readers everywhere. These are not necessarily *pleasant* chords, despite occasional peaceful and harmonious lyrics, for Baudelaire distrusts prettiness. He tries to shock us into clearer insights by undermining conventional attitudes: addressing his beloved as a potentially rotting carcass in *A Carcass*, or accusing his reader of being—like himself—full of vices and fundamentally hypocritical. Baudelaire's modern appeal, however, derives from more than shock effects. Speaking from his own anguished subjectivity, the poet describes broadly human concerns: the fear of death and decay, the need for love, a painful alienation from others and from society. In response, he desires to create beauty, to understand the relationships between things ("correspondences"), and to find answers. Such themes are reinforced by a precise and disciplined style that coordinates classical meter and rhyme schemes with extraordinarily subtle interrelationships of images, associations, and logically developed argument.

To the Reader functions as a traditional preface, introducing the book's themes and establishing a common ground with its reader; however, there convention stops. This preface is also a direct attack on the reader, who is included—along with the poet—in a lurid sermon on human sin. The catalogue of sins culminates unexpectedly in "BOREDOM," seen as a destructive apathy that is worse than conventional vices because it refuses to become involved and merely "swallows the world in a yawn" (see note 5, p. 1384 in the anthology). Images of the devil as scientist in his laboratory boiling off human willpower, or as puppet master controlling our strings, underscore this fundamentally religious vision in which free will is of paramount importance. The riddling eight stanza launches a long, five-line sentence suggesting that one supreme sin remains to be mentioned. That sin is finally identified as boredom, described literally as a chain-smoking beast. In a line that continues to be quoted to this day, the poet accuses himself and his reader of complicity in this worst of evils.

Correspondences is an anchor point in Baudelaire's work, a classically perfect alexandrine sonnet proclaiming that everything is interconnected (corresponds) at a subterranean level that the poet, a seer, is specially qualified to perceive. Baudelaire insists on connectedness throughout, repeating the French word *comme* ("like" or "as") six times in the two middle stanzas; moreover, he strengthens the impact of this link-work by giving the word two syllables instead of the usual one. (In classical French verse, the mute *e* is sounded separately when it precedes a consonant.)

The sonnet develops its argument in logical stages of hypothesis, explanation, and illustration. At the beginning, nature is seen as quasi-divine, a living temple in which only humankind wanders blindly. In this basic unity of all life, explains the second stanza, the senses—or, more specifically, "scents and sounds and colors"—are fused (literally, "answer one another"). The third stanza offers examples of these five reciprocal senses in perfumes (*smell*) that are fresh as (literally) a child's flesh (*touch*), sweet as oboes (*taste* and *hearing*) and green as prairies (*sight*). The overwhelming tones of youth and immaturity in these images prefigure the maturing of perfume images into rich, overripe ("corrupt"), expansive odors that dizzy and transport the senses. It is this ecstasy of the mind and senses that fascinates Baudelaire, and it is a motif he will evoke in different images throughout his poetry.

In the love poem *Her Hair*, Baudelaire celebrates his mistress's head of hair as another route to ecstasy. The poet's recurrent theme of the *voyage* blends with erotic escapism as Jeanne Duval's tresses become a perfumed sea of ebony, a black ocean whose sensual pleasure invites him to dream of a sea voyage to exotic tropical climes. (Compare the less erotic but similarly ecstatic voyage in *Invitation to the Voyage*.) This richly colorful dream dominates the whole situation, for clearly Jeanne herself—hair, oasis, and gourd of wine—disappears under the weight of the dream-evocation she has inspired.

A Carcass intends to shock the reader with its brutal description of an animal carcass swarming with maggots—a carcass, moreover, that the poet ends by comparing with the woman he loves. The contrast of ideal femininity and physical mortality was familiar to the Romantics; Baudelaire is treading familiar paths when he parodies Petrarchan imagery ("star of my eyes," etc.) and the *carpe diem* tradition (claiming in the last stanza that he is "the keeper for corpses of love / Of the form, and the essence divine!"). He has pulled off a surprising poetic gamble, nonetheless, in transforming images of decay into images of new life; the hum of flies and maggots into the more acceptable music of waves, running water, wind, or a thresher winnowing grain. By this transformation, the poet has demonstrated the power of artistic imagination (eight stanza) before returning to the cruder image of the hungry dog and the final, aggressive emphasis on universal decay—inevitable for all but the art of poetry.

Invitation to the Voyage, written for Marie Daubrun, is celebrated for the musicality of its verse and the peaceful beauty of its visionary trip to an idealized Holland: the Holland of Dutch interiors painted by Vermeer, for example, or the Holland that collected objects of Eastern splendor through its seafaring empire. It is a dream of harmony, as embodied by a woman addressed as "child" or "sister" rather than the erotic images of other love poems. This harmony is also the profound unity of *Correspondences*, in which beautiful sensuous images combine to address the soul in its sweet and secret native tongue.

Song of Autumn I is the first of two short poems written in October 1859; the second poem is a love poem addressed to Marie Daubrun. The scene is Paris; winter approaches, and Baudelaire (who detests cold) hears the customary October delivery of cordwood in the courtyard. Wintry passions will enter his soul. His heart, chilled to a frozen red block by despair and hard work, is compared to a setting sun frozen in its own arctic hell. The poem is especially accessible through the ascending sequence of images based on the sound of falling logs: Baudelaire imagines the regular thumps as the construction of an executioner's scaffold, the blows of a battering ram destroying a tower, or nails being driven into a coffin. Autumn's dull knocking does not announce an arrival; instead, it heralds a departure into winter and, by association, death.

The three *Spleen* poems included in the anthology evoke this same melancholy in an even more concentrated fashion. They may be taught individually or as a group, expressing different facets of the speaker's alienation and despair. You may wish to compare the bitterness of Dostoevsky's narrator in *Notes from Underground* (pp. 1307–79 in the anthology). Like *Song of Autumn I*, each *Spleen* employs both realistic details and larger abstract or fantastic visions, and each depicts a progression of images. The best-known, *Spleen LXXXI*, pursues a series of confinement images from covered pot, dungeon, and barred prison to the enclosures of brain and skull. A series of water-related images dwindling gradually from city to playing cards characterizes *Spleen LXXVIII*, while the first half of *Spleen LXXIX* accumulates images of the dead past to evoke the poet's numb despair at the meaningless passage of time. Before students become too discouraged by the theme of gray misery, remind them that these are virtuoso performances, developments on a theme, just as is the peaceful dream of *Invitation to the Voyage*. Baudelaire considers it a kind of redemption to be able "to produce a few beautiful verses" (*One o'Clock in the Morning*), and he finds in art a counterweight to the boredom and sense of helplessness called *spleen*.

The Voyage assumes a number of familiar Romantic themes, such as the deception of everyday life in a world too petty and cramped for the human spirit, the desire to escape by traveling to exotic and unknown realms, and the lure of the infinite. Although contemporary students may be struck chiefly by its colorful allegories of the human condition, its attack on organized religion (VI, lines 97–100) and on political structures (VI, lines 95–96) was so pointed that the poem was rejected by the journal scheduled to publish it. Writing to his friend Charles Asselineau on February 20, 1859, Baudelaire predicted that *The Voyage* would cause "nature to shudder, and especially lovers of progress."

The poem's eight sections fall into three general movements: the first describing a human craving (felt already in childhood) to voyage toward an intuited ideal realm (I–V), the second depicting the sin and corruption that the traveler encounters everywhere on earth (VI), and the final sequence reiterating the experienced traveler's compulsion to continue— along with the traveler's realization that the voyage leads beyond mortal experience and into the only remaining unknown region, death.

Although there are scattered examples of short poetic works written in prose before Baudelaire, the appearance in 1862 of twenty-one *Little Poems in Prose (Paris Spleen)* by the French poet marked the first time that the genre had been named as such. For Baudelaire, these poems filled a different role from *The Flowers of Evil*: based in everyday experience, they offered a broad range of "impressions of the street, Parisian events and horizons, sudden starts of consciousness, languorous daydreams, philosophy, dreams themselves, and even anecdotes." In his dedication, he envisioned the ideal prose poem as a "poetic prose that would be musical without rhythm or rhyme, supple yet irregular enough to adapt to the lyric movements of the soul, to fluctuations of reverie, to sudden starts of consciousness." The prose poem is no less poetic for not being written in verse; it manifests the same internal rhythm and intricate organization of theme and image that we associate with lyric poetry. In Baudelaire's eyes, this supple and rhythmic prose was uniquely suited to expressing shifts of consciousness. It is easy to see how not only poets but also twentieth-century novelists exploiting stream-of-consciousness techniques (e.g., James Joyce, Virginia Woolf, and William Faulkner) are indebted to Baudelaire's example.

Classroom Strategies

Two days will allow you to give a good sense of what Baudelaire is about and why he has been such a powerful influence on later literature; three days will allow you to look closely at a number of poems. There are several ways to enter the subject, depending on your own and your students' preferences. The autobiographical stance of the four prose poems makes them especially accessible to students who are "afraid of poetry," and they allow easy entry into Baudelaire's characteristic themes. The picture of the harassed poet alienated from a commercialized society (*One O'Clock in the Morning*) is a familiar theme, to be paired with the escape wish in *Anywhere out of the World* (students appreciate the humorous realism of the hospital image, too). Alternately, you may wish to begin with the longer thematic poems (*The Voyage* and *A Carcass*) and move to a selection of shorter lyric pieces. Another possibility might be to structure the days according to selected thematic contrasts ("Spleen and Ideal," a grouping in *The Flowers of Evil*; or dream and reality, beauty and ugliness, escape and a feeling of being trapped, eroticism and childlike harmony).

Topics for Discussion

1. Baudelaire combines aspects associated with realism and with Romanticism. How far can he be considered as belonging to the age of realism? In what ways may he be considered a Romantic? Discuss this in light of the general introductions to the relevant sections.
2. Discuss the theme of the *voyage* throughout Baudelaire's poetry.
3. Discuss the appearance of an urban (as opposed to rural or pastoral) sensibility in Baudelaire's poetry. Compare more modern reflections on the alienating city in poems like Alfonsina Storni's *Squares and Angles* or Pablo Neruda's record of what war does to a city, *I'm Explaining a Few Things*.
4. Baudelaire is often claimed as the first Symbolist poet, although Symbolism as such did not develop until much later in the century. What elements in his poetry support this claim?
5. Compare and contrast the world represented by Baudelaire's speaker with the world represented by 1) Petrarch's speaker, 2) Pope's speaker in *The Rape of the Lock*, 3) the narrator in *Notes from Underground*.
6. How are women imagined and characterized in the poems you read? What attitude is implied? Is it dual or contradictory? Does Baudelaire give similar weight to the description of men? Compare the picture of women in Baudelaire and in (choose) 1) Pope's *The Rape of the Lock*, 2) Voltaire's *Candide*, 3) Goethe's *Faust*. What definitions of womanliness are depicted, affirmed, or criticized in each work?
7. Discuss the themes of art and of the role of the artist in Baudelaire's poetry. You may wish to compare your findings with similar themes in Wordsworth, Coleridge, Keats, and Shelley, and the many modern poets who question the limits of their art, including Rubén Darío.

Comparative Perspectives

1. Baudelaire's self-comparison to a crammed bureau and stale boudoir in *Spleen LXXIX* recalls the link between the jumble of Be-

linda's vanity table and the contents of her mind in Pope's *The Rape of the Lock*. What are the moral implications of the inventoried objects in these two poems, or in the geisha's paraphernalia described in Kawabata's *Snow Country*? The catalog is an ancient literary strategy that goes back at least to Homer. Why does this device continue to attract writers?

[A fuller excursion on this theme might explore the special appeal the catalog has had for Japanese writers, including Sei Shōnagon and Yoshida Kenkō in volume B of the anthology and Tanizaki in volume F. Perhaps they share with writers like Homer (whom Pope, of course, imitates in making Belinda's toilet into a priest-assisted ritual) an alertness to how precious physical objects are in a world plagued by impermanence.]

2. The function of imagery in Baudelaire's poetry and in Ghalib's *Ghazals* may profitably be compared. Consider, for example, the second couplet of Ghazal XII: "You were meant to sit in the shade of your rippling hair; / I was made to look further, into a blacker tangle," where the hair is a site of infinite mystery, alongside Baudelaire's full-scale celebration of the sensuousness of hair in *Her Hair*.

[This question might also be used to introduce a general discussion of Orientalism in the poetry and visual arts of nineteenth-century Europe. The headnote (pp. 1380–83 in the anthology) mentions Baudelaire's art criticism and his championing of Delacroix. Looking at the works of other French painters, from Gérôme through Matisse, would enrich a consideration of Baudelaire's evocation of "Languorous Asia, burning Africa" in *Her Hair*. The strong German line of Orientalism that begins with Goethe and is represented in the anthology by Heine's *A Pine is Standing Lonely* traces its way through to Aschenbach's deadly attraction to Venice in Mann's *Death in Venice*.]

Further Reading

See also the reading suggestions in the anthology, p. 1383.

Auerbach, Erich. "The Aesthetic Dignity of *Les Fleurs du Mal*." In *Scenes from the Drama of European Literature: Six Essays*. 1959. Impressive stylistic analysis.

Benjamin, Walter. *Charles Baudelaire: A Lyric Poet in the Era of High Capitalism*. Trans. Harry Zohn. 1973. An imaginative theoretical treatment by a forerunner of deconstructionist criticism. See also the chapter on Baudelaire in his *Illuminations* (1968).

Bersani, Leo. *Baudelaire and Freud*. 1977. An interesting discussion of Baudelaire's poetry, arranged according to Freudian terminology.

Caws, Mary Ann, and Hermine Riffaterre, eds. *The Prose Poem in France: Theory and Practice*. 1983. Studies in the French prose poem from Baudelaire to modern times.

Eliot, T. S. "Baudelaire." 1930. In *Selected Essays*. 1932. A discussion focused on Baudelaire's religious views.

Porter, Laurence M. "Baudelaire's Fictive Audiences." In *The Crisis of French Symbolism*. 1990. Includes psychoanalytic perspectives in a discussion of Baudelaire's attempts to communicate with differently imagined audiences.

Poulet, Georges. *Exploding Poetry: Baudelaire/Rimbaud*. Trans. Françoise Meltzer. 1984. Contains an extended essay on Baudelaire's consciousness or worldview by a major phenomenological critic.

Raymond, Marcel. *From Baudelaire to Surrealism*. 1957, reprinted 1961. A major critical work that contains a discussion of Baudelaire and his influence on modern poetry.

Rees, Garnet. *Baudelaire, Sartre and Camus: Lectures and Commentaries*. 1976. A brief volume of accessible, popularized lectures.

Sharpe, William Chapman. *Unreal Cities: Urban Figuration in Wordsworth, Baudelaire, Whitman, Eliot, and Williams*. 1990. An interesting discussion of Baudelaire and other city-oriented poets of the modern age.

STÉPHANE MALLARMÉ

Like Baudelaire, whom he admired, Stéphane Mallarmé wrote in a variety of forms: verse and prose poetry, translations of Edgar Allan Poe, and theoretical works that often began as reflections on theater and ballet performances. A sociable man, he composed delightful "occasional" poems for his friends: conversational quatrains written on fans, or composed as a postal address and (successfully) sent by mail. For awhile, he even edited a small fashion magazine. A poorly paid teacher of English, he tried to earn money and gain credit in the French national educational system by writing a book on English words, a manual for the review of English parts of speech, and by translating a mythology manual for the schools. In short—and unlike his Symbolist peers—Mallarmé was embedded in the conventional society of his time: yet he was also the "Prince of Poets" and is remembered today for a small number of finely crafted poems that are the most intellectual, the most impersonal, and the most abstract of Symbolist literature. Life and beauty exist in these poems, but "elsewhere," in a new dimension of interlocking allusions that uses everyday reality only as a point of departure.

Saint, written in the same year that Mallarmé began *The Afternoon of a Faun* (1865), is a deceptively simple and appealing short lyric that hints at coexisting levels of reality. A poem of extreme delicacy, it uses subtly interwoven images to suggest alternately presence and absence—as do many of Mallarmé's poems. It was written as an occasional poem for the saint's day of a friend, Cécile Brunet, and he called it "a little melodic poem composed especially with music in mind." Indeed, it was set to music by Maurice Ravel in 1896. The anthology headnote discusses the poem's remarkable unity (one sentence from beginning to end; two overlapping scenes of contrasting nature) and the fact that the poem's original title ("Saint Cecilia Playing on the Wing of an Angel") is illustrated by the imaginary harp evoked in the third stanza. The play of presence and absence emerges from the ingenious manner in which physical images first appear and then are taken away; the viol described through the first stanza, for example, exists but cannot be seen—it is concealed by the window frame; the gilt on the sandalwood *used* to shine but is now peeling away; a mandolin and flute are mentioned, but only as accompanying the viol in *former* concerts—they also are now absent. The missal's music used to sound (or *flow*, a visual image) at services, but now it is absent; the harp evoked by the angel's wing at sunset (or by the shape of its cast shadow) exists only in the imagination. The cumulative play of all these images prepares and justifies the otherwise impossible concluding image of a "musician of silences." References to music are not casual in Mallarmé: in *Music and Letters*, major lectures delivered at Oxford and Cambridge in 1894, he explains that the aim of the new French poetry is "the musicality of everything," and adds (alluding obliquely to German idealist philosophy) "Music and Letters are the alternate face . . . of a single phenomenon I call the Idea."

The *Afternoon of a Faun*, a faun's dimly recalled erotic dream of a passionate pursuit, also treats themes of music, absence, and poetic creation. In dramatic monologue of some density, the italicized passages represent the dream itself, and the body of the poem recounts the faun's attempt to understand his situation. Awakening with troubled feelings and mysterious tooth marks on his chest, he alternately recapitulates his dream and evokes it in a musical solo on the reed pipe (16–22, 42–62). The dream is unabashedly lustful (as in conventional scenes of satyrs and nymphs): the faun remembers cutting reeds for his pipes, coming across two sleeping nymphs, and passing immediately to an attempted double rape. Awake, he lasciviously imagines seeing the nymphs naked once more, sucks the juice from clusters of grapes held high, and reeling with passion and wine, reaches a peak of desire in which he imagines seizing the goddess of love herself—only to fall back, chastised and sleepy, ready to go back into the dream and find the nymphs again.

Both *The Tomb of Edgar Poe* and *The Virginal, Vibrant, and Beautiful Dawn* are more direct in their evocation of poetic language and the plight of the poet. The anthology headnote and related footnotes cover important allusions in these poems, including a brief explanation of how Mallarmé came to write a tribute to Poe. The Symbolists venerated the American poet as a precursor: they respected his theory of willed, craftsmanlike creation in "The Philosophy of Composition" and his portrayal of beauty, excess, mystery, and death. Unlike most American readers, they also admired the rhythm and melody of his verse. (See also the headnote to Baudelaire.) Poe filled, moreover, a sympathetic role in Romantic and Symbolist tradition as the misunderstood genius, the "accursed poet" scorned by the vulgar crowd. The famous line in the *Tomb* that describes Poe's writing as "bestow[ing] a purer sense on the language of the horde" (using everyday words in combinations that together evoke a different or transcendent meaning) probably fits the Symbolists' concept of poetic language more than it does that of Poe, nonetheless. The figure of an exiled poet reigns in both sonnets; in the first, the poet is the victim of slander; in the second, more abstract poem, the metaphor of a swan represents the poet trapped in his impossible search for perfection. For the Symbolists, and especially for Mallarmé, poetic language achieves perfection through combinations and allusion—through *signs* pointing to each other and to a purer realm. The so-called swan sonnet reinforces this emphasis on poetic language when it concludes with a capitalized Swan that (in French) is simultaneously heard as Sign (*Cygne/Signe*).

Classroom Strategies

The four poems printed here are a good introduction to Mallarmé's characteristic play of images and concept of poetic language; you may also enjoy using them in a comparison of selected Symbolist lyrics. *The Virginal, Vibrant, and Beautiful Dawn, Bridges,* and *Moonlight,* for example, present three very different Symbolist landscapes. Rimbaud's *The Drunken Boat* and Mallarmé's *The Afternoon of a Faun,* both longer poems, provide differently focused narratives of poetic creation. Both Rimbaud and Mallarmé believe in the poet's prophetic role; the one ends in silence, the other in brilliant hermetic poems and the paralyzing vision of an all-encompassing Book.

A convenient way to begin is to take one of the short poems as an introduction to Mallarmé's style. *Saint* is a good choice because it is relatively uncomplicated, depending on a straightforward sequence of physical images. You may, however, wish to take advantage of your students' familiarity with Edgar Allan Poe (and all the legends surrounding him) by beginning with *The Tomb of Edgar Poe.*

When you take up *The Afternoon of a Faun,* make sure your students grasp the distinction between the italicized passages (dream memory) and the narrative portion (real time). Once the basic story line is clear, you can focus on such things as the faun's dual nature: on the one hand (and in passionate detail) the classical convention of the faun as a lascivious forest spirit, a part of nature; on the other hand, the faun as an image of the creative artist: preparing his tools (cutting the reeds for pipes), grasping after beauty, seeking meaning through art (the melodies that mingle with the landscape and become fused with the contours of the nymphs), and finally returning to the world of dream to continue his search. It is useful to select a few passages to examine Mallarmé's extended chains of images (partly to clarify those passages, and partly to show that the poet works this way). In lines 4–6, for example, the uncertain faun pursues the labyrinthine branches of his doubt only for them to dissolve into the real branches of the surrounding woods, a return to reality that proves his remembered triumph was only a dreamed (ideal) or poetic counterpart. Wind and water are mentioned, but only as absent (the same technique found in *Saint*); instead, the landscape contains the dryly flowing melody of the faun's flute—a melody that rises to the sky as a visible breath of inspiration and falls back as an arid rain. In both passages, the play of words suggests the mysterious other world that is characteristic of Symbolist imagination.

Topics for Discussion

1. How does Mallarmé use language to "bestow a purer sense on the language of the horde"? What is the "language of the horde," and how is it different when used in Symbolist practice?
2. How might one argue that all Mallarmé's poems have, as their implied subject, poetic or artistic creation?
3. Poetic language, for Symbolists, should approach the condition of music. Does "the condition of music" mean the same thing for Mallarmé and Verlaine? How does each poet represent music in his poetry?
4. Discuss the layering of real and unreal images in Mallarmé's poetry.
5. *The Afternoon of a Faun* has been set to music and also made into a ballet. What qualities in the poem contribute to such settings?

Further Reading

Porter, Laurence M. "Mallarmé's Disappearing Muse." In *The Crisis of French Symbolism*. 1990. Discusses the poet's gradual exploration of indeterminacy as the only acceptable muse.

PAUL VERLAINE

For many, *Autumn Song* expresses the quintessential Verlainean persona: a sensitive, melancholy, somewhat passive soul whose moods express alternately yearning and helplessness. While translation can only hint at the melodic delicacy of the lilting French lines, the subtly interwoven images are quite clear. At the beginning of the poem, nature is anthropomorphized and also equated with music; at the end, the speaker is equated with nature. Throughout, the mood is established by an interpenetration of images in which no one category dominates: the initial sound of sobbing (presumably human) is quickly attributed to violins, which are then attributed to autumn. This seasonal sobbing wounds the speaker with a monotonous (single-toned, like a violin string) languor. In the second stanza, a clock chime tells the hour and evokes memories in the speaker, who weeps—echoing the autumn violins. In the third stanza the initial humanization of nature is reversed as the speaker is first subject to "ill winds" and then equated with autumn's dead leaf. No specific cause is given for this melancholy; as so often in Verlaine, the reference remains open and ambiguous.

One of Verlaine's most famous poems is *Moonlight* (*Clair de lune*), in which a melancholy mood is established by a dreamlike pastoral masquerade that has been compared with the rococo paintings of similar masquerades (*fêtes galantes*) by the French artist Antoine Watteau (1684–1721). Such tableaux by various artists were popular in the eighteenth century and constituted a recognizable theme and style. Watteau's own masquerades (he had studied with the theatrical designer Claude Gillot) were notable for their overtones of theater and artifice, their ambiguous actors and melancholy clowns. Verlaine himself wrote a one-act pastoral comedy, *The Ones and the Others* (1871), that takes place in a "Watteau park."

Moonlight is a tour de force that begins with a personal address ("Your soul") but shifts into an impersonal perspective immediately after these two words. The change is all the more abrupt inasmuch as the French omits "like"; your soul *is* a landscape, not just like one. The landscape, moreover (as the translation indicates), is most likely not found in nature but is a landscape painting, which is populated by the artifice of a masquerade party reenacting pastoral romances. In this dramatic tableau, masked revelers are vaguely conscious of their own alienation. Artifice and discrepancy rule: masks, mummeries, disguises, and uncertain songs about love and happiness that combine with the melancholy half-light of the moon. Despite the charade of love in the first two stanzas, any real eroticism emerges only in the decor of the last two lines with the spurting of the tall fountains. In this play of uncertain identities, the first line's human addressee is effectively lost from sight, replaced by marble statues and ecstatically sobbing fountains at the end.

In *The White Moonglow*, written for his fiancée before their wedding, the same moon reigns as in *Moonlight*, but here the poet tries to evoke a moment of perfection: no doubts about love or happiness, but an exquisite instant of peace and harmony. The short, regular (four-syllable) lines in the French are remarkable for their subtle melody, and the poem creates an enchanted scene as it moves in swiftly noted details from woods to pond and sky, all dominated by the reflected light of the moon. The picture is complete, and some readers will wish to go no further; yet Verlaine includes some puzzing elements that may undermine this completeness. Just as in *Moonlight*, there is a sense of distance and separation, and mournful images appear. Disembodied voices flee; a willow tree (conventionally associated with mourning) is reflected, black, in the pond; the wind weeps; and the tender peace of the last stanza has nothing to do with human beings, but seems to descend from the moonlit sky. Verlaine's fiancée seems remarkably absent, and perhaps the poet is absent too—except that it is his reverie and reflects his unique sensibility.

Wooden Horses strikes a very different tone: it is set at a country fair in Belgium with merry-go-rounds, loud music, carnival crowds out to have fun and—instead of romantic shepherds and shepherdesses—soldiers and fat maids off duty and bent on sex. Driving rhythm and insistent rhymes whirl the poem along ("turn" is repeated eight times in the first [French] stanza), and the desperation of that drive is reinforced by the image of wooden horses galloping round and round without hope of hay. There are hints of an ironic contrast between physical and romantic love: the sudden elegance of the evening sky in its velvet coat buttoned with golden stars and the covert allusion to Plato's dialogue on love, the *Phaedrus* (line 21 is literally "horses of their soul"), come from a different dimension than the cruder lusts of the carnival. (Verlaine did not always write about sensitive souls, and some of his poems are gleefully pornographic.) After his conversion, the poet introduced a disapproving note to counteract the joyous drums at the end: he revised the penultimate line, "Away the lovers go, in pairs," to read "The church bell rings sadly."

The Art of Poetry, which Verlaine wrote in 1874 but published only in 1882, was a witty and humorous manifesto that quickly became a cause célèbre when it drew attack from traditionalists. Pouring contempt on the classical virtues of French poetry—clarity, precision, and intricate rhymes—it was adopted by a new generation of antiestablishment poets who called Verlaine their leader. The anthology headnote summarizes the manifesto's antitraditional recommendations and its call for liberation from conventional metrical, intellectual, and pictorial restraints. The poem itself is full of puns, humor, and surprises: "tipsy," for example (line 7), can also be translated "gray": an in-between color, foreshadowing the next line's advice to join opposite qualities. Line 5's recommendation to make mistakes in word choice not only contradicts classical academic values but implies using wordplay to suggest additional connotations. The critique of rhyme in stanzas 6 and 7 is itself loaded with excessive or grating rhymes. (You may understandably be put off by the phrase in stanza 7 "What crazy negro or deaf child / made this trinket . . ."; one can say only that Verlaine is reaching for obvious rhymes in these lines and finds them in cultural stereotypes that otherwise have no place in his poetry.) In a challenge to its readers, *The Art of Poetry* culminates in elusive images that have nothing to do with literary *form*: poetry should be pure music, or an indefinable something that wings its way toward other skies, or a fresh morning wind scented with mint and thyme. Such poetry is an immediate appeal to the senses. Words are transparent (or at least made to seem that way), and the impression is all. At the time, of course, these words were anything but transparent. The shock of irregular meter, puzzlement over ambiguous images, and the lack of an explicit message all caused contemporary readers to stop and notice the new literary style. Paradoxically echoing the Romantic prejudice against artifice while employing his own counter-canonical artifice, Verlaine opposes the impalpable spirit of *poetry* to academic definitions of *literature*. (The force of this opposition is best understood if we remember that the French Academy, a unique national institution, approved the addition of new words to the language and elected the "best" writers to its society of "Immortals.") Despite Verlaine's later admission that he treasured "irreproachable rhymes, correct French, and good poetry of any kind," the poem's last line has become one of the most famous critiques of canonically "correct" writing in any language: next to the evocation of experience, "all the rest is literature."

Classroom Strategies

These five poems make an eminently teachable cluster and, as a group, they also invite comparison with Rimbaud's different approach to autobiographical themes and imaginary scenes. At the beginning, take advantage of the personal stance of the *Autumn Song* and *The White Moonglow* to interest students in the creation of a poetic mood; then show them two different examples in *Moonlight* and *Wooden Horses*. A good way to move to *The Art of Poetry* is to bring up its last two stanzas and ask your class if the previous poems are apt illustrations. Are they "poetry" or "literature"? How does Verlaine's distinction relate to earlier poetry the class has read? As you discuss the details of these poems with your students, you can mention some of the Symbolist tactics described at the beginning of this section and begin to show how and why Verlaine's poetry is a forerunner of so much modern literature.

Topics for Discussion

1. Discuss *Autumn Song* and *The White Moonglow* as mood poems. How does each poem use natural surroundings? What mood is established?
2. Verlaine calls for nuance and ambiguity in *The Art of Poetry*. To what extent does his own work embody these recommendations?
3. Comment on the role of music in Verlaine's poetry, both his recommendations in *The Art of Poetry* and his own poetic practice.
4. Explain the opposition of "poetry" and "literature" in *The Art of Poetry*. Do you agree? What examples of "literature" and "poetry" (perhaps of poetics) do you recall from previous reading? Is Verlaine's poetry without artifice?
5. How does Verlaine's work extend familiar Romantic themes? How is it different?
6. How might *Moonlight* and *Wooden Horses* be seen as impersonal evocations of a subjective mood?

Further Reading

Porter, Laurence M. "Verlaine's Subversion of Language." In *The Crisis of French Symbolism*. 1990. A perceptive discussion of Verlaine's use of language to subvert certainty. The whole book is recommended.

ARTHUR RIMBAUD

Rimbaud's mythic status may be traced to his image as a scandalous boy-genius and visionary: on the one hand, he is a poet-prophet in the grand tradition of Romantic literature, and on the other, an adolescent rebel who attempts every mode of transgression. Yet Rimbaud's writing would not have had such impact if he had not also been a remarkably adventurous and experimental poet who, in the five years of his teenage literary production, created complex structures out of brilliant hallucinatory images and revolutionized the rhythms of poetic prose.

By the time he was sixteen years old, Rimbaud had run away from home several times, seeking to escape the boredom of small-town life and his mother's strict supervision. Paris was a magnet for would-be writers and artists, and the young poet sent several of his poems to the established poet Paul Verlaine, hoping to attrct his attention. During the summer of 1871 he worked on *The Drunken Boat*, an ambitious poem of twenty-five quatrains in perfectly rhymed alexandrines (the classical twelve-syllable line) that was to be his introduction to the Parisian literary world. In September, Rimbaud presented the poem to Verlaine personally. Its saga of adventure on the high seas was a triumph of imagination, not least because the young poet had never seen the ocean. Rimbaud was a voracious reader, and in *The Drunken Boat* he combines and transforms images taken from (among other sources) novels like Jules Verne's *20,000 Leagues Under the Sea* and James Fenimore Cooper's *The Last of the Mohicans*, the poetry of Victor Hugo and Charles Baudelaire (*The Voyage*), and a fanciful travel magazine, *Le Magasin pittoresque*. The poem has been seen as an allegorical account of his abortive attempts to escape Charleville in 1870–71; as a foreshadowing of his poetic career and disillusionment; and as a Symbolist version of the Romantic (and Baudelairean) theme of escape and adventure into the unknown.

It is a voyage of intoxicating liberation, but also one of defeat. Strangely passive at the beginning, the boat is liberated by mysterious natural forces from its ties to land and civilization. Freed of any trace of its former life, and from control of its journey as well (the steering devices and the sight of beacons), the boat plunges into a primal chaos represented by the Poem of the Sea. From this point until the last two stanzas, Rimbaud presents a dazzling display of intertwined visionary images that fuse light, sounds, taste, and touch; exotic scenes and biblical legends; brilliant colors and infinite dark; fantastic fish, animals, and birds; delirious skies and pulsating ocean depths. Violent emotions accompany these clusters of images, from the ecstasy of mystic revelation ("I have seen what men imagine they have seen") to—gradually—fear, yearning, and despair. It is typical of Symbolist writing that, in each image cluster, no one element is the key to the whole. Every set of images (for example, stanzas 7, 8, 10, 12, or 20) evokes a fantastic scene with its own unique combination of emotions and connotations; together, the sequence of scenes makes up a narrative of revelation that gradually turns menacing. Sailing on through beauty now mixed with death and decay, the boat is tossed into the sky, where it plunges on until, finally overwhelmed, it calls for oblivion and total absorption in the sea (stanza 23) or a return to Europe with its familiar fixed forms (stanza 21). Two diminished futures offer themselves at the end: a return either to childhood as a frail boat drifting in a puddle or to the—now completely rejected—role of commercial ship in a world of authorities and prisons. The formal poem is rounded off—the conclusion echoes the situation at the beginning, except that the boat has lost its indifference—but the speaker's dissatisfaction suggests that his journey is not over.

A Season in Hell was written between April and August 1873, in diverse locations in France, London, and Brussels (scene of the July gunshot that ended his affair with Verlaine). The only work that Rimbaud himself published, it is a remarkable set of autobiographical but hallucinatory prose poems arranged as a short preface and seven separate sections: *Bad Blood, Night of Hell, Deliriums* with its subsections I: *The Foolish Virgin / The Infernal Bridegroom* and II: *Alchemy of the Word, The Impossible, The Flash of Lightning, Morning,* and *Farewell.* The work is often taken as Rimbaud's farewell to poetry, and in *Alchemy of the Word* the poet makes clear that he has lost hope in his vocation as a poet-prophet: it is now "the history of one of my follies." In *Farewell* he adds, "I must bury my imagination and my memories . . . I who called myself magus or angel, dispensed of any morality, I have come back to the soil . . . Peasant!" Despite his disavowals, *A Season in Hell* is a masterpiece of poetic prose that draws much of its emotional power from the skillful counterpoint of themes and images and from the supple rhythms of language evoking a torturous stream of thought. In addition, the poet continued working on the prose poems of *Illuminations.* Nonetheless, *A Season in Hell* provides a picture of disillusionment that was followed soon after by Rimbaud's abandonment of writing.

Night of Hell, like the rest of *A Season in Hell,* is written as a monologue set in a hell with all the trappings of traditional doctrine: fire, pitchforks, poison, and Satan (who may well be the voice of his own ironic self-consciousness). The speaker is convinced of his damnation, which he blames both on his own sinful nature and on the fact that he was baptized a Catholic; for without baptism, there would be no heaven or hell. Several themes alternate throughout the section: his misery as a damned soul aware of his condition; his yearning for salvation and happier times (along with a massive skepticism that emerges in various ironic passages); the poet's miraculous creative powers and associated hallucinations. Some critics feel that *Night of Hell* evokes the summer Rimbaud spent in London with Verlaine: the "errors that are whispered to me" would be the words of the older poet (the *bell tower* phrase is actually printed in one of Verlaine's later poems), and the "glimpse of conversion to righteousness and happiness, salvation" may refer to Verlaine's summer return to Catholicism. Whether or not there is such a specific reference, the description of salvation is heavily ironic: "millions of charming creatures, a sweet sacred concert . . . and goodness knows what else." Rimbaud's impatience with insipidity, with conventional thoughts, and with the boredom of a regulated life makes him prefer the stimulation of fire and pitchfork—but it does not alleviate his anguish.

The Bridges and *Barbarian* represent the shorter, visionary prose poems that Rimbaud wrote at the end of his literary career. Most critics accept that *The Bridges* is a transposition of a real scene: the bridges over London's river Thames on a gray day. It has also been suggested that the poem describes an unknown painting. No matter what the source, Rimbaud clearly creates his own painting with words, and moreover informs us that he is doing so. The word-painting begins impersonally with geometric patterns, the angular shapes of the bridges as they appear along the river and contrast with buildings on the shore. Additional details of hovels, masts, and parapets give texture and interest to the scene. Gradually, the description is humanized: musical chords are heard, and "one detects" a note of color—perhaps even musical instruments. A question is asked: what kind of music? Once uncertainty exists, a subjective perspective has entered the picture. It is no longer an impersonal description but now a mental event. Just at this point, a ray of sun pierces the gray landscape and ends the poet's reverie—or, from another angle, the poet reveals and obliterates this game of his imagination.

Both *The Bridges* and *Barbarian* (discussed in the anthology headnote) exemplify Rimbaud's culminating work as *voyant*, a poet-seer who creates transcendent images of reality. Letters written when he was sixteen to his former teacher, Georges Izambard, and to a poet-friend, Paul Demeny, eloquently express the young poet's vision of his nature, his destiny, and the path he must take. He reproaches his teacher for having gone back into "the comfortable rut" of teaching, predicting "you will end up self-satisfied, someone who has done nothing because there was nothing he wanted to do." In contrast:

> I want to be a poet, and am working to make myself a *Seer* [*Voyant*]. . . . The sufferings are enormous, but one must be strong, be born a poet, and I have recognized that I am a poet. It is not my fault at all. It's a mistake to say "I think": you should say "I am thought."—Forgive me the play on words.
> I is somebody else. So much the worse for wood that discovers it is a violin.

Two days later, a letter to Demeny recapitulates the same ideas in more detail.

> For *I* is somebody else. If brass wakes up a trumpet, that's not its fault. This is clear to me: I am present at the birth of my thought: I watch it, I listen to it. . . . I tell you one must be a *seer*, make oneself a *seer*.
> The poet becomes a *seer* by a long, immense and reasoned *derangement* of *all the senses*. All forms of love, suffering, madness; he explores himself, he exhausts within himself all poisons in order to keep only their essences. Ineffable torture where he needs complete faith, superhuman force, where he becomes among all the great invalid, the great criminal, the great accursed—and the supreme Scholar!—For he arrives at the *unknown*!

These passages are often used to explain the basic concepts of Rimbaud's poetry: the *voyant* as a mystical or Illuminist seer; the poet as an impersonal force of nature; the artist's need to plumb the depths of human experience; and a concurrent faith that the result of such adventure will be supreme knowledge—the discovery of the unknown. Rimbaud clearly follows in the Romantic tradition of the poet-prophet, especially as it is transmitted through Baudelaire, whom he salutes as "the first *voyant*, king of poets, *a true God.*"

Classroom Strategies

Students are predictably interested in Rimbaud's vision of the poet-prophet or seer, and you can show them how he pursued that vision in three different kinds of writing. Rimbaud may also be discussed as an inheritor of the Romantic tradition of the visionary poet, or as a secular example of mystic or Illuminist literature. You may want to give them passages from his letters (see above) and remind them of Shelley's claim that "Poets are the unacknowledged legislators of the World (volume E, p. 825, *A Defence of Poetry*). Remaining within Symbolism, you may decide to show connections with the Baudelaire of *Correspondences* and *The Voyage*, or contrast Rimbaud's more impersonal style with the mood poetry of Paul Verlaine. Rimbaud foreshadows modernist style in its ruptured rhythms and rapid shifts of images, and he is also indispensable to understanding the aims and techniques of twentieth-century Surrealist poetry. The easiest way to begin is to emphasize the narrative and implied autobiographical stance of *The Drunken Boat* and, subsequently, *Night of Hell.* If you are using passages from the letters to explain Rimbaud's sense of mission, you can ask what scenes in *The Drunken Boat* illustrate the young poet's claim of making himself a seer.

Topics for Discussion

1. Choose a passage from a letter to Izambard or Demeny (above) and ask students to explain its relevance to *The Bridges* and *Barbarian.* (*The Drunken Boat* is certainly possible, but students may limit themselves to repeating its narrative line.)
2. On March 2, 1950, Balanchine's New York City Ballet performed the world premiere of a ballet based on Rimbaud's *Illuminations.* What is there in Rimbaud's poetry that makes it a candidate for modern ballet? Discuss in relation to *The Bridges* and *Barbarian.*
3. Discuss the play of thematic and pictorial opposites in *Night of Hell.*
4. Discuss Rimbaud's use of irony throughout these poems.
5. In *Night of Hell* Rimbaud states that he is a damned soul. How does he explain this condemnation, and what kind of case does he make for guilt or innocence?
6. Compare Rimbaud's sense of mission with that of his Romantic precursors (Blake, Keats, Shelley, for example). Why does he call Baudelaire "the first *voyant*"?
7. Compare the autobiographical voice in Rimbaud, Verlaine, and Baudelaire.

Further Reading

Porter, Laurence M. "Artistic Self-Conciousness in Rimbaud's Poetry."
In *The Crisis of French Symbolism*. 1990. Includes psychological perspectives in an intricate description of Rimbaud's style as a changing relationship to his implied audience.

LEO TOLSTOY

The Death of Ivan Ilyich

Backgrounds

The Death of Ivan Ilyich is the story of a Russian judge in the 1880s who, after a fall from a ladder, contracts an illness that leads to a lingering, painful death. In the course of dying, Ivan Ilyich recognizes that he has led a misguided life, yet at the very end he feels he has defeated death. There is a light—symbolizing hope in the form of another life—at the bottom of the black sack into which he is being pushed.

The story was written in 1886, after Tolstoy's "conversion" in 1879. It reflects his lifelong preoccupation with death and dying and his ambition to found a simplified religion, together with his criticism of urban civilization.

In its bald manner of telling, the story differs sharply from Tolstoy's earlier work, including the epic novels *War and Peace* and *Anna Karenina*. Its tone is rather that of a parable: "Ivan Ilyich's life had been most simple and most ordinary and therefore most terrible" (p. 1427).

Classroom Strategies

The Death of Ivan Ilyich is so unified that it is difficult to divide. If you wish to present it in two assignments, use the end of chapter III as a breaking point.

The story is so straightforward that students cannot misunderstand it. It is intended to remind us forcefully of the inevitability of death and the loneliness of every human being when confronted with his or her own death. Tolstoy brings home the contrast between the triviality of the life and activities of the average person (Ivan Ilyich in Russian is the equivalent of John Smith in English) and the sudden, awesome awareness of death and dying. One could argue that he stresses this contrast because he resents the hypocrisy with which the fact of death is usually swept under the rug.

Students may have difficulties with the harsh satire upon doctors, the institution of marriage, and the courts of law. They may also reject as not clearly motivated the final acceptance of death that Ivan achieves. Possibly an explanation of the Russian class system may help to explain details: the bureaucracy sharply divided from the peasantry, of which Gerasim, the assistant to the butler, is the lonely representative. He alone has genuine compassion for his dying master and is able to speak of death, while all the upper-class characters are hidebound in social conventions and hypocrisy.

Topics for Discussion

Compare the attitude to death and dying in the story with representative American attitudes. What do our current substitutions of *funeral director* for *undertaker*, *casket* for *coffin*, *deceased* for *dead man* or *woman*, and *passed away* for *died* have to do with Tolstoy's theme? Tolstoy satirizes the funereal rituals of the orthodox church, including the confession and the display of the corpse in an open coffin. But his harshest satire is of the hypocrisy of the people who surround Ivan Ilyich. Tolstoy exposes the selfish concern of the widow for the price of the burial plot. He also exposes the annoyance of the family at their own inconvenience (the girl is eager to marry), the callousness of the doctors interested in the diagnosis of the illness (floating kidney or vermiform appendix?) rather than in the suffering of the patient, and the hardly concealed pleasure of Ilyich's supposed friends at the news of his death, since it will vacate a position at court. But Tolstoy wants primarily to convey our need to recognize the majesty of death and the triviality of the life of the average man.

A powerful vein of realism runs throughout this story. Ugly details usually excluded from conventional fiction bring before us the smell of the disease, the processes of elimination, the sound of screaming in excruciating pain. Yet there is also a degree of contrivance almost too neat in the way the characters are typed and in the contrast between their lives at the beginning and at the end. Small satirical details like the creaking of the hassock or the "full bosom pushed up by her corset" of Ivan Ilyich's wife (p. 1452) may seem too artful, and the final image of the black sack with the light at its bottom is obviously a symbol with a manifest design on our feelings. Suspense is deliberately eliminated by the title and the first scene of the funeral service.

The story can be seen as a miniature educational novel. Ilyich slowly comes to recognize that what we all know in theory (that human beings are mortal) is going to happen to *him*. He slowly progresses not only to a recognition of the inevitability of death but to a rejection of his former life and finally to a dim hope for transcendence and even redemption.

Topics for Writing

1. What is the attitude to death and dying of the main character, Ivan Ilyich, and of the author?

   [Clues to an answer are found in the comments above.]
2. What elements in the story are unrealistic?

   [See the comments above.]
3. Trace the main events and changes in Ivan Ilyich's life discussed above.

   [Details of Ivan Ilyich's earlier life appear in the reminiscences he evokes.]

4. Describe the society implied in the story (the group in the law courts, the family doctors, the servants). What elements appear to you peculiarly Russian or representative of the late nineteenth century? What elements seem universally applicable?

[However blunt Tolstoy's attack on society and its hypocrisy, his main concern is to emphasize the universal truth of man's mortality and the falseness of living without consciousness of the end.]

Comparative Perspectives

1. Dostoevsky's main character in *Notes from Underground* was once a "nasty" and "rude" civil servant, while Tolstoy's Ivan Ilyich prides himself on occasionally letting "the human and official relations mingle." In the hands of writers such as Dostoevsky and Tolstoy, the culture of the bureaucracy became one of the great subjects of nineteenth-century European narrative. How does Tolstoy's depiction of Gerasim's relationship to Ivan Ilyich reinforce our understanding of the evils of governmental systems? Compare the degree and nature of irony in diverse texts that deal with the stifling of imagination promoted by such systems. Include, as appropriate, *A Modest Proposal*, *The Metamorphosis*, and *Ladies and Gentlemen, to the Gas Chamber*.

2. *The Death of Ivan Ilyich* offers a devastating portrait of a marriage, a topic that preoccupies modern artists much as adulterous love fascinated their medieval counterparts. What social changes are involved in this shift of interest? As appropriate, diagnose the marital difficulties of the Golovíns and compare them with those in *Hedda Gabler*, *The Dead*, *The Barking*, or *Walker Brothers Cowboy*. How do differences in taste relate to differences in class and family background, and how much do they contribute to the problems faced by the couples in these works?

Further Reading

See also the reading suggestions in the anthology, p. 1421.

Maude, Aylmer. *The Life of Tolstoy*. 2 vols. 1917.

Simmons, Ernest J. *An Introduction to Tolstoy's Writings*. 1968. Elementary and informative.

HENRIK IBSEN
Hedda Gabler

Backgrounds

This is the tragedy of a beautiful, proud woman, the daughter of a general (whose picture presides over the scene). At thirty, in straitened circumstances, she marries George Tesman, a scholar studying "the domestic industries of Brabant in the Middle Ages" (p. 1469). To further his research, Tesman takes her on an extended honeymoon trip from their Norwegian town (Christiana, now called Oslo) to the Continent. The play begins with their return home.

They have rented a splendid house in the expectation that Tesman will soon be appointed professor, but this turns out to be uncertain. A rival, Eilert Loevborg, has just published a survey of the history of civilization and might thus win in a competition for the chair. Eilert, however, who has courted Hedda in former times, has a drinking problem, from which he has (for the time being) been rescued by a former schoolmate of Hedda's, Mrs. Thea Elvsted, during a stay in the country. When he returns to town, Thea leaves her husband to follow him, fearing his relapse into alcoholism. As soon as Eilert meets Hedda, he begins to court her again passionately and abandons any idea of challenging Tesman for the professorship. He now dismisses his published work as trivial and is absorbed in writing a book on the future of mankind, the manuscript of which he carries with him.

Hedda is violently jealous of Eilert's relationship with Thea and considers the new abstinence a sign of weakness and of subservience to the other woman. A friend of the house, Judge Brack, arranges a drinking party, which Hedda taunts Eilert into joining. The party is a disaster for Eilert: he gets drunk and late in the night goes off to a brothel, losing his manuscript on the way. When Tesman finds it and brings it back to the house, Hedda in her jealousy burns it. It is somehow, she feels, Eilert and Thea's child. This striking scene ends the third act. In the fourth act, we hear that Eilert has not only gotten into trouble with the police but has killed himself with the pistol that Hedda had given him. The Judge, who also has designs on Hedda, threatens to testify that she supplied Eilert with the pistol unless she gives herself to him. Trapped by her marriage, by the prospect (which she scorns) of bearing Tesman's child, and by the fear of local scandal, she shoots herself.

In his youth, Ibsen had written romantic verse plays such as *Peer Gynt*, but established his reputation as a writer for the stage with his social plays. These advocated causes such as the emancipation of women (*A Doll's House*) or discussed taboo topics such as hereditary venereal disease (*Ghosts*). *Hedda Gabler*, unlike Ibsen's other plays, seems to have no direct social purpose, unless it is to celebrate the dilemma of the rebellious individual who must die to escape societal constraints. The play, extremely effective on the stage, has allowed many famous actresses to display their art.

Classroom Strategies

The play can be taught in two class periods.

The greatest difficulty of the play lies in explaining the character and behavior of Hedda. We must assume that she is desperate on returning home; hating her dull, somewhat obtuse, and even ridiculous husband;

and further disgusted by the prospect of bearing a child—in particular, his child. She is not, however, a blameless heroine. Her playing with the pistol in threatening Judge Brack and later giving one of the two pistols inherited from her father to Eilert, thus practically ordering him to commit suicide, forecasts her own final decision. She behaves with cold contempt toward her husband, with callousness and maliciousness toward his harmless aunt, with cattish jealousy toward Thea, and with violent, domineering passion toward Eilert, who has to prove himself in her eyes by drinking and returning "with a crown of vine-leaves" (p. 1497) in his hair. When he fails, she quite unconcernedly sends him to his death. At the same time, she is strangely hemmed in by conventions. She yearns for luxuries—a liveried footman, a thoroughbred horse, a grand piano—and has ambitions to play hostess. She is unwilling to commit adultery, though she flirts with Judge Brack, and she is deeply upset by the prospect of a police investigation and a local scandal. Her main trait is a fierce individualism: pride in her family, her beauty, and her independence. The fear that she might have to yield to Judge Brack is the last straw in motivating her suicide. There is something grotesque and a little sick in her insistence that a beautiful death consists of putting a bullet through the temple and that Eilert has bungled his by shooting himself in the abdomen. Still, we are asked to admire her beauty, pride, and yearning for freedom, and to pity her as the victim of the dull, limited, or cowardly people around her.

The only problematic character besides Hedda is Eilert. We must assume that he is something of a genius. Ibsen contrasts what Eilert sees as Tesman's dull, antiquarian subject with Eilert's allegedly brilliant speculations about the future course of civilization. At least in the imagination of Hedda, he is an almost Dionysian figure, whose collapse and ignominious end come as a terrible blow to her.

The construction of the play demands attention. We may notice the deliberately misleading optimism of the beginning. By the end of Act I, Hedda has bested both her husband and his aunt and by hypocritical blandishments extracted the secret of Thea's relationship with Eilert. In Act II, she proves her power over Eilert by inducing him to join the Judge's party. The act ends with Eilert leaving and the two women, Hedda and Thea, left alone waiting for his return late into the night. Act III is the turning point, the *peripeteia*, which ends with Hedda burning the manuscript of Eilert's new book. Act IV brings a speedy resolution: The story of the horrible end of Eilert, the disappointing recognition that Eilert's manuscript can be pieced together again from notes preserved by Thea and Hedda's own husband, and the threat of Judge Brack all add intensity and suspense to the final moment when, playing "a frenzied dance melody on the piano," Hedda ends her life with a pistol shot. The comments of the two survivors, Tesman screaming "She's shot herself! Shot herself in the head! By Jove! Fancy that!" and Judge Brack's commonsensical "But, good God! People don't do such things!" (p. 1518), make a grotesque, almost parodic point.

Comparative Perspectives

1. Hedda's idealized vision of her father deforms her life. How does Ibsen dramatize General Gabler's enduring control over his daughter? How would you compare the relationship between the Father and the Daughter in Pirandello's *Six Characters in Search of an Author?* Even if not related by blood, many of the female characters represented in the anthology experience quasi-incestuous relations with strong paternal figures. Discuss the attitude toward these relationships in, as appropriate, the *Odyssey* (Nausicaa) or Freud's *"Dora."*
2. Why does Hedda sit down to play "a frenzied dance melody on the piano" as a prelude to committing suicide? Compare the implication that there is heroic beauty in her act with the treatment of suicide in *Madame Bovary*, or with the tragic but differently motivated suicide that ends *Things Fall Apart.*

Further Reading

See also the reading suggestions in the anthology, p. 1463.

Bentley, Eric. *In Search of Theatre.* 1953. Contains a good chapter on Ibsen.

Brustein, Robert. *The Theatre of Revolt: An Approach to the Modern Drama.* 1964. A survey of modern drama containing chapters on Strindberg, Chekhov, Brecht, Pirandello, and others. Chapter 2 deals with Ibsen.

LeGallienne, Eva. "Preface to Ibsen's *Hedda Gabler*." 1953. Praise from a famous American actress.

Northam, John. *Ibsen's Dramatic Method: A Study of the Prose Dramas.* 1953. Concentrates on Ibsen's stagecraft.

ANTON CHEKHOV

The Lady with the Dog

Classroom Strategies and Topics for Discussion

Short fiction has a very long history, but the short story itself is a modern form. If your students have read some of the ancient and medieval tales in the first volume of the anthology, a good way to begin your discussion of *The Lady with the Dog* is to ask how the genre differs from its ancient precursors. The fantasy of Lucian's *A True Story*, for example, is a lot closer to a work like *Candide* than it is to Chekhov, and densely plotted fabliaux and tales like Boccaccio's do not aim at the kind of psychological subtlety we find in *The Lady with the Dog*. Other short fiction closer in time, like Pushkin's *Queen of Spades*, with its intermingling of irony and the supernatural, or *The Death of Ivan Ilyich*, with its moral agenda and visible closure, would make especially good contrasts. Discovering what makes Chekhov's story special will help students deal with the complex conciousness and unresolved plots of many recent short narratives, like those of Alice Munro. Often called *"New Yorker stories"* after the magazine that has published so much apparently indeterminate and open-ended fiction, these subtle works challenge students. Once it is understood that they portray experience in ways much more like "real life" than do the older fictional forms, your class can get to the heart of Chekhov's accomplishment.

Ask your students, too, how many of the writers in the anthology are represented by selections from two different genres; Chekhov's experience as a playwright explains much about his narrative technique. As a dramatist, he is the least moralizing of storytellers. In both genres, he emphasizes character and action in the expectation that his audience will respond to what it observes and draw its own conclusions. Unlike other dramatists, Chekhov's plays are known, as the headnote in the anthology points out, for their naturalistic scenes and their seeming plotlessness— but plot is there in abundance, waiting to be uncovered in the inner lives of his characters, if not in loud, definitive, stagy confrontation scenes. Students may first think that Chekhov's story similarly lacks form and punch.

He filters *The Lady with the Dog* through Gurov's consciousness without abandoning the objectivity of the third-person narrator and certainly uses physical detail as any conventional narrator would. It is, as always, helpful to ask your students to comment on the implications of character descriptions. *The Lady with the Dog* deals with its secondary characters in this traditional way, with the intellectual pretensions of Gurov's tall wife somehow corroborated by her dark eyebrows, and the servility of Anna Sergeyevna's husband captured by his side-whiskers, bald spot, and badge. We have no difficulty understanding why the protagonists of the story find their marriages unsatisfying. Anna Sergeyevna herself is initially subjected to this reductive descriptive technigue: her toque, her lorgnette, even—perhaps especially—her Pomeranian dog tell us that she is seen, and perhaps sees herself, in terms of social images.

Gurov himself is the center of the story, and you will probably want to spend some time on the paragraphs that establish his character as the story begins, when we still see him from the outside: "bored and ill-at-ease in the company of men," he is not particularly interested in his work at a bank. Alone at a seaside resort, he seems a typical man-about-town. His thoughts as he enters Anna Sergeyevna's room for the first time confirm this impression of him, as he idly categorizes the different varieties of women he has known. Thus well into the second section of the story, we see that Anna Sergeyevna does not mean a great deal to him.

Yet as the story develops, and Gurov ceases to be the bored, judgmental sensualist, we recall again the playwright's art. Physical details seem to become symbolic, suggestive in the way that stage effects can be. The scene changes, as in a play, deserve some attention: what is the mood of a seaside resort? Why do casual affairs characterize a place like Yalta? How do the long paragraph devoted to the roaring of the sea at Oreanda (p. 1528) and Gurov's meditation as he watches Anna Sergeyevna's train depart and feels that "he had only just awakened" (p. 1529) begin to shift the mood of the story? We realize here, in the reflections that recall so many of the great romantic nature poems that would work well in combination with Chekhov's story, that he is capable of a deep and thoughtful response to the world around him.

Were Gurov just a roué, the return to Moscow would be the end of this liaison. "It's time for me to be going north," he thinks, presumably to a colder, brisker world of reason. But the introduction to part III of the story may upset the reader's expectations; this is a Russian story, and the romance of the snow on the lime trees and birches has a spiritual resonance that undercuts the notion of a return to reality. Only when the lovers are separated do they recognize that something remarkable has happened to them.

When Gurov pursues Anna Sergeyevna in the provincial theater—a place where the playwright rules—they move out of the public eye to stand "on a dark narrow staircase over which was a notice bearing the inscription 'To the upper circle.' " How does that directional sign forecast the higher aspirations toward which their relationship has surprisingly led? How does Gurov's "double life," embarked on once Anna Sergeyevna begins her secret visits to Moscow, begin in the moment of stepping out of the stalls and into the stairwell? Why should her excuse to her husband be that she is being treated by a specialist in "female diseases"? Is this a lie?

Chekhov's story never analyzes why the feelings of these two people change, yet the weight of the transformation weighs upon us as it does on them. Ask your students to try to explain the difference between the first visit to a hotel room, where Gurov rather unfeelingly eats his watermelon, and the one with which the story concludes, in which Anna Sergeyevna weeps as she drinks tea. The parallel actions announce how much has in fact been transformed, a realization that is capped when Gurov glimpses himself in the mirror and discovers the pathos of his and his lover's mortality. The narrator then offers the simile of the migrating birds to reinforce the character's sudden perception. How much does a rhetorical device intended to explain through comparison explain? How are all human beings like migrating birds caught in cages? Why should this figure of speech lead to the information that "they forgave one another all that they were ashamed of in the past and in the present"?

Would this be a better story if it ended by telling us that Anna Sergeyevna ran off with Gurov and that they quarreled? Or that their respective spouses died and they remarried and lived happily ever after? Or that discovery brought shame to Anna Sergeyevna but only a temporary inconvenience to Gurov? Does a transcendent moment of melancholy and pity, such as that experienced by Gurov as the story closes, last?

Questions like these will probably elicit a good deal of class discussion, and in effect, that discussion will prove the wisdom of Chekhov's narrative reticence.

Topics for Writing

1. How does Chekhov use seasonal change in shaping his narrative? [If you have also assigned *The Cherry Orchard*, you can expand this topic to cover both works, of course.]
2. Both of the leading characters in this story find themselves taking steps that would have been inconceivable to them when we first meet them. Describe the ways in which Chekhov conveys their transformation. Which do you think undergoes the more profound change? Why?

Comparative Perspectives

1. Compare and contrast Tolstoy's Ivan Ilyich and Chekhov's Gurov. What are their lives initially like? How and why do they change? What is the meaning of each story's ending?
2. Compare Flaubert's novelistic treatment of adultery with Chekhov's in *The Lady with the Dog*.

   a. Look, for example, at the description of Rodolphe's way of placing Emma as one among his many conquests in chapters XII and XIII in part two of *Madame Bovary*. What does Flaubert reveal about the workings of his mind that would make it impossible for him to change, as does Gurov, although he initially "places" Anna Sergeyevna as one type of woman he has known as well?

   b. Compare the youthful Anna Sergeyevna with the equally inexperienced Emma Bovary. Which qualities does Flaubert underline in his portrait of Emma that make her so easy to corrupt?
3. Comment on the description of Oreanda in section II of *The Lady with the Dog* and compare the treatment of a similar romantic landscape in Lamartine's *The Lake*. How does the sensibility of the scientifically trained Chekhov differ from Lamartine's (as in the reflection on p. 1528 that "this continuity, this utter indifference of life and death" holds "the secret of our ultimate salvation")?
4. Compare the license afforded by the seaside resort in Chekhov's story with the liberating and then chastening impact of the Hong Kong setting in Zhang Ailing's *Love in a Fallen City* (volume F).

Further Reading

See also the reading suggestions in the anthology, p. 1523.

Johnson, Ronald L. *Anton Chekhov: A Study of the Short Fiction*. 1993. One in the Twayne's Studies in Short Fiction series, this book has a good discussion of narrative perspective in *The Lady with the Dog*.

The Cherry Orchard

Backgrounds

Chekhov's plays have the reputation of being plotless, static, a mere string of scenes held together by a mood. But this is not true of Chekhov's last play, *The Cherry Orchard*, which has a clear plot line. Madame Lubov Ranevskaya returns to her estate in the provinces of Russia after an absence of five years. With her are her seventeen-year-old daughter, Anya; a governess, Charlotta; and a footman, Yasha. They are greeted by the brother of Lubov, Leonid Gayev; a maid, Dunyasha; and a merchant, Yermolay Lopahin, who is the son of a serf on the estate, but who has made money—even become wealthy—cultivating poppies. He soon reminds the arrivals that the estate will be up for sale unless they can raise the money to pay the heavy debts. The great cherry orchard will have to be cut down to make room for country houses. It is spring now: the orchard is in bloom, all white, a symbol for Lubov of the innocence of her childhood, which she betrayed when, after the death of her husband and the accidental drowning of her other child, a son named Grisha, she left for Paris with a lover, who has since robbed and betrayed her.

The second act in the open air provides relief in an idyllic setting. The "eternal" student Petya Trofimov, who was the tutor of the drowned boy, courts Anya and grandiloquently talks about the backwardness of Russia and the bright future of humanity. The merchant Lopahin reminds Lubov of the impending sale, which she faces helplessly.

The third act is the turning point. Recklessly, just on the day of the auction, Lubov gives a dance: at the end, Lopahin comes back from town and awkwardly announces that he has bought the estate when another bidder seemed about to acquire it. He has paid ninety thousand rubles for it above the mortgage.

The fourth act returns to the scene of the first, the nursery, where the company assembles, ready to depart. Lubov and her brother have somewhat recovered from the blow of the sale. Lubov is returning to Paris to look after her ill lover, who has been bombarding her with telegrams. Leonid has gotten a job in the local bank. Anya will go to Moscow to study. The house will be locked and eventually demolished. We hear the sound of the axes cutting down the cherry orchard.

Classroom Strategies

The play has four acts; two assignments should suffice.

The most controversial question, still being debated, concerns the pervasive tone of the play. Is it a tragedy or, as Chekhov insisted, a comedy? The headnote (pp. 1519–23 in the anthology) discusses the issue at length. There is an undoubted pathos in the sale of the estate and in the situation of old Firs being left alone in the abandoned house. (It is possible but not necessary, however, to think of him as dying. We may surmise that Lopahin, who goes off to Kharkov, instructs his clerk Yepihodov to look after the house.) There is also sadness in the passing of the old order, in the destruction of the beautiful orchard, and in the acquisition of the estate by an upstart developer. The end can be seen as an example of the twilight of Tsarist Russia or, more accurately, of its landowning class.

But the economic and social themes are made purely personal and possibly trivial by the passive resignation of Lubov, who feels that she must pay for her sins, and even more by the grotesque fecklessness of her brother, Leonid. Though Lubov can say that without the cherry orchard life has no meaning for her, she accepts the solution. Her brother says that "we all calmed down, and even felt quite cheerful" (p. 1567). Lubov, in fact, is sleeping and feeling well and is now off to Paris to live on the money of a great aunt, money that she knows will not last long. There are so many comic and even farcical characters and scenes in the play that the gloom of the main event is considerably lightened.

Anya, a serious decent girl, is the only character not ridiculed. Even Trofimov, the student who courts her and who pronounces famous, grandiloquent speeches on the backwardness of Russia and the need for expiating the sufferings of the serfs in the past, is himself a good-for-nothing who has never done any work. His speech promising a bright future for mankind sounds hollow, as does his pompous assertion of being "above love." Lubov punctures this boast by scolding him: "At your age not to have a mistress!" (p. 1560). The relationship with Anya fizzles out.

Lubov's brother, Leonid Gayev, is similarly a figure of fun: effete, limited, even stupid. He drinks and eats and talks too much, telling the waiters inappropriate stories of the decadents in Paris. He plays imaginary games of billiards on all occasions, loudly giving commands in the jargon of the game. The adopted daughter of Lubov, Varya, is a poor, awkward spinster who spoils her last chance of marrying Lopahin in a painful scene in which she speaks of a broken thermometer. Charlotta, the governess, performs card tricks, practices ventriloquism, and lugs a nut-eating dog around. The neighboring landowner with the comic double name Simeonov-Pishchik (something like Squealer) is as broke and irrepressible as the owners of the cherry orchard, but is rescued by an Englishman turning up out of the blue to pay him for the lease of some white clay found on his estate. Having swallowed a whole box of pills of Lubov's, he suddenly falls asleep and talks knowingly about Nietzsche's advocating the forging of bank-notes. The clerk, Semyon Yepihodov, is an even more grotesque figure. He is unlucky; he constantly knocks over things, finds a cockroach in his drink, and irrelevantly drops the name of Buckle, a British historian. The maid, Dunyasha, is a foolish girl in love with the one definitely repulsive character, the valet, Yasha. Firs, the old man-servant who remembers with nostalgia the days of serfdom, is a pathetic figure, hard of hearing, shuffling, ludicrous in his loneliness. One has to conclude that the play is a mixture of comedy and pathos.

Topics for Discussion

1. Consider the picture of Russia at the turn of the century: the play presents the landed gentry with their hangers-on and servants, the new merchant-developers risen from the serf class, and the ineffectual, verbose student intelligentsia.

2. The technique of the play deserves discussion, especially the contrasts of the four acts. These take place during spring, summer, a day in August, and, shortly after, the day of departure. The white bloom of the cherry trees in Act I is juxtaposed against the sound of the axes felling them in Act IV. Action shifts quickly from one speaker to another, and small incidents interrupt any semblance of a continuous argument or mood.

Topics for Writing

1. Is the play a tragedy or a comedy? How does Russia look, as seen in this play? What message is implied, if there is one?

   [Chekhov's attitude is not that of a reformer or revolutionary, but is also not reactionary. It is an attitude of deep human sympathy for almost everybody, coupled with a dim hope for progress. While extravagance is obviously condemned and the merchant, Lopahin, depicted favorably (as Chekhov's letters insist), the playwright also excuses real passion, even guilty passion—or at least shows understanding for it.]

2. Can one define the role of symbolism in this play?

   [The cherry orchard dominates, obviously. More puzzling is the sound of the broken string. This, when it first sounds out of doors in Act II (p. 1553), is explained as possibly due to the fall of a bucket in a distant mine or perhaps as the cry of a heron or the hooting of an owl, but its unexplained repetition at the very end of the play (p. 1571) has a weird, ominous effect. Attempts have been made to trace it to a childhood memory of Chekhov's or more simply to the general superstition that a broken string, say on a guitar, presages ill luck or even death.]

Comparative Perspectives

1. In setting the scenes for his play, Chekhov kept the cherry orchard out of sight, yet it dominates the stage action. What exactly is threatened and then lost—and what is gained—by cutting down the cherry trees? Literature through the ages presents many other such cherished but often doomed orchards, forests, and fields. As appropriate, compare the symbolic functions of Chekhov's orchard with those of the Cedar Forest in *Gilgamesh*; the Garden of Eden in the Jewish, Christian, and Islamic traditions; the forest retreats in Indian works like the *Rāmāyaṇa* and *Śakuntalā*; the wilderness in *The Bear*; and/or the woods in *Matryona's Home*.

2. Readers (as opposed to spectators) often fail to appreciate the impact that stage music has on a theater audience. The famous "sound of a snapping string" heard in *The Cherry Orchard* is only one in a pattern of sounds and songs woven throughout. Discuss the different functions of music here and in other plays.

[Possibilities include Greek choral odes and the various musical interludes in *Śakuntalā*, *Nō* plays, *Faust*, *Six Characters in Search of an Author*, and *The Good Woman of Setzuan*.]

Further Reading

See also the reading suggestions in the anthology, p. 1523.

Barricelli, Jean-Pierre, ed. *Chekhov's Great Plays: A Critical Anthology.* 1981.

Chekhov, Anton. *Anton Chekhov's Plays*: A Norton Critical Edition. Trans. and ed. Eugene K. Bristow. 1977. Contains several useful critical essays.

Hingley, Ronald. *Chekhov: A Biographical and Critical Study.* 1950; 1966.

Magarshack, David. *Chekhov the Dramatist.* 1951; 1960. Has a chapter arguing for the comedy of *The Cherry Orchard.*

Valency, Maurice. *The Breaking String.* 1966. A general study of Chekhov's themes.

The Modern World:
Self and Other in
Global Context

THE NIGHT CHANT

Backgrounds

The ceremonial is accounted for by an origin story, not part of the per-formance, in which a young man visits the gods, learns the ritual proce-dure, and returns to teach his people. In theory the tale is connected to the traditional Navajo tribal history, known as the Emergence Story, branching off from it at a point after the people have been brought forth from inside the earth. The origin stories of ceremonials other than the Night Chant are also linked to the Emergence Story, creating a vast inter-related lore.

Since the Navajo day begins at nightfall, the ceremonial performance starts in the evening. Standing at the door of the ceremonial lodge, a crier calls out the invitation "Come on the trail of song." The first day of the proceedings, spanning the period from nightfall to nightfall, includes a sweat bath in a specially built structure to the east of the lodge. On the second day, the purifying sweat bath is to the south; on the third day, to the west; on the fourth, to the north. Thus the first four days of the cere-monial swing through the four cardinal points in a clockwise, or "sun-wise," circuit.

On each day of the second part the chanter and his assistants prepare a large sand painting, which is used therapeutically (rubbing the patient's body with pigments taken from the bodies of the depicted gods) and promptly obliterated. Such would be the program, at least, for an ordinary Navajo ceremonial. But according to the origin story of the Night Chant, one of the sand paintings was withheld or forbidden by the gods; in fact on the eighth day the ceremonial participants do not create a sand paint-ing, but use the time to prepare for the all-night activity of the ninth day, which begins at dusk.

PRAYER TO THUNDER

On the final night of the ceremonial, eight bonfires are lit in front of the lodge, four on each side of a central area designated the "dancing ground." Spectators gather on either side, beyond the fires. The bodies of four dancers, representing the four *atsálei*, or thunderbirds, are painted with white earth. Singing begins within the lodge; against this background of song, the chanter, with the patient echoing him line for line, recites the great prayer, addressing it to the first of the *atsálei*. The prayer is repeated, with minor variations, for each of the remaining three dancers.

Following a prescribed pattern of prayer-making, the text begins by describing the home of the deity (lines 1–13); note the formalistic pairing of dawn and evening, he-rain and she-rain. Observe also the important reference to the doorway and its path made of "rainbow" (the proverbial means of swift travel, used by gods).

The prayer-maker now invokes the god directly, drawing him forward; note the incremental piling up of imagery (lines 14–35), culminating in the request "I wish the foam floating on the flowing water" (line 36).

The ritual offering is named (lines 37–38), followed by an enumeration of the services to be rendered in exchange (lines 39–59). At line 60 the litany changes from overtly personal requests to more generalized requests for rain and fecundity (through line 88) and a communal blessing on behalf of men, women, and children: "may their roads home be on the trail of pollen. / Happily may they all get back" (lines 89–90).

Finally, the supplicant asks for a personal zone of protection extending before, behind, below, above, and all around (lines 91–96); the prayer ends with the formulaic closing, stated four times, "It [i.e., the prayer] is finished in beauty."

Following the prayer, the dance of the *atsálei* begins, to the accompaniment of two special songs (not included in the anthology) that include the verses "The corn comes up, the rain descends" and "Above it thunders, / His thoughts are directed to you."

FINISHING SONG

When the *atsálei* have finished, another group of dancers, the *naakhaí* (a company of twelve god-impersonators), takes the dancing ground and performs at intervals throughout the night. The *naakhaí* dance to the accompaniment of a strongly rhythmic Night Chant song built on the vocables "Ohohohó héhehe héya héya." The rain god, Tónenili, acting as a ceremonial clown, interferes with the dancers. During breaks in the dancing, singers within the lodge keep the night filled with song by reprising the song cycles that have been heard during the first eight days of the ceremony. At dawn, the special cycle of four Finishing Songs is performed— only one of which, the last, was recorded by Matthews.

Navajo songs do not rhyme, but they employ antithesis and complementarity in a manner that one writer has referred to as "rhyming thoughts." In the example, notice the pairing of "white" and "green" and of "man" and "woman."

At the close of this song, the inverted basket that has been used throughout the ceremony as a drum is "turned up." An assistant to the chanter shreds the yucca-fiber drumstick and whispers the benediction "Thus will it be beautiful, / Thus walk in beauty, my grandchild," as the patient, facing east, inhales the breath of dawn.

Note that a performance of the Night Chant song mentioned above ("Ohohohó héhehe héya héya") was included, along with works of Beethoven and other composers, in the "Sounds of the Earth" recording sent into space aboard the Voyager spacecraft, launched by the United States' National Aeronautics and Space Administration in the summer of 1977.

Classroom Strategies

The selections present an opportunity to demonstrate—clearly—the differences between two major native American genres, oratory and song (see the headnote "Native America and Europe in the New World," pp. 3063–67 in volume C of the anthology). Most students will be familiar with an entirely different kind of prayer and sacred song. Comparison (see below) could be profitable.

One's impression of the Night Chant may be deepened immediately by the sight of Edward Curtis's famous sepia-toned photographs of the Night Chant god-impersonators (see Curtis) and Matthews's full-color reproductions of the Night Chant sand paintings (see Matthews, one of the readings suggested in the headnote, pp. 1607–08 in the anthology). The volumes in which these illustrative materials originally appeared are rare and fragile; black-and-white reproductions are in the Curtis reprint and in Bierhorst.

Topics for Discussion and Writing

1. Compare the Navajo texts with the New Testament prayer given in Matthew 6 and with the Old Testament Psalms.
2. The Navajo and the Zuni are neighbors and attend each other's ceremonials. Indeed, the Zuni Shalako regularly includes an imitation of the Night Chant *naakhaí* dance, and there has undoubtedly been borrowing in the other directions as well. Yet Navajo and Zuni prayers (see "Zuni Ritual Poetry," pp. 2031–36 in the anthology) are entirely different in tone. Can you characterize this difference?

Some Comparative Perspectives

1. The therapeutic effect of *The Night Chant* depends partly on the repetition, which makes the patient an active participant in the chant. Many poets have sought to give their poems a liturgical quality by experimenting with similar repetitive elements. Compare the nature of repetition in the Navajo ceremonial, in which the desire to be inclusive plays such a central role, to its uses in, as appropriate, Yeats's *Easter 1916*, Eliot's *The Waste Land* and *Little Gidding*, Césaire's *Notebook of a Return to the Native Land*.

[Discuss the blending of religious, political, and aesthetic purposes in poetry in general, and analyze the particular emphasis in
selections such as these.]

2. *The Night Chant* concludes with a Finishing Song that may be said
   to ratify the healing powers of the chant. Chronology sets *The Night
   Chant* in close proximity to Freud's *"Dora,"* and this fortuitous juxtaposition helps us see that Freud, like the Navajo, takes advantage of
   ritual and the power of words to heal. Compare and contrast the unorthodox definitions of sickness and health that distinguish these
   two texts.

Further Reading

See also the reading suggestions in the anthology, p. 1608.

Curtis, Edward S. *The North American Indian*, vol. 1. 1907; 1970.
Description of the Night Chant with photographs of the god-
impersonators.

Reichard, Gladys. *Prayer: The Compulsive Word*. 1944. Study of Navajo
prayer.

Spencer, Katherine. *Mythology and Values: An Analysis of Navaho Chant-
way Myths*. 1957. Includes a useful synopsis of the Night Chant origin
story.

SIGMUND FREUD

"Dora"

Backgrounds

If there is a single twentieth-century figure about whom people generally feel that they should know something, that figure is Sigmund Freud.
Freud, after all, demonstrated that there was an unconscious life of the
mind governing many of our daily activities; he proposed methods for recognizing these buried impulses; he held out the possibility of a systematic
self-knowledge that was hitherto only hinted at in literary works from
Saint Augustine's *Confessions* to Dostoevsky's *Notes from Underground*.
Freudian vocabulary has become common currency for describing human
behavior; terms such as "repression," "defense mechanism," and "self-
love" have lost any visible connection to the founder of psychoanalysis but
continue to be used in describing how people relate to one another. Scrutinizing the self has become a staple of art, literature, philosophy, medicine, and science. Self-scrutiny itself cannot be attributed to Freud, of
course. Socrates claimed in fifth-century Greece that the "unexamined
life" was "not worth living," and Romantic writers commonly developed
the theme of self-knowledge, but Freud stands out as the modern figure
who most crucially symbolizes an attempt to understand the phenomenon
of human behavior.

When "Dora" (Ida Bauer) became Freud's patient in October 1900, the psychoanalyst was still indignant at the poor reception of his recently published *Interpretation of Dreams* (November 4, 1899; publisher's date 1900), which found few readers and was attacked by conservative members of the medical establishment. In the partly autobiographical study, Freud had not only reviewed previous literature on dreams and dreaming as if investigating a serious topic but—more upsetting to neurologists—he had also developed a theory of dream interpretation that included a theory of how the mind works. Dreams were a way of representing and dealing with material that could not safely be brought to consciousness; as he explained in the prefatory remarks to *"Dora"* (omitted in this selection), they were "one of *the détours by which repression can be evaded."* Freud claimed that he learned "how to translate the language of dreams into the forms of expression of our own thought-language." He intended the case study of *"Dora,"* initially titled "Dreams and Hysteria," to be read as a response to criticism of the *Interpretation of Dreams* and as a practical demonstration of its theories. Its combative preface reasserted that "a thorough investigation of the problems of dreams is an indispensable prerequisite for any comprehension of the mental processes in hysteria and the other psychoneuroses, and that no one who wishes to shirk that preparatory labor has the smallest prospect of advancing even a few steps into this region of knowledge. . . . What is new has always aroused bewilderment and resistance."

If critics attacked the *Interpretation of Dreams* as too speculative and abstract, *"Dora"* would earn their criticism for being too specific—an invasion of privacy in the particularly sensitive field of personal sexuality. Freud predicts this criticism in his prefatory remarks, and indeed he goes out of his way to justify his procedures. If, as he believes, the causes of neurosis are to be found in the patient's psychosexual life and repressed wishes, then completely elucidating such neuroses does reveal personal secrets that a "person of delicacy" would refuse to betray. However, Freud continues, "the physician has taken upon himself duties not only towards the individual but towards science as well"; thus it becomes "a disgraceful piece of cowardice" not to expose what he knows. Readers who have noted Freud's disappointment at Dora's termination of the treatment may agree with his principles but find the attitude ambiguous—the writer reminds us that he

> naturally cannot prevent the patient herself from being pained if her own case history should accidentally fall into her hands. But she will learn nothing from it that she does not already know; and she may ask herself who besides he could discover from it that she is the subject of this paper.

In the next paragraph, Freud speculates on that very matter. Although he has changed names and only his friend Wilhelm Fliess knows Dora's identity, Freud is aware that "many physicians (revolting though it may seem) choose to read a case history of this kind . . . as a *roman à clef* [a novel with 'real-life' references intended to be deciphered] designed for their private delectation."

Freud anticipates another reproach: impropriety. He expects his readers to be startled at the frankness with which he discusses sexual matters with a young woman, especially since "the organs and functions of sexual life will be called by their proper names." Scientific inquiry, however, requires such frankness; he claims for himself "the rights of a gynaecologist" and adds that it would be "a singular and perverse prurience to consider that such conversations excite or gratify sexual desire." Overall, Freud is very aware of his readers' foreseeable response as well as of his own aims; he states in a letter that "Dora" "is the most subtle thing I have yet written and will produce an even more horrifying effect than usual."

"Dora" continues to be read as a major case history, but interpretations of *what* one reads differ. In the traditional view, Freud progressively uncovers Dora's real motivations and fails to effect a cure only because she prematurely terminates the analysis. In a view gaining increasing currency today, Freud himself is implicated in the tale of Dora and the reader's analysis must be brought to bear on both the analyst, who is determined to uncover the truth and reveal it in a coherent explanatory narrative, and the analysed, who resists the author-physician's attempt to write her story for her.

There are many indications of Freud's personal interest in this story, among them his presentation of the case history as a "practical application" encompassing plot despite (or, through the interpretation of) Dora's resistance. "Story" and "narrative" are terms that recur throughout the case history. After noting his patients' generic "inability to give an ordered history of their life in so far as it coincides with the history of their illness" (p. 1617), Freud assumes the responsibility of drawing up that ordered account: "At such points the physicians is usually faced by the task of guessing and filling in what the analysis offers him in the shape only of hints and allusions" (p. 1632). An inquirer must not "rest content with the first 'No' that crosses his path" but must pursue an explanation which the patient is trying to conceal.

To a certain degree this pursuit seems only reasonable, but it is accompanied by an extraordinary insistence on the correctness of Freud's interpretation. He is hot on the trail of truth—"I was obliged to point out . . . ," "there could be no doubt . . . ," "it could be none other than . . . ," "the truth of this statement can invariably be relied upon," "I could not avoid the assumption that . . ."—while a patient ideally "arrives at a sense of conviction of the validity of the connections which have been constructed during the analysis" (p. 1667). Dora and the reader must be persuaded, as the former seems to realize toward the end: "And Dora disputed the fact no longer" (p. 1660). Readers encounter a constant obbligato of footnotes, supplemented over the years, that support Freud's argument by elaborating a particular judgment, adducing other works, or referring backward or forward in the text to confirming passages. The Postscript, added fifteen months later, proposes a further explanation. Dora's case was a failure because Freud (as he now realizes) had not taken fully into account the phenomenon of transference; Dora had transferred to Freud her feelings of betrayal by her father and Herr K. In short, it remains extremely important to Freud that this "Fragment of an Analysis of a Case," which was terminated abruptly by the patient in what he calls "an unmistakable act of vengeance on her part" (p. 1663), result at some point in a successful explanation.

Another common issue in contemporary discussion of "Dora" is the extent to which Freud's interpretation is colored by the patriarchal bias of nineteenth-century Viennese society. Although the analyst does not accept the father's view without qualification, he certainly uses it as a point of departure. Her father is "a man of rather unusual activity and talents . . . a man of some perspicacity . . . shrewdness which I have remarked upon more than once" (p. 1620, p. 1621). We hear a great deal about Dora's relationship with her father, but very little about the mother, whom both father and daughter consider "an uncultivated woman and above all . . . a foolish one," in other words a perfect example of what Freud calls the "housewife's psychosis" (p. 1619). Freud also seems predisposed in Herr K.'s favor and is quite ready to consider Dora, at age fourteen, "entirely and completely hysterical" for failing to be excited by Herr K.'s kiss. "I happen to know Herr K., for he was the same person who had visited me with the patient's father, and he was still quite young and of prepossessing appearance" (note 1, p. 1623). Small wonder that Dora should come to associate Freud with her father and Herr K.; all three represent male authority figures who challenge her credibility in a sensitive situation. That it is in fact a challenge and not merely analysis emerges from the way Freud's own image of Dora evolves according to circumstances; although he initially appreciates her intelligence and "engaging looks" (p. 1620), his descriptions become harsher and more critical the more she disputes his interpretations. While Dora's nervous disorder is undoubtedly real, and severe enough to cause physical symptoms, the rhetorical structure of this "Fragment of an Analysis of a Case of Hysteria" reveals a male-oriented perspective that can only have augmented her dilemma. The conceptual discoveries that Freud was able to make on the basis of this analysis did not accompany a successful treatment, and Dora chose to put her own end to the story.

"Dora" begins with a brief discussion of Freud's theories in The Interpretation of Dreams, followed by a relatively detailed summary of the patient's family situation. Dora's father was a well-to-do manufacturer and a dominating figure to whom she was devoted from early childhood. The father had suffered many illnesses: tuberculosis when Dora was six years old, a detached retina when she was ten, and two years later the confusion and partial paralysis for which he sought Freud's help. Freud attributed the father's illness to syphilis, a disease that the father apparently had passed on to his wife, now estranged from both husband and daughter, who spent her time obsessively housecleaning. Dora fell ill at age eight with a dyspnea (difficulty in breathing) that Freud calls an early neurotic symptom; we learn later that she also wet her bed around this time. At age twelve she began to have migraine headaches and a nervous cough, which sometimes led to a complete loss of voice for three to five weeks at a time. When she was seventeen she had a feverish attack that was diagnosed as appendicitis. All these symptoms Freud would later relate to emotional causes, and indeed Dora's father brought her to Freud when she was eighteen after discovering a suicide letter in her desk.

Dora's depression, explained her father, was due to an unreasoning dislike of Herr K., who she said had propositioned her when they were walking by a lake during summer vacation. She was also jealous of her father's friendship with Frau K. Dora's version of events was remarkably different. Herr K. had first kissed her by surprise when she was fourteen, the episode by the lake was real, and her father had been having an open affair with Frau K. ever since the latter took over his nursing during a serious illness. Dora was not only outraged by her parents' refusal to believe her, but she resented being—as she felt—bartered to Herr K. in compensation for his wife.

Freud's treatment consists largely in asking Dora to tell the story of these relationships in increasing detail, and to examine her own feelings. He comments on everything she says, interpreting her words, her actions, and the two dreams, whose words and images are given rigorous analysis. Throughout the case history, there are extended passages of self-reflexive psychoanalysis in which Freud explains Dora's behavior, his own procedures, and the various concepts he is in the process of formulating. Step by step, he obliges his patient to recognize in her actions and dreams an unconscious attraction to Herr K., as well as to her father. In an extraordinarily complex network of interrelated images, wordplay, and ambiguous associations, Freud elucidates a series of repressed desires that are at the base of Dora's depression and physical maladies. His patient, however, has imperceptibly been deciding to discontinue treatment, a decision she announces to the analyst's surprise on December 31, 1900, only eleven weeks after their first session. Freud brings the analysis to a conclusion in a final set of interpretations to which Dora listens "without any of her usual contradictions" (p. 1663), but his disappointment and hurt are evident in the Postscript. In January 1901, he wrote up the case, though its unfinished nature continued to plague him, and he published the "Fragment" and its Postscript in 1905.

Classroom Strategies

Given the cultural significance of Freud's work, and the length and complexity of "Dora," you will probably want to allot four days to this piece. Students will very likely have strong ideas about "Freudianism" even if they have not read Freud, and you may find it useful to begin by finding out what these presuppositions are. Some will know a few terms (Oedipus complex, defense mechanism, repression, narcissism, etc.); others will be intrigued by the thought of uncovering hidden motivations; others may be concerned by the preoccupation with sexuality; and still others may be acquainted with the feminist "anti-Freud" debate and be ready to denounce him.

It will probably be useful at this point to emphasize the balance of *scientific inquiry* and *fictional portrait* that will carry you through the discussion of *"Dora."* Students will be aware of Freud's standing as a scientist and founder of psychoanalysis; you can, therefore, suggest that they treat this assignment as a novel, with a given cast of characters and, in this case, a first-person narrative point of view (treating Freud, for the occasion, as the conventional "unreliable narrator"). Compare *"Dora"* with other works in the anthology that use fictional structures to describe personal or family relationships (*The Queen of Spades, The Death of Ivan Ilyich, Death in Venice*). Establish *"Dora"* as a story, and Freud as a narrator with two commitments: on the one hand, Freud has just completed *The Interpretation of Dreams* and is now working on his *Psychopathology of Everyday Life,* so he is feverishly engaged in formulating some basic insights into human behavior; on the other hand, he is consciously arranging events to tell a story while proposing a particular version of the truth. Remind your students that Freud was aware of literary structures and of the way his own case histories read like stories; encourage them to follow the thread of this "fragment" by using familiar literary-critical techniques (e.g., analyzing the narrative point of view, discussing the relationships of major and minor characters, following the cumulative stages of the plot and the duel of the two major characters, Freud and Dora).

There are many ways of organizing the material. You might use the first day to establish the setting: Freud's identity as psychoanalyst and author of *The Interpretation of Dreams*, Dora's family background, the way that she came to be Freud's patient. Ask the students what they think is going to happen, and what their evaluation of the narrator's reliability is, on the basis of this initial information. On the second day, you might begin to develop the alternate aspects of this case history: the increased understanding of Freudian psychoanalysis as it takes shape in the very course of the analysis, and concurrently, the developing picture of Dora as she becomes a flesh-and-blood character engaged in a duel of competing interpretations with her analyst. The third day might well be devoted to the dreams as examples of the dream analysis that is Freud's real interest in this work: the first, longer and more narrative, and the second, shorter and more complicated. Finally, the last day could be a wrap-up of the whole piece focused on the Postscript, which makes clear Freud's continual involvement with the case and also the way he continues writing and rewriting the story. If you have a colleague in psychology or women's studies who might be willing to join in a general discussion of *"Dora,"* this would be a good time to schedule such a visit.

Topics for Discussion

1. Why is it part of the psychoanalyst's duty, according to Freud, to compose a coherent story from the patient's disjointed memories?

[Compare, perhaps, Freud's statement that he is like "a conscientious archaeologist," one of those discoverers whose good fortune it is "to bring to the light of day after their long burial the priceless though mutilated relics of antiquity. I have restored what is missing, taking the best models known to me from other analyses . . ."].

2. How, according to Freud, do dreams allow repressed impulses and memories a way to express themselves?

3. Explain and give examples of such Freudian concepts as repression, displacement, somatic compliance, overdetermination, sublimation, symptomatic acts, and the importance of wordplay or "switchwords."

4. Why did Dora's father bring her to Freud for analysis? Did Freud fulfill his expectations? Did he intend to?

5. What does Freud mean by "there is no such thing at all as an unconscious 'No' "?

6. How many instances of betrayal would Dora have felt in the course of the case history?

7. What is "transference" and how does Freud feel that it played a part in the case history's unsuccessful conclusion? Do you agree with his interpretation, given in the Postscript, of what he should have done?

8. What evidence do you find of Freud's ability as a creative writer?
   [Among other examples, you might point to the second paragraph, in which the patient's account is described as an "unnavigable river whose stream is at one moment choked by masses of rock and at another divided and lost among shallows and sandbanks."]

9. To what extent, in your opinion, has Freud located the causes of Dora's depression and physical maladies?

10. How successful is Freud in maintaining an objective point of view?

11. Speculate on what the analysis might have looked like if Dora's mother had been the patient. What evidence do we have of Freud's attitude toward this possibility?
    [See pp. 1618–20.]

12. Comment on the following statement made by Thomas Mann in 1936:

> We shall one day recognize in Freud's life-work the cornerstone for the building of a new anthropology and therewith a new structure, to which many stones are being brought up today, which shall be the future dwelling of a wiser and freer humanity.

Comparative Perspectives

1. How we deal with dreams reveals our systems of values and beliefs. Compare Freud's methods in interpreting Dora's dreams with those of Joseph in the New Testament of the Bible or in the Koran. Why

is it significant that in each case it is another person's dreams being analyzed? What is the source of the interpreter's insight into the meaning of dreams? What role does Freud play in relation to his patients? How is the psychoanalyst like God?

2. In *The Death of Ivan Ilyich*, the title character is shocked when he perceives that the "important air" his doctor assumes in treating him resembles his own manner as an eminent judge dealing with an "accused person." How might Tolstoy portray Freud's account of his professional manner in describing his treatment of Dora? What other modern writers consider the emotional consequences of depending on an "expert" in matters of life and death?

Further Reading

See also the reading suggestions in the anthology, p. 1615.

Diacritics (Spring, 1983). This special issue, "A Fine Romance: Freud and Dora," includes Sarah Burd's translation of a short play called *Portrait of Dora* by French feminist scholar Hélène Cixous.

Forrester, John. *The Seductions of Psychoanalysis: Freud, Lacan and Derida.* 1990. Contains a section on *"Dora."*

Freeman, Lucy, and Herbert S. Strean. *Freud and Women.* 1981. An introduction with a biographical approach and brief summaries of individual cases.

Gay, Peter. *Reading Freud: Explorations and Entertainments.* 1990. Offers eight essays on different aspects of Freud's work and thought.

Mahony, Patrick J. *Freud as a Writer.* 1987. Analyzes Freud's literary style as a key to his habits of mind.

Storr, Anthony. *Freud.* 1989. Offers a brief overview of Freud's life and chief concepts, situated in critical perspective; includes a section on contemporary psychoanalysis and a short annotated bibliography.

RABINDRANATH TAGORE

Poems

Backgrounds

Thanks to the Nobel Prize for Literature the author received in 1913, Rabindranath Tagore's short stories have been rapidly and widely disseminated in translation, both in India and abroad. His poems have not been as fully appreciated, but new translations have made them much more accessible, and students who have already had some introduction to the traditional literatures of South Asia are well prepared for the ample selection in the anthology. To begin, you might ask your students to consider how Tagore has adapted the formulas of mystical contemplation (volume B of the anthology) in some of his short poems. Compare, for example, the attitude toward the ascetic life in Kabīr's *Go Naked if You Want* (volume B, p. 2397) and Tagore's *Deliverance is not for me in renunciation,* where the modern man reflects on his situation in terms quite different from the witty epigrammatic style of the fifteenth-century poet. Other interesting comparisons might be based on Tagore's use of a female voice in the first selection, *The song that I came to sing,* or the twelfth selection, *Under the cascading stream,* and any of the Bhakti poems either written by women or impersonating them (for example, any of Mira's poems or Chaṇḍidāsa's *My mind is not on housework*).

You will want also to establish that Tagore's philosophy was universal and wide-ranging; his work should not be considered parochial. Many of his longer poems in the anthology make use of symbols that resonate in a variety of cultures. The refrain of *A Stressful Time,* "yet bird, o my bird / already blind, don't fold your wings yet" would be generally understood as an emblem for the soul. Similarly, the overflowing pitcher of *Under the cascading stream* seems to function as a mystical image for the human mind that transcends any particular sect. For this reason, the longer poems are particularly attractive for extended classroom study. Students should be encouraged to use their imaginations and find their own ways of explaining the meanings potential in Tagore's images and situations.

The charming and poignant family situations explored in poems like *I Won't Let You Go* and *Hide-and-Seek* are actually vehicles for deep meditative reflections on humanity and the cosmos. Tagore's sympathetic portraits of lovingly rendered realistic children are also representations of the human soul. In the same way, *The Golden Boat,* which seems at first to be a realistic scene painting, turns out to be an allegory open to various interpretations. Some critics may see the boat as the ship of life. Why, then, is there room only for the farmer's produce, but not for him? Is it his fate—the human condition—always to be left behind? Or is a specific moral failure on the part of the disappointed farmer implied? The translator believes that "the distinction between self and soul" is examined in *The Golden Boat,* and that the farmer is being chastised for wanting too much credit for having produced his bounteous crop. Setting this poem alongside the prose poem about Sudās, the gardener, may clarify this reading (as might a reference to the biblical story of Cain and Abel).

Music is another unifying theme in many of the selections. The virtuosic *Flute Music* begins with a significant statement of location: Kinugoala Lane, or, as the footnote explains, "Kinu the Milkman's Lane," associating the flute with Krishna, the lover of dairymaids. (Note, too, these lines: "The cosmos is a field where the infinite's flute / plays a pastoral lament" in the final stanza of *I Won't Let You Go,* showing the frequency with which the flute is the instrument of divine utterance.) Thus the poem's title, like the clerk Haripada's address, alerts the reader to the way Tagore's wonderfully idiosyncratic description of a junior office worker's dilapidated lodgings becomes an emblem of life on earth: "Then in a flash I grasp / That the entire lane is a dreadful lie, / Insufferable, like the ravings of a drunk." It is not surprising, then, that the arranged marriage from which the hapless Haripada tried to escape takes on a new, mystical identity as his prospective bride seems at the last to beckon, a stand-in for union with the divine. The poem deftly fuses comic portraits of two superficially unprepossessing persons with a generous humanism, for both Haripada and Kanta Babu seem by the last lines to have demonstrated an unsuspected spiritual dimension and, if only for the moment, to have been redeemed by the power of art.

Some of the poems depart from this sort of elliptical narrative and frankly declare Tagore's philosophical beliefs. *In Praise of Trees* and *Last Honey* may look at first like the nature poems of the English Romantic school, but instead of the undertone of anxiety that one may hear in the effusions of a Wordsworth or a Shelley, these verses, with their references to Vedic ritual and the rhythms of the Bengali calendar, communicate a calm assurance that humanity is rooted in an essentially beneficent universe. *On My Birthday*, the late poem that closes the anthology's selections of Tagore's poetry, strikes a marvelous final note of affirmation. The creative power of the word springs from deep natural sources:

> The festive sound of leaves rustling in forests,
> The sound that measures the rhythm of approaching tempests,
> The great night-ending sound of day-break—
> From these sound-fields man has captured words . . . (lines 23–26)

One should not worry if art lacks clarity. Energy carries the day and even "nonsense nursery syllables" in fact bespeak poetic force: *Horselum, bridelum, ridelum, into the fray*. The effect is heroic, the battle worth fighting, and the rhythms strong.

Punishment

In fiction, the mood is quite different. While Tagore's novels are set in the context of middle-class Bengali society, many of his short stories (including the frequently anthologized *Postmaster* and *Holiday*) take place in rural Bengal.

In *Punishment*, one of the stories he wrote during his sojourn as a landlord in rural East Bengal, Tagore treats the lives of poor landless laborers with the deep concern for the dignity and value of the individual, of the human being, regardless of gender, class, or status, that characterizes all of his writing. The egalitarian, idealistic, and humanistic tendencies of the Bengal "Renaissance" of the nineteenth century appear to have found a highly personal yet universally appealing expression in Tagore's fiction. The eminent Indian director Satyajit Ray (1922–1992) based his award-winning 1954 Bengali film *Pather Panchali* ("Song of the Road") on Bibhutibhushana Bandyopadhyaya's novel of the same name, in which the author paints an unforgettable portrait of life in rural Bengal as seen through the eyes of a child. Both Banerjee and Ray were carrying forward the humanistic tradition in art and literature that Tagore had inspired in

Bengali culture. Ray's lyrical film abundantly conveys the atmosphere of life in a Bengali village, and his characters have the vitality of those in Tagore's fiction. Either *Pather Panchali*, or Ray's film based on two of Tagore's short stories (put together under the title *Two Daughters*), is worth viewing as a contextual companion to *Punishment* and an aid to a discussion of Tagore's work from aesthetic and cultural perspectives.

Essentially the story of Chandara, the young wife of a low-caste laborer, *Punishment* has the kind of immediate, universal appeal that Tagore invoked in a 1914 letter to the British poet Sturge Moore: "whatever is broadly human and deeply true can be safely shipped for distant times and remote countries" (A. Chakravarty, ed., *A Tagore Reader* [1961], p. 24). When Dukhiram Rui, the elder of the two Rui brothers, kills his wife, Radha, in a fit of anger, Chidam Rui panics and shifts the blame for the murder to his wife, Chandara. Deeply wounded at this betrayal by a husband with whom she has had a relationship of passionate attachment (intense love, colored by intense sexual jealousy), Chandara chooses to accept the accusation, and thus to court the death penalty, rather than live on with Chidam. During the court proceedings the two brothers break down and admit their own guilt, but nobody believes them. Chandara stubbornly sticks to her "confession" of murder and willingly accepts the death sentence. In this powerful story Tagore skillfully delineates universal human emotions in a tightly structured, psychologically convincing dramatic plot, which revolves around the enigmatic yet entirely convincing character of the betrayed girl.

In order to fully appreciate Tagore's achievement as a short-story writer, students will need to be reminded that *Punishment* is among the first modern short stories in the Bengali language. Although Bengali had a rich, diverse literature from the medieval era onward, and although classical and medieval Indian literature in Sanskrit and the regional languages abounds in narrative genres, until the late nineteenth century mythological themes and verse genres (see, for instance, the Songs of the Bengali Vaiṣṇava Saints, pp. 2390–95 in volume B of the anthology) dominated these traditions. While some contemporaries of Tagore in his early years wrote prose fiction, Tagore was the first author consistently to reject idealized and typecast characters, and to move from social realism to a focus on the psychology of individuals.

In *Punishment* and in other early short stories (such as *The Postmaster*) Tagore portrays villagers without sentimentality. While he continually draws attention to the oppression of marginalized groups in rural society (low-caste workers, landless laborers such as the Rui brothers, and, above all, women), his characters are fully differentiated from each other. They emerge as unique individuals, whose identities are not defined simply by their social roles. Whereas characters in the classical and premodern imaginative texts in the Indian languages are usually portrayed as fitting into particular roles (e.g., Śakuntalā as the lovelorn and desirable heroine in Kālidāsa's play, Sītā as the faithful wife and Rama as the perfect husband in the *Rāmāyaṇa*), Chandara and Chidam are portrayed as having unpredictable, dynamic personalities, and as engaging in a deeply ambivalent love/hate relationship with each other, in a way that no couple would in a classical or medieval work. The discussion of character in *Punishment* should broaden into a discussion of the modern in Tagore's fiction.

In portraying Chandara as a strong, independent, and self-confident person, Tagore goes directly against stereotypes of the heroine in much of Indian literature. Although the young woman has been deeply wounded by her husband's abandonment of her, she is not crushed by this betrayal, but retaliates in the only way left open to her: that is, by treating her death sentence not as a punishment imposed upon her but as an *act of choice*. By making her statements at the trial entirely independent of the statements of both her accusers and her defenders, Chandara resists the oppression she suffers under various interrelated systems of male domination. In fact, at the end of the story, when she exclaims "*maran*," which literally means "death to him," it is she who pronounces a death sentence on her husband, and on the society that nurtures and condones such inhuman behavior. She has the last word, both metaphorically and literally, in the narrative. By refusing to bend with the men's changing positions, she turns self-sacrifice into triumph and revenge. She is dignified to the end, but the tragedy is that she can triumph only in death.

Students should be encouraged to think about the skill with which Tagore combines his exploration of human psychology with a keen critique of the social and economic aspects of the oppression of the powerless. Tagore is equally unsparing in his criticism of the callous neglect suffered by the landless laborers and of the exploitation of women by men in the patriarchal family. The entire British colonial judicial system, with its alien machinery of "justice," is evoked by the police, the sessions court, and the civil court, each of which plays an important part in the story. At the end of *Punishment*, the young female victim's being led to the gallows illustrates that the system of justice collaborates with the logic, the unwritten laws, and the mechanisms of patriarchal oppression. The title of the story itself suggests the close connections Tagore sees among all these forms of oppression. Weighing the "punishment" the court levies on Chandara against the one that she directs against her betrayers, the reader is left to reflect on the many ways in which the individual, and human emotions in general, exists outside and triumphs over the most elaborate of institutions.

In *Punishment* Tagore combines humor, irony, pathos, and authorial comment in a typically Tagorean stylistic mix. As in all of his work, the human lives in this story are integrally linked with the natural landscape. Thus, like Mark Twain's Mississippi, the great Padma river bears witness to the human events in the story, including the dehumanization of the Rui men. By highlighting the link between nature and the human world, Tagore gives new life to an old feature of classical Indian literature, a feature expressed exquisitely in the drama *Śakuntalā* and other works of the fourth-century Sanskrit poet Kālidāsa. Again, the same link is illuminated in visual form in the films of Satyajit Ray.

Questions for Discussion and Writing

1. Select a poem of Tagore's that seems to you to deal with humanity's role in the natural world, and show how the poem's dramatic situation, imagery, and tone illustrate the relationship of these fundamental forms of life to a universal or divine power.
2. Examine the view of childhood articulated in *On the Seashore*, and show how the purity of the playing children takes on personality in one of Tagore's poetic portraits of individual youngsters, notably *I Won't Let You Go* or *Hide-and-Seek*.
3. Discuss the success of *Punishment* as a short story, in terms of structure, tone, character, and incident.
4. Compare Tagore's portrait of village life in Bengal with Premchand's delineation of peasant life in North India. Discuss some of the factors that account for the similarities and differences between the two portraits.
5. Compare Chandara with Jashoda in Mahasweta Devi's Bengali short story *Breast-Giver*, in terms of her awareness of oppression and ability to resist it. How do Tagore and Mahasweta Devi approach the issues of the marginalization and exploitation of women, the poor, and lower classes in Bengal?
6. View either of two films by Satyajit Ray (these have been reissued in new prints and are also available, in old prints on videotape, through most sources of world cinema): *Pather Panchali* (full-length feature film) or *Two Daughters* (two shorter films put together). How do these films illuminate Tagore's writing and Bengali humanism?

Comparative Perspectives

1. Compare and contrast the function of dramatic monologue in Tagore's *Flute Music* with the three poems by Robert Browning in the anthology. Why does *Childe Roland to the Dark Tower Came* seem closer in manner and effect to Tagore's poem than do *My Last Duchess* or *The Bishop Orders His Tomb*?

   [In the first two poems by Browning, emphasis tends to be on exposing a single human personality. In the enigmatic *Childe Roland*, however, we seem to be reaching toward a statement about more universal truths, as do all of Tagore's apparently realistic monologues.]
2. Compare the aging poet's affirmation of the power of poetry in *On My Birthday* with the view of words and thus of the poet's vocation expressed in Darío's *I Seek a Form* or Walcott's *North and South*.
3. Tagore's story seems to incorporate some of the central motifs of the ancient Indian epic the *Mahābhārata*. In what way does the introduction of Chandara echo the introduction of Draupadi in "The Game of Dice"? Compare the reasons why wives and brothers are caught in a web of deceit in both the ancient and the modern works.
4. Compare the approach taken by Premchand and Tagore in criticizing traditional Indian values and mores.

5. Chidam "realized that if he kept to the story he would have to wrap it in five more stories if his wife was to be saved." Show how this idea of wrapping stories inside of stories, central to ancient Indian narrative and the framed tales it influenced, may also be seen as a technique of modern writers, as demonstrated by Borges in *The Garden of Forking Paths*.

Further Reading and Viewing

See also the reading suggestions in the anthology, p. 1673.

Ray, Satyajit. *Pather Panchali* ("Song of the Road"). 1954. Feature film (111 minutes), available on videotape.

———. *Two Daughters*. 1963. Feature film (114 minutes), available on videotape.

Tagore, Rabindranath. *Glimpses of Bengal*. 1921.

WILLIAM BUTLER YEATS

Backgrounds

We continue to read W. B. Yeats because he wrote incontestably great poetry of widely differing types for over fifty years, because the various phases he passed through mirror the course of modern poetry as a whole, and because his work both charms the unsophisticated reader and challenges the sophisticated. He is the modern poet who most forcefully suggests to students something of the possibilities of poetry. The nine poems selected here are among the most famous and most representative of his work.

WHEN YOU ARE OLD

When You Are Old is one of the five love poems that Yeats copied out in manuscript and presented to Maud Gonne, who inspired many of his poems and much of his imagery. The central themes of the five poems have to do with threats to love—pity, tears, exhaustion, death, and, in the case of *When You Are Old*, age.

The poem is relatively straightforward until the last stanza, when the speaker of the poem presents the figure of Love pacing upon mountains and hiding "his face amid a crowd of stars." Here, the figure of Love has fled from the physical realm to the Olympian—the realm, that is, of poetry. Like other poems of Yeats's, this one features the sad recollection of the physical passion of youth from the perspective of wise age, which must replace sweet but fleeting passion with the eternal beauty of art. *Sailing to Byzantium* raises similar issues, as does Keats's *Ode on a Grecian Urn*.

The author expects us to see that he has based his poem on one by the sixteenth-century French poet Ronsard, but with a difference. Whereas the speaker in Ronsard's poem stresses the fast-fading joys of youth to strengthen his argument that the beloved should yield to him now, Yeats takes the argument to an entirely different plane of feeling, with a love that has fixed itself forever among the stars.

EASTER 1916

To convey the state of mind—and of Ireland—out of which this poem rises, it may be useful to hand out copies of Yeats's *September 1913*, in which the poet insists that the money-minded middle class (the paudeens) have so completely taken over that the romantic spirit of the Irish revolutionaries is dried up: "Romantic Ireland's dead and gone / It's with O'Leary in the grave."

By the time of *Easter 1916*, an appropriate time of year for thoughts of rebirth, Yeats's views have changed. The Irish spirit and what Yeats refers to in *September 1913* as "all that delirium of the brave" have revived with the Easter Rebellion. And for Yeats, all has "changed, changed utterly: / A terrible beauty is born." The first stanza of the poem delivers an Ireland reminiscent of *September 1913*—it seems a fool's country, meaningless, a "casual comedy" in which all heroism is dead. The second stanza enlists a number of Yeats's friends and acquaintances who played prominent roles in the Rebellion—Con Markiewicz, Patrick Pearse, Thomas MacDonagh, even John MacBride (the estranged husband of Maud Gonne)—to suggest how the meaningless Ireland of *September 1913* has been transformed utterly.

The third stanza is truly extraordinary. It contrasts mutability with stasis, the living stream and the seasons with the "stone" that the poet associates with the fatal revolutionary purpose of his friends. The imagery of the stanza seems governed by the compelling forward-motion of the changes these friends brought about. The stanza surges with activity, plunging forward with increasing speed and power, dazzling the ear. The whole of the natural world participates in this motion, enchanted into action, so to speak, by the singlemindedness of the revolutionary vision— perhaps in the same way that a stone in a stream generates ripples, eddies, even cascades.

But the singleminded passion necessary to create such an active transformation can "make a stone of the heart." In the fourth stanza Yeats raises the questions that must be asked about the consequences of any passionate action, especially revolutionary action. Where will it end? Was it necessary? Was it excessive? Was it worth it? Yeats raises the questions, but—we can be thankful for this—declines to answer them. That, Yeats says, "is Heaven's part, our part / To murmur name upon name" and to "know their dream; enough / To know they dreamed and are dead." Yeats's response to the Easter Rising is, then, complex. The last lines of the poem, the refrain, shift from a comparatively simple celebration of change into something celebrative but simultaneously deeply ambivalent. The words "terrible" and "beauty" in the refrain have picked up important

new connotations; they are now as highly charged with apprehension as
with celebration.

THE SECOND COMING

With the possible exception of *Sailing to Byzantium*, this may be Yeats's
most famous poem. To expound its implications fully it will be necessary
to introduce a brief description of Yeats's theory of history, which is discussed in the headnote (pp. 1699–1702 in the anthology). But this introduction should be kept brief and pithy, or the poem will get lost in theory.
It is enough to say that here Yeats implies a second coming is at hand, not
literally the coming of the biblical Antichrist, but of a new era that will
have characteristics opposite to those of Christianity—an era that Yeats
imagines beginning around the year 2000. The first stanza describes the
disintegration of the Christian era, which has lost coherence, unity, order. The "centre cannot hold; / Mere anarchy is loosed upon the world";
the falcon whirls beyond the control of its master. At the end of this era,
then, the order and ceremony of Christianity will be reversed. Lines 5 and
6 suggest an explosion of violence—an inverted baptism, with inverted results; the innocent will be drowned in their own blood.

The second stanza declares the meaning of this incoherence: "Surely
some revelation is at hand; / Surely the Second Coming is at hand." As a
symbol of the new era Yeats imagines a kind of Sphinx, a "shape with lion
body and the head of a man," which is just beginning to move as "indignant desert birds" reel above it. Their presence recalls the uncontrolled
falcon that begins the poem, and thus confirms the link between the end
of the old era and the beginning of the new. The poet's ability to visualize
this new beginning then ends: "The darkness drops again." But he knows
what he has "seen," and he knows its meaning. The new pitiless cycle of
history has been waiting its turn, "vexed to nightmare" by the twenty centuries of the Christian era. Its time now has come; and Yeats leaves us
with his final question: "what rough beast, its hour come round at last, /
Slouches toward Bethlehem to be born?"

There is no definitive answer, of course. But the implications of *The
Second Coming* are that the new order will reverse the values of the exhausted Christian era; the new era will be violent, "blank and pitiless,"
where only "the worst" will have the intensity to carry out their convictions. And, since the traditional answer to the riddle of the Sphinx has always been "man," the "rough beast" may be humanity itself. Yeats does
not like the look of what he sees.

LEDA AND THE SWAN

The Second Coming deals with the end of the Christian era and the beginning of a new one. *Leda and the Swan* deals with the beginning of the
classical era that preceded the Christian, but a classical era that many
take to be a metaphor for our own. As the descent of the dove upon Mary
announces a scheme of things that in *The Second Coming* is nearing the

end, so the rape of Leda by the Swan announces a scheme of things that includes the Trojan War (fought for Helen, one offspring of this union) and the murder of Agamemnon by Clytemnestra (another of its offspring). You may well find that your students are concerned by this mythologized glorification of what is, in fact, the rape of a terrified girl. The powerfully sensual description of that rape is pursued right up to the last two lines, when attention is directed to a more abstract issue: did she foresee the future? How far in *this* instance did the divine suffuse the human? The combination of these two aspects can be a strong catalyst for class discussion.

SAILING TO BYZANTIUM

Again, with the possible exception of *The Second Coming*, this may be Yeats's best-known poem. Except for Eliot's *The Love Song of J. Alfred Prufrock* and one or two of Robert Frost's pieces, it is perhaps the best-known modern poem in English. Although *Sailing to Byzantium*, like *The Second Coming* and *Leda and the Swan*, requires some knowledge of Yeats's personal mythology to be fully understood, you must again be on guard against losing the poem amid symbolic baggage.

A reading of the poem is best begun by comparing "that" country which the speaker is leaving (Ireland, perhaps) with the place to which he is going—Byzantium. Both are symbolic places, and idiosyncratically so, since the meaning Yeats means to give them is true only insofar as we accept the poet's claims for them. They cannot be better understood by reading more about Byzantium or the mating habits of the early-Modern Irish; they can be understood as symbols only by reading more Yeats. "That" country is the country of the young, the passionate, the fertile; it is a place "caught in the sensual music," a place of generation and, therefore, of the inevitable decay that comes with mortality. Byzantium, on the other hand, is a city of the soul, especially of the artist's soul; it suggests changelessness and immortality. It is that place where the spiritual and secular meet in art.

The second stanza establishes the poem's speaker as an "aged man" who must "sing louder," that is, insist on the primacy of spirit over body as he becomes older. And since the spirit is best represented in art, the speaker has "sailed the seas" to reach Byzantium. Once there, in the third stanza, he asks the city's "sages" to instruct him, to become the "singing-masters" of his soul, to gather him into the "artifice of eternity" that only art can make.

In the last stanza, the speaker makes known his desire—that he shall never again take bodily form except, perhaps, as a work of art, a golden bird upon a golden bough who will sing "To lords and ladies of Byzantium / Of what is past, or passing, or to come." Thus if the poem concentrates on the speaker's desire to leave the world of mortality in order to achieve an immortality of the spirit through art, the last line suggests its opposite—the world of mortality, the very world the speaker has renounced.

(Likewise in *Lapis Lazuli*, the Chinese elders look out upon a world in turmoil from their secure place in art, and their glittering eyes are untroubled, tranquil, gay.) The last line echoes "Whatever is begotten, born, and dies" in the first stanza and thus serves to remind us, as Yeats always reminds us, that when something is gained, something is lost. *Sailing to Byzantium* looks back at earlier poems such as *The Stolen Child* and *The Dolls* (both of which might usefully be handed out to students), and ahead to *The Circus Animals' Desertion*, in which Yeats insists that the ladder of his vision, and of all art, starts in the "foul rag-and-bone shop of the heart." Like Keats in *Ode on a Grecian Urn*, Yeats recognizes that the immortality of art is cold; it derives from and serves life—the one thing it cannot be. *Sailing to Byzantium* can very easily be read as being "about" the desire of the aged to transcend the decay of the body in favor of the eternality of art, but the ambiguity of the poem should not be ignored.

AMONG SCHOOL CHILDREN

This poem, like *Sailing to Byzantium*, begins with the question of old age, the contrast between current decrepitude and remembered youth, and then moves to a consideration of how age and final decay come to everyone, no matter how wisely one has worked to find an ideal world to pit against the imperfections of reality. Plato, Aristotle, and Pythagoras, like the speaker and the rest of us, become old scarecrows—"Old clothes upon old sticks to scare a bird."

As if to mock humankind's inevitable decay and to put off thoughts of it, "nuns and mothers worship images"—nuns worship religious icons as mothers worship idealized versions of their children. The invocation of these visions (both icons and fantasies are a kind of art) leads Yeats to his final stanza. Here Yeats again insists on the necessity of combining real and ideal, mortal and immortal, life and art. The ideal worlds of Plato and Aristotle are achieved only by denying an important part of what life is; they bruise the body to "pleasure soul." Instead, Yeats appears to say, images and theories cannot be separated from life itself—"How can we know the dancer from the dance?"—and the actual world and the visionary world, the world of mortal imperfection and artistic perfection, must exist in concert. The "comfortable kind of old scarecrow" and the child he once was are one thing, much as the chestnut tree is always its past and future as well as its present, a synthesis of leaf, blossom, and bole.

BYZANTIUM

In this poem Yeats stresses particularly the mutual dependence of the changeless, perfect world of Byzantium and the mortal world of "all that man is . . . The fury and the mire of human veins." *Byzantium* exploits the same contrast as its predecessor, but what existed as a rather ambiguous implication in *Sailing to Byzantium* becomes the central issue here.

After four stanzas that describe the spirit world of Byzantium, and how the mortal becomes immortal, Yeats gives the final stanza over to images, as one critic puts it, "not only of the eternal world, but also of the world of nature which is feeding it." In this poem, then, the natural and spiritual are inseparable; one can never be entirely abandoned for the other.

Students will find Yeats's imagery—the dolphins, the mummy, and so on—significantly more problematic here than in *Sailing to Byzantium*, but most of their troubles will be addressed in the footnotes.

LAPIS LAZULI

When *Lapis Lazuli* was written in 1936, Europe was both emerging from an economic depression and heating up for war. Hitler and Mussolini were gaining power in Germany and Italy, and the Spanish Civil War was running its course toward Franco. It was not just "hysterical women" who must have told Yeats that they were sick of art, or that he should use his considerable powers for political purposes. In these years, public affairs were intruding on private visions so forcefully that almost all of the important young British poets and novelists of the period (Auden, Spender, Day Lewis, MacNeice, Isherwood, Orwell, Warner, etc.) were engaged in writing books that were emphatically political. Poetry, especially as it was being written by High Modernists, was seen as a kind of luxury, too obscure and resistant to the needs and desires of the public to do the work in the world that these writers, and Yeats's "hysterical women," thought needed to be done. *Lapis Lazuli* constitutes Yeats's answer to them.

The first stanza presents the accusation: art is no longer enough. Commitment is needed, because "if nothing drastic is done" war will break out. Yeats's use of a popular seventeenth-century ballad to describe war has enticed some critics to claim that Yeats was ignoring political realities. Indeed, the scornful phrase "King Billy bomb-balls" does have the effect of deflating the seriousness of what might, and did, happen. But Yeats surely intended this deflation, because it serves to place the war to come in the larger context of all wars, in the larger context of the rise and fall of civilizations (many of which are now remembered or understood only through, and because of, their art), a subject with which Yeats, like Eliot and Pound, was much obsessed.

The second stanza suggests that in the play of civilizations even the greatest of actors do not betray the tragic parts they play, though they and we know they are participating in tragedy. Instead they retain a "gaiety" that "transfigures all that dread." They commit themselves but remain themselves. They empower the play they are in and, at the same time, transcend it by displaying the proper heroic reaction to catastrophe. And these "actors," Yeats suggests in the third stanza, are the ones who make civilizations. Their work may fall, may not last out the day, their "wisdom" may go "to rack," but "All things fall and are built again, / And those that build them again are gay."

The fourth and fifth stanzas locate that transcendent gaiety in one seemingly unspectacular work of art, a piece of lapis lazuli "carved by some Chinese sculptor into the semblance of a mountain with temple, trees, paths and an ascetic and pupil about to climb the mountain." In it, Yeats discovers all their civilization, now available only through art. He imagines them seated between mountain and sky, surveying "the tragic scene" below. And their "ancient, glittering eyes, are gay." They have, through art, survived, immortalized, and thus transcended the civilization from which they emerged. Through them, through art, their civilization retains the only meaning left to have. If King Billy's bomb-balls are pitched in, if Yeats's civilization is "beaten flat," his art—if it really is art— will remain, preserving its world for the instruction and delight of future men and women, perhaps even "A young girl in the indolence of her youth, / Or an old man upon a winter's night" (*On Being Asked for a War Poem*, lines 5–6).

THE CIRCUS ANIMALS' DESERTION

This poem was written in the last year of Yeats's life, and it serves as a kind of final survey of his career, a map of his imagery and thinking, and a declaration about the source of his art. The "circus animals" are, of course, the images that Yeats has used throughout his poetic life, during that "winter and summer till old age began." Here again are all the "stilted boys" of his imagination: Oisin, Niamh, Countess Cathleen, Cuchulain, the various faces of Maud Gonne, "Lion and woman and the Lord knows what." In his insouciant litany of his "masterful images," Yeats admits—a bit sadly, one feels—that it was the images themselves that finally en-chanted him, not "those things that they were emblems of."

In the final stanza, Yeats speculates, as he had so often in his earlier work, about the source of his art. And he discovers it, as we knew he must, in the "mound of refuse," the noisy and filthy thing, that life is. No matter the heights to which imagination may climb, the ladder of vision necessarily stands planted in the mire of earth. And now that the ladder is gone, he "must lie down where all the ladders start, / In the foul rag-and-bone shop of the heart."

Classroom Strategies

If you plan to teach all nine of the poems, you should probably allow at least two—better yet three—days for the purpose. Yeats's poems tend to build on themselves, the meaning and imagery of one informing the meaning and imagery of the next. Hence it is wise to keep them in their chronological order, though it will be difficult not to make *Sailing to Byzantium* and *Byzantium* into a matched pair.

Should you choose to teach a representative sample of the poems, I would recommend *Easter 1916*, *The Second Coming*, *Sailing to Byzan-tium*, *Among School Children*, and *Lapis Lazuli*. The middle three poems here are among his most famous as well as his best, and introduce some of his most persistent poetic concerns, while at the same time providing a kind of unity to your students' experience of his work.

The most difficult immediate problem for students will lie with the "allusive imagery and symbolic structure" (see the headnote, p. 1700) of Yeats's work, especially his best work. Not only are many of his most suggestive images and symbols derived from sources well out of the mainstream of Western thought—occult texts, Irish myths and legends, personal friends and unrequited lovers, and so on—but they are also filtered through Yeats's own fertile imagination and given their applicable meanings *only in the context of Yeats's own work*. That is to say, the only way students can fully understand Yeats's images and symbols is to read more Yeats, though as suggested in the critical discussions above, these can be understood and appreciated without plunging deeply into Yeats's personal mythology. A brief description of his most important mythical structure—Yeats's cyclical model of history—appears on page 1700. Yeats's historical "gyres," or spirals, might best be represented in the following way:

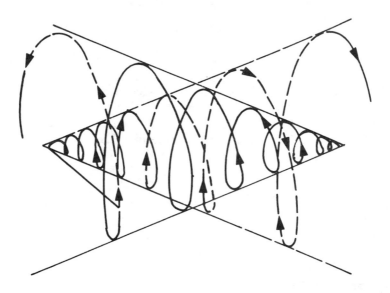

It is important to notice that the gyres interpenetrate, that a new one begins only as its opposite concludes, that each gyre represents a cycle of history covering approximately two thousand years, and that—though one is always dominant—the opposing gyres exist simultaneously, one always implying the other. (His "Byzantium," therefore, exists at that midpoint—A.D. 1000—of the gyres' interpenetration.) Yeats's use of this model, as well as his related use of the "phases of the moon," is personal in the extreme, but can be related to other cyclical versions of history, such as those of Vico, Spengler, and Toynbee.

To get students in the mood to discuss such matters, it is useful to point out that all of us have and maintain versions of history, whether we realize it or not. To mention some of them—the Christian version; the "wave"; evolutionary meliorism, or the idea of progress; the strictly linear (Aldous Huxley's "one damn thing after another")—will always evoke discussion and soften up the doubters. Teachers who wish to know more about Yeats's particular version should consult *A Vision*, surely one of the most arcane and, in some ways, difficult books ever seriously offered by a major writer.

Students will very likely recognize Yeats's technical prowess after they are advised of it, but they are unlikely to respond to it on their own. Yeats himself once said that poems should be "packed in ice or salt," meaning that they should retain traditional, formal structures. Like Frost, he felt that writing poems without formal complications was like playing tennis without a net. It should come as no surprise, then, that each of the poems here is highly structured.

Sailing to Byzantium uses four stanzas of eight lines apiece, and each stanza maintains a rhyme scheme of *a b a b a b c c*. This very tight formal structure is at the same time relaxed in the sense that it is almost invisible; it seems not to intrude at all on the development of the poem's meaning. Each stanza suggests a movement in space, from "that country" to "Byzantium," which corresponds to the speaker's movement of mind, from engagement in nature to engagement in spirit. The first stanza, one of Yeats's most memorable, is as rich and sensual as the natural world it observes. The phrase "Those dying generations" calls up one of the central issues of the poem—that in the world of nature whatever is born must inevitably die, in fact is always in the process of dying. This phrase, and the notion it suggests, is immediately called up again by the "salmon-falls," which salmon climb to spawn and die. The richness of organic life, "fish, flesh, or fowl," reechoes in a phrase summarizing its rich but also limiting processes: "Whatever is begotten, born, and dies." And this is echoed again, with extended meaning, in the last line of the poem. Thus the first stanza describes the "sensual music" of the natural world while it sings the very music it describes.

In *Among School Children* (eight stanzas of eight lines each with a rhyme scheme of *a b a b a b c c*), the formal structure of the poem again reflects its interwoven thoughts and images. The movement of the thought is supported by recurring imagery—the scarecrow, Leda (and swans), history, Plato, "image," and "dream." Thesis and antithesis (age/youth, reality/dream, mortal/immortal) finally achieve synthesis. The assurance of Yeats's formal structure gives a certain credence to the assurance of the poem's final resolution.

Topics for Discussion

1. In what ways is *When You Are Old* like *Sailing to Byzantium*?
   [See "Backgrounds," *When You Are Old*.]
2. What is Yeats's attitude toward the Easter Rebellion of 1916 and the people who were involved in it? Are his feelings mixed? How do we know?
   [See "Backgrounds," *Easter 1916*.]
3. How do the images in stanza three of *Easter 1916* relate to the poem as a whole?

[See "Backgrounds," *Easter 1916*, third paragraph.]

4. How does the second stanza of *The Second Coming* answer the first stanza?

[See "Background," *The Second Coming*.]

5. What are gyres? What have they to do with Yeats's idea of history? How are they used in the poem? Does Yeats seem to think that the coming era will be better or worse than the last? How do we know?

[See "Backgrounds," *The Second Coming*, and the third and fourth paragraphs of "Classroom Strategies."]

6. What is going on in the first stanza of *Leda and the Swan*? How long does it take to realize that Yeats is alluding to a classical myth? What use does he make of that myth? What do the last two lines mean, and why is the beak finally "indifferent"?

[See "Backgrounds," *Leda and the Swan*.]

7. What is the crucial difference between "that" country and Byzantium? Why does the speaker wish to sail to Byzantium in *Sailing to Byzantium*? What does he want to do once there?

[See "Backgrounds," *Sailing to Byzantium*.]

8. Through what details does Yeats conjure up the natural world in the first stanza of *Sailing to Byzantium*? Why these details? What are his feelings about the world of "sensual music" that he renounces? From what evidence in the poem do we infer these feelings?

[See "Backgrounds," *Sailing to Byzantium*, and the seventh paragraph of "Classroom Strategies."]

9. How are Keats's *Ode on a Grecian Urn* and *Ode to a Nightingale* similar to *Sailing to Byzantium*?

[Both contrast the sensual, temporal world with a world of immortality and timelessness. Both use a bird as a symbol of that immortality.]

10. What is Yeats's point in *Among School Children*? How are the images worshipped by "nuns and mothers" similar? What other poems by Yeats help us to understand this one?

[See "Backgrounds," *Among School Children*, as well as the last two paragraphs of "Classroom Strategies." *Leda and the Swan*, *Sailing to Byzantium*, *Byzantium*, and *The Circus Animals' Desertion* can all be usefully related to *Among School Children*.]

11. How does *Byzantium* answer *Sailing to Byzantium*?

[See "Backgrounds," *Byzantium*.]

12. What would Yeats's answer be to those who want him to write poems about present-day concerns? What does Yeats mean by "gaiety" in *Lapis Lazuli*? Does this poem reveal that Yeats does not take the possibility of war seriously?

[See "Backgrounds," *Lapis Lazuli*.]

13. In what ways is *The Circus Animals' Desertion* a review of Yeats's poetic career? Where does it locate the source of art?

[See "Backgrounds," *The Circus Animals' Desertion*.]

14. What are the major thematic concerns in Yeats's work? Is he consistent in the positions he takes on matters that concern him? Where can apparent contradictions be found? Is he ambivalent about many of these matters? Should Yeats be consistent or certain?

Comparative Perspective

Admitting that art can be vulnerable to time, Yeats notes that Callimachus's renowned classical sculptures have not survived. As proof that nevertheless art endures, he cites instead a small Chinese carving in *Lapis Lazuli*, marveling at the skill with which the carver made a virtue of every flaw in the stone. How do you react to this juxtaposition of Western and Asian art? How would you compare Tanizaki's comments on Western art later in this volume with Yeats's characterization of the small but charming effects he admires in the carving?

[This is perhaps a delicate matter to pursue, but the issue of aesthetic cultural stereotyping may be broached at this juncture and developed at length if *In Praise of Shadows* or *Notebook of a Return to the Native Land* is to be studied later in the semester.]

See also comparisons suggested to *The Night Chant* and to the poems of Victor Hugo, Walt Whitman, and Rainer Maria Rilke.

Further Reading

See also the reading suggestions in the anthology, p. 1702.

Archibald, Douglas. *Yeats*. 1983. An overall study, but especially interesting on Yeats's work with regard to politics and public life.

Bloom, Harold. *Yeats*. 1970. Yeats's achievement discussed and judged in the context of the Romantic tradition, especially the work of Blake and Shelley.

Diggory, Terence. *Yeats and American Poetry*. 1983. The impact of individual poems on the "tradition of myself" in American poetry. Poets discussed include Eliot, Stevens, Tate, Ransom, Warren, MacLeish, Roethke, and Robert Lowell.

Donoghue, Denis. *William Butler Yeats*. 1988, © 1971. A fluent, generalized thematic discussion of Yeats's relationship to European Romanticism, exploring ideas of self, imagination, will, action, symbol, history, world, vision, and self-transformation.

Ellmann, Richard. *Yeats: The Man and the Masks*. 1948; 1978. A very fine, short critical biography.

Finneran, Richard J. *Editing Yeats's Poems: A Reconsideration*. 1990. A scholarly companion to Finneran's 1989 revised edition of Yeats's *The Poems*, containing new material.

Henn, T. R. *The Lonely Tower*. 1950. A thorough and influential study of all of Yeats's work.

Kinahan, Frank. *Yeats, Folklore, and Occultism: Contexts of the Early World and Thought*. 1988.

Longenbach, James. *Stone Cottage: Pound, Yeats, and Modernism*. 1988. Situates Yeats inside the modernist movement.

Lynch, David. *Yeats: The Poetics of the Self*. 1981. A more specialized psychoanalytic study emphasizing the analysis of the self practiced by Heinz Kohut.

Pethica, James, ed. *Yeats's Poetry, Drama, and Prose: A Norton Critical Edition*. 1999. A comprehensive selection of Yeats's major writings spanning his entire career.

Stallworthy, Jon. *Between the Lines: Yeats's Poetry in the Making*. 1963. Displays various drafts of Yeats's work in process.

Stanfield, Paul Scott. *Yeats and Politics in the 1930s*. 1988. Another discussion of Yeats's relation to politics.

Timm, Eitel. *W. B. Yeats: A Century of Criticism*. Translated by Eric Wredenhagen. 1990. A survey of Yeats criticism structured according to early, middle, and late works that describes critical tendencies and approaches and includes debates over specific works.

Zwerdling, Alex. *Yeats and the Heroic Ideal*. 1965. Yeats's vision of heroism and its expression in his poetry.

RUBÉN DARÍO

Backgrounds

In his essay on the poet, Octavio Paz comments: "A name like that is like an expanding horizon: Persia, Judea—" and indeed, true to his *nom de plume*, Rubén (as in the biblical tribe) Darío (for the Persian conqueror Darius), writes with a full command of the classical inheritance of the West even as he champions the indigenous peoples of Latin America who had been ignored—or worse—by the European invaders of their homeland. The poems in the anthology are likely to engage your students, who will find in them the comfort of allusions they will have learned to recognize, the pleasure of sensuous form (even in translation, the musicality and structure of these verses comes through), and the challenge of exploring the new perspectives that Darío brought to this inheritance.

SONATINA

The exquisite fairy tale world evoked by this poem should be easy for your students to describe. Ask them to notice Darío's palette: like a visual artist, he balances the delicate hues associated with the pale Princess and the brilliant colors of the garden and the court. How do the color contrasts suggest why the Princess feels imprisoned? What kind of experience will the joyous knight who rides toward her bring to fulfill her indistinct longings? The title of the poem is worthy of some discussion, as it invites a consideration of the poem's formal properties. Darío has not written a full-blown sonata, with several movements in contrasting modes, but a slighter composition, appropriate for its wan heroine. So melodic and hypnotic is *Sonatina* that it is regularly assigned to young children studying Spanish; it would be helpful to have students who know Spanish read it out loud and comment on the way Darío plays with sound as if he were indeed a musician—which, of course, he is.

Blazon

Here we move from gauzy adolescent daydreams to a world of mature poetry. The poem is a compliment to a lady (the wife of the Costa Rican ambassador to Spain when Darío was in Europe) and the presentation gift is the swan in all its iconographic glory. Following the references from stanza to stanza allows us to see the interweaving of cultures implicit in Darío's name. The classical references—Olympia, the Greek amphora, Leda and her swan—all mingle with the Christian symbolism of Eucharist and Easter lamb. The whiteness of the swan stands for both purity and royalty; witness the *fleur-de-lis* of France and the dreamlike castles of the Bavarian Alps.

The artistry of Leonardo (whose legendary painting of Leda and the Swan, executed in 1504, has been lost, although drawings remain) was apparently important to Darío, who wrote a poem called *Greetings to Leonardo*. The reference here takes us to the Italian Renaissance, even as the reference to Lohengrin points to the heights of German Romanticism. (Darío had seen performances of Wagner's *Lohengrin* and *Parsifal* in Chile; the musicality of his verses has been called Wagnerian, presumably for its use of leitmotivs and the virtually orchestral powers of his sonorities.)

I seek a Form

This is the last of the selections in the anthology from the *Profane Hymns*; like the two preceding poems, it frames aesthetic issues in a luscious diction. Significantly, Darío chooses a sonnet to contain his quest for appropriate form. Full of dreamlike images, the octave shimmers in moonlight, with the white stone of the Venus de Milo and the "bird of the moon," the great white swan. In the sestet, the search for the word that could make the bud blossom into a rose fails, but the mood remains elegant and removed from any harsh reality. You might inform your students that in a letter to a Cuban writer, Darío had expressed "appreciation . . . [for his] loyalty to the Purity of Art in the midst of life's ugliness. There are so many toads and so few swans!" How does that sense of the world's dichotomy inform Darío's poetry?

TO ROOSEVELT

Here Darío raises his voice and shifts his emphasis. The Spanish-American War had led to the occupation of Puerto Rico and the Philippines by United States military forces, and Darío wrote this powerful indictment of American cultural imperialism while he was in Malaga, Spain, in early 1904. His concern was a poet's: "Will so many millions of us be speaking English?" he asked. At the same time, the conclusion of *To Roosevelt* seems to admit that Spanish too was the language of the conqueror. After all, as the poem admits, Moctezuma and Atahualpa, natives of the Americas, were tortured and defeated many centuries before Roosevelt's war.

The diction here is dramatically different from that employed in the *Profane Hymns*. Here is the biblical, oracular side of Darío's chosen name. By invoking the figure of Nimrod, Darío classes American military might with the brutal phase of civilization that led God to make his covenant with Abraham and to choose the children of Israel (among whom was Reuben) to counteract. "Naive" Spanish-speaking America represents Christian piety; Roosevelt becomes the epitome of a complex modern civilization, "cultured and able." The culture, however, is that of an arid science and the multital-ented American president a "Professor of Energy" devoted to the rule of the bullet. Indeed, the poem ends in an implicit threat, for the lion cubs of Spanish-speaking America will have to be eliminated if the North American colossus is to prevail. In its ambivalent, half-admiring density of reference (Walt Whitman and the Statue of Liberty, wealth and vigor all elicit tacit approval), Darío's poem is a harbinger of the postcolonial literature that was to distinguish writing in Spanish and many other languages in the twentieth century—a new form that was just beginning as *To Roosevelt* was written.

LEDA

Swans in general and Leda in particular are themes to which Darío kept returning. As the headnote suggests, comparing this poem with Yeats's *Leda and the Swan* would be a useful exercise for your students. Yeats sets the myth within the context of the Trojan War and looks beyond the event itself, which is communicated with some horror. Darío has no philosophy of history in mind, but aesthetic concerns in *Leda* draw the Spanish poet's attention away from the suffering victim to the bystander Pan, a lubricious demigod but also a musician. The water sings and nature screens the rape in complicity with Zeus, condoning the masculine sensualist "wounded by love." Darío (well known for his many affairs with beautiful women) acknowledges the suffering of the "naked and lovely" woman, but his sympathy is with the swan.

FATALITY

In 1909, Darío wrote his own commentary on this tragic poem:

In "Lo fatal" [*Fatality*], against my deep-rooted religion, and despite myself, a phantasm of desolation and doubt rises like a fearful shadow. Certainly, there has existed in me, from the beginning of my life, a profound preoccupation with the end of existence. . . . I have been filled with anguish when I examined the basis of my beliefs and discovered my faith to be neither solid nor well-founded enough when conflicting ideas have made me waver, and I have felt myself lacking a constant and firm support. I have known the cruelty and idiocies of men. I have been betrayed, repaid with ingratitude, slandered, misinterpreted in my best intentions by the evil-minded, attacked, vilified. And I have smiled sadly. . . .

In this Sophoclean poem, which records a moment of existential crisis, one hears a Shakespearean note as well: "To be, and to know nothing, and to lack a way, / and the dread of having been, and future terrors" seems to paraphrase Hamlet's famous soliloquy. For once, the world of sensual beauty cannot avert the intellect from confronting mortality: "the flesh that tempts us with bunches of cool grapes" can only lead to "the tomb that awaits us with its funeral sprays." There is no color in *Fatality*, only painful thought. For human beings, as opposed to other orders of the natural world, the very ability to think is the source of torment.

Topics for Discussion and Writing

1. Why is the swan a universal symbol of beauty? Discuss some of the values that Darío attaches to it in the poems included here.
2. Show how Darío mixes references to classical and biblical themes and to ancient and contemporary history in his poems.

Comparative Perspectives

1. In the nineteenth and twentieth centuries, poets greatly enlarged the range of themes investigated in the sonnet form. Compare and contrast sonnets by writers like Wordsworth, Keats, Rilke, Yeats, and Darío. How does the fourteen-line structure make it a flexible vehicle for contemplating a lyric subject?
2. Darío revises an old poetic form in *Blazon* by offering the Countess of Peralta a series of aesthetic icons; the medieval blazon more typically catalogues the lady's own charms. Compare Darío's compliment with another brilliant revision of the form, André Breton's *Free Union*. The Surrealist poet writes to his wife: what kinds of imagery does he use to praise her? Discuss the range of associations treasured by Darío and explain how they differ from those conjured up by Breton both in form and content.
3. *To Roosevelt* looks forward to a century of poems attacking the United States and the imperial powers of the West. Compare Darío's strong but nuanced view of Teddy Roosevelt as the epitome of North American culture with poems like Césaire's *Notebook of a Return to the Native Land* or Walcott's *North and South*.

Further Reading

See the reading suggestions in the anthology, p. 1715.

LUIGI PIRANDELLO

Six Characters in Search of an Author

Backgrounds

Pirandello's plays are so important to modern drama as a whole that it is almost impossible to imagine what it would have been like without him. His theoretical concerns—the inability of language to say what one most wants to say; the difficulty a person has in establishing germane communication with another; the variability of personality; the relation of life-illusion to stage-illusion; the relativity of perception to time, place, mood, personality, and even the state of one's digestion—anticipated almost every important development of the modern theater. He is humorous, exasperating, fascinating, profound—a true genius of the theater.

Six Characters is about fictional and dramatic "characters." These differ from human beings in that they are embodiments of feelings, ideas, or overpowering emotions and are trapped in their embodied roles. Unlike human beings, they are also possibly immortal; "whoever has the luck to be born a character," says the Father in *Six Characters*, "can laugh even at death. Because a character will never die" (p. 1731). Thus characters have a life of their own—they live on eternally but only so far developed as their creator has made them. Our six characters, having been abandoned by their author, are so overpowered by emotion that they are compelled to come to the theater and plead with the professional actors (who are rehearsing Pirandello's play *The Rules of the Game*) to reenact their drama. The Father says: "The play is in us: we are the play . . . the passion inside us is driving us on" (p. 1732). The characters have been created but left stranded, with no play or novel to house them; their vitality has no context in which to live. They can reach their completion only as parts of a play.

Discovering a ready-made setting for their "existence," they insist that their tragedy is more important, more urgently in need of expression, than the Pirandello play being rehearsed. The drama of their lives is simple enough, though complicated at the end by the question of what has happened as opposed to what is happening. What has happened takes up almost the entire first act and can be outlined as follows: the Father is a rationalist who married beneath himself. He notices the interest that his secretary takes in his wife, and that it is returned. It is a platonic relationship, but the Father senses their love and sends them off together, though he keeps his young Son with him. The wife obediently leaves with the secretary and they raise three children of their own. The abandoned Son grows up resentful and arrogant; he has been raised away from his father by a wetnurse. The Father keeps up with his wife's new family, even going so far as to watch the Stepdaughter as she comes and goes from school. The secretary eventually takes his family and leaves town. Years pass and the secretary dies. His wife and children, destitute, move back to their original town, but they do not contact the Father. The Mother gets a job with Mme. Pace, a dressmaker who runs a call-girl ring from her shop. Mme. Pace lures the Stepdaughter into her service. The Father patronizes the establishment and unwittingly ends up in the arms of the Stepdaughter, only to be interrupted by the screams of the Mother ("just in time," according to the Father; "almost in time," according to the Stepdaughter). The Father is horrified and reunites the family under his roof. His own Son opposes the reunion, and becomes excessively bitter toward all of them, especially his Mother. There is an explosion of emotions in the house; the Mother agonizes over her Son's bitterness, and the Boy—the wife's middle child by the secretary—despises being what he sees as a charity case.

But this is not all. To this point, we know the history of the family by watching it filled in, piece by piece, by the characters. The inner action now merges with the outer action of the play (Act Three) when the wife's youngest child falls into a garden fountain and drowns, and the Boy, who watches in horror as it happens, draws a revolver and shoots himself. Because this last event takes place after the actors and the Producer (who were rehearsing the Pirandello play) have prepared the scene for the play the characters want to perform, the question of what is "real" and what is "illusion" becomes even more tenuous. The characters "perform" the final acts of their history, but when the shot rings out confusion reigns; the Boy lies on the ground while some of the actors cry, "He's dead!" and others claim, "It's all make-believe. It's a sham!" The Father rejoins: "What do you mean, make-believe? It's real" (pp. 1765–66).

The play deals with various planes of "reality" and does so in such a way as to place the entire notion of reality under suspicion. That the theater is an illusion is not at issue here, although the degree to which the theater is simply unable adequately to reflect reality certainly is. When the actors, who have adopted conventional stage mannerisms, attempt to act out the parts the characters have provided for them, the characters—whose "real" drama is about to be enacted—can hardly recognize themselves; they laugh satirically.

FATHER [*Immediately, unable to restrain himself.*] Oh, no!
[*The* STEPDAUGHTER, *watching the* LEADING ACTOR *enter this way, bursts into laughter.*]
PRODUCER [*Furious.*] Shut up, for God's sake! And don't you dare laugh like that! We're never going to get anywhere at this rate.
STEPDAUGHTER [*Coming to the front.*] I'm sorry, I can't help it! The lady stands exactly where you told her to stand and she never moved. But if it were me and I heard someone say good afternoon to me in that way and with a voice like that I should burst out laughing—so I did.
  (p. 1752)

Pirandello is suggesting the wide gulf that inevitably separates life from its recreation on stage. Robert Brustein has pointed out that when the "Producer transforms the sordid, semi-incestuous happening in the dress shop into a romantic and sentimental love scene between the Leading Man and the Leading Lady . . . the Father understands how the author came to abandon them—in a fit of disgust over the conventional theatre."

But if one of Pirandello's central concerns is the theater's inability to catch reality as it is, an even more central concern is his seemingly paradoxical notion that theater is "truer" than life. He expresses this by contrasting the fixed reality of literary characters with the ever-changing reality of human beings. Fictional characters are "less real," perhaps, "but truer." It is the characters' tragedy that they are fixed within immutable bounds, often in one disastrous moment of their lives, or that, like the Boy and the Little Girl in *Six Characters*, they may have personalities and histories that are barely developed. Still, though they may be frustrated by their ineffective attempts to extend their fixed identities, they do not—like the human beings they imperfectly imitate—have to experience the yet more frustrating attempt to unify the multiple aspects of their personalities. As the Father tells the Producer in the play:

> But [our reality] doesn't change! Do you see? That's the difference! Ours doesn't change, it can't change, it can never be different, never, because it is already determined, like this, for ever, that what's so terrible! We are an eternal reality. That should make you shudder to come near us.
>   (p. 1759)

The Father's argument here is also Pirandello's: human beings—unlike the imaginative creations of human beings—are merely a series of moods, impressions, beliefs, idiosyncrasies, and social masks that can never be fully integrated. The human tragedy—and comedy—is that we keep trying to unify these disparate elements, and are disconsolate at our failure.

Many of the most important of Pirandello's works, including *Six Characters*, were written during the most insecure and troubled period of his life. His wife's insanity began in 1903, after the birth of their third and last child and the loss of the family fortune. Pirandello refused to institutionalize her. She remained at home torturing the family with her insane rages while Pirandello suffered in silence, his wife beating at his door while he wrote. Among other things, she accused him and their daughter of incest, an accusation that so unsettled the daughter that she attempted suicide.

It is not difficult to imagine why artifice held such attraction for him, or why it struck him as being so obviously different from reality. His writing was his only release. Pirandello once wrote to a friend that he would sometimes sit in his study all day "at the service of the characters of my stories who crowd about me, each one wanting to come to life before the others, each one with his particular unhappiness to make public." His "madmen" characters provided a way to shout and revolt at his predicament. *Six Characters* is one of many plays that reveal Pirandello's torment as well as his genuine pleasure in the immortal fixity of his creations, creations that would not cringe at his wife's accusations, and that could strut, immortally undemoralized, out the door and into an eternal future.

Two of the most significant influences on Pirandello were Henri Bergson (1859–1941), with his theory of "psychological" time and his emphasis on the mutability of personality, and Henrik Ibsen, with his grasp of the inner life. More interesting, perhaps, is the degree to which Pirandello himself has touched subsequent dramatists and fiction writers. Only Shakespeare and Ibsen, it has often been said, have been more influential. Anouilh, Sartre, Camus, Beckett, Ionesco, Giraudoux, O'Neill, Pinter, Stoppard, Albee, Wilder, Wesker, and Genet all show Pirandello's influence in one way or another.

Classroom Strategies

Because of the peculiar problems of Six Characters, it may need to consume two class periods and for best effect, should be taught in tandem with other self-reflexive works.

Like the stories of Borges, John Barth, or Robert Coover, Pirandello's play will be a fascinating puzzle to some and a positive headache to others. It will be important to establish the context of Six Characters before discussion of its theoretical implications swamps the class. We have "real" actors putting on a "real" play in a "real" theater, interrupted by "fictional" characters who want to act out their "real" "fictional lives," or to have them acted out by the "real" actors. The melodrama of these characters' lives can, and should, be outlined for the students—perhaps in a handout distributed at the first class. During the first day of discussion, this melodrama—what we have here called the "inner action" of the play—should be established. Since the characters' story is mainly revealed in Act One, you may wish to limit discussion to that act on the first day. Acts Two and Three will provide discussion of the "outer action" of the play, with the theoretical and philosophical implications it raises. Although there are many possible approaches, the central theme of reality and illusion—in part because it is so thematically central to much modern drama—will probably be the most fruitful. The last few paragraphs of "Backgrounds" are intended to suggest some of the most significant theoretical questions raised by Pirandello.

It may be difficult to persuade students of Pirandello's humor, in part because it does not translate very well and in part because students are unlikely to be amused when they are confused. The notion of humor was basic to his writing (he wrote an essay on the subject in which he insists on its importance in comprehending and coping with suffering), and will be basic to students' enjoyment of the play. You should read appropriate passages or, perhaps more effectively, have students take parts and do a reading in class. There is a 52-minute videotape available from Films for the Humanities, a compressed but lively version of the play, which would be extremely useful for students to see, and an excellent 1993 film, starring John Hurt, Tara Fitzgerald, and Susan Fleetwood. Their bravura performances in the leading roles make the miracle of theatrical transformation viscerally intelligible to students with little playgoing experience.

Topics for Discussion and Writing

1. In the original stage directions Pirandello says of the characters:

A tenuous light surrounds them, as if radiating from them—it is the faint breath of their fantastic reality.

In the revised edition he states that in order for the six characters to be distinguished from the actors of the company, the characters should wear semi-masks:

The CHARACTERS should not appear as ghosts, but as created realities, timeless creations of the imagination, and so more real and consistent than the changeable realities of the ACTORS.

Why did Pirandello make this change? What does it have to do with his theory of characters and his notions about human personality? In what ways can a character achieve independence from its author? Is this just a literary notion or does it have some application to everyday life?
[Characters are fixed while human beings are not, and it is human beings who feel cheated and disappointed at their predicament.]

2. In what ways is the play about the problem of illusion and reality? What is "real" in the play? Are there *degrees* of "reality" in *Six Characters*?
[See "Backgrounds" for discussion.]

3. What purpose does the "play-within-the-play" serve? What other plays use this technique?
[A look back at *Hamlet* may be useful here.]

4. What do you make of the end of the play? Is the Boy dead? In what ways is he dead? In what ways is he not *dead*?
[We cannot, perhaps, definitively resolve the question of the Boy's death. We can say that he is dead insofar as the play ends, that he is not dead insofar as the play may be put on again.]

Comparative Perspectives

1. Discuss the contrast between the aggressively "realistic" opening scene, in which the actors are rehearsing a play by one Pirandello and the appearance of the Six Characters in masks and under special lights. Compare the Prologue of *The Peach Blossom Fan*, in

which the Master of Ceremonies and an offstage voice chat about a remarkable play called *The Peach Blossom Fan*, which then begins in earnest. What is the purpose of calling attention like this to the fact that theatrical performance takes place in a constructed world? How might this device remind the members of the audience of ways in which their own lives are also full of acting and the playing of roles?

2. The Father speaks of the "disaster" that comes upon characters who have been created and then abandoned by their creator. How might one link this situation to the modern fear that God is dead? Discuss the resemblances between the Father's anguish and the disastrous experience of Gregor Samsa, whose progenitors abandon him to the junk room that his room becomes, or to Tennyson in *In Memoriam*, seeking reassurance that God "will not leave us in the dust." In what ways does the limbo in which the Six Characters exist become a metaphor for the existential anxiety so typical of twentieth-century art?

See also comparisons suggested to *Child's Play*, Goethe's *Faust*, *Hedda Gabler*, *The Peach Blossom Fan*, *Śakuntalā*, *The Sultan's Dilemma*.

Further Reading

See also the reading suggestions in the anthology, p. 1725.

Bishop, Thomas. *Pirandello and French Theater*. 1960. Contains a helpful chapter, "Ideas in Pirandello's Theater."

Brustein, Robert. *The Theatre of Revolt*. 1964. An illuminating and cogent discussion of the play.

Giudice, Gaspare. *Pirandello: A Biography*. Translated by Alastair Hamilton. 1975. A good, short biography.

Lorch, Jennifer. "The 1925 Text of 'Sei Personnaggi in Cerca d'Autore' and Pitoëff's Production of 1925." *Yearbook of the British Pirandello Society* 2, 1982, pp. 32–47. Gives a detailed discussion of Pitoëff's innovative production of *Six Characters* and its impact on later versions of the play (see Introduction).

Oliver, Roger. *Dreams of Passion: The Theatre of Luigi Pirandello*. 1979. Discusses *Six Characters* and four other plays, as well as Pirandello's aesthetics.

Stone, Jennifer. *Pirandello's Naked Prompt: The Structures of Repetition in Modernism*. 1959. Discusses Pirandello's plays in relation to modernism and especially cubo-futurism.

Vittorini, Domenico. *The Drama of Luigi Pirandello*. 1957. A thorough study, first published in 1935, that Pirandello approved.

MARCEL PROUST

Remembrance of Things Past

Backgrounds

In the eyes of many, twentieth-century writing after 1913 is merely a footnote to Marcel Proust. It was Proust's massive novel, *Remembrance of Things Past*, which gave literary definition to the concept of "human time"—a subjective or *bodily* experience of living in time that would represent human existence far more accurately than the "clock" time of exterior, scientific measurement. Proust shows his narrator, Marcel, carefully building a picture of his "whole" self out of layers of buried memory. Each glimpse of an earlier "Marcel" brings with it a forgotten world of experience and makes clear the emotional and intellectual links between past and present identity. The detailed description of sense perceptions (the smell of a book or stairway, the taste of a small cake and tea) becomes a key to uncovering a past that is actually a series of layers creating the present. Proust's ability to convince us of the reality of these experiences derives in large part from his use of concrete details—details that follow a stream of psychological association and seem to espouse the rhythms of the remembering consciousness itself. Both the richly remembered scenes and the example of the narrator's associative memory have provided a compelling example for later writers, themselves haunted by the question of knowing the self and the difficulty of representing it in language. The extraordinarily complex architecture of this multivolume novel, and its complex symmetry of themes and metaphors, has also proved a fruitful example for modern novelists who emphasize organization by themes or mental associations rather than by linear or chronological construction. While the appreciation of Proust's aesthetic constructions will take more than one reading, students usually feel— often to their surprise—a strong identification with his description of sensuous memory, and with the search for the past as a way of giving meaning to the present.

The title *Overture*, introducing a book whose title translates literally as "In Search of Lost Time," sets the tone for a chapter that examines the meaning of memory itself. Marcel's process of associative memory is at stake, from the beginning where he talks about the state of half-consciousness and blurred perceptions when he is going to sleep, to the end where he describes the successful recall of his childhood world. Marcel is attempting to "gradually piece together the original components of my ego" (p. 1773), and he finds that the memory of physical sensations is an indispensable part of this process. His dreams and confused memories are shaped by the physical position of his limbs in bed; later on, it will be the taste of madeleine soaked in tea that calls up a world the conscious mind has forgotten. "My body . . . faithful [guardian] of a past which my mind should never have forgotten . . . " allows the narrator to recapture scenes, events, and emotions that were otherwise lost to consciousness.

After the introduction, in which the older narrator recalls (among other things) his childhood experience of going to sleep, we move into the years at Combray when Marcel's bedtime hours were dominated by his Mamma's goodnight kiss. The child Marcel appears as a sensitive, highly nervous boy whose devotion to his mother is coupled with a lively imagination and the need for reassurance and familiar surroundings: he is disturbed by the way the slide-projected story of Golo and Geneviève de Brabant becomes superimposed on the appearance of his familiar bedroom, and confused by the way Golo's cloak or face seems to share the reality of down-to-earth objects like the doorknob.

The initial description of the narrator's ambivalent state of consciousness now moves to a series of embedded stories that center on themes of love and loss: Marcel's anxious wait for Mamma's kiss, and Swann's similar anxiety during his earlier love for Odette (a piece of information known to the older Marcel, and alluded to here as he narrates events in full perspective). The narrative center of these tales is the dinner party from which Marcel is sent to bed without his accustomed goodnight kiss—a dinner in which Proust's famous capacity for character sketches and social satire emerges especially strongly in the portraits of the two sisters, Flora and Celine, and their inability to thank Swann directly for his present of a case of Asti wine. Throughout the evening, Marcel undergoes alternating hope and despair as he appeals to his mother through a message carried by Françoise, is humiliated when she refuses to respond, decides to stay up for her no matter what the cost, and is unexpectedly allowed her company for the night when his indulgent father recognizes the child's real misery. The *Overture*, however, is not merely a story of Marcel's successful attempt to obtain his goodnight kiss. The sequence of memories also culminates in Marcel's first realization that his mother is excusing him as a "nervous" child, not truly responsible for his actions and psychologically flawed. This realization, which is accompanied by feelings of guilt at having thus "traced a first wrinkle upon her soul" (p. 1797) but also by Marcel's determination to enjoy the evening's unrepeatable indulgence to the hilt, forms a climax after which there is a sudden break, and the narrator concludes with a meditation on the role of memory.

The picture of Proust that remains in the mind is of an extraordinarily sensitive aesthete and intellectual who lived most of his adult years shut up in a heated, cork-lined room in Paris because he suffered from asthma. The disease that attacked him at the age of nine sharply limited his activities; nonetheless, he was able to transform personal experience—seaside vacations at Cabourg, country visits to Illiers and Auteuil, a year's military service at Orleans, participation in Parisian salon society, protests during the Dreyfus affair, and his relationship with Albert Agostinelli—into a complex panorama of Parisian society around the turn of the century.

Many readers like to compare Proust and the philosopher Henri Bergson, author of the influential *Essay on the Immediate Data of Consciousness* (1889). Bergson stressed the importance of "duration," or lived time, as the direct intuition of consciousness—to be valued over the sterile mathematics of measurable "clock time." While the comparison is often illuminating because of the similarity between Proust's and Bergson's rejection of positivist explanations of human experience, it remains a comparison rather than a causal link.

Classroom Strategies

Your students will enjoy Proust more if you devote two class periods to the *Overture*—one discussing the psychological drama of Marcel's going to bed, another examining the famous Proustian style that calls up buried memories. Since Proust is traditionally associated with the project of recapturing forgotten layers of memory, we recommend using this aspect as an opening wedge. Here there are two easy approaches: examining a short but significant passage as a "laboratory sample," and asking students to think about the processes of memory—their own and those described at the beginning of the book.

You may find it useful to start with the last sentence, and read aloud the famous description of the Japanese flowers that are only crumpled bits of paper until they expand in water and become a miniature landscape. Some students may have seen these flowers, and those who have not can still appreciate the gradual unfolding of the description as the bits of paper "become wet, stretch and twist and take on colour and distinctive shape, become flowers or houses or people . . ." (p. 1803). You may then wish to read back into the preceding page and take up the episode of the madeleine, and its contrast between the "memory of the intellect" that preserves "nothing of the past itself" (p. 1801) and the memory of the senses—"taste and smell alone" (p. 1803) that enables one to call up buried worlds.

Another possibility is to examine the description of consciousness and memory at the beginning, asking students to compare their own experiences with the narrator's account, and pointing out the use of this relaxed or open consciousness to link different stages of life: "I had drifted back to an earlier stage in my life . . . only the most rudimentary sense of existence . . . (I) would gradually piece together the original components of my ego" (p. 1773). Once you have established the role of involuntary (bodily, sensuous) memory in calling up past experience, you are ready to describe the rest of that experience: Marcel's adoration of his mother, his misery as he ascends the staircase, his alternate hope and despair as he waits for her kiss, and the rest.

A number of passages lend themselves well to discussion: the magic lantern, the dinner party, the sending of the letter via Françoise, Marcel's mixed feelings as his father tells his mother to stay with the boy, the descriptions of the grandmother (her love of the outdoors, her relationship to the great-aunt, her choice of books).

The chief difficulty that students encounter is the length of the sentences and paragraphs. Perhaps they should be reassured that the long sentences are not a quirk of translation but an integral part of Proust's style—a style that consciously sets out to imitate the rhythms of a mind caught up in its many memories. Encourage them to read fast and to read aloud. They should not stop and wonder about each image and allusion (on first reading, at least), but read quickly through the sentences and paragraphs to get the drift of the whole. Once they realize, for example, that the first two pages are a series of associations by a mind drifting in and out of sleep, they will be more comfortable about the shifting, digressive pattern of the prose. Only then should each image be taken up for what it contributes to the whole picture.

A second difficulty may come with Proust's habit of embedding stories within stories. Students may be confused by what seems constant digression from the topic, and they should be encouraged to read quickly through to the end of the passage where the disgression finally makes thematic sense. You may wish to meet the problem head-on by examining the embedding or associative technique with the class. Two useful examples come in the passage where Marcel's anguish is compared with that of Swann's unhappy passion for Odette (which then becomes a generalized description of unrequited love in Parisian society), and the description of the grandmother's character in the midst of a scene in which Marcel's mother reads him a book (pp. 1797ff.).

Topics for Discussion and Writing

1. What are the two kinds of memory, according to Proust, and how do they work?

    [The "voluntary" or intellectual memory and the "involuntary," spontaneous memory associated with the senses. See the first and second paragraphs of "Backgrounds."]

2. In what sense is Marcel a "nervous" child? How does his account of the evening illustrate this quality? Will he outgrow it?

    [See the third and fourth paragraphs of "Backgrounds." "Nervousness" in this sense is the quality of being high-strung and overimaginative. It appears in Marcel's sensitivity to colors and smells and in his anxiety over the ambivalence of reality and fantasy in the magic-lantern picture on his wall, as well as in his anxious dependence on his mother. The adult Marcel—our narrator—seems equally sensitive to sense perceptions and the nuances of memory.]

3. Comment on Proust's use of digression.

    [See the fifth and sixth paragraphs of "Classroom Strategies." Digression is not only a technique of the associative memory, but also an excellent way to introduce short sketches of intrinsic interest that add to our knowledge of characters or situations.]

4. From what point of view is the story told?

    [See the third paragraph of "Backgrounds." Proust blends the

still-naive experiences of the younger Marcel with the informed perspective of the older Marcel who is narrating the novel.]
5. Are there any comic elements in the story?

[See the fourth paragraph of "Backgrounds." In addition to the almost caricatural pictures of the two sisters, students may note the
constant frustration of any conversational thread, and the way the
grandfather is thwarted in his desire for gossip.]
6. Compare Proust's associative technique with that of other writers
known for use of the "stream of consciousness."

[In this anthology, the selections by Woolf and Joyce provide examples.]

Comparative Perspectives

1. In the years of his youth, according to Marcel, middle-class people
of the older generation took "almost a Hindu view of society, which
they held to consist of sharply defined castes." What errors do Marcel's great-aunts in particular fall into because of their rigid sense of
class distinctions? Compare Proust's attitude toward social rank
with that of other authors whose work you have read this term. Why
have so many writers been preoccupied by the different manners
and attitudes with which it is associated? How important do you
think social background really is?

[If appropriate, start with Voltaire's witty dissection of Cunégonde's brother in *Candide*, or Dorine's acid comments on the social
background of Tartuffe. Other good candidates include *The Queen
of Spades*, *Hedda Gabler*, *The Cherry Orchard*, and the Indian short
stories, where caste is still caste, most dramatically in Mahasweta
Devi's *Breast-Giver*.]
2. Toward the end of the *Overture*, surprised by his father's unexpected
kindness, Marcel likens him to "Abraham in the engraving after
Benozzo Gozzoli." Explain the application of the biblical story of
Abraham, Isaac, and Sarah to the events here recalled, and comment on Proust's reason for introducing it through an involuntary
visual memory. Compare the very different allusions to the sacrifice
of Isaac in *Things Fall Apart*.

[This admittedly tangential link between two novels central to
their respective cultures can lead to a discussion of the flexible uses
to which tradition may be put.]

Further Reading

See also the reading suggestions in the anthology, p. 1770.

Bloom, Harold, ed. *Marcel Proust*. 1987. More general, with some overlap, than Bloom's collection, *Marcel Proust's* Remembrance of Things
Past; it contains some useful essays.

Bowie, Malcom. *Freud, Proust, and Lacan: Theory as Fiction.* 1987. Discusses and compares the theories of knowledge underlying each writer's work.

Deleuze, Gilles. *Proust and Signs.* Translated by Richard Howard. 1972. Post-structural, semiotic criticism of the novel as a "machine producing signs of different orders."

Ellison, David R. *The Reading of Proust.* 1984. A more specialized theoretical discussion of the narrative self, questions of readability and influence, and Ruskin's influence on Proust.

Fowlie, Wallace. *A Reading of Proust.* 1963; reprinted 1975. A useful guide.

Painter, George. *Marcel Proust: A Biography.* 1959; new edition, 1989. A readable, anecdotal biography.

Poulet, Georges. *Proustian Space.* Translated by Elliot Coleman. 1977. A study of Proust's fictional world-vision in terms of time and space.

Proust, Marcel. "On Reading." Translated and edited by Jean Autret and William Burford. 1971. Proust's views on the psychological experience of reading.

———. *Selected Letters.* Translated by Ralph Manheim; edited by Philip Kolb. 1983.

Zurbrugg, Nicholas. *Beckett and Proust.* 1988. An interesting source of comparative topics for discussion, despite a rather mechanical organization of ideas.

HIGUCHI ICHIYŌ

Child's Play

Backgrounds and Classroom Strategies

Child's Play is a popular story with students. They like its energy and they like its subject: the growing pains of becoming an adult. However, they sometimes miss the irony and, surprisingly, the message that there is no innocence in the world of adults.

A thematic approach will therefore be productive. Ask students how adults are depicted in the story, and begin by looking at the ninth section ("Thus have I heard it spoken . . . "). In its tone, economy, and rhythm this is a masterpiece of characterization. Ichiyō depicts the gross appetites of the parents of her main male protagonist, Nobu, and contrasts them with his youthful, sensitive ways. Nobu's father is a Buddhist priest whose tastes are far too corporeal for a man of the cloth. At every turn, the narrator's ironic stance exposes the gap between the stated and the signified, so that we see before us a man whose greed and hunger undercut any claim to moral authority. Not only is he a fish-eater (which, as note 8, p. 1824, explains, would still have had a taint of the proscribed), but he goes in for broiled eel—"the big oily ones"—a dish associated with enhancing sexual prowess. Even if Nobu is too young to be conscious of the connotation, he knows there is something fleshly about the food, and that is why he is embarrassed to be sent out for it.

And so when the section opens by interrupting the priest's intoning of the sutras to tell us that "smoke rose from fish broiling in the kitchen" and "in the cemetery diapers had been seen drying over tombstones (p. 1824)," both the priest's lax character and the narrator's irony are instantly established. To signal that the irony is intended and will sustain itself, Ichiyō adds, "Nothing wrong here in the eyes of the Order, perhaps; those who fancied their clerics above worldly desires, though, found the doings at Ryūge Temple rather too earthly for their tastes."

Ask students what kind of image they suppose was standard for a Buddhist priest, and then what sort of physical picture emerges in this instance. The answer to the first question is that, until the modern period, the Buddhist clergy in all but one sect subjected themselves to even more austerities than their Catholic counterparts. They were celibate, vegetarian, and in general led lives of denial and asceticism. What we see here, however, is a man with a nice round belly from years of good eating, so well fed that his complexion glows "like burnished copper." Even his eyebrows, bushy and grizzled, seem intemperate. And in place of the quietude of devout meditation, we hear raucous laughter so loud that the "excess could have toppled Buddha from the altar" (p. 1824).

It is true that in the history of Japanese Buddhism temples were landowners and even moneylenders. Nonetheless, Nobu's father takes the entrepreneurial to new heights, having established his comely daughter in a tea shop where she can trade on her looks, and sending his wife out as a huckster on festival days. Ichiyō adds:

> But his holiness was the busy one. Loans to collect, the shop to oversee, funerals to arrange, not to mention all the sermons every month. When he wasn't flipping through accounts, he was going through the sutras. If things didn't let up, he'd wear himself out, he would sigh as he dragged his flowered cushion onto the veranda, where he fanned himself, half-naked, and enjoyed his nightly hooch.

That enumeration of his responsibilities has them in about the right order: religion takes a back seat to business. Referring to this greedy, gin-swilling gourmand as "his holiness" is almost too rich in irony.

It is certainly too much for Nobu. The self-conscious introverted youth is dismissed by his father as a dour naif. Poor Nobu—suffering already from shyness and the raw tortures of adolescence—finds himself completely isolated, even in his own family.

There was nothing in his upbringing to make Nobu such a gloomy child. He had the same parents as Ohana. They were part of the same cozy, self-contained family. Yet he was the quiet one. Even when he did speak, his opinions were never taken seriously. His father's schemes, his mother's conduct, his sister's education—to Nobu everything they did was a travesty. He had resigned himself to knowing that they would never listen. How unfair it was. His friends found him contrary and perverse, but in fact he was a weakling. If anyone maligned him in the slightest, he would run for the shelter of his room. He was a coward utterly lacking in the courage to defend himself. At school they called him a brain; his family's station was not lowly. No one knew how weak he really was. More than one of his friends considered Nobu something of a cold fish.

This last paragraph of the section is wrenching because we know that things will never get better. The whole point of the story is that they will get worse. Look at the other adults in *Child's Play*: Sangorō's father, "Groveling Tetsu" (tenth section); Shōta's skinflint grandmother (fourth and sixth sections); Midori's parents, who sell their daughters into prostitution (third and seventh sections). Only the woman at the paper shop, the implied narrator, appears unblemished—but then she seems somehow marginal, on the fringes of the community. In growing up, these children are leaving innocence behind them. They will become the same adults their parents are. In the process, they will lose their friends, their ideals, their security. They will slip into a mode of moral compromise. They will learn to become opportunists. If they retain a shred of sensitivity, they will be utterly alone.

Topics for Writing and Discussion

1. Discuss local color in *Child's Play*. Why does the author set the story near the red-light district? Why does she spend almost the entire first chapter describing the customs of the neighborhood?

2. *Child's Play* is both playful and elegiac. Give examples of both moods and discuss whether you think Ichiyō is successful in balancing them.

3. The plight of the outsider, cut off from his or her surroundings by moral scruples, has been a recurring theme in modern Japanese literature. How is it dealt with here? Who is the outsider?

4. Discuss the operation of symbolism in this story.

5. What is your understanding of the changes in Midori's character, and what motivates them?

6. Analyze the narrative tone, including the place of irony.

7. Although children occupy center stage in this story, adults have an important role to play. Discuss that role and its thematic significance.

8. According to the headnote, one of the remarkable aspects of *Child's Play* is that it never patronizes its young subjects. Do you agree? If so, give examples of how this is accomplished.

Comparative Perspectives

1. Compare the point of view and the range of protagonists in Ichiyō's treatment of childhood with, as appropriate, Wordsworth's *Ode on Intimations of Immortality* (philosophical abstractions), Proust's *Remembrance of Things Past* (intensity of first-person, essentially autobiographical focus), or Munro's *Walker Brothers Cowboy* (rueful consciousness of others' inner lives). Discuss whether Ichiyō's account of the collective growing pains of four young people, may reflect views of community and selfhood different from those of the self-conscious, art-fixated Western authors listed above.

2. *Child's Play* demonstrates that "there are times when daughters are more valuable than sons." What times are those? Compare the experience of, as appropriate, Sor Juana, Hedda Gabler, Freud's "Dora," the Stepdaughter in Pirandello's *Six Characters in Search of an Author*, Grete Samsa in Kafka's *Metamorphosis*, or Liu su in *Love in a Fallen City*.

Further Reading

See the reading suggestions in the anthology, pp. 1806–07.

THOMAS MANN

Death in Venice

Backgrounds

Thomas Mann often used the figure of the artist in society as a vehicle for examining cultural crisis, and *Death in Venice*—describing the fall of writer Gustave von Aschenbach—is a complex tracery of political, artistic, psychological, and ethical issues. Published two years before the beginning of World War I, portraying a cosmopolitan Europe that is already collapsing under the weight of economic and political rivalries, the novella describes in realistic detail a particular moment of European society. Yet this historical aspect fades into the background before larger themes: the role of art, the role of the artist, and the balance that human beings must preserve between reason and impulse, discipline and spontaneity, conscious and unconscious life. Mann himself noted that an important turn in his work had occurred with the writing of *Death in Venice*. Works after this period regularly incorporate a dual meaning-structure, a system of entwined references that endow characters and events with both psychological and broad historical or mythic significance.

Mann wrote *Death in Venice* in 1911, shortly after he had taken a brief vacation in Venice to recover from nervous exhaustion. Correspondence with his older brother, the already established Heinrich Mann, shows that he was frustrated at being unable to finish a series of planned works, much less the masterwork of which he felt himself capable. Obsessed by his image of the artist's tormented but prophetic role, struggling to define his own lofty concept of art over and against contemporary stress on innovative form, Mann produced the story of a writer many of whose anxieties are close to his own. Yet Aschenbach is not a hero, and while Mann sympathizes with his predicament, he also criticizes him for several kinds of betrayal.

The Gustave von Aschenbach who is introduced at the beginning has earned his respected position (and the honorific *von* before his name) by hard labor at his craft, by a search for dignified expression, and by the repudiation of uncontrollable depths—that is, the fatal knowledge and profound emotions of the "abyss." (Compare Baudelaire's *The Voyage*, in which the true artist plunges "to the bottom of the abyss" to find something new.) Mann's ironic description of the way this "master of his trade" has fought his way to a conventional, uninspired style in a quest for perfection prepares the ground for a shattering reversal. Challenged by the sight of a pugnacious traveler outside the mortuary chapel, the exhausted Aschenbach starts thinking about a foreign vacation to reinvigorate his creative powers. He imagines escaping from the monotonous, confining routine of his European life and sees that escape in Eastern landscapes with lush swampland, tigers, and bamboo thickets. Venice, finally, is the place to which he retreats: "half fairy tale and half tourist trap" (p. 1876), combining East and West, past and present, art and commerce, all with an odor of corruption—an "impossible destination, forbidden to him" that "enchanted him, relaxed his will, made him happy" (pp. 1864, 1866).

The happiness that Aschenbach encounters in Venice is accompanied by a complete disorientation that begins on the initial ferryboat ride, when he feels "that things were starting to take a turn away from the ordinary, as if a dreamy estrangement, a bizarre distortion of the world were setting in" (p. 1850). He beholds with horror a garishly painted and bewigged old man among a crowd of young excursionists—yet he himself will later undergo a similar cosmetic rejuvenation when he pursues the Polish youth Tadzio.

Aschenbach's relationship with Tadzio fuses two main themes: erotic love and the artist's worship of beauty. He is drawn to the youth's classic beauty, which recalls the perfection of Greek sculpture and especially busts of Eros, the god of love. Gradually, as Aschenbach watches Tadzio on the beach and in the dining room, the references to godly beauty increase; so, too, does his attraction, which he now defines as a "paternal kindness . . . the attachment that someone who produces beauty at the cost of intellectual self-sacrifice feels toward someone who naturally possesses beauty" (p. 1861). Only when the writer is accidentally prevented from leaving Venice does he realize that he is in love with Tadzio. It is worth noting that Mann does not criticize Aschenbach's love itself but rather his response to it. The writer accepts doom for himself and for others rather than separation from Tadzio and a return to a life of humdrum toil; even after discovering that plague has stricken the city (and that the authorities are concealing it), he does not warn Tadzio's mother. His obsession with Tadzio also leads him to define a despairing view of art—and a personal submission—that precisely negates the Platonic position he appears to adopt.

References to Greek culture permeate *Death in Venice*, partly because they express Aschenbach's traditional German admiration for Greek art and philosophy and partly because the web of allusions supports the development of other themes in the novella. Eros (the Roman Cupid), god of love; Hermes, patron of travelers and "soul-summoner"; Semele, who perished in the flames of her lover Zeus, king of the gods; Helios, fiery god of the sun that "turns our attention from intellectual to sensuous matters" (p. 1868); the boatman Charon, who ferries souls to the world of the dead; Narcissus, who drowned in his own reflected image; Hyacinthus, doomed object of Apollo's love; Dionysus, the "stranger god" whose orgiastic revels drive out reason; Eos; Pan; Poseidon; and others all have symbolic roles in Aschenbach's journey towards death. The allusions become more significant toward the end, as he seeks to understand his attachment to Tadzio in terms of Greek homosexual love (the *pederasty* that is literally the love of an older man for a youth, generally with implications of leading the youth toward adulthood) and especially Platonic views of art.

Aschenbach's discourse on love and the artist, in which he imagines himself speaking to the young Phaedrus of the Platonic dialogue, derives from several sources. The most obvious reference is clearly the *Phaedrus*, in which Socrates counters a speech on love by the sophist Lusias with two of his own. Another well-known Socratic speech on love occurs in Plato's *Symposium*—a much-annotated copy of which was found in Mann's library after his death. The philosopher Arthur Schopenhauer, whose discussion of the artist's nature greatly interested Mann, linked both dialogues with Plutarch's *Erotikos* (*Dialogue on Love*) in the forty-fourth chapter of his *The World as Will and Representation*. Despite apparent similarities, however, there are sharp differences between Socrates' address to Phaedrus and that of Aschenbach. Where one talks about the artist, the other talks about knowing the beautiful. Aschenbach focuses on the necessary "self-debauchery" of the artist, who is doomed by a knowledge and understanding that sympathizes with the abyss through intoxication with sensuous beauty (see p. 1888). Socrates, conversely, interprets physical beauty as a sign of the ideal and describes how love of a beautiful youth can draw the mind to contemplate concepts of ideal beauty and moral perfection. Aschenbach's despairing conclusion in *Death in Venice* is that the world of the senses will inevitably lead the artist astray. It is a conclusion prefigured by his earlier dream of a Dionysian orgy, when his last effort of will is insufficient to protect him against the onslaught of the Stranger-God, "the enemy of the self-controlled and dignified intellect" (p. 1885). From then on, he is enslaved by the world of earthly experience, submitting to the barber in an attempt to make himself more attractive and pursuing Tadzio wherever he goes. Aschenbach dies in his beach chair with the ambiguous image of Tadzio-

Hermes before his eyes, trying vainly to follow the "pale and charming psychagogue" (p. 1890) into the immensity before him but sinking back into mortality and death.

Mann employs a series of leitmotifs and oppositions to organize thematic patterns throughout *Death in Venice*. There are smaller recurrent themes, such as the leitmotif in Tadzio's "twilight-gray eyes," the reddish hair and snub nose that belong to an obscurely menacing character, or Aschenbach's repeated eating of strawberries that, shortly before the plague strikes him down, are "overripe and soft." More prominent themes include the figure of a traveler-guide, beginning with the traveler by the mortuary and continuing in the ship's purser, the Charonlike gondolier, and the various references to Hermes. There are also individual passages that echo each other, such as the description of the painted old man on the ferry and Aschenbach's transformation by the barber; or the writer's return to the little square where he rests again on the edge of a fountain; or his early "affinity for the undivided, the immeasurable" echoed in the ending scene, in which he recognizes Tadzio-Hermes beckoning him into "an immensity full of promise" (p. 1890). Yet the broadest and most persistent contrast is that of Apollo and Dionysus as opposed rational and irrational forces—a famous opposition that Mann would have known from Friedrich Nietzsche's *Birth of Tragedy*. Reinforcing this contrast is a second thematics, of East and West, in which the West is associated with order and discipline, with bourgeois habits and dignity, and with Apollo as the god of light and rationality. Conversely, the "stranger-god" Dionysus comes from the East (as is clear in Euripides' play *The Bacchae*, which Aschenbach's dream recalls). Death also comes from the East; the plague afflicting Venice is an Asiatic cholera originating in the Ganges delta (pp. 1882–83). *Death in Venice* is a highly structured composition that demonstrates Mann's desire to create, in prose, a "musical complex of associations."

Classroom Strategies

Death in Venice can be taught in two or three days, depending on how thoroughly you wish to explore its thematic patterns. It is probably easiest to begin by considering Aschenbach the man—his dedication to his work, his ambition, the willpower and self-control (and repression) that have come to dominate his life—before moving into questions of literary style and its implied moral choices. Once students have a good picture of what Aschenbach has become, and what he has sacrificed to reach that pinnacle, you can ask them if they have any predictions about what will happen to him, and whether his "moral resoluteness" indeed signifies "a reduction, a moral simplification of the world and of the human soul and therefore also a growing potential for what is evil, forbidden, and morally unacceptable" (p. 1847). Get them to talk about their ideas of art (e.g., its moral and social function, the importance of form, the relative importance of spontaneity and discipline) and you will be launched into the second strand: Aschenbach the writer, who has devoted his life to a certain concept of beauty.

It may be interesting at this point to broaden the discussion with references to other works in the volume, comparing different styles and concepts of art (see the introductions to "Realism, Naturalism, Symbolism in Europe" and "The Modern World" for discussions of realism, naturalism, symbolism, modernism, and postmodernism). At this level, it is not merely Aschenbach's concept of art that is relevant, but Mann's own practice: his psychological realism, use of myth, almost musical organization of themes and motifs, *and* critical distance from Aschenbach himself.

The stages of Aschenbach's infatuation with Tadzio are relatively clear. What remains to be explored is the degree of self-knowledge (or delusion) the writer attains, and also the secondary mythic plane of interpretation created by classical allusions having to do with human nature and the search for absolutes. Students may find the picture of Aschenbach repellent, but they should recognize that he constantly attempts to deal with fundamental issues. They may find the opposition of Dionysus and Apollo oversimplified, too (one hopes); this in itself is another subject for discussion.

Since Mann is such a complex writer, it will be helpful to focus on certain key passages as microcosms of intertwining themes. The most obvious possibilities are the Dionysian dream and the final "Phaedrus" soliloquy. The latter may be difficult for students to follow without guidance, not only for its philosophical distinctions but also because they may be expecting a more direct description of Aschenbach's death from plague at that point. There are, in addition, many useful passages or symbolic scenes throughout the novella, some of which are mentioned in the last paragraph of "Backgrounds."

Topics for Discussion

1. Why is it important that Aschenbach see Tadzio first as an incarnation of ancient Greek sculpture?
2. How does Mann bring out the *successive* stages of Aschenbach's infatuation with Tadzio?
3. Do you agree that the artistic form has "two faces," that it is "moral and amoral at the same time" (p. 1847)? How does this concept determine Aschenbach's career as a writer?
4. What are several reasons for Aschenbach's unwillingness to tell Tadzio's mother about the plague?
5. Describe and contrast the two "Phaedrus" passages (p. 1869, 1888).
6. Discuss the importance of mythological references for an understanding of *Death in Venice*.
7. How does Mann's description of Venice make it an appropriate place for Aschenbach's downfall and death?

8. Where else have you seen the concept of "abyss" used in reference to art?

[See "Backgrounds," third paragraph.]

9. Describe the combination of psychological realism, historical detail, and symbolic allusions in *Death in Venice*.

10. How does the contrast of East and West, Dionysus and Apollo, underlie issues in *Death in Venice*?

11. Discuss the theme of the traveler throughout *Death in Venice*; in what sense does Hermes preside over Aschenbach's journey into infatuation and death?

Comparative Perspectives

1. Aschenbach's illicit sexual desire is linked to the onset of plague. How does Mann's treatment of this connection compare with Boccaccio's introduction to the *Decameron* or Chaucer's *The Pardoner's Tale*?

[After the stark realism of Boccaccio's opening pages, the plague recedes from view. If feasible, a comparison between Mann's novella and *The Pardoner's Tale* would allow for some surprising parallels. In each case, the protagonists search for death. The Pardoner, who may without knowing it be expressing his own anxieties in his depiction of the doomed rioters, must confront his own confused sexuality in the Host's angry expostulation in the epilogue. Aschenbach undergoes a similar confrontation, couched in modern rather than medieval terms.]

2. Contrast the imagery and tone of the vision that seizes Aschenbach with "hallucinatory force" in chapter 1 of *Death in Venice* with the imagery and tone of the scene described in stanza VII of Wallace Stevens's *Sunday Morning* or of the section of *Notebook of a Return to a Native Land* in which Césaire celebrates the "Tepid dawn of ancestral heats and fears." How does each writer challenge the modern Western pose of separation from such antiquated, distant ritual practices?

Further Reading

See also the reading suggestions in the anthology, p. 1839.

Bloom, Harold, ed. *Thomas Mann*. 1986. Twenty-one essays on themes, texts, and techniques in a range of Mann's work, including two pieces on *Death in Venice*.

Ezergailis, Inta M., ed. *Critical Essays on Thomas Mann*. 1988. Fourteen essays on a range of broadly focused topics.

Hatfield, Henry. *From* The Magic Mountain: *Mann's Later Masterpieces*. 1979.

Jonas, Ilsedore B. *Thomas Mann in Italy*. Trans. Betty Crouse. 1979. A discussion of Mann's use of Italy and his depiction of Italians throughout his work.

Lesser, Esther H. *Thomas Mann's Short Fiction: An Intellectual Biography*. 1989. The stories read individually and as part of Mann's intellectual development.

Lukács, Georg. *Essays on Thomas Mann*. Trans. Stanley Mitchell. 1965; reprinted 1979. Important essays by a major twentieth-century critic.

McWilliams, James R. *Brother Artist: A Psychological Study of Thomas Mann's Fiction*. 1983. Especially relevant to the theme of the artist in Mann's work.

RAINER MARIA RILKE

Backgrounds

Rilke's exceptional lyric gifts make him the most prominent German poet of our century. His work, *The Duino Elegies* especially, speaks to the modern sense of a fragmented universe with "all that was once relation so loosely fluttering hither and thither in space"—a universe in which communion constantly gives way to solitude. Yet Rilke's vision is redemptive as well as tragic. Sharing with Joyce a highly developed sense of the artist's mission, he sees art as a way to combat chaos by lending shape to the invisible, and to transform suffering and unify life and death in the context of eternity.

ARCHAIC TORSO OF APOLLO

Apollo is just one of the statues in Rilke's poetic museum, but as god of poetry and light he assumes pride of place. *Archaic Torso of Apollo* displays for the first time the typical Rilkean sonnet form: *abba abab cddc cdcd eef gfg*. The volume it begins is dedicated to Auguste Rodin, and in fact it can be said that the poem aspires to the condition of the statue it describes—seeking heft, palpability, the power to confront its observer directly and irresistibly (its second-person form of address at the close has this effect) and to move him out of complacency: "You must change your life." The maimed statue embodies both the incompleteness of human art and its transcendence in spite of all: "We cannot know his legendary head / with eyes like ripening fruit. And yet his torso / is still suffused with brilliance from inside, like a lamp."

Light, Apollo's attribute and imperium, endows this stone with being. The glow of life, of animal warmth and sexual heat, irradiates the poem, shining from breast bone and shoulder, from the center of procreation (at the poem's physical center), its exuberance finally breaking out "from all the borders of itself" and spilling beyond form. Such is the role of art, creating a beauty whose impact reaches beyond its own formal boundaries.

In connection with *Archaic Torso of Apollo* it is important to remember Rilke's long association with Rodin, who served as patron, employer, friend, and exalted example. Rodin's enormous industry and initiative provided a model that Rilke—plagued as he was with an impossible double hunger for solitude and love, barraged by the shapes of his fevered imagination—could not hope to match. The sculptor, according to one of the characters in Rilke's story "The Last" (not in the anthology), enjoys special mastery:

> A song, a picture you notice, a poem you like—all have their significance and value, the same, I think, for him who first creates it as for him who re-creates it. The sculptor creates his statues only for himself: but . . . he also creates space for his own statue in the world. . . . Art raised man to God.

Rilke's poem can be said to re-create the sculptor's creation. To it belongs the joy of renewing the triumph of light (form, life) over chaos.

Other influences on Rilke include Poe (particularly his linkage of terror and beauty, as seen in the opening of the first elegy) and Baudelaire (see the headnote, pp. 1890–93 in the anthology). Rilke also admired the lyrics of Hölderlin and translated Valéry. Impressionist painting—Cézanne's work in particular—affected his way of seeing as well as his energies. Of Cézanne he wrote:

> I notice by the way Cézanne keeps me busy now how very different I have grown. I am on the road to becoming a worker, on a long road perhaps and probably only at the first milestone. . . . This consuming of love in anonymous work, which gives rise to such pure things, probably no one has succeeded in doing so completely as old Cézanne.

THE PANTHER

This poem, written in Paris in 1902, provides an excellent example of the "new kind of literary and artistic inspiration" (see headnote, p. 1891) that Rilke gained there. A favorite of Rilke's among his own works, *The Panther* demonstrates the power of intense visualization through which he found the means to objectify his art and go beyond the cultivation of sensation that typifies the Romantic lyric. Beginning with the panther's exhausted gaze, so concentrated on the bars that entrap him, the poem seems to merge the observer and the panther as they enter into each other's visual fields. Deeply empathizing with the pacing animal, the poet makes him into an image of ritual. Circular movement becomes a dance, an art form that takes its energy from the animal's "mighty will" even in paralysis.

The poem makes of this double seeing an engagement between audience and object when "the curtain of the pupils / lifts, quietly." As if in the theater, the observer glimpses the reality behind the façade and the panther, like an actor, seems to absorb the observer's interest. So profound is this exchange that the image of the human being outside the bars "enters in"; and, removed from the scene, readers may feel that they merge spiritually with the powerful, entrapped animal, whose situation can be interpreted as a metaphor for our own lives.

THE SWAN

Ask your students to count the number of lines in *The Swan*, which is a truncated sonnet: the opening sequence of the poem, as in any sonnet, introduces a proposition that will lead to some kind of turnaround in the concluding sestet. At the start, where we expect quatrains, the last lines drop off and Rilke leaves us with two tercets instead, as if to mimic the swan's uncompleted labors. The swan out of water, the proverbial ugly duckling, is like the poet who has not yet achieved his vision. The release into the medium in which he flourishes is, tellingly, likened to giving in to death.

The fully articulated sestet embodies the poet's mastery of form as it records the swan's majestic command of his true element. A rich comparison can be drawn to an image of swans in *The Half of Life* by Hölderlin, whose work Rilke admired. Found on p. 836 of volume E of the anthology, that poem links the "gracious" movement of the swans to youth and life; Rilke's swan represents "the essential unity of life and death" discussed in the headnote (p. 1892), a state of quiet triumph rather than loss.

SPANISH DANCER

Titles are important in Rilke's work. One needs the title of this brilliant poem to make sense of the daring introductory image, which, much like the extended similes of ancient epic, takes on a life of its own before it reveals its relevance to the subject at hand. Note the footnote explaining the derivation of the term *flamenco* from the verb meaning to flame and have your students work through stages in the life of the flame described here as a metaphor for the creative work the dancer is engaged in—and perhaps for human life itself. How does Rilke's use of imagery here resemble that of the Surrealists? How many meanings can we ascribe to the act of extinguishing with which the dancer concludes her performance?

Classroom Strategies

It would be helpful to start with *Archaic Torso of Apollo*, not only because it is first chronologically but because its relative compactness and formality make it most manageable. This poem can serve as a convenient introduction to Rilke's conceptions of the artist and of art. Students who are able to read the original German text (p. 1894) should be encouraged to read aloud to the class and to comment on any effects (rhythmic, verbal, imagistic) that they find specific to the German original.

Topics for Discussion and Writing

1. What is the role of light in *Archaic Torso of Apollo*?
   [See "Backgrounds" for further discussion.]
2. Why does Rilke choose to emphasize the sexuality of the statue?
   [In a letter to Kappus, Rilke says that "artistic experience lies so

incredibly close to that of sex, to its pain and its ecstasy, that the two manifestations are indeed but different forms of one and the same yearning and delight." See "Backgrounds" for further discussion.]

3. What does *Archaic Torso of Apollo* say (and demonstrate) about the role of art?

   [See "Backgrounds" for discussion.]

4. How should we interpret the famous command at the end of *Archaic Torso of Apollo*?

5. If you read German, you may wish to read aloud or compare passages from the translation with the original poem (p. 1894). Students may also be encouraged to try reading the original text on their own and to comment on the way the translation has or has not succeeded in grasping the German original. Some of the bolder ones may attempt their own translations, which will bring them closer to the text at the same time that it induces a healthy respect for the difficulties of translation.

Comparative Perspectives

1. Compare the high expectations of art that inform Rilke's celebration of the "archaic torso of Apollo" with García Lorca's tragic recollection of the "marble torso" of Ignacio Sánchez Mejías. If Rilke's poem is by definition an Apollonian view of art, does García Lorca's horror at the blood of the fallen toreador offer a Dionysian view? Where would Yeats's meditation, in *Lapis Lazuli*, on the art that finds beauty in flawed stone fit in this continuum?

2. *The Spanish Dancer*, *The Swan*, and *The Panther* make meaning out of the special way that their subjects move; in *Archaic Torso of Apollo*, the statue seems full of motion. Compare and contrast the qualities attributed to each and consider Rilke's sensitivity to motion with the predilections shown by other poets for other sensory details.

   [Note, for instance, the significance of stasis in Wordsworth's lyrics and of light in Dickinson's verse, and try to define the writers' different poetic sensibilities in terms of these attractions.]

3. Compare and contrast the terrifying visions of created life embodied by Rilke's panther and Blake's tyger.

4. Swans, like nightingales, are interpreted by poets in a number of ways. Comment on the different uses of these two avian metaphors for poetry, and compare Rilke's vision of the almost mystical swan with that of Hölderlin in *The Half of Life*, the figure of the bird imagined in Yeats's *Leda and the Swan*, or Darío's reiterated visions of the swan in the anthology.

   [Nightingales, from Ovid onward, seem to be associated with the idea that expressive beauty comes from a tragic wound. By contrast, despite the popular image of "the dying swan," the poets cited above develop ideas about the grace and the power of the swan.]

Further Reading

See also the reading suggestions in the anthology, p. 1893.

Lehnert, Herbert. "Alienation and Transformation: Rilke's Poem 'Der Schwan.' " In *Rilke: The Alchemy of Alienation*, eds. Frank Baron, Ernst S. Dick, and Warren R. Maurer. 1980. An excellent discussion of *The Swan*, alluded to in the comments above.

Mandel, Siegfried. *Rainer Maria Rilke: The Poetic Instinct*. 1965. A useful introduction to Rilke's work.

Mason, Eudo C. *Rilke, Europe, and the English-Speaking World*. 1961. Mason discusses both Rilke's view of the English-speaking world and its views of him.

Shaw, Priscilla W. *Rilke, Valery, and Yeats: The Domain of the Self*. 1964. Shaw discusses the relationship between self and world in Rilke, with particular reference to his view of the body and the world of objects.

WALLACE STEVENS

Backgrounds

Stevens is a poet of the drama of the mind, caught in its "double fate of self and world." He can be difficult, arcane, and even precious, but at his best he is elegant and resonant. He makes use of images, parables, anecdotes, lectures, dialogues, monologues, aphorisms, and so on, to promote the life of the imagination. As Northrop Frye has said: "His poetic vision is informed by a metaphysic; his metaphysic is informed by a theory of knowledge; his theory of knowledge is informed by a poetic vision." But always in Stevens we come back finally to "poetry itself, the naked poem." It is the poet's responsibility, as he sees it, to renew a world under the constant threat of imaginative impoverishment, and he fulfills that responsibility in poems of extraordinary range and speculative brilliance.

SUNDAY MORNING

Sunday Morning is Stevens's most famous poem and perhaps his best. It is a poem of contrasts—the female subject of the poem confronts two opposing views of paradise, neither of which is immediately satisfying: the earthly paradise, which she finds decadent and empty, and the mythological, religious paradise, to which she cannot commit herself. The woman, in whose highly civilized rooms we find ourselves, is too sensitive to content herself with the decadent pursuit of earthly pleasure and too sophisticated to accept the religious idea of heaven. Her meditation on the matter, Stevens tells us, "is anybody's meditation."

The first stanza contrasts a luxuriously sensual natural world with "silent Palestine." But the objects of the sensual world—"late [c]offee," "pungent oranges," the "green freedom of a cockatoo"—"[s]eem things in some procession of the dead." She is unable, emotionally, to commit herself to the physical or to the spiritual. The second stanza develops the questions raised in the first. What does the natural world offer that can be "cherished like the thought of heaven"? The answer is that "Divinity must live within herself," through her experiences, and the memory of those experiences, in the natural world.

But if the earth—the natural world, the world of physicality—is to be, as the third stanza puts it, "all of paradise that we shall know," she must then wonder what is to happen when the world of nature passes, to remain alive only in memory and desire. The sky may seem "friendlier" if paradise is invested in earth, but she still feels "the need of some imperishable bliss."

The sixth stanza reconsiders the traditional view of paradise in a way that recalls Keats's *Ode on a Grecian Urn*. In this view, paradise is static, a "cold pastoral" (Keats's term), where rivers "seek for seas / They never find." It lacks beauty because it lacks death, and "Death is the mother of Beauty." Without death there can be no passionate pleasure.

In the last stanza, the woman relinquishes her desire for the paradise promised by religion; she finds that "The tomb in Palestine / . . . is the grave of Jesus, where he lay"—nothing more. We, however, must continue to live in "an old chaos of the sun," where death makes for beauty and sponsors the only paradise available to us, a place where:

> in the isolation of the sky,
> At evening, casual flocks of pigeons make
> Ambiguous undulations as they sink.
> Downward to darkness, on extended wings.

> (lines 117–120)

PETER QUINCE AT THE CLAVIER

Stevens wrote *Peter Quince at the Clavier* during the same period in which he wrote *Sunday Morning*, and both poems evidence concern with the cyclical process of life and death in the natural world. In this poem, however, physical beauty becomes immortal not only through the memories of the living, but also by its transubstantiation into art. "Music is feeling," not mere sound, and it is music that in the first stanza brings the speaker to desire. The speaker compares his awakened desire for an unidentified woman of his memories to the "strain / Waked in the elders by Susanna," a "strain" that made their thin blood "Pulse pizzicati of Hosanna." The second and third stanzas recreate the biblical story in a way reminiscent of paintings by Rembrandt and Tintoretto.

The last stanza recognizes that the passionate throbbing brought on by such beauty must, inevitably, die: evenings, gardens, seasons, maidens—all die. "Susanna's music touched the bawdy strings / Of those white elders; but, escaping, / Left only Death's ironic scraping." But in memory, as in art, Susanna's music—her beauty and the desire it awakens—is immortal, and "makes a constant sacrament of praise."

ANECDOTE OF THE JAR

Anecdote of the Jar can be, and has been, interpreted in two mutually exclusive ways. One view of the poem finds that the jar represents the imposition of form by intellect, and that its introduction onto the hill destroys the "natural beauty" of the surrounding wilderness. Another view, perhaps less dedicatedly Romantic, notes that the wilderness is "slovenly" at first, but that the jar—which has form and is therefore representative of art—takes "dominion" and establishes order where before there was merely "wild" chaos. This second interpretation of the poem has the advantage of having a basis in Stevens's aesthetics—his insistence that art, because it has form, produces order and beauty in a world where flux and chaos otherwise predominate.

Both interpretations, however, assume that Stevens means to evaluate the wilderness, as well as the jar, either positively or negatively. Through the introduction of form, however undistinguished ("The jar was round upon the ground" hardly seems to suggest a particularly significant form), our perception of nature is inevitably altered.

THE EMPEROR OF ICE-CREAM

With the cold-blooded assurance of the child, the speaker of *The Emperor of Ice-Cream* registers the meanness and finality of death, and urges the reader to recognize that "The only emperor is the emperor of ice-cream." The ministrations over the dead become a kind of ugly carnival; the attempt at decorum is exploded by the recognition that it is, after all, merely empty formality—a pathetically inadequate illusion unappreciated by the one for whom it is being performed. Death is final, the hands that once embroidered fantails are still, the horny feet are cold. Death should be the end of the charade: "Let be be finale of seem."

THE IDEA OF ORDER AT KEY WEST

The Idea of Order at Key West illustrates the ascendancy of the poetic mind over the chaos and strength of the natural world, represented here by the sea. As in *Peter Quince*, music is related to the desire to impose order upon the world. In *The Idea of Order*, however, the female singer creates the world in which she exists through her song and, more important, changes the world significantly for those who hear her. Nature attains a higher order of reality when it is organized by the artist, who speaks to and for her audience.

In the first line of the poem, it is apparent that the singer has powers greater than those of the sea. The sea possesses no ordering imagination; it moves and makes sounds, but they are movements and sounds without direction. It is the woman's song—not the "grinding water and the gasping wind"—that commands the speaker's attention. In comparison, the sea becomes a mere backdrop, a "place by which she walked to sing." The fourth stanza further emphasizes the idea that nature, without the creative imagination to order it, is beautiful but meaningless. Her voice gathers together not only the sea, but all that the sea apportions.

> It was her voice that made
> The sky acutest at its vanishing.
> She measured to the hour its solitude.
> She was the single artificer of the world
> In which she sang. And when she sang, the sea,
> Whatever self it had, became the self
> That was her song, for she was the maker.
>
> (lines 34–40)

Because the singer is the "single artificer" of her world, the sea becomes, both for the singer and for her audience, her particular vision of the sea. There is no "world for her / Except the one she sang, and singing, made."

When the singing ends, the speaker finds the world arranged, organized gorgeous, in such a way as to be beyond the understanding of the aesthetician ("Ramon Fernandez"). The last stanza is a coda that pays tribute to the "rage for order" and to the inspirational quality of the art such a rage produces.

THE MAN ON THE DUMP

Once again, the central interest in *The Man on the Dump* is art—specifically the creation of poetry, and the problems of the poet as he imaginatively creates his world. "The dump is full / Of images," but these images are mainly exhausted, timeworn, obsolete, laughable; the poet sits atop the mound of the tradition's imagery and takes inventory—sifts, mocks, rejects. If the moon is going to come up at all in a poem, it will have to come up "as a moon" (not as a stale image of the moon) in an "empty sky" (a sky swept clean of all the trash the poet must reject). The process of rejection, the sloughing off of the trite, purifies and renews the imagination, and the poet is able to begin a new cycle of creativity. He beats "an old tin can" in order to create a fresh version of reality: "One beats and beats for that which one believes."

The poem ends with a series of questions that ask, essentially, why the poet has rejected certain images and why he continues to sit among them. The answer, if there is one, appears in the last line: the discarded images that now "torture the ear" were once fresh, once a direct apprehension of reality, the truth—the thing itself. It is still the poet's job of work to find or refind the image that offers the thing itself—"The the"—and reorder the world into beauty.

Classroom Strategies

The six poems can be covered in two class periods. The most difficult aspects of Stevens's aesthetics and poetics are contained in *Sunday Morn-*

ing and *Peter Quince*, so it would be useful to concentrate on these two during the first class meeting. If you can spend only one class period on the work, *Sunday Morning* and *The Idea of Order at Key West* are the most representative, significant, and telling poems to discuss. *The Emperor of Ice-Cream,* however, is perhaps the most accessible.

Stevens's work offers both concrete imagery and abstract speculation, and the abstractions will cause most of the difficulty for students, who will want a definite meaning assigned to lines such as "Let be be finale of seem," phrases such as "The the," the images such as the jar in Tennessee. The more elusive these things are (and are intended to be) the more the student will insist on an assigned meaning—and decide, in its absence, that the poems are "not worth the trouble." This tendency will be exacerbated because of Stevens's continual use of art itself as his central subject. Some students find this fascinating, but many tend to doubt that it is an important enough subject for a poem, finding in it a certain self-absorption and an illusory self-importance. A discussion of literary language—tending as it does toward multiple meanings, as opposed to scientific language, which tends toward a sole meaning—can be useful in this context. So can the fact that Stevens worked as a successful insurance executive. Students find this duly surprising, but admirable. If a hardheaded businessman thinks poetry is so important, then . . .

Students might be directed to notice that quite often in Stevens's work a line in the poem presents a truth demonstrated by the poem as a whole. In *Peter Quince*, for instance, the speaker's claim that "Music is feeling, then, not sound" is confirmed by the poetic music that envelops each of the poem's characters. The coarse elders, for instance, are characterized by coarse poetic rhythms and images ("A cymbal crashed, / And roaring horns") or else pizzicati plucking intended to suggest their glandular excitement. The simpering Byzantine maids come and go with "a noise like tambourines." Susanna's music, however, is as "clear and warm" as she is.

In *The Idea of Order at Key West*, visual and auditory imagery fortify Stevens's notion that the natural world, however beautiful, remains meaningless without the ordering power of the artistic imagination. The sea can only cry, grind, and gasp until it is transformed by the woman's song. Once again, the poem demonstrates its own claims.

Topics for Discussion and Writing

1. What kinds of contrasts can be found in *Sunday Morning*? What purpose do they serve? How does Stevens exploit the traditional activities of a Sunday morning?

    [See "Backgrounds" for discussion.]

2. How does music function in *Peter Quince at the Clavier*? What is meant by "Music is feeling, then, not sound"? How is this thought demonstrated in the poem as a whole?

    [See "Backgrounds" and the third paragraph of "Classroom Strategies."]

3. What aesthetic position is suggested by *Anecdote of the Jar*? What other poems suggest a similar aesthetic position?
4. Both *The Emperor of Ice-Cream* and *Sunday Morning* concern themselves with death. How do they differ? Have they any similarities?
5. How does *The Idea of Order at Key West* illustrate the artist's ability to order the natural world? Do you believe any of this? Can you name any examples of art that has caused us to reperceive the nature of the world? What did Oscar Wilde mean when he said that "Nature imitates art"?
6. Why does the poet in *The Man on the Dump* need to discard used-up images? Why do they become exhausted? Why would Stevens insist that it is important to discover new, fresh images?
7. Why does Stevens make such use of contrast? Locate and discuss examples of contrasting images, voices, settings, and points of view (see especially *The Idea of Order at Key West*, *Sunday Morning*, *Anecdote of the Jar*, and *The Man on the Dump*).
8. Discuss Stevens's idea of the poet as creator of reality in light of Baudelaire (see especially *One O'clock in the Morning*, *Windows*, *A Carcass*, *Her Hair*, and *Correspondences*).

Comparative Perspectives

1. Compare the contemplation, in *Anecdote of the Jar*, of a simple object and its impact on its surroundings with similar meditations in Tanizaki's *In Praise of Shadows*. To what extent do Stevens and Tanizaki introduce humor into their aesthetic considerations?

   [See the headnote to Tanizaki (especially the material concerning Japanese toilets) and the deadpan humor of Stevens's last line in this poem.]

2. Although Stevens gives *The Idea of Order at Key West* a contemporary setting, the poem conjures up images of the ancient Greek world, and virtually any historical period or cultural tradition offers examples of the "rage for order" described here. Reviewing the reading you have done this semester, discuss a text in which you see the human mind struggling to make sense of experience. Do you find art as successful at imposing order as this High Modernist vision implies it to be?

   [Works that challenge that assumption may be proposed for students to analyze. Good choices from the modern period include Freud's frustrated efforts to make sense of Dora's experience, Kafka's *The Metamorphosis*, or Beckett's *Endgame*. If appropriate, consider selections from package 1 as well, including, but not limited to Job, the *Chuang Tzu*, the essays of Montaigne or *Hamlet*.]

Further Reading

See also the reading suggestions in the anthology, p. 1899.

Bloom, Harold. *Wallace Stevens: The Poems of Our Climate*. 1977. Intriguing commentary on his work, noting the "anxiety of influence" caused by similarities to Emerson, Whitman, Tennyson, Shelley, and others.

Doggett, Frank. *Stevens's Poetry of Thought.* 1966. Clear, straightforward discussions of the poems.

Morse, Samuel French. *Wallace Stevens: Poetry as Life.* 1970. An extended critical biography.

Pearce, Roy Harvey, and J. Hillis Miller, eds. *The Act of the Mind: Essays on the Poetry of Wallace Stevens.* 1965. The essays by Morse, Pearce, Vendler, and Macksey are particularly useful.

Stevens, Wallace. *Letters of Wallace Stevens.* Edited by Holly Stevens. 1966. Interesting letters that also contain observations on Stevens's own poetry.

———. *The Necessary Angel: Essays on Reality and the Imagination.* Edited by Holly Stevens. 1951. Stevens's own discussions of poetry and poetics.

Vendler, Helen H. *On Extended Wings: Wallace Stevens' Longer Poems.* 1969. A discussion of poetic and critical attitudes for and against Romantic norms.

PREMCHAND (DHANPAT RAI SHRIVASTAVA)

The Road to Salvation

Backgrounds and Classroom Strategies

In the short-story genre, Premchand's contribution to modern Hindi literature is similar to Rabindranath Tagore's contribution to Bengali literature. When Premchand began writing, modern Urdu prose fiction barely existed, and Hindi had only recently emerged as a literary language, replacing Braj, the major literary dialect of earlier north Indian literature. Premchand was the first major Hindi author to write short stories, that is, short realistic fiction with social themes, as opposed to narratives in the older tale and romance genres such as the Urdu *dāstān* and *qissā.*

Class discussion of *The Road to Salvation* should include some discussion of the writer's engagement with the great national and international ideological currents of his time. For Premchand writing was an integral aspect of social and political activism, and fiction was both a critique of social ills and an instrument of social change. The author was directly involved in India's struggle for freedom from British rule and particularly in Mahatma Gandhi's anticolonial movement for social change. In 1921 Premchand resigned his government job, mainly in response to Gandhi's call for noncooperation with the British regime; in 1930 his wife, Shivrani Devi, an activist in the Indian National Congress, went to jail for her antigovernment work. Premchand's life and writings were also deeply influenced by socialist and Marxist ideals, which he affirmed in his alliance with the Progressive Writers' movement in Europe and India toward the end of his life. The Marxist and socialist sources of Premchand's focus on the Indian peasant as the representative of the oppressed classes are readily apparent. Yet we must bear in mind that the author was also inspired by Mahatma Gandhi's arguments for social justice as a precondition for liberation from colonial rule, and for a village-based social and economic system as the desirable model for India. While Premchand openly criticizes the exploitation of peasants by landlords and others in *Godan*, his best-known novel, in many of his short stories, as in *The Road to Salvation*, he couches his critique in the form of a portrait of peasant life.

Premchand's brand of social realism cannot be traced to any single literary influence. Although he was greatly influenced by major European (and especially Russian) writers, including Tolstoy, Chekhov, and Galsworthy, his stories reveal a distinctly Indian sensibility and a deep feeling for the realities of life in the north Indian heartland, which he knew firsthand. Born in a village in Uttar Pradesh (then United Provinces), Premchand lived in smaller and larger towns in north India (such as Allahabad, Gorakhpur, and Banaras) during his career as schoolteacher and journalist. He thus was able to portray peasant life, rural society, and rural poverty in an authentic manner to his audience of educated readers—to intellectuals as well as to individuals from the growing middle classes of the towns and cities. Premchand, more than any other writer, has influenced, educated, and raised the consciousnesses of the north Indian elites and middle classes regarding social problems, and has often moved them to action.

Premchand's portrayal of the underclasses, like that of Mulk Raj Anand and other Indian Progressive writers of the 1930s, can often be sentimental, but in the best of his short stories he imaginatively represents the lives of oppressed north Indian peasants and the poor with a devastating clarity of vision. *The Road to Salvation* exemplifies the author's interest in the mechanics as well as the psychology of the exploitation of the underclasses. The moralizing tone of the earlier stories gives way, as in this story, to irony and black humor, and he exposes the folly of the self-delusion of the powerless as pitilessly as he indicts the rich and the powerful. Premchand repeatedly returns to the questions of why the exploitation of the weak persists in Indian society, and why those who are exploited acquiesce to such oppression, sometimes even colluding with their oppressors. The stories do not offer answers. At the end of *The Road to Salvation*, Buddhu and Jhingur learn of the treachery by which each has brought ruin upon the other. Yet the title must be read ironically: this is no road to salvation, no moment of redemptive love or transcendent understanding, just an instance of the resignation of defeated human beings.

Premchand's short stories are notable particularly for the author's adaptation of aspects of the vivid everyday speech of rural north India to modern literary Hindi. While "today his lamp is burning in the skies" is a common idiom, "to take vengeance on a farmer is easier than slicing a banana" is more likely Premchand's coinage; however, both expressions convey the authenticity of living speech. Such colloquial-sounding sentences, at the same time, dovetail with passages displaying a pedigree in classical literature. For instance, when Premchand devotes an entire paragraph to a description of wealth personified as the goddess Lakshmi, the fully worked-out metaphor is an outgrowth of similar tropes in older Indian literature, both in Sanskrit and in the regional languages. Finally, the class will want to know more about the general statements and moral dicta in which the story abounds. You might explain to students that such statements as are found in the opening sentence of the story ("The pride the peasant takes . . .") and in the paragraph on the love of evil (beginning with "It's a mystery why there is as much love among the wicked as malice among the good") are characteristic of Premchand's personal sensibility and style, as well as part of an ancient tradition of didactic writing.

Topics for Discussion and Writing

1. Discuss Premchand's style and voice. Do you find them effective? Discuss the didactic/moralizing aspects of The Road to Salvation, keeping in mind Indian literary conventions and the context of Hindi fiction of the 1920s and '30s.
2. Discuss the story as a sketch of peasant life in north India. What does Premchand want to convey about the village economy and society, and about the peasants' own view of the natural and social orders? How does he accomplish this portrait?
3. Discuss Premchand's portrayal of "tradition," especially as embodied in caste relations and religious ritual, both essential aspects of Hindu society.
4. Discuss the ending of the story. Is it convincing?
5. Compare Premchand's attitude toward the chief characters in his story with those of Mahasweta Devi in Breast-Giver and Tagore in Punishment. Account for the similarities and differences among these authorial stances.

Comparative Perspectives

1. By noting that Jhingur beats Buddhu's "army" of sheep "with the prowess of an epic hero," Premchand's narrator sets the tone for the rest of this story. Describe the ways in which The Road to Salvation blends mock epic, satire, and modern realism, and compare the range of effects with those deployed in another work of mixed genres, Don Quixote, the protagonist of which does battle with another army of sheep.
   [See Part I, chapter 18, of Cervantes's novel.]
2. Like Premchand, in Pedro Páramo Juan Rulfo makes the poverty of agrarian workers painfully clear, but the two writers view their characters in very different ways. Compare the ambitions of the short-

story writer and the novelist. To what extent may cultural differences contribute to the distinctive manner of each writer?

Further Reading

See the reading suggestions in the anthology, p. 1909.

LU XUN (LU HSÜN)

Diary of a Madman

Backgrounds

The polite, excessively formal introduction creates a level of social
falseness that is essential contextualization for reading the diary. The introduction notes that the mad younger brother has been "cured" and is
now awaiting appointment in the Chinese bureaucracy. As the alternative
to madness offered within the text, it confirms some of the paranoid suspicions of the diarist and invites us to find a truth in the young man's
madness. The introduction seems to confirm the diarist's final anticipation that he will be eaten (or, perhaps, become one of the cannibals
himself), and this gives us a strong indication of the metaphorical implications of this cannibalism.

Stories of cannibalism were, in fact, common in China (as in most cultures, the rumors were far more prevalent than was credible evidence of
the practice). As Lu Xun's story suggests, in times of famine families were
rumored to have exchanged babies for food; stories of filial children cutting off pieces of their own flesh to feed hungry parents were common;
and eating the internal organs of a slain enemy was both the ultimate revenge and a means to assimilate the enemy's power. Taken together,
these and the other legends recounted in the diary create a figurative
world in which the young are sacrificed to the old and the individual is
sacrificed to the group. Society grows strong by devouring the young and
the independent. It should be added here that, in reaction against China's
traditional veneration of age, revolutionary China of the 1920s had a virtual cult of youth: young people were supposed to have been purer and
wiser than their elders. Here, of course, Lu Xun is satirizing the traditional view.

If the introduction presents a social world of false politeness, the madman sees beneath its surface to the animal violence that sustains society.
The farmers of Wolf Club Village gang up on a "bad" man, kill him, and
eat him. In the same way Elder Brother approves whenever the madman
writes an essay finding fault with some figure in the past. Beneath the pious lies of traditional morality, the society seeks out any deviation and is
ready to devour such a person to enhance its own collective strength.
Once he realizes this, the madman realizes that he is a potential victim.
The more frightened he becomes, the more he draws the attention of his
brother and the community, until at last he is locked away—to later

emerge, after the completion of the diary, "cured" and a well-behaved, properly assimilated member of society.

Lu Xun places the reader in the position of the community, encouraging us to see the writer as mad. We appreciate the humor as the young man raves to his brother and draws the attention of bystanders, who seem to the young man like cannibals. Lu Xun sustains that "common-sense" perspective, while forcing us into a critique of it.

At the end the young man understands that he lives in a world of cannibals, the end product of a long history of cannibalism, and that his very body has been formed out of a lineage of eating others. He wonders if, unknowingly, he himself did not eat some of his sister's flesh. Cannibalism —and the kind of society for which it is a figure—is more like an infection than a willful choice of evil. Once a person participates in it, it defines the person. The only hope seems to lie in the children, the ones who have not yet tasted human flesh. The implications are that a person is corrupted by participating in a society that "feeds on its young," a society that coerces the young to conform to the values of the group and their elders and punishes independence and deviation.

Upstairs in a Wineshop

Backgrounds

Although the term had not yet been invented when Lu Xun was writing, Lu Xun's work represents "Third World" literature, a literature shaped by the experience of colonialism and the destruction of traditional culture. However grounded in a particular place and time, the work of the European writer often lays implicit claim to universality, just as European nations laid territorial claim to most of the globe. The colonial subject, by contrast, is shaped by the experience of being excluded from the center, with its claims on universality. No matter how much that is universal we may find in Lu Xun, in some essential way he is writing about China and the very particular experience of Chinese civilization. This is all the more remarkable when we reflect that a hundred and fifty years earlier (a brief span in the Chinese sense of history), Chinese writers were writing "universally." They maintained a sense of Chinese ethnicity and knew that China had borders, but Chinese culture was the medium in which they wrote rather than the subject about which they wrote.

Upstairs in a Wineshop is poised between traditional China and modern China. Since China has changed so dramatically since then, students must be reminded that during this period Chinese intellectuals like Lu Xun often despaired that China could ever be changed. These thinkers feared that the country was trapped in permanent inertia.

In *Upstairs in a Wineshop* the narrator's friend explicitly compares his own return to that of bees and flies: "When I was a kid, I used to think that bees and flies were absurd and pathetic. I'd watch the way they'd light someplace, get spooked by something, and then fly away. After making a small circle, they'd always come back again and land just exactly where they had been before" (p. 1932). In fact, the story includes many variations on being trapped in repetition and, after brief dreams of going elsewhere, getting nowhere. Though this theme may be seen as universal, the focus here is on the inertia of Chinese culture at a particular historical moment. Cultural forms that once had meaning, such as filial compliance with a mother's request and tending the grave of a brother, are emptied out; quite literally nothing remains. The narrator's friend goes through the motions and buries an empty coffin in a new location: "This time I had the coffin enclosed in bricks to make a good tight seal" (pp. 1933–34).

The center of the story is the account of the friend's futile effort to make contact with Ah-shun. Shyness and awkwardness destroy all hope of human contact, and a general ineffectualness leads to wasted lives. With Ah-shun dead, the friend will have the velvet flowers delivered to her unworthy sister, Ah-zhao, just so he can tell his mother that she was delighted. The act of kindness becomes as hollow as the reburial—as hollow a ritual as the friend's reversion to teaching Chinese classics rather than Western learning.

Wild Grass

Backgrounds

Written between 1924 and 1926, *Wild Grass* introduces a new, surrealistic note to Lu Xun's oeuvre. These moody prose poems evoke a dark moment in the writer's life. Having quarreled with his brother and sister-in-law, he fell ill. He then took part in a student rebellion at Peking Women's Normal University, where he was teaching. In August 1925, the student leaders of this movement were expelled, and Lu Xun temporarily lost his job at the Ministry of Education.

The Epigraph announces the pattern of cyclical alternation that dominates these pieces: fulfilled/empty, death/life—neither closure nor satisfaction can be sustained. Rather than contemplate a deep river or timeless mountains, the poet sees wild grass, which "drinks in dew and water, sucks in the flesh and blood of long dead corpses" and has no permanence. *Wild Grass*, of course, is a euphemism for *weeds*.

The anthology prints the opening selections, which are short and accessible enough for students to analyze and can profitably be set against other poems in the anthology for comparison. *Autumn Night* moves into an imaginary realm of personified nature: the sky begins to wink lewdly at life on earth, a tiny flower dreaming of "a skinny poet wiping his tears on her last petal" fails to enjoy full bloom, and the date trees, wounded by boys in quest of fruit, reject the optimism of easy cyclical promise. If winter comes, and spring is not far behind, we know that autumn too is on its way.

Thinking these thoughts, the poet begins to hear laughter. In his self-alienation, at first he fails to recognize the source of the sound—it is his own. He leaves the backyard, yawns, and lights a cigarette, moved by the drama of heroic self-annihilation that he comes upon inside as he watches insects throwing themselves against the lampshade.

Topics for Discussion

1. It is hard to read *Diary of a Madman* and not think of films such as *Invasion of the Body-Snatchers*, or numerous others about were-wolves or vampires. In these films a community of ruthless, sometimes animal-like beings seeks to assimilate one or more normal "others" (who are inevitably young). Consider the implications of this almost mythic pattern.

2. Lu Xun gives symbolic prominence to flowers and insects in *Upstairs in a Wineshop* and *Autumn Night*. Discuss the patterns of life and death, persistence and failure, with which he associates them, and comment on the difference between the ways in which Lu Xun's prose fiction and prose poems treat the "real world."

Comparative Perspectives

1. Compare the narrative strategies Lu Xun employs in the effort to reform society with those used by other politically motivated writers, including, as appropriate, Frederick Douglass, Premchand, Aimé Césaire, Kojima Nobuo, Nadine Gordimer, and A. B. Yehoshua.

   [Ask your students to consider the different ways in which direct exhortation, personal memoir, ironic fable, and other tactics may excite moral responses in readers.]

2. Lu Xun was apparently familiar with Swift's *A Modest Proposal*. Compare the way each uses the idea of cannibalism as a satiric indictment of human behavior.

   [Episodes of and references to cannibalism are part of Chinese traditional lore; thus Lu Xun's madman may be paranoid, but his fears are not without foundation. Swift, by contrast, works in metaphor.]

3. Many masterpieces of the modern era try to assess the impact of the past on the present. Discuss Lu Xun's approach to this issue in the madman's references to the account books of Mr. Antiquity, the return to the South in *Upstairs in a Wineshop*, and the missions his mother sends Weifu to fulfill. How would you compare this aproach to the view of the past in T. S. Eliot's *The Waste Land* or in Proust's *Remembrance of Things Past*?

   [Compare the Western modernists' nostalgia for a better time with Lu Xun's portrait of a culture that needs to disentangle itself from a past too powerful to elude.]

4. Compare the personification of the tiny flower in *Autumn Night* and the personification of Heine's lonely pine tree. Do you see any difference between the German Romantic and the modernist Chinese perspectives?

5. Autumn is one of the great poetic themes. Characterize Lu Xun's

treatment of the season in *Autumn Night* and compare, as appropriate, the views of autumn in selections from the *Kokinshū*; Keats's *To Autumn*; Shelley's *Ode to the West Wind*; Hölderlin's *The Half of Life*; Verlaine's *Autumn Song*; Tagore's *Golden Boat* and *I Won't Let You Go*.

Further Reading

See the reading suggestions in the anthology, p. 1920.

Alber, Charles. "Wild Grass, Symmetry and Parallelism in Lu Hsun's Prose Poems," in *Critical Essays on Chinese Literature*. Edited by William H. Nienhauser, Jr. 1976. Pp. 1–29. A good discussion of the dichotomies to be observed in *Autumn Night*.

Hsia, T. A. *The Gate of Darkness: Studies on the Leftist Literary Movement in China*. 1968. Provides a nuanced account of Lu Xun's relationship to the Communist party and the influence of his political associations on his state of mind.

JAMES JOYCE

The Dead

Classroom Strategies and Topics for Discussion

This long short story demonstrates the fullness of vision that a focused episode can take on when described by a master writer. Every detail counts; every reference expands beyond its immediate relevance. While *The Dead* would repay intensive word-by-word scrutiny, you will do better to choose a few key moments to highlight without exhausting your students. Beginning with its title, one useful approach is to examine how *The Dead* simultaneously evokes and embraces opposites: life and death, the present and the past, the individual and the community.

A natural place to start is with the community gathered in the opening section of the story. The Misses Morkans' annual dance is, on the one hand, a ritual celebration, a New Year's revel. On the other hand, the specter of death hovers over the party, and the jollity is in fact rather forced. As several critics have remarked, the aunts' genuine hospitality issues not only from the goodness of their hearts; the party also serves as an advertisement for Mary Jane's music school. Who are the members of the family? Much may be made of the dominance here of the elderly maiden aunts living in a "dark gaunt house." Ask your students why, as the headnote points out, Joyce should have changed the married state of the Misses Morkans' real-life prototypes.

The characters collected here are of course the most prosperous of Dublin's bourgeoisie. This information is provided by the street names in the second paragraph of the story: note that most of Mary Jane's students live in a fashionable part of town. Ask your students how this piece of information subtly contributes to our understanding of the role class plays in *The Dead*: how has the Morkan family changed since the days of Johnny the millhorse? What has happened to the people who still work in the mills? It may be helpful to explain at this point that except for enclaves such as these, Dublin in Joyce's day was an exceedingly poor city that had not participated in Ireland's rising economy: one third of the inhabitants in the central part of the city lived in slums, and only one in five workers had a full-time job.

Early in your discussion, you will also want to sensitize your students to the way the narration incorporates different characters' points of view, moving from the community to the individual. From whose perspective does the opening paragraph show us the world of the Misses Morkan? It is presumably Lily's voice being echoed, with its use of "literally" when "figuratively" would be the more accurate word choice. Critics have pointed also to Joyce's decision to name the caretaker's daughter Lily, a flower with funereal associations; alert your students to the significance of names in Joyce's fiction, most dramatically demonstrated in the final sequence.

Gabriel Conroy, the first man to enter the story, is eagerly awaited by his aunts; the expectations that eagerness may have raised in the reader are somewhat deflated as we observe his difficulty in finding the right tone in which to address Lily and his self-conscious concern that he has offended her. Moreover, he is wearing galoshes: punctilious, nervous, anxious Gabriel hardly provides the anticipated virile masculine presence. (Note his position in his nuclear family; the favored nephew, he is nevertheless the second son of his demanding mother, who gave her children imposing names. Gabriel's elder brother bears the name Constantine, the first Roman emperor to convert to Christianity. Like "Gabriel," to be discussed further below, it sets a high standard for a child.) In fact, none of the men at the annual dance seems particularly prepossessing. Freddy Malins, drunk and self-indulgent, who has failed to button up his fly, looks and acts rather like a big baby, rubbing his eye with his knuckles and giggling before he reaches the punchline of his own story. Likewise, the formidable Mr. Browne has been a trial to the aunts, "laid on here like the gas" (p. 1964) as Aunt Kate complains—again, a whiff of death enters the story.

After the opening glance through Lily's eyes, we see most of the rest of the story through Gabriel's—that is, from the perspective of an individual who lacks the ability to get along easily with others. His insistence on wearing galoshes like everyone "on the continent" (p. 1949), which amuses his wife, takes on new importance in his encounter with Miss Ivors, the champion of Ireland's indigenous Gaelic culture (only Gretta, born in the West of Ireland herself and demeaningly labeled "country cute" by Gabriel's mother, calls this brusque, amused, and well-educated woman by her comfortable, unpretentious name, Molly). It is worth pausing at this point in the story to review the crisis of Irish politics embodied in the conversation between G. C., the author of literary reviews for a conservative paper, and Molly Ivors, who takes him to task for neglecting his own country. Joyce here fastens on issues that still divide compatriots around the globe and that deeply affected his own life. What are the sources of personal authenticity? Must an individual represent a community? Your students will probably have strong feelings about whether or not one should define oneself primarily as a product of race, religion, or national affiliation. What have been the consequences of "identity politics" in the twentieth century? How does the choice of the place to spend one's summer vacation dramatize the conflict between Gabriel and Miss Ivors?

Gabriel finally has the limelight all to himself in his much-prepared-for after-dinner speech. Working through this speech carefully, you can show your students how Joyce uses Gabriel's remarks to organize many of the oppositions so central to *The Dead*. He praises life-affirming, positive qualities—the generous array of food (so sensuously described by Joyce); the hospitality of his aunts; the beauty of their music; the traditions of his country. Yet each affirmation is undercut by details mentioned elsewhere, details that bring the dead of the title before the reader and rob the present of its superficial vitality. Irish hospitality is also demonstrated by the monks of Melleray, who supposedly sleep in their coffins (p. 1961); music is no longer as well performed as it used to be (p. 1960); Ireland is riven between Celtic roots and European sophistication.

The way Joyce handles these points of contention may be most easily exemplified by the constant presence of music in the story: Aunt Julia's triumphant singing of Bellini's aria, a coloratura showpiece, is only one of the story's many containers, as it were, of the theme of death in life. Although her voice still rings true, she has aged perceptibly, and her closeness to death is emphasized by the contrast between her person and the music she chooses (*Arrayed for the Bridal* is an ebullient expression of the virginal hopes of the heroine of Bellini's opera *I Puritani*). The joy in the music sung by the heroine, Elvira, functions ironically both in the opera, for she is about to go mad, and in Joyce's knowing use of it. (Joyce was an opera lover and once famously took second prize in a singing competition that the great professional Irish tenor, John McCormack, won.) And the brilliance of Aunt Julia's performance, so unexpected in one so old, makes all the more fierce Aunt Kate's anger at the pope's decision "to turn out the women out of the choirs that have slaved there all their lives and put little whipper-snappers of boys over their heads" (p. 1957).

This theme of displacement echoes throughout *The Dead*. In the second of the three phases of the story to which the anthology headnote refers, the anecdote about Johnny the millhorse encapsulates many complex attitudes toward Ireland and the condition of its people. Your students should have no trouble elucidating the significance of Johnny's "tragic" experience once you call it to their attention: Patrick Morkan's pretensions to grandeur cannot survive the force of habit and the call of the past that lead his workhorse to circle the statue of "King Billy" rather than conduct his owner to join with "the quality [at] a military review in the park" (p. 1964).

Art and music provide the transition that links the powerful third section of *The Dead* to the story's initial stages and sets up the culmination of all its themes in the hotel room to which Gretta and Gabriel Conroy repair as the night draws toward day. The artist in Gabriel sees his wife listening intently to Bartell D'Arcy's voice in the next room as he sings "The Lass of Aughrim." The tenor (unlike Aunt Julia) is not in his best voice; he is separated from his audience, and the sight of Gretta in the shadow, straining to hear him, suggests itself to Gabriel as a painterly composition that he would call *Distant Music*. "He asked himself what is a woman standing on the stairs in the shadow, listening to distant music, a symbol of" (p. 1966). The clumsy syntax of that sentence conveys the workings of Gabriel's mind, a mind that feverishly reviews moments of intimacy between husband and wife as the Conroys approach the hotel. When they reach their room, Gabriel's expectations as lover and artist are overturned.

The Dead ends with Gretta's revelation of her past intimacy with Michael Furey, in a brilliant coda that fully exposes Gabriel's inherited snobbishness and debilitating sense of inadequacy. Bristling at his wife's recollection of a former romance, he at first goes on the attack: "—What was he? asked Gabriel, still ironically" (p. 1971). Used to dealing with others in terms of occupation and status, Gabriel is properly humiliated by Gretta's simple answer. The seventeen-year-old Michael Furey "was in the gasworks" (p. 1972), here a pathetic reference that offsets Aunt Kate's exasperated mention of the gaslike pall that Mr. Browne has cast over the Christmas holidays.

Your students should have no difficulty hearing the pun in Michael Furey's last name; those who are familiar with the archangels Gabriel and Michael should be able to explain the contrast between Gabriel, the angel of the annuciation charged with conveying a difficult message to a young woman, and Michael, the leader of God's armies. Michael Furey, eternally young and passionate, stood in the rain for a last glimpse of Gretta; Gabriel Conroy, declining into middle age, does not venture out into snow without galoshes.

Moving toward the Joycean epiphany in the final paragraphs, however, Gabriel appears to achieve a sensitivity to the feelings of others of which he has not shown himself capable until now. The narrative takes us into Gabriel's mind processing the events of the day as he tries to sleep. His awareness of his own ridiculousness and pomposity is mitigated by the "generous tears" that fill his eyes, and we remember that Gretta had quite sincerely praised his generosity, thinking better of him for lending Freddy money than he himself does in the internal monologue that precedes her comment (p. 1970).

The oppositions that are everywhere to be found in *The Dead* typically complicate its conclusion. He will be making a journey "westward": is he foreseeing his death, or will he be revisiting the sources of Irish identity? Is he recognizing a common humanity as he muses (in another example of odd syntax) on the "snow that was general all over Ireland," or do the chill images of dissolution and mortality symbolize the final destruction of a self that was none too sturdy to begin with? Is the "swooned" of the final sentence a token of authorial sentiment or is it a vocabulary choice meant to mark the limitations of Gabriel's late-Victorian aesthetic? In debating unanswerable questions such as these, today's readers can still test their own sensibilities by looking into the vistas opened up by one of the great modernist writers.

Topics for Writing

1. How does the seasonal setting of the Misses Morkans' annual dance mirror the thematic concerns of *The Dead*? Does the party celebrate an end or a beginning? How does the falling snow add to the mood and development of the story?
2. Discuss the importance of music in *The Dead*.

   [If you have access to a tape of John Huston's 1987 movie version, your students can hear the melodies and grasp the way music permeates the story. You can also ask your students to note ways in which the movie distorts the story; one is by having Aunt Julia sing in an off-key, wavering voice.]
3. How does the story of Johnny the horse express Joyce's conviction that Dublin is the "centre of paralysis"? What other evidence is there of that problem in *The Dead*?

Comparative Perspectives

1. What kind of character is Gabriel Conroy? Compare him to the protagonists of other modernist works, such as Eliot's J. Alfred Prufrock or Mann's Gustav von Aschenbach.
2. Compare and contrast Joyce's view of Irish politics in *The Dead* with those expressed in the poems of Yeats.
3. Fiercely critical of Dublin and Ireland, in *The Dead* Joyce writes of characters trapped in routine lives in a moribund society and therefore as good as dead; some, like Aunt Julia, are on the verge of death. In *Pedro Páramo*, Juan Rulfo writes of characters who are literally dead, but haunted even in the afterlife by the experiences that drove them into early graves. Compare and contrast the worlds created by these two authors. What faults do they see in their countries and their inhabitants? Does either work leave open a possibility for renewal and regeneration?
4. Molly Ivors is a literary type unencountered in earlier selections: the well-educated, politically active, independent woman. Compare and contrast Miss Ivors with a character like the beautiful lady in Tawfiq al-Hakim's *The Sultan's Revenge* or the narrator of el Saadawi's *In Camera*. What qualities do these very different characters share? How do their compatriots respond to them? Discuss the accuracy of these portraits in relation to some real-life counterparts of these socially committed women.

Further Reading

See also the reading suggestions in the anthology, p. 1945.

Leonard, Garry M. *Reading* Dubliners *Again: A Lacanian Perspective.* 1993. Densely argued, with interesting close readings.

Williams, Trevor L. *Reading Joyce Politically.* 1997. A materialist interpretation that offers close analyses of the text in terms of power structures and economic difference.

VIRGINIA WOOLF

A Room of One's Own

Classroom Strategies and Topics for Discussion

This wonderful, totally idiosyncratic work, a landmark of twentieth-century cultural criticism, can serve a variety of purposes in your course. You might begin by asking students to what genre *A Room of One's Own* belongs. Is it a lecture? Is it an essay? Is it fiction? That one can say yes to each of these suggestions, without excluding the others as equally valid designations, immediately should establish the fluidity of Woolf's prose and the way it mirrors human thought. *A Room of One's Own*, like so many of Virginia Woolf's novels, breaks down conventional boundaries and in its own elusiveness embodies one of her core perceptions—that consciousness is neither fixed nor static.

Woolf herself would probably have been amazed by the changes wrought by *A Room of One's Own*. This witty and heartfelt analysis of (among other things) the influence of gender and poverty on human creativity has transformed the literary canon in English. Generations of university women have responded to the lecturer's exhortation to the young women of Newnham and Girton and in fact recovered poets and even playwrights who wrote alongside Shakespeare. Their existence takes away nothing from the bravura of Woolf's imagined tragedy of Judith Shakespeare; in fact, the recovery of these writers is one proof of the power of Woolf's fiction.

The array of women writers with which the anthology concludes may suggest that the material preconditions for art that Woolf lays out here have finally been achieved. It would be worth pursuing this hypothesis: outside of Proust, how many writers have ever had the benefit of "sound-proof rooms" (p. 1994)? If women are no longer laughed at when they proclaim a desire to write, have they ceased to be the looking glass that reflects and enlarges the image of the men to whom they are attached? (We live in an era when a political spouse may be male rather than female, yet it is the rare husband of the candidate or office holder who sits in photogenic, wide-eyed wonderment as his wife speaks.)

Certainly the very presence of women students in your own academic institution bears witness to how the world has changed since Woolf wrote, but the prose in which she captured the world has not grown stale.

Woolf is such a keen observer of quotidian detail that you might ask your students to sharpen their own eyes and look around themselves: "London was like a workshop. London was like a machine" (p. 1978). The pace of the modern city has accelerated since 1928, when Woolf wrote these words, but the sense of rupture with the past implied by those terse sentences fuels much of her work and is one of the marks of the modernist movement. At a time when New York's Museum of Modern Art has had to give up drawings by Van Gogh and Manet on the grounds that these works have ceased to be "modern," you could anchor an inquiry into the meaning of "modern" and "modernism" in a discussion of *A Room of One's Own*. In what ways are Woolf, Joyce, and Proust more "modern" than many writers of the last few years whose novels turn up on the best-seller lists? (Most popular fiction of the day treats readers like consumers by providing them with detailed inventories of characters' possessions and thus tends to be much closer, at least in this attention to the external world, to ninteenth-century realism.)

There is no question that *A Room of One's Own* mirrors its own time—a time when a writer could speak of Mussolini without having a political ax to grind, or complain about having to work for a living without acknowledging a worldwide depression (which began in 1929, a year after Woolf delivered her lectures, and lasted in many cases until 1939). It may, in fact, be helpful to review some of the history of Europe between the wars with your students: ask whether anyone can identify Mussolini (1883–1945), who was much admired at the time Woolf wrote *A Room of One's Own*. By 1920, Mussolini had established a fighting force called a *Fasci di Combattimento*, using the ancient Roman symbol of authority, the *fascinae*, to anchor his party's claims to lead the Italian people to greatness. As the first Fascist dictator in a fractured Europe, Mussolini was credited with "making the trains run on time." In the 1930s, of course, Mussolini began on a program of imperial conquest and collaboration with Hitler. He would not then have been casually mentioned by Woolf, who writes in her diaries of the horror of the Fascist bombardment of England and feared the consequences of a Nazi invasion, a real threat in the early years of World War II.

Yet *A Room of One's Own* also transcends its historical context and even its declared subject, for what Woolf described here is a quest as relevant at the end of the twentieth century as it was at the end of its third decade: she looks for the "pure fluid, the essential oil of truth" (p. 1978). She understands that anger, like any emotion, colors and distorts truth. As the English publisher of Freud's works and a woman painfully self-aware of the way childhood shapes the adult consciousness, she knows firsthand how being laughed at "in his cradle by a pretty girl" (p. 1982) may have twisted the professorial mind so that it is incapable of arriving at an objective view of experience. For all this sophistication about the impact of forgotten irritants on the way we think and feel and the concomitant implication that nothing stable exists outside the mind of the beholder, the selection in the anthology suggests that the essential oil can be found in the greatest art, represented here by the "incandescent" mind of Shakespeare. Readers of Shakespeare may wonder about the meaning of that "incandescent," and many artists and critics would challenge the apparent implication of a single standard of art or truth. Especially if you are going on to read writers such as Beckett or Robbe-Grillet, you may want to use Woolf's text to prepare your students for current doubts about the existence of immutable, objective truth.

Woolf's "evocations of states of mind," as the headnote describes them, have lost none of their innovative freshness. The long paragraph that dominates chapter 2 (pp. 1982–85) is a good laboratory for scrutinizing the transitional strategies that create a rhetorical unity out of so apparently random a sequence. Beginning in the library, reflecting on the anger of the professors who write books about women, the would-be lecturer goes off to lunch, where she comes upon an abandoned newspaper. Have your students look closely at the headlines that lead her to announce that "this scattered testimony" demonstrates that "England is under the rule of a patriarchy." What is it about topics ranging from the Shamelessness of Women to the dangling film actress, from a scene of violence in a cellar to the sports score that bespeaks masculine dominion? Sitting in a lunchroom and staring out the window, the narrator reflects in an elliptical way on the sources of masculine power. Throughout these chapters, she prefers ironic obliquity to direct attack, but the scorn for male chauvinist pretension is not hard to track: "How much thinking those old gentlemen used to save one!" (p. 1990).

Not until she pays her check does a new paragraph begin: it is money that frees her from the power of patriarchy. Her aunt who "died by a fall from her horse when she was riding out to take the air in Bombay" seems almost an antidote to the Hollywood actress suspended in air. For this woman died exercising her independence, not acting out a film producer's fantasy of female daring. (Perhaps Judith Shakespeare, who "let herself down by a rope one summer's night" [p. 1991], makes a third female acrobat seeking freedom at great cost to herself.)

Woolf's walker through the city returns to the question of patriarchy with her brilliant suggestion that "Anon . . . was often a woman" (p. 1992). She draws a line between the male ego and the female "desire to be veiled" (p. 1992) that culminates in a remarkable equation drawn between British imperialism and men's quest of fame. As in her insistence that social class makes a difference—"genius like Shakespeare's is not born among labouring, uneducated, servile people" (p. 1991), Woolf does not shrink from separating persons by race and gender. In a sentence that calls for analysis of her attitudes toward race, class, and gender, those three central categories of contemporary critical discourse, Woolf's narrator dryly notes: "It is one of the great advantages of being a woman that one can pass even a very fine negress without wishing to make an Englishwoman of her" (p. 1993). (It would be interesting to teach A Room of One's Own in close proximity to Ingeborg Bachmann's The Barking, another reflection on connections between patriarchy and the social aberrations it breeds. Writing a generation after Virginia Woolf, Bachmann sees egotistical masculine behavior as an arbitrary social form and an implicit cause of fascism.)

Today's critics have pursued the significance of similar passages, questioning the extent to which this daughter of privilege (if not of great wealth) understood the crushing social and economic pressures that continue to deprive human beings of the ability to realize their talents. As influential as Woolf's work has been, it is important to point out that she was also deeply influenced by her contemporaries. The most obvious contemporary influence on Woolf was Marcel Proust, whose *Remembrance of Things Past* was, perhaps, her favorite book. Although she is often linked with Joyce, she did not—at least in her public statements—much like his work, which she called "indecent." Joyce was mainly interested in using stream-of-consciousness techniques as a way of exploring the conscious mind; Woolf was interested in life below the level of consciousness, emotional life, and she used all of her considerable creative powers to render and articulate that life. Woolf was also influenced by Henri Bergson's discussions of the immediate data of consciousness as it exists outside of clocktime. Dorothy Richardson, whose experiments in stream-of-consciousness predated Woolf's, and Katherine Mansfield, whose sensibility and insight made Woolf envious, were also significant influences.

Woolf was at the center of what was perhaps England's most influential group of intellectuals during the 1920s and '30s—the Bloomsbury group. It has often been noted by biographers of the group and its individual members that their principles were derived from the Cambridge philosopher G. E. Moore, who argued, among other things, that "aesthetic enjoyment and the pleasures of human intercourse include *all* the greatest, and *by far* the greatest, goods we can imagine." Woolf went some distance in expressing these principles in life as well as in literature.

Topics for Writing and Comparative Perspectives

1. Find evidence in *A Room of One's Own* of Virginia Woolf's novelistic talents. Can this text be categorized as fiction?
2. How does the lecturer use irony and humor as devices to advance an argument?

    [If you wish to expand this topic, you might have your students compare the argumentative strategies of Sister Juana in the other great feminist treatise in the anthology, the *Reply to Sor Filotea de la Cruz*: how does each writer use autobiographical detail? How would you characterize the tone of their respective attacks on male-dominated societies?]
3. Show how Woolf makes the case that women express themselves in ways that are natural to them and not available to men. Do you agree with her?

    [Compare Dorothy Wordsworth's style in her *Grasmere Journals*, Clarice Lispector's in *Daydreams of a Drunk Woman*, Mahasweta

Devi's in *Breast-Giver*, or Anita Desai's in *The Rooftop Dwellers*. Each writes with exquisite attention to detail. Do they all see the same things? Would they see differently if they were men?]
4. Compare ideas about opportunities for women to create fiction explored by Leslie Marmon Silko in *Yellow Woman*. How do their cultural situations contribute to Woolf's and Silko's understanding of their own freedom to create?
5. Moyna, in Anita Desai's *The Rooftop Dwellers*, achieves a room of her own, and longs for a career in publishing. How might Woolf analyze the frustration of Moyna's literary ambitions?

Further Reading

See also the reading suggestions in the anthology, p. 1977.

Bell, Quentin. *Virginia Woolf: A Biography*. 1972. The definitive biography of Woolf, written by her nephew (the son of Clive and Vanessa Bell). It has been criticized for being too sympathetic with the Bloomsbury sensibility, but no one knows more about Woolf than Quentin Bell.

Colburn, Krystyna. "Women's Oral Tradition and *A Room of One's Own*." In *Re:Reading, Re:Writing, Re: Teaching Virginia Woolf*, eds. Eileen Barrett and Patrick Cramer. 1995. An explanation of the choice of "Mary Beton," "Seton," etc., which derive from "The Ballad of the Four Marys," an old folk song.

Duisinberre, Juliet. *Virginia Woolf's Renaissance: Woman Reader or Common Reader?* 1997. Although there is little of direct relevance to *A Room of One's Own* in this book by a well-known feminist critic of Shakespeare and his contemporaries, it brings together Woolf's various comments about Renaissance figures like Montaigne, and forms a background against which one can better appreciate the genesis of Woolf's searing vision of Judith Shakespeare.

Gordan, Lyndall. *Virginia Woolf: A Writer's Life*. 1985. This biography moves back and forth between the life and the work, with special attention to the latter.

Woolf, Virginia. "Mr. Bennett and Mrs. Brown." In *Collected Essays*, vol. I. 1966. An extremely important essay for understanding Woolf's approach to character in fiction, especially insofar as it differs from the English Edwardian realists.

FRANZ KAFKA

The Metamorphosis

Backgrounds

Even now, nearly ninety years after *The Metamorphosis* was written, students find it as fresh and contemporary as the latest story by Joyce

Carol Oates, and as baffling and troubling as the last stories of Jorge Luis Borges. What still interests and excites contemporary readers and writers about Kafka is his ability to force us to look beyond the seemingly calm surface of the story for a symbolic or allegorical meaning, along with his persistent refusal to deliver such a meaning. As soon as we try to nail down Kafka, he gets up and walks away with the nail. Kafka frustrates our expectation that there is a final, unequivocal meaning to be found anywhere. Nevertheless, students will find Kafka's prose precise and objective, and they will find it especially enchanting because it appears to be in service to the inner life—dreams, fantasies, unconscious fears and desires—without straining their ability to understand what is being said. As baffling as Kafka often seems to be, he manages in his best work to present his world with the humanity, humor, and power that we expect from great writers of any era.

To say that someone is "like" a vermin, an insect, a bug—or to feel "like" that ourselves—is to say something we all understand, metaphorically. The metaphorical basis of Kafka's tale is rather simple; it is Kafka's matter-of-fact, almost journalistic, insistence on the *reality* of the metaphor that strikes us as being curious. In *The Metamorphosis* Gregor Samsa has been transformed into a metaphor that states his essential self, but this metaphor in turn is treated as an actual fact. Gregor does not just call himself a vermin; he wakes up to find himself one. Kafka has transformed the metaphor back into fictional reality, and this counter-metamorphosis becomes the starting point of his tale. Such a fictional act seems simple enough, but it is extraordinarily radical, one of the most radical beginnings of any story anywhere.

Kafka confirms his intention to insist on the *fact* of Gregor's metamorphosis by his use of absolutely ordinary language, a language purged of surprise, to describe it. The first two paragraphs of the story tell us a great deal about Kafka's method in *The Metamorphosis*. In the first paragraph, Gregor is introduced already transformed—but he is introduced by a narrator who seems absolutely unsurprised by what has taken place, a narrator who presents this extraordinary moment with the cold objectivity and precision of a visiting zoologist. In the second paragraph, we notice that the narrator remains separate from Gregor's consciousness (and is thus able to make factual comments such as "Samsa was a traveling salesman"), but still identifies almost completely with Gregor, sees through his eyes and ears, removed only slightly farther away from things than the character himself. Such a narrative stance makes it impossible for us to read the story as if it were merely a hallucination or a dream. As importantly, and more intriguingly, the narrator seems curiously unhurried to explain what we are most interested in. When the narrator *does* evidence astonishment, it is not over Gregor's transformation at all, but instead over a vaguely erotic picture, from an illustrated magazine, that hangs on the wall of his room. "The picture showed a lady sitting there upright, bedizened in a fur hat and fur boa, with her entire forearm vanishing inside a heavy fur muff that she held out toward the viewer" (p. 1999). The narrator refuses to be impressed by the same things we are, and the frustration of our expectations—expectations we probably did not know existed—is curiously humorous.

The Metamorphosis is also a family drama, a drama about the relationship between Gregor and his sister, his mother, and—especially—his father. Indeed, if we forget for a moment that Gregor is now a monstrous insect (although Kafka clearly doesn't want us to forget), his behavior resembles nothing so much as that of a monstrous infant, struggling unsuccessfully to establish a functional identity in an environment with which he is unequipped to cope, and in a family situation that continually reconfirms his lack of status. Gregor's family depends on him for their welfare, but as a "father"—the breadwinner, the one economically responsible for the family's welfare—Gregor feels himself to be a failure. He is such a minor functionary in his company that he can be mercilessly assailed by its manager, who arrives at the Samsa home only a few minutes after Gregor should have arrived at work. The manager berates Gregor "on behalf of your parents and the director of the firm" (p. 2004)—the two sources of authority, and therefore of punishment, in the story—in full view of his family, accuses him of doing unsatisfactory work, implies that he may have stolen money from company funds entrusted to him, and reminds him how easily he could be fired. He treats Gregor like the vermin that Gregor has in fact become, and exposes Gregor's sense of vulnerability and guilt.

The world of officials and the world of fathers appear to be essentially the same. Both worlds have authority and use that authority to punish Gregor, whose guilt attracts their attention and their desire for power. This is exacerbated by Gregor's own sense of insufficiency, which has stultified him spiritually long before his physical transformation. His literal imprisonment—in the body of a vermin, locked in his room, with employers and family members as jailers—is made even more intolerable by his horrible awareness of it. It has been suggested that Gregor's acceptance of his metamorphosis occurs because he recognizes that his present status as insect is about the same as his former status as human being.

In *The Metamorphosis,* every weakening of the son's position results in the strengthening of the father's. In the end, one will triumph, the other will die. Gregor makes three forays out of his room and into the world of his family, and these three forays constitute the central events of the three sections of the story. In part I, Gregor struggles to open his door with his jaws, but when he emerges from his bedroom, he frightens away the manager and is finally driven back by his infuriated father, who wields a walking stick and a newspaper and stamps the floor in anger. In part II, Gregor is overtaken by the desire to see his mother, but when his angry and exultant father, now wearing a uniform that suggests his newfound authority and power, discovers him outside his room, he drives him back by pelting Gregor with apples. In part III, the starving, wounded Gregor comes out while Grete—the only one in the family who has shown anything resembling sympathy for his plight—is playing the violin. He is entranced by the music, but is driven back this time by a different, and more devastating, kind of attack: the stark indifference of his family. His mother sits still, her "eyes almost shut in exhaustion" (p. 2027), and Grete, who has had enough of tending her brother, locks his door behind him and cries, "Finally!" Gregor dies alone, to be discovered in the morning by the charwoman. His father delivers Gregor's epitaph: "now we can thank the Lord" (p. 2028).

Gregor's treatment by his family—especially his father—is progressively more violent, fueled by their increasing disgust and annoyance at having to put up with such a creature in their house. In many ways, they become as monstrous, as parasitical, as Gregor looks. As long as Gregor filled the role of breadwinner, the family (especially the father) was moribund, but as soon as Gregor is reduced to a vermin, the family comes alive. In fact, Gregor's diminishment is in direct proportion to his family's advancement. For the family to thrive, Gregor must die. After his death, the family—suddenly and happily free of the burden that was their son—decides to leave the apartment, which is "something they had not done in months," to take the tram excusion into the country. The last paragraph of the story is written in Kafka's most lilting cadences. It is springtime; the tram is "flooded with warm sunshine"; they are free; and Grete, under the admiring gaze of her mother and father, demonstrates her own metamorphosis. Like a butterfly emerging from a cocoon, she has "blossomed into a lovely and shapely girl." Mr. and Mrs. Samsa come to the conclusion "that it was high time they found a decent husband for her. And it was like a confirmation of their new dreams and good intentions that at the end of their ride the daughter was the first to get up, stretching her young body" (p. 2030).

It is easy, perhaps too easy, to read the central metaphor in *The Metamorphosis* as Gregor = vermin = modern man and to insist that it is a parable about the human condition in the modern world. In many ways such a reading is perfectly justifiable; in other ways it extends the story's implications beyond what it can be reasonably expected to suggest.

Kafka's inability to assert himself and his overwhelming sense of shortcoming and consequently of guilt mark everything he ever wrote. Although he was a brilliant graduate in law, he never practiced, taking instead a position as a civil servant in the Austrian government. He was engaged several times and had several affairs (his meeting with Felice Bauer led directly to his writing *The Metamorphosis*) but could never bring himself to marry. Kafka even asked that his unpublished writings be destroyed upon his death. Fortunately for us, Max Brod, his literary executor, published them anyway.

Any analysis of Kafka's work must take into account the peculiarly poetic and tormenting character of Prague. As all biographers of Kafka agree, his Prague was perfectly suited to reflect his disposition—a place of Slavonic melancholy, weighed down by its history, where different traditions and tongues competed and where desire for the unequivocal is persistently met by recognition of its impossibility. Because Kafka was a

German-speaking Jew living in Prague, he felt even more powerfully the burden of his separateness, which reveals itself also in the very form of his stories. In his work—as in the Jewish tradition—time is a dimension that fuses past and present, eternity and the instant, just as it fuses the extraordinary and the mundane, the ultimate and the immediate. Authority is not represented by fathers alone, but also by Gentiles, who may turn from allies to enemies at any given moment. For Kafka's characters the world of authority—of Law—is closed but ambiguous, and nothing can be finally resolved. In the Jewish tradition, full resolution can take place only with the decisive return of the Messiah; until that time everyone lives in the middle of an inconclusive history. We find this same "in the middle" effect in Kafka, where the story typically begins *after* the decisive event has taken place, where characters go through a gradual shifting of states of being but are never granted a conclusive resolution to their problems.

The Metamorphosis was written in late 1912. It is one of the very few stories that apparently satisfied Kafka to the point that he wanted to see it published. Though it would be a mistake to interpret the story merely as a coded autobiographical document, *The Metamorphosis* does, of course, have personal significance for its author. It quite evidently reflects his sense of personal inadequacy in comparison to his father—a strong-willed, self-made authoritarian—who, as we know from reading Kafka's *Letter to His Father*, once likened his son to a vermin. Kafka's tenderness toward his sister, Ottla, can be felt in his depiction of Grete, as can his frustration over his mother's inability to deal with his psychological difficulties.

After Kafka wrote *The Judgment* in 1912, a few months before he began *The Metamorphosis*, he wrote in his diary, "Thoughts of Freud, naturally." And it *was* natural: Kafka was intensely aware of the work of Freud and others working in the developing field of psychoanalysis, and he sometimes claimed that "the therapeutic claims of psychoanalysis" were an "impotent error" and that he was "nauseated" by them. Kafka had read some of Freud's work, had heard him discussed in various intellectual circles, and was personally acquainted with Otto Gross, a member of Freud's inner circle. The impact of Freud is evident in the importance Kafka attaches to the images of his inner life (as well as his talent for portraying them), his extraordinary interest in childhood experience and in the Oedipal situation in particular, and his awareness of his own neurotic symptoms.

The climate of thought that made his work possible is also evident in expressionism, one of the most influential aesthetic movements of the early twentieth century. Its central tendency is to distort or magnify the shape of reality in order to suggest a higher order of emotional reality beneath the surface. It assumes, like many of the major movements of modern art and literature, that art based predominantly on visible reality is inadequate. If Robert Wiene's film *The Cabinet of Dr. Caligari* (1919) is available, it might be useful to screen it for the class, since it quite dramatically and enjoyably reveals a number of German expressionism's essential features: the distortion of surfaces, the obsession with the inner life, and the relationship between individual and authority (especially the conflict between fathers and sons).

Classroom Strategies

The Metamorphosis can be taught in as few as two class periods. The first discussion of the story could emphasize the nature of its narrative, while the second might concentrate on the relations between Gregor and his family, his feelings of guilt and inadequacy, the ambiguity of self-knowledge and values, and the relationship between the individual and authority.

The narrative of The Metamorphosis exploits the gap between a reader's expectations and his or her findings. Inevitably, then, students will find Kafka's narrative curious or even unacceptable. Though they may not know exactly why they find it so (they often accept events far more outlandish in a science fiction story), a close examination of the events described and of the tone the narrator uses will allow them to move beyond their initial confusion. In order to press the point home, it might be useful to read from other writers who use similar narrative strategies—Beckett, Borges, Donald Barthelme, Robert Coover, or Peter Handke, for instance. But perhaps the most telling comparison might be made between Kafka's narrative and everyday newspaper reports, which often describe the most extraordinary events in a tone of detached, journalistic objectivity. The cool, detached quality of such reports on unlikely events makes them bleakly humorous. In The Metamorphosis, the effect of such a narrative is first to establish the fictional reality of the metaphor: Gregor is an insect. But like the newspaper stories, it also delivers humor, deriving, for the most part, from the apparent disjunction of the tone of the narrative from the events it describes. Teaching humor, beyond insisting that it is there, is very difficult, perhaps impossible. But there are particular moments in the text that might be used to establish Kafka's humor: Gregor's difficulty over getting up for the first time after his transformation and feeling "anything but fresh or sprightly," along with his attendant worry over lying idle in bed and getting behind in his work (p. 2000), Gregor's attempts to speak, which come out in "a painful and insuppressible squeal" (p. 2001); the manager's lecture on the nature of business (p. 2004); the three lodgers, who behave like performers in a vaudeville routine; or the cleaning woman, who appears to respond to Gregor as if he were nothing more than a ridiculous obstacle to completing her work.

Henri Bergson—with whose work Kafka was familiar—has claimed that "we laugh every time a person gives us the impression of being a thing" and that the comic produces "something like a momentary anesthesia of the heart," which is brought on by "looking at life as a disinterested spectator." In The Metamorphosis Kafka meets these requirements, and our response is precisely what Bergson might have expected. Invariably, Kafka's grotesquely extravagant vision of people enmeshed in the sad absurdity of the universe evokes in us an uneasy laughter.

Topics for Discussion and Writing

1. How does Kafka use his central metaphor in *The Metamorphosis*? In what ways is his use of it different from what we might expect to find?

   [Kafka's central metaphor, Gregor = vermin, is insisted upon as being literally true. The metaphor is treated as an actual fact. To get the response he evidently wants, Kafka exploits the gap between what the reader expects and what he finds. The reader's objections to Gregor's transformation into a monstrous vermin are undermined by the literalness, the journalistic objectivity, of the narrative.]

2. How does the apparent disjunction between tone and event create humor in *The Metamorphosis*?

   [See the second paragraph of "Backgrounds" and the second and third paragraphs of "Classroom Strategies."]

3. What is the relationship between Gregor and his family? What clues in the story suggest that his relationship with his family, particularly his father, is unsatisfactory?

   [See "Backgrounds," from the fourth paragraph through the seventh. Besides the many evidences of Gregor's indifferent treatment in the story, students should note details such as his father's use of a newspaper (something we typically use to squash bugs) and a walking stick (a traditional symbol of paternal authority) to drive Gregor back into his room during their first confrontation. It is also worth noting that Gregor apparently feels it necessary to lock his room in his own home.]

4. Discuss the central events in each of the three sections of the story. In what ways do these events suggest that the weakening of Gregor results in the strengthening of the family as a whole?

   [See "Backgrounds," the sixth and seventh paragraphs.]

5. What significance is attached to food in *The Metamorphosis*?

   [Kafka often uses food as an image of spiritual, psychic, or artistic fulfillment in his stories, just as he uses hunger and starvation to suggest unfulfillment. *The Hunger Artist* is the most famous example of his use of this formula. In *The Metamorphosis*, Gregor is first offered fresh food, which does not satisfy him. His sister, "in the goodness of her heart," then tries to satisfy Gregor by offering him half-decayed food from the family table. As his family becomes more indifferent, his sister merely shoves "any old food into Gregor's room with her foot," then clears it out "with a swish of the broom," heedless of whether it has been tasted or left untouched. Soon after, Gregor eats almost nothing while, by contrast, his family and the three boarders stuff themselves with meat and potatoes and make much of their satisfaction. Gregor thinks: "I do have an appetite . . . but not for these foods. How well these boarders eat, and I'm starving to death!" (p. 2024). On his last foray out of his room, Gregor trails "hairs, threads, and scraps of leftover food" to listen to his sister play the violin. The music affects him greatly, and he feels "as if he were being shown the path to the unknown food he was yearning for" (p. 2025). But it is too late. When Gregor's flat and dry corpse is discovered, the rotting apple thrown by his father still imbedded in his back, Grete says, "Just look how skinny he was. . . . The food came back out exactly as it went in" (p. 2028).]

6. What is the significance of the minor characters in the story—the manager, the three boarders, and the cleaning woman?

   [See the fourth paragraph of "Backgrounds." Note that the family feels itself independent enough to dismiss the three boarders, and their demands, only after Gregor's death.]

7. What is the importance of the final scene in the story, the family's trip to the country? Why is it written so lyrically in comparison to the rest of the text?

   [The lyricism of the last scene reflects the family's new dispensation, the revival of their prospects. Gregor's death allows them their release, and the language of this final scene embodies their new hopes. See the seventh paragraph of "Backgrounds."]

8. *The Metamorphosis* has been read and interpreted in many ways—as an example of existentialist philosophy, a depiction of humanity's condition in the modern world, a presentation of psychological neurosis, and a theological parable. Discuss these various interpretive possibilities.

Comparative Perspectives

1. In *Notes From Underground*, part II, chapter I, the Underground Man announces that "every decent man of our time is and must be a coward and a slave." To what extent does this description fit Gregor Samsa before he turns into a dung beetle? Is it true of him in his metamorphosed state? Is it true of his entire family? How many other protagonists of the modern period could be similarly characterized? What sets of circumstances are involved in each case?

   [Consider, among others, Prufrock metaphorically transformed into an insect, "formulated, sprawling on a pin," Weifu in *Upstairs in a Wineshop*, or Isa in *The American School*.]

2. Listening to his sister play the violin, Gregor—who had not particularly appreciated music before—is deeply affected. "Was he a beast to be so moved by music?" This difficult sentence makes us reread it: it seems to ask whether a dung beetle could have this capacity to respond to high art and therefore to throw Gregor's identity into question once more. What sensibilities are ascribed to animals in

other modern texts like Rilke's *The Panther* or Faulkner's *The Bear*? Why is it easier to accept the idea of a powerful animal's alertness to his surroundings? Compare the nobility imparted to animals in essentially oral works like *The Boy and the Deer* and *Mother Crocodile*. Would Kafka's story be as unsettling to a reader raised in Reynetsa's or Diop's milieu as it is to an audience of Western readers?

3. What other texts in the anthology might bear significant comparison to *The Metamorphosis*?

   [One might usefully compare *The Metamorphosis* with *The Death of Ivan Ilyich*. In both works we are told of a character who moves toward death; in Tolstoy that death is redemptive, and it provides the central meaning of the text, but in *The Metamorphosis,* Gregor's death is remarkable precisely because it is without redemption. Comparisons also can be drawn between *The Metamorphosis* and *Notes from Underground*, especially with regard to the depiction of a psychological condition that suggests self-hatred. In *Endgame* we experience the same discrepancy between extreme unreality and the dry precision of its presentation, and we laugh with a similar uneasiness. In *The Love Song of J. Alfred Prufrock* the title figure sings of his own insufficiency. And texts as different as *A Modest Proposal*, *Candide*, and *The Garden of Forking Paths* all use a similar kind of narrative strategy to provoke the reader's response. It is important to note, however, that Swift and Voltaire both assume a firm and commonly understood series of values against which they measure their irony, whereas Kafka has no such center and no such certainty.]

Further Reading

See also the reading suggestions in the anthology, p. 1999.

Anders, Gunter. *Franz Kafka*. Trans. A. Steer and A. K. Thorlby. 1960. A well-known analysis of *The Metamorphosis* that examines Gregor's transformation as an extended metaphor for Kafka's view of the world "as it appears to a stranger."

Anderson, Mark, ed. *Reading Kafka: Prague, Politics, and the Fin de Siècle*. 1989. Useful study of Kafka's relation to his time.

Benjamin, Walter. "Franz Kafka. On the Tenth Anniversary of His Death." In *Illuminations*, ed. Hannah Arendt, pp. 111–40. 1968. Benjamin describes clusters of related images, gestures, and motifs in order to suggest the nature of Kafka's world.

Bernheimer, Charles. *Flaubert and Kafka: Studies in Psychopoetic Structure*. 1982. Employs contemporary critical theory to describe aspects of Kafka's work.

Corngold, Stanley. *The Commentators' Despair*. 1973. A useful annotated bibliography of works on *The Metamorphosis* (up to 1972).

————. *Franz Kafka: The Necessity of Form*. 1988.

Deleuze, Gilles, and Felix Guattari. *Kafka: Toward a Minor Literature*. Trans. Dana Polan. 1986. An important study of Kafka's many-sided alienation from his linguistic and social context.

Gray, Ronald. *Franz Kafka*. 1973. Useful brief studies.

Koelb, Clayton. *Kafka's Rhetoric: The Passion of Reading*. 1989. Employs critical theory to describe aspects of Kafka's work.

Lawson, Richard. *Franz Kafka*. 1987. Biographical study.

Robert, Marthe. *As Lonely as Franz Kafka*. Trans. Ralph Manheim. 1982. Psychoanalytic criticism.

Robertson, Ritchie. *Kafka: Judaism, Politics, Literature*. 1985. Describes Kafka's emerging sense of Jewish identity.

Sandbank, Shimon. *After Kafka: The Influence of Kafka's Fiction*. 1989.

Stern, J. P., ed. *The World of Franz Kafka*. 1980. Contains portraits and photographs.

Stric, Roman, and Yardley, J. C., eds. *Franz Kafka (1883–1924): His Craft and Thought*. 1986. Collected essays.

Thiher, Allan. *Franz Kafka: A Study of the Short Fiction*. 1990.

Udoff, Alan, ed. *Kafka and the Contemporary Critical Performance*. 1987. Collection of essays.

ZUNI RITUAL POETRY

Classroom Strategies

Zuni prayers seek a relationship with the natural world in which longevity is purchased through a system of prescribed payments. Although human sacrifice in the literal sense is unknown in the North American Southwest, the symbolic sacrifice of effigy wands and the stringent programs of ritual duty amount to a considerable expenditure of human resources. In the excerpt from the *Scalp Dance*, which serves as the most pointed expression of the underlying theory, death and life are balanced in a single equation. Whatever is relinquished, in other words, will return. The corollary is that natural energy flows in a closed circuit from which nothing may be subtracted without payment.

This basic idea, with its profound implications for conservation and human responsibility, is at the core of what is vaguely perceived by the outside world as the Native American nature ethic. Use the texts to illuminate the theory, calling attention to the details of duty and benefit, investment and return.

Topics for Discussion and Writing

1. How many nonhuman persons can you detect in the excerpt from *A Prayer at the Winter Solstice*? What are the personifying features of each?
2. Divide the *Dismissal of the Koyemshi* into its three constituent parts: the statement of the occasion (lines 1–3), the description of duty (lines 4–29), and the request for blessing (lines 30–40). Note that more specific blessings are enumerated in the other selections. What do these blessings have in common?

   [General requests for "life," "old age," "that we shall always live"; specific emphasis on rain, crops, and fecundity.]
3. Discuss the texts in light of the relationship between human duty (e.g., "Tirelessly, unwearied, / We shall pass his days") and natural resources (e.g., "His seeds we shall win").

   [See "Classroom Strategies."]

Comparative Perspectives

1. These selections from Zuni ritual poetry emphasize communal experience. These authentic expressions of still-vital traditions make a fascinating counterpart to T. S. Eliot's *The Waste Land*. How effectively does Eliot summon the kinds of powers called on with confidence by the Native American orators?

   [Compare the impact of the spare rhetoric of *A Prayer at the Winter Solstice* with the densely knitted imagery of earth and regeneration in "The Burial of the Dead."]
2. The Scalp Dance assumes a reciprocity between the dead and the living that many modern artists have wanted to believe in. Compare the conviction that "The enemy, / Reaching the end of his life, / Added to the flesh of our earth mother" (lines 34–36) with García Lorca's fantastic vision of the "moss and the grass" opening the "the flower of his skull" in *Lament for Ignacio Sánchez Mejías*.

Further Reading

See also the reading suggestions in the anthology, p. 2032.

Tedlock, Dennis. *The Spoken Word and the Work of Interpretation*. 1983. Includes an essay on Zuni prayer with observations on the style of performance.

Wilson, Edmund. *Red, Black, Blond and Olive: Studies in Four Civilizations—Zuñi, Haiti, Soviet Russia, Israel*. 1956. Wilson's personal response to Zuni culture is woefully out of date, yet he offers a memorable description of the Shalako he witnessed in 1947.

INUIT SONGS

Classroom Strategies

In an age when the reading public increasingly doubts the connection between life and poetry, it is refreshing to stumble upon a tradition in which the two are virtually one. Orpingalik's song *My Breath* introduces the point dramatically. As he states in his prefatory remark, "it is as important for me to sing it, as it is to draw breath." But even without this cue, the immediacy of his experience can be felt by the reader/hearer as though he or she were listening to a news report. The same is true of the songs by Uvlunuaq and Kibkarjuk. This, apparently, is art without varnish. Yet we have no difficulty in recognizing it as genuine poetry. Students rarely fail to respond. The suggestions offered below may help them to verbalize their reactions.

Topics for Discussion and Writing

1. At least three of the songs, especially Uvlunuaq's, are intensely personal, even revelatory. The term "confessional poetry," often encountered in twentieth-century literary criticism, carries a somewhat distasteful connotation. But does it apply here? Why not?

   [Observe that there is no exhibitionism, no apparent intent to shock, and no request for sympathy either stated or implied.]

2. A well-known Inuit song collected by Rasmussen contains the lines "And yet, there is only / One great thing, / The only thing: / to live to see in huts and on journeys / The great day that dawns, / And the light that fills the world." Take the statement at face value and relate it to the songs by Orpingalik, Uvlunuaq, Netsit, and Kibkarjuk.

   [Observe how an image drawn from nature, revealed in the final stanza of each song, elevates the text to a higher level of meaning.]

3. Attempt to characterize the song by Uvavnuk. In a word, describe its tone (idyllic? ecstatic? hypnotic?). Now consider the occasion that brought forth the song, minutely reported by Rasmussen, and decide whether this colors your reaction to it:

   Uvavnuk had gone outside the hut one winter evening to make water. It was particularly dark that evening, as the moon was not visible. Then suddenly there appeared a glowing ball of fire in the sky, and it came rushing down to earth straight toward her. She would have got up and fled, but before she could pull up her breeches, the ball of fire struck her and entered into her. At the same moment she perceived that all within her grew light, and she lost consciousness. But from that moment also she became a great shaman. She had never before concerned herself with the invocation of spirits, but now the spirit of the meteor had entered into her and made her a shaman. She saw the spirit just before she fainted. It had two kinds of bodies, that rushed all glowing through space; one side was a bear, the other was like a human being; the head was that of a human being with the tusks of a bear.* * *

Every shaman has his own particular song, which he sings when calling up his helping spirits; they [the shamans] must sing when the helping spirits enter into their bodies, and [they must] speak with the voice of the helping spirits themselves. The song which Uvavnuk generally sang, and which she sang the first evening, without knowing why, after the meteor had struck her was as follows.

(*Intellectual Culture of the Iglulik Eskimos*, pp. 122–23)

Comparative Perspectives

1. These poems offer powerful images of the snowbound North, a source of stability (Orpingalik's "firm and safe as the winter-ice") and beauty (the Rejected Woman's nostalgia for hunting inland "under falling snow") for native peoples who have survived in it for centuries. In contrast to the many seekers after the warm South, some of the fictional protagonists in this volume visit the cold North and bring different interpretations to bear on the region and its climate. Compare the lure of *Snow Country* for Kawabata's Shimamura, or of the central Asian region of *Matryona's Home* for Solzhenitsyn's narrator.

   [Shimamura brings his own inner frigidity to a matching scene, while the mathematician seeks the real Russia in the provinces.]

2. In *Song of a Mother* Uvlunuaq expresses complex feelings toward her reprobate son. Compare the sentiments of the young Pedro Páramo's mother and grandmother in Rulfo's novel or of Frau Jordan in *The Barking*.

Further Reading

See also the reading suggestions in the anthology, p. 2037.

Cavanagh, Beverley. *Music of the Netsilik Eskimo: A Study of Stability and Change*, 2 vols. 1982. English-Inuit texts with music scores and commentary.

Freuchen, Peter. *Book of the Eskimos*. 1961. Classic account of Inuit life by a comrade of Rasmussen's; includes a chapter on poetry.

McGrath, Robin. *Canadian Inuit Literature: The Development of a Tradition*. 1984. Includes two chapters on poetry.

TANIZAKI JUN'ICHIRŌ

In Praise of Shadows

Backgrounds and Classroom Strategies

With the rising trend in cultural studies first in Great Britain and more recently in the United States, *In Praise of Shadows* could become an important text for Western readers. An eloquent and waggish piece of cultural criticism by one of Japan's most gifted writers, this errant essay has the added attraction of introducing a genre inherently noncanonical to Eurocentric eyes.

Students will be unfamiliar with its playfulness (unless perhaps they have been reading Nabokov), as well as with its form. The first thing to do, probably, is remind them of its antecedents. *In Praise of Shadows* belongs to the tradition of discursive essays known as *zuihitsu*, established by Sei Shōnagon in the eleventh century. Ideally, students will have read selections from her *Pillow Book* (see pp. 2273–300 in volume B) and its fourteenth-century successor, Yoshida Kenkō's *Essays in Idleness* (pp. 2328–42 in volume B). For background on the form, see the headnotes to these two works (pp. 2270–72; 2326–27) and the comments on them in the instructors' guide to volumes A, B, and C. Historically, the *zuihitsu* was a loosely, even miscellaneously, organized prose form. The random structure of this form gave it its name—literally "following the brush"—and allowed a subjective, impressionistic reflection on the author's feelings, experiences, opinions, or tastes. This medium lends itself to an apparently offhand and candid presentation and to the impression that reader encounters writer warts and all. It goes without saying that such a work may be a good deal less casual than it seems, and the author's persona contrived.

Once one accepts the genre's assumptions, initial impatience with a perceived wayward narrative succumbs to charm (if that doesn't sound too patronizing) at the plastic possibilities of the form. In this regard it is eye-opening to compare the current translation of the essay with an earlier English version by Edward G. Seidensticker, one half of the translating team that produced the selection in the anthology. In 1955 Seidensticker published an "adaptation" of *In Praise of Shadows* in *The Atlantic Monthly*. What he there offers American readers is an abridged version that omits all digression. Translated are only those passages perceived by Seidensticker as central to the main theme: "that the traditional Japanese arts thrived in the shade" (Seidensticker's words).[1] These excerpts are threaded together with a summary of the remaining contents, but even in this digested form Tanizaki's "digressions" are ignored. There is no mention of Albert Einstein's visit to Kyoto, the novelist Takebayashi Musōan's trip to Paris, or the newspaper article about old women in England. One is left with the impression that initially Tanizaki's translator understood his writer's project no better than an American freshman, who might be forgiven for opining that once the essay reaches its crescendo with that incredible set piece on a Kyoto geisha being swallowed up by the dark ("The darkness wrapped her round tenfold, twentyfold, it filled the collar, the sleeves of her kimono, the folds of her skirt, wherever a hollow invited" [p. 2067]) the essayist should have known when to quit and cut to the final paragraph (fifteen away).

Twenty-two years later it is remarkable how much better Tanizaki's translators understand his work. In an Afterword to the 1977 translation,

1. *The Atlantic Monthly* 195, 1 (January 1955), pp. 141–44.

Thomas J. Harper provides a subtle account of the *zuihitsu* as cultivated by Tanizaki:

> One of the oldest and most deeply ingrained of Japanese attitudes to literary style holds that too obvious a structure is contrivance, that too orderly an exposition falsifies the ruminations of the heart, that the truest representation of the searching mind is just to "follow the brush." Indeed it would not be far wrong to say that the narrative technique we call "stream of consciousness" has an ancient history in Japanese letters. It is not that Japanese writers have been ignorant of the powers of concision and articulation. Rather they have felt that certain subjects—the vicissitudes of the emotions, the fleeting perceptions of the mind—are best couched in a style that conveys something of the uncertainty of the mental process and not just its neatly packaged conclusions.[2]

It would be a shame, then, if students mistook this essay for an old reactionary's rambling tract on dead values. Having worked through with students the ways that the stray structure of the essay is actually a virtue, you might turn next to aspects of its artifice. "I am aware of and most grateful for the benefits of the [modern] age," Tanizaki says in his conclusion. "No matter what complaints we may have, Japan has chosen to follow the West, and there is nothing for her to do but move bravely ahead and leave us old ones behind" (p. 2071).

This particular old one was forty-eight. The exaggeration typifies the rhetorical strategem. Yes, there is a genuine nostalgia for the baby thrown out with the bathwater. And, to put the essay in its historical perspective, Tanizaki's cultural critique coincides with an emerging nativism in the 1930s, a movement that transmuted as the decade wore on into virulent nationalism. Tanizaki is not totally removed from contemporary currents. But neither is he one for ingesting ideology. This is no more an anti-Western tract than it is the voice of superannuation. What it really seems to be, as the headnote has already suggested, is a meditation on the folly of letting others set one's standards. All the rest is simply metaphor.

Topics for Discussion and Writing

1. What is the central metaphor in this essay? How does it operate?
2. Do you think Tanizaki can be accused of exoticizing the past, or, in an odd role reversal, of peddling the cliché of a "mysterious Orient"?
3. Some critics have said that *In Praise of Shadows* finally amounts to no more than wistful nostalgia. Do you agree?
4. How does Tanizaki alert the reader to his ironic intent?
5. According to *In Praise of Shadows*, what is the real problem with Western influence?

---

2. Thomas J. Harper and Edward G. Seidensticker, trans., *In Praise of Shadows*, New Haven, 1977, p. 45.

Comparative Perspectives

1. Tanizaki alerts us to both the practical and the symbolic implications of the spaces in which we live. Compare his remarks on the provisions for privacy and meditation made by the placement of the toilet in Japanese architecture with the lack of privacy afforded by apartments and houses in many of the fictional selections in the anthology.

   [Good choices include Kafka's *Metamorphosis*, with its precise outline of the peculiar layout of Gregor's room, vulnerable to intrusion from every side; Proust's *Remembrance of Things Past*, with the series of rooms in which the unhappy Marcel tries to find comfort; Amichai's poems, especially *Of Three or Four in a Room* or *Sleep in Jerusalem*, in which private rooms seem always vulnerable to the outside world.]

2. Compare Tanizaki's ruminations on skin color with those of the Caribbean writers in this volume, especially in Chapter 35 of Walcott's *Omeros*; or in Lorna Goodison's *Guinea Woman*. How does personal experience condition the various attitudes expressed? Do you find any of these sentiments troubling? Can you explain why?

Further Reading

See the reading suggestions in the anthology, p. 2048. The brief Afterword quoted above (see note 2) is highly recommended.

T. S. Eliot

T. S. Eliot is probably the best-known and most influential twentieth-century poet writing in English. He believed that great writers represent their time, and his own poems, plays, and criticism have given modern Western society a characteristic voice. When we read *The Love Song of J. Alfred Prufrock* we find ourselves engaged with a vulnerable, self-conscious presence that has become so central to twentieth-century literature that it is hard to imagine the modern consciousness without him. *The Waste Land*, with its insistent depiction of a civilization in fragments and its dramatic litany of the symptoms of the collapse, is, for many, the central statement of modern culture's obsessions and fears. Eliot did not stop, however, with the bleak vision of these earlier poems. *Little Gidding*, from the *Four Quartets*, attempts to redeem the earlier despair; it is a redemption conjured out of the language itself, grave and endlessly fascinating. The range of Eliot's vision and the power of his language make the poet a dominating presence in modern literature.

The Love Song of J. Alfred Prufrock

Backgrounds

The opening three lines of *The Love Song of J. Alfred Prufrock* raise significant questions as to just exactly what kind of poem it is. The "I" of the first line does not at first present any particular problems; it appears to be the shadowy, wispy figure of J. Alfred Prufrock. The "you," however, is a different matter. Is it the reader? If so, then the poem is a monologue: the speaker alone, addressing an audience of readers. The monologue depends on its honesty, because we tend to believe that what the speaker has to say, especially about himself, is true.

But perhaps the "you" is another person in the poem, someone whose silent companionship calls forth Prufrock's poetic speech? If so, then the poem is a dramatic monologue, and we are invited to look beyond the spoken words for sources of psychological motivation. In such a case we are not dealing with a private self, but instead with a self on public display, subject to the usual distortions and camouflages associated with the social self. But who then is this "you"? Eliot himself said that it was an unidentified male companion. But it has also been suggested, with considerable plausibility, that the mysterious "you" is simply Prufrock's public self, which can be differentiated from the sensitive, thinking, inward Prufrock who is the "I" in the poem.

In any case, what we clearly have in the poem is a central figure driven by a psychic unrest toward action (to break away from a meaningless life? make a proposal of love? upset the universe?), yet dissuaded from action by a psychic terror of the unfamiliar, the new, the upsetting. So the poem dramatizes in its narrative, its images, even its rhythms, a tug of war between impulses of restlessness, anticipations of a movement toward a goal, enticements vaguely erotic and sexually arousing (like light brown hair on the woman's arms), and impulses of escape through anesthesia (the etherised patient), through acceptance of defeat ("And would it have been worth it, after all"), and through nostalgia for more primitive states characterized by uninhibited instinctual drives. In one part of himself, Prufrock longs for the fatal interview with its moment of truth; in another part of himself he fights it with every ounce of his rational and rationalizing brain. Such a sketch is far too simplistic to contain the poem, but it may serve usefully as a scaffold for approaching it.

Prufrock's world has three main features. It is trivial and full of trivialities like marmalade and tea. It is in part a metaphor or symbol of Prufrock's own frustrated interior consciousness. It is, in addition, a sort of Dantesque Inferno. The Dantesque qualities are not to be overlooked. The epigraph (and we should always pay close attention to Eliot's epigraphs) is from *The Divine Comedy*, and suggests the degree to which the landscape of the poem is to be seen as hellish and the speaker of the poem as one of the damned. From the first stanza, with its sinister litany of "half-deserted streets" and "sawdust restaurants with oyster-shells," through the feline "yellow smoke that slides along the street," and so on, we are aware that the modern city has become one of the circles of Hell for Prufrock—as in the poetry of Baudelaire, whose Paris is also a derivative of Dante's Hell.

If the first few stanzas of *Prufrock* use a modern cityscape to mirror interior psychic states, the remaining stanzas elaborate the triviality of

Prufrock's existence in that setting. It is a setting shorn of heroes; Prufrock is "not Prince Hamlet, nor was meant to be." Should he rise from the dead, like Lazarus, the response would be indifference. He is not only unable to answer the "overwhelming question," he is unable even to ask it. Questions of real depth can lead only to speechless ellipsis. In an environment where the only great issues are issues of etiquette ("My necktie rich and modest"), who would dare "Disturb the universe?"—and what would "they" say if someone did? Since the women "in the room" can reduce even so extraordinary a figure as Michelangelo to a subject of tea-party conversation, Prufrock can guess what short work they would make of *him*.

Shrunk to the dimensions of the world that up to now has contained it, Prufrock's life is "measured out" with "coffee spoons"—has become a meaningless round of meaningless activity; after "tea and cakes and ices" he wonders if he has the "strength to force the moment to its crisis." The "crisis," we suspect, is *any* moment of significance, but Prufrock seems to situate it specifically in a proposal to a woman. Somewhere in this suffocating void, then, there is a woman whom Prufrock wishes to approach, perhaps seriously—for this is a "love song," after all. But the possibilities of success are almost nil. Prufrock's prospects are dimmed by his own shyness, by his morbid consciousness of "them," and by the ways of a world over which he cannot even presume to have control. His fantasies and desires, his vision of the romantically heroic self that he longs to be, are inevitably intruded upon by the "real world," a world in which he grows old and wonders if he dares to "eat a peach." In his fantasies, he may have "heard the mermaids singing." He cannot, however, "linger in the chambers" of his romantic wishes for very long before "human voices"—the voices of the world he actually inhabits—drown him and his fantasies together.

Eliot wanted, as he once said, "an expression of *significant* emotion, emotion which has its life in the poem and not in the history of the poet." The way emotion could be born inside the poem, without turning loose what were merely personal—and therefore idiosyncratic and trivial—emotions, was through an "objective correlative":

> The only way of expressing emotion in the form of art is by finding an "objective correlative"; in other words, a set of objects, a situation, a chain of events which shall be the formula of that *particular* emotion; such that when the external facts, which must terminate in sensory experience, are given, the emotion is immediately invoked.
> —*Hamlet and His Problems* (1919)

Prufrock, especially, presents Eliot's use of this method to good advantage.

Eliot quite consciously left few biographical clues behind him. Until recently, we had no published collection of letters, and there are no diaries, memoirs, or autobiographical writings to work from. Hugh Kenner has called him "the invisible poet," and Eliot himself was pleased to be called "Old Possum."

We do know that he was, from the first, much disturbed by the conflict between his supersubtle and refined intelligence and what he apparently felt were the demeaning distractions of his physical life. Similarly, he felt the sanctuary of the inward self to be under constant stress from the insistent social and material facts around him—shabby streets, sickness, the social round, the dance of courting. He was inhibited and perhaps afraid when in the presence of women; yet he desired them, and the resulting struggle often left him feeling inadequate, irritated, and distressed. All of these impressions find their way into *The Love Song of J. Alfred Prufrock* and suggest some of the reasons for the poem's tonal interplay of self-mockery and despair.

In the poem we find adaptations of Dante, Baudelaire, and Jules Laforgue, whose presentations of interior landscapes of atomized consciousness were particularly important to Eliot during the period in which he wrote the poem. He was also influenced by the dramatic monologues as well as the crisis-ridden personae of Browning and Tennyson. Henri Bergson's notion of life as a succession of psychological states, memories, and roles has possibly left its mark on the poem, as have Dostoevsky's portrayals of characters with significant psychological disabilities, and Henry James's analysis of the unlived life, especially in *The Beast in the Jungle* and *Crapy Cornelia*. Influences from the seventeenth-century English metaphysical poets (particularly Donne) and the nineteenth-century French symbolist tradition tradition may likewise be traced.

Classroom Strategies

The Love Song of J. Alfred Prufrock will take a full class period, since you will likely be inclined to discuss not only the poem, but the characteristics of modern poetry generally. Even if other modern poets—from Baudelaire through Rilke and Stevens—have been covered, you may feel the need to review or qualify earlier remarks and to make direct applications to Eliot. Beginning with *Prufrock*, in which some of the problems of reading Eliot appear in reasonably simple form, seems the best approach to take, no matter whether you teach all three poems or not.

When approaching *The Love Song of J. Alfred Prufrock*, familiar though that poem has now become to most teachers, it is worth remembering that early readers of the poem often found it obscure and incoherent. Arthur Waugh, father of Evelyn Waugh, reviewed it with the verdict that "the state of Poetry is indeed threatened with anarchy which will end in something worse even than 'red ruin and the breaking up of laws.' " Most students coming to Eliot for the first time are "early readers." For many, establishing the "I" and the "you" will be the most helpful step. Although it can plausibly be argued that Prufrock has no fixed identity and, additionally, that the entire poem takes place not in the real world but in his tormented subconscious, students will grasp the poem more clearly on a first reading if they view the speaker of the poem as a middle-aged man named Prufrock and the "you" as the reader. The first line then becomes an invitation to go with the speaker on his outward and inward journey. The point that what we "see" in the poem has more to do with Prufrock's consciousness than with any material facts can be established on a second reading by the implications of lines 2 and 3. The evening is "like" an anesthetized patient because Prufrock himself is "like" one. Students are likely to understand this poem long before they comprehend it. With a bit of help they will enjoy it immensely.

Topics for Discussion and Writing

1. What kind of a poem is *The Love Song of J. Alfred Prufrock*? Is it a monologue? A dramatic monologue? An inner monologue? What difference does such an identification make?

   [See the first three paragraphs of "Backgrounds" for discussion.]

2. How is description—especially of the cityscape—used in *Prufrock*?

   [See the fifth and sixth paragraphs of "Backgrounds" for discussion.]

3. What sort of person is Prufrock? What does his full name suggest about him? What is he afraid of? In what ways is his life trivial or meaningless? To what extent is the title of the poem ironic?

   [See "Backgrounds" and "Classroom Strategies."]

The Waste Land

Backgrounds

Experience shows that students attempting to cope for the first time with the flurry of allusions, the imbedded meanings, the tone, and the structure of *The Waste Land* are soon out of their depth. You will be well advised to read as many of the commentaries listed below as you have time for.

Underlying myth. It is important, first, for students to understand a background that the poem takes for granted. The following summary by Cleanth Brooks of the myth that underlies the poem is perhaps the clearest to be had:

> The basic symbol used, that of the waste land, is taken . . . from Miss Jessie Weston's *From Ritual to Romance*. In the legends which she treats there, the land has been blighted by a curse. The crops do not grow and the animals cannot reproduce. The plight of the land is summed up by, and connected with, the plight of the lord of the land, the Fisher King, who has been rendered impotent by maiming or sickness. The curse can be removed only by the appearance of a knight who will ask the meanings of the various symbols which are displayed to him in the castle. The shift in meaning from physical to spiritual sterility is easily made, and was, as a matter of fact, made in certain of the legends.

Eliot once remarked of Joyce that his use of the *Odyssey* as background in *Ulysses* gave him "a way of controlling, of ordering, of giving a shape and a significance to the immense panorama of futility and anarchy which is contemporary history." Where Joyce used Homeric myth as a parallel, Eliot used anthropology (Jessie Weston's book, behind which lies Sir James Frazer's immensely influential *The Golden Bough*) as well as a succession of key works in the Western literary tradition. In this way he transforms the original anthropological vegetation myth into one that has symbolic application to the modern world.

Voices. Eliot's original title for the poem was taken from Dickens—"He Do the Police in Different Voices." And, indeed, there are many different voices in the poem, many different speakers. Some have names (Tiresias, Madame Sosostris), most have not—but all are clearly "characters" in the poem. There is the sledding "I" of lines 8–18; the grave "I" of lines 27–30; the "hyacinth girl" (lines 35–41); the friend of Stetson (lines 60–76); the nervous speaker and her respondent (lines 111–38); Lil's friend and advisor, who tells her story (lines 142–72); the Spenserian/Marvellian speaker (lines 173–201); the object of Mr. Eugenides's desire (lines 207–14); the "typist" (line 252); the visitor to the church of St. Magnus Martyr (lines 257–65); the three "Thames daughters" (lines 292–95, 296–99, 300–305); and the (apparently) single voice of section V of the poem.

All of these different voices are, however, absorbed into the one comprehensive voice of the poet through which the other voices speak. Eliot himself named Tiresias (who clearly speaks lines 215–56) as the "most important personage in the poem, uniting all the rest. . . . What Tiresias *sees*, in fact, is the substance of the poem." It is a good choice: Tiresias— witnessing prophet, seer of past, present and future, with experience as both man and woman—connects the fragments of a civilization scattered through time and space. In Tiresias (see the *Odyssey* X and XI, and *Oedipus the King*) past and future are always present, contained in a single consciousness. Had Eliot left the matter open he would have allowed us to assume that the all-comprehending voice in the poem was his own, an idea that he probably thought presumptuous.

Tone. Despite the competing voices of the poem, it sustains a singular tone—urbane, grave, dry, abrupt, poignant, slightly sinister, and suffering, vibrant with something very like Old Testament prophetic despair. This is the tone of the poet in the poem, who does not take lightly what he sees.

Structure. The poem means to appear as disjointed as the world it describes, and we are left to put the pieces together, to make sense of them, just as we are in the "real world." Most poetry, like most fiction, is linear: one stanza leads to the next with a kind of inevitability, and the poet usually takes pains to lead the reader from one part of the poem to the next. Words and stanzas rush—and then, and then, and then—to an inevitable conclusion. The "meaning" of *The Waste Land*, on the contrary, is lodged in the spaces between the lines, where the suggestions of the poet and the responses of the reader mix to make sense of the material at hand. The central theme of the poem is the breakdown of civilization, the resulting death-in-life that is a consequence of that breakdown, and the difficulties of cultural regeneration from this death-in-life. Each of the five sections (or movements) of the poem cleaves closely to this theme.

Section I, "The Burial of the Dead," introduces the reader to the underlying myth of the poem, presents the first image of the waste land, offers the controlling images of water and dryness, explores the difficulty of being aroused from death-in-life, and suggests the false avenues—such as the occult—that might be taken to establish meaning in an otherwise meaningless world.

Section II, "A Game of Chess," again gestures toward the notion of death-in-life, but this time by exploring the failure of love due to emotional impotence; the emptiness of marriage, shown especially through the rejection of offspring; and the suggestion that nature itself has become perverted or artificial.

Section III, "The Fire Sermon," again presents the failure of love, but this time by emphasizing the emptiness of sexual relationships outside of marriage; it explores the automatism of lust, and the "mind-forged manacles" (see Blake's *London* [volume E, p. 787]) that debase societies and individuals alike.

Section IV, "Death by Water," though extremely brief, enforces the notion that the forces of life (water) easily become the forces of death (by drowning). We are left uncertain whether the death is regenerative or sterile; whether it is real or an image reflecting the speaker's longing for oblivion.

Section V, "What the Thunder Said," continues to insist on the harsh, stony, wasted landscape of the present, but also offers the prospect of regeneration and inner peace through the avenues of giving, sympathy, and self-control. The incantatory "Shantih shantih shantih," which comes directly after the thunder speaks, literally *means* something like the "peace which passeth understanding," but it has also been thought to suggest the sound of the much-desired rain.

The comparison of past and present. Past and present in the poem are meant to be simultaneous; they are both contained in the poem's central consciousness. Eliot, like Yeats, was aware in his work that present experience is merely the sum of past experiences. Thus the past may allude to a similar condition in the present, serving as a prophetic warning to contemporary readers:

> What is the city over the mountains
> Cracks and reforms and bursts in the violet air
> Falling towers
> Jerusalem Athens Alexandria
> Vienna London
> Unreal

(lines 372–77)

Or the past may emphasize the comparative decadence of the present. Eliot uses direct quotations, half-quotations, parodies of well-known texts, and allusions through tone, rhythm, and imagery to register the existence of a once vital tradition that has been either corrupted, forgotten, or ignored in the modern present. A few significant examples of various kinds follow:

Lines 1–7: lines meant to bring to mind the vital, regenerative April and the pilgrimage to a holy place in the Prologue to Chaucer's *Canterbury Tales*.

Lines 31–34, 42: from Wagner's opera *Tristan and Isolde*, a story of tragic passion, the lines evoke a kind of passion no longer available in the modern world, and also, however, an enhanced awareness of the aridity of *mere* passion, which is further suggested by the image of desolation and emptiness in line 42.

Lines 60–68: Baudelaire's "unreal city," Dante's souls awaiting transport to the various circles of Hell, Joyce's Dublin graveyard scene in *Ulysses*, and Blake's vision of the city in his poem *London* are used here to suggest the infernal quality of modern life in the modern city.

Lines 77–110: the opening is a parody of Enobarbus's speech describing Cleopatra in Shakespeare's *Antony and Cleopatra* II.ii, and it registers a comparison between a gloried past and a tawdry present. In Shakespeare, the queen is a kind of magical goddess, and her barge and the surrounding seascape suggest harmony with the natural world. In Eliot, the scene is a sexual and natural waste land; the woman can muster no magic without the most artificial aids, and she is surrounded by painted images of rape and violence. Yet here too a melancholy hint remains of the destructive capacities of passion and of the *likeness* of that world to ours.

Line 172: Eliot's use of Ophelia's mad farewell in *Hamlet* IV.v makes even more sinister the pub story told about Lil and Albert and provides ironic commentary on the "sweet ladies" involved.

Lines 173–84: Spenser's image in his *Prothalamion* of the "sweet Thames" covered with flower petals for an impending double marriage stands in stark contrast to the modern Thames described by the speaker.

Lines 266–78, 279–91: again, Spenser's *Prothalamion* is invoked in order to contrast the sweating, polluted river of the present with the sparkling "sweet Thames" of the past.

Lines 306–311: these lines combine the words of St. Augustine, recalling his youthful days of "unholy loves," with those of the Buddha, denouncing desire in his *Fire Sermon*. Carthage, like London, was a commercial center and was, as London might be, destroyed. Conceivably, Virgil's *Aeneid* is also suggested here: Carthage was the site of Dido's funeral pyre, again a monument to passion that ends in death.

After reading *The Waste Land*, one of Eliot's friends declared that it was his "autobiography." But the autobiographical elements of the poem are so deeply imbedded, and we know so comparatively little about Eliot's life, that to unearth what is strictly personal in the poem will probably take years of rather difficult excavation.

Some personal facts are relevant. During the final period of the poem's composition, Eliot's troubled marriage with his wife Vivien was collapsing. She suffered one of her many nervous breakdowns in 1921, and her crises, combined with the strain of his monotonous clerk's job at Lloyd's Bank and a persistent lack of funds, drove Eliot to a breakdown of his own later in that year. He wrote much of the poem during a period of recuperation at Margate ("On Margate Sands. . . . I can connect / Nothing with nothing" [lines 300–02]) and in Lausanne. Vivien had suffered from bouts of mental illness ever since their marriage in 1915. They had been married under rather mysterious circumstances and without the blessing of his pious and still influential parents. Contemporary rumor suggested that Eliot, in the "awful daring of a moment's surrender / Which an age of prudence can never retract" (lines 404–05), had "compromised" Vivien and then felt obliged to marry her, but this has never been verified. Whatever the case, Vivien's behavior, especially during her bouts of nervous illness, alarmed Eliot and others. One account describes her this way: "She gave the impression of absolute terror, of a person who's seen a ghost, a goblin ghost, and who was always seeing a goblin in front of her. Her face was all drawn and white, with wild, frightened, angry eyes. . . . Supposing you would say to her, 'Oh, will you have some more cake?' she'd say, 'What's that? What do you mean? What do you say that for?' She was terrifying." Very possibly her accents can be heard in lines 111–38 of the poem.

Like all other Europeans and a large number of Americans, Eliot found World War I and its exhausting aftermath a sign that civilization as it had been lived for five hundred years or so was collapsing. Images from the war, or having to do with war, infiltrate *The Waste Land* at every point: the dehumanization of the people of London, the continued references to collapsing or inverted towers and bridges, the "rats' alley" (a term used to describe the trenches as well as urban blight), the allusions to the Russian Revolution in lines 367–77, and the vision of the waste land itself. The Great War had changed everything, and Eliot's poem registers that change and suggests its effects.

In an essay on Philip Massinger (1920), Eliot writes:

> Immature poets imitate; mature poets steal; bad poets deface what they take, and good poets make it into something better, or at least something different. The good poet welds his theft into a whole of feeling which is unique, utterly different from that from which it was torn; the bad poet throws it into something which has no cohesion.

Though these comments may be self-serving, there is no doubt that Eliot's own use of his predecessors is transformative.

The direct influence of Ezra Pound on the final version of *The Waste Land* must be mentioned. In January 1922, Eliot showed the manuscript of the poem to Pound, who remarked that it was impressive enough "to make the rest of us shut up shop." Even so, he felt it could be improved; he slashed out whole sections of the poem and tightened others. The poem we have is, in fact, so heavily indebted to Pound's editorial skills that it is almost a collaboration. Eliot's dedication of the poem to Pound, *il miglior fabbro* ("the better craftsman"), is as justified a dedication as ever appeared on a work of literature. The nature and extent of Pound's editing can be viewed firsthand in the *Facsimile and Transcript of the Original Drafts* of the poem, edited by Eliot's second wife, Valerie.

Classroom Strategies

The Waste Land will take a minimum of two class periods, perhaps more. Students will not follow Eliot's poems effectively without your aid and generosity—generosity in establishing the general meaning (without sounding pedantic) of individual allusions, lines, images, and symbols. *The Waste Land,* especially, can be turned into a kind of poem-encyclopedia—a great off-putting puzzle—if you do not keep the whole poem continually in focus.

How do you teach *The Waste Land?* Two warnings may be useful:

1. Do not attempt to go through the poem line by line, allusion by allusion, reference by reference. Students will be impressed by Eliot's knowledge, and no doubt by yours, but they will miss the poem altogether and worry overmuch about which of Eliot's allusions is to appear on their next exam.
2. Do not pretend that the poem is simple once one has some sort of "key," or that there *is* a key. Eliot once told a group of students at Harvard that *he* thought everything about it was pretty clear. He was reportedly disturbed by their laughter.

Some suggestions of procedure may also be helpful:

1. Begin with *Prufrock.* Some of the difficulties of Eliot's poetic method in *The Waste Land* clear up in advance on students' encounter with this poem.
2. Place *The Waste Land* in the context of modern thought and writing—its major themes, images, techniques—already encountered by the student in previous assignments. Useful contextual remarks on the modern era will be found in the Introduction, "The Modern World: Self and Other in Global Context" (pp. 1579–99 in the anthology), which students should be asked to review.
3. Make sure the underlying myth of the poem is understood (see "Backgrounds": *Underlying myth*). If you are well grounded in the

Arthurian legends you will find they buttress the discussion, since students usually have some knowledge of these legends and of quest narratives in general, owing to the proliferation of films and books such as J. R. R. Tolkien's *Lord of the Rings* or Frank Herbert's *Dune*. Easily called up too are the many quest narratives students have met with earlier in the anthology: the *Odyssey*, *The Divine Comedy*, *The Canterbury Tales*, *Don Quixote*, *Gulliver's Travels*, *Candide*, and *The Death of Ivan Ilyich*, to mention only a few. The particularities of the myth as used by Eliot will be new to the class, but not the basic form of the quest.

4. Emphasize that the poem's "voices," however numerous, belong to a presiding, comprehending consciousness (which may be called either Tiresias's or Eliot's) and that the story told by each voice contributes to Eliot's overriding theme.

5. Analyze briefly the way the fragments of the poem hang together and make its central themes resonate. Since each section of the poem emphasizes something different, yet contributes to the emotional and intellectual effect as a whole, it will be wise, early on, to discuss what each section individually is about, but without going into detail.

6. At about this point, if time permits, it pays to let the class hear the poem in Eliot's own rendering of it on Caedmon records or cassette tapes, with its grave Anglo-American twang. This will not only enhance the fascination of the poem, it will also register unforgettably the myriad interconnections of sound and sense within the poem and provide a dramatic background for the next procedure.

7. Pick one section for extremely close examination. Section II, "A Game of Chess," is perhaps the easiest to deal with in this way. Section III, "The Fire Sermon," also offers comparatively easy opportunities for close scrutiny. Section I, "The Burial of the Dead," and the concluding section V, "What the Thunder Said," generally strike students as the most difficult.

8. Discuss the range and character of critique within the poem. The way that Eliot manages the devaluations of the present by implicit comparisons with the past can best be demonstrated by looking at lines 77–105 in section II, lines 173–202 in section III, and lines 266–91 in section III. To convince students of the persuasiveness of this technique, you might consider invoking the way politicians imply a decline in current conditions by evoking past stabilities, or the way teachers condemn present educational standards by comparing them to the standards in place when they were in school. The point is not that any of these speakers, including the poem's speaker, expects to recapture the past. It is simply that the past, seen as golden, makes a persuasive point of reference for inciting improvements in the future. In *The Waste Land*, however, one must remember also that the past functions as evidence that basic human frailties do not greatly change.

Topics for Discussion and Writing

1. What is the underlying myth of *The Waste Land*? Where does it come from? In what other works do we find it? How does the poem use it to comment on our world?
   [See "Backgrounds": *Underlying myth.*]
2. Discuss the use of different speakers in *The Waste Land*. How does their use mirror the disjointedness of modern experience? In what way is Tiresias important?
   [See "Backgrounds": *Voices.*]
3. How does Eliot compare past with present in the poem? To what purposes?
   [See the appropriate section in "Backgrounds" and suggestion number 8 in "Classroom Strategies."]
4. Describe the controlling images of *The Waste Land*: water and dryness, the seasons, and so forth. How do they interrelate in the poem?
5. Define the attitudes toward love and sex expressed in the poem. How do they relate to a waste land?

Four Quartets: Little Gidding

Backgrounds

As with each of the *Four Quartets*, *Little Gidding* is written in a form that its author liked to think of as analogous to Beethoven's late quartets. It has five movements: an introduction and a statement of theme, a lyrical development of that theme with a meditation on it, a metaphorical journey that suggests the theme of exploration, a shorter lyric, and a summary of the whole that echoes the opening movement.

The first movement is set in midwinter at Little Gidding, a seventeenth-century Anglican religious community, a time of year that suggests the coldness of old age and oncoming death, a time when the "soul's sap quivers." But the first movement emphasizes the possibilities of renewed life, a springtime that, for the speaker, must take place outside of time—it is "not in time's covenant." Pentecostal fire gleams in the poem in the same way the "brief sun flames the ice." Little Gidding, where the eternal ritual of prayer and worship persists and remains valid, becomes symbolic of a place outside of time, a spiritual realm that is "the intersection of the timeless moment," is "England and nowhere," "Never and always." It is the place, the speaker suggests, where all travelers must come and that will "always be the same." Little Gidding exists in an order of reality beyond the world.

The second movement begins with three rhymed stanzas that suggest the hopelessness of mere earthly existence by lyrically detailing the death of the four Heraclitean elements—air, earth, water, and fire—and the civilization that these earthly elements make up. These are followed by a long narrative section in which the speaker, walking in the "waning-dusk" on fire patrol during the London blitz of World War II (during which the poem was written), encounters "a familiar compound ghost / Both intimate and unidentifiable." This "ghost" both is and is not the speaker; it is himself and everyone. The meeting is much like that of Dante the pilgrim's meeting with Virgil in *The Divine Comedy*. Thus, the ghost in *Little Gidding* has the "look of some dead master" and is the speaker's guide and kindred spirit. This kindred spirit rehearses the futility, isolation, and guilt that, in the end, are all that life has brought him. He has found that what he once took for "exercise of virtue" came to nothing but the "bitter tastelessness of shadow fruit" because his work and life were not in service to spiritual values.

The third movement attempts to establish a set of values alternative to those cited by the "ghost." Those who once lived these alternative values are our inheritance; they have become for us a "symbol perfected in death," and we, like Little Gidding itself, can be united with them in a common spiritual present.

The pentecostal experience is the central theme of the two-stanza lyric that makes up the fourth movement. It is about the gorgeous terror of being "redeemed from fire [Hell] by fire [the pentecostal flame]." The movement insists that such an experience consumes like love, a love that surrenders all to a spiritual principle beyond us.

> We only live, only suspire
> Consumed by either fire or fire.
>
> (lines 212–13)

The final movement echoes all the previous themes and images and attempts to reconcile them. Here, the past is reconciled with the present, the poet is reconciled with his work, "the fire and the rose are one." All takes place in symbolic Little Gidding on "a winter's afternoon, in a secluded chapel" where "History is now and England." The poem, like the life of the spirit, finds that:

> . . . the end of all our exploring
> Will be to arrive where we started
> And know the place for the first time.
>
> (lines 242–44)

Little Gidding contains what many find Eliot's best poetry and his most profound and generous thought. The poem finds life in death, spring in winter, the flame in the ice. And it was the last major poem that Eliot would write—finding, perhaps, that the end *was* his beginning.

Eliot was received into the Anglican Church in 1927, an answer to his own despair in *The Waste Land* and the basis for his work in *Little Gidding*. The conflict between the life of the spirit and the life of the body found its resolution in *Little Gidding* and in the other *Four Quartets*.

Little Gidding is, as we might expect, soaked in the Anglican liturgy, its images and its rhythms. Beyond that, there are explicit references to Dante (especially in the second movement), to the mystical visions of Dame Julian of Norwich, and to the anonymous fourteenth-century *Cloud of Unknowing*. The influence of W. B. Yeats is evident throughout, most notably in sections having to do with the decrepitude of old age. The major accents in the poem, however, apart from the liturgical ones, come from Eliot's own earlier poems, particularly *The Waste Land* (see *Little Gidding*, lines 64–71, 80–89, and 100, for instance), which quite understandably were at the back of his mind during the writing of *Little Gidding*.

Classroom Strategies

Little Gidding will require at least one class period. You might find it useful at the beginning of your discussion of *Little Gidding* to consider it in relation to *The Waste Land*, since what Eliot despaired over in *The Waste Land* is resolved in *Little Gidding* through his acceptance of the spiritual life—which in the earlier poem is seen as only a remote, perhaps unattainable, possibility. His vision of a civilization in decline, his insistence on the importance of the past as a comment on the present, his sense that the past and present exist simultaneously—all are found in *Little Gidding* just as they are in *The Waste Land*. The speaker's encounter with the "compound" ghost can almost be seen as the Eliot of *Little Gidding* talking with the Eliot of *The Waste Land*. What needs to be pointed out, of course, is Eliot's change of attitude: the state of civilization may be precarious, but it can be redeemed. The past cannot be reclaimed entire:

> We cannot revive old factions
> We cannot restore old policies
> Or follow an antique drum.

> (lines 187–89)

It can, however, be reclaimed in our lives by our participating in its best values. In *The Waste Land* Eliot's attitude is one of revulsion; in *Little Gidding* he experiences revulsion, but moves beyond it toward acceptance and love. *Little Gidding*, unlike *The Waste Land*, wants to be a generous poem.

Topics for Discussion and Writing

1. Why does *Little Gidding* take place in midwinter? How does the opening remind us of *The Waste Land*? In what ways does *Little Gidding* constitute an "answer" to *The Waste Land*?

    [See the second paragraph of "Backgrounds" and "Classroom Strategies" for discussion.]

2. Who is the "compound ghost" in *Little Gidding*? Of what elements is he "compounded"?

[See the third paragraph of "Backgrounds" for discussion.]
3. Why is the historical Little Gidding an appropriate setting for this poem?

[See the second paragraph of "Backgrounds."]

Comparative Perspectives

1. *The Waste Land* probes the mixture of "[m]emory and desire," a preoccupation that applies equally well to the writing of European modernists and to the oral art of Africa and native America. Try to characterize the distinctive understanding of memory that motivates Eliot and, as appropriate, the writing of Proust, Joyce, and Freud, and compare Birago Diop's discussion of memory throughout *Mother Crocodile* (the title character of which may be seen as a counterpart to Eliot's Tiresias).

   [Perhaps it is fair to say that the modernists struggle to reclaim memory as a way of analyzing the self-conscious individual's experience of desire, an intensely private culture, while the oral realm offers easy access to historical memory that preserves the common culture.]

2. *Little Gidding* takes its name from an English village and seems deeply rooted in local soil. At the same time, as in *The Waste Land*, Eliot's familiarity with non-Western sources leaves an imprint on the poem that lifts it into a "timeless moment" beyond parochialism. Drawing on your reading of other religious poetic texts in this anthology, discuss the "intersection" (line 54) of mystical themes that transcend specific rites and suggest a common human longing for union with the divine.

   [If appropriate, consider the *Bhagavad-Gītā*, especially the similarities between the opening of part III of Eliot's poem and the reflections on action in Krishna's second teaching, the poems of Rumi and Basavanna, the *Ghazals* of Ghalib, *The Night Chant*, Zuni ritual poetry, and *Zaabalawi*.]

Further Reading

See also the reading suggestions in the anthology, p. 2075.

Ackroyd, Peter. *T. S. Eliot: A Life.* 1984. A full-length biography.

Behr, Caroline. *T. S. Eliot: A Chronology of His Life and Works.* 1983.

Bloom, Harold, ed. *T. S. Eliot's* The Waste Land. 1986.

Boernstein, George. *Transformation of Romanticism in Yeats, Eliot, and Stevens.* 1976. Describes similarities and differences in relation to Romantic norms.

Brooker, Jewel Spears. *Reading the Waste Land: Modernism and the Limits of Interpretation.* 1990.

————. *Approaches to Teaching Eliot's Poetry and Plays.* 1988. Published as part of the Modern Language Association's series "Approaches to Teaching World Literature."

Brooks, Cleanth. *Modern Poetry and the Tradition.* 1939. Chapter 7 contains Brooks's clear discussion of the underlying myth in *The Waste Land.*

Davidson, Harriet. *T. S. Eliot and Hermeneutics: Absence and Interpretation in* The Waste Land.1985.

Eliot, T. S. *Selected Essays.* 1950. "Tradition and the Individual Talent" remains a crucial essay for understanding Eliot's work.

Eliot, Valerie, ed. The Waste Land: *A Facsimile and Transcript of the Original Drafts Including the Annotations of Ezra Pound.* 1974. An indispensable aid to understanding *The Waste Land.*

————, ed. *The Letters of T.S. Eliot.* 1988.

Gardner, Helen. *The Composition of Four Quartets.* 1978. An important aid to understanding *Little Gidding.*

Gish, Nancy. The Waste Land: *A Poem of Memory and Desire.* 1988.

Gordon, Lyndall. *Eliot's Early Years*, 1977, and *Eliot's New Life*, 1988. One of the few detailed biographical studies of Eliot.

Harding, D. W. "Little Gidding." In *T. S. Elliot: A Collection of Critical Essays*, edited by Hugh Kenner. 1962, pp. 125–28. The best short discussion of *Little Gidding.*

Kenner, Hugh. *The Invisible Poet: T. S. Eliot.* 1959. Particularly interesting on tone and language.

————, ed. *T. S. Eliot: A Collection of Critical Essays.* 1962.

Longenbach, James. *Modernist Poetics of History: Pound, Eliot, and the Sense of the Past.* 1987. Draws on contemporary philosophical approaches (Gadamer, Nietzsche, DeMann).

Menand, Louis. *Discovering Modernism: T. S. Eliot and His Context.* 1987. Discussion of Eliot in the context of modernism.

North, Michael, ed. *The Waste Land*: A Norton Critical Edition. 2001. The most comprehensive edition available.

Schwartz, Sanford. *The Matrix of Modernism: Pound, Eliot, and Early Twentieth-Century Thought.* 1985. Systematically describes the relationships between twentieth-century philosophers and modernist poets to construct an intellectual-historical model of modernist thought.

Smith, Grover. *T. S. Eliot's Poetry and Plays.* 1956. A highly detailed and thorough investigation of the work, particularly useful on influences and sources.

Spender, Stephen. *T. S. Eliot*. 1976. A readable short introduction to Eliot, written by another poet of considerable accomplishment.

Sultan, Stanley. *Eliot, Joyce and Company*. 1987. Contains a discussion of *The Love Song of J. Alfred Prufrock* and *The Waste Land* as "exemplary shapers" of English modernism.

Tramplin, Ronald. *A Preface to Eliot*. 1988. Gives a full overview and interpretation.

ANNA AKHMATOVA

Requiem

Backgrounds

Anna Akhmatova (pronounced Ahk-*mah*-tov-a) is one of those writers who testify, who bring to light a painful dimension of social reality in the twentieth century and impel us to a deeper understanding of our era. Like T. S. Eliot denouncing the loss of values in *The Waste Land*, or Kafka portraying the dehumanization of industrial society in *The Metamorphosis*, the Russian poet mourns the death of individual freedom and the negation of family ties during the most famous political purges of modern totalitarian society. For each writer, modern society is sick or wounded. Akhmatova's testimony, however, strikes a personal note from the beginning, unlike the more distanced and often symbolic perspectives of Kafka, Eliot, Mann, Brecht, or Beckett. Her readers are immediately confronted by a subjective "I" speaking throughout, whether in individual short poems or in a longer cycle like *Requiem*. There are clearly historical reasons for the subjective "I" in *Requiem*, for the cycle refers directly to the poet's own experience during the purge. However, this "I" whose mounting emotions reach out to the reader is not exclusively Akhmatova's own, for it is gradually equated with the voice of her people. Like Dostoevsky and Tolstoy in the nineteenth century and Solzhenitsyn in the twentieth, Akhmatova is part of a Russian tradition that expects its major authors to be more than subjective individuals and ultimately to bear witness for the national conscience.

Requiem took its current shape over more than twenty-five years. The central (numbered) poems appear to be the first ones written, as if to express her immediate personal shock at the arrest and imprisonment of her husband and son. The first numbered poem is dated 1935 and describes her husband's arrest that year. Numbers V and VI are dated 1939, the year after her son, Lev, was arrested for the second time and then imprisoned for the seventeen months Akhmatova mentions in the "Preface." Number VII, which announces the son's condemnation, is dated Summer 1939. The following invocation to Death is dated August 19, 1939 (from their home in Fontanny Dom), and Number IX, which describes her mad despair, is dated May 4, 1940. Nineteen forty appears to be the year in which Akhmatova began to cast her personal tragedy in larger terms, for the "Dedication," and the two epilogues, all of which link her fate to that of her people, are dated March 1940, and the tenth numbered poem (*Crucifixion*), which invokes a religious parallel and consolation, is dated 1940–43. Akhmatova herself gave the dates for these poems and for the prose *Preface* (April 1, 1957) and introductory epigraph (1961), as if to reaffirm the historical authenticity of what she says. Nonetheless, she has not forgotten the inner constraints of poetic form, for it seems likely that other poems—written later but reflecting situations earlier in the cycle— were left undated so as not to contradict the sense of chronological development from one stage to another.

In the years when the first poems were written, life was precarious indeed. Manuscripts were often confiscated and examined by the secret police for indications of subversive thinking, and Akhmatova reportedly destroyed the manuscripts of individual stanzas of *Requiem* after they were committed to memory. Political censorship had existed for decades and writers did not stop writing, but they often turned to scenes from history, mythology, or the Bible in order to be able to comment obliquely on situations that could not otherwise be addressed. Thus Akhmatova in the thirties wrote an "Armenian" fable in which she took the role of a bereaved ewe asking the shah (and any image of a ruler would evoke Stalin) "Have you dined well? . . . was my little son / To your taste, was he fat enough?" *Requiem*, however, was too open in its condemnation to be published or even acknowledged in Stalin's lifetime; in fact, the subject of the Stalinist regime was such a sensitive topic that the entire cycle has never been published in the Soviet Union.

The epigraph and *Preface* to the cycle introduce Akhmatova to us in three ways: as a person who refused to seek refuge in other countries (she sharply criticized those who did), as a woman waiting numbly outside prison for news of a loved one inside, and as a writer asked by her fellow-sufferers to bear witness to what happened. As the poet begins to speak in the "Dedication" and "Prologue" she evokes their common situation but still sees herself as an individual, a person separate from "my chance friends / Of those two diabolical years." It will take the development of the poem itself, and a crisis of mounting personal agony that cannot be faced alone, for the speaker to identify herself with other sufferers in Russia and throughout history.

Religious and patriotic images are present from the beginning. The women waiting before the prison rise each morning "as if for an early service"; other religious references appear in the icon kissed in the first numbered poem, the invocation to "Say a prayer for me" in the second, the swinging censers in the fifth, the transcendent cross in the sixth, and the culminating projection of the bereaved mother's plight onto a biblical level in the last numbered poem, *Crucifixion*. A broad sense of Russian history and culture provides another framework transcending current events: age-old "innocent Russia" is the true victim of the present regime ("Prologue"), contemporary tyrannical murders have an historical precedent (the 1698 execution of the Streltsy in the first poem), and a projected image of the

Russian people of "folk" underlies the lilting melancholy of the second poem, which echoes both the simplicity and metrical form of a Russian folksong. Shattering as their individual experiences may be, these women are not alone in either divine or human history.

Classroom Strategies

Requiem can be taught in one period. You may help your students focus their reading if you suggest ahead of time that they read the numbered poems as the diary of a mother who is grieving—perhaps to the point of madness—over the arrest of her son. In class, this personal focus can be situated in the larger perspective of the public poet through examining the "Preface" and, later, the frame of "Dedication" and epilogue. *Requiem* takes its place in the stream of literary works that evoke a moment in history, such as works by Dostoevsky or Chekhov in the preceding section, or by Mann, Kafka, Camus, and Solzhenitsyn in this section. You may wish to comment on the way the Russian authors especially take it upon themselves to speak for their country, and to ask whether students can think of American authors who do the same. It may bring the poem painfully alive if you draw parallels with the vigils of bereaved mothers in Argentina during the military dictatorship: the thousands of women called simply "The Mothers," who gathered each week in the large public square of Buenos Aires, holding the photographs of the "disappeared": their husbands, children, and grandchildren who were taken by the secret police.

While students will probably be drawn by the image of the grieving mother and imprisoned son, they may have some trouble in linking the perspectives in the "story" poems of the core section. Part of the poem's interest, of course, lies in the rich variation of lyric forms in the different parts, but at the beginning it is probably best to emphasize that these shifting and fragmented perspectives are so many glimpses, over time, into the mind of a woman who is greatly shaken by grief and fear. The "Prologue" and the first numbered poem are spoken in the first person, using a relatively objective style to describe painful events. In the second numbered poem, however, the pain has apparently dominated the speaker to the point that she is no longer capable of using the subjective "I," but imagines a scene in which she is seen only from outside, part of a strangely alienated landscape. That such alienation is real becomes apparent in the following poem, which returns to the "I" but claims incredulously "No . . . it is somebody else who is suffering." In the fourth poem, the "I" restored to her full sense of self looks back on her early carefree life, and compares with it her current misery as she waits outside prison on New Year's Day. In the next two poems she is increasingly fearful as she addresses her son; tinges of madness enter, both in her confessions of mental confusion, and also in images of the stars staring down like predatory hawks. By the seventh poem, the sentence has been passed, and she speaks in frantic contradictions of the need to adjust, to kill memory, or to live before moving to the eighth poem's invocation to Death and images of the swirling Yenisey River and glittering North Star. She sinks openly into madness in the ninth poem, but only for a moment: madness means forgetting, and it is clear from the poignant images of the latter half of the poem that the speaker cannot and will not forget. The tenth poem, however, marks another significant break in perspective as the poet ceases to speak in subjective terms and withdraws personally from the scene, which is now transformed into a biblical drama. As the epilogues show, the speaker's development throughout the cycle has purged her of a purely separate subjective identity and united her with all those who suffer.

Each poem in the cycle also has its own formal and thematic unity, usually involving the development of a particular dramatic scene. A close reading of two or three individual poems will allow you to discuss them as independent works and will give students a sense of how Akhmatova varies her style. For example, the "Prologue" is a brief evocation of an historical period whose horror is emphasized through images of contradiction, madness, or inverted proportions. The first numbered poem is more intimate and focuses on a poignant domestic scene, as did Akhmatova's early work. The second numbered poem uses simple folktale imagery and folk rhythms to present a landscape of alienated identity. The seventh poem, "The Sentence," conveys a state of shock through the speaker's alternating and contradictory moods. You will find your own favorite examples, which may also serve to explore more fully a particular issue.

Most students will have some sense of the secret police systems in dictatorships and totalitarian countries, but they will probably not be acquainted with the geographic references coordinating the setting of *Requiem*. It may be useful to bring or sketch a map of the former Soviet Union in order to situate references to Leningrad and the Neva River, and to the Royal Gardens at Tsarskoe Selo close by; to Moscow (home of the Kremlin), to the Don River, to the Yenisey River in Siberia, where many concentration camps were located, and to the Black Sea.

Topics for Discussion and Writing

1. Why does the woman in the "Preface" ask Akhmatova, "Can you describe this?" Why is she happy at the poet's response? What aspect of Russian literary tradition is involved in both question and response?

    [See "Backgrounds," the discussion of the second epilogue and the tradition of the writer as national conscience.]

2. How does the figure of the narrator change over the course of the cycle? Does she lose or gain a sense of identity (or both)?

    [See the headnote, on pp. 2098–2101 in the anthology, and "Backgrounds" for the poet's identification with the community of suffering women and with the biblical mother of Christ.]

3. What coherence do you perceive in the numbered poems taken as a group? What themes or strategies hold them together?

[See "Classroom Strategies" for a discussion of the fragmentation of narrative perspective.]

4. To what extent do the individual poems stand on their own, as independent pieces?

   [See discussion in "Classroom Strategies."]

5. Why does the tenth numbered poem suddenly present a biblical scene? What previous elements prepare this shift in setting?

   [See the headnote and the discussions of religious imagery and narrative perspective in "Classroom Strategies."]

6. Does the United States have "national writers"? Regional writers? Are American writers and artists expected to act as a "national conscience"? In what way?

   [Answers will vary.]

7. How are frame and core related in the cycle? Does one develop into the other, or were both conceived at once? Explain.

   [See the headnote and "Backgrounds" for a discussion of the chronological development of the cycle. This question assumes you will have mentioned that most of the inner poems were composed before the "Dedication," "Prologue," and epilogues of 1940.]

8. How effective do you find the poem as a political protest? *Requiem* was not published until well after the purges were over and Stalin was dead; is it, then, totally lacking in influence?

   [Answers will vary. Some students will be content with intrinsic aesthetic value, while others may find the poem too specific and therefore dated. You may wish to suggest—in line with traditional "masterpiece" values—that as long as situations of repression and political censorship exist anywhere, such a poem is potentially explosive in its assertion of civil rights and human values; it witnesses movingly to feelings that are timeless as long as children die and mothers grieve, even in a world of perfect freedom.]

Comparative Perspectives

1. Poets frequently claim to lack the words they need, yet in the face of more personal punishment than that experienced by most of the writers in the anthology. Akhmatova replies "Yes, I can," when asked, "Can you describe this?" How does she use poetry to objectify her experience and thus relieve her suffering even while recording it? How would you compare this approach to pain with that of Tennyson in *In Memoriam A. H. H.*, or García Lorca in *Lament for Ignacio Sánchez Mejías*?

2. In the second epilogue Akhmatova makes poetry a political testament; because "the list has been confiscated," her statement seems all the more necessary. Compare the spare means she chooses to voice her outrage with the different rhetorical strategies chosen by other politically committed poets in the anthology. Consider, for example, the way Césaire adapts the imagery of Baudelaire and the

French surrealist tradition in *Notebook of a Return to the Native Land*, the way Neruda gives voice to the oppressed workers of Macchu Picchu, or the way Amichai alludes to biblical and liturgical models in his interweaving of personal and national concerns.

Further Reading

See also the reading suggestions in the anthology, p. 2101.

Akhmatova, Anna. *Poems*. Translated by Lyn Coffin. 1983. The introduction is written by Joseph Brodsky, who knew Akhmatova.

Contemporary Poetry and Poetics. Fall 1988. Several papers from a symposium on Akhmatova appear in this issue (pp. 7–44).

Driver, Sam. "Directions in Akhmatova's Poetry since the Early Period." *Russian Language Journal*, Supplementary Issue: *Toward a Definition of Acmeism* (Spring 1975), pp. 84–91. Notes as a "new thematics" Akhmatova's increasing sense of "nostalgia for European cultural history." (Note that Russian citations are not translated.)

Ketchian, Sonia. "Metempsychosis in the Verse of Anna Akhmatova." *Slavic and East European Journal* 25, 1 (1981), pp. 44–60. Examines the complex layers of reference in Akhmatova's poetry as coordinated with a theme of metempsychosis or the transmigration of souls.

Ketchian, Sonia, and Julian W. Connolly, eds. *Studies in Russian Literature in Honor of Vsevolod Setchkarev*. 1986. In "An Inspiration for Anna Akhmatova's *Requiem*," Sonia Ketchian argues that the aspects of a Requiem by Armenian poet Hovannes Tumanian influenced Akhmatova's poem.

McDuff, David. "Anna Akhmatova." *Parnassus: Poetry in Review* 11, 2 (Spring–Summer 1984), pp. 51–82. Provides a perceptive, focused, and well-documented overview of Akhmatova's work in the context of political, personal, and literary events.

Rosslyn, Wendy. *The Prince, the Fool, and the Nunnery: The Religious Theme in the Early Poetry of Anna Akhmatova*. 1984. A discussion of Akhmatova's early religious poetry.

Soviet Literature. June 1989. This issue, devoted to Akhmatova, contains many interesting essays and also a translation by Sergei Roy of *Requiem* (pp. 67–73) that reproduces the poem's metrical and rhyming patterns. Roy also discusses the cultural context of these literary patterns and how they would have been perceived by the Russian reader.

Terras, Victor. *Handbook of Russian Literature*. The entry by Sonia Ketchian is a compact and lucid overview of the poet's work.

Verheul, Kees. *The Theme of Time in the Poetry of Anna Akhmatova*. A detailed discussion of many important themes, formal strategies, and historical contexts in Akhmatova's poetry, coordinated through their relationship to the concept of time. (Note that Russian citations are not translated.)

DADA-SURREALIST POETRY: A SELECTION

Backgrounds

Dada-Surrealism is now situated as the most radical element in twentieth-century modernism, even though its rebellious founders rejected the possibility of becoming part of a canon. It is in fact two movements, the one more performance-oriented and revolutionary and the other—after a bitter break with Dadaism—emphasizing the consistent exploration of the "revolution of the mind" in any medium. Single or double, Dada-Surrealism takes many modernist themes and techniques to the edge of possibility, emphasizing the role of antilogic and the unconscious in performance as well as in written and artistic form. Most readers find Dada-Surrealism fascinating and even familiar, nonetheless, since the tactics of oddly juxtaposed images, rapid unexplained shifts in point of view, sequences patterned by emotions and not logic, and the will to shock or at least startle the audience form such a large part of contemporary film, TV, advertising, and avant-garde writing and theatrical performance. To make the point that Dada-Surrealism is part of an evolution rather than a completely alien phenomenon, one has only to bring in the reproduction of a Surrealist painting (René Magritte or the early Salvador Dalí, for example) and compare it with major earlier works. It is likely that the Surrealist painting, with all its distortions or startling perspectives, will seem part of contemporary culture in a way that the earlier stylized realism is not.

Tristan Tzara, the best-known figure of Dadaism, is often identified with his *Seven Dada Manifestoes* (1924). His later work extends beyond Dada polemics, however, and includes a major poem, *Approximate Man* (1931), whose nineteen sections explore, in subjective and lyrical tones, the uncertainty of language and personal identity. Poetry and polemics are represented equally in the works printed here. Both the *Proclamation without Pretention,* given complete, and *Dadaist Disgust*, the culminating section of the *Dada Manifesto 1918*, are manifestos issued in 1918, and both use poetic effects as part of their attacks on art and society. *Dadaist Disgust* is more broadly aimed and attacks all the icons of conventional society in the name of spontaneity, vitality, and intense feeling. The *Proclamation without Pretention* focuses on conventional art—or, more precisely, professional formulas for the production and appreciation of "the Beautiful." It is worth remembering that the Dadaists' disgust is historically quite specific: reacting against the "Papa's Europe" that brought on World War I, they reject what they see as its arrogantly destructive mindset. If family, morals, money, logical systems, social hierarchies, respect for the past, faith in progress, and the individual's duty to society are all shibboleths of nineteenth-century respectability, the *Dada Mani-*

festo 1918 will pour scorn on them in the name of individuality, equality, intensity, spontaneous and even contradictory emotions, immediate experience, freedom, and, finally, LIFE.

In the passages leading up to the final paragraph, which is titled *Dadaist Disgust*, Tzara justifies his distrust of scientific and moral pronouncements by saying "everyone has danced according to his own personal boomboom . . . Logic is always false. It draws the superficial threads of concepts and words toward illusory conclusions and centres." It "asphyxiates independence," while morality "infuses chocolate into every man's veins." Tzara protects himself by not accepting any predetermined values: "I am against systems; the most acceptable system is that of having none on no principle."

The very form of these manifestos demonstrates the Dadaist's break with conventional patterns: the *Dada Manifesto 1918* includes scribbles as part of the text, and both manifestos play merrily with typographical conventions; contraries and contradictions are gleefully thrown in the reader's face or glide suddenly into bizarre and disproportionate images. Yet there is a certain cumulative pattern to each piece. Rapid shifts of subject and tone gradually establish their own alternating rhythm and reinforce the work's rebellious tones. Coming at the end of the manifesto, *Dadaist Disgust* pulls together themes from previous passages (*rejection* of family, compromise and sociability, logic, hierarchies of any kind, knowledge of the past, authority and progress; *approval* of shock, spontaneity, word associations, individuality, contradictions, anarchy, intensity, and living in the present) in a condensed summary that races on, through increasingly vivid capitalizations, to its shouted conclusion: "shrieking of contracted pains, intertwining of contraries and all contradictions, grotesqueries, nonsequiturs: LIFE." *Proclamation without Pretention* is even more traditionally organized, in two parts: an attack on professional artists (the "druggists" who assemble their works calculating the rules and prescriptions of pretentious experts) and the proclamation of a natural "antiphilosophy" that is nihilist, vital, spontaneous, gaily contradictory, whimsically illogical, and full of dynamic images that escape academic control. The poem-manifesto ends in a final (boldface) dig at the druggist-artists as narcissistic runts who are still staring at their navels.

As the headnote states, Dadaism was a decentered movement whose adherents often disagreed violently over ideology and action. Kurt Schwitters, for example, once proposed joining the Berlin Dada circle but was rejected by its leader, Richard Huelsenbeck, because he was "too aesthetic" and not sufficiently active in politics. Schwitters is often considered on the outskirts of Dada because he never joined an active Dada group and spent most of his life in Hannover producing artworks that usually took the form of collage (the *Merz* pictures) or gigantic constructions that grew by accretion. While he is usually known as a visual artist, he also composed remarkable sound poems (combinations of sounds organized as pieces of music) and wrote a collection of prose and poetry, *Anna Blume*, which is known chiefly for the title poem, printed in the anthology. (There are, in fact, several *Anna Blume* collections, for the first edition of 1919 caused a sensation and Schwitters published various sequels; later, he and the Dadaist poet Raoul Hausmann even collaborated on a proposed novel.)

Schwitters' writing style evolved as much as his collage art and constructions; the lyrical *Anna Blume* is still close to the expressionist poetry he produced in his youth, predating the abstract word poems of subsequent years. It can be and is usually read as a love poem—unlike two pieces in the later, retitled collection *Blume Anna* that print the alphabet backwards (one in capital letters, the other lowercase; the poet insisted on German pronunciation). Huelsenbeck attacked the lyrical *Anna Blume* because it *could* be read as a bourgeois love poem, "a typical idealist product prettified by craziness." Nonetheless, Schwitters' own crisp, chilly readings of the poem show that he considered it an experiment with rhythm and sound patterns as much as anything else.

Anna Blume is most easily approached as a humorous, ecstatic, happily illogical expression of love. The five senses of normal experience are multiplied to twenty-seven (not a specific allusion, but simply a joyful expansion), and grammar soon falls by the wayside: "I love your!" Here the English *your* should not be interpreted as an adjective for which we can imagine a following noun (such as *eyes*): the German text fractures grammatical logic with a declined form of the pronoun (*Dir*). Schwitters' English adaption, *Eve Blossom Has Wheels*, proposes "thine!," which appropriately startles the grammar-conscious reader and leads into grammatical forms of *I* and *you* until they propose a merger as "*We?*" (*Wir*, rhyming with *Dir*). Puns and free association achieve a subconscious meaning that coexists with surface nonsense: the "uncounted female," for example, is a play on the German *Frauenzimmer*, a familiar term for woman that includes the word *room* (*zimmer*). Rooms have numbers, Anna is unique or unnumbered among women, and thus the phrase offers a tribute that seems, on the one hand, totally gratuitous and, on the other, validated by a play on words. Mocking common sense—in the color contradictions ("Blue is the colour of your yellow hair"), in the image of Anna walking around on her hands, in the prize question's parody of a syllogism—and using increasingly sensual images that are anchored in Anna's name, Schwitters manages to express the delirium of love and also an unwillingness to subordinate its spontaneous emotion to any regulation or restraint.

The simple vocabulary and emotional directness of poems by Paul Eluard make him the most intuitively accessible Surrealist poet. From his early experiments with automatic writing to his resistance poetry during World War II, Eluard emphasized primary emotions and the elemental power of *sight*. "To see is to understand, to judge, to distort, to forget or forget oneself, to be or to disappear." His poetry is charged with visual images that interpret the world of experience, whether it be love, sadness, confusion, or anger—and love is almost uppermost. Like Rimbaud, he believes in the artist as *voyant* or seer: poetry is "a lesson in things," and *see-*

ing (here he refers to visual artists) bridges the gap between the material world and human experience and also between individual human beings. "The role of the artist," he says, is "to teach how to see"; it is a "nostalgia for total light." The mystic overtones of these assertions correspond to the descriptive style of Eluard's poetry, in which everyday scenes are *not* reproduced realistically. Instead, these scenes are reconfigured into dreamlike settings that expose the poet's emotions—perhaps his relationship to a woman—and, throughout, his experience of the world at that precise moment.

Woman in Love (1923) begins with a shocking image ("She is standing on my eyelids") that is typical of such transfiguration. The picture is painful or grotesque unless one interprets it as a metaphor for the poet's obsessive dreaming about his beloved. Such a realistic explanation may be useful, but it also loses the force of the original picture, which is pursued throughout various images of overlap to evoke the absolute fusion of two lovers. Much of Surrealism's appeal depends on this ability to evoke startling, impossible, but subconsciously meaningful images. The *First Manifesto* quotes Pierre Reverdy's 1918 definition of a desirable image as "bringing together two more or less distant realities. . . . The farther they are away yet still connected, the stronger the image." In the second stanza, the sequence of images that describe this apparently dominant woman ("Her eyes are always open," for example) culminates in another impossible but powerful scene: her dreams overcome daytime reality, dissipating plural suns (*plural* demonstrating the continued dominance of dream) rather than being dissipated in broad daylight. The last two lines, however, break the illusion and return it to the poet's control as he comments on his emotional state and the nonsense he has just uttered: speaking "without anything to say."

The three shorter poems pursue similar themes of love and mingled identity, but they also introduce elements of pain and loss. Eluard had married his first wife, Gala, in 1917, and their relationship was not simple: in 1929, she left him for the painter Salvador Dalí. The epigraph to *Dying for Not Dying* (1924, included in *Capital of Pain*) refers to the volume as "his last book," and Eluard took a boat for Tahiti the day before publication. Some felt that he intended to follow Rimbaud's example and abandon literature; others claimed the influence of Breton's poem *Let Everything Go!* Less literary explanations have been found in Gala's affair that year with the artist Max Ernst; months after Eluard's departure, she located the poet in Singapore and brought him back to Paris. The poems are deceptively simple: brief, spare scenes delineated by spare yet precise images. This simplicity encloses complex and poignant emotions, whether it be a sense of cosmic interconnectedness in the lover's gaze his fearful glimpse of her damaged and damaging nature, or his utter desolation as he watches himself lose a dreamed-of ideal partner.

Vision is emphasized in the other two poems: the first set in an ordinary restaurant where the poet is torn between two dimensions of life, and the second using images of time as a mirror (or mirrored time) to raise questions of appearance and reality. In the restaurant, the poet annoyedly denies his difference from other people—his special acquaintance with mystery—and tries to discard the fragments of his dreams; at the same time, he is pulled toward the rich "inward language" of sleep and wonder, to which he finally submits, as the ending series of visionary implosions shows.

André Breton employs a more measured, even logical framework in his poetry. *Free Union* takes its point of departure in the traditional *blason* form, in which a person or object is described (positively or satirically) through a list of qualities: one of the most popular was the "blason of the feminine body." The modern poet presents an encyclopedic list of associations, some of which are easily visualized ("mist on the window-panes," "thoughts like flashes of heat lightning"), while others are responses to intuition ("eyes of water to be drunk in prison") or word associations ("a neck of impearled barley": pearl barley": pearls in a necklace). Each image implies a perspective or emotion ("with the back of a bird in vertical flight"), and the detailed list builds through its own series of internal associations to culminate in the picture of his wife as an embodiment of all nature.

Vigilance is structured as an autobiographical narrative, but a strange narrative in which the speaker turns out to be asleep and describing his journey into a further dimension of dream. Breton moves from relatively familiar images at the beginning—the tower's reflection in the river Seine—to large abstract images of "the heart of things" at the end. Differing from Eluard's more intuitive approach, he adopts a logical perspective to explain his vision's separate stages. As a dream figure, the narrator sets fire to the bed in which he is sleeping, and burns away all vestiges of cooperation with the everyday world (compare the oceanic purge in Rimbaud's *The Drunken Boat*). Dual images emphasize the shift from one to another dimension of reality, as the bedroom furniture metamorphoses into animals: chairs into lions, sheets into white-bellied sharks, imagined flames into the beaks of ibises (the hieratic bird of the Egyptian *Book of the Dead*). Like Eluard in *To Be Caught in One's Own Trap*, the narrator leaves behind the "passersby" of everyday life, "whose shuffling steps are heard far off," to pursue a larger mystery. The lace shell in the shape of a breast reminds us that the experience of "mad love" (undiluted passion) was among the Surrealist's favored routes to inner vision and the state they called the "sublime point" or "the marvelous."

Aimé Césaire and Joyce Mansour, poets a generation after Breton and Eluard, make use of Surrealist perspectives and techniques in their own very different ways. Césaire's connections with Surrealism are confined to the 1940s and linked to a concurrent exploration of black Caribbean identity, an exploration to which he subsequently devoted himself in plays, poetry, essays, and the celebrated *Discourse on Colonialism*. In 1945, however, an essay by Césaire, "Poetry and Knowledge," published in his journal *Tropiques*, clearly echoes themes and images familiar from Surrealism—some of them evident in the Breton and Eluard poems printed here. Summarizing his views in a series of concluding "Propositions," Césaire states: "Poetry is that attitude that by the word, the image, myth, love and humour places me at the living heart of myself and of the world" and "On the marvellous contact of the interior totality and exterior totality, perceived imaginatively and simultaneously by the poet, or more precisely within the poet, marvellous discoveries are made." The ending "Corollary" asserts: "The poet is that very old and very new, very complex and very simple being who—within the lived confines of the dream and the real, day and night, between absence and presence—seeks and receives, in the sudden unleashing of internal cataclysms, the password of complicity and power." Whether in the automatic writing of *Day and Night* or the more focused and coordinated address of *Do Not Have Pity and Sun Serpent*, these poems show an eagerness to use Surrealist tactics of free association, startling juxtapositions, and reversals to liberate thought processes and enable a fresh look at the world of the Caribbean. The tropical landscape of these poems differs sharply from the sketched-in symbolic settings in Eluard and even from the proliferating but intellectualized cosmos of Breton's *Free Union*. Césaire's poet is barely distinguishable from a landscape that undergoes upheaval and revolution, rediscovering its relationship to a basic "ancestral heritage / the invincible zeal of acid in the flesh of / life—sea swamps—."

Mansour's poetry returns to an inward and personal vision, one that uses but radically subverts core Surrealist themes of mad love, absolute freedom, dream life, the search for the marvelous, and transfiguring experience. Where the early Surrealists emphasize male love for a woman who is per se a route to the marvelous, Mansour asserts a female perspective and predatory fantasies that turn romantic love on its head and point to more difficult emotions. *Men's Vices* approaches parody in its picture of the predatory female—the femme fatale of male iconology—who revels in the power given her by men's own fantasies. *I Opened Your Head* is a far cry from Eluard's *Woman in Love*, whose structure it nonetheless recalls. Instead of the earlier poet's tender, even abstract picture of inseparable lovers, Mansour gives the scene in visceral, impossible physical details that evoke a brutal will to dominate one's partner. It does not really matter whether the victim is male or female (in her plays, Mansour sometimes destabilizes gender identity by giving the same attributes to both male and female characters), but rather what kind of emotional or existential plight is being defined. For it is a plight: the agony of the shared nightmare in *I Saw You through My Closed Eye*, or the symbolic vision of *Empty Black Haunted House*, in which rooms are crowded with unfinished visions and objects beyond reach. Mansour's scenes remain rooted in mundane interpersonal reality even when they are most fantastic and dreamlike. She does not take the prescribed Surrealist route of escaping to the *marvelous*, but accepts the reality of "eternal inedible bread" and opens herself to the night.

Classroom Strategies

The nine pages of Dada-Surrealist poetry presented here present selections from six different writers but may easily be treated as the development of a single evolution in art and literature. As previously suggested, one way to introduce this evolution is to bring in examples of Surrealist painting and contrast them with earlier works. You may want to lead off discussion of the poetry by looking at the turn away from previous practice in Tzara's *Dadaist Disgust* and examining the Dadaists' specific attacks of the society of their time (whose mindset and conventions they blamed for World War I). Tzara's *Proclamation without Pretention* is an amusing parody of pompous proclamations that satirizes the claims of conventional Great Art to immortality and the Beautiful, and it sets the stage for writing that looks to different goals. Schwitters' sensuously lyrical, absurdist *Anna Blume* is an appealing example of this differently oriented poetry, and it also leads into the following Surrealist love poetry. Links are easily made between Eluard and Breton, and then continuities and contrast appear in the differently focused poets of the next generation, Césaire and Mansour.

Not to be overlooked, however, is the opportunity to introduce selections from these poets in other periods: for example, the rebellion of Tzara's *Dadaist Disgust* with Heine's *The Silesian Weavers* or Shelley's *England in 1819*; or, in love poetry, the fusion of woman and nature in Eluard's *Woman in Love* and Lamartine's *The Lake*. Breton called Surrealism the "prehensile tail of Romanticism," and Surrealism's visionary qualities suggest comparisons with Romantic and Symbolist literature as well as with modernist avant-garde techniques.

Topics for Discussion

1. Both Dadaists and Surrealists point to Rimbaud as a precursor. Which work or works by the earlier poet might explain their interest?

   [The easiest responses for Dada will be found in *A Season in Hell*, for Surrealism in the *Illuminations* or *The Drunken Boat*.]

2. Dada is a movement of pure revolt, and Tristan Tzara sums up the themes of that revolt in *Dadaist Disgust*, the conclusion to his *Dada Manifesto 1918*. What specific elements in contemporary society did the Dadaists find disgusting, and why? What political impetus for that disgust in suggested by the date of the manifesto and the fact that the original Dadaists gathered in Zürich, Switzerland, between 1916 and 1918?

   [See pp. 2112–13 of the anthology.]

3. Dada has been described as simultaneously "Art and anti-art." How does Tzara's *Proclamation without Pretention* describe the weakness of conventional or canonized art, and what does he wish to put in its place? Is his own *Proclamation* devoid of artistic techniques?

4. Discuss the love poems by Kurt Schwitters, Paul Eluard, and André

Breton; what image of the beloved do they propose, and how is that image rejected in poems by Joyce Mansour?

5. An ideal Surrealist image will bring together two distant realities that are somehow felt to be connected (or are shown, by the poet, to be connected). In what way do Breton's *Free Union*, Eluard's *Woman in Love*, and Césaire's *Sun Serpent* illustrate this principle? [Note: any one of these poems can be used in itself.]

6. How do Eluard's *To Be Caught in One's Own Trap*, Breton's *Vigilance*, and Mansour's *Empty Black Haunted House* evoke a sense of supreme mystery, each in its own way?

7. Breton's *Free Union* and Aimé Césaire's *Sun Serpent* and *Day and Night* are crammed with wide-ranging, almost encyclopedic details. What function do these details fill in each poem? How is it the same, and how different?

Comparative Perspectives

1. Each of the targets of *Dadaist Disgust* can be related to one or more works in the anthology. Pick any one of Tzara's manifestos and compare and contrast them with a related example. For instance, discuss Tzara's preference for "abolition of logic . . . abolition of future" with Darío's ambivalent rejection of progress in *To Roosevelt*. Or consider what Tzara means by "the trajectory of a word tossed like a sonorous cry of phonograph record" in connection with Bécquer's *I Know a Strange, Gigantic Hymn*. Which poet has greater faith in the possibilities of verbal art? In relation to both such questions, finally, one might ask how seriously we should take the Dadaists' statements.

2. Joyce Mansour deals with a number of themes and images that also concern Alfonsina Storni. Compare some of Storni's earlier poems with Mansour's; *Empty Black Haunted House* and *Squares and Angles*, or *Men's Voices* and *Little-Bitty Man* make interesting companion pieces. How is Mansour's imagery in these examples more surrealistic than Storni's? In Storni's later work, where do we see surrealistic elements?

3. Compare the vision of the natural world in Aimé Césaire's Surrealistic poems with Lu Xun's in the excerpts from *Wild Grass*. Does Lu Xun's statement of personal emotional involvement disqualify his work from being considered Surrealistic?

Further Reading

See also the reading suggestions in the anthology, p. 2112.

Bradley, Fiona. *Surrealism*. 1997. Offers a useful, illustrated short introduction to Surrealist art that includes the contributions of women.

Camfield, William A. *Max Ernst: Dada and the Dawn of Surrealism*. 1993. Sheds light on early Dada.

Chadwick, Whitney. *Mirror Images: Women, Surrealism, and Self-Representation*. 1998. Presents an interesting perspective on the situation of women in Surrealism.

Elderfield, John. *Kurt Schwitters*. 1985. Discusses the artist's work with some attention to his writing.

Hubert, Renee Riese. *Magnifying Mirrors: Women, Surrealism, & Partnership*. 1994. Presents another interesting perspective on the situation of women in Surrealism.

Naumann, Francis. *New York Dada 1915–23*. 1994. Sheds light on early Dada.

Richardson, Michael and Kryzysztof Fijalkowski, eds. *Refusal of the Shadow: Surrealism and the Caribbean*. 1996. Assembles contemporary essays chiefly by Caribbean Surrealists that demonstrate Surrealism's impact and its relation to colonialism in the Caribbean.

Schmalenbach, Werner. *Kurt Schwitters*. 1967. Discusses the artist's work with some attention to his writing.

Suleiman, Susan. *Subversive Intent*. 1990. Chapters offer valuable theoretical insights into the role of Surrealist women writers in relation to the French avant-garde.

ALFONSINA STORNI

Backgrounds

The poems in the anthology illustrate well the evolution of Storni's work outlined in the headnote. Students should have little difficulty with the first few; having become familiar with Storni's idiom and concerns, they will be able to work through the longer, more complex late poems with your assistance.

SQUARES AND ANGLES

There should be no problem identifying the kind of world this witty poem depicts. You might want to ask why the geometric architectural forms described here are identified with the modern world. Although Storni is hardly a contemporary, *Squares and Angles* has lost no currency in today's world of modular housing. What were the economic and ideological reasons for the cookie-cutter shapes embraced by so many early modernist architects? Why does Storni reject the presumably egalitarian ethic of the squares and angles that typify the kind of twentieth-century design that she turns into a metaphor for lazy stereotypical thinking? Today's students speak of "nerds" while earlier generations spoke of "squares." You might ask what those words mean, and ask how they relate to "Ideas in a row / And an angle on the back." If your classroom facilitates board work by students, you might invite someone to draw the shape that typically represents a tear and then elicit from your students why its ovoid contours suggest greater depth and human emotion than the square tear that Storni conjures up here in mock horror.

You Want Me White

This poem starts with an indignant survey of similes (white as dawn, foam, pearl, snow) typically used to signify passive female chastity. It then progresses to a more vigorous representation of masculine debauchery based on actions accomplished:

> You have held all the wineglasses
> In your hand,
> Your lips stained purple
> With fruit and honey

and so on. In the last long stanza, the tables turn, and the speaker throws out a challenge to the man who has kept only his "skeleton . . . intact." The woman who cannot regenerate her virginity is no worse than the man who has lost his connection to nature. Implicit here, it appears, is an accusation of sterility and bad faith. Let this man renew the vital earthiness that ought to accompany the human experience of love, a richer contact with sensuality than the hypocritical playboy's entanglement "In all the bedrooms." Not until he can achieve this miracle and integrate flesh, body, and soul does he have a right to demand her miraculous conversion.

Little-Bitty Man

This short poem shows the power of repetition. The title issues another one of Storni's challenges: one is used to hearing about "the little woman." What is the effect of calling a member of the male sex "little bitty man"? How many meanings circulate in the familiar figure of the bird in the cage? As in You Want Me White, the female speaker ends up in a surprisingly strong role in an age-old debate. A standard complaint ("you don't understand me") becomes an affront to the male ego: "Nor do I understand you." Nor does she seem to want to; it's traditional to hear of men who seduce and abandon, but here the woman has had her fill of the man and seeks her freedom. Half an hour has been enough for her.

Ancestral Burden

Addressed to her mother, this poem makes a good companion piece to Little-Bitty Man, for it is another one of Storni's statements of essential female strength. Despite the conventional characterization of women as "weak," they have learned to carry the burdens of emotional stress that men have been taught to hide. Storni describes her mother's tear as a poison drink—all the more potent because it is the distillation of the pain that men apparently diffuse by projecting it onto women.

THE WORLD OF SEVEN WELLS

This poem may initially seem difficult to your students, but the head-note provides the necessary clue to understanding. As a woman's poem, *The World of Seven Wells* upsets the masculine tradition of Petrarchan compliments to the lady. For example, in Ariosto's *Orlando Furioso*, Alcina's facial beauty is described in typically decorative terms:

Her serene brow was like polished ivory, and in perfect proportion. / Beneath two of the thinnest black arches, two dark eyes—or rather, two bright / suns; soft was their look, gentle their movement. . . . Below this, the mouth, set between two dimples; it was imbued with native cinnabar. Here a beautiful soft pair of lips opened to disclose a double row of choicest pearls. (Canto 7)

By contrast, the grotesque imagery of Storni's poem sets the body within the cosmos and the natural world. The perspective is oddly off-center; "There above" suggests a low vantage point, and a certain tenuousness is communicated by "on the neck, / is balanced the world / of the seven doors," as if the neck might not be strong enough to support so monumental a burden. We begin with "two planets" and a nucleus, apparently the two lobes of the brain. The scalp and hair are bark and forest.

While the description of the eyes with their "tender doors" and marine blue glance seems far more inviting, the prospect in which they are situated remains disturbing. A broad seascape over which "butterflies and insects hover" may call up halcyon days at the seashore. But who wants butterflies and insects hovering above their eyes? Similarly, the elegance of "snails of mother-of-pearl" associated with the ear is undercut by references to "antennae" (as of hovering insects or technological appurtenances?) and "catacombs," which lead to the convolutions of the middle and inner ear ("tubes located to the right and to the left"), intricate mechanisms that even the most fervent lover is unlikely to include in an admiring catalogue of female charms.

The perspective keeps shifting without any clear sense of a line to connect the views. How do we get from the distant "mountain / over the equatorial line of the head" to "the wax-like nostrils" that promote olfactory perception of pretty "flowers, branches, and fruit," and then back off again to contemplate what sounds like scorched terrain that gives the lie to all verbal pretensions?

> And the crater of the mouth
> with raised edges
> and dry chapped walls;
> the crater which spouts forth
> the sulphur of violent words,
> the dense smoke which comes
> from the heart and its turmoil. . . .

The struggle within the head of beast and angel is too much for poet to control, "and the human volcano erupts."

The last stanzas are marked by a peculiar incongruity that undermines what seems at first a return to convention. Praising a rosy complexion, instead of the traditional damasked roses we confront "mossy cheeks"; and instead of a beauteous forehead, "a white desert, / the distant light of a dead moon." The cheeks seem about to metamorphose into some vegetable form and the forehead to radiate not saintly intellect but a lunar catastrophe. For the sublunary reader, the effect is foreboding.

PORTRAIT OF GARCÍA LORCA

The World of Seven Wells is a kind of puzzle that students can usefully take apart and examine; although its images are, to say the least, unorthodox, its method of producing them is intelligible. At any point in the poem, one knows which of the head's orifices have been reached. The poem signals a profound change in Storni's use of imagery that becomes even more pronounced in her *Portrait of García Lorca*, which soon abandons any pretense of linear logic. This portrait too starts at the top of the head, but the tour of a face is almost immediately obscured: "a curtain of death is drawn," and in moving down from forehead to eyes to cheekbone to mouth to throat, the poem superimposes disconnected, often threatening scenes on the facial contours it ostensibly portrays.

A tribute from one Spanish-speaking artist to another, with its references to violence and death, it brings to mind the Surrealist films of a third such figure, Luis Bunuel, and the earlier traditions of the Spanish Baroque. The famous image of an eyeball being slashed in Bunuel's *Un Chien Andalou* is evoked in the mind of the reader by the horrific fifth and sixth stanzas; but in the spirit of Surrealist experimentation, there is nothing personal about the imagery in the movie or in Storni's poem. The effect is more to alienate than engage. At a moment when modernists were getting inside the heads of their characters through stream-of-consciousness narration, Storni is writing poems that literally get inside the heads of her subjects.

The poem seems at its conclusion to cast García Lorca as a titan of Renaissance exploration, bridging Atlantic and Pacific with his eyes "like lost ships" sailing an endless ocean. His intellectual power seems perversely to precipitate the ominous suggestion to "Let the head fly / (only the head)." Perhaps the animal references that link García Lorca's brilliant energy to that of powerful birds and animals of prey prepare us for the paradox that the poem seems to explore: so great a figure can only realize his transcendent gifts by a violent separation from the material world.

This poem makes a fascinating companion piece to García Lorca's *Lament for Ignacio Sánchez Mejías*, for both offer homage to a heroic being who unites past and present through his creative powers. The classical references here include the suggestion of "Grecian eyes," perhaps as in ancient statuary, and the vision of him acting in some undefined theatrical ritual, with "the mane of the satyr . . . on the face / of an ancient mask." His facial bone structure connects him to the Andalusian hills and valleys. The very traits for which García Lorca praised Sánchez Mejías are praised here: a deep evocation of a primal Spain, an outsized embodiment of antique virtues. García Lorca, however, is writing out of tremendous personal and national pain, mourning the death of a beloved celebrity; Storni had met García Lorca, but she was not an intimate of his. Moreover, *Portrait of García Lorca*, as the headnote in the anthology informs your students, is visionary rather than reactive. It was written two years before García Lorca's murder.

DEPARTURE

This is another poem with an eerie prophetic force, since it seems to prefigure Storni's suicide. Yet *Departure* does not speak of despair. In fact, the images of "golden dust" and coral brought up from the sea may owe something to the optimistic spirit of Shakespeare's last plays. Storni knew these works well, having written a farce called *Cymbeline in 1900* that transposes this redemptive romance to a modern setting. In the original, of course, the long-lost brothers of Imogen sing the beautiful dirge that includes a famous couplet:

> Golden lads and girls all must,
> As chimney-sweepers, come to dust.

Death seems beautiful here, as it does in Ariel's song in the second scene of *The Tempest*:

> Full fathom five thy father lies;
> Of his bones are coral made;
> Those are pearls that were his eyes:
> Nothing of him that doth fade
> But doth suffer a sea-change
> Into something rich and strange.

Perhaps it is not too far-fetched to hear an echo of these sentiments in Storni's *Departure*, a poem full of light and air, in which the sea elevates rather than immerses.

Certainly, there is a sense of mystical elation in this poem. *Departure* shares the Surrealistic impulse that becomes so prominent in *The World of Seven Wells* and *Portrait of García Lorca*, but it presents a landscape of dream rather than nightmare. By concluding with the spinning spindle enveloped by the rays of the sun, Storni remakes the classic female image of the distaff into an emblem of ecstasy. If there are hints of opiates administered to a body in pain in the references to poppies and "the sky [rolling] through the bed / of my veins," the overall effect nevertheless is exhilarating. The departure seems clearly to bring the speaker to a better place.

Topics for Discussion and Writing

1. Identify some of the images traditionally associated with women in Storni's poems and discuss her use of them. Is she using them in conventional ways?
2. As her poetic style evolves, Storni depicts the world as a place of dislocated parts. What is the emotional impact of her references to the body and the landscape?

Comparative Perspectives

1. Compare the color schemes of Darío's *Sonatina* and *Leda* with the values ascribed to white, red, and black in Storni's *You Want Me White*. In what ways do Darío's poems reflect a masculine perspective that Storni rejects in her poem?
2. Compare *The World of Seven Wells* with Emily Dickinson's poem 632 ("The Brain—is wider than the Sky—") or Virginia Woolf's depiction of the mind at work in *A Room of One's Own*. Are their concerns with the process of human consciousness marked in any way as gender-related?
3. Describe some of the dislocations of scale and imagery in *The World of Seven Wells* or the *Portrait of García Lorca,* and compare the impact of these incongruities with those encountered in Canto 4 of *The Rape of the Lock* or in *Gulliver's Travels*. How do the eighteenth-century satirists' descriptions of freakish bodies in inappropriate roles comment on their own societies? Do you think that Storni is writing satire in these poems?
4. Compare Storni's *Portrait of García Lorca* with Lorca's *Lament for Ignacio Sánchez Mejías*. How does Storni's invocation of the "wild animal" that "snarls in [García Lorca's] face / trying to destroy him / in its rage" contrast with García Lorca's portrait of the bull that gored Sánchez Mejías?

Further Reading

See the reading suggestions in the anthology, p. 2123.

WILLIAM FAULKNER

Go Down, Moses

THE BEAR

Classroom Strategies and Topics for Discussion

Like other great modern writers, Faulkner hungered for a mythology; like other great American writers, he created his own. Drawing on classical, biblical, and Native American motifs, Faulkner transformed a little corner of north Mississippi into Yoknapatawpha, a land both real and imagined. However odd and idiosyncratic they may at first appear, events and persons in Faulkner's Yoknapatawpha County reflect a powerful and universal image of the human condition.

Students who encounter Faulkner as they reach the end of a year-long survey of world masterpieces will recognize at least some of the myriad and masterful ways in which *The Bear* appropriates many of the archetypal themes of Western culture. Following up on the reference in the headnote, you can make this art of appropriation clear immediately by asking your students about the complex associations raised by the title of the entire volume: *Go Down, Moses*. Like the Negro spiritual for which it is named, Faulkner's work mines the biblical past for its relevance to the quintessential American tragedy—slavery and the ever-elusive goal of freedom for all. You may find that today's students will catch this reference most directly through their recollections of Martin Luther King, Jr.'s "I Have a Dream" speech: American and human history are full of towering figures who never made it to the Promised Land.

As you begin your reading of Faulkner's text, it will be helpful to ask how these imposing themes find expression in a hunting story. What kind of meaning is invested in the bear? Faulkner had been reading *Moby-Dick* to his daughter while he was writing *The Bear*, and Old Ben is as formidable a figure as the white whale, rich with the kind of symbolic possibilities that you will want your students to look for as they read. The opening paragraph identifies three "taintless and incorruptible" figures in the story: the great bear himself; Lion, the dog who will help bring him down; and Sam Fathers. But none of these figures is sentimentalized, and Faulkner's several comparisons of the bear to a locomotive (pp. 2137, 2146, 2160) deserve some discussion, especially because the incursion of the locomotive into the woods is one sign of the corruption of the wilderness. If the bear can be called, in the story's words, the "epitome and apotheosis of the old wild life" (p. 2137), it may also be, as Richard H. King suggests, "the same kind of amoral force as old Carothers represents." Thus the bear hunt in sections 1, 2, and 3 of *The Bear* is analogous to the hunt conducted in section 4, where Ike McCaslin pursues the truth about his family heritage as persistently as Major de Spain, General Compson, and their company pursue the bear, season after season until the ancient creature finally meets its demise.

Some time needs to be devoted to Ike himself, who is hardly ever named in Faulkner's narrative. To be recognizably the "he" so frequently invoked is a perverse mark of Ike's centrality to the story, for his consciousness lies at its core. Ike enters "his novitiate" (p. 2138) under Sam's tutelage. Significantly, and unusually for a hunting story, Ike's maturing in *The Bear* does not center on his shedding of animal blood. This takes place in *The Old People*, a story in *Go Down, Moses* that fits chronologically between sections 1 and 2 of *The Bear*. There, the orphan Ike kills his first deer and adopts Sam (who bears a significant surname shortened from "Has Two Fathers") as an ideal paternal model.

Parts 1, 2, 3, and 5 of *The Bear* offer a classic tale of adolescent development, and one sure way to engage your students is to ask them how Ike grows in the course of the story and how he distinguishes himself among the hunters. The beautifully structured sections chart Ike's maturation. By the end of section 1, he is already a better woodsman than most of the older men. You might ask your students to mark the stages of Ike's advancement, as Sam introduces him to the use of the rifle and teaches him to listen for the telltale sounds of the bear. Only when Ike has become so adept that he can relinquish his gun, watch, and compass does he actually see the bear whose presence he has previously felt. This relinquishing will take on another dimension in the great fourth section of the novel, and it is worth eliciting from your students the way that Faulkner signals approval of Ike's learning to risk himself, unarmed and innocent of technological assistance, in the wilderness. Here, his disregard of all prerogatives is a great virtue.

In section 1, the ten-year-old Ike is seen by and then himself sees the bear; in section 2, the thirteen-year-old boy watches Sam cultivate the mongrel hound, Lion, the agent of destruction of the bear at which Ike himself is unwilling to shoot. Three times the narrator repeats the formulaic comment "So he should have hated and feared Lion" (pp. 2145–53). But Ike does not, for the boy accepts the mythic, fated quality of the mutual destruction of beast and hunter to which this story inexorably leads.

In section 3, when the final confrontation of man, bear, and dog occurs, we realize that Faulkner has made the hunt a metaphor for the mutual destruction that lies at the heart of the history of the American South as well. The very first paragraph of the story telegraphs this by speaking of blood lines as it forecasts the meeting of two beasts and two men. Each of the participants in the killing of the bear is of mixed parentage: Boon Hogganbeck, who will stab Old Ben rather than kill him with the hunter's rifle he can never control, is the "grandson of a Chickasaw squaw" (p. 2154). Lion is "part mastiff, something of Airedale and something of a dozen other strains probably" (p. 2149). And Sam Fathers is the "son of a negro slave and a Chickasaw chief" (p. 2143). Perhaps more to the point, each is celibate. So *The Bear* is simultaneously, and almost paradoxically, a tale about a boy's growing up and a tale about the end of a civilization, as the reference to "old Priam reft of his old wife and outlived all his sons" that caps the first description of Old Ben himself—"solitary, indomitable, and alone; widowered childless and absolved of morality"—indicates (p. 2138).

Before moving on to section 4, where these issues are tortuously explored, you may want to look closely at the brilliantly visualized moment of the kill, which Eric Sundquist has called "the celibate marriage of hunter and beast." Boon, a case of arrested development who is incapable of complex human interaction, has shared a bed with Lion. Such cohabitation, however innocent, nevertheless carries with it a sense of norms violated that prepares us for the revelations to come in section 4 and reinforces our understanding of the disturbing mythic dimensions of the story's action. When Boon sees that Old Ben has "caught the dog in both arms, almost loverlike" (p. 2161), he leaps at the bear and stabs him. "For an instant they almost resembled a piece of statuary: the clinging dog, the bear, the man stride its back, working and probing the buried blade." From this curiously intimate and asexual congress comes death.

When Ike and McCaslin talk in the commissary, the sculptural image reemerges. The older man asks Ike why he didn't shoot the bear when he had the chance; answering his own question, he takes a book of poems down from the shelf and reads Keats's *Ode on a Grecian Urn*. Cass and Ike grope toward an articulation of the connection between Keats's affirmation of beauty and truth and the beauty and truth implicit in Ike's inaction. Faulkner's narrative, by focusing on two lines in the poem in particular, insists on the linkage between the boy's refusal to shoot and the perfect Keatsian moment before consummation:

> She cannot fade, though thou hast not thy bliss,
> Forever wilt thou love, and she be fair!

If we read the bas relief on the Grecian Urn mentioned in section 4 back onto the statuesque scene of bodies intertwined in the wilderness at the height of section 3, we can infer another nexus between the hunting of the bear in the first sequence of *The Bear* and the hunting of the past in the more complex narrative of the ledgers. Both lead from the heat of passion to a static sterility. Deciphering the meaning of the events catalogued in the ledgers kept by his father and his uncle, Ike refuses the various legacies of those events. Faulkner underscores the significance of Ike's breaking the chain of family inheritance by ending section 4 with a scene between an older Ike and his unnamed wife. She wants him to lay claim to the farm that is the cousins' joint inheritance. McCaslin is working it; Ike will not. Out of this refusal grows his wife's taunting laughter: lying naked before him for the first time, she announces, "If this dont get you that son you talk about, it wont be mine" (p. 2200). Ike never has a son. His marriage disintegrates, as we learn while he is immersed in parsing the ledgers and the narrator projects us foward in time: "and that was all: 1874 the boy; 1888 the man, repudiated denied and free; 1895 and husband but no father, unwidowered but without a wife" (p. 2182). Like old Ben (who was "widowered"), like Sam Fathers, Ike has no children. As the headnote suggests, one of the unanswered questions in this story is how we are to respond to the barrenness that grows out of Ike's repudiation of his heritage.

Once you have established this overview of Ike's initiation, you will probably need to spend a good deal of time helping your students deal with the formal difficulties of section 4. Before moving into a discussion of the ledgers per se, you may want to raise the general question of form as Faulkner invents it for his own purposes throughout *The Bear*. The shapeliness of the three opening sections is accentuated by the short declarative sentences that open them and to which the headnote will have drawn your students' attention. Although they are deceptively simple, they set a clear frame for the well-defined action that occurs in the wilderness. Significantly, however, unlike the first two, section 3 ends with a dramatic outcry, as will sections 4 and 5. The careful framing can no longer contain the meaning of events. Why does Ike scream at Cass when he asks Boon whether he has helped Sam Fathers die (p. 2168)? What is important here is not so much whether Boon hastened Sam's end or not but that Ike asserts himself against his older cousin, another paternal figure whom he is now prepared to challenge.

That self-assertion leads directly into the statement, issued without benefit of capital letter or paragraph indentation, that begins the great 4th section: "then he was twenty-one." The chronological promise that may seem implicit there is, like so much else in Faulkner's narrative, delusory, as the scenes in the commissary weave back and forth between eras and encounters. It is probably a good idea to ask your students to try to pin down the shifting time scheme of this section, as it is a good idea to ask them why it is set in the commissary. Faulkner's evocative scene-painting of the wilderness is one of the glories of this novel; so is his decision to have the two cousins debate the meaning of and their relation to the wilderness in the business office out of which the property of old Carothers McCaslin has been run for roughly a hundred years.

The first paragraph of section 4 speaks of the slave economy that was put into place to turn the wilderness into a profitmaking machine. The commissary is "not the heart perhaps but certainly the solar plexus of the repudiated and relinquished": this brilliant metaphor locates the ruthlessness of the business of slavery in the nervous system that controls the abdominal region. Appetite and visceral impulse rather than love allow a human being to think he has a license to keep other human beings in bondage and exploit their frailties even when that bondage has technically ended (as the phrase " '65 or no" makes clear).

Ask your students to keep a bookmark on the genealogical table provided on p. 2135 of the anthology as they work through this section of *The Bear*. Ike penetrates the family secrets by close reading of the older ledgers kept by the twin sons of old Carothers. (This should encourage your students, of course—Ike would have received an A in Advanced Ledgerology.) With their Greek and Latin names, both of which signify "love of god," and their virtually—but not totally—indistinguishable handwriting and moral outlook, Uncle Buck (Ike's father) and Uncle Buddy themselves struggled with the corrupt paternal legacy that Ike, more like Buddy (who did not fight in the Civil War, and who is the first to understand the cryptic note about a drowning) than Buck in this respect, will relinquish. He too will be known later as Uncle, despite McCaslin's efforts to impress a sense of curatorial responsibility upon his younger cousin, scion of the legitimate male line, while Cass, though older, is further from the source, born in a later generation through the female line.

The genealogy will be very useful here, as will a careful stepping through of some of the key ledger entries. Following Faulkner's own ordering of items makes sense. The first that Ike reconstructs are comic.

The grandiosity of Southern nomenclature that Faulkner delights in deserves special comment in the person of Percival Brownlee. Percival, named for the pure knight of the Arthurian legend, proves no savior. A good reading assignment to help students along at this point would be to ask for an elucidation of the entries on p. 2175 detailing the fiasco of this purchase. After this lighthearted prelude, Ike struggles to comprehend the tragic meaning behind notes that record the purchase and suicide of Eunice.

Remind your students to watch for the dual chronology of Ike's encounter with these materials and of the chronicled events themselves. He has been staring at these crumbling ledgers from an early age, as he had first entered the wilderness at an early age. Sam Fathers nurses him along until he becomes a superior woodsman; Ike has to educate himself in this subtler hunt in the commissary on his own. "Then he was sixteen. He knew what he was going to find before he found it" (p. 2175). This is the point, mentioned in the headnote, at which the long sentence that begins on p. 2172 ends; in a spectacularly complex example of stream of consciousness, Faulkner has taken his reader into Ike's anguished thoughts. You may want at this juncture to ask your students whether this technique unnecessarily obfuscates meaning, or whether the stuggle to follow the character's mental processes deepens a reader's experience of the text. Legitimate arguments can be made on both sides of the issue.

What Ike deciphers here may be thought of as the equivalent of the Laocoonlike statuary image that brings together the great bear, the leonine dog, and the frenzied, bewildered Boon Hogganbeck. Old Lucius Quintus Carothers McCaslin was prolific rather than celibate, and Ike fights through to a recognition of the incest and miscegenation that taint the heritage he will refuse as he laboriously reviews the references to the birth of a son to Tomasina called Tomy, the daughter of Eunice, in June 1833, "Y[ea]r stars fell" and six months after Eunice drowned herself. On pp. 2176–77, Ike sees the pattern clearly. In 1807, Old Carothers had sought Eunice out, having already seen and desired her. He makes an uncharacteristic trip to New Orleans to buy her for a huge sum—$650. In 1832, Eunice drowns on Christmas Day. Tomasina, the daughter of Eunice and Carothers, dies in childbirth in June 1833; and on June 21, Ike's Uncle Buddy first writes "Drownd herself," having made the connection between the mother's discovery of her white master/lover's impregnation of their own child in December, when the pregnancy would have become manifest, and her decision to kill herself.

Here Faulkner's mythology achieves classical and biblical proportions. His work lives not only as an analysis of the crisis of the Old South but also as an acknowledgment of the enormities of universal human history, punctuated by a cataclysm in offended nature: "yr stars fell." Old Carothers with his monstrous ego has blood on his hands, and rather than admit it or try to expiate it, he bequeaths a sum of money to each of his descendants, legitimate or illegitimate, white or of mixed blood. Uncle Buck and Uncle Buddy accept this responsibility in the same ambivalent spirit in which they deal with the old plantation they inherit. They move into a simple log cabin and leave the big house to the manumitted slaves who will not leave the place they know as home, while refusing to supervise them (p. 2172). They faithfully record the debt to their father's many heirs, but it is Ike who takes it upon himself to deliver it.

Confused, idealistic, and ineffectual, "an experienced traveller by now and an experienced bloodhound" (p. 2180), Ike eventually hunts down Fonsiba (have your students find her on the genealogical table) and her Northern Negro husband and tries to give her the inheritance that she refuses. Announcing "I'm free" (p. 2182) to her distant cousin Ike, Fonsiba will instead become the recipient of a monthly check, doled out by a local banker to whom Ike turns in frustration. But the youngest child in the family, who changed "Lucius" to Lucas, "himself selfprogenitive and nominate, by himself ancestored," demands the money that is due him on his twenty-first birthday and receives it.

With this bequest, the McCaslin monies are accounted for; but Fonsiba's "I'm free" resonates throughout the remaining portion of section 4, as does the idea of self-genesis. Ike argues with Cass, who mounts a careful defense of the Southern past. Citing Genesis again, Ike seeks to distance himself as a latter-day Isaac entitled to turn from sacrifice, "fatherless and therefore safe declining the altar" (p. 2183). You may want to have your students search out the references to the Bible, the "harsher book" (p. 2187) that underlies the tension between the second cousins, who disagree about the nature of their responsibility to the land and to the McCaslin inheritance. They grapple with hard questions about race that this society has still not found a way to resolve. The dream of the new world in which Europeans could reinvent themselves turned to nightmare, as Faulkner's review of the history of the United States shows. Fonsiba's husband speaks of "the new Canaan" (p. 2181) that he believe the Reconstructionist era will usher in, but earlier McCaslin has stated, with considerably more accuracy, that the family (and by extension the country) are "dispossessed of Eden. Dispossessed of Canaan" (p. 2170), the promised land beyond reach.

At the core of their debate is the false freedom of Emancipation and the inability of Southern blacks to take advantage of their new status, not because of their race (it is important to emphasize this) but because they have not been prepared. Faulkner's tragic vision is not limited, however, to any single race's failure to live up to the divine inheritance: in the post-Civil war period, blacks "misused it as human beings always misuse freedom" (p. 2187). Ike insists that blacks "are better than we are" (p. 2189), a view that McCaslin rejects as superficial and sentimental. A critical word emerges here, as Ike affirms the "endurance" of the Negro. As the headnote remarks, it is difficult to say who prevails in this discussion, in which Ike in effect justifies his relinquishing of family responsibility. As an aside, you may want to point out that in his celebrated speech of acceptance of the Nobel Prize for Literature in 1950, Faulkner spoke movingly of the strength of the human spirit in the face of all odds—a strength that will "endure."

Section 4 moves to closure with a glance at Ike's other inheritance, from his mother's family, the Beauchamps. Paralleling the ledger entries is a series of cryptic notes, IOUs that Ike's Uncle Hubert has substituted for the gold pieces he once had placed in the silver cup that was to be Ike's inheritance. In a daring move, Faulkner has earlier allowed Ike to re-iterate Fonsiba's claim, "I am free" (p. 2192), although she will depend on the three dollars per month that Ike arranges for her, as Ike will on the thirty-dollar dole that McCaslin arranges (p. 2197). Thirty pieces of silver are fraught with Christian meaning, of course, and the narrative goes even further, informing us that Ike becomes a kind of Jesus figure, with "brand-new carpenter's tools" (p. 2192) like those used by "the Nazarene" (p. 2197). How many fatherless sons are here being betrayed?

With the end of Ike's line forecast by the conclusion of section 4, the narrative returns to the wilderness and retreats chronologically to tell of one more bear, a half-grown creature frightened twenty years earlier by the train that dug into the forest that has been sold to a lumber company (p. 2202). In a foreshadowing of the very end of the story, the men pro-tect this bear, with Boon particularly singled out. Two years after the deaths of Old Ben, Lion, and Sam, Ike goes to bid them a last farewell. In one final scene that merges Edenic and Native American allusions, Ike's homage is interrupted by the appearance of a great snake, very much like the serpent in *Paradise Lost* (see 9.494 ff., p. 3034, volume C of the an-thology): "The elevation of the head did not change as it began to glide away from him, moving erect yet off the perpendicular . . . an entity walk-ing on two feet" (p. 2207). Speaking in "the old tongue," Ike echoes the words of Sam Fathers in *The Old People*. To voice his deepest respect for the spirits in the woods, Ike salutes the snake, which seems to be the em-bodiment of Sam, as Sam had shown him the great buck that embodied his ancestors.

This moment of communion with the natural world that he is going to abandon, as the white men who shortsightedly claim ownership have al-ready abandoned it, is broken by one more dramatic story-ending out-burst. Hysterically, Boon shrieks his possession of the squirrels, the only creatures he has ever been able to hunt. This limited human being, com-rade of the hound and protector of the half-grown bear, has gone mad. Thus *The Bear* at its conclusion dwindles down to mock-heroic and irony, mirroring the decline of the irredeemably flawed society that it re-creates.

Topics for Writing

1. Attitudes toward Ike.
2. Attitudes toward slavery.
   a. Evidence of the ledger entries.
   b. Buck and Buddy and the big house.

3. The meaning of bloodlines in the story.
4. The symbolic import of the animal world of the wilderness: Old Ben, the fyce, Lion, the half-grown bear, the snake.

Comparative Perspectives

1. Compare the references to "truth" in Keats's *Ode On a Grecian Urn* and in the conversation of Cass and Ike in which the poem is quoted.
2. Compare the portrait of the wilderness in *The Bear* with an ancient view, such as that offered in *Gilgamesh* (in volume A of the anthology) or in a modern work about the encroachment of modernity on the pristine forest, such as *The Cherry Orchard* or *Matryona's Home*.
3. Discuss the literary response to violations of the family, such as incest and miscegenation, in *The Bear* and in works as diverse as *Oedipus the King, Phaedra, Narrative of the Life of Frederick Douglass, An American Slave,* or *Pedro Páramo*.
4. Modernists are obsessed by the sense that the culture in which they were raised has reached its end. Compare Faulkner's treatment of this theme with the poems of Yeats and Eliot; with Joyce's *The Dead*; or with Achebe's *Things Fall Apart*.
5. Drawing from the evidence in *The Bear*, how would you characterize Faulkner's view of women? How would Virginia Woolf, in light of *A Room of One's Own*, evaluate it?
6. Compare the treatment of animals as superior to human beings in Peynetsa's *The Boy and the Deer* or Dadie's *The Hunter and the Boa* to the ethic that Sam Fathers teaches Ike, and discuss Faulkner's insight into the cultural significance of animal life in non-Western societies.

Further Reading

See also the suggestions in the anthology, p. 2134.

King, Richard H. *A Southern Renaissance.* 1980. The chapter called "Working Through: Faulkner's *Go Down, Moses*" offers a psychoanalytically informed discussion of Ike's failures, locating their source in the loss of a series of primal father figures.

Kinney, Arthur F. Go Down, Moses: *The Miscegenation of Time.* 1996. The latest of Kinney's many encounters with Faulkner, with an emphasis on racial issues in contemporary America.

Rollyson, Carl E. *Uses of the Past in the Novels of William Faulkner.* 1984. In the chapter called "Evolution of History in *Go Down, Moses*," this lucid book discusses the way in which the ledgers represent the kind of primary materials out of which historians construct their interpretations of human experience.

Sundquist, Eric. Faulkner: *A House Divided.* 1983. An extremely useful study, particularly good on the Keats connection.

Volpe, Edmund. *A Reader's Guide to William Faulkner*. 1964. A cogent examination of Faulkner's works.

BERTOLT BRECHT

The Good Woman of Setzuan

Classroom Strategies and Topics for Discussion

With Ibsen, Chekhov, Strindberg, and Pirandello, Brecht belongs on any list of influential modern playwrights; like Chekhov and Pirandello, Brecht, a talented poet and writer of fiction, worked in more than one medium. His reputation, however, rests on his dramatic innovations, deriving not only from his own practice as a playwright but also from his theoretical writings on theater. Many of the best young dramatists working today consciously emulate Brecht, seeking to further their social and political goals by distancing audiences from the staged performance that manifests the importance of these goals. With a leading character whose plight could bring an audience to tears in the hands of a more traditional dramatist, *The Good Woman of Setzuan* vividly demonstrates the paradox inherent in the Brechtian mix of ideological engagement and emotional alienation (see the headnote, pp. 2208–12).

Today's students may be familiar with contemporary plays that break the fourth wall, in which actors step out of character and speak directly to the audience; they will surely recognize these techniques from many popular television series in which the leading character (Garry Shandling, for example) offers ironic commentary on the events just "imitated." This breaking of dramatic illusion is a typical modernist device, most easily recognized in theater or the visual arts. You might show your students a reproduction of Picasso's famous painting *Les Demoiselles d'Avignon*, which introduces multiple perspectives and transforms human faces into African-masklike visages, to demonstrate the way an artist purposely set about fracturing the single-point perspective that was the artistic legacy of the West. One of the challenges in reading (as opposed to seeing) a play by Brecht is to watch how the planes of reality shift before our eyes and ultimately to articulate what this shifting of planes achieves.

Like so many modernist techniques, Brecht's playing with perspectives has ancient roots in other periods and cultures. Originally published in a volume called *Two Parables for the Theatre, The Good Woman of Setzuan* and *The Caucasian Chalk Circle* were inspired by a fourteenth-century Chinese play *The Chalk Circle*, by Li Hsing-tao. The play retells an old Chinese folk tale that resembles the biblical story of the judgment of Solomon (1 Kings 3.16–28). Each of two women insists that she is the mother of a child. To choose between these contesting maternal claims, the judge threatens the child; the real mother gives up her claim rather than see her baby killed. One of the rivals in the Chinese play is a prostitute named Chan Hai-tang: in her goodness, this character inspired Brecht's Shen Te.

The Chalk Circle was richly produced by Max Reinhardt in a German adaptation by Klabund in Berlin in 1924; it was done in an English translation in London in 1931. In 1932, in reaction to the saccharine quality of the Klabund version of *The Chalk Circle,* a writer named Friedrich Wolf wrote a play about the Chinese revolution, *Tai Yan Wakes Up,* set in modern Shanghai and enacted in a spare modern production by Erwin Piscator. Wolf's technique, however, was to engage the audience's sympathy.

Equally dissatisfied with the synthetic sweetness of Klabund's adaptation of the old play and the intense dramatic engagement of Wolf's modern response, Brecht went on to write two of his most popular and influential plays. Both *The Caucasian Chalk Circle,* mainly through its plot, and *The Good Woman of Setzuan,* primarily in its leading character, draw upon the six-hundred-year-old Chinese *Chalk Circle.* In both plays, Brecht is intent on demystifying what Western bourgeois audiences might perceive as its Oriental charm by resetting it in a shabby twentieth-century Asian locale.

Even before his visit to Moscow in 1935, where Brecht saw authentic Chinese theater (see the headnote, p. 2211) he had been exploiting anti-illusionist devices: in 1931, for example, his *A Man's a Man* used masks to demonstrate a character's personality change. Some devices may have been suggested by Meyerhold's revolutionary theater (p. 2210), others are already part of early Western tradition. The direct address to the audience, interpolated songs, and masks to indicate identity appear in Greek and Roman comedy (see the selections by Aristophanes and Plautus in vol. A.) Ancient theater also employed mechanical stage devices: if your students have studied Greek tragedy, you will want to remind them that when the gods remove themselves from Setzuan in a "cloud" (p. 2266), as Brecht's stage directions specify, they occupy a *mechane* very much like the one in Euripides' *Medea.* (A photograph of this moment showing Karl von Appen's design for the Berliner Ensemble's production of the play in 1957, after Brecht had died, is reproduced in many of the books in the headnote's bibliography, including *The Cambridge Companion to Brecht.*) Nonetheless, Brecht's recent exposure to the stylized drama of traditional Chinese theater, with its masks, songs, and the amazing adaptability of the actors to a variety of roles (including gender impersonation by the celebrated Mai Lan-fang), clearly made its mark on *The Good Woman of Setzuan.*

The modern "half-Westernized city of Setzuan" is the scene for our play. As note 1 on p. 2213 points out, the choice of Setzuan, properly a province rather than a city, indicates that we are in a geographical limbo rather than a historically specific site: the real location is "wherever man is exploited by man." Ask your students what Brecht gains from juxtaposing Eastern and Western motifs here. Would the visit from the gods work as well if the play were set in a contemporary, fully Westernized city? How does his habitual choice of nonrealistic stage pictures of exotic or premodern geographical locations contribute to the distancing effect that Brecht works to achieve in the theater?

You will probably want to return to the question of locale every time the scene shifts. This is easily done if you spend some time discussing *The Good Woman of Setzuan*'s episodic structure, which is again typically Brechtian. Why does he purposely avoid a fluid, chronologically seamless presentation of events? Here is another means by which Brecht constantly jolts the audience out of complacency. Notice in particular the subsidiary skits attached to several scenes (3a, 4a, etc.); having your students identify and explain these additions would be a good preparatory assignment to accompany a first reading of the text, since the students should have no trouble discerning their function.

The prologue, in which Wong speaks directly to the audience and greets the itinerant gods, is in effect the first of these anti-illusionist commentaries. Moving in and out of the action of the play, Wong serves as the audience's ambassador. He is equipped with two props worth some discussion: the cup with the false bottom (p. 2214) and the carrying pole. Ask your students to interpret the stage image of his balancing the pole with one hand, his other having been smashed by the irate barber's curling iron (p. 2234). Literally singlehandedly, throughout the play, Wong mediates the action, trying to put the best face on human failings when the gods accost him and to persuade them to reconsider the demands of orthodoxy: "Maybe a little relaxation of the rules, Benevolent One, in view of the bad times" (p. 2254).

The prologue resembles also the opening chapters of the Book of Job (pp. 77–93 in volume A) and the *Prologue in Heaven* to Goethe's *Faust* (pp. 681–780 in volume E), in which divine powers question the sustainability of human virtue. The larger texts then proceed to test that virtue, as does *The Good Woman of Setzuan*. By setting his play in a semimythical, semi-Westernized China, Brecht can allude to the Judeo-Christian tradition (which includes, as the headnote indicates, the angelic visit to— and the ultimate destruction of—the corrupt cities of Sodom and Gomorrah in Genesis 18–19) without directly impugning the ways of God to men. The three Chinese gods pictured here are infirm and old-fashioned when the play begins and, despite Wong's excellent advice to them when they appear to him later in dreams, increasingly out of touch with reality. (When the Father in *Six Characters in Search of an Author* speaks of the "disaster it is for a character to be born in the imagination of an author who then refuses to give him life" [p. 1760], Pirandello, like Brecht, presents the audience with a devastating image of divine impotence.)

The argument of the atheists that confounds the gods lies at the heart of Brecht's ideology: "The world must be changed because no one can *be* good and *stay* good" (p. 2214). The gods don't want to be bothered, but only change will save the world. Wong himself, a beleaguered water seller, exemplifies the economic roots of human suffering. *The Good Woman of Setzuan* examines the failures of the capitalist system by focusing on the effort to support oneself by the sale of commodities; in this case water and tobacco. Students will easily understand the contrast between the two, one essential to life, the other a narcotic. An extended discussion of the way each figures in the play can help you organize many of the ideas Brecht examines here.

The opening lines of the play lay out the law of supply and demand ("When water is scarce, I have long distances to go in search of it, and when it is plentiful, I have no income"). Only half-Westernized, Brecht's Setzuan does not boast a modern system of water supply. Wong lives in a "den in the sewer pipe down by the river" (p. 2233), the site of the five dreams in which the gods appear to him. Civil engineering is sufficiently advanced to channel wastes that pollute the river, but indoor plumbing has not yet been provided for Setzuan. At the end of scene 1, Shen Te already sees how little refuge her tobacco shop will offer her and tellingly uses a watery image to express her consternation: "The little lifeboat is swiftly sent down / Too many men too greedily / Hold on to it as they drown" (p. 2222). In scene 3, she meets her suicidal pilot on a rainy day in the park; using another watery metaphor, Yang Sun explains his friends' lack of concern:

> they don't want to hear I'm still unemployed. "What?" they ask. "Is there still water in the sea?" (p. 2231)

There are too many mail pilots for them all to be employed (p. 2229), and illustrating the same universal law of oversupply, Shen Te weeps, adding water to the rainy day. Wong wanders through the park to sing "The Song of the Water Seller in the Rain," complaining that no one wants to buy water in the rain. Shen Te's goodness, however, compels her to buy a cup for Yang Sun, who has fallen asleep by the time she reaches him with this sustenance. And the audience has observed a series of lessons elucidating the economic imbalances that drive human beings to theft and suicide.

The tobacco shop thrives, however, once Shen Te's alter ego, Shui Ta, comes to stay. You may want to ask your students why Brecht chose tobacco and explore with them the reasons why it sells better than life-sustaining water. Note how many of the stage directions indicate who smokes what, and how: no sooner has Shen Te opened her shop than the Unemployed Man comes to beg for a cigarette butt, scandalizing the wife of the "family of eight" listed in the dramatis personae, the parasitical past owners of a tobacco shop who will contribute the sacks of (apparently) stolen tobacco that ultimately makes Shui Ta's fortune.

> WIFE   What nerve, begging for tobacco. [*Rhetorically.*] Why don't they ask for bread?
> UNEMPLOYED MAN   Bread is expensive.   (p. 2218)

In "The Song of the Smoke," sung by members of this greedy family of former tobacconists (p. 2221), the insubstantiality of smoke stands for the vacuity symbolized by the commodity they sold and the impossibility of being good in a world where there are no options for intelligence or goodness to succeed.

When Shui Ta arrives, in scene 2, he puts himself on the right side of the law by informing on the petty theft of baked goods by the son of the family of eight, magnanimously looking on while the policeman takes two cigars and puts them in his pocket (p. 2227). Shui Ta's ultimate success is signaled by his smoking of a cigar (p. 2256), a simple act with which an inventive actor can stop the show. In other words, tobacco products affirm social status and have long served as props on which self-doubting or self-aggrandizing smokers equally rely. More fundamentally, of course, you may analyze their addictive properties and the profound social dislocations they cause, exemplified here by the Unemployed Man's predicament.

Students today are likely to perceive the shadow of illegality that hovers over Shen Te's shop more quickly than Brecht's first audiences, for whom smoking had a carefully nurtured romantic aura. Ask your students what roles cigarettes play in films of the 1930s and '40s. Think of the uses of celebrities in advertising campaigns for cigarettes in the 1950s. Smoking has similarly been associated with artistic creativity (note the prominent cigar in Brecht's hand in Rudolf Schlichter's portrait of 1926, reproduced on the cover of *The Cambridge Companion to Brecht*). Nevertheless, *The Good Woman of Setzuan* clearly links tobacco with criminality. When the Husband and Wife of the family of eight drag in the sacks that they ask Shen Te to hide for them, they do so "furtively" and "cryptically," according to the stage directions (p. 2251). It is interesting to note that when Brecht adapted the play for a possible production in the United States, he changed the contents of these sacks to opium. In today's antitobacco climate, it should be easy for your students to see that the play, even in its original version, treats tobacco as a drug, a source of different fetishes and fascinations, the sort of item that an unscrupulous capitalist can turn to profit.

Once you have set up this conceptual background, you will probably want to talk about character, the dramatic element toward which students most naturally gravitate. You might begin by noting the perennial challenge that Brecht's protagonists present to audiences and performers. Despite his ability to imagine outsize theatrical personalities, his theoretical aim is to deflate them, to keep us from sympathizing with them. In his early sketches for *The Good Woman of Setzuan*, he is preoccupied with the pitfalls that await the actor who assumes the title role: "the girl must be a big powerful person," he writes, fearful that impersonating Shen Te as a delicate Chinese beauty will undercut his efforts.

Ask your students to give their opinions of the love story of Shen Te and Yang Sun. What is the attitude toward women here? Why does Shen Te fall in love with a suicidal pilot? How does Brecht use this kind of masochistic relationship, a staple of conventional romance narratives, to further his political agenda? Yang Sun's brutal explanation of his power over Shen Te is the cause of Shui Ta's momentary dropping of the mask in scene 5 (p. 2241). He seems to be a total cad, and he will become a willing capitalist functionary in the tobacco factory (see "The Song of the Eighth Elephant," p. 2256). Yet Brecht allows him to express just enough sentimental concern for Shen Te to keep her love for him from seeming utterly ridiculous. He claims to have bought two tickets to Peking, for example, at the abortive wedding celebration (p. 2247), but he is not above paying court to the landlady on behalf of the tobacco factory. Then again, he threatens to blackmail Shui Ta since his "interest in this young woman has not been officially terminated," p. 2259), but he speaks in Shui Ta's defense when he testifies that he has not killed his cousin, since he has heard Shen Te sobbing in the back room.

How genuine is Yang Sun's attachment to Shen Te? Brecht does not wish to portray complex, psychologically coherent characters; Yang Sun is full of contradictions, and different productions could show diametrically different versions of his romance with Shen Te. At no point, however, are we allowed to lose sight of the pilot's primary concern, which is for himself. Like every other human being—except the good half of the good woman of Setzuan—Yang Sun is ruled by his own self-interest.

Although Brecht did not live long enough to produce *The Good Woman of Setzuan* with the Berliner Ensemble, and therefore to tackle firsthand the paradoxical nature of the double character of Shen Te/Shui Ta, the list of actresses who have taken the role is impressive. In 1956, Uta Hagen and Peggy Ashcroft, two highly intelligent players with a wide emotional range, each a famous Desdemona but capable of tough and unsentimental acting, put their imprint on the role in the first productions in New York and London, respectively. Interestingly, Brecht did not consider casting the role with a man, in the style of the Chinese theater, although that might be an ideal solution to the dilemma he foresaw.

In order not to sentimentalize Shen Te it is helpful to remember what her occupation is. To the commodities for sale in the play, one must add the female body. Shen Te's goodness is not automatic, since before she can offer hospitality to the gods, she has to get rid of a client (p. 2215). And Wong's recommendation of Shen Te is, of course, a joke. She is a prostitute; "she *can't* say no." When she falls in love with Yang Sun, she has to put up with the casual insults that spring to his lips, even as he is about to throw a rope around the tree to hang himself. She enters the park as one of three whores to walk through it while the pilot seeks privacy; she has to insist that she has avoided the occupational hazard of being bowlegged (p. 2229) and to defend herself against the charge of nymphomania:

YANG SUN   What do you know about love?
SHEN TE   Everything.
YANG SUN   Nothing. [*Pause.*] Or d'you just mean you enjoyed it?
                                              (p. 2231)

Prostitution for Brecht is just one more metaphor for life in a capitalist society. When the landlady, Mrs. Mi Tzu, talks of Shen Te with Shui Ta, she is about to call her a prostitute when the "cousin" intervenes: "Pauper. Let's use the uglier word" (p. 2226). That word explains why persons —of whatever sex and in whatever manner—prostitute themselves. Brecht wants Shen Te to be a "big powerful person," a woman who can impersonate a man, not a tragic whore with a heart of gold. Remind your students of the significance of the play's German title, which is not gender specific: the title character in *Der Gute Mensch von Sezuan* endures the compromised existence that any person caught in the essential contradictions of the capitalist West must deal with. Presumably to inoculate the role against the threat of prettiness, Brecht has Shen Te immediately act on the suggestion of the hardened Husband and Wife that she has to learn to say no and that the easiest way to do that is to invent "some relative who insists on all accounts being strictly in order" (p. 2218).

This device allows the playwright to have his cake and eat it too. It makes Shen Te/Shui Ta a virtuoso turn for a major actor, but splitting her/him into two halves runs the risk of obscuring the character's struggle. Shen Te, "The Angel of the Slums," whose name means *divine virtue*, is also the hard-nosed businessman, Shui Ta, whose name means *flood tide*. The image again is of water, here as a symbol of fate. As Shakespeare's Brutus says,

> There is a tide in the affairs of men
> Which, taken at the flood, leads on to fortune;
> Omitted, all the voyage of their life
> Is bound in shallows and in miseries.
> > (*Julius Caesar* 4.3.216–20)

To succeed, one must be an opportunist. The Angel of the Slums is an opportunist; but because she puts on a mask that allows her to express the opportunistic side of her character as if it were someone else taking advantage of others' ill fortune (as Shui Ta does with the sacks of contraband tobacco), Brecht makes possible the very prettifying of Shen Te and divine virtue that he ostensibly sets out here to unmask.

Divine virtue is literally on trial in the final episode of *The Good Woman of Setzuan*. Courtroom scenes always make for good theater, and you may want to ask your students why this is so. In a way, the trial epitomizes Brecht's dramaturgy: out of the conflicting testimonies of accuser and accused, truth should emerge—and the observers must make a judgment. In Setzuan, as elsewhere, justice is easily bought and sold. Wong expresses delight when he sees who the new judges are, thinking that the power of the political establishment has been quelled now that the gods replace the pillars of the community whom Shu Fu and Shui Ta have corrupted. Note that Shui Ta is about to "open twelve super tobacco markets" (p. 2261) if you are so inclined, you may encourage your students to reflect on the recent decisions in suits brought against the major tobacco companies in the United States. Who profits? Who ultimately pays? How are strong rulings diluted when appeals courts review them? How do lobbyists influence tobacco legislation? Analyzing judicial and legislative politics would be an eminently Brechtian exercise.

Within the play itself, corruption is not so easily expunged. The divine judges have their own biases. To be sure, they show their independence of the ruling classes when they discount the rich barber's testimony in favor of the defendant:

> SHU FU   Mr. Shui Ta is a businessman, my lord. Need I say more?
> FIRST GOD   Yes.   (p. 2262)

But when the court is cleared and Shui Ta tears off his clothes and his masks and becomes Shen Te, the gods refuse to hear or understand or help her. Brecht insists that it is up to us to fix the problems that conventional bourgeois religion and politics sweep under the rug. Directly addressing the audience in the epilogue, Shen Te bluntly asks if the world can be changed.

> *You* write the happy ending to the play!
> There must, there must, there's got to be a way!
>   (p. 2267)

Topics for Writing

1. Brecht called *The Good Woman of Setzuan* a parable, the formal genre that Jesus used for teaching his disciples. How would you characterize the theological content of *The Good Woman of Setzuan*? What kind of religious questions does Shen Te's life raise?

2. Why does Shen Te fall in love with Yang Sun? Do her feelings for him demonstrate her essential goodness?

3. What view of women emerges from the splitting of the good person of Setzuan into male and female halves? How would you compare Shen Te to the other female characters in the play?

4. Discuss the songs in this play, explaining how they relate to the scenes in which they are sung.

5. Give as many examples as possible to demonstrate the view of capitalism expressed in this play. Do you think Brecht fairly presents the workings of a modern economic system?

Comparative Perspectives

1. Compare the descriptions of poverty offered in Swift's *Modest Proposal* and Brecht's *Good Woman of Setzuan*, and the solutions proposed in each. How do you think each writer would react to the other's work?

2. Compare other trial scenes in the anthology to that in Brecht's play. How is Melville's approach to his material in *Billy Budd* fundamen-

tally different from Brecht's? How is judicial practice represented in each case? What definitions of goodness are at stake? How does the trial that is the substance of *In Camera* take further the cynical deconstruction of justice that Brecht dramatizes here?

3. After viewing Chinese theater on a visit to Moscow in 1935, Brecht wrote an approving essay called *Alienation Effects in Chinese Acting*. What similarities do you see between Brecht's play and the scenes from *The Peach Blossom Fan?* Examine in particular the impact of the songs and the episodic structure in each work, explaining whether they "alienate" you from the characters's dilemmas and help you focus on the political problems their experiences illuminate, or if you identify with the characters anyway.

[See also comparisons suggested with *The Cherry Orchard* and *The Sultan's Dilemma*.]

Further Reading

See also the reading suggestion in the anthology, p. 2212.

Bartram, Graham, and Anthony Waine, eds. *Brecht in Perspective.* 1982. A collection of thirteen essays on historical, literary, and theatrical perspectives, including a discussion of Brecht's legacy for German dramatists and the English theater.

Brecht, Bertolt. *Collected Plays.* Annot. and ed., John Willett and Ralph Manheim. 1970 and continuing. In the English edition, published by Methuen, volume 6.i (1985) contains *The Good Person in Szechwan* (not the translation in use here). The introduction and notes differ somewhat from those in the American edition; sparse but extremely valuable, they are worth seeking out.

Brustein, Robert. *The Theater of Revolt.* 1964. The chapter on Brecht is particularly well written and enlightening.

The Drama Review 12, 1 (Fall 1967). A special Brecht issue.

Eaton, Katherine Bliss. *The Theater of Meyerhold and Brecht.* 1985. Considers Brecht's relationship to "epic theater" and twentieth-century experimental theater techniques.

Fuegi, John. *Bertolt Brecht: Chaos, According to Plan.* 1987. Provides a general view of Brecht's work with actors in concrete theatrical situations.

Gray, Ronald. *Bertolt Brecht.* 1961. A good short introduction.

Kiebuzinska, Christine Olga. *Revolutionaries in the Theater: Meyerhold, Brecht, and Witkiewicz.* 1988.

Lug, Sieglinde. "The 'Good' Woman Demystified." *Communications from the International Brecht Society* 14, 1 (November 1984): 3–16. Uses a feminist approach in discussing three plays by Brecht.

Pike, David. *Lukács and Brecht.* 1985. Discusses the famous Brecht-Lukács debate over experimental versus conventionally realistic form.

Willett, John. *The Theatre of Bertolt Brecht: A Study of Eight Aspects.* 1959. Very good on theatrical influences and stage practice, with a useful discussion of Brecht's use of music.

————. *Brecht in Context: Comparative Approaches.* 1984. Diverse interdisciplinary topics.

Witt, Hubert, ed. *Brecht As They Knew Him.* Trans. John Peet. 1974. Short memoirs of Brecht.

Wright, Elizabeth. *Postmodern Brecht: A Re-representation.* 1989. A valuable study that rejects period-oriented views of Brecht's career and demonstrates the continuing importance of his theorectical pieces and early works.

FEDERICO GARCÍA LORCA

Lament for Ignacio Sánchez Mejías

Backgrounds

Federico García Lorca is a poet of myth, of emotion, of rhythmic language, of the earth. The most internationally famous Spanish writer since Cervantes, his visionary poetry and his death at the hands of Franco's militia have already made him a symbol of the artist's opposition to the sterility of the modern industrial West and to the impersonal repressions of the fascist police state. Lorca's imaginative roots reach into the past and the countryside: into the folklore and folk imagery, gypsy legends, ballad rhythms, and pastoral landscape of his native Andalusia. He maintains the mysterious life of nature and the subconscious in the midst of a highly civilized—perhaps overcivilized—society and seems to speak directly from the life of his dreams and personal emotions. To a reader of Spanish, Lorca's lyric rhythms and the dense network of his allusive imagery compose a poetic voice unique in modern literature.

Death is the central theme in *Lament for Ignacio Sánchez Mejías,* as it is in all of Lorca's work. One critic calls him "the poet of death" and notes that Spain has an ancient popular tradition of the "culture of death," which Lorca continually, and naturally, exploits. The bull has long been the characteristic symbol of death in Spain—as in other Mediterranean cultures—and in the *Lament* it possesses the terrors of darkness that gather around the finality that everyone must face. The confrontation with death is, for Lorca, at its most impressive and spectacular in the bullfight: the "greatest poetic and human treasure of Spain" and "the most cultured pastime in the world today; it is pure drama . . . the only place where one can go and with certainty see death surrounded by the most astonishing beauty."

In *Lament,* bulls and bullfighting, death and the spilling of blood permeate every passage, and Sánchez Mejías's death takes on the power of a religious sacrifice. In section 1, "Cogida and Death," the bull invades Sánchez Mejías's body ("a thigh with a desolate horn. . . . the bull was bellowing through his forehead") and the images of the bull ring merge with those of the hospital ("the bull ring was covered in iodine") in which Sánchez Mejías lies dying. In section 2, "The Spilled Blood," Lorca invokes the bulls of Guisando, "partly death and partly stone," which bellow "like two centuries / sated with treading the earth." Later in the same section, as the moment of the goring approaches, "secret voices" shout to "celestial bulls." Overseeing, all is the "cow of the ancient world"— mother of bulls, mother of men—who passes her "sad tongue / over a snout of blood / spilled on the sand."

For Sánchez Mejías, as for Lorca, the bullfight is like a religious ceremony in which priest and congregation alike take part: he has gone "up the tiers / with all his death on his shoulders" and spilled his blood before "a thirsty multitude." The blood—always a symbol of vitality and passion in Lorca's work (the "nightingale of his veins!")—is the medium of sacrifice, a blood so marvelous and potent "[n]o chalice can contain it."

In section 1, the poet encounters the moment of death at the instant of its happening. Section 2 presents his rejection of it ("No . . . I will not see it!") and his simultaneous attempt to universalize it: to give it a meaning beyond itself. In section 3, "The Laid Out Body," the poet attempts to come to grips with death, to accommodate its finality. The section is calmer, more resigned, less hyperbolic. The poet encounters the niggardly meanness of death and asks for answers. There are none, and his final claim—"even the sea dies!"—is cold consolation.

The elegiac occasion gives full play to Lorca's mythmaking, surrealistic imagination. That he called it a lament assures us, says one critic, that it will depend heavily on Lorca's personal emotions. And indeed, though Sánchez Mejías is always at the center of the poem, forever praised, its most powerful presence is the despairing and urgent voice of the speaker. It is through the speaker's impassioned response and poetic insistence, his ability to involve the bullfighter in a larger drama of universal feeling, that Sánchez Mejías will be remembered. He may well have been "a great torero in the ring," and a "good peasant in the sierra" but only the poet can make his strength "like a river of lions" and his blood sing "along marshes and meadows." In section 4, "Absent Soul," Lorca recognizes the oblivion to which death consigns us, how in death we are forgotten "in a heap of lifeless dogs." And so the poet must sing in an effort to defeat oblivion, even though he knows that his song will be but "a sad breeze through the olive trees."

Ignacio Sánchez Mejías was severely gored in Manzanares on August 11, 1934, and died two days later in Madrid. He was one of the most eminent bullfighters in Spain at the time and a man of surprising talent as a dramatist. His intellectual interests were wide ranging, a fact that no doubt contributed to Lorca's powerful sense of loss upon his death.

The bullfight—in which the bullfighter quite literally faces death in a mounting sequence of dangerous ritual actions—and the *cante jondo,* the traditional music of Andalusia, are the primary cultural influences on the *Lament.* In one of the most famous of his essays, Lorca attempted to find the essence, the "marrow of forms," of successful art in the "dark sounds" of what the Andalusians call *duende,* the "spirit of the earth," the "mysterious power that everyone feels but that no philosopher has explained":

> The *duende* is a power and not a behavior, it is a struggle and not a concept. I have heard an old guitarist master say: "The *duende* is not in the throat; the *duende* surges up from the soles of the feet." It is not a matter of ability, but of real live form; of blood; of ancient culture; of creative action.

It was in his native culture, in its traditional forms and feelings, that Lorca located the *duende* he wanted to infuse into his own verse.

Classroom Strategies

Lament for Ignacio Sánchez Mejías can be taught in one class period. You may wish to compare Lorca with other poets—Rilke, Stevens, and Baudelaire come to mind—to suggest the range of modern poetry and poetics. Students who are able to read the original Spanish passages printed in the text (p. 2277) should be encouraged to read aloud to the class and to comment on any rhythmic effects or verbal associations that they feel are lost in translation.

In general, American students will have little understanding of the bullfight as such. The bullfight is *not* a sport; it is a ritual. For Lorca's poem, it is the basis from which the action starts, like the appearance of the ghost in *Hamlet* or Agamemnon's sacrifice of his daughter Iphigenia in the *Oresteia.* Students will be impressed with the play of Lorca's imagination over the event. They will also be impressed by the way the poem follows the stages that psychologists say all of us go through when we encounter death: recognition, refusal, questioning, resignation, and acceptance.

They may not always be able to "follow" the language line by line. Lorca's use of archetypal and Spanish imagery in the loosely connected way associated with surrealism will be especially obscure for many. But one of the extraordinary powers of surreal imagery is that it becomes more effective as it accumulates. Surrealism exists to locate and make articulate that place where the conscious intellect cannot go. Lorca's surrealism works in the sense that it soaks in before it is questioned.

Because each section of the poem is different in form and tone, it helps to discuss them separately. With the refrain of section 1 students will be on familiar ground, not necessarily from Andalusian gypsy ballads, but from contemporary popular music, where again the refrain serves as a kind of "hook" to arrest the listener's attention. Section 2 is probably for most students the most immediately accessible; Lorca's refusal to "see" his friend's spilled blood is simultaneously poignant and insistent. For students who are having difficulty with the poem, concentration on section 2 will help define its tone, demonstrate its emotional power, and clarify its surrealistic mode of meaning.

Topics for Discussion and Writing

1. Why is the death of a bullfighter a particularly appropriate occasion for Lorca's lament about death in general?

    [See the second paragraph of "Backgrounds," and the headnote to Lorca, in the anthology, for further discussion.]

2. How does Lorca use images of bulls in the poem? What do they suggest? What other important images are connected with bulls?

    [See the third and fourth paragraphs of "Backgrounds" for a discussion of bulls. You might also wish to point out the way Lorca associates the moon (traditionally female, like the "ancient cow" of section 2, and connected with notions of fate) with bulls. Critics have noticed that the moon, its crescent shape perhaps suggesting the bull's horns, presides "with a fatal glow" over Sánchez Mejías's death.]

3. Is there any logical organization apparent in the poem? If so, what is it? How does it bear upon the central theme of death?

    [See the second paragraph of "Classroom Strategies" as well as the headnote for further discussion.]

4. What are the conventions of the elegy in poetry? In what ways is this a traditional elegy? In what ways does it differ from the traditional elegy?

5. What is *duende*? Does this poem have it?

6. Compare Lorca's attitude toward death with that of García Márquez in *Death Constant Beyond Love*.

7. If you read Spanish, you may wish to read aloud or compare passages from the translation with the section of the original text given in the anthology (p. 2277). You may also encourage students to try reading the original text on their own and to comment on the way the translation has or has not succeeded in grasping the original. Some of the bolder ones may attempt their own translations, which will bring them closer to the text and, at the same time, induce a healthy respect for the difficulties of translation.

Comparative Perspectives

From the beginning of time, poets have sought ways to come to terms with violent death. Lorca's poem may usefully be compared to early epics, like *Gilgamesh* and the *Iliad*, in which the death of an exemplary friend fuels passionate mourning and desperate action. What issues that concern Gilgamesh and Achilles obsess the speaker here as well? By what means does the modern poet distill such intensity of feeling into 221 lines?

See also comparisons suggested with Tennyson's *In Memoriam A. H. H.*,

Rilke's *Archaic Torso of Apollo,* Zuni ritual poetry, Akhmatova's *Requiem,* and Alfonsina Storni's *Portrait of García Lorca.*

Further Reading

See also the reading suggestions in the anthology, p. 2271.

Adams, Mildred. *García Lorca: Playwright and Poet.* 1984. Fuller general study.

Allen, Rupert C. *The Symbolic World of Federico García Lorca.* 1972.

Binding, Paul. *Lorca: The Gay Imagination.* 1985.

Colecchia, Francesca. *García Lorca: An Annotated Bibliography of Criticism.* 1979. A guide to reference material before 1979.

Cannon, Calvin. "Lorca's 'Llanto por Ignacio Sanchez Mejias' and the Elegiac Tradition." *Hispanic Review* XXXI (1963), pp. 229–38. Demonstrates the *Lament's* place in the tradition of the classical elegy.

Davies, Catherine, and Garry Marvin. "Control of the Wild in Andalusian Culture: Bull and Horse Imagery in Lorca from an Anthropological Perspective." *Neophilologus* 71, 4 (October 1987), pp. 543–58. An anthropological perspective.

García Lorca, Federico. "Theory and Function of the *Duende.*" In *The Poetics of the New American Poetry,* edited by Donald M. Allen and Warren Tallman. 1973. One of Lorca's most important prose statements, it provides great insight into what Lorca is after in his work.

García Lorca, Francisco. *In the Green Morning: Memories of Federico.* Translated by Christopher Maurer. 1986.

Gershator, David, ed. *Selected Letters.* 1983.

Londre, Felicia Hardison. *Federico Garcia Lorca.* 1984. Fuller general study.

Loughran, David K. *Federico García Lorca: The Poetry of Limits.* 1978.

MacCurdy, Grant G. *Federico García Lorca: Life, Work and Criticism.* 1986. Brief overview.

Morris, C. Brian. *"Cuando yo me muera . . .": Essays in Memory of Federico García Lorca.* 1988. Collects seventeen papers from a symposium on Lorca; the essays are chiefly in English while the poetry is cited in Spanish.

Oppenheimer, Helen. *Lorca, the Drawings: Their Relation to the Poet's Life and Work.* 1986. Reproduces drawings from different periods in the poet's life along with valuable commentary on their historical context and personal significance; appendices contain Lorca's slide lecture entitled "Thoughts on Modern Art" and a film script.

Rees, Margaret A., ed. *Leeds Papers on Lorca and on Civil War Verse.* 1988.

Salinas, Pedro. "Lorca and the Poetry of Death." In *Lorca: A Collection of Critical Essays,* edited by Manuel Duran. 1962, pp. 100–107. Discusses Lorca and the Spanish "culture of death."

Stanton, Edward. *The Tragic Myth: Lorca and the Cante Jondo.* 1978. See pp. 46–51 for a short but persuasive discussion of bulls, bullfighting, and native Andalusian traditions as mythic elements in Lorca's work, especially *Lament.*

TAWFIQ AL-HAKIM

The Sultan's Dilemma

Backgrounds

The play begins with a lengthy exchange between two characters whom we quickly learn are an executioner and a condemned man facing execution. This is not heavy drama, but a kind of vaudeville turn in which the executioner begs for sympathy due to his hard lot, sings a song concerning the poignancy of mortality, and wheedles a glass of wine from his victim. The executioner needs the wine, he explains, so that his hand won't tremble at the crucial moment. The prospect of a slip is presented as more comic than gruesome, but the condemned man pays up. And so a wine merchant is drawn into the dialogue, as are, when their exchanges become too loud, a woman—the beautiful lady—and her maid. The former is assumed to be a prostitute by the merchant and the executioner. Nonetheless, she proves to be a shrewd and kind-hearted woman: when she learns that the man has been condemned without a hearing, she thinks of a ruse to save his neck. He is to be executed at dawn, but the actual wording of the order is "when the muezzin gives the call for morning prayer." The muezzin arrives, she invites him in for a warming drink, and since he does not give the call, at least not so it can be heard, the man is spared. She also saves the executioner, or calms his fears of punishment, by pointing out to him that he has adhered to the strict letter of his responsibility (no call for prayer, no execution). Her actions initiate the drama to follow, for at this point the Sultan and his entourage enter. The condemned man, very much alive, clamors for the trial he was denied, and so by degrees the Sultan's terrible secret is revealed. The remainder of the play is taken up with working out the consequences of the failure to execute this slave merchant.

The vizier and the chief cadi embody the two possible solutions to the dilemma that the Sultan's slave status poses both for him and for the state. On the one hand the vizier urges a simple, arbitrary execution that will bury the problem by burying the man. The chief cadi balks at this solution and offers an alternative, namely trust in the law. The debate between them is prolonged, but it does eventually resolve itself into a simple confrontation between the use of force and reliance on law. The Sultan, despite the fact that he is a general first and foremost and more at home on the battlefield than in the court, courageously and uncharacteristically chooses the law. His decision is made easier by the assurances of the vizier and the chief cadi that they can arrange for him to be purchased and freed at one and the same moment.

As the third act begins, the wine merchant and his neighbor the shoemaker speculate on what they would do if they could buy the Sultan. They clearly have no idea who or what the Sultan is, but their banter suggests that whoever offers the highest bid may well not be willing to give up his purchase as freely as the officers of the court expect. In any event, the beautiful lady thwarts their plans and precipitates a second crisis in the play. For reasons of her own she both buys the Sultan and refuses to free him. The Sultan must choose to continue to trust the law or fall back on the arbitrary violence. He continues to trust the law. After some pleading the lady is persuaded to free the Sultan, but only after he has served her for one night. He agrees, and what follows is both chaste and surprising. The vizier tries once more to gain mastery of the situation by using on the lady the same trick that she used on him, but the Sultan, who has grown wonderfully in wisdom throughout the play, gives him a short lesson in the real nature of justice.

Topics for Discussion

The Sultan's Dilemma is a comedy, but as often with comedy, the questions it raises are thoughtful. Is it possible for a ruler to put aside the arbitrary use of force and trust entirely to the law when his own well-being is at stake? The answer that al-Hakim gives through his play is an emphatic yes. But he has loaded the dice in his favor by making the Sultan a wise and just ruler—or more accurately, the tetchy and confused military hero at the start of the play is transformed into a wise and far-seeing statesman by the end. Other substantial issues are raised along the way, but again with the same lightness of touch. Should we respect the letter of the law or the spirit? That is, what conclusion are we to draw from the two appearances of "dawn" as the moment when the muezzin gives the call for the morning prayer? And is benign deceit acceptable because it is benign? Both the lady and the vizier have the best intentions when they persuade, or coerce, the muezzin to not give his call, or to give it out of season.

Are the common people—represented here by the wine merchant and the shoemaker—able to appreciate a ruler who chooses law over force? The trivial employments they would find for the Sultan if they owned him suggest anything but a population committed to law or justice. But is that really an issue? Can a ruler excuse the use of unjust force by saying that the people are not ready for anything better?

And what are we to make of the lady? She is, aside from her bullying servant, the only female character in the play, yet she is second only to the Sultan in importance. Historically there were wives and queen mothers who were extremely powerful in Islamic courts, even though they were restricted to the women's quarters and had to exert their influence through intermediaries. What is the purpose of making her a character who can have so admirable a life only by enduring public scorn? Is she more or less believable than the Solomonic Sultan? Isn't there something of Shahrazad here in her risking so much personally to educate the monarch?

Topics for Writing

1. Al-Hakim claims not to have read Pirandello before he wrote *The Sultan's Dilemma*, but it is possible to detect certain qualities in his play that seem to echo themes of *Six Characters in Search of an Author*, especially the puzzling and intricate relation between what is real and what is fictional. A Sultan cannot be a monarch and a slave at the same time, yet this sultan is a very effective ruler so long as he is perceived as legitimate. Even after the slave trader blows the whistle on him he is still treated by his ministers as their ruler, though now, technically, he cannot be so. The lady is another character who has both a real identity and a fictional identity that are at odds with each other. She cannot be both a whore and a virtuous woman, yet in order to be one she must appear to be the other. Then there is the question of what is meant by "dawn."
2. Do modern rulers trust entirely in the law? Could this play be rewritten in a contemporary setting with, say, a president having to choose either to make an appearance in court to defend himself against charges of having violated the law (Watergate, Iran/Contra, Whitewater) or to fall back on executive authority to avoid a trial?
3. This is a serious play, but not a solemn one. How does al-Hakim manage to keep the play humorous and serious at the same time?
4. How persuasive is al-Hakim in creating plausible characters that embody particular points of view? Or, put another way, do the requirements of believability work against the need to maintain a consistent point of view?

Comparative Perspectives

1. In *The Sultan's Dilemma* Tawfiq al-Hakim investigates ideas about cost and value. Compare Brecht's examination of similar economic concepts in *The Good Woman of Setzuan*.
2. How does our understanding of the life led by the enigmatic beautiful lady change in the course of the play? Compare and contrast the sexual and social expectations that shape her to those influencing the development of, as appropriate, the Stepdaughter in *Six Characters in Search of an Author* or Komako in *Snow Country*.

Further Reading

See also the reading suggestions in the anthology, p. 2281.

Abdel Wahab, Farouk, ed. and trans. *Modern Egyptian Drama: An Anthology*. 1974. Includes the work of other good Egyptian dramatists, such as Mikhail Roman, Rashad Rushdy, and Yusuf Idris.

Al-Hakim, Tawfiq. *Plays, Prefaces and Postscripts of Tawfiq al-Hakim*. Volume I: *Theatre of the Mind*. Volume II: *Theatre of Society*. Translated by William M. Hutchins. 1981; 1984. Especially valuable for the generous sampling of al-Hakim's comments on his own work.

KAWABATA YASUNARI

Snow Country

Backgrounds and Classroom Strategies

Snow Country tends to fit everyone's idea of what Japanese literature should be. What people seem to mean is that it reminds them of *haiku*. In describing the ambiguities of love and the imperfection inherent in human attachment, and in placing mere mortals in a moment larger than themselves, the novel's lyric, imagistic narrative, like *haiku*, works in ways surprisingly nondiscursive, elliptical, quiescent. And hovering over all is the most refined of artistic temperaments. The net result is that of a miniature—a delicate, fastidious recreation of the experience of resignation.

Your challenge is to take readers beyond what has become almost a cliché. After all, *Snow Country* is an extended narrative, not a poem, and seeking to define a Japanese quintessence (as the Nobel Prize committee sought to do) will probably amount to an exercise in tautology. This is not to say that if students want to pursue the novel's links with its heritage fruitful topics are not at hand. A comparison of love as depicted in *The Tale of Genji* (volume B, pp. 2182–2270), for example, or in classical Japanese poetry (*The Kokinshū*, volume B, pp. 2163–74), with its depiction in *Snow Country* would be interesting, as would a responsible examination of specific ways that the novel is evocative of *haiku*. How does Kawabata employ juxtaposition in place of linear exposition? How does he use natural imagery? And how does he sometimes tip the balance between characters and background for an effect comparable to the speaker's submersion in *haiku*?

Ultimately, however, the careful reader is drawn back to persistent themes—longing, wasted effort, time—that give Kawabata's novel a power beyond its slender proportions. You will probably want to address each of these themes.

The first, longing, is in fact one of Kawabata's favorite words. Life to him is like a fire, fueled by a distant, often unattainable ideal; it kindles until it attains that ideal, or it ends by burning itself out. A colder version of this yearning, appropriate to the setting, opens *Snow Country*. Perhaps the most famous thing that Kawabata ever wrote is the train scene, in which Shimamura observes Yoko by watching her reflection in the window. At first he is startled that, as night comes on, his window functions as a mirror. He is intrigued by this woman, whose name he learns only much later, and by her relation to the sick man she is tending. And so he studies her through his furtive "mirror."

> Since the girl was thus diagonally opposite him, Shimamura could as well have looked directly at her. When the two of them came on the train, however, something coolly piercing about her beauty had startled Shimamura, and as he hastily lowered his eyes he had seen the man's ashen fingers clutching at the girl's. Somehow it seemed wrong to look their way again. (p. 2344)

The "mirror," however, allows him to play the voyeur.

> In the depths of the mirror the evening landscape moved by, the mirror and the reflected figures like motion pictures superimposed one on the other. The figures and the background were unrelated, and yet the figures, transparent and intangible, and the background, dim in the gathering darkness, melted together into a sort of symbolic world not of this world. Particularly when a light out in the mountains shone in the center of the girl's face, Shimamura felt his chest rise at the inexpressible beauty of it. (pp. 2344–45)

Just as the woman and the landscape are superimposed in the window "like motion pictures . . . one on the other," Kawabata achieves a nimble overlay of emotional and lyrical description. He creates a visual scene so beautiful and dreamlike and so moving (in both senses) that the reader experiences almost the same yearning as Shimamura. Discuss with students how Kawabata's technique succeeds here in ways that a more direct subjective expression would not. Discuss, too, how the scene establishes the paradigm for Shimamura's passive behavior throughout the novel. And discuss the ways that ambiguity figures in the type of longing that Kawabata depicts. The indeterminate relation of Yoko to the sick man, the contrast between the narrator's decision to call her a girl but describe her as a woman, and, most of all, the feminine presence that is more ethereal than physical as it floats over the evening landscape work together to create something closer to chimera. Similarly, it is the ambiguity in Komako, the *geisha*, that arouses Shimamura. One moment she is childlike and the next mature; first she is passionate, then reserved; sometimes she is elegant, sometimes unrefined. The sheer disparity tantalizes him. Ambiguity exerts for Shimamura almost as great an attraction as the unattainable.

Wasted effort, the second theme, plagues every character in the story. Shimamura is so detached from life that everything seems unreal. He sees Komako, with whom he becomes involved, "as somehow unreal, like the woman's face in that evening mirror" (p. 2350) and even his greatest interest, his "taste for the occidental dance had much the same air of unreality about it." Without engagement, all effort is wasted. His hobbies; his affair with Komako; his attempt to recover a kind of purity, or honesty with himself (as the narrator puts it), by periodically retreating into the snow country—in the end nothing comes of anything.

Komako's life, as the country *geisha* squandering her looks, is equally misspent. She acknowledges as much to Shimamura: "I could go pleasantly to seed here in the mountains. It would be a fine, quiet feeling." Her youth, her beauty, her musical talents are all being wasted. Again Kawabata, like the *haiku* poet, speaks most eloquently through natural description:

> Each day, as the autumn grew colder, insects died on the floor of his room. Stiff-winged insects fell on their backs and were unable to get to their feet again. A bee walked a little and collapsed, walked a little and collapsed. It was a quiet death that came with the change of seasons. Looking closely, however, Shimamura could see that the legs and feelers were trembling in the struggle to live. For such a tiny death, the empty eight-mat room seemed enormous. (p. 2393)

Time, then, is the third theme. The novel covers a period of about twenty months, as Shimamura travels three times to the snow country. But its back-and-forth structure—winter, spring, winter, fall—employing flashbacks and frequent references to earlier events, makes the period seem much longer. More important, the construction creates in the reader's mind an illusion of the flow of time, so that Kawabata's supposedly loose structure is actually used very effectively to thematic ends. Among other things, *Snow Country* is a modern variation on an old Japanese theme, as old as the first Japanese poetry: we ephemeral humans are carried by the current of time, our blessing when it confers youth and affection, our bane when it snatches them away.

Near the end of the novel, as autumn is about to yield to winter, Shimamura sits ruminating by a charcoal brazier, wondering "what was lacking in him, what kept him from living as completely":

> He leaned against the brazier, provided against the coming of the snowy season, and thought how unlikely it was that he would come again once he had left. The innkeeper had lent him an old Kyoto teakettle, skillfully inlaid in silver with flowers and birds, and from it came the sound of wind in the pines. He could make out two pine breezes, as a matter of fact, a near one and a far one. Just beyond the far breeze he heard faintly the tinkling of a bell. He put his ear to the kettle and listened. Far away, where the bell tinkled on, he suddenly saw Komako's feet, tripping in time to the bell. He drew back. The time had come to leave. (p. 2403)

Kawabata perfectly captures the flow of time through a structure and a style that are both lyrical.

Topics for Discussion and Writing

1. Longing for the unattainable is a frequent theme in Kawabata. Critics have interpreted Komako's behavior as the result of disillusion when the unattainable becomes attainable. That is, when Shimamura—a man from distant parts, as out of reach as a *kabuki* actor—turns out to be too easily within her grasp, Komako's love loses its purity, and from there the novel traces her degradation. Do you agree?

2. In what ways could the unattainable also be said to be a preoccupation of Shimamura's? How is it related to the tentative quality of his temperament?

3. *Beauty and Sadness* is the title of one of Kawabata's later novels. How well does it describe the theme of *Snow Country*?

4. In an essay on the art of fiction, Kawabata maintained that the value of a novel resides in its plot. Yet elsewhere he said that his novels could end at any point, or even that they never really have an end. How do you reconcile these two statements?

5. Kawabata characterized his writing habits and the resulting narrative structures as "lazy and unmethodical." But could we not attribute them to certain continuing traditions in Japanese literature? Think of *haiku* and *zuihitsu*, for example, and of classical Japanese poetry.

6. Both Tanizaki's essay *In Praise of Shadows* (pp. 2049–71) and *Snow Country* have been described as works of stream-of-consciousness. Compare the two with respect to this. Compare them to Western works employing stream-of-consciousness.

7. A sense of Kawabata's style comes through remarkably well in English translation. It tends to simplicity in diction and syntax but complexity in meaning and connotation. Select some examples and discuss them. Are there other aspects of his style that should be mentioned?

8. Yoko may be the most enigmatic character in Kawabata's enigmatic novel. Do we understand her better if we view this somewhat disembodied woman as the symbolic other half of Komako?

9. In Japan's classical, or court, poetry, nature is commonly employed as an objective correlative, the external equivalent for an internal state of mind. Due to court poetry's incredibly strong legacy in the Japanese literary tradition, the lyric tendency to see emotional affinities in nature has continued into modern times. There is probably no better representative than the work of Kawabata. Discuss with reference to *The Man'yōshū* (volume B, pp. 2152–60) and *The Kokinshū* (volume B, pp. 2163–74), if you have read them. If not, discuss in general terms the ways that nature assumes emotional value in *Snow Country*. Are there other ways that natural imagery functions in the novel?

10. A feminist reading of *Snow Country* might call Shimamura to task

for objectifying Komako. But does he totally succeed? Can a coun-
terargument be made that Kawabata creates a female protagonist
who resists by asserting her own subjectivity?

Comparative Perspectives

1. Why was the invention of the railroad such a boon to writers?
   [The scene in the railroad car offered a natural setting for thrust-
   ing fictional characters into intimate contact with each other.]
2. Part of the brilliance of *Snow Country's* first section derives from
   the complex set of relationships guessed at by Shimamura as he
   observes Yoko and her sick charge opposite him in the car. How do
   the ruminations their presence sets in motion prove to be central
   to our understanding of Shimamura's character and his relationship to Komako? Compare the use made by other writers of the
   journey as a catalyst for unsought revelations.
   [A good candidate includes *The Death of Ivan Ilyich*. For earlier
   examples of chance travel encounters, consider the shipboard connections struck up in *Candide*. For a later, parodic glance at the
   convention so dear to writers of mystery stories, see *The Garden of
   Forking Paths*.]
3. Why are several pages of *Snow Country* devoted to a discussion of
   Chijimi linen? Discuss the symbolic resonance of this apparent digression and compare similar moments in other narratives you
   have read this semester.
   [Possibilities include *Remembrance of Things Past* or *Walker
   Brothers Cowboy*.]

Further Reading

See the reading suggestions in the anthology, p. 2342.

JORGE LUIS BORGES

The Garden of Forking Paths

Backgrounds

Borges is perhaps the most extraordinary labyrinth-maker in contemporary literature. For him everything—the nature of time, of space, of
knowlege, of the self, of literary form—is problematic. He looks at the
world as a "puzzle" that compels examination even while it resists solution. Nothing can be proved, but nothing can be disproved. Borges combines his immense narrative skill with the qualities of a metaphysician,
fantasist, scholar, detective writer, theologian, and ironist. He is very
much like the metaphysicians in one of his own fictional places, Tlön,
who "seek neither truth nor likelihood; they seek astonishment." In all of
his major stories, Borges is intent upon making a coherent fictional world
almost entirely out of his intelligence and out of his imagination playing
over other intelligences.

   The Garden of Forking Paths is a detective story, but one in which the
reader, finally, is the detective, and time is the solution to the mystery.
On the level of plot, the story is reasonably simple: Yu Tsun, a Chinese
spy grudgingly working for the Germans during World War I, has to transmit an important message to his chief in Berlin. Since Yu Tsun's identity
has been discovered by the British, he must transmit the message before
he is caught, and he must do so without letting the British know he has
done it. He travels to a suburb of London, to the house of a sinologist
named Stephen Albert. Yu Tsun and Albert discuss the nature of a manuscript written by Ts'ui Pên, one of Yu Tsun's ancestors, and then Yu Tsun
shoots Albert, who dies instantaneously. In the last paragraph we discover
the reason for Yu Tsun's actions: the message he must convey to Berlin is
the name of a French city the Germans must attack. The city's name is
Albert, and by killing a man of that name Yu Tsun both fulfills his mission
and condemns himself to be captured and, ultimately, hanged.
   The story, however, is full of coincidences, analogies between characters, and resonances and suggestions of ideas that are more important
than the simple plot. The central idea of the story is the labyrinth, which
is both the story's subject and its structure. The labyrinth is presented in
a number of ways: an actual labyrinthlike walk through English suburban
life that Yu Tsun takes on his way to Albert's house; the literary labyrinth
constructed by Yu Tsun's ancestor, Ts'ui Pên; and the formal labyrinth of
Borges's story itself. The implications of all three are the same: to suggest
the infinite possibilities—the "various futures"—of any human action in
time, and the consequent shrinkage in the importance of that action
when we think of it as just one possible outcome among many. Borges
presents a fictional reality that has as its center the death of Stephen Albert at the hands of Yu Tsun, but he implies that there are other conceiv-
able centers, other possible dimensions, other possible times. As Albert
tells Yu Tsun, "We do not exist in the majority of these times; in some you
exist, and not I; in others I, and not you; in others, both of us. In the present one, which a favorable fate has granted me, you have arrived at my
house; in another, while crossing the garden, you found me dead; in still
another, I utter these same words, but I am a mistake, a ghost" (p. 2420).
The story refutes the notion of present time as the only one that contains
"reality" and, therefore, the only significant time.
   The Garden of Forking Paths effectively blurs most of the categories we
use to "know" the world—especially the distinction between reality and
fiction. The story begins with Borges blurring the traditional distinctions
between author, narrator, and character. We are told in no uncertain
terms by someone who appears to be the author of an historical essay that
on "page 22 of Liddell Hart's *History of World War I*" we will read about a
particular military attack, "planned for the 24th of July, 1916" which had
to be postponed until the morning of the 29th because of "torrential
rains" (p. 2414). The scholarly authority of the voice in this opening
passage—the voice of the historian—suggests that the information delivered belongs to the world of fact, outside of fiction altogether. Further,

the matter-of-fact authority of this narrative voice tends to make the sections that follow, consisting entirely—except for a footnote—of Yu Tsun's narrative, into a revelation important only in that it "throws an unsuspected light" on the postponement of the battle. The "author" of the "essay" reveals no interest whatsoever in the extraordinary qualities of Yu Tsun's narrative.

If we look at Liddell Hart's book, we notice that what our "scholar" says is not what Liddell Hart reports: there was such a battle, but there is no mention of its postponement, and the torrential rains did not fall until November. The "author," then, is as much a fiction as Yu Tsun, Stephen Albert, Captain Richard Madden, Ts'ui Pên, or any other character in the story. Even the "editor," presumably the "editor" of the "journal" that published our "author's" scholarly revelation, is exposed as simply another character in Borges's story when he is offended by Yu Tsun's version of Viktor Runeberg's death and proceeds to comment authoritatively on the "real" events behind that death. The language is heavily loaded: one representation of the German agent identifies him as a "Prussian spy" who "attacked with drawn automatic," and his opponent is identified both as "Captain" and "the bearer of a warrent" acting in self-defense; moreover, he did not actually kill Runeberg but merely "inflicted a wound" that led to death. Who is to say whether Yu Tsun or the editor is closer to the truth? What we have, then, is a fictional editor taking offense at a fictional account of a fictional death of a fictional spy in a footnote to a fictional historical essay called *The Garden of Forking Paths* written by a fictional author who was created by Jorge Luis Borges in a piece of fiction called *The Garden of Forking Paths*.

The ramifications of Borges's story lead us back to the relation between historical events and historical narratives of those events, that is, between reality and fiction. Borges suggests that Liddell Hart left out something important when he rendered the battle of July 24, 1916, in his history of World War I. And of course he did. Liddell Hart, like any historian, must leave out more than he puts in; he must make selections based on his own fallible interpretation of what is significant and what is not in the series of events he presents as historical "fact." Historians, then, are writers of fiction who use their intelligence and imagination to create a coherent narrative based on reality. The "reality" of that battle ended when it ended; what is left of it is in books like Liddell Hart's, or further emendations like Yu Tsun's tale and even a biased footnote. The disorder and contingency of reality have been replaced by fiction.

Unlike almost all of the other major writers of Latin America—Gabriel García Márquez, Pablo Neruda, Carlos Fuentes, Alejandro Carpentier, Cesar Vallejo, and so on—Borges appears to be adamantly apolitical in his work. (This despite the fact that Borges was briefly a *cause célèbre* in the 1940s because of his public opposition to Peron.) His life was devoted to books, to writing them, reading them, even cataloguing them, and since his early years—when he was much interested in Argentina's past and its folk literature—his mind took up residence in a country without national boundaries. In *The Argentine Writer and Tradition,* Borges argues that the real Argentine tradition is "all of Western culture . . . our patrimony is the universe."

Although Borges's reputation in Argentina stresses his poetry rather than his fiction, his influence on contemporary fiction has been exceptional. Almost every postmodernist writer is in some way in Borges's debt.

Classroom Strategies

You can discuss *The Garden of Forking Paths* in one or two class periods. If you use two periods, you might devote the first to disentangling the plot and Borges's narrative strategy, the second to disentangling the implications of the plot and the implications of that narrative. At some point, you might draw a "tree" formation on the board (which mathematics and linguistics students will immediately recognize) to illustrate how various alternative possibilities can exist simultaneously. Students usually enjoy hearing the ancient Chinese riddle about the man who dreamed he was a butterfly dreaming he was a man—who woke up. The question then follows: who is he? Is he a butterfly dreaming he is a man (who was dreaming he was a butterfly) who has just woken up, or . . .

The Garden of Forking Paths is the kind of story that can make students' heads hurt. Encourage them to see its playing with reality as part of modern literary techniques: Kafka's *The Metamorphosis,* for example, or Pirandello's *Six Characters in Search of an Author.* You may want to draw comparisons with later modern works, such as Julio Cortázar's *Hopscotch,* in which the reader is invited to rearrange the order of chapters, or John Fowles's *The French Lieutenant's Woman,* which includes different endings among which the reader may choose. Emphasizing the detective-story qualities of the piece, or noting that it bears significant resemblances to many science-fiction stories (stories about parallel times or alternate worlds, for instance), will also help your students enjoy *The Garden of Forking Paths* before they begin to worry about whether they have completely understood it. On the other hand, one of the things that differentiates Borges's piece from a typical piece of science fiction is the economy and complexity of the narrative. Only a few pages long, the story nevertheless dizzies the reader with continually expanding implications and suggestions. You will find that an exploration of the way Borges uses analogies—between events and between characters—makes his narrative economy more evident. The various kinds of labyrinths suggested by the story have already been noted, and the analogies between them should be obvious. It will also be worth noting the following:

1. Ts'ui Pên was murdered by the hand of a stranger, just as Stephen Albert, the only person to decipher Ts'ui Pên's novel, will be.
2. Ts'ui Pên closed himself up for thirteen years in the Pavilion of Limpid Solitude to write his novel, and Stephen Albert greets Yu

Tsun by saying "I see that the pious Hsi P'êng persists in correcting my solitude?" (p. 2417).

3. Albert reads a section from Ts'ui Pên's novel that has to do with armies marching to battle. He also tries to explain the implications of the novel by describing a scene in which a stranger calls at a man's door and, in one possible outcome, kills him.

4. Stephen Albert—a Westerner who is ostensibly Yu Tsun's enemy— restores the good name of Yu Tsun's ancestor, while Yu Tsun—an Easterner who teaches the languages of the West—kills Albert to prove to his Chief that "the innumerable ancestors" who merge within him are worthy of respect. "I wanted," says Yu Tsun, "to prove to him that a yellow man could save his armies" (p. 2415).

5. Yu Tsun, like his ancestor Ts'ui Pên, is faced with transmitting a message. Both must do so through indirection. Paradoxically, Ts'ui Pên invents something traditionally made for the many—a novel— which can be decoded by only one, while Yu Tsun invents for one— the Chief—by addressing the many through the newspapers.

6. Yu Tsun and Richard Madden are paired as spy/counterspy, but both are distrusted aliens who must prove themselves to their chiefs.

Topics for Discussion and Writing

1. Discuss the ways Borges uses the labyrinth as the central idea and image of *The Garden of Forking Paths*.
   [See the third paragraph of "Backgrounds" for discussion.]

2. Discuss the implications of Borges's narrative technique in the story. Who is the narrator? In what guise does he present himself? How does Borges blur the traditional distinctions between author, narrator, and character in *The Garden of Forking Paths*?
   [See the fourth and fifth paragraphs of "Backgrounds" as well as "Classroom Strategies" for discussion.]

3. Discuss analogies between characters and between events in the story.
   [See the third paragraph of "Backgrounds" as well as "Classroom Strategies" for discussion.]

4. What kinds of questions does Borges raise in *The Garden of Forking Paths* about the nature of time?
   [See the third paragraph of "Backgrounds" for discussion.]

5. What relationship between reality and fiction is suggested in *The Garden of Forking Paths*? What conclusions might we draw about the writing of history?
   [See the fourth, fifth, and sixth paragraphs of "Backgrounds" for discussion.]

6. What clues are given at the beginning of the story, and how are we misled by them?
   [The name of the person "capable of transmitting the message" is

usually interpreted as the name of another agent. The single bullet in Yu Tsun's revolver may suggest that he will commit suicide if captured. Generally overlooked is the fact that the Chief in Berlin spends his time "endlessly examining newspapers" while waiting for his agents's reports.]

7. How does Borges base his story in observable documentary facts in order to lend solidity to the idea of alternate worlds?

[See, in addition of Liddell Hart's book, the following references: the actual town of Albert, located on the Ancre River (near the Somme) and therefore close to the bloodiest battles of World War I; the existing countries of Staffordshire (western England) and Fenton (eastern England); the German writer Goethe (see pp. 678–780, volume C of the anthology); the Latin author Tacitus; a famous Chinese novel, the *Hung Lu Meng* (*The Story of the Stone*—see pp. 148–279, volume D of the anthology); *The Thousand and One Nights* (pp. 1569–1618, volume B of the anthology); recognized pottery styles and a real (though lost) encyclopedia from the Ming Dynasty; physicist Isaac Newton and philosopher Arthur Schopenhauer.]

Comparative Perspectives

1. Dr. Yu Tsun arranges his complicated exploit "to prove . . . that a yellow man could save" the armies of a "barbarous country" that held his "race" in contempt. Within this brilliant parody we hear a serious note that links Yu Tsun to many characters in the anthology who are painfully conscious that others consider them inferior beings. How would you compare Yu Tsun's announced motive to that of the characters in Kojima's *The American School*, or the chief in Lessing's *The Old Chief Mshlanga*? Compare the moral vantage points from which these different writers address the fact of cultural difference.

2. Stephen Albert's elucidation of the novelistic method he discerns in Ts'ui Pên's "garden of forking paths" is more than a witty postmodernist conceit. Over the past few years, hypertext fiction has put exactly such forking paths at the fingertips of computer-using readers who choose the turns they wish to take and thereby determine the outcome of the story, allowing it to mutate constantly at their wills. Similar experiments have been made with films that viewers control from handsets embedded in the arms of the seats in theaters. Look at the opening chapter of *The Story of the Stone*, the novel Borges's narrator refers to by its Chinese title, *Hung Lu Meng*. How does the introduction to Cao Xueqin's eighteenth-century work prefigure these technological devices? Why are the tales of *The Thousand and One Nights* also mentioned in Borges's story? What perceptions concerning the nature of reality may make authors shrink from exercising too much "authority" over their creations?

Further Reading

See also the reading suggestions in the anthology, pp. 2413–14.

Alazraki, Jaime. *Borges and the Kabbalah.* 1988. A collection of essays on various aspects of the writer's fiction and poetry.

Balderston, Daniel, ed. *The Literary Universe of Jorge Luis Borges: An Index to References and Allusions to Persons, Titles and Places in IIis Writings.* 1986.

Bell-Villada, Gene H. *Borges and His Fiction.* 1981. A particularly useful discussion of Borges's use of simultaneous times in *The Garden of Forking Paths.* See especially pp. 93–96.

Bloom, Harold, ed. *Jorge Luis Borges.* 1986. Fifteen essays by different scholars, and a chronology.

Borges, Jorge Luis. *Other Inquisitions, 1937–1952.* Translated by Ruth L. C. Simms. 1964. Discussions of *The Garden of Forking Paths* will be aided by reading *A New Refutation of Time* and *The Argentine Writer and Tradition.*

Burgin, Richard. *Conversations with Jorge Luis Borges.* 1969. A useful discussion of Borges by Borges.

Foster, David William. *Jorge Luis Borges: An Annotated Primary and Secondary Bibliography.* 1984.

di Giovanni, Norman Thomas. *In Memory of Borges.* 1988. Seven essays, including a 1983 address by Borges on his work and an anecdotal essay by di Giovanni as Borges's translator.

Rimmon-Kenan, Shlomith. "Doubles and Counterparts: Patterns of Interchangeability in Borges' 'The Garden of Forking Paths.'" *Critical Inquiry* 6, 4 (Summer 1980), pp. 639–47. An interesting discussion of Borges's use of analogies between characters and between events in the story.

Rodriguez-Monegal, Emir. *Jorge Luis Borges: A Literary Biography.* 1978. The only full-length biography of Borges in English.

Stabb, Martin. *Borges Revisited.* 1991. A useful introduction organized by perspectives on Borges's work; includes "The Canonical Texts," "The Critical Trajectory," "Borges in Perspective," and a chronology.

ANDREW PEYNETSA

The Boy and the Deer

Backgrounds

Like other traditional narratives from a wide variety of cultures, the story of the adopted Deer Boy is framed by a formulaic opening and a standard closing. Typical of Zuni openings is the obligatory localization. Zuni listeners expect to be told at the outset where the action will take place.

Thus, in the village of He'shokta a young virgin well secluded (in a room on the fourth level down from the roof entrance) is reached by a ray of sunlight, which magically impregnates her. Having hidden her pregnancy, she gives birth secretly at the riverside, abandoning the child—though not without preparing an earthen bed, nicely lined with leaves, for him to lie in.

A family of deer, two fawns and their mother, discover the boy. He is adopted by the doe, who nurses him with her own nipples and cuddles him at night "the way deer sleep." To make sure the child stays warm through the day, since he is without fur, the deer mother goes to Kachina Village to request human clothing from the kachinas, or spirits of the dead. While she is gone, young men from He'shokta come into the hills looking for deer. The fawns and the little boy apparently escape detection.

Now properly clothed by his deer mother, the adopted boy plays with his fawn siblings during the day and grows safely to maturity in the company of his deer family—despite the presence of would-be hunters in nearby He'shokta. At last one of the hunters, the boy's own uncle, catches sight of him and notices, significantly, that the boy runs faster than the deer.

News of a human among the deer, a human presumed to be someone's relative (" 'Who's child could this be?' " [line 186]), causes a stir in the village. The report is taken as a sign that a deer hunt is to be organized—finally. (Note that through all this time no successful hunting, no killing of deer, has been mentioned.)

The evening before the hunt, the deer mother informs her human child that his relative, the uncle, will be coming with other hunters on the following day because the boy has been spotted. ("Tomorrow we'll be chased, the one who found us is your uncle. / When he found us he saw you, and that's why" [lines 259–60].) Foretelling the entire episode of the hunt, the deer mother calmly explains to the boy that she and her deer children will be killed, while the boy, running ahead, will be captured live and brought back to He'shokta.

The next day the chase begins. The boy, as predicted, takes the lead, separating himself from the deer, who are killed and promptly gutted. The boy runs on. But seeing his uncle behind him, he stops and allows himself to be caught. "So you've come," says the boy (line 431). "Yes," replies the uncle.

Back at the village, the deer corpses are dressed in turquoise necklaces and the boy, confronting his human mother, is reluctantly acknowledged by her. Four days later she sends the boy on an errand, which results in his death.

Classroom Strategies

It may be helpful to see two separate plots intersecting. In one, a young woman made fearful by the birth of a child she cannot explain takes concerted measures to hide the fact of her motherhood. In the other, hunters and deer are brought together by the newly established bond of a common relative.

Why is it necessary to human survival for men and deer to become kin? And what are the costs? Without promising definitive answers to these questions, one may may lead students toward a deeper appreciation of the story by taking up the following suggested topics in order.

1. A near-universal element of native American theory is that deer and other game animals give themselves willingly, provided hunters treat them with respect. Where do you see this in the story?
   [Refer to "Backgrounds," as well as to Joseph Peynetsa's commentary in the second-to-last footnote to the text.]
2. What human traits and sentiments are ascribed to the deer? Do these imagined qualities make it difficult to use deer for food, and is there an element of human guilt?
   [Consider such affecting passages as "Well, why shouldn't we / save him? / Why don't you two hold my nipples / so / so he can nurse?" (lines 60–64)]
3. Who is to blame for the boy's death? Consider the human mother, the uncles. Consider also the deer mother and the kachinas.
   [Take into account the attenuated search for guilt mentioned in the headnote (pp. 2421–23 in the anthology).]
4. If the boy is a suicide, what might be his motive?
   [Refer to Andrew Peynetsa's commentary quoted on p. 2422 in the anthology.]
5. If you have studied the selections under the heading *Zuni Ritual Poetry,* review the discussion of human sacrifice and ask whether this relates to *The Boy and the Deer.*
6. Compare the taming of Enkidu in *Gilgamesh* to the hunters's capture of the child in *The Boy and the Deer.* The Western view of nature as a thing to be tamed—expressed also in of Genesis 1 ("subdue it: and have domination")—may be contrasted with the cooperative approach revealed in native American thinking. Recognize that the latter approach is neither simplistic nor free of responsibility.

Topics for Discussion

See topics listed immediately above.

Tedlock's method of translation has been widely imitated by linguists working with Hopi, Inuit, Nahuatl, Navajo, Tlingit, and other native American languages, as well as, to a lesser extent, native languages of Africa, Australia, and Oceania. Stories created in English could be published in the same manner, yet few have. Cultural differences permit less display of theatricality in English; consequently there is less to show in a "scored" text. On the other hand, certain English-language genres, such as sermons and political oratory, lend themselves to the treatment. Can you think of others? If you are aware of issues that concern avocational and professional storytellers in the United States today, you know there is disagreement as to whether an emotive delivery is tasteful or even effective. If you have heard an author (who writes in English) reading from— or let us say, performing—his or her work, consider whether the author would appreciate seeing a "scored" text of that performance in print.

Topic for Writing

See number 6 under "Classroom Strategies."

Comparative Perspectives

1. In *The Boy and the Deer,* however violent and painful the deeds in which they are involved, the members of the Zuni community and the deer comport themselves with beautiful manners and serene dignity. How do Andrew Peynetsa's narration and Dennis Tedlock's translation achieve this exquisite poise?

    [Force of prophetic foresight strengthened by repetition; ritual quality of greetings, invitations to sit and eat—a way of life governed by order and respect.]

2. Of particular interest in Tedlock's translation is the reliance on the word "dropped" to describe both the act of childbirth and the destruction of the deer (see especially the insertion "voice breaking" when Peynetsa speaks of the third uncle who "dropped his elder sister" [line 411]). Why should the boy's mother be linked to his uncle by this repeated verb? What effect does the ambiguity of the pronoun "his" in the quoted line seem to promote? How would you compare the role of the boy's uncle with that of the father in *Geriguigatugo?*

    [In each of these coming-of-age stories, the paternal/avuncular older male seems vengefully caught up in an effort to punish the boy and the nurturing female who comforts him.]

Further Reading

See also the reading suggestions in the anthology, p. 2423.

Briggs, Charles L. "Metadiscursive Practices and Scholarly Authority in Folkloristics." *Journal of American Folklore,* vol. 106 (1993). Pp. 387–434. Bristles with technicalities but offers a penetrating critique of the methods used by Tedlock and his colleagues (as well as earlier translators in the fields of anthropology and folklore), suggesting that the unexamined search for "authenticity" may lead to the exercise of subtle Western "dominance" over non-Western texts.

Pablo Neruda

Backgrounds

Pablo Neruda was an extremely prolific poet and he had a remarkably wide range of subjects and styles. If there is one consistent note throughout his work, it is in the wild abundance of the things that he sees and can describe in totally unorthodox and original ways. Several critics have pointed to Neruda's admiration for Walt Whitman. Certainly, he shares with Whitman a penchant for cataloguing everything as well as an endlessly inventive management of the poetic line. Both their openness to all experience and their transcendence of academic form may be understood as profoundly democratic. These traits also pose a tremendous challenge, to Neruda as to Whitman and ultimately to the reader. Our goal is to find coherence in this abundance by defining the sensibility that notices and celebrates so much, so often seemingly at random. It will be important to reassure your students that they need not "get" every word, or even every line. Probably Neruda himself would have been hard pressed to deliver a lucid exegesis of every one of his poems. Better to try to identify in each piece where the speaker has situated himself and why he notices the things of which he writes. Finally, even in English translation, readers should allow themselves to be swept up in the flow of imagery and sound, to feel as well as think. (Indeed, this advice should be a constant in our efforts to teach verse.)

Tonight I Can Write

Your students will probably be familiar at this point in the semester with the Romantic arguments about the relative claims of art and nature. This early poem finds the speaker caught between his one-time love for a woman he has lost—his natural feelings—and his artistic curiosity about how to write verses about that love. Can one separate the lover from the poet? The poem begins with the writer's preoccupation: "Tonight I can write the saddest lines." What are the saddest lines? Only by trying them out can he discover. How about "The night is shattered / and the blue stars shiver in the distance"? The love lost has a cosmic significance, we gather, and approximately, nature plays a dominant role in the poem: the endless sky has been shattered; the night wind sings; there are trees.

The poem veers between lines that capture the immensity of night, the backdrop for this love, and other lines in which the speaker seems to be taking his own emotional temperature. "I loved her, and sometimes she loved me too," he says, but then he tries again: "She loved me, sometimes I loved her too." The pain, however, seems less compelling than his effort to write about it. "I no longer love her, that's certain, but how I loved her." His "soul is not satisfied that it has lost her," yet poetry nurtures: "the verse falls to the soul like dew to the pasture."

The form mimics the speaker's tense indecisiveness in its elegant structure, which forestalls the luxury of sustained self-inquiry. It begins with a stanza of one line, then two, then another single line, before settling into its pattern of unrhymed but intricately patterned couplets that keep going back to the original premises, slightly altering them with each repetition. Nevertheless, the poem finds its conclusion: however unsatisfied his soul may be, he will move on. If she will be "Another's," these will be the last verses that he writes for her.

WALKING AROUND

After the slender elegance of the first poem, we move on to new terrain. Here is twentieth-century man in a state of urban fatigue, rejecting the modern bourgeois world of tailor's shops and barber shops. Instead of the romantic night of *Tonight I Can Write* we have the mundane reality of merchandise, elevators, and shoes. The third and fourth lines announce a poetic crisis. The speaker is desiccated. Far from the symbolic equivalent of a shapely white bird, he is a simulacrum made of cheap materials: "a felt swan." Far from skimming a reviving sea, he is "navigating on a water of origin and ash," a densely packed image that recalls the stuff of which man was made in Genesis 2: life leads inevitably to ashes and dust, and highfalutin poetry cannot change that. (One translator captures that sense of poetic irrelevance by rendering this line "awash on an ocean of therefores and ashes.")

The speaker's malaise is more than that of a bored *flaneur*, strolling in a boring cityscape. It goes to the root of his art and his physical being. Everything is ennervating:

> It happens that I am tired of my feet and my nails
> and my hair and my shadow.
> It happens that I am tired of being a man.

For all that, in the delightful fourth stanza (the first of three six-line stanzas in a poem basically built of quatrains), the speaker is capable of relishing the idea of affronting the bourgeoisie. There is a Surrealistic touch to the deliberately provocative imagery here. A notary becomes a symbol of dull legalism; lacking a sense of beauty, "a cut lily" would scare him, as organized religion, in the person of a nun, could be knocked out with "one blow of an ear." Imagining himself on a rampage "through the streets with a green knife," the speaker takes comfort in the inherent menace of vital ("green") life in the face of the moribund surroundings he deplores.

The next stanzas, however, return to the hopelessness of his natural state: he imagines himself in downward motion, "a root in the dark . . . in the wet tripe of the earth," a tomb as well as a root, "a cellar full of corpses." Monday is singled out, the day that starts the week (ask your students if they ever cheerfully reflect, "Thank God it's Monday"). As the speaker conjures up grisly images of the quotidian city, you may want to mention J. Alfred Prufrock's depressed view of the cityscape he crosses as

he moves toward—and then retreats from—the overwhelming question
that he fears.

> And it [Monday] shoves me along to certain corners, to certain damp
> houses
> to hospitals where the bones come out of the windows,
> to certain cobblers' shops smelling of vinegar,
> to streets horrendous as crevices.

Neruda's walker in the city ends with two long stanzas that describes an
increasingly disgusting place. Passing hospitals confirms his "fury" and
"forgetfulness." All around him he sees evidence of human weakness and
bodily decrepitude that only affirms his previous disaffection with the fee-
ble efforts people make to keep themselves functioning. Neruda presumably refers to way trades people signal prospective customers with
"birds the colour of sulphur, and horrible intestines [one translator says
"tripe"] / hanging from the doors of the houses which I hate." This is the
semiotics of shop owners who need no poetic vocabulary to advertise their
wares. There are brilliant sequences in these stanzas, mixing categories
and crossing boundaries of animate and inanimate, normal and
grotesque. You should ask your students to explain the goads to "shame
and horror" encountered on the speaker's stroll: "umbrellas all over the
place, and poisons, and navels" or "orthopaedic appliances" and intimate
laundry weeping "slow dirty tears." The speaker seems furious with himself for somehow being complicit with all the tawdry devices on which human dignity relies: after all, he is wearing shoes.

I'M EXPLAINING A FEW THINGS

The point of view in *I'm Explaining a Few Things* is chillingly clear. The
arresting opening lines dare the reader to complain that the poem doesn't
seem poetic: "where are the lilacs?" Now the bourgeois images that engendered disgust in *Walking Around* become gauges to measure what has
been lost in the first attacks of Franco's forces on the innocent people of
Republican Spain. Neruda's virtuosic management of form—the varying
length of stanzas, the strategic placement of half lines, the incantatory
voice—all converge to make this a fiercely powerful political and moral statement. The deceptively calm description of suburban life, "with
bells, / and clocks, and trees," with wonderful markets and flowers all
around, is shattered in the sequence that begins "And one morning." Nor
is this a merely personal response; Neruda here speaks as a poet among
poets, the artistic conscience of a nation betrayed. He speaks to "Raul"
Gonzalez Tunon, to "Rafael" Alberti, and to "Federico" García Lorca,
anti-Fascist comrades, the second of whom had been exiled, the third of
whom was to be executed.

It would be a good idea to examine a copy of Picasso's *Guernica* and
ask your students to compare Picasso's visual depiction of the aerial

bombing of Spanish cities with Neruda's furious apostrophe to the "Treacherous generals" who are worse than jackals. The Surrealistic quality of the painter's and the poet's images deserves detailed discussion. Traditional verse forms break down in the face of this enormity. Out of the death of children, a terrible retribution is sure to come:

> from every socket of Spain
> Spain emerges
> from every dead child a rifle with eyes
> and from every crime bullets are born
> which will one day find
> the bull's eye of your hearts.

The simple repetitions of the final stanza would overwhelm anyone with a conscience. But the wrong people were listening.

GENERAL SONG: THE HEIGHTS OF MACCHU PICCHU

This meditation on a lost civilization was written in August and September, 1945—in the aftermath of the bombing of Hiroshima and Nagasaki. Neruda actually made the ascent to the heights of Macchu Picchu described here in the fall of 1943. The opening lines of the selection follow him up "the ladder of the earth," a literal description of the incised steps that ascend the cliff. The term may also be a deliberate reminder of Dante's climb out of the Inferno, for we are on a visionary journey to weigh the sins and the accomplishments of the past. (Note that Dante and Virgil pull themselves up by grasping the hair of Lucifer "as a ladder" in a poem divided, like Neruda's, into Cantos [*Inferno*, Canto XXXIV.119].)

Macchu Picchu was a pre-Columbian fortress, but it was more than a military redoubt. The Inca site was built in the mid-fifteenth century and escaped the Spanish Conquest that began in 1532. An architectural symbol of a complex culture, it was raised "like a chalice in the hands / of all" (VII.23). While you are studying Neruda's poem, it would be interesting to have your students read the excerpts from the *Popol Vuh* in volume C, a document produced by the inhabitants of another high citadel that did not escape conquest. Neruda's imagination of the making and inhabitation of Macchu Picchu echoes many of the terms of the Quiche epic. Neruda begins with a kind of creation myth, as does the *Popol Vuh*:

> This was the dwelling, this is the site:
> here the full kernels of corn rose
> and fell again like red hailstones. (VI.13–15)

Life in these early South and Meso-American cities blended ritual and sacrifice, agriculture and war. These interwoven activities capture the imagination here:

> Here the golden fiber emerged from the vicuna,
> to cloth love, tombs, mothers,
> the king, prayers, warriors. . . .
> I behold vestments and hands. . . . (VI.16–18, 25)

The speaker's Whitmanesque greeting to his "brother" in Canto XII recalls the work of the artisans who are the gods of the Maya "Bible"—
"Maker, Modeler . . . Bearer, Begetter" (in Dennis Tedlock's translation)
and who were engaged in the same crafts that Neruda salutes:

> laborer, weaver, silent herdsman:
> tamer of the tutelary guanacos:
> mason of the defied scaffold:
> bearer of the Andean tears:
> jeweler with your fingers crushed:
> tiller trembling in the seed:
> potter split in your clay . . . (XII.9–15)

Where the Maya epic celebrates the arts and crafts by attributing to the
multiple Quiche gods the talents of their local craftsmen, Neruda, from
the vantage point of twentieth-century politics, speaks of the cost to the
human beings who wrought their arts and crafts for the terrifying rulers
of Macchu Picchu. He declares his solidarity with "Juan Stonecutter . . .
Juan Coldeater . . . Juan Barefoot," the common ancestors of "American
love" (VIII.I).

> Bring me back the slave that you buried!
> Shake from the earth the hard bread
> of the poor wretch, show me
> the slave's clothing and his window. (X.29–31)

The call for social justice, however, is not the sum of this remarkable
poem. In *The Heights of Macchu Picchu* Neruda confronts the powers of
nature, the cosmic setting that he invoked in his early love poetry too. Images pour out of the speaker as he looks around him, inviting the great
rivers of the Andes (Urubamba and Wilkamayu) to help him penetrate to
the creative core of this magnificent ruin. Like William Blake wondering
at the sinister perfection of the tiger, Neruda wants to understand how
vegetable life came to exist among the stones ("the void of the grapevine /
the petrous plant, the hard wreath" [VIII.5–6]). Where is the language
that can explain the mysteries of Macchu Picchu? We can only read the
stones, for the Incas were a people without writing.

> Who seized the cold's lightning
> and left it shackled in the heights,
> dispersed in its glacial tears,
> smitten in its swift swords,

> hammering its embattled stamens,
> borne on its warrior's bed,
> startled in its rocky end?
>
> What are your tormented sparks saying?
> Did your secret insurgent lightning
> once journey charged with words?
> Who keeps on shattering frozen syllables,
> black languages, golden banners,
> deep mouths, muffled cries,
> in your slender arterial waters? (VIII.23–36)

The creative energies of the individual and of the universe provoke a paean to love, but there is great danger. Canto VIII ends with a cryptic reference to what may be a stone altar where the sun worshipers of the Incas made their sacrifices. Built in sacrifice in part to isolate a place for sacrifice, Macchu Picchu fascinates not only the man who approaches it up the ladder in the cliff, but also the scavenging birds that fly above it: "And over the Sundial the sanguinary shadow / of the condor crosses like a black ship" (lines 63–64).

In 43 separate lines, Canto IX enumerates myriad ways of capturing the essence of Macchu Picchu, finding words to which its builders and inhabitants had no access. The entire range of sense experience and the variety of the created universe come together here—eagle, mist, and silver wave, somehow fused with the manmade work of Macchu Picchu—"entombed ship" (8) or "patriarchal bell of the sleeping" (21) and the symbols of the South American gods—"Andean serpent, brow of amaranth" (31–32). This extraordinary roll call is simultaneously exhilarating and daunting. You might ask your students to think of the way some documentary films survey a massive structure like a Gothic cathedral, lingering lovingly on a gargoyle here, then a segment of a stained-glass window there, without attempting to link the individual splendors on which it focuses. There is no verb in Canto IX to render a judgment or suggest a way of connecting these disparate views of a dead city that still lives in the dazzling facets that flash before the eye of the poet's mind.

The following Cantos, already mentioned above, turn to the human beings who suffered and built. The splendor of the structures and the headiness of the heights cannot keep the poet from looking down as well.

> Give me your hand from the deep
> zone of your disseminated sorrow.
> You'll not return from the bottom of the rocks. (XII.2–4)

How many people plummeted from those heights accidentally? How many were thrown over the cliff? How many were offered at the cruel altar? In sympathy with these lost workers, the speaker bares his own breast to the knife, pledging what a poet can. In single separated lines that emphasize the equality of the transaction between the living artist and the dead who inspire him, Neruda in effect promises the poem that he has just concluded:

> Give me silence, water, hope.
>
> Give me struggle, iron, volcanoes.
>
> Cling to my body like magnets.
>
> Hasten to my veins and to my mouth.
>
> Speak through my words and my blood. (XII.41–45)

ODE TO THE TOMATO

This charming final selection from Neruda's massive oeuvre takes us from the sublime to the delicious. Here, too, the knife looms and will assassinate. Yet the victim of this attack is only a tomato, and if red pulp is spilt, there will be progeny to come: the tomato "beds cheerfully / with the blonde onion." The very short lines here deserve some comment. Is this really a prose poem? What is the impact of separating these salad ingredients out so that each component commands our attention on its own terms? How refreshing to realize that the sensuous voluptuary can revel in "convolutions / canals and plenitudes" that do not stand in for the eternal feminine, but are adored for themselves. Even this deliberately simplified poetic mode gives us one more example of Neruda's gift for evoking the riches of the earth.

Topics for Discussion and Writing

1. The headnote proposes multiple designations of achievement: "Love poet, nature poet, political poet, and poet of common things." Discuss the ways in which Neruda's poems demonstrate his various interests. Comment on the ways in which *The Heights of Macchu Picchu* may be read as uniting all these poetic personae.
2. What is wrong with being "a felt swan / navigating on a water of origin and ash"? How does *Walking Around* enlarge the poetic vocabulary and suggest the limitations of classical references?
3. In what ways may *Ode to the Tomato* be considered a love poem?

Comparative Perspectives

1. What view of the city emerges from *Walking Around*? Compare the selection of details that arouse the speaker's disgust with the details that J. Alfred Prufrock notices as he makes his way through the insidious streets.
2. How is Walt Whitman a presence in Neruda's poetry? Discuss the

contribution made to Neruda's developing style by the fluidity of line lengths, the poetic persona, and the range of imagery in *Leaves of Grass.*

3. Many poems in the anthology concern the ruins of the past. Compare and contrast this aspect of *The Heights of Macchu Picchu* with the views of a lost culture in a variety of poems, including "Poem written by Kakinomoto Hitamaro when he passed the ruined capital at Omi" (*Man'yoshu*, 29–31), Eliot's *The Waste Land*, and Walcott's *Omeros.*

4. Compare the questions posed in Blake's *The Tyger* with those articulated in Canto VIII of *The Heights of Macchu Picchu*. What assumptions does Blake make about the creator that Neruda seems unable to make?

   [Blake seems to know the answer to his question—"Did he smile his work to see? / Did he who made the Lamb make thee?" Neruda seems unsure that there is any articulate presence behind the majesty and cruelty of the rivers of Macchu Picchu: "Who keeps on shattering frozen syllables, / black languages, golden banners, / deep mouths, muffled cries, / in your slender arterial waters?"]

Further Reading

See also the reading suggestions in the anthology, p. 2442.

Gugelberger, Georg M. "Blake, Neruda, Ngugi wa Thiong'o: Issues in Third World Literature." *Comparative Literature Studies* 21 (1984): 463–82. Suggests that Neruda's translating of a few of Blake's socially radical poems (*Visions of the Daughters of Albion* and *The Mental Traveler*) in 1935 may have contributed to his move away from French symbolist influence and toward the engaged poetry of his later years.

SAMUEL BECKETT

Endgame

Backgrounds

Beckett's world is the world of last things—stark, bare, gray from pole to pole—in which characters are bitterly self-conscious and the activity of life is reduced to mere waiting and game-playing. As Tom Stoppard has said, Beckett redefined the minima of theatrical validity. His world is refrigerated and tends toward silence, yet he wrote an extraordinary number of plays, novels, short fictions, and poems that examine such silence in a language as suggestive and penetrating as the language of any writer of his time.

The headnote to Beckett (pp. 2455–59 in the anthology) points out almost all of *Endgame*'s central obsessions: the dead world inside, the deader world outside; the four barren characters absolutely restricted in both time and space; the notion of life as a game that cannot be won, only cruelly played; the master-slave relationships of the characters, the struggle of body and soul within each of them.

In *Waiting for Godot,* Vladimir and Estragon play games to endure; game-playing structures their wait. In *Endgame,* game-playing, or the game itself, becomes the central metaphor for existence. Games have no meaning outside of themselves (except indirectly); they are morally and practically superfluous; rule-governed; repetitive; independent of the immediate satisfactions of wants and appetites; dependent on the virtuosity of the players, some of whom dominate while others are dominated; confirmative of role and the stabilizing of position. Games create a world of meaning that is entirely self-reflexive, a dead end. One of the most elaborate of all human games is the play, the drama, which provides an actively present metaphor within the larger metaphor of *Endgame.*

Endgame is aware of itself as a text performed in a theater, and the characters are aware of themselves as characters on stage; they flaunt their consciousness that the whole business is a performance. Their essential traits are those that have been devised in previous plays: Hamm, whose name recalls the term referring to a bad actor, is also Hamlet, who, to quote Hugh Kenner, is "bounded by a nutshell, fancying himself king of infinite space, but troubled by bad dreams." He is also Prospero, but one whose kingdom is without magic, except perhaps the magic of power. Hamm's relationship with the other characters is one of domination and cruelty. He is the hammer to Clov's nail; the Prospero to Clov's Ariel *and* Caliban; the king to Clov's knight; the master to Clov's dog. Both Hamm and Clov continually suggest that they are on stage alive, only because they have roles to perform in a play, a dramatic game—roles that they cannot stop playing because there is no alternative but to play them. When Clov threatens to leave Hamm, he asks, "What is there to keep me here?" Hamm replies, "The dialogue" (p. 2479). Hamm, Clov, Nagg, and Nell say what they say as if they have said the same things many times before. (Note particularly Hamm's story and Nagg's joke about the English tailor [pp. 2466–67].) The characters are burdened with a blinding self-consciousness, an awareness of the eternal, repetitive monotony of being trapped in their roles in a game that, when there is nothing outside from which to differentiate it, is meaningless.

When the curtain (if there is a curtain) rises on *Endgame,* it is as if all the characters are just waking up—preparing themselves for another day (another performance), which they hope will soon be finished. The furniture is covered in sheets, suggesting both storage (for the night, between performances) and the covering of the dead. Clov opens the play by performing his ritual actions (he must, according to the script, do this *every* performance) until Hamm removes his personal curtain and announces that he is ready "to play." The stage is their shelter and their gameboard; it is the space in which they do their "living."

In this space there is no future, since the future can be only a mere repetition of the present. Nor can there be a past, except as it persists in memory—the memory, that is, of a life "outside" the stage, a life that seems only disturbingly ironic when compared to present circumstances. The characters live in the hell of an eternal present, but outside is the "other hell." The waves of the sea are like lead, the sun is "zero," there is "no more nature" except the characters's natural tendency to grow old and dwindle toward a death that neglects to come:

> HAMM   But we breathe, we change! We lose our hair, our teeth! Our bloom! Our ideals!
> CLOV   Then she hasn't forgotten us.
>   (p. 2463)

The "little round box" of the universe was once full, perhaps, but now is empty.

Any suggestion of life outside Hamm's kingdom (the flea, the rat, the small boy) terrifies and thrills for the same reason: "humanity might start from there all over again" (p. 2470). Clov, at least, can conceive of a renewal, regeneration, a new play with new roles. But he, like Hamm, can also imagine that new life would mean only a continuation of life as it now exists, a life so checkmated that "a world where all would be silent and still and each thing in its last place, under the last dust" offers itself as a desirable end, the final "pain-killer" to the prison of endless time the characters now inhabit.

Beckett is rumored to have remarked that in *Waiting for Godot* the audience wonders whether Godot will ever come, while in *Endgame* they wonder whether Clov will ever leave. The "small boy," if there is one, intensifies the question, suggesting both the horror and potentiality of new life. At play's end, Clov is "dressed for the road," suggesting the possibility that he intends to carry out his threat and leave Hamm, perhaps to take in the small boy (as Hamm, apparently, once did) and play Hamm's role himself. Or perhaps Hamm dismisses Clov because he himself intends to take in the small boy, a new player in his game, making Clov no longer necessary. In any case, Clov (who can imagine both "I'll never go" and "I open the door of my cell and go") is still there at the end, "eyes fixed on Hamm." Hamm's final two monologues (p. 2482 and pp. 2486–87), with all of their rhetorical flourish again suggesting scriptedness, are derisive parodies of Jesus' words: they suggest both death and regeneration. Whether regeneration can come in a form other than the play's being enacted again, tomorrow night, is left ambivalent. Hamm finishes where he began, his bloodstained handkerchief over his face, motionless—waiting, perhaps, for the curtain to rise once more.

It has been suggested, by Lionel Abel among others, that Hamm is based on James Joyce—the almost-blind master for whom Beckett worked as a secretary in the late 1920s—and that Clov is based on Beckett himself. Indeed, Joyce (like Hamm) was working on an interminable story, *Finnegans Wake,* during the time Beckett worked with him, and Beckett (like Clov) was very much under Joyce's influence and in Joyce's debt during those years. Even if there is some truth to the claim, however, the play can by no means be read merely as a thinly disguised examination of the conflict between a literary master and his gifted pupil.

Commentators on Beckett often locate him in a tradition that includes Dostoevsky, Gogol, Goncharov, Andreyev, Musil, and Kafka—writers who were interested in the "marginal self," and who find modern men eaten up by consciousness. Dramatically, he has long been included in the "theater of the absurd" with Eugene Ionesco, Jean Genet, and Fernando Arrabal, who certainly belong in such a context, and Harold Pinter, who perhaps does not, but who avails himself of many of the techniques we find in Beckett and the others.

Ruby Cohn has outlined a number of evident allusions, parodies, and influences in *Endgame*. She notes Beckett's use of the Bible, especially the Gospel of Saint John; James Joyce, the labyrinth-maker and word-man who may have been a model for Hamm; Shakespeare's *The Tempest* and *King Lear*; Baudelaire, whom Hamm quotes at the end of the play; and Tiresias and Oedipus, blind prophets of suffering.

Classroom Strategies

Endgame can be taught in two class periods. The first should probably examine the thematic implications of the play by exploring the various plausible interpretations that offer themselves to the reader. The second might concentrate on the richness of Beckett's wordplay, his humor, and the way his language lends itself to multiple readings.

You might begin by discussing the implications of the stage setting. It is depressingly bare, enveloped in gray light; the offstage scene is brutally excluded except for the two small windows so high that they can be reached only by ladder. There will be no entrances by persons un-known; only Clov can use the door, which in one production was so nar-row that the actor playing the part of Clov thought of himself as a rat squeezing into its hole. The stage certainly appears to be sym-bolic, though precisely what it symbolizes is a matter of considerable de-bate. The headnote discusses a number of the possibilities: the stage as the inside of a skull, suggesting that Hamm and Clov are two aspects of a single personality, while Nagg and Nell are suppressed earlier selves; as a last refuge of those who have survived an unnamed catastrophe (perhaps a deluge or nuclear holocaust), making Hamm—to quote Katharine Worth—"lord of the ark of survivors, with his human family and a selection of animals"; as a metaphor for the twilight of civilization, in which Nagg and Nell's ash cans come to represent the dustbin of modern civilized values; as an image of purgatory, or purgatorial consciousness; as a womb, from which the characters are eternally hoping—and fearing—to emerge. Beckett has said of his imaginings of life in the womb:

> Even before the fetus can draw breath it is in a state of barrenness and of pain. I have a clear memory of my own fetal existence. It was an existence where no voice, no possible movement could free me from the agony and darkness I was subjected to.

Hugh Kenner adds another possibility, describing the stage as a chessboard and the characters' actions as a game of chess, in which Hamm is the king, Clov the knight, and Nagg and Nell are pawns. The point here is that Beckett has constructed his play so brilliantly and ambiguously that, as Kenner has said, "The play contains whatever ideas we discern inside it; no idea contains the play."

Beckett's refusal to assign a definite meaning to his evidently symbolic characters, setting, and dramatic "action," combined with his denial of the rich inner life that students have come to expect from traditional drama, make some students uneasy. But this uneasiness can be turned to your, and the play's, advantage. Just as we recognize the terrifying sense of no exit, we are—like Clov—drawn almost irresistibly to see out, to make the laborious climb up the ladder of vision to a world less claustrophobic, fresher than the one Beckett's characters inhabit. Students may resist the notion that there is "an absence of meaning at the core" of the world. They can, however, imagine it, and with their imagining comes a shock of recognition. The game metaphor is of particular use here: any game that has no reference to anything outside itself, that *is* life rather than a *recreation* in it (or re-creation of it), can be imagined as a kind of purgatory—repetitive, monotonous, endless.

Students need to be aware of Beckett's extraordinary wordplay as well as his humor. Certain scenes might be read out loud in class, with students taking the parts, in order to emphasize these qualities. The pace of the repartee, which sometimes—though not as often as in *Waiting for Godot*—approaches a vaudeville routine, will become immediately accessible. The opening dialogue between Hamm and Clov (beginning with Clov's "I've just got you up," and ending with his "There's nowhere else" [p. 2460]) will serve you well. Also useful is the repartee beginning on p. 2463 (Hamm: "Every man his specialty") and ending on p. 2464 (Clov: "Something is taking its course"); Nagg and Nell's dialogue (pp. 2466–67), which includes Nagg's joke; and Hamm and Clov's discussion on pp. 2470–71, beginning with Clov's "Why this farce, day after day?" and ending with Hamm's long, bitter speech.

Topics for Discussion and Writing

1. What is the significance of the stage setting? What does it symbolize? Why doesn't Beckett certify any particular interpretation?
   [See the second paragraph of "Backgrounds" and the second paragraph of "Classroom Strategies" for discussion.]
2. Why is the play called *Endgame*? What do games have to do with it? How does Beckett use play (including "drama" as "play") in *Endgame*?
   [See the headnote and the second, third, and fourth paragraphs of "Backgrounds" for discussion.]
3. Characterize the relationship between Hamm and Clov; between Hamm, Nagg, and Nell. Why is Nagg called "accursed progenitor"?

[See the headnote and the second paragraph of "Backgrounds" for discussion.]

4. If "waiting" is the controlling verb in *Waiting for Godot,* what is the controlling verb in *Endgame?*
   [Ending? Gaming? Playing? Finishing?]

5. In what ways does *Endgame* suggest the ending of things? In what ways does it suggest a possible beginning? Can it suggest both?
   [See "Backgrounds" for discussion.]

6. How is Prospero a useful analogue for Hamm? How is King Lear? The biblical Ham? James Joyce?
   [See "Backgrounds" for discussion.]

Comparative Perspectives

1. "Ask my father if he wants to listen to my story," Hamm instructs Clov as he launches into a long narrative excursion. While the words the characters speak may be difficult to fathom, the rhythms of Beckett's dialogue represent intergenerational conversations that we all can recognize. How well do family members listen to each others' stories in "real life"? Compare *Endgame*'s postmodernist dramatization of parental indifference and obsessive childhood memories to the treatment of these concerns in some of the family-centered works in this volume.

2. During his lifetime, Beckett exercised total control over the production of his plays. Now that he has died, his executors have sued directors who have deviated from his detailed and specific stage directions and prescribed scenic designs. How central do you think such physical circumstances are to the success of this play? What would happen if Nagg and Nell were not housed in their ash cans, for example? Discuss the role of stage setting and action in other plays you have read this term, including, if appropriate, *nō* dramas, Moliere's *Tartuffe,* Chekhov's *The Cherry Orchard,* and Brecht's *The Good Woman of Setzuan.* Which playwrights seem to place the greatest premium on precisely defined production techniques? Why?
   [See also the comparison suggested to Stevens's *The Idea of Order at Key West.*]

Further Reading

See also the reading suggestions in the anthology, pp. 2458–59.

Ben-Zvi, Linda, ed. *Women in Beckett: Performance and Critical Perspectives.* 1990. Although not specifically related to *Endgame,* this collection is interesting as a particular examination of Beckett's dramatic work. It contains twelve interviews with actresses from seven different countries (Part I: "Acting Beckett's Women") and nineteen essays using modern critical approaches, arranged in order from fiction to drama and radio-television (Part II: "Reacting to Beckett's Women").

Bloom, Harold, ed. *Samuel Beckett's* Endgame. 1988. Assembles a range of essays on the play.

Brater, Enoch. *Why Beckett.* 1989. A brief illustrated biography with 122 illustrations, chiefly photos.

Burkman, Katherine H., ed. *Myth and Ritual in the Plays of Samuel Beckett.* 1987. Eleven essays, including a study by Susan Maughlin based on anthropologist Victor Turner's concept of liminality: "Liminality: An Approach to Artistic Process in *Endgame.*"

———. *Just Play: Beckett's Theater.* 1980. A thorough study of the dramatic works, particularly interesting on Beckett's language.

Esslin, Martin, ed. *Samuel Beckett: A Collection of Essays.* 1965. Contains a particularly fine essay on *Endgame,* "Beckett's Brinkmanship," by Ross Chambers.

Kalb, Jonathan. *Beckett in Performance.* 1989. An excellent dramaturgical discussion of actual performances as interpretations; includes interviews with eight actors and directors.

Kane, Leslie. *The Language of Silence: On the Unspoken and the Unspeakable in Modern Drama.* 1984.

Pilling, John. *Samuel Beckett.* 1976. A general study, useful on the intellectual, cultural, and literary background to Beckett's work.

Sheedy, John J. "The Comic Apocalypse of King Hamm." *Modern Drama,* IX (December 1966). Pp. 310–18. A close analysis that suggests both comic and apocalyptic dimensions in the play.

Worth, Katharine, ed. *Beckett the Shape Changer.* 1975. Worth's essay, "The Space and Sound in Beckett's Theatre," is illuminating on *Endgame* and his other plays.

BIRAGO DIOP

Classroom Strategies

The Bone and *Mother Crocodile* share with the epic of *Son-Jara* a common background of historical and cultural references. This is a circumstance highlighted by the second part of *Mother Crocodile,* which owes its epic resonance to its terse and dramatic reconstruction of the conflict between Arab invaders and indigenous African populations in West Africa that marks the history of the region throughout the Middle Ages. Many of the observations on orality as a determining factor of the structure of the Son-Jara epic also apply to Diop's tales. You should point out to students, however, that in the latter case it is a question of secondary orality, obtained by a creative adaptation of traditional oral form to the demands of the written medium. As with the Son-Jara epic (in volume C, pp. 2415–62), visual aids such as photographs and video clips will be helpful in providing an idea of the landscape that plays so important a role in Diop's tales.

In terms of content and structure, Diop's tales bear a minimal resemblance to certain European folktales with which students may already be familiar. However, the most convenient approach to these tales is to relate them to the Brer Rabbit stories, which are directly derived from the African folktale tradition. These stories, which were collected early in this century among the rural black folk in the American South, form part of the cluster of African cultural survivals in the New World. They provide an excellent illustration of the themes and structure of African folktales. The rapprochement between the African and African-American traditions indicates that Brer Rabbit is manifestly a reincarnation of Leuk-the-Hare, the main protagonist in the cycle of animal tales of the Wolof people in Senegal and Gambia. The existence of similar cycles in other parts of Africa should be pointed out to students. In many respects, the Wolof tales correspond to the cycle of animal tales among the Akan of Ghana and the Ivory Coast, centered on the figure of Anansi the Spider (Kacou Ananze in Dadié's *The Black Cloth*); this cycle is the source of the "Nancy" tales in Jamaica and other parts of the Caribbean. The trickster element in these tales is brought out even more prominently, further east, among the Yoruba, in the cycle of tales devoted to the adventures of Tortoise, the equivalent to the Wolof hare and the Akan spider. We might remark, in passing, that the Yoruba cycle of the Tortoise is considered the most comprehensive cycle in Africa. However, as the roll call of animals in Diop's *Mother Crocodile* indicates, the trickster figure is only one among many animal characters in the corpus of traditional folktales across the continent. These animal characters provide the anthropomorphic basis for the preeminent didactic function of the folktales; through a psychological and moral interpretation of their physical aspects and habitual demeanors, these animals came to represent human types and moral values.

Birago Diop's association of Amadou Koumba, his family *griot*, with these tales makes clear that he is consciously deriving his own work from the indigenous tradition. It is important to point out, however, that the tradition is only a point of departure for an imaginative enterprise that seeks to extend the habitual themes of the tales and the allegorical significance of the animal characters into a new sphere of modern African awareness. Attention should therefore be drawn to the originality of Diop's handling of the traditional form. Equally original is the perspective of personal experience within which Diop sets the narration of this model of the etiological tale, the ironic outcome and moral significance of which depend on the marked asymmetry between the obsessive directions taken by its two female characters. In *The Bone*, the integration of a realistic social setting with a satiric portrayal of an obsessive character trait provides us with another example of Diop's departure from the conventions of the traditional form. Finally, in *Mother Crocodile*, while remaining faithful to the formal demands of the genre, Diop succeeds in expanding the range of the traditional folk tale through the interaction of the animal world with the human universe toward which the moral intention that informs the tale is ultimately directed.

These tales demonstrate that the particular interest of Diop's work resides in his creative deployment of the folktale material. In this respect, he may be compared to the seventeenth-century French writer, La Fontaine, whose adaptations of Aesop's fables have obviously exerted a direct influence on Diop. But perhaps the most important attraction of the tales is their dramatic potential, demonstrated by the enormous popular success of Diop's stage adaptation of *The Bone*. Encourage students to read the tales aloud, accompanied by the gestures and dramatic devices associated with oral performance, in order both to stimulate interest and to bring out the dramatic quality inherent in Diop's re-creations, through a blend of realism and fancy, of the African folktale tradition.

Topics for Discussion and Writing

1. Humor and satire in Birago Diop's tales.
2. A comparative study of animal characters as allegorical figures in Diop's tales and in the fables of either either Aesop or La Fontaine.
3. A study of the narrative progression in the three stories, with a view to exploring Diop's various approaches.
4. Research on folktale as universal form; students could be referred to the classic Arne-Stith-Thompson Index of folktale motifs.

Comparative Perspectives

1. Compare the humorous depiction of self-destructive greed in *The Bone* with earlier allegorical treatments of the theme in *The Pardoner's Tale* or *The Jātaka Tales*, if appropriate. What lands of connotations accompany the idea of appetite for food in such stories?
2. *Mother Crocodile* brilliantly sketches the bloody history of West Africa from the perspective of an amphibian river-dweller. Explain the moral of the story, discuss the pathos of the short final paragraph through which it is conveyed, and evaluate the cultural backdrop that gives such resonance to Diop's use of a crocodile's eyewitness view of events. How would you compare this adaptation of the traditional beastfable for serious political purposes with the perspective brought by other writers trying to express the tragedy of the African experience?

   [Explore the different means of, and effects achieved by, Diop's adaptation of the *griot*'s idiomatic treatment of the animal world and, as appropriate, the Westernized models that inform Césaire's angry invective; Achebe's and/or Gordimer's nuanced, detailed narratives; Soyinka's fusion of Yoruba and European dramatic modes.]

Further Reading

See also the reading suggestions in the anthology, p. 2490.

Bascom, William Russel. *African Folktales in the New World.* 1992. The introductory essay combines an overview of the folktale genre with an analysis of theme, structure, and atmosphere in African tales.

Scheub, Harold. *The African Storyteller: Stories from African Oral Tradition.* 1990. The introductory essay combines an overview of the folktale genre with an analysis of themes, structure, and atmosphere in African tales.

LÉOPOLD SÉDAR SENGHOR

Backgrounds

In the Afterword (*Postface*) to his third collection of poems, *Ethiopiques* (1956), Senghor summed up the creative tension central to the inspiration of modern African literature in the European languages, at the head of which his own work stands so prominently: "Our ambition is modest: to be precursors, to pave the way for an authentic black poetry which, nonetheless, does not deny its claim to be French." Although Senghor's statement here concerns his own poetry and that of the French-speaking black poets represented in his historic *Anthologie de la nouvelle poésie nègre et malgache* (1948), it applies equally to African writers working in other European languages, such as Chinua Achebe and Wole Soyinka writing in English. For these writers, the impulse to imaginative expression has involved the adaptation of a European language—imposed by the historical happenstance of European colonialism—to the expressive needs of the individual writer's exploration of the African experience. Because of the circumstances of its genesis, modern African literature emerged primarily as a testimony to the historical stress provoked in Africa by the encounter between Africans and Europeans, and as a mode of self-repossession by the divided African who appears as the ambiguous product of this encounter.

This double impetus to the development of modern African literature is well illustrated by Senghor's work. It is what gives meaning to the concept of Négritude, with which his writing and career have been so closely associated and the immediate bearing of which upon his poetry can hardly be exaggerated. Négritude represents primarily a response to the pain and humiliation of colonial domination, and especially to the negative representations of Africa and the black race in general by which the colonial order itself was rationalized in Western ideological literature. In its more specific character as a literary movement, Négritude relates to the cultural and spiritual malaise of a whole generation of French-speaking black intellectuals, of which Senghor himself is perhaps the outstanding representative. It testifies to a collective condition engendered by the French cultural policy of assimilation, with its contradiction between the selective promotion of a few chosen individuals on one hand, and the general devaluation of the race to which they belonged on the other.

This militant aspect of the Négritude movement is reflected in the bitter note that underlies *Letter to a Prisoner,* one of the most striking of Senghor's poems based on his wartime experience in France. The movement's theme of racial commitment and its critical stance toward the West are motivated by an imperative need to challenge European colonialism in both its effects and its ideological premises. This challenge is complemented by a sustained endeavour to foster a new vision of Africa in order to rehabilitate the black race, which has been demoralized by the constant denigration of its human worth and its essence through Western racism. The acute sense of racial solidarity involved in this process is well exemplified by the poem *To New York,* its rhetorical flourish and hyper-romanticism testifying to a well-defined ideological purpose.

At the same time, the terms of Senghor's expression in this and other poems suggest that their essential impulse corresponds more profoundly to a quest for identity. They testify to a process of self-discovery on the part of a Westemised and assimilated black elite, leading ultimately to a heightened and even exacerbated self-consciousness. Senghor has invested considerable effort in promoting Négritude not simply as a form of cultural nationalism, with its plea for the recognition of the validity of African forms of cultural expression, but as a pronounced strategy of self-differentiation. In this regard, Négritude denotes the unified concept of an essential Africanism, serving as the principle of the collective personality of black people. Senghor's frequent definition of Négritude as "the sum total of African values" ("l'ensemble des valeurs de la civilisation africaine") posits a collective ethos distinguished by modes of feeling and doing and, above all, by a unique manner of relating to the world.

Despite its racial underpinnings, Senghor's Négritude needs to be understood as essentially a concept of culture, designating an autonomous area of human expression, with its distinctive forms of life informed by a coherent vision of the world. In its specific relation to his poetry, it represents an imaginative ideal, derived from a new feeling on the part of the poet for his African homeland, an ideal that comes to serve as a spiritual reference for his poetic universe. This is the perspective of Négritude that makes Senghor's poetry so interesting, for it is the increasing elaboration of the elements of his African background that has determined the thematic progression of Senghor's poetry, the extension of its references beyond the contigencies of a personal historical situation, and a corresponding deepening of its tone. *Letter to a Poet* can be considered the ground plan of this development, a manifesto outlining the thematic direction and aesthetic implications of the new expression to which Senghor has been fundamentally committed. The poem, conceived in terms of the feeling for nobility in traditional cultures, represents a statement by Senghor of the sources of his inspiration and of the conception he held, at the very outset of his writing career, of his own mission as an African poet.

Classroom Strategies

Discussion of the selections may start with a consideration of the ways in which Senghor endows Africa with poetic significance. *Night in Sine* employs a highly wrought evocation of the African landscape to create a distinctive atmosphere and a contemplative mood associated with the poet's continent. The African references serve more than the requirements of local color; they collaborate to sustain the structure of thought within the poem. An appreciation of the emotional register and symbolic resonance of the poem will thus depend to some extent on an understanding of the system of belief on which the theme of devotion to ancestors is based, of the privileged place ancestors are thought to occupy in the chain of existence linking them to the living and the unborn. This mystical conception of the human community lends force to the organizing image of night by which the enduring cycle of nature and the intuition of cosmic renewal are expressed. Similarly, the affirmative tone of *Black Woman* reflects the strong valuation of the feminine principle evident in ritual and other expressive schemes of traditional African societies. It must be stressed that this poem, which combines the enumerative style of the Western canticle (as in the Catholic litany to the Virgin Mary) with that of the African praise poem, is not a love poem in any conventional sense of the term, but a rhapsodic celebration of the poet's organic bond with the Africa that gave him birth. The woman addressed in the poem is not an individual person, object of the poet's devotion, but rather a symbolic figure, a "generic" African woman, bearer of the race and embodiment of a universal principle of life. The refrains introduce impressionistic invocations through which Senghor develops a succession of ecstatic images, culminating in the exultant affirmation of the vital significance of the poetic calling.

These examples demonstrate the way in which Senghor integrates his personal intimations of life and experience into a more comprehensive African framework of vision and sensibility. This process can be illustrated by the way in which, in *Elegy of the Circumcised,* Senghor identifies his passage through life with the various rites of passage in traditional society, of which circumcision is a key one, determining the transition from the innocence of childhood to the maturity and experience of adulthood. The meaning of the theme expands to denote the passage of time as a fundamental element of human apprehension, and the fact of mortality as an inescapable aspect of the human condition. The meditation in this and other elegies is developed by reference to an African scheme of symbolic meanings.

Topics for Discussion and Writing

1. Is it possible to draw a parallel between Senghor's recourse to African systems of belief and the deliberate appropriation of myth in modern poetry, for example in Eliot's *The Waste Land?*
2. Another parallel may be suggested by the role of poetry in the forg-

ing of national consciousness. Consider Senghor's Négritude in light of American cultural nationalism, for example, as expressed by Emerson's *The American Scholar* and exemplified by Whitman's *Leaves of Grass*.

3. The Négritude movement deserves to be studied as an important modern literary movement. Students may be asked to research the literary and intellectual history of the movement and to assess Senghor's contribution to its formulation.

Comparative Perspectives

1. In *Letter to a Poet*, Senghor addresses Aimé Césaire in terms that recall the dialogue between Coleridge and Wordsworth implicit in *Dejection: An Ode*. What does Senghor seem to be requesting of Césaire? How would you compare the center of interest in Coleridge's poem? Where is the poems of these two sets of friends can we see evidence of their commitment to similar ideals and the development of a shared vocabulary in which to express them?

   [Senghor calls Césaire back into action, thinking of his friend's importance to their common cause, whereas Coleridge, measuring himself against other poets, laments what he perceives to be his own imaginative failure to write it all. See the footnotes to Coleridge's *Dejection: An Ode* and the material on that poem in this manual.]

2. Compare Senghor's imagery throughout this poem with that of *Notebook of a Return to the Native Land*. Pay special attention to the impact of the closing section, in which Césaire understands that "it is not true that the work of man is done," on some of Senghor's other poems in this volume.

   [Imagery of Africa's indispensable nurturing—the navel (*Letter to a Prisoner*); the dance (*Prayer to the Masks.*)]

3. In *Prayer to the Masks*, Senghor invokes the spirits of the ancestors in a medium typical not only of African but of native American rites as well, where masked kachinas dance and grant seeds. Discuss the power of the mask for ritual purposes, with reference to the selections of Zuni ritual poetry, or the horrible consequences that result from the unmasking of the *egwugwu* in *Things Fall Apart*.

   [For an interdisciplinary assignment, discuss questions raised about exhibiting African masks, which are ritual objects, as if they were artworks.]

Further Reading

See also the reading suggestions in the anthology, p. 2505.

Blair, Dorothy. *African Literature in French*. 1976. Useful as general introduction to the field.

Irele, Abiola. *The African Experience in Literature and Ideology*. 1980. Reprinted 1990. The three essays that constitute the middle section of this collection are devoted to the Négritude movement and aspects of African Nationalism. (See also my chapter on Senghor in Brian Cox, ed. *African Authors*, forthcoming.)

July, Robert. *The Origins of Modern African Thought*. 1968. Essential for the intellectual background to Senghor's work.

Rubin, William. *"Primitivism" in 20th-Century Art*. Vol. I. 1984.

Senghor, L.S. *Selected Poetry and Prose*. Translated by James Reed and Clive Wake. 1976. Contains a selection of Senghor's essays in translation, useful for gaining a general idea of his ideas on African culture and for his formulations of the concept of Négritude.

Spleth, Janice, ed. *Critical Perspectives on Léopold Sédar Senghor*. 1993. A collection of essays that illuminate various aspects of Senghor's poetry.

RICHARD WRIGHT

The Man Who Was Almost a Man

Classroom Strategies and Topics for Discussion

Originally published in the magazine *Harper's Bazaar*, this brief, powerful story has many affinities with the outer stories of initiation contained in the anthology, but Wright here manages the difficult task of making articulate the emotions of an inarticulate youth. By using dialect and taking us into Dave's mind, Wright scrupulously records his protagonist's limits. As the headnote and the title suggest, this is a coming-of-age story in which the hero fails to come of age. Its poignancy stems from the truncation of the natural arc of development that the reader expects from such a story, a literary embodiment of Dave's lack of options.

Your students should have little difficulty understanding the means by which Wright captures his protagonist's personality and dilemma. The story, divided into three sections, begins and ends with the boy on the move: Dave's restlessness determines his fate. In the first part, with great economy Wright shows us Dave's sense of inadequacy. The men with whom he works are bigger than he is and "talk to him as though he were a little boy" (p. 2518), his mother and father treat him as a boy too, as does the white storeowner, Joe: "You ain't nothing but a boy. You don't need a gun" (p. 2519).

That the gun functions as a phallic symbol is quite clear—Dave sees it as the validator of his manhood, fondles it as he awakes in the morning, and ties "it to his naked thigh while it was still loaded" (p. 2522). Hoping to achieve through it a virility he cannot yet claim, Dave ultimately finds that he has instead been betrayed on all sides. Joe sells him a virtual antique, too heavy and erratic for an inexperienced seventeen-year-old boy to manage. In the classic Oedipal scene on pp. 2521–22, Dave seductively persuades his mother to give him money for the gun. This hard-pressed woman sees only an immediate use for the catalog her son brings to the house ("We kin use it in the outhouse"). Against the odds, Dave seems to be asserting his masculine powers in this encounter with the dominant figure in the household. The reader recognizes, however, that Mrs. Saunders relents only when she satisfies herself that the gun will really be for her husband. And later on, trying to get her hapless son to confess the truth, she will reveal his secret and expose him to his father's fury and the laughter of the crowd.

Note what Wright does not include in his narrative: he fastens on Dave's humiliations rather than his successes. We do not see the acquisition of the gun, for example, nor do we hear how he tells the story of Jenny's that is at least tentatively accepted. The harrowing central section of *The Man Who Was Almost a Man* concentrates instead on the mule's suffering, and in the last section of his narrative, Wright carefully draws the connection between Jenny and Dave: "They treat me like a mule, n then they beat me" (p. 2526). If in some recesses of his subconscious mind Dave seeks to exert his authority over the one creature he can command, Jenny the mule, when he raises his gun the shots rebound in more ways than one. He makes himself even more the laughing stock of the community he hoped to impress; he not only "bought a dead mule" (p. 2525), but also, in some subtle way, perhaps, destroyed himself. In an odd reversal of the sexual imagery traditionally associated with the shooting of a gun, Dave takes his own innocence when he opens the bloody hole in the flank of the desperate mule. Many initiation stories revolve around the youthful protagonist's first kill; *The Man Who Was Almost a Man* may be read at least in part as a bitter parody of romantic accounts of that epic encounter. Still not mature, Dave fantasizes about making an impact on the world after he has fired the gun with such horrendous consequences; significantly, we learn his full name only in the course of these thoughts: "Ah'd like t scare ol man Hawkins jusa little . . . Jusa enough t let im know Dave Saunders is a man" (p. 2526).

The mule's terrified galloping after the gunshot seems one more symptom of Dave's restlessness; it is perhaps significant that Wright evokes the sound of the train bearing down on the railroad tracks at the end of the story by writing "*hoooof-hoooof,*" as if to suggest some equation with the animal. In tones very much like those he has used in condescending to Jenny in the woods before shooting the gun, Dave impatiently awaits the train: "Here she comes, erron the ben . . . C mon, yuh slow poke! C mon!"

The headnote comments on the haiku that Wright was working on in his last years; in 1998, some four hundred of these poems were first published. Even in this early story, we can see evidence of the delicate observation that we associate with Japanese verse. Ask your students to watch the way in which Wright bathes the grim reality of Dave's plight in a transfiguring light. *The Man Who Was Almost a Man* begins in "paling light" (p. 2518); the next section starts in "the gray light of dawn" (p. 2522); the last begins "It was sunset" (p. 2524) and ends when Dave digs up the buried gun in "silence and moonlight" and pulls himself onto a railroad car traveling the rails "glinting in the moonlight" (p. 2527). With such descriptions, Wright stresses the gap between the boy's constricted circumstances and the radiance with which an indifferent universe illuminates them.

The glamor of that last image, however, and the sense that the boy is "getting on with his life," may delude students into seeing Dave's leap onto the train as a triumphant conclusion. Ask them to consider the indeterminacy of Wright's last sentence and the import of the story's title: where is the "somewhere where he could be a man"? What are the boy's prospects? Can we run away from the problems that we create for ourselves?

Topics for Writing

1. Why does Dave want a gun? Discuss the connection between the gun and his relationship with his mother and father.
2. How do the whites in this story treat Dave? How large a role does Wright give to racial tensions in his descriptions of Dave's problems?
3. Discuss the significance of Dave's final decision. Will he be better off because he runs away from home? Is he liberating himself, or will his life be more difficult when he is on his own?

Comparative Perspectives

1. Compare and contrast Frederick Douglass's description of his struggle with a recalcitrant team of oxen in chapter X of his *Narrative* with Dave's disastrous encounter with Jenny in *The Man Who Was Almost a Man*. What does each scene tell us about the contest between a young man and an animal that has been trusted to his care? How is the character of the protagonist revealed by the way he conducts himself?
2. Compare and contrast Faulkner's description of man and beast in Mississippi in *The Bear* with Wright's treatment of this theme in *The Man Who Was Almost a Man*. How does each author relate the human world to the animal world?
3. Explain how Dave convinces his mother to let him buy a gun, and compare the tensions in his family role to those experienced by other fictional sons in this volume, including Marcel in *Swann's Way*, Gregor in *The Metamorphosis*, and the several sons of Pedro Páramo.

Further Reading

See also the reading suggestions in the anthology, p. 2518.

Hoeveler, Diane Long. "Oedipus Agonistes: Mothers and Sons in Richard Wright's Fiction." *Black American Literature Forum* 12,2 (1978):

65–68. This article makes no direct reference to *The Man Who Was Almost a Man,* but it provides a useful contact for discussing Dave's relationship with his strong mother.

Loftis, John E. "Domestic Prey: Richard Wright's Parody of the Hunt Tradition in 'The Man Who Was Almost a Man.' " *Studies in Short Fiction* 23 (1986): 437–42. A neat comparison between Ike McCaslin's coming of age in Faulkner's *The Old People* (published in late 1940) and Dave's failure to do so in Wright's story (published in the beginning of that year). In other words, Loftis does not argue for any explicit influence of one on the other, but his discussion accentuates the differences between the two boys and their communities: where Ike is supported, Dave is thwarted.

NAGUIB MAHFOUZ

Zaabalawi

Backgrounds

Several years after publishing *Children of Gebelawi,* in which the history of a family descended from Gebelawi was also an allegorical history of religions, Naguib Mahfouz published a collection of stories called *God's World* (1963). If the patriarch Gebelawi (often transliterated Jabalawi) is to be allegorized as God, the almost-homonymic Zaabalawi of *God's World* is at least a close relation. The story *Zaabalawi* can easily be read as a mystic vision of the modern quest for God: as the allegorical rejection of a decadent society that has forgotten religious faith and that claims, in Nietzsche's words, that "God is dead." Yet Mahfouz concurrently provides a realistic picture of the middle-class Cairo society he knows best. Although he is not recognized in his native Egypt as a "committed" realist writer—indeed, the more militant younger novelists feel that he has worked too much inside the establishment and become a canonical figure—he has developed his own complex way of representing reality. Mahfouz's criticism of moral weakness or social wrongdoing is not limited to a single dimension: it functions on individual, national, and religious levels. Nor has he gone unscathed. The movie made from *Miramar* was initially banned because it criticized Nasser's régime, and Mahfouz received death threats from religious fundamentalists after publicly criticizing Khomeini's call to murder Salman Rushdie.

Indeed, in October 1994, while sitting in a car outside his home in Cairo, Mahfouz was stabbed in the neck by a follower of the radical Egyptian cleric Sheik Omar Abdel Rahman. Mahfouz survived the attack, but an Egyptian military court sentenced two militant Muslims to death, two other defendants to life imprisonment, and nine other defendants to extended prison terms for their roles in the attempted murder.

Despite his status as the Grand Old Man of Egyptian letters and the first Arabic writer to receive the Nobel Prize in Literature, as of this writing neither *Children of Gebelawi* nor the story *Zaabalawi* has been pub-

lished in his native Egypt: both works have shocked people with traditional beliefs about the representation of religious figures.

Allegorical literature is certainly not new with Naguib Mahfouz, but
students may find it an unfamiliar mode inasmuch as the best-known
Western examples of religious allegory lie further in the past: Dante's *Divine Comedy,* the medieval drama *Everyman,* Spenser's *Faerie Queene,* or
Bunyan's *Pilgrim's Progress.* Modern literature—certainly modern Western literature—tends to provide different kinds of symbolism rather than
religious allegory, and it presents realistic details more often than personified concepts. One could argue that Beckett's *Endgame* and Solzhenitsyn's *Matryona's Home* are modern versions of religious allegories, but
the argument would have to take into account on the one hand a different
philosophical basis and on the other a different fictional strategy. Mahfouz's personification of religious history in *Children of Gebelawi,* and the
protagonist's quest for a cure in his *Zaabalawi,* are clearly closer to familiar models of religious allegory insofar as they employ a set of symbolic
characters acting out a drama with specific religious significance.

Yet it would be a mistake to stop here and to ignore the fact that Mahfouz's stories are firmly rooted in the material world of modern Egyptian
society. The religious allegory may itself be an allegory of modern Egypt's
struggle to keep its bearings when faced with sudden industrialization and
with what Mahfouz sees as the commercialization of spiritual values. His
characters are contemporary individuals trying to survive in urban society,
and their acts all have realistic motivations and consequences. The clerk
protagonist of *Respected Sir* (1975), for example, gives up love, friendship, and his own personal life in a dogged attempt to achieve the hal-
lowed position of Director General. The narrator of *Zaabalawi* is not just
looking for a saintlike figure; he is desperately trying to find a cure for his
terminal illness after modern medicine has failed. Everyday life, not an
abstract or transcendental other world, is the arena in which these struggles are played out. For Mahfouz, *social* existence dramatizes spiritual fulfillment or its lack:

> But the tragedy of life is a complex, rather than a simple one. . . . When we
> think of [life] as social existence, we discover in it many artificial tragedies of
> man's own making, such as ignorance, poverty, exploitation, violence, brutality.
> . . . These are tragedies that can be remedied, and . . . in the act of remedying
> them we create civilization and progress. (*Atahaddath Ilaykum* [I Speak to You],
> 1977)

Not surprisingly, the story *Zaabalawi* has both social and religious significance. The elusive, otherworldly figure of Zaabalawi exists in a materialist society of ambitious bureaucrats, dilapidated houses, street vendors,
policemen, and bars. Zaabalawi's house still exists, although it is no longer
inhabited: "time had so eaten at the building that nothing was left of it
save an antiquated façade and a courtyard that . . . was being used as a
rubbish dump" (p. 2532). The narrator's illness likewise has a dual inter-

pretation. On the one hand, it is introduced as a physical ailment, a serious condition following a series of minor illnesses that were successfully treated. Most readers would associate this "illness for which no one possesses a remedy" with cancer, and they would find it quite comprehensible that the narrator seeks alternate treatment when medical science cannot help. Many cultures, too, have traditions in which one seeks out holy men to heal intractable illnesses. On the other hand, there are also intimations that the narrator's illness transcends physical definition. The ambiguity of the pain that afflicts him in mid-life (the point at which Dante's *Divine Comedy* begins); the repeated sense that only God (pp. 2534–35) or Zaabalawi will be able to cure him; the various hints that " 'suffering is part of the cure' " (p. 2535); and that Zaabalawi cures those who love him (p. 2538), all imply a larger explanation that has to do with spiritual crisis.

Reinforcing this shift from the physical to the transcendental plane is the narrator's progression from interviewing materialistic characters who have completely lost touch with Zaabalawi to others with different values who are closer to the saint. Here Mahfouz employs a sequence of representative figures—lawyer, bureaucrat, artist, and musician—like those in traditional allegories of the human condition (or, given another focus, in the Balzacian novel with its panorama of social types). If the narrator's quest can be read as the search of the soul for God, it also suggests a contemporary Egyptian society that is gradually losing touch with the faith of its ancestors. Some people remember Zaabalawi but don't know where to find him; many don't even know his name; and still others assert that the saint is a charlatan and advise the narrator to turn to modern science to cure his malady (p. 2533). The lawyer with whom the narrator first speaks used to practice in the religious courts, but "[h]e left the quarter ages ago" (p. 2532) and devoted himself to making money. It is a scathing portrait, especially in terms of traditional Arab values: Sheikh Qamar wears a Western lounge suit instead of the traditional *galabeya*, he receives clients (including "a beautiful woman with a most intoxicating perfume") in a luxuriously carpeted office with Western-style furniture, he makes it plain that his only interest in his visitors is whether or not they will be profitable, and he virtually dismisses the son of his former friend Sheikh Ali al-Tatawi. The lawyer has moved heart and soul into the modern age, as he makes clear in the verb tense of his description of Zaabalawi: "We used to regard him as a man of miracles" (p. 2532).

Other portraits fill a similar symbolic function. The local sheikh or district officer is more cooperative than the lawyer: he is only half-Westernized ("wearing a jacket over his striped galabeya," p. 2533), and once the narrator has ingratiated himself the sheikh helps to the best of his ability. Yet he also has grown away from Zaabalawi ("I myself haven't seen him for years, having been somewhat preoccupied with the cares of the world"), and his only help is a map of the physical quarters in which Zaabalawi might be found. Modern technical expertise is not the best route to locate an elusive figure who "may well be concealed among the beggars," among dervishes, or in cafés and mosques. Neither office-worker has the time for human relationships, as is indicated by their complete lack of hospitality when the petitioner arrives.

In contrast, both the calligrapher Hassanein—who is inscribing the name "Allah" when the narrator arrives—and the composer Sheikh Gad immediately receive the visitor "with unaffected gentleness" and "understanding and kindness" (p. 2535). Both men also know Zaabalawi well and have done their best work under his inspiration. The arts, it appears, lead one closer to the elusive saint than do commerce or technology, but they remain an indirect route and Zaabalawi is not actually *there*. Sheikh Gad gently reproves his disappointed visitor for complaining that his visit has been of no use, and he reminds him of the value of simple human relationships ("God forgive you . . . " p. 2535).

The climax at the Negma Bar is both appropriate and problematic. Given the allegorical overtones of Zaabalawi's description, it is not likely that the narrator will meet him in person until the moment of death. Only indirect acquaintance has been possible up to now, and this situation continues when the narrator wakes from a drunken stupor to find that Zaabalawi has been present while he slept. The paradisiacal vision that he enters under Zaabalawi's influence confirms earlier indications of the saint's holiness. Strangely enough, the description of the drinking bout reinforces the vision's otherworldly stature since the narrator must divest himself of earthly consciousness before he can enter the dream of "harmony between me and my inner self, and between the two of us and the world, everything being in its rightful place, without discord or distortion" (p. 2537). On a level of realistic description, the presentation of Mr. Wanas as a hardened drinker who insists that his visitor get drunk with him is a credible explanation for the narrator's losing consciousness. Indeed, Mahfouz believes that the reason the story is banned in Egypt is that he offended religious traditionalists by placing the saintly Zaabalawi in a bar (Islamic religion forbids drinking alcohol). Yet the stages of this intoxication also suggest the peeling-away of ties to "normal" consciousness that is associated with mystic vision. The wine has an initial fiery effect; with the second glass the narrator loses "all willpower"; with the third glass, he loses his memory, and with the fourth, "the future vanished." Mr. Wanas and the world around him are no longer recognizable; they become an abstract picture, "a mere meaningless series of colored planes." Ordinary perceptions of space and time have disappeared as the narrator succumbs to a vision of eternity. When the narrator returns to consciousness he is convinced that Zaabalawi exists and is the key to his cure. In the ending pages, the possibility of a material explanation still exists but it has receded into the background. "I have to find Zaabalawi" has taken on a much larger meaning than it had in the beginning.

Classroom Strategies

Zaabalawi can be taught in one class period. Students should have no difficulty with the plot or with the religious symbolism of the quest for

Zaabalawi. Compare, if appropriate, *Gilgamesh* (in volume A) or the *Divine Comedy* (in volume B) or the Arthurian romances of the Holy Grail. You may wish to point out the relationship of *Zaabalawi* with Gebelawi (or Jabalawi), and remind students that the story is found in a collection titled *God's World*.

What is more easily overlooked—at least on first reading—is the story's social criticism. Here it may be useful to talk a bit about Mahfouz as an Egyptian writer (the first writer in Arabic to win the Nobel Prize for Literature), and to remind students that despite the universal themes addressed in *Zaabalawi*, the story reflects a specific cultural setting. Located in Cairo, constantly referring to the context of Islamic religious tradition, it uses the interaction of characters to express a real social dilemma between different generations or ways of life in modern Egypt. No one will find the rude and unfriendly lawyer, Sheikh Qamar, an attractive figure. Your students may nonetheless accept his luxurious office with thick carpet and leather-upholstered furniture as merely signs of upward mobility, instead of an implied critique of Westernized bureaucracy. Examine with them such things as the use of Western or traditional Egyptian clothing to suggest opposing value systems: in contrast with the lounge-suited lawyer, for example, Hagg Wanas wears a silk galabeya and a carefully wrapped turban. (See "Backgrounds," fifth and sixth paragraphs.) The local sheikh comes in for similar criticism, for his gift of a map shows that he thinks in terms of technical expertise when such is clearly not the way to locate the saint. Neither the lawyer nor the local sheikh welcome casual visitors; for them, "business is business" and that governs their daily life. In contrast, the warmly hospitable artists (the calligrapher Hassanein and the composer Sheikh Gad) are much closer to Zaabalawi. (See "Backgrounds," seventh paragraph.)

It is possible that some students will be as disturbed as the Islamic fundamentalists to find that the narrator's vision of paradise is reached by drinking himself into unconsciousness in a bar. If so, you will want to examine with them the significant emphasis on the stages of the narrator's loss of consciousness. Everyday categories of time and space are successively demolished in order to reach a mystic vision, a process that may be compared with techniques of meditation to arrive at a special inner consciousness. (See also "Backgrounds," last paragraph.) On the level of realistic description, moreover, the bar scene makes a logical conclusion for a plot that starts with scenes of self-serving, calculating rationality and technical expertise and works towards an ecstatic vision in which rational consciousness is submerged.

Topics for Discussion

1. Discuss the picture given of Zaabalawi in the course of the story. How does this picture relate to concepts of religion, to society, and to modern society in particular?
2. Why does the narrator want or need to find Zaabalawi? What is "that illness for which no one possesses a remedy"?

3. Discuss the relationship of the lawyer Sheikh Qamar and the district officer to Zaabalawi. How do the artists, the calligrapher Hassanein and the composer Sheikh Gad, differ in their perception of him?

4. How are elements of realism and mysticism combined in *Zaabalawi*?

5. Describe the stages of the narrator's quest for Zaabalawi. Why does the quest culminate in the dream in the Negma Bar?

6. What kinds of people does the narrator encounter during his search for Zaabalawi? Are you surprised at the character of Hagg Wanas?

7. What relationship does Zaabalawi have to art? to commerce? to the police?

Comparative Perspectives

1. The four glasses of wine that intoxicate the narrator take on a richer significance if we see them as extensions of the imagery of the *Ghazals* of Ghalib and the poetic tradition of the Sufis. Examine the details of the dream in light of the recurrent references to wine and flowers, gardens and fountains in the mystical literature of Islam.

2. Mahfouz's protagonist seeks a cure for an unnamed malady (see the discussion of his illness in "Backgrounds"). Sickness drives many fictional characters to look for help. Compare the attitudes toward conventional medical remedies and other healing arts in stories like *The Death of Ivan Ilyich*, *The Barking*, and *Breast-Giver*. Why is the physician so often a compromised figure in works like these?

Further Reading

See also the reading suggestions in the anthology, pp. 2530–31.

Beard, Michael, and Adnan Haydar, eds. *Naguib Mahfouz: From Regional Fame to Global Recognition*. 1992. A valuable collection of eleven essays on themes, individual texts, and cultural contexts in Mahfouz's work. Bibliography.

Gordon, Haim. *Naguib Mahfouz's Egypt: Existential Themes in His Writings*. 1990. Considers existential identity for individuals and for Egyptian society throughout Mahfouz's work; literary analysis and anecdotes stemming from many interviews with Mahfouz. The appendix reviews works in English on Mahfouz (up to 1984). Gordon is an Israeli scholar who praises Mahfouz's universal themes but makes pointed criticisms of Egyptian society.

Mahfouz, Naguib. *Respected Sir*. Translated by Dr. Rasheed El-Enany 1986. Translator's introduction is particularly interesting on the connections between Mahfouz's themes and the evolution of his style.

Ostle, R. C., ed. *Studies in Modern Arabic Literature*. 1975. Hamdi Sakkout's "Najib Mahfuz's Short Stories" argues for the importance and separate identity of Mahfouz's stories; correlations drawn between selected stories and political events.

Aimé Césaire

Notebook of a Return to the Native Land

Backgrounds and Classroom Strategies

Aimé Césaire's *Notebook of a Return to the Native Land* has a reputation for being a difficult text, but ever since its enthusiastic reception by André Breton, the leader of the Surrealist movement, the poem has been recognized as a masterpiece of modern literature. Moreover, the fact that it has acquired classic status points not only to its historical interest and thematic significance but also its considerable level of literary achievement. It is a work that rewards critical attention. For one thing, there is an obvious relation between the charged utterances in the poem and the intensity of feeling that animates its theme of black racial consciousness and collective self-assertion. From a strictly literary point of view, the extended range of Césaire's poetic language and the complexity of his imagery make for a richness of texture that alerts us to the quality of imaginative life from which the poem derives its essential power.

These features contribute to the effectiveness of *Notebook* as a lyrical statement of the poets—that is, the poet-as-historical-subject's—existential condition. Césaire's peculiar idiom, deriving from his affiliation with Surrealism, makes many of the poem's important passages difficult to comprehend, and thus precludes immediate entry into the system of references that sustain the unfolding of the collective and personal drama the poem enacts. This difficulty must be reckoned with in teaching *Notebook*; students are likely to find the poem discouraging at first. Although the notes that accompany the text in the anthology go some way toward making the work accessible, students will require further guidance. Close attention to the text is necessary to understand the full meaning of the poem.

Notebook does not offer the linear progression of a narrative poem, but it is composed of a recognizable sequence of phases and episodes, often signaled by the refrain "At the end of the wee hours," that mark the ebb and flow of its movement from an engagement with a collective agony toward a vision of liberation and spiritual fulfillment. The poem opens, appropriately enough, with a panorama of the depressed condition of the West Indies. The graphic realism of this passage calls attention as much to the pathetic quality of the social situation that inspired the poem as to the poet's emotional involvement in his subject. This involvement becomes increasingly evident as the lyrical voice grows in intensity, and the poem's thematic references extend from the immediate situation to the background of Caribbean history. Here, the memory of slavery emerges as the poem's organizing experience: the recollection of the horrors of the

Middle Passage and of the degradations to which the transplanted African was subjected in the New World become central to the sentiment of historical grievance that propels the poem's most telling formulations and arresting metaphors.

The poet's personal predicament derives from his unhappy consciousness as an individual severed from a sense of self and community, a condition to which the tramway incident, recounted with such verve and bitter irony, serves as poignant testimony. The resentment brought about by his psychological and spiritual discomfort accounts for the impassioned accents of the poet's indictment of Europe and his rejection of the cultural and moral constraints of Western civilization, associated with colonial domination and a life-denying technocracy. The stances adopted by the poet in his revolt revolve around a truculent nihilism that owes much of its energy to the critical current of modern expression: to the satanism of Baudelaire and the aggressiveness of Rimbaud or Lautréamont, and ultimately to the revolutionary aesthetics of Breton and his fellow Surrealists.

The passages in which the theme of revolt is articulated form the central section of the poem. This theme culminates, a little more than halfway through the text, in the celebrated proclamation of négritude in terms of a triumphant messianism, which is presented through an image of a totemic tree conflated with the Christian cross: "my negritude is not a stone, its deafness hurled against the clamor of / the day. . . . it takes root in the red flesh of the soil / it takes root in the ardent flesh of the sky / it breaks through the opaque prostration with its upright patience" (lines 813–20). This passage marks the high point of the poem, which thereafter moves resolutely toward the apprehension of an order of reality that transcends the contingencies of history. The poem's references to concrete life henceforth evoke a moral resource that triumphs over the vicissitudes of a limited earthly experience. Its ritualistic tenor, intimated in isolated passages earlier, becomes intensified so that the poem comes to focus upon the theme of rebirth as a condition for the poet's integration into the universe.

The summary of the poem offered above suggests a thematic framework for close readings of selected passages that reveal their place in the overall structure of the poem. The extended homage to Toussaint L'Ouverture (lines 341–74) is an obvious choice for such an exercise, as it offers the possibility of observing the relation between theme and language in Césaire's poem. In its specific reference to the historical background of the Haitian revolution whose hero the passage celebrates, the homage is contextually bound to the rest of the poem, but it stands out as an independent unit of poetic expression that merits special attention. Similarly, the passage in which an uprising on board a slave ship is reenacted (lines 660–68) deserves scrunity for its dramatic quality and may be compared to Herman Melville's *Benito Cereno* in order to clarify the symbolic import of Césaire's text. Students will benefit from this exercise in *explication de texte*, which will make clear to them that the language of *Notebook* is far from arbitrary or gratuitous, that the words of the poem make up a unique structure of expression and, in so doing, create significance.

Césaire's style and diction proceed from a conscious engagement with his means of expression—a determined reconversion of language to his ideological and imaginative purpose. The abundant lexicon and the often formal diction, along with the recondite allusions and ironic reversals, provide a rhetorical foundation for a poetic idiom marked by remarkably compact thought and, in particular, especially dense imagery. It is the highly allusive character of the imagery that accounts for the hermeticism of Césaire's poetic diction. This hermeticism is more apparent than real, however, and requires no more than focused analysis to be dispelled. Indeed, as with the rest of Césaire's poetry, Notebook derives much of its coherence from the associative pattern of its imagery. Thus the theme of social and metaphysical revolt is sustained through a well-defined scheme of violent images drawn from the poet's Caribbean environment and its fauna and flora. The most prominent element of this scheme is that of turbulence in nature, represented by the image of the volcano. This theme is reinforced by the animal imagery and numerous references to toxic plants, a symbolism of aggression that informs the poem's agitated movement. The values of opposition elaborated by this symbolism are constantly balanced by their positive equivalents, so that, for instance, Césaire also employs vegetal imagery in its more conventional connotation, to register the cycle of growth in nature. Césaire's imagery derives its full import from the poet's effort to redirect the suggestive potential of language toward his vision of universal renewal.

The various aspects of the poem touched upon here indicate the thematic range of the poem and the resources Césaire brings to the multiple experiences it represents. As a protest poem, Notebook is the vehicle of Césaire's advocacy, in political and social terms, of a collective cause. Its Caribbean emphasis suggests that it may be read as a nationalist work. The vehemence of its language is likely to bewilder a younger generation of readers, who may need to have the historical and social context of its inspiration recalled for them. Euzhan Palcy's film Sugar Cane Alley will prove especially helpful in this respect. The film depicts the social situation in Martinique during a period roughly equivalent to that covered in Notebook and thus represents an admirable visual complement to Césaire's poem. It may also be useful to relate the poem to the struggle for civil rights in the United States, as presented in the PBS documentary Eyes on the Prize.

It is perhaps not too much to affirm that the psychological significance of the poem ultimately takes precedence over the political and ideological. The presiding idea and dominant theme of the poem are related to the poet's project of self-reconstruction. Notebook may thus be read as a poem of introspection, in which the native land of the title emerges as a central reference to the poet's quest for authentic selfhood. His concern with moral and spiritual values, and even his prophetic vision, can be seen, in the final analysis, to be bound up with the impulse toward the recovery of an essential humanity.

Topics for Discussion and Writing

1. *Notebook* as an example of "resistance literature"; the tension between aesthetics and commitment.
2. Césaire and Surrealism. (Consider here the antecedents in post-Romantic French poetry).

Comparative Perspectives

1. Compare Césaire's *Notebook* and another long poem of introspection in the anthology: for example, Eliot's *The Waste Land*.
2. Césaire's harrowing vision of his "inert town" gradually gives way to a short autobiographical interlude of Christmas memories. How joyful is this respite as seen retrospectively? What effect do you think Césaire creates by inserting the Greek phrases central to the Christian rite ("KYRIE ELEISON . . . LEISON . . . LEISON")? Christmas memories are also pivotal in the *Narrative of the Life of Frederick Douglass, An American Slave*. Compare the grown writer's perceptions of the role religion played in permitting or even fostering oppression and humiliation in their communities.
3. *Notebook of a Return to the Native Land* describes a complicated journey of the poet's imagination. Chart the stops along the way, in which Césaire develops a "special geography" that transforms his loathing for his small Antillean town as he sees how it came to be and where its true roots lie. Compare the motif of the mental "return" from a kind of exile to some of the other travels recorded in this volume, in *Pedro Páramo* or *Omeros* or, going further afield, Candide's circuitous route to the garden in Constantinople or Bashō's refining pilgrimage.

Further Reading

See also the reading suggestions in the anthology, p. 2542.

Césaire, Aimé. *Cahier d'un retour au pays natal*. Edited, with introduction commentary, and notes, by Abiola Irele. 1994. This edition, which contains a comprehensive bibliography on Aimé Césaire, is intended as a complete working guide to the poem. Although the editorial matter, in English, is keyed to the French text, the edition should prove useful for studying the poem in the English translation printed in the anthology.

———. *Discourse on Colonialism*. Translated by Joan Pinkham. 1972. Notable for its polemical denunciation of European colonialism and its expression of a determined moral vision.

Kesteloot, Lilyane. *Black Writers in French*. Translated by Ellen Conroy Kennedy. 1991. An excellent historical and critical review of black literature in French, the study contains many passages devoted to Césaire's poetry in general and *Notebook* in particular.

ALBERT CAMUS

The Guest

Backgrounds

Camus is known as the great "moralist" of twentieth-century French letters: "moralist" in a very special French sense that describes a philosophical writer who examines the everyday ethical and moral implications of what it means to be human. Despite the technical brilliance of his work in novels, plays, short stories, and essays, Camus is usually remembered first for his pictures of human beings struggling to understand themselves and the critical circumstances in which they exist. Two elements complement each other in his moral vision: the consciousness of the "absurd" (the discrepancy between our desire for meaning and the actual non-sense of material reality), and a subsequent voluntary "engagement" or devotion to liberty and justice "as if" the world made sense. From the starkly brilliant images of *The Stranger* to the labyrinthine half-dialogue of *The Fall*, Camus's fiction asserts an aesthetic dimension that goes far beyond the philosophical and political frameworks often chosen to discuss it. Nonetheless, his enormous popularity with students continues to be based on his moral insight, a context in which they find him vital and even ennobling.

The Guest is one of Camus's most successful short stories and contains a number of ideas that obsessed him in all his work. Daru lives alone in a vast landscape that suggests a total physical and moral isolation. In many ways, it is similar to Beckett's empty landscapes—absurd, stony, inimical to man—but, unlike Beckett's, it is strikingly beautiful. It is, in any case, the only landscape in which Daru does not feel himself an exile. But into this landscape come men, with their "rotten spite, their tireless hates, their blood lust," their political and cultural ties and assumptions. It is these ties that cause Daru the difficulty he must confront in the story.

Balducci brings the Arab to Daru on the assumption that since Daru is European he will complete the process of justice set out by Europeans for Arab offenders. The attitude of the *gendarme* toward Daru is one of condescension, the kind of condescension that comes with assumed cultural bonds. Balducci calls Daru "son" and "kid," and simply commands the schoolteacher to act as desired: "You must take him to Tinguit tomorrow before the day is over" (p. 2576). Daru is clearly sympathetic to the natives of his area (he teaches them, speaks the language, distributes food during the drought, and will treat the Arab as a guest), and it is not his job to deal with prisoners. But, as Balducci says, "If there's an uprising, no one is safe, we're all in the same boat" (p. 2577). His demands of Daru, however friendly, are based on the assumption that Daru will act as a European, that he is obliged to accept the prisoner because cultural bonds are stronger than any individual objections Daru may reasonably have. And, when it comes down to it, Daru *is* obliged, he *is* a European: the four rivers of France on the map in his schoolroom are the appropriate backdrop for his actions as well as his moral quandary. Balducci sees his world as *us* and *them*, and so does Daru ("Is he against us?" [p. 2576]), although his feelings about *them* are mitigated by his sympathies and his own desire not to be complicit in taking action against them.

When Daru tells Balducci that he will have no part in turning in the Arab, it is not because he thinks the Arab has been unjustly treated (he is, apparently, guilty of a murder), but because Daru does want to act in a way that will appear to be *for* the Europeans and *against* the Arabs. Essentially, Daru doesn't want to have to commit himself to any course of action, since any such course will suggest to others that he has political sympathies that he does not, in fact, have.

Daru's situation is impossible: though he hopes to evade misunderstanding, he is bound to be misunderstood no matter which option he chooses. The world he lives in guarantees it. Daru attempts to make a choice *not* to do anything, to let the Arab choose freedom or prison for himself; Daru wants to wash his hands of complicity one way or the other. But a man living in a world of "rotten spite" and undeniable allegiances must discover that even not choosing constitutes a choice. Daru has responsibility for the Arab's fate because of his birth and circumstance. He cannot disclaim it.

The end of the story is usually interpreted as an unfortunate misunderstanding, but this interpretation does not do justice to the complexity of Camus's tale. Those who scrawled "You handed over our brother. You will pay for this" (p. 2582) understand Daru perfectly well, though they do not, and cannot, fully appreciate his position. What they understand is that Daru handed over their brother when Daru was born—that the message is written on the map of France confirms why they feel as they do. Daru's solitariness at the end of the story, then, is the solitariness of a man trapped in a universe in which no act is without its moral implications and in which there is no way to elude complicity.

Daru's position may be impossible, as is the Arab's, but this does not mean that he cannot treat the prisoner well as long as the Arab is his guest. Something like brotherhood and a "strange alliance" is established between them, but Daru must recognize that he lives in a world in which brotherhood can simultaneously mean betrayal. Still, the brotherhood developed between Daru and the Arab is necessary and heroic. However small a gesture, it is perhaps all that can be done; like the title character of Camus's essay *The Myth of Sisyphus* one must willingly—even joyously—push the boulder up the mountain knowing full well that it will roll back down again.

Camus was born to European parents in Algeria, then a colony of France, and lived and worked there exclusively until he was twenty-seven. Friends and family continued to live in Algeria throughout his life. His interest and concern in the Algerian Question, as it was then called, are perfectly understandable. What was not understandable to many French intellectuals, including Jean-Paul Sartre (with whom Camus had had a spectacular public quarrel in 1952) and Simone de Beauvoir, was Camus's consistent call for tolerance and understanding, and his refusal to back wholeheartedly any movement that called either for violent rebellion or the restriction of individual freedoms. During the Algerian conflict, Camus was hardly silent—in 1956 he flew to Algiers in order to address both French and Moslem citizens, although he was constantly under threat of his life—but he adopted the comparatively safe position of concentrating on the effort to spare innocent civilians: "Truce until it is time for solutions, truce to the massacre of civilians, on one side and the other!" Camus, like Daru, clearly hated having to be put in the position of taking sides. And because he was without question the most powerful Algerian-born voice capable of being heard in France, his position carried with it enormous responsibilities—responsibilities that both those on the Left and those on the Right felt he was shirking or misusing. *The Guest* appears to be, in part at least, an attempt to express the personal difficulties he felt in judging the Algerian situation.

Camus often insisted that he was not an existentialist, and he and Sartre were reportedly surprised, and sometimes disturbed (especially after 1952), at seeing their names constantly linked. At one point they jokingly agreed to sign a statement claiming that neither could be held responsible for the debts incurred by the other.

Classroom Strategies

The Guest is teachable in one class period and can be linked with a number of other texts in which characters must make difficult moral choices: *Medea, Antigone, Hamlet, Billy Budd* (Captain Vere).

The major problem that students will have with *The Guest* is selling the story short. Daru's "quiet heroism" is evident, so students will tend to see him as a quiet hero, severely misunderstood and unjustly accused by the Arab rebels at the end of the story. They will compare him with Balducci, clearly a man involved—though not happily—in a master/slave relationship with his prisoner, and find him heroic in comparison. It is more difficult to see him as heroic when we realize that his heroism is not nearly enough. He goes far enough with Balducci to satisfy the letter of the law and far enough with the Arab to satisfy the demands of his sympathies. He is not heroic because he sets the prisoner free. In the first place, he doesn't free him—he only gives the Arab the chance to take his freedom. Second, the Arab's crime is not a political crime—it is a murder, which Daru (as well as Balducci) finds repellent; it is much to Camus's credit that he has not made the prisoner's guilt or innocence an issue. Third, he is complicit, whether he likes it or not, in the system that, perhaps justly, has ensnared the prisoner, but that also, perhaps unjustly, has also ensnared the prisoner's countrymen. Daru is heroic not through heroic action, but by suffering the inevitable fate that awaits human beings in an absurd universe—and doing it with civility, sympathy, and the desire to be nice.

Students will not always understand why the prisoner does not escape during the night, or why he chooses the road to prison rather than freedom at the end of the story. One reason is given in the headnote: the "host's humane hospitality has placed a new burden and reciprocal responsibility on his guest" (p. 2573). There are, however, other possibilities. One has its basis in the master/slave relationship that even a night of humane treatment cannot erase: the Arab simply cannot believe that a European *really* means to set him free. We must remember, as the prisoner no doubt remembers, that Daru still has his gun, just as he still has the power to give or deny freedom at a whim. We know, but the prisoner does not, that Daru is uneasy with such power; that he has it whether he wants it or not is, however, undeniable. Teachers may find their position in the classroom analogous to Daru's position. We do not always want the power we have; we may even seek to diminish or deny it. But we give A's and F's and Incompletes, and as long as we stand in front of the classroom we are collaborators in a structure of evaluation that is impossible to disregard.

Another plausible reading is that the prisoner takes the road toward prison because prison is precisely what he deserves. He is, after all, a murderer. If Daru, in his role as a teacher, is interested in "conveying to a fellow human being the freedom of action, which all people require" (from the headnote, p. 2573), the Arab may very well be capable of learning it. To freely choose to be punished for a crime he has committed is just as admirable, and perhaps more admirable, than eluding the punishment that is due him.

Topics for Discussion and Writing

1. Why does Camus set the story on a remote outpost in Algeria, just after a freak snow has isolated it even more profoundly than usual? How does Camus use descriptions of the landscape to confirm Daru's isolation? Do the descriptions of the landscape suggest its beauty? Why?

   [See "Backgrounds" for discussion.]

2. What is the point of Balducci's rather long conversation with Daru? Why does Balducci think he can leave the prisoner with Daru? Why does Daru keep him? Why does Daru say he will not take him to prison? What is Balducci's attitude about this?

   [See the third, fourth, and fifth paragraphs of "Backgrounds" and the third paragraph of "Classroom Strategies" for discussion.]

3. Why does Daru give the Arab the opportunity to escape? Why does he choose not to escape? Why does he choose not to take the road to the Arab lands at the end of the story?

   [See the fourth and fifth paragraphs of "Backgrounds" and the fourth and fifth paragraph of "Classroom Strategies" for discussion.]

4. In what ways is the Arab treated as a guest by Daru? In what ways is Daru a guest in Algeria?

   [See the seventh paragraph of "Backgrounds" for discussion.]

5. How can this story be seen as an expression of Camus's personal position on the Algerian Question?
   [See the eighth paragraph of "Backgrounds" for discussion.]

Comparative Perspectives

1. Daru is frustrated by the Arab's reluctance to seize the opportunity
   he gives him to escape. Compare Candide's frequent escapes in
   Voltaire's satire, the deer mother's instructions about escape in *The
   Boy and the Deer,* Isa's repeated escapes in *The American School,* or
   the impossibility of escape in *In Camera.* What kinds of cultural situations produce narratives in which chase and escape figure so
   prominently? What kinds of personality traits are required for a successful escape? What accounts for the tonal differences in the way
   escape is treated in each of these works?
2. Camus's story of Algeria and A. B. Yehoshua's *Facing the Forests*
   each revolve around a dilemma faced by an intellectual alone in a
   room, delegated to guard against the Arabs whose territory he is in-
   habiting. Compare the kinds of responsibility with which these intellectuals are charged and the different ways in which they defy
   their orders. How may these stories reflect their creators's conceptions of the moral efficacy of the scholar in an immoral political situation? How is each story a product of a particular philosophical
   disposition as well as of a specific political moment?

Further Reading

See also the reading suggestions in the anthology, p. 2573.

Amoia, Alba della Fazia. *Albert Camus.* 1989. An introductory study with a
short biography and discussion of individual works organized by genre.

Bloom, Harold. *Albert Camus.* 1989. A selection of critical essays.

Cruickshank, John. *Albert Camus and the Literature of Revolt.* 1959.
Reprinted 1978. A useful general study.

Ellison, David R. *Understanding Albert Camus.* 1990. A perceptive, readable overview of Camus's work that describes individual works (*The
Guest,* pp. 194–99) and interprets according to structure, historical
context, and themes.

Sprintzen, David. *Camus, a Critical Examination.* 1988.

Suther, Judith D., ed. *Essays on Camus's* Exile and the Kingdom. 1980.
Contains "The Symbolic Decor of 'The Guest' " by Paul A. Fortier and
Joseph G. Morello, pp. 203–15.

Thody, Philip. *Albert Camus.* 1957. A short but cogent study of the works,
including a discussion of *The Guest.*

KOJIMA NOBUO

The American School

Backgrounds

Students will probably need a short history lesson before you can effectively begin discussing Nobuo's brilliant dissection of the Japanese psyche in the aftermath of a disastrous war. You will want to make sure that they know who fought whom in Asia in World War II. Remind (inform?) them that the war in Europe came to an end in April 1945, while the war in Asia continued. In order to bring hostilities to a halt, in August of that year the United States dropped atom bombs on Hiroshima and Nagasaki, with devastating results. The defeated Japanese people were hungry and humiliated. In *The American School*, Kojima manages a difficult balancing act. As a military veteran, he could not have been immune to the feelings of resentment that still, to this day, persist in Japan. As an observer of his own society, however, he demonstrates a wry awareness of the kinds of behavior that made it important for the United States to foster a new culture through the Occupation, which lasted from 1945 to 1952. Be sure that the class reads the discussion of the American Army of Occupation's role in the headnote to Kojima's story: it is important to stress the benign motives of the American occupation, which resulted in the adoption of a new Constitution and a democratic form of government. Kojima's story, published in 1954, is set in 1948, as we learn at the end of the second paragraph.

In choosing language teaching as the subject of this story, Kojima not only reflects his personal background and experience. Inextricably linked to one's sense of identity, language is deeply tied to the self. The conquering Americans make little effort to learn the language of the people whose country they temporarily inhabit. (Especially in a world literature course, a discussion of the monolinguistic complacency demonstrated by the Americans in *The American School* and the transformations currently at work in an increasingly multicultural society would be of great interest.) Kojima's story, however, deals primarily with the way their attitudes toward language reveal the personalities of his central characters. Writing for his home audience, he is interested in the dynamics of Japanese social relations and the ways in which the injection of American power and wealth ironically serves to bring out Japanese characteristics even more emphatically than would be the case had the Japanese been left to their own devices. In this context, the ability to speak English well complicates one's sense of nationality and belonging. Isa, the beleaguered hero of Kojima's story, has a profound insight: "It is foolish for Japanese to speak this language like foreigners. If they do, it makes them foreigners, too. And that is a real disgrace" (p. 2596).

The Japanese devotion to group identity is sketched out at the very beginning of the story: everyone is on time (if not early), as ordered. Within the group, nevertheless, certain personalities stand out. For the Japanese reader, the combative Yamada would probably have been the easiest character to understand. He regards language as a tool of aggression, a continuation of war by other means. Reflecting on the contrast between the way American and Chinese prisoners reacted to his grim ministrations, Yamada displays the racial pride that fuels his actions throughout: the Yanks lack "what you might call Oriental philosophy" (p. 2592). Michiko, who emerges as the normative figure in Kojima's satire, speaks a fluent, unaccented English, but already marked as the only woman in the group, she does not want to draw attention to herself or her good English. Isa is the subtlest of the three main figures, the ineffectual but oddly appealing male protagonist for which Kojima's fiction is particularly well known. He is certified to teach English, yet he has come to grief when required to act as an interpreter for the American election observers. The funniest scenes in this very funny story are those in which he desperately tries to evade anyone who threatens to engage him in an English conversation.

The goal of the American Occupation of Japan was to educate a nation. For the American student, *The American School*'s greatest interest may lie in the way it contrasts the cultures of America and Japan by illustrating their very different educational philosophies. Methods of language instruction reveal a great deal about a society. The American system emphasizes fluency; small classes ("the ideal is seven-*teen*," p. 2601) encourage individuality and self-expression. The Japanese system emphasizes accuracy and efficiency; high enrollments ("seven-*ty*") discourage efforts to let individual students practice speaking the language. The clever and subversive cartoon drawings of the visitors quickly sketched by the American students in their art class exemplify the American style; Yamada fails to see the humor. Not only has he personally been insulted by their caricatures, but he also has no appreciation of the students' capacity for free-form and spontaneous performance. Yet the Japanese English teachers have a command of English grammar that appears to elude the native American speakers.

Kojima's portrait of Yamada causes us to rethink the impact of the American Occupation. His toadying only reaps contempt; nevertheless, his martial mode has also been adopted by the Americans. Why must the Japanese teachers walk four miles each way along an asphalt road to reach their destination, as if they were "a chain gang" (p. 2589)? The American school toward which they march is in itself an affront to Japanese sensibilities, since the U.S. Army base is a totally self-contained community. The children of the occupying force are sheltered from any contact with the people in whose land they are quartered; adding insult to injury, we learn that Japanese funds paid for the construction of the school. Yet the principal complains about its shortcomings. The terrible sense of humiliation felt by the Japanese teachers when they contemplate the spacious compound should be noted and discussed.

William's dry reference to "The old Kamikaze spirit" at the story's conclusion indicates how difficult it is to return to normal relations after years of war. The Americans will not easily forget the ferocious dedication with which their Japanese adversaries forestalled the ending of a war that they knew they could not win. Some of your students will probably be able to explain what the Kamikaze pilots did, but a full explication of the term will be useful. The word literally means "divine wind," implying a sacred mission on the part of the solo pilots who dropped from the sky on enemy targets, crashing bomb-filled planes that simultaneously destroyed them and their carefully selected targets. Similar acts of self-immolation continue to occur in other parts of the globe, which may provide for your students a frame of reference to assist them in analyzing the "heavy irony" of the principal's comment that "was lost on Yamada, who took . . . it as a compliment" (p. 2606). Whether it was his original intention or not, Kojima's story today forces his readers to reflect that much depends in life on where one stands.

Standing, rather than flying or walking, is the posture that Yamada's antagonist, the shy Isa, prefers. The significance of shoes in *The American School* deserves a great deal of discussion. Told "to dress impeccably" (p. 2588), the Japanese English teachers also are informed that they will have to walk eight miles in the course of their day. These instructions seem internally inconsistent; Michiko wears a suit, a hat, and high heels, but she has had the foresight to pack a pair of sneakers for the walk. Shoes, of course, are expensive, and it should be remembered that they are dispensable items in traditional Japanese society; one removes them before entering a house. In borrowing a pair of leather shoes, Isa has violated some part of his identity and soon finds himself in pain as the miles stretch out before him. When he is not running away from the Negro soldier who knows that he cannot speak English, Isa is desperately trying to protect his feet. With the relentless logic of comedy, after trying to walk barefoot, Isa finds himself picked up in a jeep by this very officer.

Kojima explores the difficult topic of national and racial character with considerable shrewdness in *The American School*. If Yamada feels "pride of race" (p. 2597, a term rather sadly used by Isa as he looks at the splendiferous Miss Emily, whose features "spoke of an ample diet, material well-being"), the black soldier is sensitive to every hint of a racial slur. His initial encounter with Isa had led him to suspect "overtones of a personal animus against himself" (p. 2595) and indeed, as Isa watched the soldier coming after him, he thought the Negro soldier's "beard contributed an incongruously civilized air" (p. 2587). Asserting his own pride, the soldier enjoys the opportunity to take "a little revenge" for their earlier contretemps; presumably in an unconsious play on stereotypical African-American behavior, the soldier threatens Isa with a toy gun and hums a jazz tune as he drives him to the school. Kojima manages to make fun of the foibles of his American characters even as he demonstrates their essentially good intentions. Attracted by the well-spoken and personable Michiko, soldiers give her chocolate and cheese, lavishing these gifts of affluence that became the signature gesture of American troops abroad. Acutely aware that her peers must be monitoring her every move, Michiko observes social propriety by giving Isa one can of cheese before she will take the other for herself; when she receives two bars of chocolate, she breaks one up to share with others, carefully omitting Isa the second time around.

The contrast with Miss Emily, the English teacher who smokes behind closed doors, could not be more marked. If Michiko wants to avoid being noticed, Emily has a disconcerting habit of popping up just when she seems to have left the scene. She absolutely terrifies Isa with her podiatric efforts on his behalf. It is typical of Kojima's satire that the one American soldier who emerges as an individual is a Negro and the only teacher to do the same is "a beautiful tall lady of a type one often sees in American movies" (p. 2596).

Deriving much of its humor from the clash of these stereotyped figures, *The American School* also exploits the purest forms of physical comedy. The juxtaposition of the small man and the buxom female appears to be a universal a source of laughter, as is the triumph of the little man beset by a bully. The uproarious finale that precipitates the reference to Kamikazes comes about because of the awkwardness felt by the Japanese teachers in alien surroundings. Michiko seems both to pity and admire Isa. She is reminded by Isa's stubborn resistance to her help of her dead husband's departure for the war, when, in the long march to the station, he doggedly refused to look at her or say goodbye properly. Perhaps because at some level she identifies with Isa and his cautious desire to shrink from notice, she has made up her mind to ask him to lend her a pair of chopsticks, the "missing article" that you will need to be sure your students can identify. Only upon reflection does one realize what desperation this need to share the most intimate of utensils must reflect.

Back in her high-heeled shoes, Michiko furtively reaches for the chopsticks, but Isa has moved before she can securely take the package from him. In a sequence of movements out of ancient stage comedy (be it Kyogen or Plautus), this self-possessed woman trips and falls. A commotion follows, and Yamada proffers the ludicrous explanation that Isa's and Michiko's zeal to present a demonstration class had led to Michiko's collapse: "It all proceeded from their pedagogical dedication" (p. 2606). Yamada's plan to trap Isa into showing that Japanese language teachers teach English better than Americans is foiled. At the end of the story, he is on the run and Isa trails behind, isolated still, but victorious. He has not compromised his essential Japanese soul. His hatred for the English language has been turned by Kojima into a mark of distinction and his separation from the group into a paradoxical confirmation of his integrity in a society that prizes conformity.

Topics for Discussion and Writing

1. Japan was an occupied country after its defeat in World War II. What tone does Kojima take toward the Allied Forces in *The American School*?

2. How do the relationships of the Japanese English teachers reflect the workings of Japanese society in microcosm? What continuities

between their behavior in war and peace does *The American School* suggest?

3. What is a forced march? Why do the Japanese teachers have to walk to the American compound?
4. How do gender relations complicate the problems in this story? How does Isa regard Michiko? How does Yamada? How would you characterize the way the American schoolteacher, "Miss Emily," is portrayed here?
5. What is "the missing article" that Michiko searches for with such diligence? What is its significance in the story?

Comparative Perspectives

1. "Racial" characteristics and cultural difference preoccupy the Japanese teachers of English in *The American School*. Why is Isa so intimidated by his contact with the Negro soldier? Why is so much emphasis placed on the statuesque glamor (and bad grammar) of Miss Emily? What is the "homely artifact of their native land" that Michiko borrows from Isa? Compare the attitudes toward culture and race in Tanizaki's *In Praise of Shadows*, Darío's *To Roosevelt*, or Walcott's poems.
2. *The American School* explores the ways in which human beings use language as a weapon. Note the frequency with which the aggressive Yamada in particular uses metaphors of war and the martial arts when he insists on demonstrating his command of English. Compare Kojima's essentially comic vision of dueling teachers with other writers's explorations of the aggressive uses of language.
   [Interesting choices include *Gulliver's Travels*, *Narrative of the Life of Frederick Douglass*, *Endgame*, or *Facing the Forests*.]

Further Reading

See also the reading suggestions in the anthology, pp. 2584–85.

Beasley, W. G. *The Rise of Modern Japan.* 1990.

Keene, Donald. *Dawn to the West: Japanese Literature in the Modern Era.* Volume 1: *Fiction.* Volume 2: *Poetry, Drama, Criticism.* 1984.

Lewell, John. *Modern Japanese Novelists: A Biographical Dictionary.* 1993.

Rogers, Lawrence. "Long Belts, Thin Men: The Short Stories of Kojima Nobuo." *Japan Quarterly* 41 (Jan./Mar. 1994), pp. 77–88.

Sansom, George B. *The Western World and Japan.* 1949.

BERNARD DADIÉ

Backgrounds

These tales illustrates how a modern sensibility can both revive and invigorate a traditional form. Dadié is a self-conscious literary artist. An admirer of Victor Hugo and Guy de Maupassant, he cites in particular his appreciation of de Maupassant's stories "because of their structure, their depth of meaning, and their form." At the same time, in *The Black Cloth* he honors his primary inspiration, the rich heritage of the African *griots*, with a wealth of the devices that typify oral narrative. As described in the headnote, these include the integration of songs, repetition, and onomatopoetic effects. Thematic motifs also provide connections among our three selections, which, like so many examples of folklore, involve journeys to strange lands and impossible tasks that challenge the protagonists to make a leap of faith if they are to succeed.

THE MIRROR OF DEARTH

This story opens with a powerful assertion, rather than the formulaic "Once upon a time" used in *The Black Cloth*. With his "psst!" the narrator immediately makes his listeners complicit with him. The audience is directly addressed, establishing the possibility for dialogue that will be capitalized on in the tantalizing final sentence. In between, Kacou Ananze, the trickster spider whose self-admiration gets him into trouble, takes center stage. Anticipating that the audience will express shock when Kacou Ananze decides to do the one thing he knows he must not do— that is, look in the eponymous mirror—the narrator reminds us that we are all "in the same boat and just as curious." (If we have been exposed to biblical instruction, as has Dadié, a Christian, surely we will notice a link here to the story of Eden.)

The story proper begins after several paragraphs about Kacou Ananze, with the announcement of a great famine "in the village." The scale will become greatly enlarged as the tale develops. The famine begins to spread and everyone looks in vain for a scapegoat to blame. Ever the canny Kacou Ananze has to take up fishing as a means to feed himself. At first, this activity only deepens our understanding of the calamity; a sequence of long, bravura descriptive paragraphs reminds us of the centrality of water in a hot climate and the consequent personification of the rivers and lagoons, which are also struggling to survive. Dadié raises the rhetorical stakes with a brilliant alternation of the orotund and the straightforward. Sentences become shorter, expressing increasing desperation: "the float still did not budge." Finally, Kacou Ananze catches a pathetic little fish, and then tension mounts. Only by having compassion for the baby fish and allowing it to live, despite his own hunger, will Kacou Ananze thrive. By trusting the tiny fish, suddenly grown to enormous size, and taking the prescribed leap from a tall tree, Kacou Ananze suddenly finds himself in an urban utopia, an "Eldorado" where he grows rich and fat and becomes the minister of a queen who warns him of one taboo. That, of course, is never to look in the mirror of dearth. And this is what he inevitably does, so that he finds himself once again fishing in a time of famine. The second time he encounters the fish, no miraculous transformation recurs.

What is the moral of this tale? Your students will have little trouble discussing its meaning. But Dadié's ending makes it clear that more than simple lessons may be learned from this venture into storytelling. Kacou Ananze does not die, but we hear no more about this episode. "And like all lies, it is through you that mine will be thrown out to sea, to roam the world over. . . . " We are now, perhaps, in the position of Kacou Ananze, needing to trust the teller and take a metaphysical leap by spreading the truth of this fiction if we are to survive.

THE BLACK CLOTH

This story begins in classic fairy tale fashion, but those who are used to laundered versions of this literature may be surprised by its grim introduction to Aiwa's "Calvary." The high incidence of death in childbirth has always been behind the emphasis on orphans in these stories for children, but as in the description of famine in *The Mirror of Dearth,* Dadie seems especially frank about the pain of existence in general, and in Africa in particular. Aiwa's stepmother has "coals in the heart," and she sets an appropriately dark task for the beautiful, smiling child whose gentle manner is an affront to this competetive foster parent, a fixture of stories like *Cinderella* and *Snow White* that students will easily recognize. Her charge to her suffering stepdaughter—to wash a black linen cloth to white—seems a symbolic challenge. How can one cool the fire of those black coals and transform a jealous heart?

Aiwa sets off on a journey through strange lands; at each watering place, she sings to her mother, who fails to materialize. Presumably this is because the first three water sources exist in settings filled with vitality. The first is a river in a normal world, surrounded by fish and flowers. This water will not wet her cloth, and so Aiwa moves further away from normal life, into a frightening scene where death is awaited by a vulture. But well-organized ants are at work and a huge silk-cotton tree harbors clear water, which also fails to wet her cloth. Aiwa then travels for countless months across territories with fruit and dew that sustain her, next arriving in a village where chimpanzees give her access to a spring. Here, too, the cloth remains dry.

The final "truly strange place" is the land of the dead: as in *The Mirror of Dearth,* the searcher takes a leap into salvation. At the foot of the ancestral banana tree of African legend, Aiwa finally finds water that will wet the cloth. Once again, she sings to her mother, and here, in the land where her mother now lodges, Aiwa receives the maternal care of which she has been deprived. Significantly, the black cloth cannot be scrubbed clean; her stepmother's cruel heart cannot be softened. Instead, her mother hands her a white cloth that is substituted for the stepmother's linen.

What is the moral here? For Africans, it is imperative to honor one's ancestors. Boundaries between life and death are porous. Trees and rivers symbolize and embody the links between generations and the environment that sustains life. The terrified stepmother realizes that Aiwa has been helped by the hand of the dead, a power beyond the reach of her malevolence. At last, Aiwa has something to smile about.

The Hunter and the Boa

This tale begins with another scene of poverty and deprivation. As it develops, Dadié introduces another version of the little fish in *The Mirror of Dearth*. Like Kacou Ananze, if he is to survive, the hunter must forego instant gratification and trust the promise of a creature of a lesser order. The division between the human and the animal realms comes into play here, with the animals demonstrating clear superiority to the self-absorbed hunter and his material concerns.

> "If I release you, will you harm me?"
> "Since when have the bush animals behaved like you?"
> (p. 2617)

In time, the hunter's domesticated animals observe his behavior as he enjoys the riches made available to him by releasing the boa from his grasp, noting that the once desperate man turns into an oppressor of other men as he gains in power. After twenty years, however, a new dilemma echoes the situation of Kacou Ananze. The hunter's luck has run out. Famine returns. Even the traps that the hunter regards as his instruments have a life of their own, and in failing to catch any food, they have in a sense rebelled against him.

The boa had given the hunter two gourds; upon throwing the first to the ground, he has been rewarded with power and plenty. The second, which he retains, has made it possible for him to understand the language of animals, a valuable skill that allows him to anticipate and profit from events to come (he has insider information). When disaster looms, the hunter learns from listening to his animals' conversation that he can survive only if he returns the remaining gourd. He has to decide whether a long but impoverished future is worth more than the shorter span on earth that he has now completed and in which he has luxuriated in plenty.

This dilemma clearly has a long history. One hears a distant echo of ancient Greek mythology here, for the two gourds resemble the two urns to which Achilles refers in his penitent conversation with the aged Priam in Book 24 of Homer's *Iliad*. Like Achilles, required to choose either a short glorious life or a long inglorious one, the hunter must decide what he values most. Achilles makes his choice without much debate; honor is supreme in the old warrior cultures. But what choice does the hunter make? This is a topic that students will have fun debating. Dot-coms or graduate school?

Topics for Discussion and Writing

1. In what ways do Dadié's tales reflect the reality of life in Africa?
2. In what ways do Dadié's tales bridge the gap between literary and oral narrative traditions?

3. Why is the orphan so frequently a focus of interest in pre-modern narratives? How do the complexities of contemporary family life make the experience of stepfamilies still relevant?

Comparative Perspectives

1. The narrator in *The Mirror of Dearth* reminds the audience that "one is not an idiot if he is called Kacou Ananze." What traits of behavior and intellect distinguish him? What other works have you read that celebrate wily tricksters?

   [The anthology offers many examples, from *The Jātaka Tales* and *The Pañcatantra* to *Monkey* and *Mother Crocodile*.]
2. Compare the treatment of the river in Diop's *Mother Crocodile* and in Dadié's *The Hunter and the Boa*. To what information does it give access? Why is it the carrier of news?
3. Compare the view of the dead and their continuing involvement in the affairs of the living in Soyinka's *Death and the King's Horseman* and/or Achebe's *Things Fall Apart* and *The Black Cloth*.
4. Discuss the similarities between Dadié's fables and *The Thousand and One Nights*. What do the similarities suggest about the ultimate sources of narrative materials?

   [The fantastic landscapes in *The Mirror of Dearth* and *The Hunter and The Boa* recall the land of the colored fish and the wonders it leads to in *The Story of the Fisherman and the Demon*; the talking animals of *The Hunter and the Boa* recall the Vizier's *Story of the Ox and the Donkey*. Note that *The Hunter and the Boa* takes us to "the forest of genies."]

Further Reading

See also the reading suggestions in the anthology, p. 2608.

Bettelheim, Bruno. *The Uses of Enchantment: The Meaning and Importance of Fairy Tales*. 1976. This classic psychological analysis of fairy tales has broad application and is worth consulting whenever one encounters a story that begins "once upon a time."

JUAN RULFO

Pedro Páramo

Backgrounds

Pedro Páramo draws the reader into its orbit before it becomes clear that it is not an easy book. It is therefore probably best to plunge right in with a careful analysis of the compelling opening sections and only then to stand back and provide an overview of the text's unique qualities. By taking stock of the import of what they have learned after every few paragraphs, students discover that they can follow this book's "story" if they concentrate; the footnotes provide a valuable guide to crucial shifts in voice until Rulfo's narrative strategies become familiar. Not a novel to skim, *Pedro Páramo* is immensely rewarding to those who proceed slowly. With some encouragement, your students can keep their bearings even in a first unguided reading by paying attention; subsequent re-readings deepen both understanding and admiration for the achievement of this brief, stunning, and complex work.

The very first words of the book engage us in a close relationship with the person we will eventually discover to be Juan Preciado. One crucial fact is immediately divulged: the eponymous Pedro Páramo is the unnamed narrator's father. Then we are in the midst of a death scene, as the mother elicits a promise from her son as she has done before. The paragraph ends with her death. Chronological order is now upset: "Still earlier she had told me. . . . " Surprised by the dreams that "swim" in his head and that lift his imagination, the narrator is filled with hope. The first section reaches completion with the last sentences, which essentially repeat the first. The book's beautifully crafted shape is thus adumbrated: *Pedro Páramo* is a book about family, death, and the human mind in which dreams swim and imagination takes flight, leading us to re-examine our experiences, compulsively turning them over again and again in a quest that we do not fully will or understand.

In the second section, we once more go back to the beginning: we have enough information to understand by the middle of the section that the italicized comments are the words of the mother who was Pedro Páramo's wife. In this section, we also realize that we are on a journey and that the road to Comala, explicitly compared to the mouth of hell, runs in a significant direction. *"If you are leaving, it's uphill; but as you arrive it's downhill."* The dialogue between two of Pedro Páramo's sons is launched at a crossroads called "Encounters": here you may want to review with your students the significance of crossroads meetings in world literature. Where did Oedipus strike the man who turned out to be his father? How is the meeting of two (or more) roads a metaphor for all human choice?

We are gradually accumulating a great deal of important information about the landscape as well, but the novel describes its speakers' subjective perceptions of their physical surroundings rather than indulging in objective scene-painting. The line of imagery that began with the swimming of dreams in the opening section is reinforced by the shimmering sunlight and dissolving mists that the narrator notices as he talks to his half-brother. These visual effects recur throughout *Pedro Páramo*, where clarity is hard to come by. Birds pass over the two men—crows, birds of death (in Sayula, where Juan Preciado had been the previous day, doves rather than crows flapped their wings)—and everywhere the patriarchal presence is felt. Pronouncing his definition of the man ("living bile"), the son of Pedro Páramo "for no reason at all" strikes his burros, connecting the name and the hate to a strain of violence and aggression that will define one part of Pedro Páramo's personality. We next spy his property: the Media Luna ("Half-Moon"). Despite the vastness of Pedro Páramo's holdings, the women who bore his children were poor; despite their father's subsequent indifference, he carried them to be baptized. There are mysteries and incongruities to be plumbed, and the second section ends as does the first—with death: "Pedro Páramo died years ago." So the errand on which the journeyer has come is frustrated before he even reaches his destination. But the still nameless speaker walks on.

In the latter part of his career, Juan Rulfo wrote several film scripts, and many of his stories were made into movies. His fiction has a strong cinematic quality, and *Pedro Páramo* has twice been filmed. One can see why: images flicker before our eyes as on a screen, and they return, with each iteration and reiteration assisting us to make connections among the novel's characters and events. Certain atmospheric qualities (especially of light, wind, land, and water), details of costume, and notable gestures define idiosyncratic characters and places. Alert your students to watch for these repeated visual motifs. Consider, for example, the woman in the rebozo, seen early on (p. 2628), who may be identified with Damiana Cisneros's long dead sister, Sixtina, of whom we hear about a third of the way into the story (p. 2647). It is she who points the way to the house of Doña Eduviges Dyada, where Juan Preciado will lodge. Having been told that he has entered a ghost town, he notes that the woman in the rebozo seems alive; this unsettling reflection prepares the reader for revelations yet to come. Students who are used to horror movies with their ghostly apparitions will pick up on these details. Eduviges has just spoken with Dolores Preciado, who has been dead for a week, Juan is told: "I wondered if she were crazy" (p. 2630). But the reader is catching on.

It dawns upon the reader at about this point that Rulfo uses an omniscient narrator as well as the idiosyncratic voices of the people of Comala, whom we are still only starting to meet. The storyteller takes us back to the youth of Pedro Páramo, although he is not fully identified for us immediately; by the time we recognize him, a surprisingly sympathetic character has already been sketched. The shift in narrative perspective is heralded by the sound of water dripping ("Plink! Plink!"). The birds surrounding us now are hens. We are in a domesticated space, a world of mothers and grandmothers, and the boy into whose thoughts we are about to enter can think private thoughts only in the privy (pp. 2630–31). "As the clouds retreated the sun flashed on the rocks, spread an iridescent sheen" and again the shimmering light of the landscape brings dead memories to life. Pedro remembers flying a kite (a "paper bird") with someone named Susana. By now, we have perceived that Rulfo's book communicates a great deal about scenes and people by noting what kind of birds fly over them. Susana's elusiveness is like that of the paper kites, which "disappeared into the green earth" (p. 2630). Her sensuousness obsesses the boy—her "moist" lips, her "aquamarine eyes." We begin to understand that the presence of water often indicates that Pedro Páramo is the speaker, and that water is Susana's medium as well.

The next section describes the economic plight of the Páramo family. The church is demanding: "with all the money we spent to bury your grandfather, and the tithes we've paid to the church, we don't have anything left" (p. 2631). Pedro's grandmother has known better times, and she and Pedro's mother are used to buying things on account. Pedro goes around the village asking for credit; instructed by the women, he changes one coin for the next higher denomination as he makes his way out of the house: "Now I have enough money for anything that comes along." More rain accompanies the young man's nighttime brooding about the kite-flying Susana. He hears the women of the house praying for his dead grandfather's soul. His mother stands in the doorway, casting a shadow toward the ceiling. She was in the doorway when he left the privy as well; we will see her similarly placed again. Doorways are by definition liminal spaces, where we cross a threshold from one domain to the next. And *Pedro Páramo*, full of images of melting, dissolution, and shifting boundaries, is a novel about liminality—about the blurring of the transition between life and death, home and journey, love and hate.

The end of this sequence seems a good point to stop and consider with your students what they have learned. What kind of childhood has Pedro had? What priorities and values are being shaped by his youthful penury and infatuation? It is significant that the boy's full name is not divulged (although the title leads the reader to assume that this Pedro is indeed Pedro Páramo) until he complains about the terms of his apprenticeship to his grandmother, who counsels patience. "You and your wild ideas! I'm afraid you have a hard row ahead of you, Pedro Páramo" (p. 2635). Just prior to this face-on identification, we have heard Eduviges explaining to Juan Preciado how his mother hated her husband, Pedro Páramo. And just after it, again through Edugives, we first encounter the one son whom Pedro Páramo recognized, Miguel, a murderer and rapist who is the living embodiment of the chastised grandson's wild ideas. Thus carefully piecing together the juxtapositions and recollecting repeated details, we start to grasp the architecture of Rulfo's book.

If one had enough time, it would be tempting to keep us this pace and savor section after section. Since you are unlikely to have such leisure, however, *Pedro Páramo* may be an ideal text to assign to teams of students, each being responsible to report back to the class on their area of study for a session in which the overlapping evidence that they will have assembled should allow them to see the shape of the book as a whole. Here is a suggestion for how you might organize this activity. Divide the students into small groups for one or two class sessions. Ask each group to concentrate on one of the major characters by working their way through this brief novel and taking notes on any appearance of or reference to the character. Like many other modernist writers (T. S. Eliot, for one, in writing *The Waste Land*), Rulfo spent years eliminating details and paring his novel down to its essentials. Your students will appreciate his economy as they catalogue and collate the accumulating information about personalities provided by references to distinctive visual auras, speech patterns, and gestures. By such slender means, Rulfo endows the population of his ghost town with enduring literary life. Instruct the groups to prepare a précis of their findings for presentation to the entire class during the penultimate class that you plan to devote to *Pedro Páramo*. Then each student can contribute a piece of the puzzle and the overlapping information that they have assembled will fit together.

The list of characters can be tailored to fit the number of students involved. Here are some of the leading figures to choose among, with some brief suggestions of points to emphasize.

Pedro Páramo: Start with the opening sections already reviewed, to raise the question of Rulfo's mastery of tonal adjustment as we see this lovesick boy harden into an unscrupulous murderer. Then move to p. 2637, where "Drops are falling steadily on the stone trough," signaling another entry into Pedro's consciousness. The boy wakens to hear his mother weeping at the news of his father's death. "And inside, the woman standing in the doorway, her body impeding the arrival of day: through her arms he glimpsed pieces of sky and, beneath her feet, trickles of light" (p. 2637).

We see the child his father had scorned as a "born weakling" (p. 2644) transformed in the sections narrated by Fulgor Sedano (pp. 2642–56). Fulgor's signature gesture appears in this sequence: "He used the butt of his whip to knock at Pedro Páramo's door" (p. 2643). He remembers having seen Pedro Páramo as an infant, and is taken aback by the ease with which this novice takes command. Like Fulgor, the reader takes the full measure of Pedro Páramo's villainy in piecing together the details of the planning and execution of the murder of Toribio Aldrete, who "falsified boundaries" (another example of indeterminacy in a liminal space) and claimed ownership of territory that Pedro Páramo wants. It is typical of the novel's convoluted structure that we have already heard echoes of the agonized screams of Toribio Aldrete, hanged by Pedro Páramo's flunkies in the room in which Eduviges had put Juan Preciado; see p. 2642, which directly precedes Fulgor's recollection of the way he lured Toribio Aldrete to his death.

From Fulgor's narration, we also learn why Pedro married Dolores Preciado. After his father's death, the boy who had gone through the town buying his mother's small purchases on credit determines to cancel all the Páramos' debts by whatever dishonest schemes are required. He instantaneously sees his way toward taking formal claim of the land owned by the Preciado family. Without even needing to pay court to the woman himself, he seduces Dolores by sweet-talking her through Fulgor. "You string Lola a line, and tell her I love her. That's important, Sedano, I do love her. Because of her eyes, you know?" (p. 2644.)

Fulgor reports his successful embassy to Dolores and to Father Rentería, who will marry the couple in unorthodox haste, without having called the banns, for a monetary contribution "to fix the altar" and for a new dining table for his own use. He notes that there are "only a few clouds in the still-blue sky. Higher up, air was stirring, but down below it was still and hot" (p. 2646). We are in an infernal environment, where brutal means prosper; aptly, Fulgor announces himself again by knocking on the door "with the butt of the whip." Further evidence of the total lack of scruples with which Pedro Páramo takes command comes a few sections later, with a choral sequence; on p. 2649, we hear the voices of nameless townspeople who are about to be robbed of their property and murdered ("Night. Long after midnight. And the voices . . . ") Considerably later, we go back further in time, as Juan Preciado and Dorotea, who buried him and with whom he lies buried, hear the murmuring of the dead: "What happens with these corpses that have been dead a long time is that when the damp reaches them they begin to stir. They wake up" (p. 2667). The water that is associated with Pedro Páramo precipitates a description of the wholesale slaughter of an entire community that harbored his father's murderer. Significantly, Lucas Páramo was killed at a wedding.

Susana San Juan: Pedro Páramo married Dolores Preciado for her father's land, hurrying her to the altar while she was menstruating (p. 2645). Early in the novel, we hear Eduviges Dyada explaining how she substituted in Pedro Páramo's bed on the first night of his marriage to Dolores (p. 2633); shortly after that, we learn of Dolores's unhappiness and her self-exile from Comala. By the middle of the book, we have sufficient understanding to trace the connections between these scenes. Marriages in Pedro Páramo's burnt-out Comala bear bitter fruit, the mark of his own frustrated love for Susana San Juan.

In general, the women of Comala flow into each other in *Pedro Páramo*. None of them has the strength or, it would seem, the will to resist the advances of the Páramo men. As in a movie, the image of Eduviges Dyada dissolves and Damiana Cisneros takes her place (p. 2642), even as Eduviges herself had substituted for Dolores. Damiana in her youth once kept her door closed when Pedro Páramo came knocking, and has regretted this refusal ever since. Like all the other women associated with the Media Luna, she closes her eyes to the corruption around her, deriving secondhand pleasure from the sexual predations that she cannot help but notice. This pattern of voyeuristic passivity is repeated by Dorotea, who wanted children she could not bear and procured women who did bear them for Miguel Páramo. Dorotea lies buried beside Juan Preciado and from her grave listens intently to the murmurings of Susana San Juan, relishing sensual experience through the actions of others in death as in life. Susana, who has defied her father in declaring her willingness to marry Pedro Páramo, nevertheless in her madness denies him.

Susana's own voice is first heard late in the novel—"I am lying in the same bed where my mother died so long ago" (p. 2665)—and these first words seem to support a reading of Susana's relationship with her father Bartolomé as an incestuous one. The return of the San Juans to Comala is the event for which Pedro Páramo has waited for thirty years (p. 2669). Left a widow by Florencio, whose embraces she cannot forget (p. 2679), Susana has retreated into her own mind to escape from the demands initiated by her father when she was a child, when he lowered her down into a part of the mine he works, where only a small body can fit, to recover buried gold. All she can find there, however, are skeletal remains

(p. 2674). When father and daughter come back to Comala, Fulgor reports to Pedro Páramo, mistakenly describing them as husband and wife (p. 2669).

This misconception recalls the case of Donis and his sister, siblings who sleep together (pp. 2650–51). The novel's way of interpreting characters' actions by connecting motifs rather than offering explicit explanations is well illustrated by the repeated figure of the writhing body, introduced as Donis's sister watches the sleeping Juan Preciado, whom the brother and sister have taken into their hut. She sees her own image in Juan Preciado's agitated motions: "when I see him tossing in his sleep like that I remember what happened to me the first time you did it to me. How it hurt, and how bad I felt about doing it" (p. 2651). By contrast, when Pedro Páramo sits vigil at Susana's bedside and watches her "toss and turn in her sleeplessness until it seemed she was being torn apart inside" (p. 2676), he does not realize that voluptuous memories of her life with Florencio have virtually possessed her.

The power of sexual impulse overwhelms the inhabitants of Comala and the consciousness of sin sits heavily upon them in their purgatorial agonies. Rulfo invites compassion for their human frailty in remarkable passages like Juan Preciado's acknowledgment of his transgression in the bed of Donis's sister:

> The heat woke me just before midnight. And the sweat. The woman's body was made of earth, layered in crusts of earth; it was crumbling, melting into a pool of mud. I felt myself swimming in the sweat streaming from her body, and I couldn't get enough air to breathe. (p. 2655)

This sounds like a creation story played backward; the divine spirit has deserted the body, which melts into its earthy form. This bodily dissolution, related to the blurring of boundaries that permeates Rulfo's novel, will be seen again in the description of Pedro Páramo's own death. We also hear an echo of Juan Preciado's words quoted above when Father Rentería tries to prepare Susana San Juan for her death. He urges her to contemplate her mortality: "My mouth is filled with earth." She goes to her grave, however, wrapped in her own rapturous vision of the flesh, addressing Florencio rather than God: "My mouth is filled with you, with your mouth. . . . He sheltered me in his arms. He gave me love" (pp. 2686–87).

Father Rentería: Rulfo's profound understanding of the failed priest typifies his treatment of religious themes in *Pedro Páramo*. Corrupt, weak, and self-lacerating, Rentería seeks redemption as the book comes to a close by fighting with the revolutionaries. Pedro Páramo has no real interest in politics—he just wants to be on the winning side—and it is not absolutely clear who fights with whom. It would nevertheless be understood by Rulfo's original readers that one important outcome of the Revolution was to curb the power of the Church.

Father Rentería's tortured relation to the Church is immediately made manifest. Rentería enters the narrative with the death of Miguel Páramo;

Father Rentería's voice opens this sequence, which directly follows the scene in which Pedro Páramo's father's death is announced, with a sweeping, almost benedictory, vision: "There is wind and sun, and there are clouds. High above, blue sky, and beyond that there may be songs; perhaps sweeter voices. . . . In a word, hope. There is hope for us, hope to ease our sorrows" (p. 2637). We remember that Juan Preciado began his journey in the spirit of hope. Is there hope for the evil in this book as well as for the penitent? The priest lacks the courage to refuse Miguel's increasingly powerful father. The poor boy who carefully put down his grandmother's smaller coin when he found the peso his mother left for him to use for errands (p. 2632) now has a ready stock of gold coins to buy pardon for the crimes of his unpardonable son.

The death of Miguel Páramo precipitates Father Rentería's deepest investigation of his own corruption. As he walks away from the Media Luna, the lights in the village are going out; the driver of a passing cart asks whether someone had died. "He felt like answering, 'I did. I'm the one who's dead.' But he limited himself to a smile" (p. 2663). The information that Miguel Páramo has died sends "a lot of women" to confession, but Father Rentería, having been refused absolution by his superior, lacks the authority to give absolution. Sitting in the confessional, his spiritual crisis produces an hallucinatory experience: "Then came the dizziness, the confusion, the slipping away as if in syrupy water, the whirling lights; the brilliance of the dying day was splintering into shards. And there was the taste of blood on his tongue" (p. 2665).

"Father" means one thing when it is used of a priest and another when it is used of an ordinary man; *Pedro Páramo* purposefully blurs this distinction. Susana San Juan angers her father by refusing to call him by that title: "This world presses in on us from every side; it scatters fistfuls of our dust across the land and takes bits and pieces of us as if to water the earth with our blood. What did we do? Why have our souls rotted away? Your mother always said that at the very least we could count on God's mercy. Yet you deny it, Susana. Why do you deny me as your father? Are you mad?" (pp. 2670–71)

The novel seriously questions the Catholic world view in which a merciful Father rules. As Susana San Juan lies dying, with the wind lashing around her, mysterious emanations come to her bed; it is not at all clear whether she is being visited by the ghost of her father, or of Florencio, her first husband, or by the living Pedro Páramo, watching over her in despair. Her Indian maidservant, Justina, allows her cat into Susana's room, and the cat (the familiar of witches) seems to embody these various presences as it sleeps, suggestively, between her legs (p. 2672). Father Rentería comes to bring her comfort, but when Susana asks, "Is that you, Father?" Bartolomé seems subsumed into Father Rentería (p. 2675): "Why do you come to see me, when you are dead?" We know that both Bartolomé San Juan and Father Rentería are dead, the one physically, the other spiritually. To Susana, the heavenly Father is also dead: "I only believe in hell" (p. 2684). Father Rentería himself seems unsure; in his con-

versation with the censorious priest in Contla, he reveals his despair.
Sweet fruit cannot grow in Comala, he informs his colleague.

"And yet, Father, they say that the earth of Comala is good. What a shame
the land is all in the hands of one man. Pedro Páramo *is* still the owner, isn't
he?
"That is God's will."
"I can't believe that the will of God has anything to do with it. You don't be-
lieve that, do you, Father?"
"At times I have doubted; but they believe it in Comala."
"And are you among the 'they'?" (p. 2664)

Miguel Páramo: Although Father Rentería has been systematically undermined by the father, Pedro Páramo, he is most directly victimized by
Miguel Páramo, whom he has protected all his life. The son's brutal career is telegraphed by the motion of his newly born body, carried by the
priest from the mother who has died in childbirth to his uncaring father:
"Tiny as he was, the infant was writhing like a viper" (p. 2662). (In a related instance, Fulgor remembers that he first saw Pedro Páramo as an
infant.) The motif of uncurbed sexuality elsewhere linked to the writhing
body is prophetic in this case. The uncurbed adolescent that baby grows
up to be sleeps with scores, if not hundreds, of the village's daughters.
Not only does he rape Rentería's niece Ana, he also murders her father,
the priest's brother. Miguel's unbridled virility is expressed most dramatically in the shape of his racing chestnut stallion, just as Pedro's is expressed through Miguel. The novel's cinematic technique emphasizes this
equation of father and son by indicating the way in which each one hur-
tles into a virgin's bed through her open window (pp. 2635–36).

The details enumerated above are only some of the salient details that
your students are likely to have discovered in their investigations of the
text. Their immersion in such details will give them a strong sense of the
development of plot and character. In your last class, you may want to review the novel's elliptical final scenes, and then go on to consider the implications of Rulfo's extraordinary novel. You could trace the decline of
Pedro Páramo's fortunes from the moment of Susana San Juan's death,
an occasion which Pedro has marked by causing the church bells to ring
for miles around. People from neighboring villages mistake his private obsession for a festival, and instead of public mourning merriment prevails.
"Susana San Juan was buried, and few people in Comala even realized it"
(p. 2688). Pedro Páramo's life is over too, although he lives on.
As his viciousness was embodied in the rapacity of his son, Miguel, his
despair at the loss of his wife is embodied in the wild fury that another
son, Abundio Martínez, experiences when his beloved wife dies. Drunk
and dizzy in his mourning, Abundio comes upon Pedro Páramo. He begs
for money with which to bury his wife and, apparently refused, lashes out
at Pedro Páramo and Damiana Cisneros, the housekeeper. The attack is

blurred, but the outcome is clear: Abundio stabs them both to death. Damiana's screams deafen him, adding a complication to an unexplained and disputed reference to Abundio's loss of hearing much earlier in the book (p. 2632). A kind of closure is achieved as he vomits "something yellow as bile" (p. 2691) after murdering his father, the embodiment, as he told Juan Preciado at the novel's beginning, of "[l]iving bile" (p. 2627).

Pedro Páramo allows himself to be killed because he cannot sustain an unwanted life any longer. When Miguel died, his father had understood what was happening: "I'm beginning to pay" (p. 2661). Is this a novel about the restoration of justice or does it present us with a bleaker vision? The changing sky may be read as divine commentary on events below, or as a sign of abandonment. When Lucas Páramo died, "there were no stars" (p. 2637); when Miguel Páramo dies, the night sky lights up: "Shooting stars. They fell as if the sky were raining fire" (p. 2640). Pedro Páramo dies in daylight, watching "the leaves falling from the Paradise tree" (p. 2691). In Spanish, the last sentence of the novel ends with the noun from which Pedro (Peter) derives: Pedro strikes the earth "y se fue desmoronendo come si fuera un monton de piedras"—"he eroded as if he were a heap of stones" (trans. Thomson; see below under "Further Reading").

In "Landscape and the Novel in Mexico" (see reference below), Octavio Paz makes much of the character's name and, by implication, of *Pedro Páramo's* Christian motifs:

> The title is a (unconscious?) symbol: Pedro, Peter, the founder, the rock, the origin, the father, the guardian, the keeper of the keys of Paradise, has died; Páramo (the Spanish word for wasteland) is his garden of long ago, now a desert plain, thirst and drought, the parched whispers of shadows and an eternal failure of communication. Our Lord's garden: Pedro's wasteland. (Pp. 15–16)

Juan Rulfo is hardly likely to have been unaware of the symbolism Paz outlines in this passage, but the novel as a whole does not seem to be about a return to Paradise. The book ends, but it offers no closure. Unlike Dante, Juan Preciado does not climb out of the valley to see the stars. The dominant imagery of dissolution is captured in the final sentence's "desmoronendo"—"erosion" rather than "collapse," a blur rather than a definitive ending. For what is accomplished by this death? The action of the novel does not lead in linear fashion to the death of Pedro Páramo; he has been dead from the start, as Abundio tells Juan Preciado in the opening section of the book. Rather, it appears that the entire novel takes place in purgatory, in a place where time and space overlap without clear demarcations. This characterization seems closer to the experience of reading *Pedro Páramo*. Alternative explanations for certain phenomena co-exist. Did Abundio Martínez lose his hearing? If so, how? Is the echo of a scream heard by Juan Preciado at Eduviges Dyada's place that of Toribio Aldrete or is it the sound of Eduviges's suicidal cry? Or are both explanations equally true?

Modernism, of course, thrives on such unresolvable dilemmas. If God has died, then nothing makes sense except perhaps for sensation itself. Like Gabriel García Marquez, Juan Rulfo had read Faulkner, and the comparison between *Pedro Páramo* and the Southern writer's work, well illustrated by *Go Down, Moses: The Bear* in the anthology, seems instructive. Faulkner's gloriously complicated sentences ultimately do tell all; Juan Rulfo's brief and haunting sentences are syntactically much easier to read, but their import may ultimately be more puzzling. When Ike McCaslin finds a reference reading "yr [year] stars fell" in his grandfather's ledgers, the information yields a valuable clue that helps him understand a pattern of sinful behavior for which he atones. When shooting stars accompany Miguel Páramo's death, we are at a loss to know whether God is in his heaven and is sending a message to mankind below. A townsman named Jesus has another opinion: "Must be celebrating Miguelito's arrival" (p. 2640). If that is the case, we are in a malign universe. It would appear that the collapse of the stony Pedro Páramo at the novel's end simply adds another intractable layer to the parched, burnt-out wasteland of Comala.

Topics for Writing and Discussion

1. What do we learn about relationships between parents and children in *Pedro Páramo*? Are there any examples of happy family life in the novel? How would you compare the importance of fathers and mothers in the formation of their children's characters and personalities here?
2. How are the four elements—earth, air, fire, water—used in *Pedro Páramo*? Pick one of the four and demonstrate how it helps to define the nature of a character or a place in the novel.
3. Discuss Father Rentería's problems. Is he a bad man? How important are his actions in Pedro Páramo's rise to power? Do you think Father Rentería could have saved Comala if he had resisted Pedro Páramo's requests?
4. Toribio Aldrete is charged with falsifying boundaries. How is that symbolic of the quality of the narrative in Juan Rulfo's novel?

Comparative Perspectives

1. Compare and contrast Rulfo's treatment of evil in the person of Pedro Páramo with the depiction of paternal villainy in some of the great works of the past, like Dante's *Inferno* (Ugolino, Cantos 32–33), *The Tale of the Heike* (Kiyomori), or Browning's *The Bishop Orders His Tomb at Saint Praxed's Church*. Is there a strong countervailing force for good in any of these texts? Does the modern novel view the world from the same perspective that governs these earlier works?
2. Why is incest considered such a heinous crime? How do we feel about the relationship of Donis and his sister in *Pedro Páramo*?

Compare and contrast the moral significance of incest in Pirandello's *Six Characters in Search of an Author* or Faulkner's *Go
Down, Moses: The Bear*.

3. Compare and contrast the way T. S. Eliot in *The Waste Land* and
Juan Rulfo in *Pedro Páramo* distinguish among different speakers in
these texts. What do you make of the similarities between the titles
of these two landmarks of modernism? How does the multiplicity of
voices in each text contribute to the sense of a burnt-out landscape?

Further Reading

See also the reading suggestions in the anthology, p. 2624.

Cosgrove, Ciaran. "Abstract Gestures and Elemental Pressures in Juan
Rulfo's *Pedro Páramo*." *Modern Language Review* 86 (January 1991),
pp. 79–88. An elaborate argument designed to show how Rulfo deploys
references to the four elements in his novel.

Paz, Octavio. "Landscape and the Novel in Mexico." *Alternating Current*.
Trans. Helen R. Lane. 1973. See discussion above.

Thomson, Eoin S. *The Distant Relation: Time and Identity in Spanish
American Fiction*. 2000. Elaborates on Rulfo's statement that the structure of his novel is one "where everything occurs in a simultaneous
time which is a no-time."

ALEXANDER SOLZHENITSYN

Matryona's Home

Backgrounds

Solzhenitsyn's work centers the ways that modern Soviet society affects
its citizens. Many of his characters, Matryona among them, are good people victimized by their society, who manage to rise above their predicament and demonstrate an endurance and personal integrity that cannot
be destroyed by circumstances. Awarding Solzhenitsyn the Nobel Prize
for Literature in 1970, the committee recognized Solzhenitsyn for the
"ethical force [with] which he has pursued the indispensable traditions of
Russian literature." The choice of the word *Russian* is significant here,
since Solzhenitsyn is infinitely more Russian than Soviet. He has condemned the Soviet system from the outset of his career, just as he has
condemned what he sees as the corrupt values of the decadent West. In a
letter to the Soviet Writer's Union, from which he was expelled in 1969,
he wrote: "Literature that does not warn in time against threatening
moral and social dangers—such literature does not deserve the name of
literature." His unwavering concern for truth and his earnest unwillingness to compromise his beliefs—both maintained at great personal cost—
define his reputation as a major literary presence in the last half of this
century.

Matryona's Home involves a favorite Solzhenitsyn theme—the righteous person forced to deal with corrupt and difficult circumstances. Matryona is an illiterate peasant who nevertheless faces her circumstances with an almost saintly wisdom. She becomes, in Solzhenitsyn's hands, a testimony to the good that survives in the best of human beings.

Readers of Tolstoy's *The Death of Ivan Ilyich* will have seen something of Matryona's kind of simple wisdom in the servant Gerásim. Other readers may be able to compare Matryona to Dostoevsky's Prince Myshkin in *The Idiot,* Jaroslav Haahasek's Good Soldier Schweik, or Isaac Bashevis Singer's Gimpel the Fool. Solzhenitsyn's story will not bear, or need, a great deal of analysis. In form it is a hagiography—the story of the life of saint. Like all saints, Matryona is unappreciated, misunderstood, belittled, bedeviled, taken advantage of, and abandoned. She dies while sacrificing herself for others. Her story is told with understated directness by a narrator who, we must understand, knows something about suffering and patience. But even he comes to recognize the spiritual greatness of Matryona:

> . . . the righteous one without whom, as the proverb says, no village can stand.
> Nor any city.
> Nor our whole land.
>   (p. 2722)

Matryona does not need material comforts beyond those necessary for survival, and she makes her home available to all the creatures of the earth—itinerant schoolteachers fresh from prison camp, lame cats, mice, cockroaches. Her home is *open* to the natural world and, as always in the pastoral tradition, at her death the natural world mourns her passing.

> The mice had gone mad. They were running furiously up and down the walls, and you could almost see the green wallpaper rippling and rolling over their backs.
>   (p. 2717)

She owns no suckling pig because she would have had to nurture it only to kill it. She owns no cow because she could not have fed it well enough. Her pathetic and filthy goat suits her needs, and she does not ask for more. She is supremely competent at the business of survival, though that competence is entirely unappreciated. She weathers sickness, physical hardship, bureaucracy, and the age of machines with uncomplaining dignity. The narrator is in search of "deepest Russia" (p. 2697); and in Matryona he finds its very core.

Two other central concerns of Solzhenitsyn are evident in *Matryona's Home*: the inefficiency and callousness of the Soviet bureaucracy, especially the cooperative farm system, and the inability of the "machine age" to fulfill the essential needs of human beings. The Soviet system is the target of Solzhenitsyn's narrative wrath on a number of occasions in *Ma-*

tryona's Home. The lack of peat, which Matryona must have for fuel during the insufferably cold Russian winter, is particularly suggestive, because it forces the old women of the village to gather their courage and steal it from the bogs—where it is being kept for more privileged members of the Soviet classless society. Matryona's vain and exhausting attempts to get her pension ("They shove me around, Ignatich. . . . Worn out with it I am" [p. 2703]) reemphasizes the point, as does her experience trying to get train tickets.

Solzhenitsyn's disgust with the "machine age" takes a number of forms in the story, but the most effective and suggestive is the manner of Matryona's death, which is an antimachine parable. Matryona is so afraid of trains that they have a demonic kind of horror for her:

> "When I had to go to Cherusti, the train came up from Nechaevka way with its great big eyes popping out and the rails humming away—put me in a regular fever. My knees started knocking. God's truth I'm telling you!"
> (p. 2706)

It is ironically appropriate, then, that she should be killed by a train, literally dismembered, as she helps her rapacious and callous relations cart away the pathetic fragments of her own home. The machine she so despised is the agent of her death:

> When it was light the women went to the crossing and brought back all that was left of Matryona on a hand sledge with a dirty sack over it. They threw off the sack to wash her. There was just a mess . . . no feet, only half a body, no left hand.
> (p. 2717)

Matryona's death is a testament to the inevitable destruction of the simple values that she embodies and that we are being asked to embrace. Her body, like her life, ends in pieces. The blossoming "red-faced girl clasping a sheaf" cannot survive a system and a way of life that can no longer appreciate her virtues. Once, the narrator insists, "there was singing out under the open sky, such songs as nobody can sing nowadays, with all the machines in the fields" (p. 2710).

Like the narrator of *Matryona's Home,* Solzhenitsyn spent time (eight years) in a Soviet prison camp. He had been exiled there in 1945 for creating anti-Soviet propaganda and agitation, after a letter in which he made remarks critical of Joseph Stalin was intercepted by a government censor. After he was released Solzhenitsyn, again like the narrator, took a job as a schoolteacher in rural Ryazan, near Moscow. During his tenure in Ryazan, Solzhenitsyn apparently became friendly with a person who was the basis for Matryona. The train accident that appears in *Matryona's Home* is said to be based on what happened to that friend.

Matryona's Home was one of the very few works by Solzhenitsyn actually published in the Soviet Union. On its publication, the story was attacked on the grounds that if misrepresented Russian peasants. They were not, said the critics, greedy and rapacious, as are Matryona's relatives in the story. They were, instead, as cooperative as members of a collective farm are supposed to be. Solzhenitsyn was denied the Lenin Prize, for which he had been enthusiastically nominated, and his novel *The First Circle* was rejected. (The novel was finally published in the West, as were all of his subsequent works.)

Classroom Strategies

Matryona's Home can be taught in one class period, though you may need to stretch that period if you provide much background information on the Russian Revolution and the nature of the Soviet Union under Stalin. You may wish to compare Solzhenitsyn's picture of Stalinist society with the more urban and personal experience described in Akhmatova's *Requiem* (pp. 2102–08 in the anthology).

The major problem here will not be to convince students of the "truth" of Solzhenitsyn's tale, since they will more than likely be all too happy to accept it as "truth." Because the story answers to most of the myths and preconceptions Westerners already have about Soviet life, the problem will be to make sure that students read it with the same degree of resistance with which they would normally confront any other piece of fiction. Students may well find some of Solzhenitsyn's operating notions—the saintly peasant and the evident superiority of the pastoral life, for instance—difficult to swallow once these themes are disassociated from his more explicit condemnations of the Soviet system. It will need to be pointed out that for Solzhenitsyn the universal problems of greed, indifference, misunderstanding, and the desire for unnecessary luxury do not by any means disappear beyond the boundaries of the Soviet Union.

Topics for Discussion and Writing

1. The narrator tells us that he wishes to find "deepest Russia." Does he? In what ways?

   [See the third and fourth paragraphs of "Backgrounds."]

2. What constitutes Matryona's goodness? Would the virtues she exhibits serve her in an urban or technologically sophisticated environment? Does Solzhenitsyn appear to be suggesting that we should return to a life of rural simplicity?

3. How is irony used in the story? What is ironic about the nature of Matryona's death? What is ironic about the things people say about her after her death?

   [See the sixth and seventh paragraphs of "Backgrounds" for discussion.]

4. How is narrative understatement used in the story? Is it effective? What would be the effect of writing about such a saintly woman in inflated language?

Comparative Perspectives

1. Solzhenitsyn treats the railroad as a malign mechanical intrusion on the natural Russian landscape in *Matryona's Home*. Compare and contrast the image of the railroad in Solzhenitsyn's hands with its functions in stories as diverse as *Snow Country, The Bear, The Garden of Forking Paths, The Man Who Was Almost a Man,* and *Ladies and Gentlemen, to the Gas Chamber.*

    [Emphases include, in the order of the stories listed above, the railroad as a source of profit, the railroad car as a place of social interaction, the rails as a symbol of adventure, and the transport car as an instrument of dehumanization.]

2. Analyze the symbolic significance of the tearing apart of Matryona's home. For what original purpose had the top room been built? Compare the use of architecture and setting in other texts, including *The Cherry Orchard, The Old Chief Mshlanga, The Secret Room,* or *The Rooftop Dwellers.*

Further Reading

See also the reading suggestions in the anthology, p. 2696.

Burg, David, and George Feifer. *Solzhenitsyn.* 1972. Discusses *Matryona's Home* as purely documentary, perhaps underrating the fictional elements of the story.

Curtis, James M. *Solzhenitsyn's Traditional Imagination.* 1984. Literary traditions and individual writers (Russian and non-Russian) that influenced Solzhenitsyn's novels.

Labedz, Leopold. *Solzhenitsyn: A Documentary Record.* 1970. A collection of comments, reports, reviews, and extracts of documents and interviews. Interesting for Solzhenitsyn's own comments.

Moody, Christopher. *Solzhenitsyn.* 1973. Contains a short but informative discussion of *Matryona's Home.*

Scammell, Michael. *Solzhenitsyn: A Biography.* 1984. Comprehensive and detailed.

Solzhenitsyn, Alexander. *Solzhenitsyn: A Pictorial Autobiography.* 1974.

———. *The Oak and the Calf: A Memoir.* Translated by Harry Willets. 1980.

DORIS LESSING

The Old Chief Mshlanga

Backgrounds

Lessing is one of the most intensely committed of contemporary writers in English. Individual freedom and fulfillment return over and over again as her chief theme, together with a concern for social justice. Only when human beings are full members of society, she suggests, will human society be truly harmonious—or sane. These concerns pervade not only the novels and stories set in England but also the African stories, in which black and white characters alike are molded by their position in society. Lessing's own point of view, she notes, emerges from her experience as the daughter of white settlers in Rhodesia, and her African stories describe different facets of the blocked (or budding) consciousness of that socially privileged class.

Although there is a clear historical context for these stories, they demonstrate the *functioning* of colonialism rather then specific locations, people, or events. Lessing writes about a "Zambesia" that is a "composite of various white-dominated parts of Africa and, as I've since discovered, some of the characteristics of its white people are those of any ruling minority whatever their colour." Her British characters are typically alienated from the Africa they colonize: they cling to their British or European identity, and to the habits of their homeland, as an anchor of security in the midst of a country that remains remote and strange. Now and again there are friendships (e.g., between Tommy and Dirk, Mr. Macintosh's bastard son in *The Antheap*) or inconclusive attempts by newcomers to set things right (Marina Gile's effort to reprove her neighbors and reform her servant Charles in *A Home for the Highland Cattle*), but these relationships are psychologically demanding, often frustrated, and invariably complicated.

There is a harsh economic history behind the social relationships and final conflict of *The Old Chief Mshlanga*. In many ways, the story encapsulates the successive stages of European colonization. In the typical pattern of colonial invasion, commercial companies moved in to an area and established *de facto* dominance before their overseas government took official control (sometimes in apparent response to glaring abuses of power). Southern Rhodesia was administered until 1923 by a British Chartered Company that divided all land into "alienated" property (owned and occupied by white settlers, or occupied by Africans who paid a tax to the settler and to the Company) and "unalienated" African property (which could be appropriated by whites if the Company approved). There were native "Reserves" on "unalienated" land, and the African who lived on such Reserves also paid taxes to the Company. The Company yielded control to the British government's Land Apportionment Act effectively reiterated the old distinctions by establishing areas called "Native" and "European." Africans continued to be pushed off "European" land into "Native" country, and in 1956 Lessing wrote after revisiting Southern Rhodesia that only 46 percent of the land was still owned by Africans. The figure of the Old Chief Mshlanga thus telescopes a moment of history: at one time ("not much more than fifty years before") he ruled the whole region inside which the Jordan farm occupies a small portion, but now he is reduced to presiding over a single village. Subject to alien laws and a foreign economic system, he and his people are finally pushed off the last segment of their ancestral territory, which will be "opened up for white settlement soon."

Lessing's view of African politics is clearly grounded in a European perspective, as she herself recognizes. The focus of her story—despite the title image of Chief Mshlanga—is the evolving experience of a young British girl growing up on an African farm. The protagonist's attitude towards European and African traditions, her confused discomfort as events contradict expectations, and her progressive awakening to the beauty of the African countryside may all be compared with Achebe's picture of African life in *Things Fall Apart* (included in this anthology).

Like so many stories of adolescent coming-of-age, *The Old Chief Mshlanga*, is structured by the various stages of the young girl's gradual insight. At the beginning, she is presented as totally removed from the African landscape and its people; she lives in a fairy-tale world of medieval castles, oak trees, snow, and Northern witches. The hot African countryside is unreal and its people an amorphous, faceless mass, "as remote as the trees and rocks" (p. 2727). Even the narrative perspective is external, presenting the protagonist in the third person as "a small girl," "a white child," and a "she" who teases and torments the natives as if it were her inborn right. Mr. Jordan's young daughter is insulated from any contact that might arouse insecurity or fear; she "mustn't talk to natives" (p. 2727), and she walks around fortified by two dogs and a gun.

Change and a series of more personal encounters are signaled by an abrupt introduction of the subjective "I." In her own voice, the protagonist tells how she encountered a dignified old man and was put to shame by his pride and courtesy. Chief Mshlanga, she learns later, used to rule the entire country; this extraordinary fact awakens the girl's interest in her surroundings, and she begins to experience the African countryside first as a physical reality and second as a heritage to be shared between her own people and the blacks. "It seemed quite easy—too easy, as she finds when wandering beyond the farm to visit the Chief in his village. Suddenly the landscape is unfamiliar, even menacing, and she is intensely afraid. The women and children of the village do not respond to her questions, she herself does not understand why she has come, and the Old Chief and his attendants are not pleased by her intrusion. Returning home through the newly hostile landscape, the little Chieftainess can no longer pretend to be an innocent bystander; as the land seems to tell her, she is one of the destroyers.

The end of the story comes quickly and painfully. After an argument over crops trampled by the Chief's goats, her father confiscates the animals and threatens the Chief with the police when he complains that the tribe will starve. Proudly reminding Mr. Jordan that the farm and indeed the whole region have been usurped from the tribe, Chief Mshlanga walks away, followed by his son, who has been Jordan's cook. Pride, however, is a less tangible commodity than the settler's acquaintance with the local authorities, and the Chief and his tribe are soon uprooted and moved to a Native Reserve. The young girl's reaction is not fully visible at this point; she merely reports the quarrel and its aftermath and, a year later, visits the decaying village. The people are gone; their houses are mounds of mud topped with rotting thatch and swarms of ants. Conversely, the land is a riot of triumphant colors and lush new growth. The tone of the final paragraph has changed, voicing an older and more distanced perspective that may or may not be that of the narrator—yet it still views the African landscape from outside, and still with a buried question.

Classroom Strategies

The Old Chief Mshlanga can be taught in a single period. The easiest way to coordinate discussion is to begin with the familiar narrative pattern of "coming-of-age"; in this case, the main character evolves toward an increased understanding of her African environment. The first page sets up the contrast between a European heritage that is jealously cherished (she reads European fairy tales, medieval romances, and archaizing Victorian literature) and an actual African setting that appears to be—both people and landscape—quite unreal. "The black people on the farm were as remote as the trees and the rocks. They were an amorphous black mass . . . who existed merely to serve" (p. 2727). At this point, you will want to introduce some historical background on European colonization of the eighteenth and nineteenth centuries. This background can be as broad as you wish, with examples from Africa, India, both Near and Far East, and the Western hemisphere, but it will be especially useful to describe Lessing's "Zambesia" in terms of the actual history of Southern Rhodesia (reminding students that Rhodesia is now Zimbabweh). The split between European and African, black and white, that is so much a part of this story has demonstrable roots, and the familiar theme of coming-of-age is paired with a poignant description of *what* the child comes to sense: her own cultural alienation, and the irreparable damage done to "her" country by colonization and the forced resettlement of an occupied people. Two comparisons are appropriate here: Albert Camus's *The Guest* (included earlier in the anthology), for another example of the colonial predicament seen through European eyes, and Chinua Achebe's *Things Fall Apart* (included later) as a black African perspective on the same conflict.

The fact that this *is* a European perspective is brought out by the contrast between the title image of the African "Old Chief" and the fact that the narrative recounts the experience of a young settler girl. The presence of the Old Chief is crucial but (in terms of the story) only as a symbolic figure who crystallizes questions the girl is beginning to ask. Ask the students to imagine how the story would seem if told from the perspective of the corresponding (somewhat older) child: Chief Mshlanga's son, who works in the Jordans' kitchen.

You may want to take advantage of recurring themes when you examine significant passages with your class. Lessing has clearly used different descriptions of landscape for symbolic purposes. There is the cold and snowy Northern landscape to which the child escapes in her reading, contrasted with Africa's "gaunt and violent" scenery; the contrast of the Jordans' farm and the well-kept, colorful African village; the bigness and silence of Africa with its "ancient sun," "entwined trees," lurking animals, and "shapeless menace"; and the final scene, in which nature has taken over and erased the village after its inhabitants have been sent away. These settings are also linked with different stages of the young girl's awareness. At the beginning, she is armored against fear by her two dogs and the gun she carries; later, she is panic-stricken and lost when walking alone in the immense and alien landscape. The African landscape tells her, "you walk here as a destroyer" (p. 2733)—she is an integral part of the colonial presence; it teaches her that she cannot "dismiss the past with a smile in an easy gush of feeling." The ending paragraph brings out this sense of impalpable loss in its direction of the "unsuspected vein of richness" that persists, buried, in the deserted ancestral ground in the Old Chief's village.

Topics for Discussion and Writing

1. Why is the story titled *The Old Chief Mshlanga*? In what sense is the story both *about* and *not about* the chief?
2. The narrator mentions "questions, which could not be suppressed" and "questions that troubled me." What might be some of these questions, how and by whom are they suppressed, and at what points in the story do they come to the fore?
3. Discuss the various references to fear in the story and the way that they are associated with the narrator's awareness of her surroundings.
4. How does Lessing establish the dignity and importance of Chief Mshlanga? Cite several passages.
5. What does the loss of the goats mean to Chief Mshlanga? to Mr. Jordan? What is implied when Mr. Jordan says "Go to the police, then"? Why is there no further discussion?
6. Describe Lessing's use of symbolic landscapes.

   [Note the contrast of North European and African landscapes in the opening paragraphs; the untouched landscape during the child's trip to and from Chief Mshlanga's kraal (its beauty and strangeness, the sense of menace); the Jordans' farm with its "harsh eroded soil," twisted trees, and migrant workers' compound that was "a dirty and neglected place"; the harmony of the African village with "lovingly decorated" huts and the "enclosing arm" of the river; the final scene of the abandoned kraal.]
7. What signs of colonial government are included in the story? Why are they not given more prominence?
8. Discuss the implications of the last scene: the "festival of pumpkins," the exceptionally flourishing plants, the area's "unsuspected vein of richness." What is this richness? Whose point of view governs the ending paragraph? Can you tell?

Comparative Perspectives

1. The moment when the fourteen-year-old Jordan daughter takes control of the narrative of *The Old Chief Mshlanga* is marked linguistically by her use of the first-person pronoun and socially by her possession of a rifle (see the first paragraph on p. 2728). As she matures, her need for the gun changes: "I used it for shooting food and not to give me confidence" (p. 2729). Compare and contrast the relation of protagonist and gun in this and other stories of initiation in the anthology (consider Ike McCaslin in *The Bear* and Dave Saunders in *The Man Who Was Almost a Man*), and comment on the significance of Lessing's having her story center around a girl, rather than a boy, with a gun. What kind of knowledge does Lessing's female narrator gain? What do boys with guns learn?

2. At the end of the twentieth century, many artists have tried to come to terms with genocidal assaults on despised cultural communities. Compare and contrast the view of the oppressor and the oppressed in stories such as *The Old Chief Mshlanga*, *The Guest*, *Ladies and Gentlemen, to the Gas Chamber*, *Things Fall Apart*, and *Facing the Forests*. What kind of dominance is sought? To what degree do the victims collaborate in their own destruction? What kind of future do the literary works in question seem to predict?

Further Reading

See also the suggestions in the anthology, p. 2726.

Bloom, Harold, ed. *Doris Lessing.* 1986. A collection of essays, arranged chronologically, that discusses Lessing's novels as well as broad issues of ideology and philosophy. In contrast, the editor's introduction sharply criticizes Lessing for emphasizing issues and lacking stylistic mastery.

Gardiner, Judith Kegan. *Rhys, Stead, Lessing, and the Politics of Empathy.* 1989. Discusses concepts of identity in Lessing's short fiction; contains an interesting analysis of gendered rhetoric used to describe the child in *The Old Chief Mshlanga*.

Knapp, Mona. *Doris Lessing.* 1984. An informative general introduction to Lessing's works, arranged chronologically. Describes individual works and offers a chronology.

Zhang Ailing

Love in a Fallen City

Backgrounds

In the chapter of *A History of Modern Chinese Fiction* that first brought general attention to Zhang Ailing's work, C. T. Hsia likens her to the leading women writers of the mid-twentieth century, including Katherine

Anne Porter and Eudora Welty. He also sees another resemblance: "As with Jane Austen, her uncynical detachment and comic brilliance are possible only because of her serious and tragic view of life." This is good company to be in. *Love in a Fallen City* is simultaneously a perfect piece of modern realistic fiction and a dazzling satiric romance, full of the "regulated hatred" that careful readers have long recognized in Austen's work. Students are comfortable with these related narrative genres and one may capitalize on their intellectual readiness to discuss *Love in a Fallen City* by eliciting from the class a list of the critical categories usually investigated in the study of such texts—setting, characterization, dialogue, narrative perspective, symbolism, tone—and then inviting comments on the way each functions here.

To begin with the setting, you may wish to remark that this is a tale of two cities. How do Shanghai and Hong Kong differ from the rest of China? Like ports the world over, they were more open to outside influence than interior cities. The situation in Hong Kong was even more complicated, of course, because in 1842, at the end of the Opium War, the defeated Chinese ceded this offshore island to Britain. As a consequence, Hong Kong became both a center of international trade and a gathering place for adventurers of all kinds. The blatant commercialism of the city announces itself as Liusu looks out at the billboards along the pier at which her ship from the mainland docks. The colors of the ads—"their reds, oranges, and pinks reflected in the reverse in the lush green water"—correspond to those of the vivid natural terrain: "the road was flanked by cliffs of yellow or red soil, with ravines that revealed the dense green of the forest or the aquamarine of the sea." Garish but alive, it is, as Liusu reflects, "a city of excesses . . . [in which] the smallest slip would lead to a painful fall." (It is worth pausing here to note the deftness with which the narrator foretells her heroine's ultimate success without emphasizing the point at all. In the paragraph that follows this reflection, Liusu maintains her balance even as she is almost toppled by one of the children whom she is watching out for as the boat docks.) As Zhang Ailing's story shows us, in the wake of the Japanese attack on Pearl Harbor, Hong Kong itself "fell" once more to Japanese aerial bomb attacks.

Shanghai, the heroine's home, is situated on the mainland, but when *Love in a Fallen City* takes place it too had long been a cosmopolitan center. The leaders of the revolutionary May Fourth movement, for example, had gravitated toward Shanghai; if you have read Lu Xun's work, you may wish to mention that he moved there in 1927, when China was in turmoil. In rapid succession, Shanghai passed in and out of Nationalist, then Communist control. In the late 1930s, after the Japanese annexed Manchuria, they attacked Peking and Shanghai, effectively becoming the rulers of these cities too. So Zhang Ailing sets her story in an unstable and dangerous environment.

In a preface written in the mid-1940s, Zhang Ailing makes explicit the historical crisis that forms the backdrop for *Love in a Fallen City:*

> Our age plunges forward and is already well on its way to collapse, while a bigger catastrophe looms. The day will come when our culture, whether interpreted as vanity or as sublimation, will all be in the past. If "desolate" is so common a word in my vocabulary, it is because [desolation] has always haunted my thoughts.

The looming catastrophe was the victory of Communism in China, but the desolation that Zhang Ailing paints in this story is deeply personal. For the main characters in *Love in a Fallen City*, its heroine in particular, do not know whether to interpret their world as vanity (a moral judgment) or sublimation (a psychological one), although they reject the past. Despite the profound influence of global conflict on the sequence of events in the story, its causes are never specifically addressed; here, perhaps is another similarity to Jane Austen, who acknowledges the waging of the Napoleonic Wars in *Pride and Prejudice*, for example, by noting that the regiment will be moving out when the weather improves.

Liusu's family, however, tries to keep to the old ways. Ask your students to explain the symbolic import of the first piece of information we get: Shanghai was on Daylight Savings Time, rushing forward to seize the day, while the Bai residence kept its clocks an hour behind. Since time is of the essence in this story, it is a good idea to spend some of it calling attention to such details and alerting the class to watch for subsequent references, like the broken cloisonné chiming clock flanked by hanging "crimson-red paper scrolls, embossed with gold 'Longevity' characters over which the verses ran in big, black streaks." You may also want to ask whether your students have ever heard the sound of the *huqin*, the plaintive string instrument associated with traditional Chinese music, with which, ironically, the dissolute Fourth Master accompanies his songs of "fealty and filial piety, chastity and righteousness."

This tension between old and new is on view everywhere. So formal is the household that family members are referred to by numbers: birth order is the most obvious sign of the hierarchical organization that governs the Bai family, in which everyone defers to the matriarch. But Sixth Sister—Bai Liusu—has been divorced, and the narrative is launched by the request of her ex-husband's family that she return to assume the role of widow now that he has died. It is an idea that her brothers seriously entertain. The bruising dialogue between Liusu and Third Brother swiftly reveals her sharp tongue and her family's crass desire to profit from her return to a humiliating state of servitude.

Have your students search for the small details that dramatize the heroine's painful situation. For instance, she is embroidering slippers when we first meet her, like a dutiful daughter; when the family turns on her, she pierces her hand with the needle. The unintentional self-inflicted wound is emblematic of her dilemma. Her essential passivity has kept her from trying to resolve her problems, as Mrs. Xu complains. Why had Liusu not come to her for matchmaking before?

The two leading characters, each caught between two worlds and clearly marked for each other, should be discussed in detail. Is it an accident that their names are so similar? What do we learn about their personal histories and how do they influence the lovers' behavior? You will want to be sure that students understand the uncertain prospects of a concubine's children. *Love in a Fallen City* presents us with many ironies, not the least of them that Liuyuan, the son of a "secondary wife," inherits his father's fortune in an arrangement that somewhat resembles the deal that her deceased husband's family has offered Liusu. Heirs may be chosen as well as born, but daughters need not apply.

The omniscient narrator allows us to understand more about Liuyuan and Liusu than they will ever fully understand about each other. Generally, the story emphasizes Liusu's point of view, and Zhang Ailing does not sentimentalize her. We are told that she exhibits some of her deceased father's capacity for risk-taking. It would seem that she also is capable of crass calculation; occasionally we suspect that she projects so much of her own cynicism onto Liuyuan's actions that she fails to credit his real feelings for her. It comes as a surprise, for example, after he pleads with Liusu "I don't understand myself—but I want you to understand me!" to read the narrator's comment: "He spoke like this, but in his heart he had already given up hope. Still he said stubbornly, plaintively, 'I want you to understand me!' "

Even in relatively liberated Shanghai, most Chinese marriages were arranged by families with the help of matchmakers like Mrs. Xu. One reason why it is such a pleasure to read *Love in a Fallen City* is that, like Jane Austen's novels, it allows us to watch two attractive human beings get to know each other, to fall in love, and then—to please themselves—marry. In the process, the lovers enter into a remarkably chaste intimacy: Liusu recognizes "that what Liuyuan cared about was spiritual love." Liusu reads his sexual restraint as stratagem. She must be partially right; but his restraint may also bespeak a degree of delicacy and sentiment that she cannot—or she refuses to let herself—appreciate. Typically, the narrator forces us to confront the calculation that this discovery awakens in Liusu, but it also engenders on Liuyuan's part a genuine courtship.

Throughout her first visit to Hong Kong, Liusu sleeps alone in her hotel bedroom, which nevertheless (or, more likely, *therefore*, as in Jane Austen's world) becomes the site for a series of deeply emotional scenes. In some consternation, when she is left alone in this room with Liuyuan and her unpacked trunks upon her arrival, "Liusu bowed her head. Liuyuan laughed. 'Did you realize? Your specialty is bowing the head.' " In this posture he discerns her essence—a shy refinement that goes deeper than her defensive sarcasm. The narrative's purposeful juxtaposition of these old-fashioned Chinese manners and the cosmopolitan glamor of the Princess Saheiyini, whom we first encounter right after this scene, embodies the choice that Liuyuan quickly but deliberately makes.

The bowed head will return as a kind of leitmotif that records the hesitations of Liusu's inner self. In the same way, Liuyuan's habit of quoting from *The Book of Songs* (the canonical text also known as *The Classic of*

Poetry, selections from which are to be found in volume B) establishes his own old-fashioned habits. Their frankest discussion occurs over the phone, speaking from their separate bedrooms, divided architecturally by a wall but spiritually by much more. The love dialogues of the ancient poems inform this modern scene. Deeply distraught, Liusu has hung up on Liuyuan, who dials the phone again and persists in letting it ring until she answers: "Liusu, from your window, can you see the moon?" The next day, still tense from the unresolved struggle that their midnight phone conversation has brought to the surface, Liusu wonders if she did not dream the entire exchange.

Not until they meet again after a hiatus that Liuyuan breaks do they make love. Finally, about to sleep together in the same room, they acknowledge for the first time to each other the importance of that nighttime telephone call. Still unwilling to give herself to Liuyuan and thus cheapen herself, Liusu takes out her hairpins but keeps her hair net on; when Liuyuan embraces her, the hairnet slips away. In this scene, Zhang Ailing's command of symbolism and fantasy, as well as her exquisite rendering of realistic detail, give rich romantic power to what could have been the sordid coupling that Liusu so feared. With the moon reflected in the windows and onto the bedroom mirror, as the couple about to become lovers hover over the bed, they fall against the mirror, "into another shadow world." They are entering a new reality, one into which Liuyuan had tried to usher Liusu earlier, when he held up to the light a glass from which he had drunk tea: "the leaves looked like a flourishing plantain tree, while the tea-leaves that were piled along the bottom in a tangled swirl looked like a knee-high grass and undergrowth." He wants to break down her defenses, "to take [her] to Malaya, to the forest of primitive peoples."

Only when the city falls can they let go of their citified inhibitions and act on the love they have both acknowledged. The end of the story is the stuff of high romance, with the knight in shining armor returning to save the damsel in distress. This is a state they cannot reach until Liusu has allowed herself to be outmaneuvered and Liuyuan has been constrained by geopolitical reality from treating her like a concubine. They put into practice the words of an ancient poem, even as the ancient world that it represents crumbles around them. "Life, death, separation—with thee there is happiness; thy hand in mine, we will grow old together."

Zhang Ailing's tonal control and mastery of symbolic detail indicates that these are two complex, inordinately self-conscious individuals. They watch themselves performing in glasses and mirrors, and the frame of the story insists that we understand it as meta-narrative. The hotel room is not only a place with a pre-conjugal bed; it is also a staging ground for an aesthetic vision, a theatrical set that allows the lovers to rehearse their roles. The first time they enter this fateful room, Liusu walks to the window. "It was as if the whole room were but a dark picture-frame around the big painting in the window. The roaring ocean-breakers spilled right onto the curtains, turning their edges blue." When the city is under attack, lying low in the truck that removes the lovers from the danger of their rented house and brings them one more time to the protection of the old hotel room, Liusu has a melodramatic intuition: "If you were killed my story would be over. But if I were killed, you'd still have a lot of story left!" As the strays who have taken refuge in the hotel huddle together while cannons fire across the bay, the narrator invokes other stories:

> That dark scene looked like an ancient Persian carpet, with all kinds of people woven into it—old lords, princesses, scholars and beauties. The carpet had been draped over a bamboo pole and was being beaten, dust flying in the wind. Blow after blow, it was beaten till those people had nowhere to hide, nowhere to go.

Human lives as figures in the carpet: Who wove the pattern? Is there a pattern? The deadpan ending of the story seems to play with the riddle Zhang poses in her preface: culture is the product of both sublimation and vanity. Seeing the world through Liusu's eyes, the narrator toys with the notion that *Love in a Fallen City* has the status of legend, as if all culture sublimates the ordinary and raises it to vain heights:

> Hong Kong's defeat had given her victory. But in this unreasonable world, who can say which was the cause and which the result? Who knows? Maybe it was in order to vindicate her that an entire city fell.

The heroine, now a married woman, can relax. "Liusu did not feel that her place in history was anything remarkable. She just stood up smiling, and kicked the pan of mosquito incense under the table."

Like every great writer of realistic fiction, Zhang Ailing is a consummate manipulator of symbols—every detail tells. References to mosquitoes punctuate the narrative throughout, as does the wailing sound of the *huqin*, mentioned in the story's very first and very last paragraphs. After returning from the evening outing during which Liuyuan dances repeatedly with Liusu rather than with her stepsister, for whom he had been intended, a pensive Liusu strikes a match to light a stick of mosquito incense. Overhearing her family's spiteful remarks, embittered and isolated, she refuses to give up. Mosquitoes are bloodsucking pests, like her brothers and sisters; the insect repellent, that which drives the bloodsuckers away, is disorienting—perhaps like Liuyuan.

When Liusu becomes comfortable enough to sit with Liuyuan on the beach in Hong Kong, she complains of having been bitten by a mosquito. Liuyuan corrects her: "It's a little insect called a sand fly. When it bites it leaves a red mark, like a mole on your skin." As they bake in the sun, she feels another insect bite and twists to slap her own back. He volunteers to watch hers and she his; "They started hitting and slapping, and then they broke into laughter. Suddenly, Liusu took offense, stood up, and walked back towards the hotel." Although no sexual relationship has yet been initiated, they have got under each other's skin. Their intense awareness of the other's physical presence upsets them both and they stop seeing each other after this moment of aggressive tactile contact. A resumption of their friendship leads to the night of the telephone calls and what seems to be a decisive break. But they find their way to each other, as we've seen—and mosquito repellent is no longer needed.

Leavening the fraught emotions of her love story with devastating humor, Zhang Ailing skewers the members of the extended Bai family. She writes wonderful dialogue, and old China lives anew in the sententious observations and searing invective of Liusu's various adversaries. The vernacular vigor of Fourth Mistress's curses should ward off any momentary lapse into nostalgia. But at least a woman who can say "You've got a heart smeared with pig fat" is not a hypocrite, as Fourth Master certainly is. It comes as no surprise at the end of the story to learn that this marriage could not be saved. For the last time, Liusu visits her relatives and hears of their divorce: "Liusu crouched in the lamplight, lighting mosquito incense. When she thought of Fourth Mistress, she smiled."

Zhang Ailing's comic gifts, as C. T. Hsia suggests, put her in the same league as Jane Austen and Eudora Welty. She wrote her later fiction in English and lived her final decades in the United States; yet the power of *Love in a Fallen City* derives from her insight into the culture that she left behind. In view of her scholarly researches into *The Story of the Stone*, one might say that Zhang Ailing brought the trials and anxieties of the eighteenth-century novel's Prospect Garden into the twentieth century. Like so much modern art, this story is exquisitely poised between past and present. Its exposure of a dying world's petty corruption is no less ferocious for its ability at the same time to appeal to the timeless images of its mythical past: even as Hong Kong sinks into inglorious defeat, the moon reigns supreme and the dragon winds sigh.

Topics for Discussion and Writing

1. Discuss the family situations of Liusu and Liuyuan and explain how they influence their behavior with each other.
2. Contrast Liusu and Princess Saheiyini. Why are they both in Hong Kong? What are their physical and aesthetic styles of self-presentation? What values do they represent? Which of their qualities interests Liuyuan?
3. Discuss the significance of landscape and setting in *Love in a Fallen City*.
4. How much of this story seems culturally specific? How much seems universally applicable?

Comparative Perspectives

1. Compare Grandmother Jia in *The Story of the Stone* with Liusu's mother in *Love in a Fallen City*. What is their relation to their fam-

ilies? How do they spend their days? How is each framed by the furniture design of the traditional Chinese home?

[Note the references to their great redwood beds, from which they make their pronouncements.]

2. Why is it so important that Liusu and Liuyuan dance with each other the first time they meet? Compare the symbolic function of social dancing in other texts you have read this semester. Good choices include *Madame Bovary, The Dead, Death and the King's Horseman,* and *Walker Brothers Cowboy.*

3. How do references to traditional Chinese opera and verse help us understand the nature of Zhang Ailing's characters? Do they function in the same way in classical Chinese texts such as *The Story of the Stone* or *The Peach Blossom Fan*? Compare the significance of Japanese cultural traditions in Kawabata's modern romance, *Snow Country.*

Further Reading

See the reading suggestions in the anthology, p. 2737.

TADEUSZ BOROWSKI

Ladies and Gentlemen, to the Gas Chamber

Classroom Strategies and Topics for Discussion

This powerful short story may be approached as an inquiry into the human desire to impose form on experience. In many ways, *Ladies and Gentlemen, to the Gas Chamber* is a typical initiation story, one of the staples of modern short fiction. But where the narrator of such stories usually ends up gaining knowledge and self-understanding, the narrator here works to repress such insight.

Careful discussion of the opening of Borowski's story will help you establish the kinds of ironies with which the piece records the totalizing dehumanization that is its subject. The polite locution of the title mocks the activity that the story describes even as we are actually shown the elegantly accoutred Nazi guards in strange moments of politesse, as when they exchange the Fascist salute with each other, awaiting the arrival of the transport. Without comment, the narrator notes that the church bell can be heard in the distance. Even before that, we are admitted to the sociable world of the "Canada" veterans, companionably feasting together, friends of a sort, although they often do not know each other's names. The forms of civilized life, even of the sacred, somehow persist, making the enormity of the concentration camp and the entire Nazi program even more obscene, if that is possible.

Borowski's narrator is as deadpan as he can manage: he wants to avoid offering judgments. The details he supplies, however, evoke the horror he tries to ignore. With the story's very first sentence, we are reminded of the reversal of all human norms in the camps. As one critic notes, nakedness is our Edenic state; indeed, as they march through the camp, the laborers have a surreal vision of a paradisal landscape: "the apple and pear trees . . . the exotic verdure, as though out of the moon" (p. 2776). But this is emphatically a postlapsarian world. For one thing, the linguistic chaos is described as "the babel of the multitude." The notion that human beings might work together in purposeful concert has been squelched, as in the story of the Tower of Babel; worse, the human has become the animal. In fact, as the headnote suggests, delousing is a metaphor for the whole story: Birkenau (Auschwitz II or Auschwitz-Birkenau, where Elie Wiesel, with whose work your students may be familiar, was sent) was an *extermination* camp. The vermin are being expunged.

Ladies and Gentlemen, to the Gas Chamber makes it clear that the Nazis did not dedicate themselves to the merely "negative" project of extermination. Borowski shows us, through the narrator's first experience with "Canada," that the death camps had a "positive" goal as well: they were moneymaking operations, through the use of forced labor and by the collection of gold and jewels that we watch so scrupulously pursued. The profit motive is grotesquely exemplified here in the ravenous feeding of the waiting laborers. Since what they eat comes from those who will be exterminated, they are really feeding on humanity. The contents of the transports, "the goods," are listed indiscriminately: "lumber, cement, people . . . " (p. 2776). The laborers fear that they will "run out of people." Those who ingest human flesh ought to sicken, but with time, the digestive system is trained. The Greeks "gobble up everything they lay their hands on" (p. 2781), as if they were somehow untouched by the horror all around them; yet the narrator has earlier noted that "like huge, inhuman insects they move their jaws greedily" (p. 2777). Though they eat, they still share the insectlike existence of all the camp inmates, and Borowski's narrator predicts that "half of them will die tomorrow of the trots" (p. 2781). His body still betrays the feelings he will try to conquer: his vision blurs, his mouth dries. Later, having seen death and human suffering in the railroad cars from which he has unloaded food and goods, the narrator will himself retch (p. 2785). The beginner cannot yet control his sympathetic nervous system.

Fighting off nausea is one way of coping with the reality of what he is engaged in. To survive in the extermination camps, one had to become callous. Annoyed by the sound of a rabbi's "loud and monotonous lament," the narrator's companions virtually blame the suffering of the Jews on their religion: "If they did not believe in God and in a life beyond they'd have wrecked the crematorium long ago" (p. 2775). But they themselves will take no such action, unbelievers though they are. The easy hypocrisy of the Frenchman described here as "a communist and a *rentier*" is merely a symptom of the contradictions that had to be embraced in order to live.

Probably the narrator's most consistent way of protecting himself from his surroundings is, as noted above, to refuse all editorial comment. In one remarkable paragraph (middle of p. 2780), what sounds like another voice offers us the hindsight of history, placing these events in context: "When the war is over, the cremated will be counted. There will be four and a half million of them," and so on, until the "accomplishments" of the perfected Nazi machine have been tallied. This documentary overview, curiously inserted in midstory, is like a marker in the narrative, followed by a paragraph that begins, "The cars are already empty." Perhaps because his most painful task is to describe what happens to the persons pouring out of the cars, the narrator needs to pull back in the midst of it.

From the mixture of tongues comes one word of Yiddish: *"Mamele!"* (p. 2779). This is the voice of the child whose mother has reached for a handbag and been trampled for her pains. The fate of the women and children dominates the narrative; those who are weak or unable to work are packed off to the left, into the trucks. From the infant corpses, the maddened, and the maimed, Borowski gives us one searing image after another. Perhaps the hardest to place is the frightened mother brought to the point of denying her child. Infuriated by this apparent moral depravity, a drunken Russian sailor curses her Jewishness and brutally throws her on the truck. Applauded by the SS-man, his action demands a more complicated response of the reader.

In this episode we see one of the reasons why the Nazis were able to exterminate so many members of hated minorities. Stripped of all their own resources, the Nazis' victims gained some measure of superiority by denying their human connection with other victims. This determined isolation of the Other, is, of course, the means by which all prejudice thrives and the root of the mentality that allows the narrator and his comrades to survive: Henri explains this self-defensive mechanism in answer to the pathetic question "are we good people?" (p. 2781).

The one moment when the narrator allows himself to make eye contact with the human cargo he is unloading shakes him profoundly and alters the moral equation that Henri expounds. The beautiful blonde-haired young woman who asks "Where are they taking us?" reminds him of a girlfriend who has a watch like hers. Knowing the answer to her own question, the young woman "boldly . . . ran up the steps into the nearly filled truck," defiantly going to the death that she could have avoided for at least a time (p. 2783): Here, for a moment, we see a human being not yet corrupted by the system of the camps, making a tragic choice to maintain dignity even though it means death.

Ladies and Gentlemen, to the Gas Chamber does not end with this small moment of heroism, however. Pointedly, it moves deeper into infernal imagery, as the narrator crawls under the rails. A little girl runs mad, a dead hand clutches his—he vomits, and the story's pace shifts again. Stopping for another impersonal documentary look at what will happen to the people herded off the train, the action then draws to its conclusion. The narrative, like classical tragic drama, has taken precisely a day to unfold.

Smoke rises with the dawn: as in ancient rites, the sacrifice has been offered up. Order returns, but it is the malign order of the Fascist state: "*Ordnung muss sein*" (p. 2780). The troops march. Borowski's story, like so much twentieth-century literature, is antitragedy. Little is ennobled, nothing is affirmed.

Topics for Writing

1. By suggesting the kinds of defense mechanisms that deadened human responses to horror, *Ladies and Gentlemen, to the Gas Chamber* helps us understand how the Nazis managed to dominate so much of the world for so long. Choose an example of such defensive behavior to analyze.
2. Discuss the use of animal and insect imagery in this story.
3. Do you sympathize with any of the people described here? Explain your reactions.

Comparative Perspectives

1. That "the systematic dehumanization of the camps" mentioned in the headnote succeeded for so long has often been ascribed to the unthinking obedience to which workers in an increasingly bureaucratized Europe had become habituated. Discuss the relationship between the dehumanizing behavior of lawyers and physicians described in *The Death of Ivan Ilyich,* or the office mentality in *The Metamorphosis,* and the administration of the extermination camps here.
2. "Look here, Henri, are we good people?" Goodness is a category explored in a number of twentieth-century texts. Explain why goodness is problematic in *Ladies and Gentlemen, to the Gas Chamber* and in other modern and contemporary works, such as *The Good Woman of Setzuan* and/or *Matryona's Home.* What do "good" and "bad" connote in the contrast between "good" and "bad" natives in *The Old Chief Mshlanga* or between "good" and "bad" women in *Love in a Fallen City?* If goodness can be defined in these texts, of what does it consist? If not, is the impossibility of achieving goodness due to social or personal shortcomings?

Further Reading

See also the reading suggestions in the anthology, p. 2773.

Langer, Lawrence L. *Versions of Survival: The Holocaust and the Human Spirit.* 1982. A helpful analysis of the "world of choiceless choice" and Borowski's way of forcing readers to reevaluate their assumptions about life and art.

ALAIN ROBBE-GRILLET

The Secret Room

Backgrounds

Robbe-Grillet is one of the most influential postmodern novelists and theoreticians. His fiction and theory have influenced French writers such as Nathalie Sarraute, Claude Simon, and Michel Butor; American writers such as John Barth, William Gass, and Donald Barthelme; the Austrian Peter Handke; and a host of others. Reading his work requires us to rupture our previous assumptions about what fiction "means" and to participate in a nonreferential world of pure fictionality. Yet this fictional world is not at all "unreal," in Robbe-Grillet's view. Instead, it reflects an understanding of the real opaqueness and contradictions of the world in which we live. As Robbe-Grillet says, "If the reader sometimes has difficulty getting his bearings in the modern novel, it is the same way that he loses them in the very world where he lives, when everything in the old structures and the old norms around him is giving way."

It is appropriate that Robbe-Grillet should link a sense of dislocation in the modern novel with the same dislocation in everyday life. The challenge that his works represent to literary criticism is akin to the challenge they pose to contemporary norms and cultural habits, much as it may seem that the enormous technical intricacy of his fiction removes it from real-life considerations. In fact, once students realize that the elaborately shifting scene of *The Secret Room* replays themes that would be called sadistic or pornographic if published in a newspaper, they may have real questions about the significance of this story and the nature of Robbe-Grillet's work. One way of addressing this problem is to begin by discussing the experimental innovations of new-novel technique, and then to consider the ways in which this revolutionary technique causes us to reexamine not just the way we *see* the world, but also the way we think and act in it. The "new novelists" are proposing a metaphysical and social argument, as well as a revolutionary aesthetic strategy. Robbe-Grillet's 1961 essay *New Novel, New Man* describes preparing the citizen of the future by clarifying that most basic level of social relationships: literally, how we "look at things."

Traditional modes of literary analysis are paralyzed when we come to Robbe-Grillet, and that is precisely the way he wants it. Following a linear plot or the protagonist's psychological development will not help us in *The Secret Room* as it would, for example, in *Death in Venice*. To understand Robbe-Grillet's fictions, we turn immediately to his theories and especially the essays collected in *For a New Novel* (from which the following quotations are taken).

Robbe-Grillet makes one basic assertion everywhere in his theoretical writing: that the conventions we ordinarily find in fiction are, in fact, conventional ways of looking at the world, derived from a world view that we no longer share, a world that "marked the apogee of the individual," and in which "personality represented both the means and the end of all exploration." Such a world required that all the technical elements of narrative—"systematic use of the past tense and the third person, unconditional adoption of chronological development, linear plots, regular trajectory of the passions, impulse of each episode toward a conclusion, etc."—tended to impose the image of a stable, coherent, continuous, unequivocal, entirely decipherable universe. Fictions, indeed words themselves, "functioned as a trap in which the writer captured the universe in order to hand it over to society."

For Robbe-Grillet, there are two problems with this conventional mode of literary representation. First, it is not true to our contemporary understanding of reality, and second, it does not help bring about a new order. The contemporary world is "no longer our private property." Nor is it appropriate any longer for human beings to *impress* themselves upon nature, to mold and shape it in their own image. The modern world is "less sure of itself, more modest perhaps, since it has renounced the omnipotence of the person." Where the traditional language of fiction assumed a "nature," and our superior place in it, we can now make no such assumption. For Robbe-Grillet, the world is not "moral." It is neither "significant nor absurd. It *is* quite simply." This new reality must be explored, but traditional modes of representing reality are ill-suited to the task. Robbe-Grillet's "new-novel" techniques aim to reflect the *is*-ness, the quiddity, of things. He wants to "record the distance between the object and myself, and the distances of the object itself," for this kind of narrative aims to show that "things are here and that they are nothing but things, each limited to itself." Linked to this recognition that things "are" in themselves, separate from us, is the realization that we still *perceive* them from our own angle of vision: hence Robbe-Grillet's emphasis on shifting perspective of what *is*, reminding us that any perceiver is limited and that point of view changes in time. The writer is free to invent, without preconceptions. "What constitutes the novelist's strength is precisely that he invents quite freely, without a model."

The political implications of Robbe-Grillet's position are important. In a world no longer "stable, coherent, and continuous," traditional modes of operation—including the ways we relate to others, to things, and to institutions—must be revised. Consequently, the writer revises expectations throughout his career and especially in later work that destabilizes any attempt to find a constant center. The beginning of *The House of Assignations* (1965) announces contradiction as its theme, and thereafter provides merging but contradictory versions of events: different people are given identical defining traits or are made to speak identical lines, and short passages frequently do not quite fit into the tentatively established story lines. Action in *Project for a Revolution in New York* (1970) sometimes progresses by verbal echoes, or anagrams of a few key words (*rouge* connected with *rogue, urge, roue, joue*) rather than by logical plot sequence; the narrative persona may shift in the midst of a passage, and that same shift indicates (in French) a sudden shift of gender, too—*he* becoming *she*, for example. *Project for a Revolution in New York* is not a political tract, despite its title, but an experimental revolution of "revolving" nightmare scenes that could almost be taken from pulp novels depicting the depersonalized violence of the modern city—the "New York" of popular mythology.

On the technical side, this increasingly impersonal juxtaposition of elements suggests artistic *collage* processes. Robbe-Grillet was well acquainted with avant-garde artists Robert Rauschenberg and Roy Lichtenstein; he produced collages himself and also collaborated on a 1978 text with Rauschenberg, *Suspect Surface Traces. Topology of a Phantom City* (1975) and *Memories of the Golden Triangle* (1978) display collage assembly techniques, coordinating a series of texts (some printed elsewhere and by other people) with new prose links, or setting them in patterns of mathematical repetition. *Memories of the Golden Triangle* may be read as any one of several overlapping stories, and each newly chosen protagonist will suggest a different slant on the same events (like interactions in "real life"). Less technical or impersonal are the underlying themes of all these works: the murders, rapes, torture, anxious pursuit, and general violence portrayed throughout variations on the basic detective-story form. Here the political significance is more ambiguous. On the one hand, these sado-erotic fantasies (already present in *The Secret Room*) can be interpreted as the aggressive free play of an author's libidinous imagination; on the other, as parodic recognition of similar pervasive themes in contemporary culture, whether in fiction, advertising, newspaper reporting or— most recently and most strikingly—on MTV.

The "new novel," then, reflects this new state of affairs. It reflects the isness, the quiddity, of things, since it is by firmly establishing their *presence* that "objects and gestures establish themselves." The only reality we can discuss, without becoming complicit in an outmoded system of explanatory references ("whether emotional, sociological, Freudian, or metaphysical"), is a reality that simply *is*. In his work Robbe-Grillet wants only to "record the distance between the object and myself, and the distances of the object itself (its *exterior* distances, i.e., its measurements), and the distances of objects among themselves, and to insist further that these are *only distances* (and not divisions)." He wants to do this because this kind of narrative establishes that "things are here and that they are nothing but things, each limited to itself." Linked to this recognition that things "are" in themselves separate from us, is the realization that we still *perceive* them from our own angle of vision: hence Robbe-Grillet's emphasis on shifting perspectives of what *is*, reminding us that any perceiver is limited and that point of view changes in time.

The most obvious influences on *The Secret Room* are films, paintings, and popular fiction, especially thriller fiction. Robbe-Grillet's associations with filmmaking and filmmakers (particularly Alain Resnais) are many and obvious. The images of *The Secret Room* are snapshots, and *Snap-*

shots is the title of the 1962 collection in which *The Secret Room* appeared, but they are snapshots given movement by their juxtaposition, creating a kind of montage effect. One critic has noted that whereas traditional fiction "renders the illusion of space by going from point to point in time," Robbe-Grillet's fiction—like a film—renders time "by going from point to point in space." The overall effect of the cinema on Robbe-Grillet's fiction is clarified by thinking of his narrative point of view as a camera eye, which captures what there is to see without necessarily linking what it sees in space *or* time. Readers will recall the extent to which Eliot, Pound, Joyce, and Beckett use similar techniques.

Robbe-Grillet's "verbal art" also emulates "painterly style," and *The Secret Room* pays artistic homage to the symbolist painter Gustave Moreau. Robert Rauschenberg, Jasper Johns, and René Magritte have also strikingly influenced his recent fiction, and one senses that Marcel Duchamp's success in transforming our perceptions of objects by revising their context equally left its mark. The painterly notion of collage is evident in *The Secret Room* and elsewhere in his fiction. Finally, the notion that a single "scene" may be presented from a number of perspectives simultaneously, or almost simultaneously, was one of the crucial discoveries of painters such as Cézanne, Braque, and Picasso. It also finds its way into writing by, for instance, André Gide, Gertrude Stein, Wallace Stevens, Jorge Luis Borges, and Lawrence Durrell.

The Secret Room begins as a painterly description from which human characteristics are absent; the stain is a "rosette" and not blood, and it stands out against a "smooth pale surface," not a body. It is a theatrical setting, and "space is filled" with colonnades, an ascending staircase, and a mysterious silhouette fleeing in the distance. The body itself—when finally recognized—is described with excessive surface detail as if the painter's eye registered only the shapes and textures of flesh, hair, velvet, and stone. Human emotions are depicted as compositional elements: the victim's mouth is open "as if screaming" while the murderer's face reveals a "violent exaltation." Thus far, the scene is a static tableau about which the reader receives progressively more and more information, but Robbe-Grillet invests it with puzzling movement by describing the victim as both wounded and intact, and the caped figure in four different, incompatible poses. First seen near the top of the stair and facing away, the murderer has next moved several steps back and appears on the first steps, turning to look at the body. Later he appears standing only a yard away from her, looking down, and finally he is kneeling close to the woman as she breathes convulsively, is wounded, and dies. It is as though time has moved backwards, reviewing the stages of the murder and flight before they become fixed on the artist's canvas. Beginning and ending as a painted scene, *The Secret Room* extends the spatial reality it describes by attributing movement and different position to figures on the canvas. One of Robbe-Grillet's early works, it already demonstrates the writer's ability to offer the most precise details within a calculatedly ambiguous and disturbing perspective.

Classroom Strategies

Despite the complexities noted above, *The Secret Room* can be taught in one class period, though its implications—once discussed—might require more time to examine. Students will have problems, to begin with, because they will not understand what to expect on the basis of the initial painterly description. None of the usual clues is present: no indication of plot, no character interaction, no hints about the direction of the story. (You may wish to contrast the informative beginning of *The Guest*). Try pointing out that this *lack* is precisely the point: the sole focus is a minutely described, yet mysteriously evocative *setting*—the "secret room" of the title. What secret does it hold? How well does it keep its secret?

By the third paragraph it is clear that someone has been killed in this room. The following paragraphs describe the murderer fleeing the scene, and the scene itself is more fully described. Still, there is an uncanny emphasis on physical details and a lack of information about the deed itself or the motive for it. At this point you might ask the students to imagine a murder scene, with the caped figure as murderer/torturer and the woman as victim, just as Robbe-Grillet has presented it. Then have them imagine that the entire action has been filmed from beginning to end. Next ask them to suppose that someone selects four frames from that film and places them side by side without regard to chronology, enlarges each so that we can see every detail, and then paints equally large pictures—identical to the cinema frames—on canvas. Finally, this someone describes in prose what those paintings look like, without telling us until the very end that he or she is describing a series of paintings, not the "real" murder scene itself. This strategy is not particularly fair to the sophistication of Robbe-Grillet's narrative technique, but the analogy makes his method less alien to some students.

Short though it is, *The Secret Room* and its implications will require some reference to the author's literary theories. If you are unaccustomed to discussing theory in class you may well be surprised at how interesting it can be to students, especially when combined with a short example of that theory (successfully? unsuccessfully?) put into practice. Besides, the implications of what Robbe-Grillet has to say extend prose fiction to politics, social assumptions, psychology, and personal relations—aspects of experience that students, late in the term, often tackle with some eagerness. In any case, students are usually willing to have their assumptions questioned, since it is during their college years that they are questioning the assumptions of everyone and everything around them. Ignoring Robbe-Grillet's theories while teaching *The Secret Room* can turn out to be more confusing, and considerably less interesting, than offering them for student consideration.

One of the most interesting topics for discussion is the degree to which the story seems to depart from the theories. Insofar as Robbe-Grillet means to turn our attention toward the object, he certainly succeeds, but if we understand that he believes in creating "objective literature"—in the sense of creating a literature that is impassive, impartial, and entirely un-cluttered by subjectivity—he just as certainly fails. A couple of examples might illustrate this point: in the story's third paragraph we are told that the victim's body "gleams feebly, marked with the red stain—a white body whose full, supple flesh can be sensed, fragile, no doubt, and vulnerable" (p. 2790). Later we are told of her "full buttocks, the stretched-out legs, widely spread, and the black tuft of the exposed sex, provocative, prof-fered, useless now" (p. 2791). Not only is this material blatantly sensa-tional, it is also filled with subjective judgment and evaluation. How would a fully "objective" narrator know that the flesh was "supple," "fra-gile," or "vulnerable"? And who, exactly, "senses" these things? The phrase "no doubt" immediately suggests the possibility that there might *be* a doubt, even as it registers that the narrator's opinion is contrary to such a possibility. To whom, exactly, is the victim's exposure "provocative"? And who judges that her sex is being "proffered," or decides that it is "use-less now"?

The point here is not so much that Robbe-Grillet's theory is not really "objective," however, as that a fully "objective" narration is always impos-sible—and that Robbe-Grillet knows perfectly well that it is impossible. How, then, are we to interpret the nonobjective "objectivity" of *The Secret Room*: as unconscious self-betrayal, as a parody of thriller novels and *film noir*, as an exposure of sexual and erotic stereotypes, or as simply another layer of representation?

Topics for Discussion and Writing

1. How does this story differ from conventional narrative fiction? Con-trast with a story of your choice.
2. What is Robbe-Grillet's theory of fiction? How does it apply to *The Secret Room*?

   [See the second through the sixth paragraphs of "Backgrounds" for a discussion of theory, then the seventh and eighth paragraphs of "Backgrounds" and the third through the fifth paragraphs of "Classroom Strategies" for application to *The Secret Room*.]
3. What four stages (or scenes) can you discern in the course of the story? Do they make any logical sense? What impression is made *on the reader* by having events presented in this sequence? How would the effect be changed if a single version of events was presented in chronological order?
4. In what ways is the narrative technique of the story affected by cin-ematic techniques? Painting techniques?
5. Why does Robbe-Grillet use such loaded images of sexual victimiza-tion and violence—images that remind us, moreover of much popu-lar films and fiction? To what extent do you believe that this sensationalism is intentional?
6. How far can one proceed in interpreting this story? Is there a point at which simultaneous interpretations become possible?

7. *The Secret Room* is dedicated to Gustave Moreau. Discuss the painterly qualities that you notice in Robbe-Grillet's description. On the basis of this story, can you visualize the picture as Moreau might have painted it?

8. Edgar Allan Poe stated that a good short story should achieve a "unity of effect or impression," or "a certain unique or single *effect*." To what extent has Robbe-Grillet succeeded in this task?

Comparative Perspectives

1. Robbe-Grillet's narrator becomes more and more explicit in his close, detailed, and repeated descriptions of the murder victim's breasts. Compare Mahasweta Devi's clinical reports on the cancerous lesions and morbid symptoms that Jashoda suffers in *Breast-Giver*. The discussion of "Backgrounds," above, considers the pornographic element in Robbe-Grillet's work. What connection, if any, do you see between the genders of the writers and their treatments of the female breast?

   [If appropriate, ask your students to compare the motif of the severed breast in the epic of *Son-Jara*, presumably written down by men but the product of a culture that ascribes enormous dignity and power to women.]

2. In an interdisciplinary context, pursue the discussion of Robbe-Grillet's affinity with modern artists and painters by asking your students to analyze and compare the peculiar spatial details of *The Secret Room* with the treatment of space in paintings by De Chirico or Magritte. Link this to Baudelaire's *A Carcass*, perhaps, and the languid odalisques of a painter like Gérôme, to see the evolution of a continental obsession with monumental architecture and sculptural feminine bodies.

Further Reading

See also the reading suggestions in the anthology, p. 2789.

Bogue, Ronald L. "The Twilight of Relativism: Robbe-Grillet and the Measure of Man." In *Relativism and the Arts,* edited by Betty Jean Craige. 1983.

———. "A Generative Phantasy: Robbe-Grillet's *La chambre secrete.*" *South Atlantic Review* 46, 4 (November 1981), pp. 1–16.

Gibson, Andrew. "One Kind of Ambiguity in Joyce, Beckett, and Robbe-Grillet." *Canadian Review of Comparative Literature/Revue Canadienne de Littérature Comparée* 12, 3 (September 1985), pp. 409–21.

Heath, Stephen. *The Nouveau Roman: A Study in the Practice of Writing.* 1972. The chapter on Robbe-Grillet discusses the relationship between author and reader.

Nelson, Roy Jay. *Causality and Narrative in French Fiction from Zola to Robbe-Grillet.* 1990. Contains a discussion of Robbe-Grillet's narrative technique.

Oppenheim, Lois, ed. *Three Decades of the French New Novel.* Contains several essays on different aspects of Robbe-Grillet's work as well as a round-table discussion on the new novel, in which the author participated.

Robbe-Grillet, Alain. *For a New Novel: Essays on Fiction.* Translated by Richard Howard. 1963. A crucial set of essays, extremely clear and concentrated, for understanding Robbe-Grillet's work.

Stoltzfus, Ben. *Alain Robbe-Grillet: Life, Work and Criticism.* 1987. A brief introduction.

————. *Alain Robbe-Grillet: The Body of the Text.* 1985. A discussion of the erotic and sadistic aspects of Robbe-Grillet's writing that recapitulates and develops the writer's own views.

YEHUDA AMICHAI

Backgrounds

Many critics describe Amichai's early works as intensely intellectual and reminiscent of the metaphysical verse of John Donne, George Herbert, and W. H. Auden. In his later poems, Amichai incorporates sensual imagery and colloquial cadences, prompting comparisons to the verse of William Carlos Williams. Edward Hirsch observed that "[Amichai] is like one of Emerson's 'representative men' transferred to Jerusalem and updated for the second half of the 20th century, a prophet who shuns the traditional role and speaks in the guise of an ordinary Jewish citizen concerned with his people and his place" (*Contemporary Literary Criticism,* volume 57).

The history of Israel during Amichai's lifetime has been one of continuous struggle punctuated by outbreaks of terrible violence. The existence of the country was perilous, menaced by the hostility of its neighbors and by the frailty of its own economy. This sense of peril and uncertainty, and the grim horror out of which modern Israel was born, provide a kind of backdrop for Amichai's poetry, present even when not specifically alluded to.

IF I FORGET THEE, JERUSALEM

Sidra De Koven Ezrahi speaks of this poem as "reinscrib[ing] the psalm of exile back into the native landscape through ironic reversals and the intrusion of private, even unspoken words into the formulas of collective memory" (p. 479).

OF THREE OR FOUR IN A ROOM

The images, of loss and mourning, remind one of how many Israelis have lost children, relatives, and friends either in the wars with the Arabs or in the Holocaust.

GOD HAS PITY ON KINDERGARTEN CHILDREN

The figure crawling on all fours to the aid station is, of course, a soldier wounded in one of the many wars between Israel and its Arab neighbors, but one can generalize the meaning of this figure to the daily struggle for existence that wounds and defeats adults. There is also something incongruous and ordinary in a God whose pity has been reduced to the comforting of lovers and the providing of shade to old men sleeping on a park bench.

JERUSALEM

Jerusalem was left divided after the Israeli War of Independence (1948). The Jewish forces captured the modern, western portion, but the Old City, which contained the Wailing Wall and most of the old Jewish Quarter, was controlled by the Arabs. In 1967, Israeli forces defeated the Jordanian army and gained control of all of Jerusalem, including the Old City, as well as all the land west of the Jordan River.

NORTH OF SAN FRANCISCO

Just north of San Francisco, in Marin County, low mountains face the sea, as they do in Israel, but the human geography is a world apart from the poet's home.

Classroom Strategies

A single day's assignment.

Topics for Discussion and Writing

1. Arabs are a recurring presence in Amichai's verse. Do they appear as a hostile and threatening presence, as just part of the landscape, or as something else? How does Amichai's perception of Arabs differ from, or resemble, the tourists's perception of them in *Tourists*?
2. Amichai's poem *If I Forget Thee, Jerusalem* is a response to Psalm 137, but what sort of a response? Psalm 137 is the Psalm of exile, and yet here it is a poem by a poet of the newly reestablished Jewish state. What is the promise made to Jerusalem here?
3. *Tourists* suggests a tension between how Israelis view their land and how tourists do. What is it that the speaker in the poem resents about his coreligionists from abroad? What is it he feels they don't understand?

Comparative Perspectives

1. Jerusalem is both a mythic presence and a domesticated landscape in Amichai's poetry. How do these two aspects of the city coexist in *Sleep in Jerusalem*? Compare the treatment of similarly symbolic places in the work of other poets, including Baudelaire's Paris, Yeats's Byzantium, and Goodison's Heartease.

   [Baudelaire's Paris is a "horrible city" that is still more desirable than Lisbon, Rotterdam, or Batavia, according to *Anywhere out of the World*. Yeats's Byzantium is a purely symbolic locale of art. Goodison's Heartease, her "Mecca," is little known to outsiders but an inspiration in foreign climates.]

2. Like A. B. Yehoshua, the other contemporary Israeli writer in this volume, Amichai is ever alert to the claims of the Arabs who live alongside him. Compare the depiction of the "enemy" in *Jerusalem* or *An Arab Shepherd Is Searching for His Goat on Mount Zion* with the old Arab in Yehoshua's *Facing the Forest*. Does either writer make you feel that these two ancient peoples may someday be able to live in peace? What evidence can you cite for your answer?

Further Reading

See also the reading suggestions in the anthology, p. 2795.

Burnshaw, S., Carmi, T., and E. Spicehandler, eds. *The Modern Hebrew Poem Itself*. 1966. Provides an outline history of modern Hebrew poetry.

Carmi, T., ed. *The Penguin Book of Hebrew Verse*. 1981. A remarkable anthology that provides a sketch of the history of Hebrew verse.

Ezrahi, Sidra De Koven. "Our Homeland, the Text . . . Our Text, the Homeland: Exile and Homecoming in Modern Jewish Imagination." *The Michigan Quarterly Review: The Middle East*, a special issue (Fall 1992). Touches on Amichai.

CLARICE LISPECTOR

The Daydreams of a Drunk Woman

Backgrounds

The opening paragraphs of this story establish both the physical environment in which the titular drunk woman must function and her quirky habits of mind. Ask your students why the first sentence is significant. Anyone who has ever lived in a city apartment will recognize the way the sounds and reflections of traffic outside can disturb persons inside their homes. The heightened sensitivity of the woman seated before her dressing table, however, magnifies the impact of the trolley cars' intrusion into her space. Known for her vivid and often unusual choice of words, in beginning her narrative, Lispector keeps returning to "trembled," "shivered," "rustled," "shimmered," and "fluttering"—terms that make palpable the veritable chain reaction of barely perceptible movements set up by the tremors of the passing trolley. We soon realize that the instability implied by this tremulousness is not simply an emanation from the outer world, but a disorder that lies deep within the consciousness of the story's focal character.

The second sentence is as telling as the first: a woman combs her hair in front of a triple mirror; she is unrushed, it is evening, and as the paragraphs unfold, it is clear that she has no appointment to keep. She simply contemplates her image, vaguely alert to the world around her, but essentially indifferent to it. Although she hears the newsboy's voice heralding the events of the day, her only use for a newspaper is to fan herself. We are introduced to her in the classic narcissistic posture—looking at herself in the mirror—and she seems totally absorbed in her own image and sensations. As the headnote points out, what the drunk woman sees when she looks at "the intersected breasts of several women" in her three-sided vanity mirror implies a crisis of identity. She seems poised, like Alice at her looking-glass, to fall into a distorted alternative universe. And, like Alice, she is open to strange perceptions because she drinks.

The dissociation of mind and body that accompanies inebriation pervades the narrative. The drunk woman shifts responsibility away from herself. She hears something heavy falling outside: "Had her husband and the little ones been at home, the idea would already have occurred to her that they were to blame" (p. 2803). The following sentence confirms her reluctance to recognize herself as a thinking agent causing action around her in any way. *She* does nothing; body parts and utensils act on their own. "Her eyes did not take themselves off her image, her comb worked pensively. . . ." (pp. 2803–04). She addresses the image in the mirror in idle social chitchat, and awaits her own thoughts as if she were not responsible for them: "Whosoever found, searched" (p. 2804), she says to herself before drifting off to sleep. The divine command is "Seek and ye shall find." Totally passive, the drunk woman initiates no activity and leaves her husband to perform the housewifely chores that would ordinarily be expected from her.

Sensuously self-involved, fixated on her plump whiteness, she resists her husband's marital caresses. The fluttering motions of the vigil at the mirror become harsh and brittle: "[W]hen he bent over to kiss her, her capriciousness crackled like a dry leaf" (p. 2804). Lispector's inventive combinations of vaguely inappropriate words define the dislocations of the central character's being, as in "Her anger was tenuous and ardent" (p. 2805). Adjectives that usually modify affectionate feelings for others describe instead the way she cultivates her inwardness. But the narrator does not spare her protagonist, whose basic bodily processes subvert her pose of dreamy airiness: she falls asleep, "her saliva staining the pillow" (p. 2804), and flops over "to snore beside her husband" (p. 2805).

The story breaks into two parts, the first the description of her languorous rejection of housewifely cares and the second of the Saturday night on the town at an expensive restaurant. Her alienation from her husband becomes more explicit here, when being entertained in public by a wealthy business associate of his. We learn that our drunk woman who lives with her family in the capital of Brazil is a native of Portugal, and presumably a bit of a snob for that reason. She defensively reminds herself of her own sophistication ("she was no provincial ninny and she had already experienced life in the capital") and wants to laugh at her husband, "stuffed into his new suit" (p. 2806), while resenting the high style of the woman with a hat at a neighboring table.

Hints of the bargain she had struck by marrying to achieve security emerge here. We notice in the opening of the story that she has "red-lacquered nails" (p. 2804), yet in her drunken satisfaction at losing her "every-day soul" on a Saturday night, she reflects that few remnants of her past, of her everyday reality, remain: "to remind her of former days, only her small, ill-kempt hands" (p. 2806). Later in the restaurant, a suggestive comparison reminds us of her hands as she congratulates herself on her artistic sensibility, the intensity of which "irritated her without causing her pain, like a broken fingernail" (p. 2806).

In Lispector's work, the body becomes the arbiter of truth. Broken or gnawed fingernails often betray people who think they have successfully masked their anxiety; perhaps that is the case here. As the story draws to its conclusion, the plump body of which the drunk woman seems so proud begins to metamorphose into something monstrous as she gets more and more drunk. There seems to be a link between these images of somatic distortion and the following statement: "words that a woman uttered when drunk were like being pregnant—mere words on her lips which had nothing to do with the secret core that seemed like a pregnancy" (p. 2806). Generally, when we speak of a "pregnant comment," we mean one that is filled with import; but the definition of a drunk woman's words here posits a gap between the external sign and the internal reality in the state of pregnancy. Yet the central character of Lispector's story is obsessed with her reproductive prowess. She feels positively tumescent as she distances herself from the "barren people in that restaurant" and announces her contempt for the flat-chested elegant woman with her slim waistline and fashionable hat: "I'll bet she couldn't even bear her man a child" (p. 2807). It becomes apparent that our heroine, the mother of two who feels "as if she still had milk in those firm breasts" (p. 2809), loathes her marriage to a man who wants children and an ornamental companion. She has produced babies, but in some frightening way they have nothing to do with her "secret core."

Increasing evidence of the dissociation of her mind from her body builds up in the final pages of *The Daydreams of a Drunk Woman*. She envisages herself as a lobster, with plump white flesh (just waiting, the reader may think, for the clamps to pull it from the carapace). Her mind begins to race ahead of her capacity to utter words:

> She talked and listened with curiosity to what she herself was about to reply to the well-to-do businessman. . . . Intrigued and amazed, she heard what she was

on the point of replying, and what she might say in her present state would
serve as an augury for the future. (p. 2806)

Later at home in bed, like Alice who has gone through the looking-glass
and hopes to be returned to normal size, the drunk woman tries to reconcile the split halves of her identity. " 'You gorge yourself and I pay the
piper,' she said sadly, looking at the dainty white toes of her feet"
(p. 2808). The full extent of her crisis then is registered in a characteristic passage of Lispector's word-conscious prose:

> She looked around her, patient and obedient. Ah, words, nothing but words,
> the objects in the room lined up in the order of words, to form those confused
> and irksome phrases that he who knows how will read. Boredom . . . such aw-
> ful boredom. . . . How can I describe this thing inside me? (p. 2808)

In the realm of a verbal artist like Clarice Lispector, this failure of
words is the human abyss. Finally, the drunk woman firmly articulates the
epiphany toward which she has approached several times in the course of
the story: "What *is* wrong with me? It was unhappiness" (p. 2808). The
story concludes with a resolution to clean the house and an apostrophe to
the moon, another reflecting surface, like the mirror before which the
story had begun. Not so much the romantic moon that encourages lovers
as a sorry emblem of feminine isolation ("poor thing"), the drunk housewife salutes it affectionately as an image of her own feckless state: "you
slut" (p. 2809). The drunk woman's self-accusations delude her into
thinking that she has got a grip on her problems and will soon take action
to remedy them. Lispector's cool observer, however, has led us to believe
that no such reformation is in sight.

Topics for Discussion

1. How does Lispector allow us to see the kind of life that her title
   character leads without assisting us with a traditional narrator's informative introduction?
2. Discuss the importance of the story's opening. How does looking in
   the mirror define the drunk woman's sense of herself? How does the
   multiple image that she sees there suggest the personal difficulties
   that she has not yet faced?
3. How important is the urban setting of this story? Would the drunk
   woman have the same problems if she were a rural housewife?
4. Why is it significant that the woman's children are visiting their
   aunts when the story begins? How important is her maternal function to the drunk woman?

Comparative Perspectives

1. The title of Clarice Lispector's first novel is taken from the writings
   of James Joyce. Compare the self-delusion of Gabriel in *The Dead*

with that of the drunk woman in Lispector's story. How do their environments contribute to their distorted self-images? What kind of epiphany does each reach? Do these stories leave us with a sense that ameliorative action will take place after the narrative ends?

2. Like Virginia Woolf, Clarice Lispector takes us inside her characters' minds. Compare and contrast the thoughts that occur to the drunk woman in the restaurant with those that the lecturer reflects on in the small restaurant somewhere near the British Museum in chapter two of *A Room of One's Own*. What is the significance of the outside world to the two women? Does the mind of a drunk person function the same way as a sober person's? Are there other differences between the representation of thought achieved by Lispector and Woolf?

3. Much of the imagery in Lispector's story deals with bodily distortion. Compare the description of the woman's gigantic body after the meal at the restaurant with Alfonsina Storni's descriptions of the body in *The World of Seven Wells* or *Portrait of García Lorca*. How would you characterize the tone and import of the imagery in Lispector's story? Is Storni as distanced from her material as the narrator of *The Daydreams of a Drunk Woman* seems to be?

Further Reading

See also the reading suggestions in the anthology, p. 2803.

Bassnet, Susan. "Coming Out of the Labyrinth: Women Writers in Contemporary Latin America." *On Modern Latin American Fiction*. Ed. John King. 1982. A general discussion that emphasizes the split between the public and the private face in Lispector's leading characters.

Sommer, Doris. *Foundational Fictions: The National Romance of Latin America*. 1991. A good chapter on Lispector, "who makes perfectly quotidian situations gnawingly grotesque by the same kind of static focusing and disturbing repetitions that can make women's lives unbearably familiar."

INGEBORG BACHMANN

The Barking

Backgrounds

The Barking comes from Bachmann's second collection of short stories, *Three Paths to the Lake* (in German, *Simultan*), published in 1972 and written over the same years that she was working on the novel cycle *Todesarten* (*Ways of Death* or *Death Styles*).

Characters from *Ways of Death* reappear in *Three Paths to the Lake*, and cross-references between the stories make it clear that Bachmann intended to provide a panorama of modern Austrian society from a perspective that questioned social relationships of gender and power, and the role of language in establishing identity. The consummate skill that she had brought to her earlier hermetic poetry reappears in the later prose fiction, with its oblique and terrifying pictures of human beings—especially women—unable to express or recognize themselves as complete individuals. The generally bleak picture of personal relationships in a covertly fascist society does not go unchallenged; it is criticized either by implication or occasionally by example. For Bachmann, the writer has both a role and a responsibility to effect social change. In a 1971 interview she commented that "society could be brought to a new form of consciousness by a new kind of writing. Of course one can't change the world with a poem, that's impossible, but one can have an effect on something. . . . " Her influence on later German-language writers and her growing international reputation attest to the impact of Bachmann's "new kind of writing," a consciously modernist style that articulates the twentieth century's "new experiences of suffering."

Readers exploring Bachmann's work may be puzzled by references to the second story collection under different titles: *Simultaneous* and *Three Paths to the Lake*. The 1989 English translation of *Simultan* takes its title from the last (and longest) story in the book, *Three Paths to the Lake*, rather than from the first, *Simultaneous*. *Simultaneous* ("Word for Word" in English translation) describes the spiritually dispossessed situation of a simultaneous interpreter named Nadja. Nadja exists in a linguistic limbo, an empty space of exchange in which she transmits equivalent meanings for other people's words while living "without a single thought of her own." Another projected title for the collection was *Women from Vienna*, reflecting the fact that all five stories describe different middle-class Viennese women who are, as Mark Anderson says, united "by what is missing from their lives." In one way or another, these women represent an alienation from reality that contrasts sharply with the precise description of apparently trivial details in their daily lives.

These are not isolated cases: instead, all five stories are linked by scattered references to figures appearing in other stories (and in *The Franza Case*) so that a broader pattern of social repression and inarticulate suffering begins to emerge. (This technique of cumulative cross-reference is found in novelist Honoré de Balzac's great nineteenth-century panorama of French society, *The Human Comedy*.) Beatrix, the narcissistic protagonist of *Problems, Problems,* who lives to sleep late and visit the beauty parlor, resents her cousin Elisabeth Mihailovics, whose murder by her husband is described in *Three Paths to the Lake*; she also asks the beauty parlor attendant about young Frau Jordan—seen characteristically not as an individual but as "the wife of that Jordan." In *Three Paths to the Lake*, a successful news photographer named Elisabeth Matrei recalls the different (complex and disheartening) aspects of love in her life; we hear at one point that one of her lovers mentioned living with "a woman from Vienna, an unbelievably ambitious woman, a simultaneous interpreter," and elsewhere that another character worshiped the actress Fann Goldman (a character in the *Ways of Death* cycle). Elisabeth herself feels deprived of speech, a spectator at the events she reports, unable to say what she really feels: "hasn't it ever occurred to anyone that you kill people when you deprive them of the power of speech and with it the power to experience and think?"

Such themes of loss and alienation are already present in Bachmann's earlier prose: the title story of her first collection, *The Thirtieth Year*, presents a narrator who reviews a life of spiritual passivity as he enters his thirtieth year and recovers from an automobile accident. Formerly "everything he did was on approval, on the understanding that it could be cancelled," but now he is no longer on the threshold of unlimited possibilities. "He casts the net of memory, casts it over himself and draws himself, catcher and caught in one person over the threshold of time, over the threshold of place, to see who he was and who he has become." The route to self-discovery dissolves in ambiguity for the narrator of *Malina* (1971), the only completed novel in the cycle *Ways of Death*. *Malina* is narrated until near the end by a writer who has a complicated relationship with two men who are conceivably also aspects of her artistic personality. Ivan is her lover and emotional reference point; Malina, dryly analytic, shares an apartment with her and encourages her to analyze her feelings. By the end of the novel, the narrator has lost Ivan and simultaneously her anchor in concrete reality. She disappears "into the wall" and the novel concludes with Malina's denial of her existence. What has happened? "An I tells its story to the end" ("Ein Ich erzählt sich zu Ende").

A complicated pattern of discovery and loss of identity is similarly visible in *The Barking*. The two protagonists share a mutual discovery in the course of their conversation about Leo Jordan: discoveries about each other, about themselves, and about Leo Jordan. Franziska (the diminutive of "Franza") comes to question her husband Leo's behavior towards his mother, towards his cousin Johannes, and eventually towards herself as she recognizes that she too is afraid of him. It is a very cautious questioning and only the beginning of judgment, for Franziska (like old Frau Jordan) is taught to believe that "Leo was just too good to her" (p. 2816). First, she is merely amazed and hurt that Leo, a psychiatrist "whose very profession obliged him to uphold a neutral and scientific attitude toward homosexuality . . . could go on and on about this cousin as though he had somehow, through his own negligence, fallen prey to works of art, homosexuality, and an inheritance to boot . . ." (p. 2816). Even later, when she hears that old Frau Jordan gave away her cherished dog, Nuri, because Leo didn't like it, she accuses both herself and Leo of cruelty: "What kind of people are we?" (2821) We never see the results of her growing comprehension, for Leo has forestalled her and the couple will soon part: "other things came to pass, events of such hurricane force that she almost forgot the old woman and a great many other things as well" (p. 2821). Unlike Franziska, old Frau Jordan does not allow herself to analyze or judge her experience. She cherishes the memory of another child, Kiki, but she represses painful recollections of Leo's childhood behavior. On the surface, she constantly effaces herself while praising her exceptional son; random thoughts, however, tell another story of a vindictive and grasping man who has abandoned his mother, is incapable of close relationships, and may have sent an inconvenient relative to the concentration camps. Old Frau Jordan is incapable of openly judging the contrast between her own sacrifices and Leo's blatant neglect, and defends herself from disillusionment by insisting that "Leo is just such a good son!" (p. 2813). When the pressure becomes too great, she recedes into hallucinations of barking dogs that blot out her real-life anxiety. Yet her buried resentment surfaces in different ways: in an implied criticism when Elfi replaces Franziska ("how many wives was that now anyway. . . . The barking was so close now that for an instant she was certain that Nuri was with her again and would jump at him and bark" [pp. 2822–23]); in self-abasing comments ("your dumb old mother can hardly read anymore anyway" [p. 2823]; in our discovery that her accusing Frau Agnes of having taken ten schillings probably displaces an earlier incident she tries to forget ("the day when the last ten schillings had disappeared and Leo had lied to her" [p. 2823]).

Throughout the story, the indirect focal point is Leo Jordan. Bachmann has very cleverly shown (rather than merely stated) how thoroughly these Vietnamese women are defined by the invisible priority of the men on whom they depend. Leo is the subject of all their conversations and a dominant figure without ever being present. His destructive impact is clearly connected with Bachmann's equation of patriarchy and fascism; Leo's authoritarian use and intimidation of others for his own purposes, his alienation from human relationships that would imply equality, and his scorn of women and homosexuals, are all reminiscent of Nazi beliefs. Bachmann evokes the Nazi connections especially strongly in the passages concerning Leo's homosexual cousin, Johannes, and the study of the concentration camps. Leo Jordan's attacks on Johannes (like his criticism of his first wife) have a suspicious and even guilty air. Johannes had paid for Leo's education, but "Leo was reluctant to be reminded of his mother and his former wives and lovers who were nothing to him but a conspiracy of creditors from whom he would escape only by belittling them to himself and others" (p. 2816). We learn from old Frau Jordan's "roundabout way of saying things" that Leo very likely denounced his cousin either out of spite or to protect himself. When his mother learns that Dr. Jordan has written a book on "The Significance of Endogeneous and Exogenous Factors in Connection with the Occurrence of Paranoid and Depressive Psychoses in Former Concentration Camp Inmates and Refugees," she is worried and recalls a mysterious "other thing" that turns out to be Johannes's detention in a concentration camp for a year and a half. Simultaneously, she notes that her son "knows how to defend himself" and that "[i]t meant a certain amount of danger for Leo, having a relative who . . . " (pp. 2818–19). Franziska, ironically, interprets the old woman's statement as referring to the wartime danger of having a relative in a concentration camp; more likely (especially given the references to barking that begin at this point) Leo had protected himself by denouncing his cousin. Does Johannes have a "paranoid and depressed" suspicion that such might be the case? If so, it would be important for Dr. Jordan to put such psychoses in scientific perspective.

One of the pleasures of reading *The Barking* lies in its indirect, enigmatic discourse and the opportunity it offers to reconstruct different characters from a variety of clues. Although the headnote on pp. 2809–13 in the anthology refers to a fuller picture of Dr. Jordan in *The Franza Case*, it is more rewarding to read *The Barking* in terms of the information given by the story itself. We know, for example, by the end of the story, that both women are dead, but we do not know precisely when or how they died. We can only guess why Leo and Franziska separate; Leo may be involved in another affair that has become serious, or he may be irritated by Franziska's signs of independent thinking. The language itself provides clues to the characters's psychological identity. Thoughts reported in a stream-of-consciousness style reveal not only information but also attitudes and anxieties: Franziska, secretly purchasing a radio for her mother-in-law, reassures herself that she "broke into the meager savings she had set aside for some sort of emergency which would hopefully never arise and could only be a minor emergency at any rate" (pp. 2814–15).

Students are sometimes puzzled by the last paragraph, which seems to have little to do with the plot except to make sure that the Pineider taxi service is paid. Yet this paragraph serves as a kind of pendant to the rest of the story. It is not necessary to know that Dr. Martin Ranner (according to *The Franza Case*) accompanied his sister to Egypt, where she died in a paroxysm of self-reproach after being raped by strangers; or that her feeling of self-worth, already severely damaged by Dr. Jordan's insidious attacks, was completely destroyed by this last assault. The last paragraph does not provide this information, but it does complete several themes and acts as a partial counterbalance to the bleak picture of old Frau Jordan's increasing paranoia and death. We learn several things: first, that Franziska is dead and her brother has a strong reason never to see Leo Jordan again; second that Leo Jordan's destructive example is not the only way of life in contemporary society: Dr. Ranner values human relationships and assumes ethical obligations beyond what is strictly necessary (this may be Bachmann's "utopian" side, although it is diminished by the fact that only the men survive); and third, that Leo Jordan had probably acted true to form by refusing, over several months, to pay the taxi bill incurred by his former wife on his mother's behalf.

Classroom Strategies

The Barking can be taught in one class period. If your students have read the story carefully and have no immediate questions, you may want to move directly to a discussion of the barking itself and its function as a psychological barrier between old Frau Jordan and a reality she cannot face. Some students may well ask you about the last paragraph—which leaves you starting at the end, with a description of the underlying themes

that come together at this point. It may be easiest, however, to begin at
the beginning, with the description of old Frau Jordan and what we learn
about the other characters through her eyes. As soon as her relationship
to Franziska is established, it will be useful to introduce the various discovery patterns that are developed throughout the story. The image of
Leo Jordan can then be brought out as the hidden, yet dominant, reference point that illustrates Bachmann's attack on the damage done to
women and other marginalized figures by a patriarchal (or fascist) society.
There are a number of useful themes or passages to consider with the
class: the various examples of old Frau Jordan's self-criticism, humility,
fear (and buried resentment) of her son; the several stages of Franziska's
recognition that the "Leo she came to know through the old woman was a
completely different Leo from the man she had married" (p. 2814); the
enigma of Leo's relationship to Johannes and his study of concentration-
camp psychoses; Leo's personality as an embodiment of fascism; the various passages describing dogs and barking. Discussion should be easy to
elicit throughout this story, whether as comments on individual passages,
on the differing reaction of Franziska and old Frau Jordan, on Bachmann's view of patriarchy and fascism, or on the recent rise of political
groups with neo-Nazi sympathies.

Topics for Discussion

1. What is the significance of the barking? What function does it serve
   for old Frau Jordan? When (and in what context) does she first mention hearing dogs barking? How does Nuri fit into the context?
2. Why is the story titled *The Barking* and not *Old Frau Jordan* or *The
   Jordan Family*? Give some examples of barking in the story and relate them to the plot.
3. Discuss the way that the characters's language (especially unspoken
   thoughts) reveal their psychological attitudes.
4. Discuss Leo Jordan's relationship to his cousin Johannes.
5. Discuss Bachmann's equation of patriarchy with fascism, using examples from the story.
6. Is Leo Jordan a good psychiatrist, in your opinion? Explain.
7. What responsibility—if any—does old Frau Jordan bear for her own
   fate?
8. Describe the various ways in which Franziska tries to help her
   mother-in-law. How do these attempts put her into conflict with her
   husband?
9. How does Franziska come to see her husband in a different light?
   Cite and discuss specific examples.

Comparative Perspective

1. Compare the narrative attitudes toward maternal figures in *The
   Barking*, *Matryona's Home*, and *Breast-Giver*. Is the point of these
   stories to make us feel sorry for unhappy mothers? Is there any

sense in which old Frau Jordan, Matryona, and Jashoda are complicit in their own fates? Did Frau Jordan have options in life that she should have explored in order to free herself from her tyrannical son? How seriously do you view Ignatich's remark that Matryona "was forever meddling in men's work" when he explains how she died? How do you interpret the last line of Mahasweta's story?

[Bachmann criticizes Leo more than she blames old Frau Jordan, and Ignatich's moments of annoyance with Matryona serve only to emphasize her selflessness. The case of Jashoda is more complex.]

2. Compare Bachmann's use of the dog Nuri's barking with other instances of similar narrative shorthand. When a pet offers testimony that helps us understand human behavior, what view of the animal world seems to prevail?

[This favorite device, which students will recognize from vampire films if from no other source, seems specific to Western authors, who tend to sentimentalize alert animals as inhabitants of a separate realm. Pets, inarticulate but expressive of their owners's inner lives, differ fundamentally from the talking, clever animals of African, Native American, and Asian storytelling. Consider, if appropriate, the information about character provided by Argos, the ancient dog who recognizes the disguised Odysseus in Book XVII of Homer's *Odyssey*; the repeated references to lapdogs in *The Rape of the Lock*; or the rebellious tomcat who adopts Moyna in *The Rooftop Dwellers*.]

Further Reading

See also the reading suggestions in the anthology, pp. 2812–13.

Achberger, Karen. "Introduction" to *The Thirtieth Year*. 1987. Situates Bachmann in twentieth-century German literature; concise discussion of the short stories.

Frederiksen, Elke, ed. *Women Writers of Germany, Austria, and Switzerland: An Annotated Bio-Bibliographical Guide*. 1989. Includes a brief discussion of Bachmann's work.

Frieden, Sandra. "Bachmann's *Malina* and *Todesarten*: Subliminal Crimes." *The German Quarterly* 56, 1 (January 1983), pp. 61–73. Considers Bachmann a precursor of German "inner-directed" novels; discusses the psychoanalytic overtones of her style.

Mahasweta Devi

Breast-Giver

Backgrounds and Classroom Strategies

Mahasweta Devi's fiction requires teachers to work with students on how to read fiction that is ideologically driven. How does the aesthetic of a story such as *Breast-Giver*, in which the political is deliberately foregrounded, differ from that of fiction in which ideological contexts are less explicit? What does Mahasweta Devi, a major figure among a number of politically engaged writers active in the regional languages of India, contribute to the fiction of "commitment"?

Mahasweta Devi writes powerful novels and short stories in which she imaginatively delineates the struggle of exploited groups in Bengal (and other eastern Indian states) to survive and overcome their oppression. She writes about women, tribals, and landless laborers because she sees them as the principal marginalized segments of Bengali/Indian society and as people who in their own ways are heroically resisting their marginalization. Students might find it useful to contrast Mahasweta's illumination of the lives of the oppressed in terms of economic oppression and class struggle with her eminent predecessor Rabindranath Tagore's primarily humanistic and psychological approach to similar themes (Tagore, *Punishment*). They should also keep in mind that the leftist stance of Mahasweta and a number of other Bengali writers of the 1960s to the present is of a piece with the political ambience of the state of Bengal, which has had a Communist government since 1967.

Breast-Giver is the story of Jashoda Patitundo, who moves from a role expected of her, that of the good wife, to that of the wage-earner in her family. When her husband, the poor brahmin Kangali, is crippled as a result of the carelessness of his employer's son, Jashoda moves into the employer's extended family household as a wet-nurse, thus allowing the Haldar women to bear children without losing their trim figures. In the course of the narrative, Jashoda's breasts—those "precious objects," which evolve from being objects of pleasure for her husband to being the family's means of livelihood—are invaded by cancer. At the end of the story, Jashoda, "mother-for-hire" and mother of "the world," dies alone and uncared for.

Mahasweta's third-person narrative clearly depicts the many ways in which familial, feudal, and patriarchal systems intersect and overlap in the exploitation of women and the lower classes of Bengali society. Details such as the mention of the Haldar patriarch's rise to wealth through participation in capitalism and collaboration with colonialism are essential to the narrative of Jashoda's life and death. No group is spared— exploitative Kali temple priests who cook up idol cults, the women of the Haldar residence, the self-centered Haldar boy, the narrow-minded hoarder collaborationist. In Mahasweta's synoptic vision the supreme irony of Jashoda's multiple motherhoods is that, by virtue of he femaleness, which is centered in her body (and above all in her breasts and womb), Jashoda is destined to be the ultimate victim of every form of exploitation, even when she takes on the role of principal wage-earner for her family. Within existing social systems role-reversals are, at best, superficial, while the deeper ideological tools of oppression continue to operate unhindered.

And yet, Mahasweta Devi's characters, particularly the women and tribal men who are the protagonists of much of her fiction, are heroines and heroes rather than victims. Few Indian writers have focused, as Mahasweta has, on women as wage-earners, professionals, and actors in history. Even Jashoda, who dies uncared for, is a subject and agent in her own life as well as an object of oppression. Students should be encouraged to discuss the manner in which Mahasweta solves the problem of a writer from the elite segment of society attempting to articulate the subjectivity of marginalized people. In Mahasweta's view, the fiction writer is also a historian, whose role is to witness the struggle of ordinary people, to listen to their voices, and to bear witness imaginatively to their everyday lives as the history of struggle and resistance.

The semidocumentary style and narrative voice that the author has invented to achieve her goals is by any measure striking and unique. Students will need to be alerted to the fact that Mahasweta is rebelling especially against the middle-class and sentimental tenor of much Bengali prose fiction (for example, in the novels of Saratchandra Chatterjee, a famous Bengali author, whose novels she mentions). The targets of Mahasweta's satire range from the good wives of Saratchandra's novels, who always feed their husbands an "extra mouthful of rice," to failed nationalism, Bengali regionalism, and the utopian humanism of the Bengal Renaissance writers and thinkers. Her unique eclecticism incorporates into her style diverse aspects of Indian literary and cultural discourse, referring in the same breath to ancient myths and modern movie queens. Nearly unique in modern Indian fiction is her bold, unsentimental, yet enormously compassionate treatment of the subjects of female sexuality and the oppression of women. Similarly, few Indian writers have succeeded as Mahasweta has in revealing the connections among the various forms of violation of human rights—political, economic, sexual. Jashoda shares the burden of the motherhood of the world not only with the Hindu Mother Goddess, but also with Mother India, a tremendously influential metaphor for the nation coined by Bengali writer and nationalist Bankim Chandra Chatterjee (1838–1894). This writing is calculated to shock the middle-class audience for Bengali fiction out of its complacency.

Topics for Discussion and Writing

1. Discuss the effect of Mahasweta's style on her goals of exposing the exploitation of the underclasses and of writing the history of struggle and resistance.
2. Compare Mahasweta Devi's style with that of Tagore, a major influence on style in Bengali fiction. Read the short story *Punishment*. Comment in particular on the use of irony by both writers.
3. Discuss the interaction between traditional Indian images of the ideal wife and mother and Mahasweta's portrayal of Jashoda. What are the roles of motherhood and the Mother Goddess in this story?
4. Compare Mahasweta's style, and her imaginative critique of social injustice, with their counterparts in the Hindi writer Premchand's *The Road to Salvation*.

5. If you have read works of fiction by other women writers, including writers who identify themselves as feminist writers, compare their representations of the female body and sexuality with Mahasweta Devi's in this story. What are the cultural factors that account for the differences, if any, in these representations?

6. Contrast Mahasweta's realism with the erotic idealization of the female body in classical Indian works such as Kālidāsa's *Śakuntalā*.

Comparative Perspectives

1. "Is a Mother so cheaply made? / Not just by dropping a babe!" What is the connection between bearing children and being a mother? Jashoda is a *professional mother*, having produced twenty children and nursed many more. Do we get a sense of a loving human connection with these children from Mahasweta's way of describing her efforts? How would you characterize the tone of these lines: "Her mother-love wells up for Kangali as much as for the children. She wants to become the earth and feed her crippled husband and helpless children with a fulsome harvest."

   [The extraordinary deftness with which slang vocabulary and direct address of the reader constantly undermine sentiment in Spivak's translation of *Breast-Giver* constantly challenges interpretation. No person, institution, or belief seems safe from the lethal aim of this dazzlingly self-conscious narrative.]

2. Consider the claims to motherhood of some other female figures in this volume, including Matryona (who gives birth to six children, only to see them die in infancy, and raises her niece in her own home—nevertheless she interests Solzhenitsyn less for her maternity than for her sanctitude); the pregnant Hedda Gabler's revulsion at the thought of impending motherhood and the contribution that thought makes to her successful suicide); and the conflict between mother and stepmother in *The Black Cloth*.

3. Most of the stories by modern feminists in the anthology pay at least as much attention to relationships between and among women in extended families as they do to the roles played by men in their lives. Yet none of these writers depicts "sisterhood" as a benign state of female solidarity. Discuss the differences between the widowed Mrs. Haldar, "constantly occupied with women's rituals," her daughters-in-law, and their daughters. Does Mahasweta see them as individual personalities or as representatives of generational change? Compare the assumptions about family life and female bonding that emerge in *The Barking* (which explores the growing sympathy Franziska feels for her mother-in-law), or the friendship of Tara and Moyna in *The Rooftop Dwellers*.

Further Reading

See the reading suggestions in the anthology, p. 2825.

GABRIEL GARCÍA MÁRQUEZ

Death Constant Beyond Love

Backgrounds

We read García Márquez for the sheer pleasure of his inventiveness, the explosiveness of his language, the lushness of his imagination. His short fiction often has the magic and energy of a good children's story, and he creates in his readers something that very few writers, even good ones, manage: wonder.

Senator Onésimo Sánchez sells illusions. He has made the same illusory promises every four years in the "illusory" village of Rosal del Virrey, a town so dreary and sordid that "[e]ven its name was a kind of joke, because the only rose in that village was being worn by Senator Onésimo Sánchez himself . . ." (p. 2849). As in all his previous campaign visits, he brings with him the illusory props of political promises: rented Indians to swell the crowds, music and rockets, cardboard facades of make-believe red-brick houses, an ocean liner made of colored paper, artificial trees with leaves made of felt, rainmaking machines, oils of happiness that will make things grow in the sterile landscape of the village. But this time, Onésimo Sánchez can only go through the motions. His awareness of his imminent death outweighs all other considerations. When he meets himself in the darkness of his own self-knowledge (in part derived from Marcus Aurelius), Sánchez recognizes that *"whether it's you or someone else, it won't be long before you'll be dead and it won't be long before your name won't even be left"* (p. 2854). He finds himself unable to sympathize with the rented Indians, barefoot on the saltpeter coals of the blistering village square; he looks upon the villagers with disdain because they are still willing to believe in his carnival of illusions, his fictional world. What Sánchez now realizes is that his marvelous world of illusions, even though it is backed by the force of money and political power, cannot defeat the reality of death, of nature, of the absolute and final solitude of every man.

On this final visit to Rosal del Virrey, Senator Sánchez encounters Laura Farina, who appears to him wearing a "cheap, faded Guajiro Indian robe" and, though her face is "painted as protection against the sun," it is such that "it was possible to imagine that there had never been another so beautiful in the whole world" (p. 2852). She embodies that which he uses to fend off the pressure of reality: beauty and love. Like the rose that he has carried with him to that sordid village, Laura's beauty promises to defeat the sterility of the landscape; her love promises to defeat death itself. But nature, and death, cannot be eluded. At the story's end, Senator Sánchez holds her "about the waist, sank his face into woods-animal armpit, and gave in to terror. Six months and eleven days later he would die in that same position, debased and repudiated because of the public scandal with Laura Farina and weeping with rage at dying without her" (p. 2855). The controlling notion of *Death Constant Beyond Love* is suggested by the blunt insistence of its title, which reverses the claims of

Quevedo's *Love Constant Beyond Death,* and acts as a kind of newspaper headline announcing the final discovery of Senator Onésimo Sánchez.

One's first impression of *Death Constant Beyond Love* may be that it functions very close to allegory—Death, Nature, Love, Beauty, and Illusion seem to be functioning in the upper case—while at the same time it retains some of the qualities of the tall tale. Though both of these elements are certainly present in the story, its method is in no way easy to describe. García Márquez's characteristic style—magical realism—provokes something that all good fiction provokes, a recognition of the infinite suggestibility of language, but does so in particularly observable and enchanting ways. García Márquez has said that everything he writes has its source in something that actually happened and that fiction is "reality represented through a secret code." One of the most observable tendencies of García Márquez's magical realism is to use the "secret code" of his language to lead the reader—within a sentence, from sentence to sentence, from paragraph to paragraph—to places that no reader could have expected to be. He has said that his "real inclination is to be a conjuror," and indeed, the effect of his writing is to levitate the reader, to lift the reader out of the world of prior expectations and let him or her float giddily for a moment before finding ground again.

Death Constant Beyond Love demonstrates García Márquez's use of the techniques of magical realism. We can see how García Márquez suggests possible stories beyond the one he is telling, while at the same time he deepens our understanding of the central character:

> Senator Onésimo Sánchez was placid and weatherless inside the air-conditioned car, but as soon as he opened the door he was shaken by a gust of fire and his shirt of pure silk was soaked in a kind of light-colored soup and he felt many years older and more alone than ever.
>   (p. 2850)

This we might break down as follows:

> Senator Onésimo Sánchez was placid and weatherless inside the air-conditioned car,

In what way can someone be weatherless? The word certainly suggests calm, but it is a calm that is almost unnatural, almost artificial. This "weatherlessness" could be attributed to the air conditioning, but it further suggests that Sánchez is, by his own choice, unaffected by the unpleasant world of hot weather and, by implication, shabby poverty through which it is his duty to ride. The suggestion is that to be "weatherless" is to be somehow separated from life in Rosal del Virrey. The opposite, then, would also be true—to enter into the weather suggests a fundamental connection with life there.

> but as soon as he opened the door he was shaken by a gust of fire

We expect "hot air" or its equivalent here; we get "fire," perhaps because it is more elemental and attacks our own senses more aggressively. The word "shaken" first suggests a physical response, but by the end of the sentence it can be seen to suggest an emotional or spiritual response as well.

and his shirt of pure silk

He is rich; he shines in the blistering heat. The shirt suggests that the Senator is used to separating himself from the conditions in which his constituents pass their lives.

was soaked in a kind of light-colored soup

The weather attacks him; it has a life of its own, its own magical properties and effects. The word "soup" is particularly suggestive. The peculiar pungency and viscosity of "soup," in this context, compels the reader to participate in Sanchez's sensations. If we assume that this "soup" is *caused* by the weather, rather than being an aspect of the weather itself, we immediately translate "soup" into "sweat." But to say "Onésimo Sánchez sweated profusely" would hardly suggest the energy with which García Márquez wishes to endow the atmosphere of Rosal del Virrey.

and he felt many years older and more alone than ever.

Sanchez's feelings appear to derive from his transition from "weatherless-ness" to his immersion in the hot, soupy, and sordid world of Rosal del Virrey—that is, from rose to Rosal, from illusion to disillusion. These feelings of age and solitude are inescapable for Sánchez in his life just as they are inescapable in this sentence.

Magical realism, in the hands of García Márquez, is a wonderfully supple kind of writing. It penetrates objective reality to reveal the mysterious and poetic qualities that underlie the daily lives of the people and communities it describes. His characters have an aura of woeful futility combined with a wonderful innocence that lends them much of their essential charm and virtue as fictional creations.

Death Constant Beyond Love is, like all of García Márquez's fiction, very much a story of Latin America. The geographical, historical, cultural, political, and climatic texture of Latin American life is central to any discussion of García Márquez's work, it is only necessary to compare his work with that of Borges to note the extent to which this is true. It might even be said that magical realism, as a mode of writing, is inextricably bound to Latin America, where the influence of French and Spanish surrealism combined with a desire to use the magical myths of an indigenous tradition to reexamine, indeed transform, an imperfect "colonial" reality.

García Márquez's political concerns are manifest in *Death Constant Be-*

yond Love, just as they are in almost all of his work, including *One Hundred Years of Solitude* and, especially, *The Autumn of the Patriarch.* He is an active socialist, but one who insists on a socialism appropriate to the cultural and historical conditions of Latin America. "I think the world ought to be socialist," he has said,

> that it will be, and that we should help this to happen as quickly as possible. But I'm greatly disillusioned by the socialism of the Soviet Union. They arrived at their brand of socialism through special experiences and conditions, and are trying to impose in other countries their own bureaucracy, their own authoritarianism, and their own lack of historical vision. That isn't socialism and it's the great problem of the present moment.

Many of the traditional concerns of socialist writing—the exposure of political corruption and oppression, the condition of the common man, the effects of power and money, among others—are evident in García Márquez's work.

Almost everyone who has read García Márquez has noted the affinities between his work and that of William Faulkner. There is the epic creation of an entire fictional world—García Márquez's Macondo and Faulkner's Yoknapatawpha—complete with geography, history, and whole populations of extraordinary characters; there is the lyrical magic of their language, including the tendency to become excessively lyrical. García Márquez has said that he found Faulkner's world, the southern United States,

> was very like my world . . . created by the same people. . . . When I traveled in the southern states, I found evidence—on those hot, dusty roads, with the same vegetation, trees, and great houses—of the similarity between our two worlds. One mustn't forget that Faulkner is in a way a Latin American writer. His world is that of the Gulf of Mexico.

García Márquez has also said, however, that Faulkner's influence was "really screwing me up" and that his problem was "not how to imitate Faulkner but how to destroy him." Although García Márquez couldn't "destroy" Faulkner, he could move in his own direction: his style is now entirely his own.

García Márquez claims that he "began to long to write," and in fact did write his first stories, under the influence of Kafka's *The Metamorphosis.* Certainly, García Márquez's use of metaphor and his tendency to insist that his metaphors be taken literally, and our sometimes befuddled attempts to discover an absolute "meaning" beneath the text may remind us of our struggles with Kafka.

Classroom Strategies

Death Constant Beyond Love can be taught in one class period. Students will probably experience it as a kind of dessert after a term full of main courses. If students have any particular difficulty with the story it will very likely have to do with their resistance to taking it seriously. García Márquez's stylistic conjuring combined with his insouciance will probably distract those students who persistently struggle to find "meaning" in the text. The "meaning" is, of course, there—but it emerges like a rabbit out of a magician's hat. Students who resist magic will resist *Death Constant Beyond Love.*

To break down this resistance it might be useful first to discuss García Márquez's magical realism and to emphasize its difference from fantasy, from the tall tale, and from surrealism. Reminding students of Kafka's *The Metamorphosis*—with its apparent discrepancy between narrative tone and the extraordinary events being described—might aid them in resolving their problems with the techniques of magical realism.

You might then emphasize Onésimo Sánchez himself: as a would-be dictator, in full control of the means by which the illusion of his benevolence can be foisted on his public, who is nevertheless foiled by death (the allusions to Marcus Aurelius might be useful here); as a human being not unlike ourselves, who must face the knowledge of his own imminent death; as a man who attempts, and fails, to reduce the terror of self-knowledge through erotic passion. Budding Freudians in the classroom will want to play with the clear suggestion of Thanatos here, García Márquez's merging of Sanchez's movement toward death with his desire for passion—especially since the object of his passion is Laura Farina, the very embodiment of earth.

Topics for Discussion and Writing

1. What is the importance of the title of the story? What does it tell us about the story's central thematic concerns?

   [See the third paragraph of "Backgrounds" for discussion.]

2. García Márquez has said that everything he has written has been about solitude. In what ways is *Death Constant Beyond Love* about solitude?

   [See the second and third paragraphs of "Backgrounds" for discussion.]

3. What is the symbolic importance of the rose, the chastity belt, the campaign props, and Laura Farina herself?

   [The rose, campaign props, and Laura Farina are discussed in "Backgrounds." The chastity belt worn by Laura Farina would appear to suggest, ironically, that Sanchez's final attempt to find love, and to fend off death, extracts a literal price. The route to beauty and love, then, is blocked by a padlock—a padlock that can be removed only when he turns one of his heretofore illusory promises into a reality.]

4. What similarities and differences can be found between García Márquez's fictional techniques and those of William Faulkner? Franz Kafka? Charles Dickens? How are these techniques similar to

those found in the *Odyssey*? How can magical realism be characterized?

[See the fourth through the eleventh paragraphs of "Backgrounds" for discussion.]

5. How does García Márquez link death with nature and illusion with
beauty in the story?

[See the second and third paragraphs of "Backgrounds" for discussion.]

Comparative Perspectives

1. "We are here for the purpose of defeating nature," Senator Onésimo
Sánchez declares in his standard campaign speech, but he speaks,
as the narrator of *Death Constant Beyond Love* informs us, "against
all his convictions." What is wrong with this statement? Why is it
worth telling us that the Senator has an honors degree in metallur-
gical engineering?

[An engineer may modify nature, but no one can defeat it, as the
senator's death sentence emphasizes.]

2. Compare the interplay of politics and nature in some other works
you have read this semester: is the effort to transform (or even defeat) nature always presented with the irony of García Márquez, or
do other writers see any ways in which public policy and human effort may genuinely ameliorate and improve the natural world?

[The Enlightenment is a good point at which to begin a review of
these questions. Compare Swift's serious proposals for improving
human nature (for example, "curing the expansiveness of pride, vanity, idleness, and gaming in our women") and Pope's assertion in *An
Essay on Man* that "Presumptuous Man" should leave nature to its
own devices. Discuss Romantic views of nature—Leopardi's, for example, or Wordsworth's. Examples from modern literature include
The Bear and *Matryona's Home*.]

3. García Márquez relies on his audience to understand the references
to Marcus Aurelius in *Death Constant Beyond Love*. Like Eliot and
Borges, he weaves echoes of past literary accomplishments into all of
his work and, like Eliot and Borges, has himself become a major influence on other late-twentieth-century authors. What is the irony of
the quotation from Marcus Aurelius? How are artists remembered?

Further Reading

See also the reading suggestions in the anthology, p. 2849.

Apuleyo Mendoza, Plinio. *The Fragrance of Guava*. Translated by Ann
Wright. 1983. A series of interviews with García Márquez.

Bell-Villada, Gene H. *García Márquez: The Man and His Work*. 1990. A
general description aimed at a broad audience.

Bloom, Harold, ed. *Gabriel García Márquez.* 1989. Collects eighteen essays on style, themes, and cultural contexts; chronology and bibliography.

Books Abroad. The Summer 1972 issue is dedicated to García Márquez.

Byk, John. "From Fact to Fiction: Gabriel García Márquez and the Short Story." *Mid-American Review* 6, 2 (1986), pp. 111–16.

McGuirk, Bernard, and Richard Cardwell, eds. *Gabriel García Márquez: New Readings.* 1987. Twelve essays plus the 1982 Nobel Address.

McMurray, George R., ed. *Critical Essays on Gabriel García Márquez.* 1987. Fifteen reviews plus fourteen articles and essays on a range of García Márquez's work.

McNerey, Kathleen. *Understanding Gabriel García Márquez.* 1989. A useful introduction with comments on the different works; includes a short biography stressing cultural context and a bibliography.

Minta, Stephen. *Gabriel García Márquez: Writer of Colombia.* 1987. An introduction.

Ortega, Julio, and Claudia Elliot. *Gabriel García Márquez and the Powers of Fiction.* 1988. A general collection that includes five essays and the 1982 Nobel lecture.

Shaw, Bradley A., and Nora Vera-Godwin. *Critical Perspectives on Gabriel García Márquez.* 1986. Nine essays on a wide range of topics with considerable textual analysis.

Williams, Raymond L. *Gabriel García Márquez.* 1984. An introductory study.

———. "The Visual Arts, the Poetization of Space and Writing: an Interview with Gabriel García Márquez." *PMLA* 104, 2 (March 1989), pp. 131–40.

CHINUA ACHEBE

Things Fall Apart

Backgrounds

"Literature, whether handed down by word of mouth or in print, gives us a second handle on reality." Achebe's belief in the social importance of literature emerges clearly in this sentence from the polemic essay *What Has Literature Got to Do with It?* Literature for him is not an ornamental fringe benefit of civilization; to the contrary, it provides a necessary critical perspective on everyday experience. By illuminating contexts and choices, literature—both traditional oral literature and the modern printed text—educates us to the meaning of our own actions and offers greater control over our social and personal lives. Achebe continues: literature works by

> enabling us to encounter in the safe, manageable dimensions of make-believe the very same threats to integrity that may assail the psyche in real life; and at the same time providing through the self-discovery which it imparts a veritable weapon for coping with these threats whether they are found within our problematic and incoherent selves or in the world around us.

Thus far, Achebe's description of the educational role of literature could be attributed to many writers in the realistic tradition: Flaubert, Dostoevsky, Ibsen, Solzhenitsyn, or Freud. Nor would his point of view be alien to other writers for whom literature expresses a kind of knowledge: the poet William Butler Yeats, for example, whose description of cultural disintegration ("things fall apart; the centre cannot hold") is borrowed for the title of Achebe's first novel. Yet the particular reality that Achebe describes is located at a specific point in history: a modern Africa whose rich variety of ethnic and cultural identities is further complicated by the impact of European colonialism.

Since the publication of *Things Fall Apart* (1958), Achebe has assumed a leading position as representative and interpreter of African culture at home and abroad. To a European audience that was accustomed to stereotypes of primitive savages in "darkest Africa" (e.g., the murderous Kali worshippers or loyal servants of Kipling's *Gunga Din*), he has emphasized the complexities of a different society with its alternate set of traditions, ideals and values. Achebe was enraged that *Time* magazine would call Joyce Cary's *Mister Johnson* "the best novel ever written about Africa" when Cary depicted Africa as a stagnant and impoverished culture whose

> people would not know the change if time jumped back fifty thousand years. They live like mice or rats in a palace floor; all the magnificence and variety of the arts, the learning and the battles of civilisation go on over their heads and they do not even imagine them. (Cited by Achebe from *Mister Johnson*)

He was dismayed that Africans themselves would internalize this kind of attitude and emulate a supposedly superior white European civilization. In *The Novelist as Teacher* (from *Morning Yet on Creation Day*), Achebe reports how a student used European seasons to describe African weather, writing about "winter" when he meant the period in which the harmattan wind blows. If he did not use the European terms, the student explained, everyone would call him a "bushman"! Achebe's mission, therefore, is to educate African as well as European readers, reinstating a sense of pride in African culture "to help my society regain belief in itself and put away the complexes of the years of denigration and self-abasement."

This educational mission is not a simple one, and Achebe has not hesitated to explore the complexities and contradictions of modern African—specifically Igbo—society. Indeed, he has found himself in conflict with several other writers who prefer a narrower or more militant perspective aimed at reconstituting an essentially "African" identity. For Achebe, this quest is ideal rather than practical, and modern African society must recognize that it has been irrevocably marked by the colonial era. He mistrusts absolutes and generalizations about "African identity," no matter how useful such concepts may temporarily be. "You have all heard of the African personality, of African democracy, of the African way to socialism, of negritude, and so on. They are all props we have fashioned at different times to help us get on our feet again." Perhaps the most famous disagreement between Achebe and his peers concerns the debate over the African author's choice of language. Should African writers use the "colonizer's language" (e.g., English or French) or should they use only their tribal tongue in order to build up an indigenous literature and reject any vestiges of colonial influence? James Ngugi stopped writing novels in English and, as Ngugi wa Thiong'o, began to write in his native Gikuyu (these novels are then translated into English for a Western audience). Achebe has a different attitude. His language is an "African English" expressing a particular cultural experience, and he sees

> a new voice coming out of Africa, speaking of African experience in a worldwide language. So my answer to the question *Can an African ever learn English well enough to be able to use it effectively in creative writing?* is certainly yes. If on the other hand you ask: *Can he ever learn to use it like a native speaker?* I should say, I hope not. . . . The African writer should aim to use English in a way that brings out his message best without altering the language to the extent that its value as a medium of international exchange will be lost. He should aim at fashioning out an English which is at once universal and able to carry his peculiar experience.
>
> (*The African Writer and the English Language*, 1964)

In addition to writing the five novels for which he is best known, Achebe has traveled widely and been an active representative of African letters. In 1962 he became the founding editor for Heinemann Books's publishing line called the African Writers Series, and he has founded and edited two journals: *Okike: An African Journal of New Writing* (1971) and the bilingual *Uwa ndi Igbo: a Journal of Igbo Life and Culture* (1986). Two books of essays, *Morning Yet on Creation Day* (1975) and *Hopes and Impediments* (1988), collect major statements such as *The Novelist as Teacher, The African Writer and the English Language, Colonialist Criticism, Chi in Igbo Cosmology, Africa and her Writers, What Has Literature Got to Do with It?* and *An Image of Africa*, as well as occasional pieces stemming from debates over African culture. Achebe's conviction concerning the importance of literature in creating a national identity led him and poet Christopher Okigbo to envisage a series of children's stories that would offer African children a better sense of their cultural heritage. Their Citadel Press was discontinued after Okigbo was killed in the Biafran war, but the novelist has nonetheless written *Chike and the River* (1966), a novella told from the point of view of an eleven-year-old boy, the animal fable *How The Leopard Got His Claws* (1972, with John Iroaganachi), and various adaptations of traditional tales for children. In fiction, poetry, essays, and lectures, Achebe returns to basic themes of human freedom and dignity for, as he says in an essay written during the Biafran war, "if an artist is anything, he is a human being with heightened sensitivities; he must be aware of the faintest nuances of injustice in human relations."

Things Fall Apart demonstrates this concern for the quality of human relations on both an individual and a societal level. Whether describing Okonkwo's family, interactions between neighbors and villages, the evolution of traditional Igbo society in response to internal and external pressures, or the arrival of British missionaries and colonial administrators, Achebe has a sharp and often ironic eye for the shifting balances of human relationships. His characters are strongly drawn but they are never simplified, from the briefly mentioned couple Ndulue and Ozoemena, whose mutual devotion amazes Okonkwo, to the complex character of the hero himself. Okonkwo is introduced at the beginning as a powerful and ambitious man who stammers under strong emotion and has recourse to his fists; he is arrogant and even a bully, yet he has an unadmitted tender side that appears in his relationship to his wife Ekwefi, his caring for Ezinma during her fever, and his attachment to Ikemefuna, whose death at his hands shatters him for days. Achebe prepares the reader to understand the contradictions in Okonkwo's personality by his extended description of the hero's shiftless father, Unoka, in the very first pages. Humiliated by Unoka's laziness, shameful death, and lack of title, compelled early to support the entire family, Okonkwo struggles desperately throughout the novel to root out any sign of inherited "feminine" weakness in himself or his son Nwoye.

This insistence on warlike masculine valor corresponds to traditional Igbo values, and Okonkwo rises high in his clan as long as these values are predominant. Nonetheless, things are already starting to fall apart. Internal pressures are at work and point to change. Obierika disapproves of the expedition to kill Ikemefuna, and he later starts to question the exposure of twins; the *osu* (outcasts) are not content with their status and will be quick to convert to Christianity; Nwoye is unhappy under Okonkwo's bullying, and he will never forget that his father killed his foster brother, Ikemefuna. The process is only hastened and distorted by the arrival of British missionaries, administrators, and the new trading stores with their flow of money. Traditional social and religious values—as well as the authority of the villages to govern themselves—are on their way out. In the first two thirds of the novel, Umuofia's elaborately harmonious society has been clearly established; in the last third, Achebe provides a contrasting description of the invasive colonial presence. These portrayals are scathing. Mr. Smith, who succeeds a more accommodating minister in the church at Umuofia, enforces a harsh and rigid view of Christianity:

"He saw things in black and white. And black was evil" (p. 2937). The British administrators rule over a populace whose language and customs they do not even try to understand and which they see as a kind of exotica about which one writes scientific books. They establish a system of "court messengers" to convey orders, and the court messengers become a second layer of corruption by using their borrowed authority to cheat and exploit the common people. The District Commissioner lies to get the village leaders in his power and throws them into jail until the villagers have paid an exorbitant fine. Okonkwo's passionate resistance to this exploitation and deceit makes him even more of a hero—or would, if his society had not changed. The Igbo community is afraid of defying raw power (the same power that has jailed their leaders), and when they meet they cannot decide how to respond. At this point, Okonkwo is ready to act alone, separate from the community that has provided context and reference point hitherto. His enraged execution of the imperious court messenger isolates him completely from the community he has just endangered, and it leads him to commit suicide. Suicide is a shameful or taboo death, just like his father's, and this abomination further separates "one of the greatest men of Umuofia" from the clan. On the last page, Obierika's emotional tribute to his friend contrasts bleakly with the suggestion that this tale of flawed epic heroism will be buried in the annals of colonial history as a "reasonable paragraph [in the District Commissioner's book] *The Pacification of the Primitive Tribes of the Lower Niger.*"

Language

Certain aspects of Achebe's "African English" are worth mentioning here. The presence of untranslated Igbo words reminds Western readers of the presence of another linguistic culture that has its own frames of thought and separate identifying words. Words such as *egwugwu* or *iyiuwa* are used repeatedly without translation, but their meaning is clear from the context, and their very presence in the English text is a constant reminder of the blend of two cultures.

On a less obvious level, there are also Igbo names whose meaning subtly reinforces themes in the story: a buried, yet real, level of significance that is available to those who take the trouble (as the District Commissioner does not do) to inquire about the African language. Footnotes here explain some of these buried meanings: the name of Okonkwo's lazy father, Unoka, means "Home is supreme"; the doomed Ikemefuna is named "My strength should not be dissipated"; and Nwoye's name (built on the non-gendered root *Nwa* or "child," and discussed in the headnote, pp. 2858–59 in the anthology) contrasts with Okonkwo's name, which combines stereotypical attributes of masculinity (Oko) and a non-Christian Igbo heritage (he was born on Nkwo, the third day of the four-day Igbo week). Ikemefuna, taken from his family and later killed by Okonkwo, whom he considers his father, sings his favorite song about "Nnadi"—whose name, pathetically, means "Father is there" or "Father exists" (note 5, p. 2875).

Finally, Achebe integrates into his narrative a characteristic aspect of Igbo speech: the common use of proverbs. As he explains in the conversation between Unoka and Okoye, "proverbs are the palm-oil with which words are eaten" (p. 2862). (Okoye, leading up to asking for his money, "said the next half a dozen sentences in proverbs.") Proverbs such as "[h]e who brings kola brings life" (p. 2861) or "the sun will shine on those who stand before it shines on those who kneel under them" (p. 2862) or "if a child washed his hands he could eat with kings" (p. 2862) are inserted into the narrative so appropriately that their nature as proverbs may be overlooked, but in the aggregate they illustrate a characteristic aspect of Igbo thought and speech.

Most of the names in *Things Fall Apart* are pronounced basically as they would be in English (e.g., Okonkwo as *oh-kon'-kwo*), once we exclude the fact that Igbo is a tonal language using high or low tones for individual syllables. (Igbo itself is pronounced *ee'-boh*.) Nonetheless, certain pronunciations, where the stress or number of syllables might be in question, are approximated below.

Agbala *(ag'-ba-la)*
Ajofia *(ah'-joh-fyah)*
Chielo *(chee'-ay-low)*
Ezeani *(ez-ah'-nee)*
Ezeugo *(e'-zoo-goh)*
Ikemefuna *(ee-kay-may'-foo-na)*
Ikezue *(ee'-kay'-zoo-eh)*
kwenu *(kway'-noo)*
Ndulue *(in'-doo-loo'-eh)*
Nwakibie *(nwa'-kee-ee'-bee-yay)*
Nwayieke *(nwah'-ee-eh'-kay)*
Nwoye *(nwoh'-yeh)*
Obiageli *(oh-bee-ah'-gay-lee)*
Ofoedu *(oh-foh'-eh-doo')*
Okoye *(oh-ko'-yeh)*
Onwumbiko *(on'-wum-bee'-koh)*
Ozoemena *(oh-zeh'-meh-na)*
Umuofia *(oo'-moo-off'-yah)*
Unoka *(oo'-no-ka)*

Classroom Strategies

Things Fall Apart may be taught in three days: more if you wish to include related cultural material. You may want to begin by giving some sense of recent African history, perhaps starting with a map of contemporary Africa and comparing it with a map of Africa in 1939, a map that shows colonial protectorates covering almost all the continent. (Both maps are readily available in a modern atlas.) Photographs or African art objects (masks, statuettes, cloth, bowls, metalwork, decorated calabash gourds) provided by you or your students will also help to convey the artistic presence and vitality of another culture—a culture opposed, in *Things Fall Apart,* to a European or "progress-oriented" system that is presumably more familiar to your class. As you evoke the particular African society that is about to "fall apart," the novel's title will acquire more and more significance. Comparisons to Yeats's view of modern European history are certainly appropriate, but it may be even more interesting to ask why a Nigerian writer discussing the African colonial experience would find it useful to draw upon a masterwork of English literature.

Things Fall Apart is Okonkwo's story, and students will be fascinated from the beginning by this combative, contradictory, and passionate character. Yet he is very much a member of his community, accepting its laws and struggling to achieve greatness according to traditional values. Achebe's hero does not define himself as a rebel *against* society, as do the heroes of so many European and American novels, from *René* to *Catcher in the Rye.* In order to understand his character, therefore, and the poignancy of his ultimate isolation, you will find it useful to consider the values of traditional Igbo society as they are introduced at the beginning of the novel. What are the customs and cultural expectations of Umuofia? How does one succeed in this society, and who is left out? What are the important crops? What is the role of war, of religion, and of the arts? How are decisions made in Umuofia, and who makes them? What differing roles do men and women play? What do we learn from the kola ceremony about hospitality and the taking of titles? The dramatic description of Okonkwo's success and Unoka's failure in the first section incorporates a great deal of information about the many dimensions of Igbo society.

Okonkwo is usually presented as a tragic hero, surmounting obstacles that would crush a weaker person, eventually defeated by the same qualities that sustain his greatness. His impoverished beginning as Unoka's son, the complete failure of his crops when he has just borrowed seed-corn from Nwakibie, and his unexpected exile for seven years after an inadvertent manslaughter are all challenges he manages to overcome. Yet there are other challenges to which his response is more ambiguous: his fear and rejection of the gentleness he associates with failure and, most specifically, the killing of his foster son Ikemefuna (when the latter runs to him for help against the villagers) because he is afraid of being thought weak. Students notice how Okonkwo resorts to violence to solve problems, and they are disturbed when he beats his favorite wife, Ekwefi, and narrowly misses shooting her. If they give Okonkwo credit for caring for Ezinma in her illness and for loving Ekwefi, they also recognize that his son Nwoye converts to Christianity (taking the name Isaac) chiefly because he seeks the security and approval that his father has withheld. Okonkwo's courage and readiness for action are prized in the old Umuofia, which sought supremacy among the neighboring villages, but this brand of warlike heroism is obsolete in the new era and certainly ineffective against the power of the colonial government. Time has passed by both Okonkwo and Umuofia: the former dies by his own hand because he is unwilling to change, while the latter is caught unprepared, weakened from within, and unable to do anything but submit. Ironically, it is the District Commissioners book title, *The Pacification of the Primitive Tribes of the Lower Niger,* that provides the last words. Only in the larger context of this book—by the Igbo Chinua Achebe—is the account rebalanced.

Topics for Discussion

1. Why does Achebe introduce the colonial presence only in the last third of the novel?
2. What motives does Nwoye have for converting to Christianity, and why does he take the baptismal name of Isaac?
3. How does Achebe create an "African English" in this novel?
4. How does the relationship of Okonkwo to Unoka help determine Okonkwo's conduct throughout the novel?
5. What function do the *kotma,* or "court messengers," fill in the new society?
6. What strengths and what weaknesses does Achebe show in Igbo traditional society?
7. Discuss Okonkwo's relationship to his wife Ekwefi and his daughter Ezinma.
8. In what way does Obierika represent a transitional figure between the old and new Igbo society?
9. How are the elders of Umuofia shown to be more "civilized" than the District Commissioner or Mr. Smith, the missionary?
10. Discuss Okonkwo's status as "one of the greatest men of Umuofia." How does he represent his society, and what is the significance of his isolation at the end?
11. Compare the two white missionaries, Mr. Brown and Mr. Smith, in their relationships to the villages of Umuofia. Is Mr. Brown's approach without danger?

Comparative Perspectives

1. All civilizations seem to look with particular horror at the father who kills his child, and many of the narratives in the anthology offer variations on this theme. Explore Achebe's treatment of this motif: how does he give psychological credence to Okonkwo's filicidal acts? Compare, as appropriate, the motives of Rostám in the *Shâhnâme*; Frederick Douglass's suspicions about his father's identity, and his discussion of the slave master's treatment of his own children (chapter I); the suffering and death of Melville's Captain Vere, likened (in chapter 22 of *Billy Budd*) to Abraham on the verge of sacrificing Isaac; the hostility toward Gregor demonstrated by Mr. Samsa in Kafka's *The Metamorphosis.*

   [See also the related discussion of this motif under "Comparative Perspectives" for Proust's *Remembrance of Things Past.*]

2. The diverse realms of the Igbo gods perturb the Christian missionaries, but they resemble the pantheons of most non-Western cultures. What functions do they serve, and how would you compare
   their responsibilities to other systems of divinity about which you
   have been learning?

   [The Sumerian gods in *Gilgamesh*, the Greek and Roman gods,
   Hindu divinities, Central American gods in the *Popol Vuh*.]

3. Why is the term "female murder" used of Okonkwo's crime? Why is
   this ironic? How does it reflect attitudes towards women in Achebe's
   novel? How does the author distance himself from his protagonist's
   views in this matter? How would you compare the view of women in
   the society described in *In Camera*?

Further Reading

See also the reading suggestions in the anthology, p. 2859.

Achebe, Chinua. *Morning Yet on Creation Day: Essays.* 1975.

———. *Hope and Impediments: Selected Essays, 1965–1987.* 1988.

Okoye, Emmanuel Meziemadu. *The Traditional Religion and its Encounter with Christianity in Achebe's Novels.* 1987. Discusses Achebe's
representation of traditional Igbo religion (including the *chi*), along
with other writers's accounts and occasional disagreement.

M. A. Onwuejeogwu. *An Igbo Civilisation: Nri Kingdom and Hegemony.*
1981. An anthropologist's detailed account of a strongly hierarchized
Igbo political, religious, and social system; useful in understanding the
traditional Igbo society of *Things Fall Apart*. Drawings, photographs,
and maps usable for classroom illustration.

Ubahakwe, Ebo. *Igbo Names: Their Structure and their Meanings.* 1981. A
sociolinguistic explanation of the complex meanings of names in Igbo
society and of the social importance of naming.

DEREK WALCOTT

Backgrounds

The poems in this volume testify to Derek Walcott's mastery of poetic
forms and diction, his painterly eye for detail, and his profound insight
into the historical situation of the Caribbean writer. Although he de-
nounces the depredations suffered by the inhabitants of the Caribbean at
the hands of the nations that colonized the region, he recognizes the en-
abling power afforded him by his deep acquaintance with the literature
produced by those nations. He is one of those poets who use themselves
and their experiences as subject matter, like Wordsworth, and in writing
about his early education, he has a Wordsworthian insight into the
growth of the poet's mind.

We knew the literature of Empires, Greek, Roman, British, through their essential classics; and both the patois of the street and the language of the classroom hit the elation of discovery. If there was nothing, there was everything to be made. With this prodigious ambition one began.

("What the Twilight Says: An Overture," 1970, p. 4.)

In the selections to be introduced below, Walcott explores all these options. Such "prodigious ambition" occasionally leads to knotty and obscure patches in the poems, especially in his earlier work. His passion for inclusion and allusion can make some passages almost unintelligible, but these difficulties recede in view of the overall sweep of his thematic concerns and the sheer excitement of his work. There should be no shame in sharing with students the difficulties Walcott occasionally gets himself into; putting two related poems against each other will allow you to discuss some of the chances these poems take and raise important questions about the degree to which neatness counts in the arts.

As John to Patmos

Like an ancient bard, Walcott begins this early declaration of poetic vocation with an elaborate simile. He wrote the poem when he was seventeen years old, and there is a certain degree of posturing here as the young initiate enters into a tradition. The first line states the comparison —"As"; the conclusion to the second quatrain provides the "So" of the simile. The lines between weave back and forth, balancing the situations of two very different but similarly dedicated writers. Saint John the Evangelist, writing in exile on the bleak, narrow island of Patmos in the Dodecanese Islands at the end of the first century A.D., is a model for the "I" of the poem, presumably Walcott himself, writing on another, far more beautiful island, his native St. Lucia, in the twentieth century.

If your students have not read any of the classical epics, they may need some general guidance about how to proceed further. Even experienced readers must be nimble to trace the elements of Walcott's syntactical construction here, which is characteristically complex. Once the readers of an epic simile have identified the two terms being compared, they should hunt for the verbs that define and clarify that which makes the comparison valid. The main verb is withheld until the sixth line: "welcomed." The first statement, unpacked, would then read: "As John [welcomed] to Patmos, among the rocks and the blue, live air, hounded / His heart to peace." If this is accurate, then the point of these lines is that it takes concentrated effort for an exile to clear the psychic space needed to work. Walcott need not be so fierce with himself. His island is beautiful, a nurturing female space, and he is at home there. The comparison is nevertheless instructive, because it implies that Caribbean identity is somehow provisional, that to live in the West Indies was never chosen by its inhabitants of color, but imposed on them.

The theme of exile is explored further in the third stanza, which expands to include a fifth line, as if the poet has too much matter to cram into the four-line format he has already established. The welcoming Caribbean island has become the home of the Africans exiled there, "and freed them of homeless ditties." The poet vows to bring solace to all the oppressed Caribbeans, who are his natural audience, as did John to persecuted Christians. And he will do it with love:

> O slave, soldier, worker under the red trees sleeping, hear
> What I swear now, as John did:
> To praise lovelong, the living and the brown dead.

Walcott's rhymes and rhythms in *As John to Patmos* are audacious and subtly off-kilter. Quatrains 1 and 2 are each organized around variations of one rhyme sound: "hounded," "surrounded," "rounded," and then, simply "dead"; "where," "air," "there," and (slightly off) "here." The fourth line of the extra-long stanza 3 picks up "surrounded" from quatrain 1, while the other four lines rhyme (sort of) "cities," "pretty is," "lit is," and "ditties." The fourth stanza brings back rhymes from the first two stanzas, as it brings back the opening statement: "As John to Patmos." The poet announces his themes—exile and the opportunities it affords for creative freedom—at the same time as he plays freely with the forms in which he addresses them.

RUINS OF A GREAT HOUSE

Here is another early poem in which Walcott masterfully combines his various heritages. *Ruins of a Great House* is a latter-day, ironic version of the "great house poem" typified by Ben Jonson's *To Penshurst* or Andrew Marvell's *On Appleton House,* brilliant examples of seventeenth-century English literature, like Thomas Browne's *Urn Burial,* from which the epithet is taken. The irony lies in the moral perspective of the poet: Jonson and Marvell celebrate the virtues of their friends and patrons by praising the architecture and landscaping of their stately homes. Walcott's poem contemplates the ruins of a house distinguished not for the virtues of its owner but for the tragic history of the slaves whose labor made it function.

The appeal to seventeenth-century models is linked to the historical moment when the Caribbean was being explored by the likes of "Hawkins, Walter Raleigh, Drake" (line 22), and the melodramatic diction of *Ruins of a Great House* echoes the language of the Jacobean revenge plays that were in vogue when the new continent was being settled. Consider the descriptions of the elaborate gate and ornamentation of the once great house:

> The mouths of those gate cherubs shriek with stain;
> Axle and coach wheel silted under the muck
> Of cattle droppings
> > Three crows flap for the trees

> And settle, creaking the eucalyptus boughs.
> A smell of dead limes quickens in the nose
> The leprosy of empire. (lines 4–9)

Students may miss the allusions to English poetic tradition, but they if they have read Frederick Douglass's *Narrative*, they should review Chapters 2 and 3, in which the Great House Farm is described. The Southern and the West Indian plantations operated on the same scale, although the crops were different. Douglass's horrifying description of his aunt's whipping at the end of Chapter 1 provides an example of the human cost exacted by the "imperious rakes" on the "bright girls" of whom Walcott writes (l. 21).

Another ironic note is heard in the description of a bone "Of some dead animal or human thing / Fallen from evil days, from evil times" (lines 17–18). The inspiration for this line is Miltonic, of course; in the invocation to Book 7 of *Paradise Lost*, as the blind poet prepares to describe the creation of the world, he reflects on his capacity for the task:

> More safe I sing, with mortal voice unchanged
> To hoarse or mute, though fall'n on evil days,
> On evil days though fall'n, and evil tongues . . . (24–26).

The difference between "from" and "on" in the phrasing of the two poets reminds us that Milton has experienced his own personal fall from better times; the mute skeletal remains of which Walcott sings never knew anything but "evil days."

The Edenic promise of the New World was corrupted at its inception because of the Middle Passage: "the world's green age then was a rotting lime / Whose stench became the charnel galleon's text" (lines 35–36). In a modulation typical of Walcott's capacity to see historical events from a broad perspective, the anger that he first voices is calmed by the reflection that the imperial British (whose legacy to the West Indies includes a still fertile language and poetry as well as the "ulcerous crime" of colonialism) were also once colonized. The concluding lines of the poem appear to conflate two different experiences of tyranny that allow for a measure of sympathy with the oppressor: "Albion" was subjected both to the rule of ancient Rome ("deranged / By foaming channels" and, given the seventeenth-century context of *Ruins of A Great House*, "the vain expense / Of bitter faction" that brought about the English Civil War. Walcott cites the oft-quoted lines from John Donne's Meditation 17, written in 1623, to remind us—and himself—that mortality levels us all.

THE ALMOND TREES

The Almond Trees responds to derogatory statements about the Caribbean made by the British historian James Anthony Froude (1818–94), who wrote in *The English in the West Indies*, "there are no people there in the true sense of the word," and by the contemporary Trinidadian novelist and essayist V. S. Naipaul (b. 1932), who states in *The Middle Passage,* "History is built around achievement and creation and nothing was created in the West Indies." Walcott, who once suggested that Naipaul should amend his comment to read, "Nothing was created *by the British* in the West Indies," has dedicated much of his own literary output to refuting these dismissive comments. *The Almond Trees* is an angry, witty description of the teeming life that may be observed as the sun heats up a West Indian beach, "this further shore of Africa" (p. 2955).

Like *As John to Patmos, The Almond Trees* draws a connection between the ancient world and the Caribbean, in both of which living flesh has been transformed by metamorphic experience. The bark of the almond trees and the bodies of the sun bathers have been cured by the sun; "they endured their furnace," emerging stronger from their ordeal as did Shadrach, Meshach, and Abednego from the fiery furnace of scriptural tradition (the Book of Daniel). Whatever Naipaul may have argued, the poem insists that history was built by searing the bodies of slaves:

> Welded in one flame,
> huddling naked, stripped of their name,
> for Greek or Roman tags, they were lashed
> raw by wind, washed
> out with salt and fire-dried,
> bitterly nourished where their branches died,
>
> their leaves' broad dialect a coarse,
> enduring sound
> they shared together.

Daphne, chased by Apollo, prayed to be spared from his embrace; her salvation was to become the laurel tree. No such shape-shifting saved the slaves trapped in the belly of the ships transporting them from Africa to the West Indies: "Their grief / howls seaward through charred, ravaged holes" (lines 46–47).

Walcott weaves a complex metaphorical equivalency here, assisted by ingenious rhyming and occasional puns; for example, "Aged trees and oiled limbs share a common colour!" (line 33). The bodies of slaves are like the trunks of trees; as leaves are to trees, excrescences with an expressive function ("broad dialect"), so the cries of slaves are expressive excrescences, howling from their cruel transport. If Daphne's cries are driven downward with her roots into the ground as she becomes an elegant tree, the cries of slaves sound out into the air. The similitudes are hard to grasp, and the rhymes struggle to find a pattern. From desultory instances of assonance as the poem begins ("early" in line 2 anticipates "surely" in line 8; "sand" in line 3 links to "stand" in line 6), the rhyme becomes easier to apprehend as the poem develops its essential correspondence: "noon / strewn" (lines 15–16) and "frieze / trees" (lines 21–22) point the way to the increasingly obvious rhymes in the lines quoted above.

The poem ends, as it begins, with a single figure in the middle of the trees. The old fisherman tossing a stick for his dog to catch in the third stanza yields to the woman spreading "her wrap within the beat arms of this grove / that grieves in silence, like parental love" (51–52). The *grove* grieves, and provides a tentative sense of closure to the eye with its all-but-rhyme with *love*. Contemplating the crescendo of activity on an ordinary beach from early morning to the heat of a day and a cooling evening, Walcott conjures up scenes from a cruel historical past that defy the obliviousness of complacent observers.

CRUSOE'S JOURNAL

The omnipresent intertextuality of Walcott's work is especially pronounced in the group of poems that were inspired by Daniel Defoe's *Robinson Crusoe*. Lecturing at the University of the West Indies in 1965, Walcott spoke explicitly of ideas that animate *Crusoe's Journal*:

> My Crusoe, then, is Adam, Christopher Columbus, God, a missionary, a beachcomber, and his interpreter, Daniel Defoe. He is Adam because he is the first inhabitant of a second paradise. He is Columbus because he has discovered this new world; by accident, by fatality. He is God because he teaches himself to control his creation, he rules the world he has made, and also, because he is to Friday, a white concept of Godhead. He is a missionary because he instructs Friday in the uses of religion. . . . He is a beachcomber because I have imagined him as one of those figures of adolescent literature, some derelict out of Conrad or Stevenson. . . . and finally, he is also Daniel Defoe, because the journal of Crusoe, which is Defoe's journal, is written in prose, not in poetry, and in our literature, the pioneers of our public literature have expressed themselves in prose. ("The Figure of Crusoe: On the theme of Isolation in West Indian Writing," available in *Critical Perspectives on Derek Walcott*)

Walcott wrote the poems in *The Castaway* while he worked alone in a beach house in Trinidad. He has explained in an interview that in that isolation he saw "an image of the West Indian artist as someone who was in a shipwrecked position" (in Hirsch; see reference below). Walcott takes the reader with him as he drives up to the isolated beach house, and (as he did with St. John on Patmos) interweaves his personal experiences with those of another exemplar of his theme to produce a dense and highly allusive exploration of that theme. "Mundo Nuevo trace" leads to the beach house in this corner of the New World where the poet will see what can be made of the most basic materials.

The speaker identifies both with Robinson Crusoe himself, and with Friday, the islander who becomes Crusoe's servant. An involuntary emissary of the West, Crusoe brought a language and a religion to the island, the archetypal green world that presents a *tabula rasa* on which an imported culture can be impressed. Christianity comes as a word and the Word, and "alters us / into good Fridays" (line 20–21). Assisted by puns, Walcott's speaker insinuates a familiar irony as he demonstrates how well the islanders absorbed the lessons that the West had to teach: "we make his language ours, / converted cannibals / we learn with him to eat the flesh of Christ" (lines 23–25). Cannibalism, like so much else, is in the eye of the beholder.

Crusoe is a useful figure for Walcott, because "the intellect demands its mask" (line 57). The essential loneliness of the creative artist, like the "one boy signaling at the sea's edge, / though what he cried is lost" (lines 38–39), leads him to take the fictional character as an inspiration and a model. Artists, then, are performers, putting on an act of sorts as does he in his isolated beach house, "posing as naturalists, / drunks, castaways, beachcombers" (lines 62–63). In the end, though, artists need audiences, however they desire seclusion and however hard all creatures try to combat "God's loneliness":

> For the hermetic skill, that from earth's clays
>   shapes something without use,
> and, separate from itself, lives somewhere else,
>   sharing with every beach,
> a longing for those gulls that cloud the cays
>   with raw, mimetic cries,
> never surrenders wholly, for it knows
>   it needs another's praise. . . . (lines 41–48)

VERANDAH

Again, a house provides the starting point for one of Walcott's poems. Apostrophizing the "grey apparitions" of colonial types who haunt the old plantation houses with verandahs, the speaker confronts the ghost of his own white grandfather. The list begins with "Planters whose tears were marketable gum," a typically fanciful and allusive phrase. As he is about to commit suicide, Shakespeare's Othello describes himself as one

>   whose subdued eyes,
> Albeit unused to the melting mood,
> Drops tears as fast as the Arabian trees
> Their medicinable gum. (5.2.357–60)

Thus Walcott ironically links the white planters and the black hero. Where Othello, returned to his idealistic grandeur in his final speech, characteristically sees the potential for healing and beauty in the oozing from the tree, the planters themselves produce the substance that they would see as an opportunity for commercial profit. Othello punishes himself for his crimes; did the white planters? The list becomes more accusatory, turning to "usurers whose art / kept an empire in the red" (lines 8–9), where we would expect *black*, because the money men were in the service of a bloody enterprise. Walcott wittily suggests the luxury that the British imperialists surrounded themselves with in the next tercet:

> Upholders of Victoria's china seas
> lapping embossed around a drinking mug,
> bully-boy roarers of the empire club. (lines 9–11)

"China" conjures up not only British imperialism in East Asia and the vast seas patrolled by Victoria's navy; the second line of the stanza also miniaturizes the marine expanse to a design on a china mug. As he does by using the mock heroic term familiar from Gilbert and Sullivan operettas—"tarantara"—to describe the sound of the bugler, Walcott evokes the inherent silliness of Victorian pageantry.

Suddenly, however, the poem's mood shifts. As in *Ruins of a Great House* and *The Almond Trees,* a broad and compassionate sentiment defuses some of the righteous anger of the colonial subject. Remembering the complexity of his own family background, the poet's respectful address to the shadow of his paternal grandfather demonstrates the beautiful manners of the children of St. Lucia. Yet Derek Walcott never knew his grandfather and barely knew his father. Charles Walcott bought a plantation near Choiseul, on the coast of St. Lucia; a white man who chose to live there, he nevertheless experienced some form of mental illness and died in a house fire that he was believed to have set himself. Warwick, his son and Derek's father, took charge of the burial. The poem ends with an outpouring of filial love for and self-identification with both his father and his grandfather. Like the almond trees cured in the fire, this house with its dark memories becomes an emblem of redemptive suffering: "The sparks pitched from your burning house are stars. / I am the man my father loved and was" (lines 31–32). Climbing the stair of the house, he greets as friends the gray apparitions of the poem's beginning, viewing them now as mortal men rather than as predatory colonizers.

ELEGY

American students will be on comfortable ground in analyzing *Elegy*, although it is probably a good idea to begin by reviewing with them the rebellious ferment of the late 1960s, an era of failed hopes that this poem commemorates. From the perspective of the Caribbean, mediating between North and South America, the speaker mulls the mood of the times. "[W]e miss you, Liberty" (line 2) presumably refers to the Statue of Liberty, that universally recognized symbol of high ideals that seemed shattered by a wave of assassinations of political figures identified with progressive causes. In South and North America, radical activists who wanted to precipitate change were cut down by an oddly assorted group of assailants. Walcott's phrase "the freeborn citizen's ballot in the head" (line 6) captures the sense, prevalent at the time, that bullets had been confused with ballots. Still the power of the American idea persisted.

Walcott's poem has no linear narrative; rather, it is a montage of popular images overlapping and ironically reflecting each other. His facility with rhyme subliminally fosters the reader's perception of the way these images comment on the lost promise of the American dream:

> Still, everybody wants to go to bed
> with Miss America. And, if there's no bread,
> let them eat cherry pie. (lines 7–9)

"Pie" rhymes with "die" in line 4, setting up through sound alone as mordant a contrast as the seque from Miss America to Marie Antoinette and all the fine Washingtonian connotations of cherry pie as opposed to brioche.

The second stanza takes up another revered American image, that of the woodsman and hunter disporting himself in the primeval forest. Students may have seen the movie version of James Fenimore Cooper's *The Deerslayer*. In a typically crabbed phrase, "Elegy" announces that romantic notions of rugged leather-clad individualism—"the old choice"—are no longer possible—"is gone" "while the white papers snow on / genocide" (lines 12–13). The phrase "white papers" seems to refer not only to a government document reporting the findings of some commission but also to propaganda leaflets dropped by airplanes, like "snow," covering the woods and/or spreading disinformation. *Elegy*, after all, was written in the shadow of the war in Vietnam, when napalm snowed from planes flying above enemy territory had permeated the national consciousness.

The Statue of Liberty appears to be the unvoiced antecedent to which the feminine pronouns in the third stanza refer: "Some splintered arrowhead lodged in her brain / sets the black singer howling in his bear trap" (lines 17–18) and "yearly lilacs in her dooryard bloom" (line 21). The litany of disappointments reaches "the assassin in his furnished room" (line 24), the archetypal figure of the assassin in the United States, who seems typically to be a lone gunman, like Lee Harvey Oswald, operating out of a personal sense of animus, rather than the European-style assassin who has been groomed by a political conspiracy. *Elegy* extends its elegiac regrets to the Trail of Tears—"the ghosts of the Cheyenne / scuffling across the staked and wired plains" (lines 26–27)—and ends with the implication that a streak of sterile self-righteousness in the American psyche, famously embodied in Grant Wood's *American Gothic,* is somehow to blame for the sad state of affairs so keenly felt in June 1968 and in Walcott's poem.

THE SEA IS HISTORY

This poem offers another answer to Froude and Naipaul. The supposedly nonexistent history of the Caribbean is to be found in the sea, in the history of the Middle Passage (a "caravel," mentioned in line 8, was a sailing vessel used by the Portuguese in the fifteenth and sixteenth centuries, when the African slave trade was established). Walcott casts the poem as sacramental history by using the names of biblical texts, from Genesis on. African Americans have long found parallels between the scriptural suffering of the ancient Hebrews and the experience of slavery and racism in the United States. Walcott explores some of these parallels through juxtaposing images that leap from one context to another:

> Then came from the plucked wires
> of sunlight on the sea floor
>
> the plangent harps of the Babylonian bondage,
> as the white cowries clustered like manacles
> on the drowned women,
>
> and those were the ivory bracelets
> of the Song of Solomon,
> but the ocean kept turning blank pages
>
> looking for History. (lines 18–25)

The poem mimics the voice of the disparaging critic, who demands to know "but where is your Renaissance?" despite the evidence of oppression buried under the ocean. The responding voice speaks in West Indian dialect, and what it says anticipates Achille's role in *Omeros*:

> Sir, it is locked in them sea sands
> out there past the reef's moiling shelf,
> where the men-o'-war floated down;
>
> strop on these goggles, I'll guide you there myself. (lines 34–37)

   History or not, with the coming of the slaves and the colonialists, life in the West Indies was transformed as crowded habitats were established on a once pristine land:

> then came, like scum on the river's drying lip,
> the brown reeds of villages
> mantling and congealing into towns . . . (lines 52–54)

The environment is polluted with oily coatings. Skipping over centuries of slavery and briefly alluding to the end of slavery and the gradual erosion of colonial rule in the West Indies, the poem ends by noting the lingering effects of that palpable but unacknowledged history on the collapse of local self-rule. Now, however, the populations of the West Indies may finally be free to begin to write their own story:

and in the salt chuckle of rocks
with their sea pools, there was the sound
like a rumor without any echo

of History, really beginning. (lines 77–80)

Like so many of Walcott's poems, *The Sea Is History* ends on a more optimistic note than the one on which it began.

NORTH AND SOUTH

This poem reflects Walcott's complicated feelings about living in the
United States in the 1970s and '80s, during which time he had plays produced in several cities and taught and lectured at universities across the
country. *North and South* finds him on a wintry evening in Manhattan's
Greenwich Village, a center for artists and intellectuals of all sorts—
poets, dancers, playwrights, painters, and philosophers, many of whom
were Jewish. Walcott's "I" feels out of place in this company:

> I accept my function
> as a colonial upstart at the end of an empire,
> a single circling, homeless satellite. (lines 4–6)

and recoils from the sordid intensity of this international city, linking it
with the dead civilizations of old. The British Empire has died, as did the
Roman Empire in an earlier millennium: "It's good that everything's gone,
except their language, / which is everything" (lines 11–12).

Yet the destructive power of those empires outlasts them. The speaker
broods on the famous phrase, "Carthage must be destroyed" (*Delenda est
Carthago*, l. 21), an oratorical tag that registered Roman paranoia about a
North African rival and led to the utter destruction of a great city. The
eradication of a thriving society is reflected here in the images of whiteness
and salt, salt being sown to prevent the earth from supporting vegetation.
Who is to say that other, contemporary societies like his are not similarly
vulnerable? The bitter New York winter is hard on the native of a warmer
climate, as "rime forms on the mouth / of a shivering exile from his African
province" (lines 38–39) and it is hard to believe that at home "they are
now talking over palings by the doddering / banana fences, or that seas can
be warm" (lines 48–49). The speaker misses home and its lack of the intellectual pretentiousness that characterizes the New York scene:

> I prefer the salt freshness of that ignorance,
> as language crusts and blackens on the pots
> of this cooked culture, coming from a raw one . . . (lines 55–57)

The speaker's knowing use of the anthropologist Levi-Strauss's terms
for high (cooked) as opposed to primitive (raw) civilization encapsulates

his ambiguous position. For he is in New York precisely because of the academic attractions of his own "cooked" writing. Thinking of the book-stores that once lined Eighth Street, where he himself took part in poetry readings and philosophical conversations, he appears to be dismissing the efforts of American poems less cooked than his.

> and these days in bookstores I stand paralyzed
>
> by the rows of shelves along whose wooden branches
> the free-verse nightingales area trilling "Read me! Read me!"
> in various metres of asthmatic pain . . . (lines 58–61)

The sly allusion here to Alexander Pope's elegant couplets (see line 200, *Essay on Man*, Epistle 1, where man is advised to be satisfied with the lim-its of his sense organs, lest he "die of a rose in aromatic pain") reminds the reader how very well read Walcott, the self-styled "colonial upstart" is, and how skilled a craftsman. Although he can't resist that little gibe at ri-val poets, his mood of exhausted alienation nevertheless overwhelms him:

> I am tired of words,
> and literature is an old couch stuffed with fleas,
> of culture stuffed in the taxidermist's hides. (lines 68–69)

If one important theme of *North and South* is a kind of latter-day "Bat-tle of the Books," another has deeper social implications. To what does the poem's title refer? If the cities of the American northeast are guilty of intellectual snobbery, they also foster a liberal climate that contrasts with the racial prejudice that was far more openly expressed in the American south. The speaker watches "Fragments of paper swirl round the bronze general / of Sheridan square" (lines 33–34), an image that echoes the "white papers" that snow on genocide in Elegy. Genocide is on the speaker's mind in *North and South* as well; there are no statues of Gen-eral Sheridan in the South, where his armies helped defeat the Confeder-acy in the Civil War.

Virginia and New York become polar opposites as the poem develops the implications of North and South. A chance observation in the warmer winter of Virginia, where autumnal leaves lie on the ground, of a spaniel pawing the leaves as chimneys emit smoke, becomes the occasion for an oddly jarring set of references to the Nazi efforts to exterminate the Jews in during World War II (if you have read Borowski's *Ladies and Gentle-men, to the Gas Chamber* [pp. 2773–86 in the anthology,] with your stu-dents, they will instantly grasp the application of Walcott's imagery in lines 87–95). Exquisitely aware of the history of the Ku Klux Klan in the South, the speaker recognizes in himself "the paranoid anxiety of the vic-tim" (line 98) that sets up the parallelism between "the races they fear and hate" (lines 108–09):

The ghosts of white-robed horsemen float through the trees
the galloping hysterical abhorrence of my race—
like any child of the diaspora, I remember this
even as flakes whiten Sheridan's shoulders,
and I remember once looking at my aunt's face,
the wintry blue eyes, the rusty hair, and thinking

maybe we are part Jewish (lines 99–105).

This disaffected meditation on life in the United States ends with a bitter memory of the casual racism that shocked him when he lived in this country and leads him to take special pride in the black component of his own mixed heritage. A multilingual pun leads him to a declaration of identity:

> *je suis un singe,*
> I am one of that tribe of frenetic or melancholy
> primates who made your music for many more moons
> than all the silver quarters in the till. (lines 128–31)

SEA CRANES

This brief poem builds on the affirmation of the artist as minstrel and mimic (as in "ape") that concludes *North and South* and provides a good introduction to the world of *Omeros*. Reading Robert Graves's dictum readies Walcott to take up the task of epic, for epic poetry is not born of cities, but in places like St. Lucia. The poet heads home to find the rhythms of a sustained verse narrative in the rhythms of everyday life in a fishing village where sea cranes thrive, part of an agrarian community in which "the whisking tails of horses" catch the eye.

OMEROS

Omeros is a capacious work that absorbs and amplifies on the preoccupations sketched out in the generous selection of Walcott's individual poems discussed above. The excerpts in the anthology have been carved out of a very long text to provide a coherent narrative that emphasizes Walcott's meditation on the African roots of West Indian culture. These selections could be studied without reference to the earlier work, although reading *Omeros* after analyzing some of the other texts by Walcott available in the anthology enhances one's understanding of key themes. *Omeros* is relatively easy to follow, since the syntax in the tercets here (a Dantean feature, one of many homages to the master poets of the past in Walcott's poem) is much more relaxed than that in the shorter lyrics.

The full poem is over three hundred pages long; it is arranged in seven books, with 64 continuously numbered chapters, each of which contains three sections of varying length, designated by Roman numerals. The narrative takes place mainly in the present, on Walcott's island of St. Lucia (also known, on account of its beauty, as "the 'Helen' of the West Indies"). *Omeros* interweaves three narrative strands, beginning with the fortunes of two Homerically named fishermen, Achille and Hector, who vie for the love of Helen, an imperious young woman who works as a housemaid for a retired British colonial officer, Major Dennis Plunkett, who has fallen in love with St. Lucia and settles on the island permanently with his wife, Maud. The couple is childless, and Plunkett, who would like to have an heir, discovers evidence of a heroic young Plunkett who died for Britain in one of the many sea battles fought against France over possession of St. Lucia in the eighteenth century. Maud will sicken and die before the poem ends. The third main narrative involves Walcott himself, as a Telemachian "I," in search of the father he never really knew. As in Homer's poems, the action switches from one arena to another, often with the help of a rosy-fingered dawn to cover the transition.

Book One, Chapter I, II

Early in the poem, Achille carves a canoe out of a laurel tree, hacking "the limbs from the dead god" (line 10). As in various West African religions, the trees are acknowledged to lodge spirits within. Christian and African beliefs intermingle throughout *Omeros*. Students should be alerted to watch for future references to the "swift" (line 3), a small dark bird with long narrow wings, which have the effect of giving the bird in flight a cruciform shape.

Although Walcott is emphatic in denying that he had read Homer's poems in their entirety before writing *Omeros*, and in insisting that his poem is not an epic, he saturates this section of the poem with references to the classical past, a tendency we have seen in *Ruins of A Great House* and *The Almond Trees*. Achille is just a poor fisherman, but he too has his link to Myrmidons (the people over whom Peleus, the father of Achilles ruled, who had metamorphosed from ants) in the "army of fire-ants" (line 27) to which the assiduous fishermen are likened.

Like Odysseus (and like Robinson Crusoe—note the reference to an "adze" here in line 45 and in *Crusoe's Journal*, line 9), Achille is a deft craftsman. Thus the poem begins with a wound (another character in the poem is named Philoctete, who suffers from a festering sore like the Sophoclean wounded bowman without whom it is predicted that the Greeks will not win Troy) and with preparations for a sea journey, blessed by the priest with "the swift's sign" (line 54).

Book One, Chapter VIII, I–II

St. Lucia has a small museum in which artifacts found in and around the island may be viewed; a wine cup purported to come from the wreck of the ship in which young Plunkett was drowned tantalizes the islanders. Desperate for money in the hope that wealth will enable him to regain Helen's love, Achille dives for treasure, looking for "salvation and change" (line 39). The pun on "change" balances pocket money against metamorphosis, and Achille knows that he is on a fool's errand. "What good lay in pouring / silver coins on a belly that had warmed him once?" (lines 43–44). This descent to the underworld is richly described and the imagery perhaps recalls Ariel's song in Act 1, scene 2 of *The Tempest*, another text that informs Walcott's poem:

> The shreds of the ocean's floor passed him from corpses
> that had perished in the crossing, their hair like weeds,
> their bones were long coral fingers, bubbles of eyes
>
> watched him, a brain-coral gurgled their words (lines 70–73).

This first of several fantastic voyages in *Omeros* tempts Achille with his hopes for a sea-change in Helen's feelings for him, but "the wreck / vanished with all hope of Helen" (II.87–88).

Book Three, Chapter XXV, I–III

This section, a dream sequence, is central to the poem. The first two books prepare us for journeys toward origins, and here Achille, guided by the providential swift (line 2), succumbs to sunstroke in the shelter of the mangroves. He has a vision of God speaking to him in patois, giving him "permission / to come home" (lines 32–33). Achille imagines himself sailing his canoe into the river of his ancestral African home, where he is greeted by his aged father. Walcott's voice interposes his own strand of the story in intense identification with this moment of return: "Half of me was with him. One half with the midshipman / by a Dutch canal" (II.58–59). Walcott's maternal grandfather was one Johannes Van Romandt, who came from Holland. His grandmothers, however, were both of mixed ancestry tying him directly to Africa.

Walcott's long experience as a playwright is brought to bear on the touching third section of this chapter. Imagery of the redemptive shipwreck and the collapsing of time prepare for a dialogue between a father and a son who never knew each other in life. As if he were Dante or Odysseus, Achille has the privilege of speaking with the dead. The father begins by giving his name: "Afo-la-be" (as the footnote explains, the name means "born with honor"). He does not recognize the name Achille, which has been given by the colonial world. Although the two men are mirror images of each other, Achille does not yet understand his identity or the nature of the bond between them. His father's concern closes the chapter:

> if you're content with not knowing what our names mean,
>
> then I am not Afolabe, your father, and you look through
> my body as the light looks through a leaf. I am not here
> or a shadow. And you, nameless son, are only the ghost
>
> of a name. Why did I never miss you until you returned? (III.128–32)

Book Three, Chapter XXVI, I; III

To regain his lost identity, Achille is introduced to African rituals and customs that will be familiar to students who have read *Things Fall Apart* or *Death and the King's Horseman*. He chews kola nut, drinks palm-wine, and hears the griot sing "to a balaphon's whine" (I.7). As Achille's story begins with the sawing of a tree, a violation that he senses but does not fully apprehend, it now comes full circle:

> . . . he climbed a track of huge yams to find that heaven
> of soaring trees, that sacred circle of clear ground
> where the gods assembled. He stood in the clearing
>
> and recited the gods' names. The trees within hearing
> ignored his incanatation. He heard only the cool sound
> of the river. He saw a tree-hole, raw in the uprooted ground. (I. 27–30).

The final section of Achille's vision of Africa has him floating across the ocean floor, observing the detritus of the Middle Passage. He has trained for this experience by diving into the wreck in search of coins for Helen. Now he reclaims the history of the entire Caribbean: "he walked for three hundred years / in the silken wake like a ribbon of the galleons" (III.38–39). Then he wakes, back home, to the realization that the African ceremonies he has envisaged have been practiced all along in St. Lucia: "the same dances / . . . the same chac-chac and ra-ra, the drumming the same, / and the chant of the seed-eyed prophet to the same / response from the blurring ankles. The same, the same" (III.69, 73–75).

Book Four, Chapter XXXV, I–II

Book Four brings Walcott to the United States, where he speaks in his own voice of his home in Brookline, Massachusetts, and describes a tourist excursion to Oklahoma and the old Indian territories that were seized by white settlers, a parallel to the colonizing of the West Indies by white Europeans. In this journey back in time into the southern United States, the assault on Native Americans parallels the other original American crime, that of slavery. Places along the way boast the same classical names and symbols that dominate the West Indian landscape:

> I thought of the Greek revival
>
> carried past the names of towns with columned porches,
> and how Greek it was, the necessary evil
> of slavery, in the catalogue of Georgia's
>
> marble past, the Jeffersonian ideal in
> plantations with its Hectors and Achilleses,
> its foam in the dogwood's spray, past towns named Helen,
>
> Athens, Sparta, Troy. (I.6–11)

He passes scenes where slaves were hunted and lynched, "the gibbet branches of a silk-cotton tree / from which Afolabes hung like bats" (I.25–26). The wounds with which *Omeros* begins have not yet healed:

> On their [churches'] verges,
> like islands reflected on windscreens, Negro shacks
>
> moved like a running wound, like the rusty anchor
> that scabbed Philoctete's shin . . . (I.29–32)

The voice we hear in section II belongs to a woman identified else-where in the poem as Catherine Weldon, a widow from Brooklyn, New York, mourning a son (like Derek Walcott of Brookline, Massachusetts, whose wife had recently been delivered of a stillborn child). Weldon has lost a husband and a son, and has alienated people she loves by speaking out for the Indians. Walcott uses her dedication to the plight of the de-feated Indians to enlarge the scope of *Omeros*, knitting her into the fabric of the poem as she speaks of watching "a swift or a swallow" fly away from the barn, "taking with it / my son's brown, whirring soul . . . More and more we learn to do without / those we still love" (II.51–52, 53–54). It is hard to tell here whether this is the voice of Catherine Weldon or Derek Walcott. Perhaps it suffices to say that the poem reminds us of the com-mon human experience of losses beyond repair.

Book Six, Chapter LII, II

The other prominent white woman in the poem is Maud Plunkett, who dies of cancer in section I of Chapter LII. Spread out before her on her bed are the letters her husband has written her, and the epic catalogue of section II given in the anthology reels off the items that were covered in their long correspondence, and that Major Plunkett recalls as he watches over his dead wife. Like Alexander Pope in *The Rape of the Lock* describ-ing the elements of Belinda's world assembled before her on her dressing table, Walcott here surveys the late Victorian colonial world in which the Plunketts moved and from which they retreated at the end, mixing regis-ters and references to brilliant effect. Out of Maud's "small tea-chest" (line 4) come all her cherished memories and nagging preoccupations, yielding at the last to a sense of the wound unhealed and the indignity of bodily pain:

> Solace of laudanum, menstrual cramps, the runnings,
> tinkles in the Jordan, at dusk the zebra shade
> of louvres on the quilt, the maps spread their warnings
>
> and the tribal odour of the second chambermaid. (lines 36–39)

In the final section of this chapter, not in the anthology, Walcott's voice returns, claiming an interest in the middle-class Plunketts, who remind him of his own parents, and speaking of "a changing shadow of Telemachus" in himself (III.7). Maud Plunkett dies without an heir and the poet reiterates his preoccupation with family ties severed too soon.

Book Seven, Chapter LXIV, I

The poem ends with an epilogue in which the poet has a vision of his own death. He celebrates the hero of his poem, "quiet Achille," the opposite of the wrathful Achilles of the *Iliad*. He predicts for Achille a fitting and Odyssean "death by water" (line 5), a phrase that purposefully recalls the elegiac fourth section of *The Waste Land*. The death with which the poem ends bring peace after a promise of healing is made in chapter LXIII, but there is no real closure. The sea goes on: "let the deep hymn / of the Caribbean continue my epilogue" (lines 36–37).

GRANADA

This vigorous poem grew out of Walcott's first visit to Spain, where he went to receive an honorary degree and to tour the Alhambra in Granada. Walcott's love for his own island engenders an imagery of metamorphic power; what he sees in Granada seems very different. The landscape of Granada communicates strength and deep-rootedness rather than lush fertility. Here the past declares itself immediately, while in the West Indies, it has been ignored (recall the refrain in *The Almond Trees*: "no visible history"):

> This is how to read
> Spain, backwards, like memory, like Arabic, mountains
> and predicted cypresses confirming that the only tense
> is the past, where a sin lies that is all of Spain's. (lines 6–9)

What is the sin that haunts all of Spain? Walcott probably means the expulsion of the Jews and Muslims in 1492 and the subsequent horrors of the Spanish Inquisition. There is too much history here. Walcott sees it in terms of artistic renditions by exemplary figures like García Lorca and Goya. The reference to Goya superimposes Walcott's memory of a great painting, *The Third of May*, on the physical landscape before him, as the idea of the "carbine-fire" trained on Lorca by his executioners reminds him of the staccato heel-clicks of the flamenco dancer. Once again, we see Walcott's obsessive fascination with the imprint of the past on the present and his instinctive sense of solidarity with the supporters of liberal ideals who have been suppressed. The most recently published of the poems by Walcott in the anthology, in its unusual directness of expression and painterly evocation of the olive-covered Spanish terrain, *Granada* demonstrates a new clarity in Walcott's style as he keeps assimilating new experiences into his verse.

Topics for Discussion and Writing

1. Explain the view of Caribbean history articulated by critics like J. A. Froude and V. S. Naipaul, and offer some examples from Derek Walcott's poetry that demonstrate his way of refuting it.

2. How does Walcott weave personal experience into his poetry? Choose one of the poems where you can identify self-referential materials and show how they function. (Good choices include *Verandah, North and South, Crusoe's Journal,* and *Omeros*).

3. How does Walcott experiment with poetic forms? How would you explain his reference to the "free-verse nightingales . . . trilling 'Read me! Read me!' " in *North and South?*

4. Examine some of the references in Walcott's poems to biblical and other religious motifs. How would you characterize his way of addressing spiritual concerns? (You may want to look closely at *The Sea Is History* or the central sections of *Omeros*.)

Comparative Perspectives

1. Give some examples of Walcott's appropriation of the work of earlier writers and consider how his incorporation of intertextual references contributes to the tone of his work.

   [Virtually all of Walcott's poems are highly allusive. In addition to *Omeros, Ruins of a Great House* and *Crusoe's Journal* offer many rich opportunities for discussion.]

   2. The penetration of time present by time past holds an obsessive interest for many modern poets. Compare the treatment of chronology and the influence of the past in *Omeros* with Yeats's in *Leda and the Swan* or *The Second Coming,* Eliot's in *The Waste Land* or *Little Gidding,* Joyce's in *The Dead,* Faulkner's in *Go Down Moses: The Bear,* or Juan Rulfo's in *Pedro Páramo.*

   3. Discuss the importance of fathers and sons in Walcott's verse and compare their importance in Achebe's *Things Fall Apart* or Soyinka's *Death and the King's Horseman.* Why is this relationship especially important in an African context? How does Walcott's sense of his mixed parentage complicate his sense of inheritance?

   4. Compare and contrast the treatment of African folk material in Birago Diop's *Mother Crocodile* or Bernard Dadié's *The Black Cloth* with Walcott's references to African ritual and the oral tradition in *Omeros.*

   5. Walcott insists that *Omeros* is not an epic. Discuss the differences between lyric, dramatic, and narrative verse, offering examples of Walcott's approach to these classically defined poetic genres, and suggest how best to understand the generic qualities of *Omeros.* Comment on the ways in which Walcott integrates references to the great epic poets of the past such as Homer, Virgil, Dante, Milton, and Pope into his work and discuss whether he seems to want to separate himself from their examples.

6. Walcott's *Granada* is the third verse tribute in this volume to Federico García Lorca (the others are by Alfonsina Storni and Pablo Neruda). Each of the three seem to pay homage to Lorca for his artistic force and personal integrity, but they may also be responding to different qualities in Lorca's work. Which sections of Lorca's *Lament for Ignacio Sánchez Mejías* seem most like Walcott's work? Which passages may especially have attracted Storni and Neruda?

Further Reading

See also the reading suggestions in the anthology, p. 2952.

Hirsch, Edward. "An Interview with Derek Walcott." *Contemporary Literature* 20.3 (1979), 279–92.

KAMAU BRATHWAITE

Limits

Backgrounds

See the headnote (pp. 2985–89 in the anthology) for background information and suggestions for further reading.

Comparative Perspectives

1. Discuss the function of the third-person plural in *The Forest* and *Adowa*. Why is it essential that the speaker participates in the dancing? Compare the vantage point of the "sixty-year-old smiling public man" watching the students in *Among School Children* and wondering "How can we know the dancer from the dance?": what is the difference between Brathwaite's use of the dance and Yeats's use?

   [One might try to assess the relative importance of the aesthetic and the political in each of the poems.]

2. In *Limits*, Brathwaite documents through place-names and nautical images the passage that brought black Africans to slave ships and "the white river." Comment on the force with which he applies these devices, noting some ways in which the poetry of Négritude has influenced Brathwaite's imagination. Compare the very different influences apparent in Lorna Goodison's *To Us, All Flowers Are Roses*, or in Frederick Douglass's appropriation of images and place-names when he apostrophizes the ships on Chesapeake Bay in Chapter X of his *Narrative*.

   [This question allows for a discussion of period style and "authenticity" of literary expression. Douglass, a slave with no formal education, records the songs of his oppressed brothers but chooses for his own narrative the grandiose rhetoric of nineteenth-century American culture. Brathwaite, a cultivated cosmopolite, reaches back to an African-inspired idiom made available by the equally well-educated Césaire and Senghor, and Goodison seamlessly interweaves classical, Caribbean, and European references. Yet each speaks in a uniquely personal voice.]

NAWAL EL SAADAWI

In Camera

Backgrounds

A prolific and controversial writer, Nawal El Saadawi has frequently been dismissed by critics who regard her work as polemical rather than creative. For all its brevity and concentration, *In Camera* provides a good test of that critique. As the headnote points out, in 1981, El Saadawi herself spent several months in prison. She wrote a fascinating description of her experience in a crowded cell full of other unjustly held political detainees. In this book, *Memoirs from the Women's Prison,* frankly working in a reportorial, autobiographical mode, she produces a lucid and detailed account of the women she met in prison and of the communal life they made for themselves in cramped and repellent physical circumstances.

Seen from that perspective, it becomes clear that *In Camera* is a work of considerable literary invention. Stream-of-consciousness techniques that writers like Joyce and Woolf pioneered in order to elicit a shock of recognition from their readers as they follow the vagaries of the ordinary mind allow El Saadawi to shock her readers by exposing them to the way extraordinary pressures affect the workings of a particular mind. Joyce's *Portrait of the Artist as a Young Man,* for example, mimics the gradual evolution of the intellectual processes by which all human beings learn to recognize and integrate the sensory world into a reasoned whole. *In Camera* mimics instead the cognitive process by which a young woman who has been tortured and sequestered until she is thrust, without warning, into public view comes to apprehend her surroundings. The opening sequence of *In Camera* is painful to read, as no doubt El Saadawi intended, but the means by which it induces pain are an artist's.

From time immemorial, tyrants have understood that dissent can most efficaciously be silenced by the application of physical agony. *In Camera* demonstrates with horrifying specificity how this insight was brought to bear on the person of one young female prisoner. Returning to consciousness, the mind of Leila Al-Fargani (we shall only later learn her name, as if when the story begins she has not yet reached the stage where she can separate her own identity from the surrounding environment) at first perceives only on the purely visceral level: she is like a newborn animal, its eyes still sealed, trying to hide from the blinding light.

The comparison to a newborn animal has soon to be reconsidered, however. As we read on, we quickly realize that this female creature has had experiences that would be foreign to a neonate and never inflicted on an animal. Leila has been subjected to different forms of torture, "dangling in the air by her feet or standing on her head in water" (p. 2999), after having been raped, repeatedly, until she had the audacity to tell her tormenters: "The most valuable thing that I possess is not between my legs" (p. 3007).

El Saadawi shows that there are indeed animal inhabitants of the courtroom and that the animal life on exhibit there is distinctly inferior to humankind. As Leila Al-Fargani gradually scans the shapes before her, her flawed eyesight reveals a classic satirical tableau. The representatives of officialdom may dress as if they were men, decorating their bodies with animal products, but they are themselves no better than animals. Your students will have no difficulty appreciating the following caricature of the judge as a simulacrum made up of mismatched, non-human parts:

> His face was as red as his head, his eyes as round and bulging as a frog's, moving slowly here and there, his nose as curved as a hawk's beak, beneath it a yellow moustache as thick as a bundle of dry grass, which quivered above the opening of a mouth as taut as wire and permanently gaping like a mousetrap.
>   (p. 3000)

Leila has trouble making out the identity of individual members of the court, with their "heads without hair, in the light as red as monkeys' rumps" (p. 3000). The formal portrait of the king in the background adds to the confusion. "Above the shoe she saw taut legs inside a pair of trousers of expensive leather or leopard skin or snakeskin" (p. 3000). Taking whatever small pleasure remains to her in being allowed to sit—"For the first time she understood that the human body differed from that of an animal in one important way—sitting. No animal could sit the way she could" (p. 3001)—Leila proves that she at least is human. Significantly, her name is first pronounced at this moment in the story.

One reason why Nawal El Saadawi is so controversial is that she is an Egyptian woman who writes of the maltreatment of women in some Islamic societies. Prophets are often without honor in their own countries. Yet she does not write in ignorance of her subject; her critique is all the more powerful because it comes from within. *In Camera* documents the degree to which her literary frame of reference derives from the theological and mythological classics of her culture: her use of animal imagery seems consistent with the imagery of the Qur'an, as her citations of mythology (Isis and Osiris, p. 3002) and village mores (the magician, p. 3006) reflect the influence of indigenous Egyptian materials on her imagination.

Her understanding of gender relations similarly reflects her own authentic grounding in the traditional Islamic world, which fosters distinct and different modes of being in the male and in the female. *In Camera* demonstrates these differences by taking us into the minds of Leila's parents once she has got her bearings in the courtroom. Leila's adoration of her mother is matched by her mother's love for her, and their experience as females is oddly congruent. The violation that Leila has endured leaves her with a gaping wound and perpetual pain in the lower abdomen. The intensity of her mother's protective yearning for her daughter springs from the same anatomical zone.

El Saadawi's fierce advocacy for women's rights seems like a natural extension of this primal bond forged between mothers and daughters. In a vain effort to save her child from arrest, Leila's mother had taken her into her bed:

> You'll sleep in my arms so that even if they come in the middle of the night, I will know it and I'll hold on to you with all my might and if they'll take you they'll have to take me as well. (p. 3002)

This sense of solidarity and common cause among women inspires admiration and hope throughout El Saadawi's work.

In Camera does not give false hope, however. Still unable to see clearly, Leila looks around the courtroom during the recess that has been called because the presiding judge has made a grave error: he has inadvertently evoked laughter from the observers when they hear that the girl on trial had called the ruler "stupid" (p. 3007). Turning our attention to Leila's father at this point, the narrator lets us see the ambivalent paternal reaction caused by this fleeting moment of public approval of his daughter's political stand. He feels on the one hand pride almost as intense as his wife's:

> I'm her father, I'm Al-Fargani who fathered her and whose name she bears. My God, how all the pain in my body vanished in one go with the burst of applause. What if I were I to stand up now and reveal my identity to them? This moment is unique and I must not lose it. Men like us live and die for one moment such as this, for others to recognize us, to applaud us, for us to become heroes with eyes looking at us and fingers pointing at us. (p. 3006)

On the other hand, he is humiliated by the treatment his daughter has suffered. Significantly, in relating this fearful rejection by a father of his child, the narrator adopts indirect discourse rather than having him speak his objectionable words in his own voice:

> He wanted to vanish so that no one would see or know him. His name was not Al-Fargani, not Assharqawi, not Azziftawi, not anything. He had neither name nor existence. What is left of a man whose honour is violated? . . . Death was preferable for him and her now. (p. 3006)

Since these patriarchal sentiments prevail in the society in which *In Camera* is set, Leila's story can have no real closure. The judicial establishment has lost one round and the judge is chastised. The arresting officers had treated Leila Al-Fargani like an animal; the judge himself is judged no better. Pleading that he may have been foolish, but not malign, in quoting the defendant's words to the courtroom, the term is defined for the judge's benefit: "Foolishness means that he doesn't think, that he's mindless, that he's an animal. That's the worst thing you can call an ordinary man" (p. 3008). The ordeal is not over; only the venue has changed. The rest of the trial will take place *in camera*. "As for her, they took her back to where she'd been before" (p. 3008).

Topics for Discussion and Writing

1. Analyze the use of animal imagery in El Saadawi's story.
2. Discuss the narrator's use of sensory detail to demonstrate the intense bond between mother and daughter in *In Camera*.
3. How do you feel about Leila Al-Fargani's father? Upon what evidence do you base your judgment?

Comparative Perspectives

1. Is rape best understood as a sexual act or as an expression of violence? Compare and contrast the depiction of rape and that which motivates it in *In Camera, Pedro Páramo,* and the *Narrative of the Life of Frederick Douglass, An American Slave.*
2. Like Leila Al-Fargani, Antigone (in volume A, pp. 658–93 of the anthology) is a young woman who rebels against the Establishment. Compare and contrast the offenses committed by these two characters in their pursuit of justice. Distinguish the way in which Sophocles' play presents the claims of Creon from the way in which El Saadawi presents the ruling power in *In Camera.* How do you account for the difference in their perspectives?
3. What is unusual about the trial in *In Camera*? Why do we not have the traditional trappings of courtroom literature here? Compare the view of judicial proceedings in *Billy Budd* or *The Sultan's Dilemma.*
4. Compare and contrast the terms in which El Saadawi criticizes her society with those of writers like Tagore in *Punishment,* Lu Xun in *A Madman's Diary,* or A. B. Yehoshua in *Facing the Forests.* How is the kind of political engagement represented by this group of writers different from that of writers like Chinua Achebe and Aimé Césaire?

Further Reading

See the reading suggestions in the anthology, p. 2999.

ALICE MUNRO

Walker Brothers Cowboy

Classroom Strategies and Topics for Discussion

There is no better place to start a discussion of *Walker Brothers Cowboy* than its beginning, which eschews all the formalities of narrative introduction and involves the reader at once in a conversational relationship with the young narrator. Using the present tense, as she does throughout except for one or two significant lapses, she quotes her father's cryptic, quirky question and immediately indicates that there are no easy certainties available in her fictive world: is the Lake still there? By the time the story ends, we come full circle back to the Lake but not to comfort, for the sky above it is perpetually overcast.

This classic story of a child's initiation into some of the mysteries of life has an almost mythic opening. Family tensions are palpable if unspoken. The narrator clearly prefers her father to her mother, who tries to make the daughter into a replica of her own wounded gentility, cutting her old clothes down to fit her child. Because it is summertime, the tailoring leaves the girl "sweaty, itching from the hot wool, ungrateful" (p. 3010). This sense of discomfort is reinforced a few pages later, when we see the girl dressed up for a shopping trip, her mother's unwilling "creation" (p. 3013). As *Walker Brothers Cowboy* starts, the girl has already separated herself from her overly punctilious mother; by the time it ends, she recognizes her distance from her genial father as well.

You will probably want to spend some time on the father's geology lesson, which simultaneously teaches how influence imprints itself upon us (the Great Lakes come from the mark left by the ice on a flat plain) and how faint are the signs of the influence (mimicking the ice's encroachment on the plain, the father's fingers make hardly any impression at all, prefiguring the faint, unreadable mark that Nora will make on the dusty car fender as the story draws to its conclusion).

Munro knows how to weave such hints through the web of details that your students will probably recognize by now as the fabric of modern realistic fiction. The cracks in the sidewalk that the child's imagination sees as "spread out like crocodiles into the bare yards" (p. 3011) prefigure her effort to imagine the plain before the Ice Age, with "dinosaurs walking on it." Between the mentions of the crocodile and the dinosaur, Munro inserts a sense of something primal and dangerous that could reemerge at any time as she describes their progress out of town by saying "the sidewalk gives up." Included in the catalog of details that marks the end of civilization as they move toward the water are "grain boats, ancient, rusty, wallowing." Time takes its toll throughout this story.

Munro's way of constructing her story also deserves consideration. Ask your students how Munro's description of her own way of reading, as quoted in the beginning of the anthology's headnote, may apply as well to her way of writing *Walker Brothers Cowboy*. The opening pages of the story apparently ramble—the habitual evening walk taken by father and mother does not open up to any clear-cut narrative event. The story stops after the geology lesson and seems to start in earnest when we read, "My father has a job, selling for Walker Brothers" (p. 3012), but that opening takes us down yet another road.

The central plot of the story—the action that leads up to the visit to Nora Cronin's home—begins with the still-unnamed Ben Jordan taking his children off for an afternoon while their mother rests. Ask your students what difference it would make if that incident had been left to stand alone: why do we need to learn about the narrator's separate excursions with her father and her mother in order for the visit to Nora to make a difference to us (and to her)?

You might point out to your students that, like the opening chapters of Genesis, *Walker Brothers Cowboy* begins with the introduction of two quite different creation stories that establish the complex world of the piece and thus bring meaning and artistic coherence to the "diversions" that take us from Tuppertown to memories of Dungannon, then out of Ben Jordan's territory, and finally back to the Lake and to Tuppertown. The father teaches his daughter a lesson cosmic in scope in his discourse on the origin of the Great Lakes. The mother, by contrast, works on a personal scale as she tries to create her child in her own image. Exiled from the fox farm, they live in a fallen world; Mrs. Jordan wants her daughter to feel me loss of their family Eden as intensely as she does herself.

Only after several pages marked by the persistent use of the present progressive, the tense for habitual, repeated actions, do we move in to the focused and singular encounter with Nora and her blind mother. For this excursion, "No roads paved when we left the highway" (p. 3014). Enigma rules; witness the architectural phenomenon the daughter ponders as they drive along: what do those second-story doors open onto? This is uncharted territory that Ben Jordan tries to make familiar to his children with his songs. These songs too are worth investigating with your students, for Ben is a kind of artist shaping recalcitrant material as best he can to hold back the dark, to keep "the wolf from the door" (p. 3017).

The headnote speaks of Munro's predilection for masks. How many masks does Ben Jordan wear as he tries to cheer his children—and himself? His comic routines are his way of transforming the indignities he daily encounters and of shielding the children from the bitterness of their disappointed mother. You might ask your students whether they have any friends or acquaintances who always make jokes. Does that mean that they are incredibly happy people? And you might have them think about what it must feel like to be a traveling salesman, having to convince people that they lack something in order to make a living. How much easier to be, in today's euphemistic phrase, "an associate" employed in a shop, catering to customers who come in quest of merchandise. Walker Brothers Cowboys are like strolling players who may end up with tomatoes or eggs in their faces (if not the contents of a chamberpot).

Much of the poignancy of this story comes from seeing, through the eyes of his discerning but not yet fully comprehending daughter, the deflation of Ben Jordan's natural buoyancy. In her understated, oblique way, Munro gives a glimpse of an everyday tragedy wrought by religious difference. Why should Munro have Ben Jordan sing a song about invisible Baptists as he drives by the Vacation Bible Camp? What significance does religious denomination have for the people of Tuppertown and environs? How does the narrator grasp the meaning of the picture on Nora Cronin's wall? What phrase echoes in her mind as she takes in the scene in the kitchen?

Your students should have no trouble delineating the contrast between the woman Ben Jordan married and the woman he could not. Why does Nora dance with the little girl? Why can Ben Jordan not follow suit when he is invited to do so? It's probably worth spending some time having your students explain the symbolic import of dancing in a time and place so straightlaced that for two people to hold each other in their arms while music played was practically equivalent to illicit sex.

The significance of narrative point of view may be emphasized by a close look at the story's four-paragraph coda. You might raise this topic by asking your student why Munro gave Nora Cronin a blind mother. Who in *Walker Brothers Cowboy* has the gift of sight? The daughter sees infinitely more than her younger, more practical brother, who "knows better" than to sound the horn when his older sister goads him on and who can be counted on not to remember anything of their visit. Intent on counting rabbits on the road, he will not give away a secret that he has not understood. The father who took his children to see the sweetheart he could not marry knows them well; his son has not seen anything worth talking about, and his daughter will not talk about what she has seen. She would not tell her mother about "the whisky, maybe the dancing" (p. 3020).

But there are deeper insights that are not so easily categorized or captured. One needs an artist working at the level of the divine creator to know why the impression of so delicate a handprint on a flat and colorless landscape changes it forever. The child's sense of discovery is tempered by her lack of total comprehension. Her epiphany defies precise description: it is telling that Ben Jordan has no songs left for the return drive, for the human artist can never make permanent sense of the infinitely changeable weather in which we live.

Topics for Writing

1. The importance of time and place: would this story have the same impact if it were not set during the Great Depression of the 1930s, in a remote Canadian area?
2. How does the family unit function in *Walker Brothers Cowboy*?
3. How insightful is Munro's narrator? Find examples of points that she understands and those that bewilder her. Would an omniscient narrator be able to tell this story as well?

Comparative Perspectives

1. Alice Munro's world seems comfortable and knowable, but it is full of mysteries. Compare Stephen Albert's observation at the end of *The Garden of Forking Paths* with Munro's treatment of time and space as exemplified by the father's description of the Great Lakes: "In contrast to Newton and Schopenhauer, your ancestor did not believe in a uniform, absolute time. He believed in an infinite series of times, in a growing, dizzying net of divergent, convergent and parallel times" (p. 2420).
2. Compare and contrast the opportunities available to talented daughters described in this series, including, as appropriate, Munro's narrator; Sister Juana; Hedda Gabler; Shakespeare's sister as imagined in *A Room of One's Own*; Liusu in *Love in a Fallen City*; and Ezinma in *Things Fall Apart*.

Further Reading

See also the reading suggestions in the anthology, p. 3010.

Carscallen, James. *The Other Country: Patterns in the Writing of Alice Munro*. 1993.

Martin, W. R. *Alice Munro: Paradox and Parallel*. 1987. This study offers a helpful reading of the discussion of the Great Lakes.

Redekop, Magdalene. *Mothers and Other Clowns: The Stories of Alice Munro*. 1992. Jargon-filled but useful in its tracing of the "paternal and maternal images of reproduction" that it identifies in *Walker Brothers Cowboy*.

WOLE SOYINKA

Death and the King's Horseman

Classroom Strategies

Students may approach the Yoruba tradition with the same bewilderment (and perhaps hostility) that Simon Pilkings expresses. You might want to split assignments, having students read Scenes One, Two, and Three for the first class period, making sure that the unfamiliarity of the Yoruba myth culture hasn't stalled them in their reading, and encouraging them to recognize the contrast between Elesin's mystical embrace of his fate in Scene One and the Pilkings's callous appropriation of sacred objects for a costume ball in Scene Two. Stopping at Scene Three also provides a dramatic break in the action and a chance for students to conjecture about the play's conclusion. Will Pilkings successfully intervene? What is the likely result? Is this play really "about" the contrast between Yoruba culture and British power, or is the colonial context a backdrop to a deeper, more metaphysical subject?

Olunde provides a bridge between the two worlds represented in *Death and the King's Horseman*, a bridge more firmly moored to his Yoruba upbringing than to the site of his formal education. You might ask students what they find most interesting about the dialogue between Olunde and Jane Pilkings in Scene Four. Do they agree with Jane's characterization of Yoruba speech as "long-winded, roundabout"? If so, do Olunde's arguments bring them closer to appreciating the tradition that Elesin, Iyaloja, the Praise-Singer, and the women celebrate and perpetuate?

The play's ending is tragic, but students may be asked to say in what way it is tragic. When a character seeks death, how are we to take his success in finding it? Significantly, the voices of Yoruba myth culture, Ivaloja, and the Praise-Singer provide the keys to understanding the nature of this tragedy.

Comparative Perspectives

1. Like Soyinka's Elesin, Achebe's Okonkwo commits suicide. Although a sense of guilt motivates each of them, Elesin's death has a

richer dimension as well. Discuss the meaning of ritual suicide among the Yoruba as it is explained in Soyinka's play. Compare the reasons for the death expected of the king's horseman with the reasons for the death of the British naval captain Jane tells Olunde about in Scene Four. Jane thinks "life should never be thrown deliberately away." Do you agree? Is it fair to say that Elesin throws his life away? Under what circumstances may suicide be the right choice?

[The suicides in *The Barrelmaker Brimful of Love* and *Hedda Gabler* might be included in this discussion.]

2. Soyinka uses Yoruba ceremonies incorporating music, dance, and mime to brilliant theatrical effect in many of his plays. In *Death and the King's Horseman,* the masquerade ball in the British Residency allows us to compare the efforts of the European colonizers to have fun by dancing in masks to the effortlessness with which such events mark the life of the "natives." Discuss the significance of the costumes that Simon and Jane Pilkins choose for their night out.

[The desecration implicit in their thoughtless choice may be compared to the scenes with the *egwugwu* in *Things Fall Apart*. A wider-ranging inquiry into the use of mime in drama may be readily pursued by students who have read *The Peach Blossom Fan* or *The Good Woman of Setzuan*; those who have studied examples of classical Greek or Sanskrit drama should be asked to think about the ways in which the performance style embedded in these plays derives from religious rituals not unlike the Yoruba practices Soyinka employs.]

Further Reading

See the reading suggestions in the anthology, p. 3024.

A. B. Yehoshua

Facing the Forests

Backgrounds

An aging and unnamed graduate student, who once showed considerable promise but who has become mired in a curious and prolonged lethargy, is offered a way out of his doldrums by concerned friends. He is to become a fire warden in one of the national forests—a dead-end job, the only virtue of which for him is that it promises to provide that long period of absolute and uninterrupted solitude he needs to regain a sense of purpose. Far from the distractions of the city and his friends he will be able to sort out his thoughts and begin the research that he has so long neglected. The forest itself, though it is a major symbol of the rebirth of Jewish culture in Israel, is of no interest to him. Indeed, he almost loses his chance at the job by his mocking indifference to the whole afforestation project.

Once he reaches his post he finds that his solitude, though considerable, is not complete. He shares his isolated residence on a hill overlooking the national forest with an Arab caretaker and his young daughter. This sharing is partial, however, since he cannot speak Arabic and they do not know Hebrew. The caretaker, moreover, is mute. The student's father and a former lover also briefly and unexpectedly intrude upon his six-month isolation, the former toward the beginning, the latter toward the end. Finally, during the summer bands of hikers from Israel and overseas come to visit the forest, intruding on his solitude yet further and reminding him both of how lonely and how cut off from the ordinary concerns of his community he is. The hikers also teach him an unexpected and crucial fact: this forest, which is seen by the Israelis as a monument to their future and an emblem of the renewal of the Jewish homeland, has been planted over an Arab village—a village that was destroyed during the War of Independence. The student realizes that the caretaker must be a survivor of that village. The mutilation that made the caretaker mute is, the student assumes, a wound he received in that war, although, significantly enough, it is not clear which side inflicted it.

The student's solitude is partial in another sense as well. The forest, the existence of which he was unaware of and the presence of which he assumed was negligible, amazes him by its extent and its luxuriance. And since the room he lives and works in is open to the forest on all sides, the forest soon fills his horizon both literally and figuratively. As the sole lookout at his station he must watch the forest virtually day and night. He sleeps fitfully and soon enters a state between sleep and wakefulness. He makes no progress with the research that is his ostensible reason for being there, but drifts instead into a symbolic drama in which he, the Arab, the Arab's daughter, and the forest are the principal players. He becomes obsessed with the ruin of the village buried under the forest and gradually descends into a madness that culminates in his collusion with the Arab in the fiery destruction of the forest he has been sent to guard. At the conclusion of the story he is once more in the city, still dirty and singed from the fire. His books have been burned up in the fire. His friends want nothing to do with him, and he is a more abject and complete failure now than when he left.

Topics for Discussion and Writing

1. At what point does the student go mad? Can you trace his progress from slothful sanity to lunatic collusion?
2. Symbolic narratives in which the characters lack psychological depth, as is the case here, demand a kind of allegorical interpretation. How elaborate and complete an allegorical reading of this story can you give? The larger symbols are easy. One doesn't have to work hard to extract the meaning from the national forest or the mute Arab, but what about smaller details like the choice of the Crusades for the student's thesis topic, the visits from his father and old lover,

the timing of those visits, and the chaining of the Arab's daughter to the watchman's post?

3. The details of this narrative fit the real contemporary situation of Israel so well. Is it possible to generalize its meaning beyond that context? Can you substitute other symbols for those in the story and still retain the essential narrative structure?

Comparative Perspectives

1. The fire-watcher in *Facing the Forests* is, in effect, an arsonist, but he is not easily dismissed as a mere criminal. Discuss the significance of Yehoshua's description of the burning "tree wrapped in prayer" in which the flames start. Compare other references in the anthology to the religious symbolism of fire, a purifying and reviving spiritual essence as much as an agent of punishment and destruction. Eliot's *Little Gidding* or Walcott's *Verandah* are good places to begin.

2. *Facing the Forests* brilliantly reproduces the paradoxical relation of the modern state of Israel to time and to the land in which the nation has deep historical roots and yet in which it is perceived as an interloper. Discuss the ways Yehoshua's story exploits the traditional image of the forest as a primeval repository of a culture's beliefs, while it simultaneously depicts a Kafkaesque bureaucracy imposing an artificial new growth on a terrain from which history has been erased.

   [See ancient texts like *Gilgamesh* or the *Rāmāyaṇa*. Contrast, perhaps, Brathwaite's *The Forest*, where it is "time to forget" the past.]

Further Reading

See also the reading suggestions in the anthology, p. 3074.

Alter, Robert. *Defenses of the Imagination: Jewish Writers and Modern Historical Crisis*. 1977. "Fiction in a State of Siege," originally published as "New Israeli Fiction" in *Commentary* (June 1969), treats *Facing the Forests* at some length.

Siddiq, Muhammad. "The Making of a Counter-Narrative: Two Examples from Contemporary Arabic and Hebrew Fiction." *Michigan Quarterly Review: The Middle East*, a special issue edited by Anton Shamas (Fall 1992). In a superb analysis of *Mr. Mani*, Siddiq develops the theme of Yehoshua's writing as subverting the master-narrative of Israeli culture.

Wachtel, Nili. "A. B. Yehoshua: Between the Dream and the Reality." *Midstream* (August–September 1979). Surveys Yehoshua's fiction through *The Lover*.

ANITA DESAI

The Rooftop Dwellers

Backgrounds

Before beginning a discussion of Anita Desai's fiction, it would be a good idea to set her work in the context of Indian fiction written in English, rather than in one of the regional languages like Bengali (used by Tagore and Mahasweta Devi) or Urdu or Hindi (Premchand's choices). Before India gained independence from British colonial rule in 1947, most fiction in English about India was written by colonial British writers, including Rudyard Kipling and E. M. Forster. From 1835 onward, however, English has been the principal language of education for the middle and upper classes in India. It is also the main language (along with Hindi) used by the government of India today, and upper-class Indians from different regions communicate with each other in English. It is therefore not surprising that, at least since the 1930s and 40s, many Indian writers whose mother tongue is not English have chosen to write in English. Their numbers continue to grow, but prime among them are Salman Rushdie and Anita Desai.

Like many contemporary Indian writers, whatever language they may choose, in her novels and short stories Anita Desai tends to focus on the small but influential group of educated middle- and upper-class Indians— the same classes who read her novels in India. She also has gained a large audience outside of India, especially after her novels received British literary prizes; one of them, *In Custody*, has been made into a movie. *In Custody* introduces its reader to one quintessentially Indian literary world, the domain of Urdu poetry, and is one of the last great practitioners of this form.

The Rooftop Dwellers takes us into another, much smaller, more derivative part of this world. The story is set in Delhi, a city that lacked sufficient literary life for Ajoy Bose, the founder of *Books*:

> He had missed the literary life of [Calcutta] so acutely, and had been so appalled by the absence of any equivalent in New Delhi, that he had decided to publish a small journal of book reviews to inform readers on what was being published, what might be read, a service no other magazine seemed to provide, obsessed as they all were with politics or the cinema, the only two subjects that appeared to bring people in the capital to life. (p. 3110).

The Rooftop Dwellers has fun with the marginality of *Books* in a culture that engages with its literary heritage by watching television serials of the great epics rather than by reading them. Desai holds up to ridicule the tastes of the comfortable but decidedly suburban middle-class Bhallas as well as those of the university men who write book reviews for a pathetically small set of readers and savage each other's writing, probably because, as the joke goes, the stakes are so small. Political tensions as well as professional rivalries fuel these tensions. Delhi is an old Moghal city, and one irate reviewer heaps scorn on the short stories of a writer whose work emanates from "the Hindi-speaking 'cow-belt' " (p. 3124), dangerously pitting Islam against Hinduism in a way that shocks the journal's politician/owner, "Bose Sahib." Desai has a wonderfully sharp eye for the pretensions of all of her characters and the groups with which they identify, but her main concern in *The Rooftop Dwellers* is with Moyna, the ingenuous heroine who has come to Delhi to free herself from her loving but overbearing family.

Desai's portrait of Moyna shapes the story; the first lines set the young woman before us in all her anxiety and modesty: "Paying off the autorickshaw driver, she stepped down cautiously, clutching her handbag to her" (p. 3102). Moyna's combination of diffidence and determination is made manifest as the paragraph continues. Beset by family noises (yelping dog, screaming children) and ignored as she rattles the latch, she opens the gate for herself and goes around in search of the front door "like a saleswoman preparing to sell a line in knitting patterns or "home-made jams."

Like the Bhallas, the story leaves Moyna waiting until the evening's episode of the *Mahābhārata* serialization concludes, and moves into a flashback that shows us how modern young women survive in the great Indian cities. The description of the women's hostel from which Moyna has been evicted typifies Desai's discreet feminism. With comic flair that does not disguise the serious sociological insights of this section of the story, she lets us see how difficult it is for the Moynas of India to live alone in a society that has no structures for accommodating single women. Students who live on campus will enjoy discussing the details of the "minimalism of these living arrangements," since in many ways it approximates dorm life. Students who commute to school can empathize with the description of "the Ladies' Special," the special bus that carries

> telephone operators, typists, desk receptionists, nurses, teachers, airline hostesses and bank tellers, without the menace of crazed young men groping at them or pressing into them as if magnetized, or even delivering vicious pinches before leaping off the bus and running for their lives. (p. 3104)

The comparison of Delhi men to those of Bombay or Calcutta that Tara, the Managing Editor of *Books*, offers later in the story is instructive (p. 3109), for it underscores Moyna's considerable daring in trying to "make it" in a perilous and inhospitable environment. In fact, most of the men Moyna meets in Delhi are of lower status than she is and hardly eligible suitors. Ritwick, the husband of her employer and friend Tara, protects her like an elder brother (p. 3108), but probably the most genuinely helpful male of her acquaintance is the "kindly Sikh" (p. 3109) who "became her private chauffeur," offering her a monthly rate to take her to her job on his autorickshaw. (You will want to be sure that your students know that an autorickshaw is a three-wheeled vehicle with one narrow passenger seat that its operator peddles through traffic. Rickshaws, conveyances popular in China and Japan, are pulled rather than pedaled. In either form, the reliance on human energy rather than gasoline gives this sort of transportation the flavor of a master-slave relationship.)

It is no accident that Moyna's sojourn at the women's hostel is curtailed by the arrival into her life of a male cat she calls Mao. Her emotional neediness leads her to accept the kitten as a permanent resident in her bedroom, as her choice of a name reflects the political position that dominates the office of *Books* (Ajoy Bose, after all, first made the acquaintance of Tara's husband Ritwick "during a conference on Karl Marx and Twentieth Century Bengali Literature" [p. 3110] and Tara and Moyna find that "the bookshop for the publications of the USSR" is particularly generous in allowing them to advertise *Books* [p. 3114]). Later in the story, when Mao grows into "a strapping young tom" who incites "feline bacchanalia" (p. 3117), we realize that this unpredictable animal embodies both Moyna's rebelliousness and her vulnerability.

Her choice of barsati living defines Moyna's capacity for adventure. In the description of these rooftop dwellings, Desai shows us their romantic attraction. For a young woman eager to declare her independence, the "sense of being empress of all she surveyed" (p. 3106) is intoxicating. Although the shortcomings of these lodging become all too clear—no water tank, no privacy, no security—they dwindle into insignificance in the shade of the glorious pipal tree "with a canopy of silvery, rustling leaves" (p. 3106). The admiration of the Nordic Simona who has moved to Delhi to be near her guru (p. 3126) for the pipal tree leads Moyna to recognize that she overlooks the indignities and crimes that rooftop life has exposed her to because of the tree. Without offering any explicit judgments, Desai makes it clear that Moyna understands that Simona, the poverty-striken acolyte of a probably suspect holy man, is the kind of foreigner whom native-born Indians scorn. Letting her be the tree's great admirer delicately reminds the reader that this tree is a sacred presence to the true believer and that in some way, Moyna's attachment to the tree may be an unconscious response to an ancient call. You can profitably spend some time with your students reviewing other similarly grand and awe-inspiring trees in South Asian literature, including the mango tree in the *Jātaka* called *The Monkey's Heroic Self-Sacrifice* or the peepul [sic] tree in Tagore's *I Won't Let You Go*.

The unplanned party beneath this tree in which Moyna ends up entertaining Tara and Adrian, the tall young man from the British Council, is a turning point in the story. Moyna's youth and innocence are not enough to offset one ill-advised evening under the stars. Having exposed herself to the eyes of neighboring roof dwellers and the righteous ire of the Bhallas, Moyna has no defenses left when Mao's raucous love life again calls attention to her unprotected home. She starts to miss portable pieces of property like her radio and goes so far as to file a complaint with the police, to no avail. Moyna has become easy prey for the Bhallas' servant boy, as this description shows:

He had always watched her with open, unconcealed curiosity, but now she felt he gave his hips an insulting swing, twitched his filthy kitchen duster over his shoulder with a flick, and pursed his lips to whistle a bar from some Bombay film tune although that was surely not fitting in a servant boy, even if employed in a household like the Bhallas'. (p. 3122)

Demoralized and ill, Moyna begins to lose courage. She longs for her mother, and, just as she is beginning to recover from a flu, her mother pays her a visit. In the final pages of *The Rooftop Dwellers*, Desai casts a skeptical eye on the Indian ideal of the nurturing mother. The story's consistently funny depiction of the hypocritical Bhallas reaches a high point when Moyna's mother comes to take care of her daughter. As the two maternal figures vie with each other in showing solicitude for Moyna, the young woman approaches full maturity:

"I don't know why you both like each other so much," Moyna said darkly. . . . "We are both mothers, that is why," her mother replied with what Moyna now found an indigestible sweetness. (p. 3126)

Still without a firm plan, Moyna nevertheless crosses the line from dependency to adulthood when she receives a letter from her mother that "craftily" mentions the son of neighbors whom she would like to have Moyna meet. Recognizing that an arranged marriage is in the offing, a marriage likely to saddle her with a mother-in-law like the "Dragon Lady" (p. 3114) about whom the married Tara has consistently complained, Moyna startles Mao by laughing out loud:

He sat by the door and watched her, his paws primly together, his tail wrapped around him, disapproving. It was clear he thought she had gone crazy. Even he, with his fine senses, could not know that the letter made up Moyna's mind for her. She was free, she was determined, she had made her decision. . . . (p. 3129)

All the self-serving pieties of India's stultifying social system are brilliantly expressed here in the now sanctimonious Mao's censoriousness. Desai's story does not tell us what will happen to Moyna. Certainly the ironic last line reminds us that hurdles remain to be overcome: "In the kitchen below, the Bhallas' servant boy turned up the music [recorded on a tape that he stole from Moyna] and sang along with it" (p. 3129). But a small victory has been won.

Topics for Discussion and Writing

1. What kind of picture does Desai paint of Indian popular culture today? Discuss the relative importance of literature and television and the different audiences to which each medium appeals.
2. What role does the cat Mao play in delineating the stages of Moyna's personal development?
3. Give some examples of the way the Bhallas treat their tenant. How

would you characterize the tone of Desai's presentation of their attitude toward Moyna?

4. How important are the men in this story? Is there a male figure
   upon whom Moyna can rely?

Comparative Perspectives

1. Like Mahasweta Devi in *Breast-Giver*, Anita Desai in *The Rooftop
   Dwellers* challenges the myth of the benign Indian mother. Compare and contrast the tone and content of the two stories. Which is
   more radical? How does each writer use humor in her attack?
2. Moyna is a familiar literary type, the young woman on the verge of
   maturity. Compare and contrast the different ways in which
   Higuchi Ichiyo's *Child's Play*, Alice Munro's *Walker Brothers Cowboy*, and/or Doris Lessing's *The Old Chief Mshlanga* treat other versions of this type.
3. How does the pipal tree contribute to the Indian atmosphere of Desai's story? Compare references to other beautiful and spiritually in-
   spiring trees in the poems of Rabindranath Tagore or in the classical
   South Indian texts of the ancient world.
4. Compare the portraits of family life in *The Dead*, or in *Love in a
   Fallen City*, and *The Rooftop Dwellers*. How much genuine affection
   do persons in these stories have for their relatives? Why do conservative societies offer writers so many opportunities for examining familial strains and hypocrisies?
5. Is Moyna's barsati the kind of space that Virginia Woolf was thinking of in *A Room of One's Own*? Compare the scope and direction of
   Desai's and Woolf's brands of feminism.

Further Reading

See also the reading suggestions in the anthology, pp. 3101–02.

Singh, Khushwant. *Delhi: A Portrait*. 1983. An introduction to the imperial Moghul civilization of Old Delhi that will illustrate how the city has
been transformed by the new suburban developments of the sort in
which the Bhallas live.

LORNA GOODISON

Backgrounds

See the headnote (pp. 3129–32 in the anthology) for background information and suggestions for further reading.

Some Comparative Perspectives

1. Like Leslie Marmon Silko, Goodison recreates the experience of a
   "yellow woman," her great-grandmother. Discuss the evolution of
   that label in both native American and Caribbean cultures and de-

scribe the ways in which Goodison uses sensuous detail, emphasizing the palette and sense of flavor that evoke "Guinea Woman's" complex inheritance. Compare the details of landscape, taste, and color through which Silko conjures up the American Southwest in *Yellow Woman*.

2. Discuss the complicated homage to storytelling Goodison spins out of her references to the African in Harvard Square and the bird trapped in the station in "Heartease New England 1987." How does being a "sojourner" increase the need for stories? What sort of "release" does telling a story afford? Why is it so hard to "get the measure of this world's structure" and where we belong in it? Compare the uncertainties and compulsions that drive other fictive storytellers who wish simultaneously to protect their identities and to tell their stories, such as Homer's Odysseus.

LESLIE MARMON SILKO

Yellow Woman

Backgrounds

The two Western Keresan dialects, Laguna and Acoma, are mutually intelligible and their communities adjacent. Relatively small in area and in population, the Laguna and Acoma communities have produced no fewer than three of the most prominent figures in the native American literary renaissance: Silko, of Laguna; Paula Gunn Allen, also of Laguna; and Simon J. Ortiz, of Acoma. Allen, a novelist and poet, is best known as a critic. Ortiz, a sometime writer of fiction, is often cited as the most gifted native American poet of the late twentieth century. The three writers have long been supportive of one another; Allen has published perceptive, appreciative criticism of Silko in *The Sacred Hoop* (1986) and her own retelling of the Yellow Woman tale in *Spider Woman's Granddaughters* (1989).

In a narrow, but useful, sense Silko's *Yellow Woman* may be seen as a miniature version of her novel *Ceremony* (1977)—with the sexes reversed. In the first instance a young woman identifying herself with the mythic Yellow Woman leaves home and is profoundly affected by a sexual relationship set in a distant landscape. Her lover she imagines as a kachina, a spirit connected to the land. In the second case a young man named Tayo, whose name also appears in Laguna mythology, leaves home and is profoundly affected by a sexual relationship, again set in a distant landscape. His lover is a woman who disappears in winter and is young in spring. Critics have paid attention to the names used by Silko, and indeed they are evocative. The kachina-lover in *Yellow Woman* is named Silva ("the forest trees of a region or country," according to *Merriam Webster's Collegiate Dictionary*). In *Ceremony* the young man's lover has the familiar Spanish surname Montaño (cf. Spanish *montaña*, "mountain," or, in Mexican Spanish, "forest"—Francisco J. Santamaría, *Diccionario de mejicanismos*).

The traditional stories of marriage, or sexual liaison, between human and nonhuman are not confined to Laguna mythology or even to the Southwest. They are prominent throughout the native lore of North America and even of Central and South America. Often the nonhuman spouse is an animal (such as a deer or a buffalo), sometimes a plant (most often corn). The sexual bond therefore establishes a valuable in-law relationship between the human community and its source of livelihood. In one of the old Yellow Woman stories from Laguna the abductor is a buffalo in the form of a man; at the close of the tale, when Yellow Woman has been reunited with her human husband, the husband finds that buffalo, as if magically, gather around his wife, allowing him to hunt with ease.

In an interview Silko was asked if the Yellow Woman tales might possibly have arisen from the ordinary woman's yearning to escape social and sexual domination. Silko's answer was an emphatic *no*: "That's not what it's about." Readers fortunate enough to be steeped in the entire lore may readily agree. But what is the gift, or power, that Silko's heroine brings back to the earthly community? Not food, certainly. (The Jell-O, already being made as she arrives home, is not of her doing.) According to one persuasive line of criticism, the gift is more subtle and decidedly Silkoesque: it is the gift of a new story. One must keep in mind that for Silko stories are a community's most precious possession. Only through stories can the old traditions remain alive. And our modern Yellow Woman, whether we fully approve or not, has brought home a new version.

Classroom Strategies

Yellow Woman is rich enough to fill a class period. Students tend to have strong personal reactions to the heroine's adventure and may not be hesitant to express them. Are the women's points of view different from the men's?

An effective way to begin the discussion is by showing in its entirety or in part the videotape *Running on the Edge of the Rainbow: Laguna Stories and Poems,* a twenty-minute presentation by Leslie Silko. Available separately, the tape is the sixth part in an eight-part series called *Words and Place: Native Literature from the American Southwest,* directed by Larry Evers, distributed by Norman Ross Publishing Co., New York. Silko's charismatic personality is well displayed as she reads from her work, discusses the importance of storytelling, and tells how what passes for ordinary gossip at Laguna (a neighbor woman runs off with another man) may in fact be a new version of an old tribal narrative.

Topics for Discussion

1. Is the landscape merely a setting for the story, or does it play a stronger role? Note the name Silva and its English-language definition. How does Silva's presumed connection with the remote forest (" 'Can you see the pueblo?' 'We're too far away' ") and the endless

mountains ("From here I can see the world") elevate the story from the category of a prose idyll or light romance? The anthology head-note mentions that Silko once studied law with the intention of fil-ing land claims; and it may be kept in mind that land, for the native American—as with civil rights for the African American—is the one overriding political issue. Is it possible to read a political interpreta-tion into *Yellow Woman*?

2. What do the stolen beef and the Jell-O have in common? How do these elements break the prevailing mood?

    [Both are nonnative.]

3. Silko has written dismissively of nonnative poets and writers who weave native American material into their own work. In so doing, "They deny their history," she observes, intimating that they would do better to "create a satisfactory identity for themselves" by incor-porating their own heritage instead of someone else's. If this seems a fair criticism, consider making a short list of traditional ethnic ma-terials that might profitably be reworked by Anglo, African, Asian, or other contemporary American writers. Choose a familiar folktale and prepare a brief, original plot summary that touches upon both the traditional story and modern experience. Or take a well-worn ex-ample, such as the Cinderella theme, and compare it to the Yellow Woman theme.

Comparative Perspectives

1. The narrator of *Yellow Woman* imagines the conversation about her absence taking place at home: "Where did she go?—maybe kid-napped." Has she been kidnapped? Why does she not immediately return to her people when she has the chance? How much psycho-logical insight does Silko give us into her heroine's thought patterns here? How would you compare the fantasies of the drunken woman in Clarice Lispector's story? Are Lispector and Silko writing about the same phenomenon?

    [See the editor's account in "Backgrounds," above, of Silko's em-phatic rejection of a feminist reading of her story.]

2. Although Silko's narrator protests to Silva that Yellow Woman sto-ries "couldn't happen now," the stories that her grandfather told her prepare the ground for her encounter with Silva. How much does our readiness to embrace experience depend on our ability to assim-ilate it to preexisting emotional and intellectual categories? How does the traditional material upon which *Yellow Woman* draws dis-tinguish Silko's storytelling from the narrative strategies employed in other works that subject their protagonists to strange events, in-cluding *Gulliver's Travels*, *The Metamorphosis*, or *Omeros*?

    [One might argue that Silko's narrator can go home again be-cause she knows how to tell her story. This return is problematic, if not impossible, for Swift's and Kafka's protagonists, whom we find so disturbing because they accept the absurd without having available to them narrative precedents that cushion the absurd. Presumably, this tells us something about the contrast between cultures that prize tradition and those that pride themselves on innovation.]

Further Reading

See also the reading suggestions in the anthology, p. 3143.

Ellis, Florence Hawley. "Laguna Pueblo." In *Handbook of North American Indians*, edited by William C. Sturtevant, vol. 9 (Southwest, ed. Alfonso Ortiz). 1979. Concise introduction to Laguna history and culture.

Hobson, Geary, ed. *The Remembered Earth: An Anthology of Contemporary Native American Literature*. 1979. Includes Silko's essay *An Old-Time Indian Attack Conducted in Two Parts*, her scornful critique of Anglo writers who pose as shamans.

Velie, Alan R. *Four American Indian Literary Masters: N. Scott Momaday, James Welch, Leslie Marmon Silko, and Gerald Vizenor*. 1982. Velie compares Silko's novel *Ceremony* to the Grail legend.

Index